COLLECTED PAPERS

VOLUME II

COLLECTED PAPERS

◻◻◻

GILBERT RYLE

*Formerly Waynflete Professor of
Metaphysical Philosophy in the
University of Oxford*

VOLUME II
COLLECTED ESSAYS
1929–1968

HUTCHINSON OF LONDON

HUTCHINSON & CO (*Publishers*) LTD
178–202 Great Portland Street, London W1

London Melbourne Sydney Auckland
Johannesburg Cape Town and agencies
throughout the world

First published 1971

*This book has been set in Garamond type, printed in Great Britain
on antique wove paper by W. Heffer & Sons Ltd, Cambridge*

ISBN 0 09 104420 0

CONTENTS

v

CONTENTS

INTRODUCTION

The pieces collected in this volume, articles, lectures, discussion-notes and symposium-contributions, are necessarily variegated. Composed at different dates, for different sorts of occasions and in different states of the intellectual climate, they could not, should not and do not convey any single message.

Certain major strands can, however, be distinguished.

(1) Especially in the earliest papers the Occamizing zeal is manifest. In part this was due to my desire to master, to explain to others and to enlarge the new treatment by Frege and Russell of assertions of existence and, especially, of denials of existence. The addiction of philosophers and logicians to the practice of hypostatising their own terms of art commonly goes with an inclination to inflate the import of 'there are so and so's' and to deflate the import of 'there are not such-and-suches.'

But behind this sophisticatedly Occamizing zeal there was in me, from quite early days, an ulterior concern. In the 1920's and the 1930's there was welling up the problem 'What, if anything, is philosophy?' No longer could we pretend that philosophy differed from physics, chemistry and biology by studying mental as opposed to material phenomena. We could no longer boast or confess that we were unexperimental psychologists. Hence we were beset by the temptation to look for non-mental, non-material objects—or Objects—which should be for philosophy what beetles and butterflies were for entomology. Platonic Forms, Propositions, Intentional Objects, Logical Objects, perhaps, sometimes, even Sense-Data were recruited to appease our professional hankerings to have a subject-matter of our own.

I had learned, chiefly from the *Tractatus Logico-Philosophicus*, that no specifications of a proprietary subject-matter could yield the right answer, or even the right sort of answer to the original question 'What is Philosophy?'; so my Occamizings had a positive pupose in them. Philosophical problems are problems of a special sort; they are not problems of an ordinary sort about special entities.

(2) Though not myself qualified to be a real logician, I had realized at an early stage that advances in Logic would and should result in

the re-shaping of the questions, answers and, especially the arguments of philosophers. Brokers were needed, as they still are needed, to facilitate transactions between Logic and the philosophy of Mind, between Logic and the theory of Sense/Nonsense, and even between Logic and the should-be theory of pedagogy.

A number of the papers in this volume were intended to facilitate such transactions. It was not due only to my notational incompetences that I chose to discuss these trans-frontier issues in unesoteric English prose. Aristotle had wisely complemented his *Prior Analytics* with his *De Interpretatione* and his *Categories*.

(3) The second half of this volume is heavily concentrated on the notion of Thinking. To a slight degree this particular interest derives from my discontentment with the things that real logicians say when they venture to connect their formalities with the live thinkings that human beings actually engage in; to a slight degree, also, it derives from my discontentment with the things said by psychologists and epistemologists when they venture to connect their proprietary topics with the formalities of Logic. Also, like plenty of other people, I deplored the perfunctoriness with which *The Concept of Mind* had dealt with the Mind *qua* pensive. But I have latterly been concentrating heavily on this particular theme for the simple reason that it has turned out to be at once a still intractable and a progressively ramifying maze. Only a short confrontation with the theme suffices to make it clear that and why no account of Thinking of a Behaviourist coloration will do, and also why no account of a Cartesian coloration will do either.

In this volume, as in the first volume, the papers are reprinted almost as they originally appeared. Accentuations and punctuations have been moderately freely emended; misprints and misspellings have been purged; word-orders have occasionally been altered; a few words and phrases have been replaced; here and there the paragraphing has been corrected.

I have refrained from charging myself or any colleague with the labour of compiling an index. Such an index could expedite the studies only, I like indolently to think, of those who will be writing Doctoral Dissertations; and for them the chore of rummaging for themselves will be more rewarding than would be their inheritance of the proceeds of other people's rummagings.

GILBERT RYLE

March, 1971

I

NEGATION

*Reprinted from 'Proceedings of the Aristotelian Society', suppl. vol. to
vol.* IX, *1929, by permission of the editor*

*I must preface this paper with an apology for much of the looseness and
formlessness of expression that it contains. The original paper was lost in
transmission to the printer, with the result that this had to be reproduced
largely from memory during the intervals of three busy days. The arguments,
however, are in all essentials the arguments that were contained in the original
paper.*

I wish to defend the position that a sentence involving a negative
may be the expression of something that I *know*—in other words, that
there are real negative facts.

In consequence, I shall have to quarrel with the theory, which
Mr Mabbott partially endorses, that almost all negative sentences are
meaningless, *or* that what they mean is either false or nonsensical, *or*
that the state of mind to which they give expression must almost
always be one inferior to knowledge. On the other hand, I am not so
far out of sympathy with the view which Mr Mabbott holds as to deny
that there is a real problem here which needs solution, or even that
in many respects his solution is on the right track. Accordingly,
I shall try to separate what I think is true and what false or irrelevant
in his theory, and give to the former element a turn and development
that seem to me to be required.

(1) First of all I am quite in agreement with what I think underlies
his dislike of the idea that what is negative is objective, or that what is
objective can be merely negative.

(*a*) If anyone wishes to maintain that reality contains a large class
of entities the essential character of each of which is that it is strictly
a *non*-entity, then he is, I agree, maintaining what is false or nonsensical. There are no such substances as 'not-triangles' or 'not-
goats', and no such qualities as 'not-green' or 'not-square'.

(*b*) Or if anyone wishes to maintain that the Method of Dichotomous Division is one that is by itself productive of new knowledge, then I think he is wrong. I learn nothing new about reality by dividing it into an ever-widening delta of, for instance, things corporeal and things not corporeal, and the latter into things animate and things inanimate, and so on.

(*c*) Or if anyone holds a theory which says or implies that a proposition of the form 'A is not B' can be the answer to the question 'What is A?' I think he is wrong, and that we don't yet know all that we might know, or (usually) all that we want to know when we know of A just that it is not B. I shall try to show later that while what a negative sentence states may be a real fact and one which is both knowable and worth knowing, it has a character which might warrant us in calling it 'abstract' (in a sense yet to be made precise); and that, commonly anyhow, it is only *useful* for us to get to know such a fact because knowledge of it will or may be instrumental to us in getting to know some further and less 'abstract' fact.

(2) On the other hand, I disagree with much that seems to underlie Mr Mabbott's statement of the problem and solution of it.

(*a*) He is all the time trying to account for negation in terms of our acts of 'excluding', 'rejecting' and 'eliminating'. But I urge that precisely the same objections hold against this sort of analysis of negation as hold against Bradley's definition of judgment as a species of 'referring'. For surely to 'eliminate', 'reject' or 'exclude' can only be to find that B is *not* (what Jones, perhaps, had asserted) the character of A. *We* are not excluding B-ness from A—the nature of A does that—*we* are only coming to know or believe that A's nature does so, i.e. that A is not B. In other words, an act of 'eliminating' or 'excluding' is either a practical act, like that of a college porter, or it is an intellectual one; and if it is the latter it is nothing unless it is at least founded in the knowledge or belief that A, say, is not B.

(*b*) And secondly, just to touch upon a matter which is too big to deal with fully, I cannot allow that an investigation of the purposes and technique of our intellectual operations can ever afford an answer to questions about the formal or categorial properties of facts. It is interesting and valuable for certain purposes to examine how we human beings do our thinking and what we do it for, but it is irrelevant and even damaging to look for help to such enquiries when what we want to know is what is the logical constitution of the real. Logic is not concerned, in my view, with how we think, but with some general features of what we know.

However, I must not here raise the general issue, 'What is logic about?' and I only mention the divergence between Mr Mabbott's view and my own in order to show why I am bound to try to prove that the negative element in negative sentences does denote, or may denote, some objective character of known facts and not merely some subjective limitations in our intellectual powers and equipment. It is essential to my position to deny what I accuse Mr Mabbott of maintaining, that while 'Yes' may be an expression of knowledge, 'No' is an expression only of doubt or ignorance.

I wish first of all to state briefly what I think positively about negation, and then to defend it against some of the charges levelled at it by Mr Mabbott.

When Mr Mabbott very sensibly and properly urges that if we are to study negation we should select for examination only such negative judgments as are *genuine* judgments, i.e. judgments which might occur or have occurred in real pieces of scientific thinking, distinguishing these from the sham, fabricated or mutilated specimens upon which Formal Logic loves to dwell, he is, I suppose, primarily trying to safeguard himself—and our discussion—from being committed to an acceptance of 'infinite negations' as real ones. And I think he is quite right in repudiating the pretence of 'Virtue is not square' and 'The soul is not a fire-shovel' to be cases of negation on all fours with 'genuine' negations.

But as I am not quite sure what his criterion is between judgments which are genuine and those which are sham, or, as I should put it, between genuine and nonsensical propositions,[1] I want just to mention the criterion that I shall be employing—the more so as the principle underlying the criterion is, I think, also one of the principles underlying negation itself.

By a genuine proposition I mean one which is an answer (*the* true answer or *a* false one) to a real question. And by a real question I mean one which can be known necessarily to have an answer, though the answer may not be known.

But some questions, e.g. double questions, are not real questions. So any proposition which is not an answer to a real question will be nonsensical, in the sense that neither it nor its contradictory is true; any answer, for instance, to 'Have you left off beating your mother yet?' is nonsense in this way. I shall apply this criterion later to alleged cases of 'infinite negation'.

And while I am dealing with the relation between propositions and questions, it is worth while to say here that just as I think some

---

[1] I wholeheartedly reject Mr Mabbott's identification of the meaningless with the nonsensical, of either or both with the false, of any of these with the useless, or any of these with the trivial and uninteresting.

negative sentences mean genuine negative propositions, so some negative interrogative sentences mean real questions. So that while certainly 'Mrs Smith's hat is not green' is not an answer to 'What colour is Mrs Smith's hat?' it is an answer to 'What colour is Mrs Smith's hat *not*?' And not only are such questions possible, but the method of elimination consists precisely in raising and solving them.

I want to come on now to assert fairly dogmatically some things which I am sure hold good of most cases of negation, and which I believe to hold good of all.

(1) When I assert 'Mrs Smith's hat is not green', I have not yet answered the question 'What colour is Mrs Smith's hat?' For 'not green' is not the name of a colour, as is shown for certain by the fact that whether her hat is in fact red or blue it is in exactly the same sense not green; but what 'red' is the name of is different from what 'green' is the name of.

On the other hand, though I have not stated what is the colour of the hat, it would be false to say that I have asserted *nothing* of the hat. For one thing, my assertion is (*pace* Mr Mabbott) true or false of the hat, which would not be the case had my assertion been that impossible thing, an assertion of nothing. Or, as I can now put it, though I have not answered the question 'What colour is Mrs Smith's hat?', I have answered, truly or falsely, the question 'What colour is Mrs Smith's hat *not*?'

Next, when I assert 'the hat is not green', not only is what I assert not an assertion of a colour, but I do not even need to know what colour her hat is in order to be able to make the assertion that it is not green. An obvious case of this arises when I discover that my ticket is not in my ticket-pocket, which I ordinarily do *before* I discover in which pocket it actually is. In other words, elimination may precede and not ensue upon the discovery of the required fact. But even when it does so ensue, namely, when what enables me to assert 'A is not B' is the knowledge that A is C, the assertion 'A is not B' is different from the assertion 'A is C'; for the former *might* have been true and the latter false, which would not have been the case had they been logically the same assertion. If a fact is necessitated by another fact, then it is not identical with it: and equally, what happens frequently, if one fact is *not* necessitated by another, they are not the same fact.

(2) A second point which brings me much nearer to the formulation of the theory which I wish to champion is this. With one class, or perhaps two, of possible exceptions, to which I refer later, it seems to be the case that if I can ever say, e.g., 'Mrs Smith's hat is not green', I can say, 'Mrs Smith's hat is not green *but some other*

colour'. The 'but some other . . .' is always there, sometimes explicitly, sometimes marked rather by tone of voice, or simply implied by the context. But I suggest that whether it is formulated in words or not it is always 'understood'.

For instance, 'Handkerchiefs are not square but some other shape', 'Medicines are not luxuries but are taken for some other purposes'.

Now the completion of a negative sentence with a 'but' clause is not, I urge, an alteration of the meaning of the sentence, but simply an explication of its expression. Without it, negative sentences are elliptical, intelligible, very often, in spite of being elliptical, since the context or the tone of voice prevents ambiguities arising, but even so what they are understood to mean must still embody the 'but some other . . .'.

I want to lay great stress on this completion of what is meant by negative sentences for several reasons—not the least being that, if I am not mistaken, Mr Mabbott, following or improving upon Bosanquet, has made the same point in another way.

For we are agreeing that when a 'predicate' is denied of a 'subject', that predicate must always be thought as one member of a disjunctive set, some other member of which set (not necessarily specified) is asserted to be predicable of the subject.

I may put the point in this way. When I say, 'The hat is not green (but some other colour)', I am (not stating but) presupposing that the hat is coloured; for the questions to be solved are (*a*) 'Which colour is the colour of the hat?' and (*b*) 'Which colour is *not* or which colours are *not* the colour of the hat?' both of which are only real questions if 'Yes' is the answer to 'Is the hat coloured?'

It is, in other words, known and presupposed that the Determinable 'being coloured' characterizes the hat, and the question is 'Which of the Determinates characterizes it?' And the denial of Determinate B is not yet the assertion of Determinate F (say), but, presupposing that *some* Determinate is the colour of the hat, asserts of this that it is *one* of the Determinates of the Determinable 'being coloured' other than the given Determinate B.

So the proposition 'Mrs Smith's hat is not green (but some other colour)' only in appearance has for its 'subject' Mrs Smith's hat; in fact, its subject is 'the colour of Mrs Smith's hat', and to this subject is ascribed the character of being one of the colours other than green.

And I think that we should have reached the same sort of conclusion by examining the form of the question to which 'Mrs Smith's hat is not green' is a genuine answer. For the question 'Which colour is *not* the colour of Mrs Smith's hat?' already in the simple word 'Which?' indicates the presence of a disjunctive set—namely, in our case, the disjunctive set of the determinate colours of the Determinable 'being coloured'.

Now there are various sorts of disjunctive sets, of which the set of Determinates of a Determinable is only one: just as there are various sorts of 'predicate' of which qualities are only one. And while, for simplicity's sake, I shall myself be drawing for examples mainly upon cases where the negated element is a determinate *quality*, I do not wish to be thought to be denying by implication that there are other sorts of things which may be negated. But I do wish to maintain the general position that whenever I assert, e.g., A is not B, I am asserting that some other member than B of the disjunctive set or logical family, of which B is one member, is that which A is.

And I wish to maintain, too, the further point, that while the denial of a certain quality to A seems to have A for its subject, exactly as an ascription of it to A does, in fact the real subject of the denial is not A but the (perhaps) unidentified quality of A. When I say 'the hat is not green' I am not ascribing a positive character to the hat, though I am necessarily presupposing that it has the positive character of being coloured; but I am positively characterizing what is a positive character of the hat. I am characterizing, namely, the determinate colour of the hat as being one of the colours other than green. This is not indeed enough, except in cases where the disjunctive set has only two members, e.g., where the Determinable has only two Determinates, to identify the character so characterized. But neither when I call Mr Smith a tradesman is my description enough to distinguish which his trade is; but it is not the less a positive character for being general. There are many real marks which are not monomarks, and many true descriptions which are not exclusive descriptions. Just so, then, I am asserting, being-a-colour-other-than-green is a real character of the colour of Mrs Smith's hat (which is, we will take it, blue); and it is not the less a real character of blue that it is also a real character of yellow, black, red, etc.

And this is, I suggest, the sense in which negative facts merit the title 'abstract'; namely, that they are *ex officio* facts about facts about things, or characters of characters of things, and not directly facts about things or characters of things.

Let me now apply this analysis to another case, and one in which the negated element is not a quality, and so the disjunctive set is not a set of Determinates of a Determinable.

Take 'Jones is not the secretary of the Club'.

First of all, the words as printed give no clue to which element in the whole is being negated; so in lieu of the elucidation that tone of voice, context, etc., would ordinarily afford, we must give a little more flesh to this typical logician's specimen.

I shall bring out four of the possible meanings by completing the sentence with alternative 'but' clauses and italicizing the negated element.

(*a*) '*Jones* is not the secretary of the Club (but some other member, Brown, say, is).'

(*b*) 'Jones is not the *secretary* of the Club (but holds some other office, treasurer, say).'

(*c*) 'Jones is not the secretary of the *Club* (but of some other body, a sub-committee, say).'

(*d*) 'Jones *is* not the secretary of the Club (but his tenure of the office belongs to some other period, last year, say, or next year).'

This brings out not simply the uninteresting linguistic fact that negative sentences may be elliptical and ambiguous, but much more: (*a*) that the full explication of what is meant by a negative sentence necessarily takes the form of an assertion of otherness; and (*b*) that the otherness asserted is not just otherness in general, but otherness as specified or made determinate by mention of the particular disjunctive set to which the 'others' belong as members. It would be labouring the point to work this out by showing to what real questions these four propositions are genuine answers.

We are now in a position to see exactly what it is that we have always felt in our bones was wrong with Bradley's cases of infinite negations, 'Virtue is not square' and 'The Soul is not a fire-shovel': and we can see that their being negative has hardly anything to do with their being nonsensical.

Take 'Virtue is not square': this can be completed either as (*a*) 'Virtue is not *square* (but some other shape)', or (*b*) '*Virtue* is not square (but some other entity is)'.

(*a*) This is nonsense, because any characterization of the shape of Virtue is like any characterization of the present King of France in not being about anything.

The questions 'Which shape is Virtue?' and 'Which shape is Virtue *not*?' could only be real questions on one condition, namely, that 'Yes' was the answer to 'Has Virtue a shape?' But as this is not the case, answers to questions 'Which is, or is not, Virtue's shape?' must be nonsensical in the sense I have described, namely, that neither they nor their contradictories can be true.

(*b*) In the second case, the sentence is not nonsensical but states an uninteresting because trivial truth. 'Yes' is the answer to 'Are

7

there entities?', 'Is Virtue an entity?' and 'Are there some entities which are square?'; and the answer 'Virtue is not square but handkerchiefs and window-panes are' only rings oddly because we do not ordinarily find occasion to class Virtue, handkerchiefs and window-panes together.

Similarly in 'The soul is not a *fire-shovel* (but some other sort of tool)', we have a nonsensical sentence, since 'No' is the true answer to 'Is the soul a tool?' and so there is no answer to 'Which sort of tool is, or is not, the soul?'

The other alternative, 'The *soul* is not a fire-shovel, but some other substance is', is another uninteresting and trivial truth.

But Mr Mabbott has an argument in store for us which bears upon this point, which, if valid, will completely undermine the whole analysis of negation that I have been trying to give. For he can say: Certainly, this is the true account of why 'Virtue is not square' is nonsensical. But my whole position is that just those reasons do in fact make all negative sentences nonsensical. For 'Mrs Smith's hat is not green' presupposes, you say, that Mrs Smith's hat is some-colour-or-other, i.e. 'Mrs Smith's hat is not green' is nonsense unless it is true that the hat is *either* red *or* blue *or* green *or* yellow ... But that is just the point. It is *not* true. A particular hat can not have a disjunctive colouring or hover between alternatives. If it is, e.g., blue, then it isn't any other colour, and so there is no 'either–or' about it at all.

The issue is, I think, a good one, and everything hinges on whether we can upset or circumvent Mr Mabbott's strictures upon the ascription of disjunctives to particulars.

I, then, have to maintain, and do in fact maintain, that a sentence of the form 'A (a particular) is either B or C or D' is not necessarily nonsense, and may be the statement of a real fact. And I may summarize my general position on this point by saying that to predicate a Determinable of a particular is not to ascribe *indeterminateness* to its character, but to ascribe to it the *sort* of determinateness that it has got; or, in other words, the affirmation of a Determinable is not the denial of any Determinate but rather the affirmation of some Determinate or other. (In other cases the 'either–or' would not be between *qualities*, and so the common principle of the disjunctive set would not be a Determinable generating Determinates, but the principle would be the same.)

Indeed, I would go even further and say that when I assert 'Mrs Smith's hat is some colour or other', i.e., 'is either red or blue or green or yellow ...', not only am I not making the false or nonsensical assertion that it has an indeterminate colouring, but I am not even asserting or implying that my state of mind is indeterminate (in the popular sense, of course, of 'undecided'). I may know which colour her hat actually is, and still the disjunctive sentence may express something that I know, namely, something rather general *about* the colour of her hat. And this known fact *about* the colour of her hat is just as much a fact about it when I know as well the further fact that it is actually blue. 'Facts about' lose their interestingness but not their status after the final discovery of 'facts of'. And I am so convinced that there may be genuine disjunctive propositions about particulars, that I accuse Mr Mabbott's theory, according to which ascription of an 'either–or' to a particular is an ascription of indeterminateness to it, of implying that the proposition 'Mrs Smith's hat is either red or blue or green or yellow . . .' is exactly equivalent to its contradictory 'Mrs Smith's hat is *neither* red *nor* blue *nor* green *nor* yellow . . .'

What exactly *is* meant, then, by the disjunctive proposition 'Mrs Smith's hat is either red or blue or green or yellow . . .'? I hold that it means just this: 'Mrs Smith's hat is coloured in some determinate way or other: and the determinate colour which is the colour of Mrs Smith's hat is one among the colours red, blue, green, yellow . . .' It characterizes the colour of the hat as being a member of a certain class: and it is true equally when we know as when we do not know which member it is.

Take another case. I judge at Reading, say, 'That train is going either to Swindon or to Oxford'; and I do so without necessarily implying that the engine-driver, the passengers, the signal-man or even I myself are in ignorance or doubt which its route actually is. Ordinarily, of course, I would not bother to *make* the statement if I was not in some doubt, since if I could identify its route it would be superfluous to mention such non-individuating facts about it. But facts do not cease to be facts or cease to be known when it becomes superfluous to mention them. The proposition, 'The route of that train is either the Oxford or the Swindon route', is not, therefore, a proposition about anybody's ignorance or indecision.

On the contrary, it both presupposes and expresses knowledge. It presupposes as a known fact that there is *a* route which is *the* route of *that* train: and it expresses as a known fact something about that route, namely, that it is, e.g., one of the class of routes away from London, one of the class of routes through Reading, etc., etc. Finally, it implies as a known fact that both the Reading–Swindon route and the Reading–Oxford route share these general characteristics as well as some more special ones, such as going through Reading station in such and such a direction, and being on such and such a track. I know, that is to say, that the Reading–Swindon and the Reading–Oxford routes share certain characters which no other routes do; i.e. that they are the only two members of a certain class. (Just as in other cases we may know of two Determinates that they are the only Determinates of a certain Determinable, as 'male' and 'female' are the only Determinates of the 'Determinable' 'having sex'.) So that in knowing 'that train is going either to Swindon or to Oxford' I am simply knowing a 'fact about' its route, namely, that it is one of two particular routes. And I continue to know this even when I know which of the two it is.

Disjunctive propositions about particulars and, in consequence, negative propositions about particulars are possible, since both are in fact descriptions not directly of the particulars but of characters of the particulars; of which characters they give descriptions which are true descriptions but not, except *per accidens*, exclusive descriptions. 'A is either B or C or D' means that the character of A is one of the characters B and C and D. And this seems to be the reason why or the sense in which negations and disjunctions are 'abstract', namely, that they ascribe characters not to things but to the characters of things, and the characters they ascribe are not individuating characters.

Negative sentences then state 'otherness'; but it is not otherness between, e.g., Mrs Smith's hat and the colour green, but otherness between the colour of Mrs Smith's hat and the colour green.

I mentioned earlier that there are one or two classes of negatives which do not seem to yield so readily the 'but some other . . .' One of these is the class to which Mr Mabbott gives a special treatment, namely, teleological propositions of the form 'Number 3 cannot row', 'Robinson is not honest'. The other, which he does not notice, is the class of negative existentials, such as 'Ghosts do not exist', 'There is no phlogiston'.

I am not easy in mind that the analysis I have suggested can be applied to either of these classes, though for the sake of the argument I am prepared to maintain that it can. I suggest, accordingly, that these are just prominent cases of bi-polar disjunctive sets, i.e. disjunctive sets containing only two 'others', familiarity with which has brought us to use the negative of the one as the name or the exclusive description of the other. Thus, while in the case of 'male' and 'female' we have separate names for the two alternatives, in the case of 'equal' and 'unequal', 'like' and 'unlike', 'existent' and 'non-existent', 'honest' and 'dishonest', the second of the pair has no official title except the negative of the other.

While I am on this point I should just like to call attention to the ingenuity of Mr Mabbott's treatment of the relation between negative and teleological judgments. His position seems to be that ordinary negative judgments are just teleological failures; they are specimens of thinking which 'miss the boat', and are in consequence to be relegated to the limbo in which reside all mistakes, sins and fallings from grace. But in some of the judgments that we make we are thinking *about* cases of failure or success, sin or virtue, missing or catching the boat. These are teleological judgments. And if I have to judge that someone has failed or sinned or made a mistake, my judgment is a teleological condemnation. And these are *genuine* negative judgments since they are judgments of negativeness.

So an ordinary negative judgment is a *mera negatio*, but the judgment that it is so is a true negation. It is not, like them, a bad judgment because it falls short of the ideal of true judging; on the contrary, it is a genuine judgment because it is a condemnation of the 'unideal'. I don't believe this theory, but I admire it sufficiently to think it well worth discussing.

One word, before I finish, upon the *use* of negation, i.e. upon the utility of knowing negative facts. I don't think Logic should concern itself with the objects for which we want or need to get to know things; but, if we may, for a moment, turn aside to consider this special psychological or economic question, it does seem to me to be true that we do usually want or need to know negative facts because we want to know further positive ones. The special province of negation is, I dare say, the method of elimination. But if we analyse the activity of eliminating we must in the end recognize that it is not without the discovery of negative facts; so that the attempt to explain negation in terms of elimination must break down. But if preoccupation with the method of elimination has led logicians to see that we can discover and chart disjunctive sets, and by the elimination of some alternatives converge upon the required one by the well-known process of 'getting warmer', we ought to thank them for what we have gained as well as criticize them for what they have missed.

In conclusion, it seems to me that the only reason that there is left us for being dissatisfied with negative facts is because they don't, as a rule, constitute all that we want to know, since they are only 'facts about' when we want to find the 'facts of'. But it is rank ingratitude to reject their gifts on the score that they are not very big ones, and fairness will compel us to concede that even negation is determination.

2

ARE THERE PROPOSITIONS?

Reprinted from 'Proceedings of the Aristotelian Society', vol. xxx, *1930, by permission of the editor*

There are not left now many philosophers, if there are any, who still champion the doctrine that 'there are' objective propositions or 'objectives'. Nor do I intend to try to rehabilitate it. But the arguments for the doctrine as well as some of the motives for accepting it are still worthy of some consideration, if only because the ambiguities and errors in the theories of judgment, of which the proposition theory was the critique, seem likely to rear their heads again. For in some quarters the term 'belief' and in others the term 'assertion' are being employed with (it seems to me) just the same looseness which originally made the term 'judgment' deservedly suspect. And the term 'belief', in particular, when used as an all-embracing title for all the sorts of apprehension the expression of which takes the form of statement, is even more misleading than the old term 'judgment'; for with the motive, I suppose, of conceding as much as possible to Protagoras or to Hume, its users actually imply by it, what was not implied by 'judgment', that there is not, at least in human experience, any such thing as *knowing*.

However, my business is not to discuss any modern theories about thinking other than the proposition-theory; and this I wish to discuss in the following way:

I want to give, as briefly as I can, a list of the main reasons for which it has been maintained that 'there are' propositions, as well as to describe the sort of being that, in consequence, they have been alleged to possess.

Next, I want to give the main arguments that are given, or should be given, against this doctrine. And finally I shall try to extract what is the main problem which the theory aimed at solving and to suggest at least a partial solution of it which does not commit us *either* to the view that 'there are' propositions *or* to the psychologistic theory of judgment which that view was designed to refute.

I begin with a résumé of the major arguments for the doctrine that propositions are genuine entities.

I. THE ARGUMENT FROM THE INTENTIONALITY OF ACTS OF THINKING

According to Brentano (though the kernel of the doctrine is explicitly formulated by Plato) it is of the essence of consciousness that acts of consciousness are *of* objects.

To see is to see something, to like is to like someone or something, to remember is to remember something; and so forth. This relation of being of an object is called by Brentano the *intentional*[1] relation.

It is just the natural linguistic counterpart to this psychological fact that the verbs in which we express acts of consciousness are transitive verbs. So that just as the verb 'to eat' and the verb 'to hit' can only occur in sentences with accusatives as their complements, so such verbs as 'to hate' and 'to recognize' and 'to represent' can only function in sentences which are complete with an accusative.

This intrinsic intentionality or 'transitivity' of acts of consciousness is, it is alleged, self-evident. It is not a mere hypothesis or a mere empirical generalization, but a property which can be directly ascertained to belong to the very nature of consciousness. And we can grant, I think, that it would be both paradoxical and in conflict with the evidence of language to assert that there may be some forms of consciousness which are not consciousness *of* something.

That which an act of consciousness has as its intentional object is, of course, not necessarily a *thing*, e.g. a real physical substance. It may be an imagined something, a past or future something, an ideal or abstract something (like a number or a law) or a negative something. In other words the term 'object' ('Gegenstand') does not mean 'entity', 'thing' or 'substance', save *per accidens*. But as there is a loophole for ambiguity here, I prefer, for my own convenience, to coin, what we lack in English, a rendering for 'Gegenstand' separate from that for 'Objekt', and I speak accordingly of the intentional '*accusative*' of acts of consciousness.

There is an important thing to notice about the analysis given by Brentano and his school of intentionality: namely, that it is at the start regarded as an advance in *psychology* and not as a premiss to or a conclusion from a Realist theory of knowledge. The result is that at

[1] This term is scholastic in origin; but all that need be said of it here is that it has nothing directly to do with *intending* in the sense of purposing to do.

the beginning it is only attempted to show that in the case of any act of consciousness there is an object or 'accusative' intended which is *other* than the act. Only later is the further problem tackled of showing whether or not the 'accusative' is *independent* of the act. That the object is generally, if not universally, other than the act is easy to show; for what I see is coloured, but seeing is not green or blue; what is remembered is of the past, but the remembering it is of the present; what is known is public property, but the knowing it is private to the knower, and so forth.

Now among acts of consciousness we may isolate a class which is often called the class of acts of Judgment, or acts of Thinking. I might echo Cook Wilson's strictures on the propriety of imputing real homogeneity to acts of knowing, opining, believing, supposing, wondering, etc., but it is enough for my purposes to point out that there is one common feature, if there are no others, which these various sorts of 'thinking' show, namely, that all alike find their expression in *statement* or in sentences in the indicative. If I know something, the something that I know is published in the form 'that X is Y'; and, equally, if I only opine or surmise something, that something is published in the form 'that X is Y'. Thus in contradistinction from those acts of consciousness the 'accusatives' of which are *things* which can in principle be named and pointed at (like my hat or Tommy), there is this class of acts which we call acts of thinking or judging, the 'accusatives' of which can be stated but not pointed at.

They too, apparently, can subsequently come to be named; for instance, having judged and stated that I am going bald, I can go on to name the baldness of my head, as when I regret the baldness of my head or judge that it is incurable.

Now of these 'accusatives' also we can see at once that they are *other* than the acts in which they are thought; and we can speculate whether they are not also independent of them. But postponing the arguing of this issue, we can say that if they are distinguishable from acts of thinking they had better have a name which advertises the distinction. And as the orthodox terms 'thoughts' and 'judgments' are equivocal, since they may equally well denote 'thinkings' as 'what-is-thought' (*cogitationes* as *cogitata*, *judicationes* as *judicata*), the 'accusatives' of acts of thinking have come to be called 'propositions'.

This intentional account of thinking is still a purely psychological one; it distinguishes *what* I know, opine, guess, etc., from my knowing, opining and guessing; and it draws attention to the fact that these 'accusatives' are of the form 'that X is Y'. But though

14

it raises, it does not answer, the further question of the *status* of the propositions which constitute the what-I-think.

However, it enables us already to make another highly important distinction. When I think something and express my thought in a sentence there are two completely different sorts of *meanings* to be read into the sentence. There is (*a*) that which the statement *states*, e.g. 'that this coin is bigger than that one', which is the proposition that I have been thinking; and there is (*b*) that of which the occurrence of the sentence is *evidence*, namely, that I have been thinking it. The sentence *states* one thing, which is a proposition about coins; it evinces or displays or is evidence of another, namely, the occurrence in me of the act of thinking. The difference can be clearly shown. For if I have uttered my sentence aloud, a listener can *both* understand what I say or grasp my meaning *and* infer to my state of mind. But he can't do the second at all if he cannot first understand what I say; and even when he does perfectly understand what I say, his inference to my state of mind can only be a *probable* inference. For I may be lying, or repeating something parrot-wise without thinking what I am saying.

But in any case the understanding is not a piece of inferring, save *per accidens*, and the inferring to the author's state of mind presupposes the understanding—for it is the enquiry 'Why was *that* said?'

I shall have to recur to this distinction between what a statement *states* and what its occurrence *evinces* later on; I mention it now because before broaching the subject of *meaning* which looms before me, I had to point out these two of the many senses which the ambiguous term 'meaning' carries—namely the symbolization of a symbol and the signification of a natural sign. Smoke *means* fire in the sense of signifying it (being evidence for it); but a statement's *meaning* is a proposition in the sense that it symbolizes it.

II. ARGUMENTS FOR THE INDEPENDENCE OF PROPOSITIONS FROM THINKING

Another interest than that (described above) in the psychology of thinking has led to more drastic conclusions—namely, the desire to refute subjectivist theories of knowledge and of reality.

Subjectivism (the theory that what I apprehend must always be my own thoughts or ideas), whether arrived at as a conclusion from metaphysical or from psychological premises, has always offended two or perhaps three classes of thinkers—those who respect the integrity of the physical sciences, those who respect the integrity of mathematics and Logic, and perhaps those who respect the integrity of Common Sense. We may, for what concerns us here, lump the first and the third classes together.

Those of the first class desire to defend the reality of the physical world, that is to prove the thesis or at least refute attempted disproofs of the thesis that the physical world has a status which is substantival and not adjectival upon the being of the 'knowing' mind. To do so they have to argue that anyhow some mental acts have physical realities as their objects, and that these exist and have anyhow some of their qualities and relations whether they are apprehended by a mind or not.

Consequently in the interests of physics they have to assert a doctrine like that of the intentional psychology in securing the *otherness* of objects apprehended than the apprehensions of them but going beyond it in maintaining also their *independence* from those apprehensions. For otherwise 'physical' objects would still be liable to be reduced to 'immanent contents' of psychical acts. Indeed the original doctrine of intentionality had been that the intentional object of an act of consciousness was a *mental* something, *other* than the act that had it, certainly, but none the less only a psychical proxy for a hypothetical external reality.

But the generalization of the Realist theory of consciousness leads at once to unexpected consequences; for if the physical world is saved, yet a lot more is saved than was originally wanted. All species of thinking are forms of consciousness; but if their objects too are to be emancipated, then 'concepts' or universals, numbers, laws and relations as well as 'judgments' or propositions, which are the objects of acts of conceiving and acts of judging respectively, must be allowed to be genuine entities. The integrity of Newton's world is guaranteed, but the guarantee covers also the world of Plato.

But it is from the second class, the champions of mathematics and Logic, that the strongest defence of the reality of propositions comes.

For instance, Bolzano and (quite independently of him) Frege saw that if the prevalent Kantian and psychologistic theories of know-ledge were true, then the objects of which mathematics is the study must be mental events and states, i.e. such things as 'ideas'. But if so, then mathematics and with it Logic, of which mathematics is a branch, could possess no objectivity, rigorousness or exactness. The laws of Logic would be of a piece with laws of association; demonstration would be subordinate to introspection, and truth, if it were anything at all, would be just a bit of human behaviour.

Consequently, on this side, too, the subjectivist doctrine had to be rejected, that judgments and inferences are and contain nothing save flashes in the brain-pan. And here, too, the alternative had to be that, in judging and inferring, what-I-judge and what-I-infer are both other than and independent of mental acts. There must be, then, objective Truths, which are true whether anyone thinks them or not, and there must be objective falsehoods which are false whether anyone thinks them or not. Certainly they do not *exist*; for they are not things in time. They are not members of the world of physical things and events, nor yet of the world of mental things and events. But they are not homeless, for the division of reality into mind and matter is not exhaustive. There is the Third Realm, in which truths, falsehoods, universals, numbers, relations and the like have their being. They *are*, but as they do not *exist* they may be said to *subsist*.

Accordingly Logic (and with it mathematics) need no longer be described as a branch of psychology. It has realities for its subject matter; it is in fact largely if not entirely the science of the forms of propositions.

But besides these general reasons for holding that what-we-think must be independent of our thinking it, there are some special ones.

(*a*) It is ordinarily allowed that judgments are either true or false. But the slightest consideration of what is meant by 'true' and 'false' compels us to say that if my judgment that X is Y is true, then it is true that X is Y whether or not I judge it; or if I think falsely that X is Z, then it is false that X is Z whether or not I think it. Truths are not made true by being believed; and not even by being vehemently believed are falsehoods made true. So that it is true (if it is true) that X is Y and false that X is Z, independently of the existence or the degree of intensity of anyone's belief in those propositions.

More, it seems clear at first sight, that if it is true that X is Y, then it always will be true and always has been true. (Of course the 'always' does not necessarily attach to X's being Y, which may very well be dated.) Similarly with falsehoods.

So truths and falsehoods seem to be eternal or (better) timeless. But beliefs belong to the biographies of persons and so are necessarily dated. Consequently, thinking acts must be regarded as temporary *visitors* to non-temporal truths and falsehoods. Propositions, then, as truths and falsehoods are objective to thinkings and not existential parts or products of them.

(*b*) The argument which Ehrlich[1] well calls 'the Operation with

---

[1] *Kant und Husserl,* by Walter Ehrlich (Niemeyer, Halle, 1923).

Identity' is used a lot by Bolzano and Frege and, after them, by Husserl and Meinong. It takes three main channels.

(1) Several persons—in principle an infinite number of persons—can think the same thing or make the same judgment. Truths are 'public'; and falsehoods are no less so. Otherwise neither sciences nor superstitions could have disciples or adherents.

But acts of thinking are the acts of persons and are as 'private' as toothaches and hiccoughs; two acts may be *similar*, but they must be numerically different or they couldn't be two—or similar. Acts of thinking must be at least as numerous as thinking persons. Obviously, in fact, they are vastly more so.

But if acts cannot be shared, the only sense in which 'a thought' may be shared, imparted or communicated, is that the same *cogitatum* is the object of numerically different acts. And this will be a proposition 'accusative' to all, but independent of any of the acts of thinking.

I don't know how to *prove* that several minds can think the same thing. Proof that we ordinarily take it for granted that this is possible is afforded by the existence of such terms as 'popular fallacies', 'wide-spread beliefs', 'teaching', 'persuasion', 'agreement', 'disagreement', 'understanding' and the like. The jury system postulates the possibility and I, even to venture to read this paper to you, must assume that the communication of thoughts is not in principle impossible.

(2) One person can think the same thing any number of times. His mental processes, however similar, will be numerous—or we couldn't use the phrase 'any number of times'—but the thing he thinks is numerically the same.

(3) One person (or any number of persons) may think the same thing in many different sorts of *attitude*. On Monday he may *entertain the idea* 'that X is Y', on Tuesday *surmise* it, on Wednesday *opine* it, on Thursday *believe* it, on Friday *know* it.

But if that which once was surmised now is known, the difference of attitude can have imparted no difference into the thing so thought.

The premisses of these three 'operations with identity' are not indeed self-evident but they are more than plausible; for their contradictions would be paradoxical. So the conclusion is that *either* there do subsist genuinely and independently such things as 'that $7 + 5 = 12$' and 'that $7 + 5 = 2$' *or* paradoxical views about the nature of thinking must be adopted.

III. ARGUMENTS FROM THE NATURE OF LANGUAGE FOR THE BEING OF PROPOSITIONS QUA SENTENCE-MEANINGS

(*a*) In the communication or expression of thought to others (or to ourselves), we employ symbols. Whether or not we always think in symbols, at least we *tell* what we think in symbols. Now, in order to be clear about the nature of symbols we have to distinguish on the one hand between the symbol and that which it symbolizes, e.g. between the sentence and what the sentence states, and on the other hand between what the symbol symbolizes and the state of mind in which the person is as he employs the symbol. In short, there are three things to be kept separate, what the person *says*, that which his sentence *means*, and what mental condition his utterance evinces or is evidence of. Philosophers commonly confuse and identify the *meaning* of a person's statement and his mental condition in which he makes the statement.

But if, as we must, we distinguish the two things, we are *ipso facto* distinguishing a mental process on the one hand and a proposition on the other.

Now if language is to be, what we must take it to be, a vehicle of inter-personal communication, it must be possible for two or any number of minds to find the *same* meaning in any given word or sentence. And this requires not merely that a linguistic code be public property, but, much more, that *meanings*, i.e. concepts ('word-meanings') and propositions ('sentence-meanings'), are public property. When a word means the same thing to Smith and to Jones we have two conceivings but only one concept; and when a sentence means the same thing to Smith and to Jones, two think-ings occur, namely, one in Smith's and the other in Jones' private life, but the proposition that they think is not the perquisite of either.

This argument from the possibility of inter-personal communi-cation can be reinforced by reference to the facts of translation and paraphrase. Different groups of noises may have the same meaning or, as in the case of puns, one noise-group may have two different meanings. But as in any case the argument is only a special applica-tion of the previous 'operations with identity', I need not develop it any further.

(*b*) But there is a special sort of apprehension which calls for examination at this point, namely, the *understanding* of what is said. If I *understand* a statement that is made, I am clearly knowing what is stated. Yet even if the statement does in reality state a *fact*, nevertheless I may know what is stated without knowing the fact. I may, for instance, very well understand Jones' statement 'the population of Rome is smaller than that of Birmingham' without knowing what the relation really is between the two populations.

The proposition theory explains this by distinguishing between what is stated and the real relation; the former is a proposition, the latter is that of which the proposition is true or, perhaps, false. So that in understanding a statement I am apprehending a real something, namely, a real proposition; but as I do not yet know whether this proposition is true, I do not know whether the population of Rome really is smaller than that of Birmingham.

IV. ARGUMENTS FROM THE SPECIAL CHARACTERS OF THE SUBJECT-MATTER THAT LOGIC STUDIES

It is argued by Husserl and (virtually) by Meinong that only if there are such entities as objective Meanings—and propositions are just a *species* of Meaning—is there anything for Logic to be about. Formal Logic can be seen, both from its title and from its performance, to be the science of the *forms* of something. But the things which have these forms are not physical substances or events nor yet mental substances or events. A stone wall does not *contradict* a wind; nor is a state of mind a conclusion in Barbara.

Logic studies the ways in which one thing follows from another, in which one thing is compatible with another, contradicts, corroborates or necessitates another, is a special case of another or the nerve of another. And so on.

But what are these 'things'?

(*a*) When we say 'It is true that X is Y', 'It is false that X is Z', by the word *it* we do not denote a belief or opinion or anything mental. If we did, we should always be able to amplify and say 'Jones' opinion' or 'Smith's belief that X is Y is true'.

But not only is it an empirical fact that we don't do this and don't mean it; but we could relatively seldom do it if we tried. For, however hard it may be to find out what is true or false about X, it must be harder *also* to find out facts about other people's state of mind bearing on the nature of X.

It is to be noted that whereas when I say 'It is fine', I am implicitly referring to a specified *it*, namely, the weather in *my* locality at the moment of my making the statement, when I say 'It is true that X is

Y', no reference whatsoever is made or suggested to any specified person as *its* author.

Of course we can and do in some cases say 'Smith's opinion that X is Y is true' or 'is false' (though we more usually employ semi-ethical adjectives like 'right', 'correct', 'wrong', 'mistaken'), but even when we do so, we should ordinarily be prepared to emend and say 'What Smith believes, namely that X is Y, is true', and so to characterize as true what he believes and not his believing it.

Similarly, we ordinarily find no difficulty in saying of a given thing that several people believe *it* and so, if we think it false, 'make the same mistake' or 'labour under the same delusion'. If then 'it' is not anyone's state of mind, and is true or is false, it can only be *the proposition* 'that X is Y'.

(*b*) And more convincing still, what else than propositions can the things be between which we find the relations, contradiction, implication, compatibility, incompatibility, condition and consequent, premisses and conclusion? Even those who find 'judgments' everywhere and propositions nowhere find that some judgments cohere whereas others are incoherent. What is the status of the terms between which these relations hold?

(1) When A is incompatible with B, A and B cannot be the names of *substances*; for substances may co-exist but they can no more be compatible or incompatible than honesty can be green or blue. Nor can they be the names of *facts*. For it must be nonsense to say 'the fact that X is Y is incompatible with the fact that X is Z'. 'Incompatibility' must disqualify at least one of the incompatibles from being a fact.

(2) Nor can A and B denote states of mind such as opining and surmising. For, though A is incompatible with B, there is no incompatibility in my opining A and my surmising B, or even between my believing A and my believing B. In other words, states of mind may very well co-exist though the things thought cannot both be true.

SUMMARY

These seem to me to be the main arguments for the proposition theory, the conclusion of which may be put as follows:

There are (at least) two main sorts of being, namely, actual and ideal being or existing and subsisting. Things in the world are existents, existing at a time and for a time and in many cases also in a place. These are sub-divided into physical things and mental things, both supporting qualities, states and relations. The system of them may be called the World.

But there is another realm of being which our 'prejudice in favour of the actual' causes most of us to ignore or repudiate. This may be called, after Frege, the Third Realm, and its members are not physical but are not, for that, any the more mental. (The only reason why people are prone to psychologize ideal entities and treat them as 'ideas in the mind' seems to be because they share with mental states and processes the negative property of being inaccessible to sense perception.) Entities in the Third Realm do not exist, for they are not anywhere or anywhen, but they *are* in some other way, for they too have qualities and relations. Their mode of being may be called *subsistence*.

There are several sorts of entities in this realm:

(*a*) There are universals.

(*b*) There are relations.

(*c*) There are numbers.

(*d*) There are objective truths and objective falsehoods or there are propositions.

Of all alike we can say:

(*a*) They are not sensible.

(*b*) They can be *thought*.

(*c*) Somehow or other they alone make anything—even what exists in the world—knowable or thinkable.

Further (to put the conclusion in a more drastic form) since these things *are*, for they have qualities and relations and possess their status and their characters independently of other entities, they may properly be called *substances*. There is no reason why the title should be reserved for those particular realities which endure through change and so *age*. Anything which is and does not depend for its being upon anything else is a substance, whether it is in the world or not.

The proposition theory holds then that propositions are 'objective' or 'genuine entities' in the sense of being *substances*. By parity of reasoning universals, relations, numbers, etc., would also be substances in the same sense.

In consequence the sentences, 'Honesty is the worst policy' and 'Honesty is the best policy', are *names* of two different substances of which one has the quality of being false, the other that of being true. Every sentence that makes sense is, then, a proper name and unambiguously denotes a substance. Probably there is an infinite number of these substances most of which never have been and never will be apprehended by any human being.

OBJECTIONS TO THE PROPOSITION THEORY

I begin with some objections which it would be natural to make, though I think them invalid.

(1) Many would object to the view that an entity may *be* without *existing*. But until a proof is given that there is no status other than the status which such things as trees and persons or toothaches and storms have, not much weight can be given to the objection. A lively sense of reality is a salutary thing, but it has to be proved and not merely felt that a Plato's sense of reality is inferior to the ploughboy's.

(2) '*Entia non sunt multiplicanda praeter necessitatem*' is also a healthy admonition to economy; but while it should encourage us to dispense with substantial propositions if we can, it cannot warrant us in dispensing with them if the arguments for them have *necessitas*.

(3) 'If propositions are substances, then they should do something.' But subsistents cannot be causes or agencies, so it is no disgrace that they do not justify themselves by works. And anyhow, numbers don't do anything, yet we don't regard arithmetic as a fairy story.

More serious objections are as follows:

(1) The objection, which, if not the weightiest, seems certainly to be the most cogent, is this, that, whereas there would be some dignity attaching to a subsistent Truth or an Eternal Verity, no such dignity could be felt to attach to subsistent falsehoods or Eternal Lies. Yet all the arguments for the subsistence of true propositions seem to hold good for the subsistence of false ones. And if Husserl and Meinong are right in asserting that there is also a third class of absurd or nonsensical propositions (the expressions of which are still not *meaningless*), we shall apparently have to find room in our Platonic Third Realm for, e.g., subsistent Irish bulls. Not only would '$7+5 = 12$' denote a substance, but so would '$7+5 = 2$' and 'some round squares are not red-headed'.

(2) I find more weight in this next argument.

Just as no theory of Representative Ideas can solve the problem of how knowledge is possible, since it both reduplicates and begs the whole question by assuming (*a*) that we can know these 'ideas', (*b*) that we can know the realities that they are representative of, and (*c*) that we can know a particular 'idea' to be representative of a particular reality, so no theory of objective propositions can help us in the least to explain how by thinking propositions we can come to know the realities that the propositions are about.

For a true proposition has to be defined as one which is in some sort of relation of correspondence to a reality or fact other than itself; and as we can think a proposition without knowing it to be true (as in false belief, opinion, guesswork, even true belief and understanding another's words), in order to know it to be true we should have also to know the fact that it corresponded with. And, if this is possible, on the one hand the proposition has not furthered the knowing of the fact but depends upon it for its own certification as true, and on the other there has turned out to be a sort of thinking, namely, the direct knowing of the fact, which does not need to have and cannot have a proposition for its intentional 'accusative'.

This argument is not final, of course, for plenty of things exist without helping to solve epistemological problems, but it weakens the argument from the intentionality of consciousness.

(3) But anyhow, if there are objective propositions, then being realities having their qualities, relations and independence of status in just the way that familiar realities like trees and persons have, the only sense in which they can be the 'accusatives' of acts of thinking is that they must be objects of *knowledge*. 'Thinking a proposition' must either consist in or embody having knowledge of and knowledge about it. And this can only mean that knowing is the presupposition of the intentional 'having' of an object, and cannot therefore be described as a species of it or explained in terms of it.

(So at least we must take it that in *knowing* we have a sort of apprehension the expression of which takes the shape of statement, and yet the object of which is not a proposition. If I know something, I express my knowledge in the form 'that X is Y'. But the meaning of the statement is simply the fact known; no intermediating proposition is required. What I know is a *fact* and not a truth about a fact, and still less a falsehood about it.)

(4) But, unfortunately, we think much that we do not know, and when we express what we believe, opine, surmise, entertain, etc., we do so in the form of statement. So it may be urged that while we do not need propositions to make possible *knowledge* and the expression of knowledge (since for that nothing between knowing and the fact known is wanted) yet we do need them to make possible the *inferior* forms of apprehension and their expression.

When I believe or guess that X is Y and express my belief in the sentence 'X is Y', we need a proposition to *be* the 'accusative' of the thinking and the meaning of the sentence. But the answer is easy. The hypothesis of substantial propositions only succeeds in giving to acts of believing something to believe, to acts of entertaining something to entertain, etc., by surreptitiously transforming all these acts into acts of knowing—knowing realities of a new sort. If, for instance, in *believing* that $7 + 5 = 12$ or that $7 + 5 = 13$, I am apprehending a genuine entity, namely, a substantial truth or a substantial falsehood, then, whatever else I am doing, I am at least having knowledge—I suppose analogous to perceptual knowledge—of these substances. True, I am not having arithmetical knowledge (as when I *know* that $7 + 5 = 12$), but I am knowing that there are these propositions and what sort of propositions they are.

In so far, then, as the proposition theory derives from the theory of intentionality, it seems to be just a new version of the old theory of Representative 'ideas'—with the two differences: (*a*) that the 'representatives' are depsychologized and are now not mental but 'neutral' entities, and (*b*) that they are no longer of the form of *terms* but of complete *judgments*. A proposition is of the form 'S-is-P' whereas an 'idea' was *either* S *or* P.

(5) If a proposition is one entity and if it corresponds to or is similar in structure to a fact, why should it be called *true* of that fact and not merely *like* it or *analogous* to it? And still more, if a proposition is unlike a fact or out of correspondence with it, why should it be called *false*? A map of Sussex is unlike the temperature-chart of an invalid, but it is not false of it; and one map of Sussex is like another, but it is not true of that other map, but only of the county.

This is one way of raising the question, What is the relation between (*a*) a true proposition and the fact that it is true of and (*b*) a false proposition and the fact or facts that it is false of? Another way would be to ask, How, if propositions are independent of other substances, are they *about* them? How can a proposition of which Julius Cæsar is the subject-term fail to be in some sort adjectival upon his being as an historical person in space and time?

And there is a special difficulty in the case of false propositions. For whereas there might well be just one fact, and one fact only, that a true proposition was like, so that the proposition could be plausibly regarded as peculiarly dedicated to it, in the case of false propositions we should have to grant not merely that it was unlike some given fact but that it was unlike *any* fact. So we could not speak of *the* fact that it was false of; and consequently we could not speak of its being false *of* anything at all.

These considerations merely advertise the fact that when we describe something as *true of* or *false of* something else, we ordinarily suppose there to be some functional relation between the somethings; as if a true proposition corresponded with the fact that it was true of not merely *per accidens* but *ex officio*. But if we once try to define a proposition as something the *business* of which is to be true of something else, we reduce it at once to some sort of a tool or instrument, and its boasted independence is gone.

(6) It seems difficult or impossible either to name or to describe propositions without borrowing either from the terminology of grammarians or from the terminology of psychologists. We have to use the names 'proposition', '*Satz*', λόγος, 'discourse', 'assertion', 'statement', '"that"- clause', 'sentence-meaning' or 'judgment', 'thought', '*Gedanke*' (Frege); and when we describe what a proposition 'does' we have to use verbs like 'declare', 'state' and 'affirm'.

(7) And, finally, when I believe something or guess something, although at the first blush I might, if pressed, certainly side with the doctrine of the theory of intentionality and aver that there is something that I am believing or something that I am guessing, I shall in the end become discontented if I find that this something is only a proposition. For I *mean* to be apprehending a fact; I didn't mean to be put off with a substitute from a different quarter of reality. The point of which is just this, that the doctrine of intentionality loses all its attractiveness if it has to maintain that believing, for instance, *is* the apprehension of a reality, only it is *another* reality than the one that I aimed at apprehending. I would as soon be told that in believing I am apprehending nothing at all as that I am apprehending a logical changeling.

I don't regard any of these objections as finally *refuting* the proposition theory. I think they impair the strength of some of the arguments for substantial propositions; and I think I can produce a positive theory which will enable us to dispense with propositions in so far as they were required in order to solve certain residual problems. And it is perhaps enough to show that substantial propositions are neither plausible nor necessary. To prove that they are *impossible* would necessitate an argument of another sort, namely, that antinomies necessarily arise from the assertion of substantial propositions. Just as Plato in the *Parmenides* (wittingly or unwittingly) shows that the theory that Eide are substances leads to antinomies, since they would then be instances of themselves or of one another; and just as Kant shows in a similar way that antinomies arise from treating, e.g. Space and Time, as substances; and just as Bradley shows that antinomies arise from treating relations as substances, so, I imagine, it could be shown that antinomies arise from treating propositions as substances. But this line of argument I do not and cannot develop.

SUBSTITUTE FOR THE PROPOSITION THEORY

In this third and last part of my paper, I am going to try to suggest a view which will enable us to solve some of the problems which the proposition theory was designed to solve.

KNOWLEDGE AND FACTS

I am going to take it that there is such a form of apprehension as knowing (in the strict sense), and that the meaning of the sentence 'I know that X is Y' differs generically from the meaning of the sentence 'I believe that X is Y'.

Next, if I know something, what I know is a fact, of which the verbal formulation takes, in the first instance, the shape of a sentence in the indicative or a statement. And the meaning of the statement, i.e. what is stated, is just the fact that I know. (The word '*fact*' does not denote any new entity or substance; if, for instance, I know that Julius Cæsar is dead, the fact that he is dead is not a new substance side by side with the substance we call 'Julius Cæsar'. Julius Cæsar's being dead in 1930 is simply part of the being of Julius Cæsar and not an entity on its own account. So the sentences 'It is a fact that Julius Cæsar is dead' and 'Julius Cæsar is dead' are equivalent in meaning; only the former needs more breath or more ink.)

In the case of knowing, then, no intermediating something, such as a substantial proposition, is lodged between my knowing and the fact. And when I state what I know, the fact that I know, and the meaning of my statement are not two things but one.

But our special problem begins here.

For (*a*) it is possible to understand a statement which is actually the statement of a fact, without knowing that fact, and (*b*) there are sorts of thinking which are inferior to knowing, in which what-is-thought is not known fact. (*c*) Consequently there are sentences expressing such thoughts which state what is not fact or what is *as far as is known* not fact, and yet seem not to be describable as *meaningless*.

If, for instance, I hear it said that the earth is round, or if I believe on my own account that the earth is round, or if, merely entertaining or supposing it, I make the statement 'the earth is round', even though it is a fact that the earth is round, yet what I apprehend in the case of understanding, what I believe in the case of belief, and what I state in the third case is not for me known fact. And this is still something 'accusative' to my thinking, and in its identity thinkable, too, to any other persons or to me on any other occasions.

I am going to reject *in its simple form* as too paradoxical the view, which I have heard, that there is no sense in which two persons *can* believe the same thing or one person believe the same thing several times, or one or several persons think the same thing in several different attitudes of mind, e.g. believing it, guessing it, opining it and entertaining it. According to this view, while the same *fact* can be *known* by several persons or by the same person several times, there is no analogous community possible of beliefs or opinions. But as the only motive for holding this paradoxical position is, I take it, the desire to reject the doctrine of objective propositions, we must try to find a way of avoiding the paradox as well as avoiding the proposition theory.

I want to begin by clearing the air.

The verb 'to think' and the more sophisticated verb 'to judge' are notoriously very ambiguous. I may be said to be thinking of X as being Y: (*a*) when I come to know that X is Y; (*b*) when I believe it; (*c*) when I opine it; (*d*) when I guess it; (*e*) when I wonder about it, question, or doubt it; (*f*) when I merely entertain or imagine it; and (*g*) when I understand it when stated by another.

I want to distinguish knowing that X is Y from all the others; so—and I think ordinary usage supports me—I shall reserve the umbrella-title 'thinking' for all these varieties of apprehension other than knowing. If I *know* that X is Y I am not to be described as *thinking* that X is Y or vice versa. We say: 'I don't *think*, I *know*', and 'I don't *know* but I *think* so and so'.

Next, I am assuming that the three applications of 'the operation with identity' are *in some sense* valid, namely, that (*a*) any number of persons can think the same thing; (*b*) one person can think the same thing any number of times; and (*c*) that the same thing may be thought by one or many persons in many *sorts* of attitude.

Here we are dealing with the last.

Now, if it is possible in any sense for A to opine identically what B believes and C guesses, we can say at once that the differences in the sort of attitude can be discounted as making no difference to the thing thought. And I want to suggest, what is certainly debatable, that the doctrine of Meinong is anyhow partly right, that there is a sort of 'thinking that' which is completely neutral and attitude-less, and that this must be present as an ingredient in all the varieties of 'thinking that'. Meinong's word 'Annahmen' has been translated 'assumption' and 'supposal', which both suffer from not being neutral enough. As regards the verb, I prefer to speak of 'entertaining' or 'imagining that' or, best of all, 'thinking of ... as'.

This seems to me the common element in all the other thinking attitudes. To believe that X is Y, opine it, guess it, question it, even probably to deny it and to want it, I must *think of* X *as* Y. Even to tell a lie, or to refute the errors of another, I must, though I know that X is not Y, think of X as being Y.

If I am right, the air is now cleared to this extent. We have only two states of mind to deal with. At the top we have knowing, the 'accusative' of which is a fact. At the bottom we have 'thinking of ... as' or 'entertaining', the 'accusative' of which is still *sub judice*.

The special characters of believing, wondering, etc., are of no relevance to our problem whatsoever.

What then am I doing when I am thinking of X as being Y? I am thinking, say, of the earth as flat, as when I want to refute a geoplanarian.

First of all, I must know what it is that I am thinking of, and what it is that I am thinking of it as being. I mean, I must know what the earth is, and what flatness is. There can be no *absolutely* unclear thinking, but if *per impossibile* there was, it would consist in thinking of P, say, as R to Q, while in *complete* ignorance of what P, R and Q were. More, I must not only know the elements, but also the sort of conjunction that they are thought of as being in. If I am thinking of Bristol as bigger than London, I must know not only what Bristol and London and bigger-than are, but also what it is for one thing to be bigger than another; and I must know that Bristol and London (unlike virtue and tomorrow) are things having a relation of size.

But I must have this much knowledge either to think of Bristol as bigger than London or to think of London as bigger than Bristol, so the *special* character of thinking of Bristol as bigger than London is not described when the knowledge is catalogued that I must possess in order to be able to think of it so.

There seems to be some respect in which thinking of Bristol as bigger than London is *analogous* to knowing, e.g., that the earth is bigger than the moon, or that London is bigger than Bristol. As in the two latter cases I am not merely knowing the natures of pairs of entities plus a relation but *a* fact about those entities *in* that relation, so in the case of thinking of X as Y we seem to be apprehending *a* something—yet it is not a fact, and we are debarred from saying that it is a proposition. X and being Y are somehow thought together, although 'that X is Y' is not, for me, the statement of a known fact.

So the question is, What *more* are we doing when we think of

X as Y or of P as R to Q, than knowing the natures of X and Y or of P, R and Q together with types of logical conjunction?

The answer that I wish to give is very tentative and involves some highly dubious dogmas.

KNOWING AND BELIEVING *versus* THINKING OF

In the writings of epistemologists, psychologists and logicians we commonly find that all such things as knowing, believing, wondering, remembering, etc., are classed together as *acts* of consciousness.

The term *act* is sometimes objected to as implying, what may not be true, that all these things are cases of *doing*, bits of *activity* as opposed to passivity. But even if the term *acts* is taken, as I think it should be, in the wider sense of *actus* rather than *actiones* to denote the actualizations of potentialities rather than the doing of deeds, it is often improperly used.

For even an *actus* is something that occurs at a moment and lasts only through a moment. But, anyhow, as ordinarily used, the verbs to know, believe, be of the opinion that, etc., denote not momentary occurrences but more or less enduring conditions. This is sometimes put by saying that these terms denote *dispositions*. When I say 'Smith knows or believes so and so', I am not saying that he is at this moment doing something or that at this moment something is happening to him, as I am when I say 'Smith is studying or considering so and so'.

When the words are used in this sense, it is possible and natural to say, 'I have known so and so for years', 'I still believe what I believed ten years ago', 'A man convinced against his will, is of the same opinion still'. As opposed to these more or less abiding 'dispositions', there certainly are also *acts* (*actus*). Thus 'I have just remembered so and so', 'I found out so and so all of a sudden', 'At 12 o'clock I was thinking of Egypt'.

I am not contented with the description of the former class as 'dispositions'. The evidence of ordinary language, anyhow, is against the view that 'having knowledge' is analogous to 'having a bad temper' or 'being subject to chilblains', and seems to denote something more akin to the possessing of property than to the liability or propensity to act or react in a certain way in certain circumstances. 'Knowledge' and 'belief' seem to denote *deposits* rather than *dispositions*.

However, whatever may be the true account of the matter, there does seem to be some sense in which one may have *known* or *believed* something for years, and only to have *thought of* it a few times, just as one may have possessed some property for years and only used it a few times. In this sense, knowing something does not involve attending to it in the way in which getting to know it or reflecting upon it does. And in this sense, too, it is possible to know or believe a great number of things at the same time while one can only attend to or think of one or two things at one moment.

It is only a pedantic way of putting the same point to say that what I know or believe is only *per accidens* 'present to my consciousness' at any given moment during my having that knowledge or belief, while it is essentially 'present to my consciousness' at the moment when I am thinking of it—for they are almost equivalent expressions.

A second difference is this: In the case of the sorts of thinking which are *acts*, it seems usually to be true not only that if I am thinking I must be thinking *of* something, but also that if I am thinking I must be thinking *in* or *in terms of* something.

I refer of course to thinking *in* images or *in* words.

The best developed and the most easily inspected class of things that we think in are words and sentences; for we talk in them too. But they are not the only class even of symbols that we think in; for much imagery also seems to be symbolic. Nor is all thinking *in* symbols. In perception, for instance, we must think as well as sense and this sort of thinking *need* not be *in* anything but the sense-data themselves. And sense-data are not symbols. Similarly, remembering involves much thinking *in* memory-images. And these too do not seem to be symbols. For symbols are artefacts and tools and they mean because they are made or selected to do so.

But I suggest that symbols, memory-images and sense-data may be classed together as different species of the genus 'presentative'— meaning by 'presentative' that which when itself directly present (in some way or other) to consciousness enables the mind to think of some *other*[1] object specially connected with it which is not in the same way directly present. But I have no special theory of the roles of either words and images, or memory-images or sense-data in thinking: I appeal merely to ordinary experience whether in fact thinking is not always *in* some one of these things.

The point that I wish to make here is that though we speak of thinking in French, we never talk of knowing or believing or opining in French. And the reason is clear. The having of knowledge,

---

[1] It may be the case that sometimes what I am thinking of coincides wholly or partly with what I am thinking *in*. In such cases the object of which I am thinking may be called Self-Presentative. I take objects of *perception* to belong to this class.

belief or opinion is not the having it present to consciousness. So it is not had *in* presentatives.

For the most part I shall be concentrating on the thinking that is in linguistic symbols, namely, words or, better, sentences, since examples can be provided and published and inspected. Where images are the symbols the account will hold without important modifications.

I can now put my whole question in this way; when I am thinking of X as being Y or of P as being R to Q in terms of the sentence 'X is Y' or 'P is R to Q', of what is the statement presentative—when it is not the statement of a fact known to me and is very likely not the statement of a fact at all?

We must resist the temptation to call this whatever-it-is an Imaginary Fact, though the temptation is a real one; since what I am thinking I am thinking as if it were a fact, even though I may not be believing or supposing it to be one. The title would be wrong because what is fact is not anything merely imaginary and what is merely imagined is *ipso facto* not known fact; so the phrase 'Imaginary Fact' would resemble the phrase 'Round Square' in necessarily not being the name of anything. I mention the temptation, however, for this reason. When I believe or surmise that the earth is flat, I naturally take this 'flat earth' to belong in the same realm of reality as the 'numerous stars' or 'populous London'. I would not accept the tepid justification that 'there *is* a subsistent proposition (a false one) which is there for me to believe'; I want what I believe to be not a falsehood and not even a truth, in a word, not a denizen of a realm of Platonized 'that'-clauses but simply a geographical fact among geographical facts.

STATEMENT AND FACTS

I want to work round to the solution of this final question by solving first a simpler one, namely, What am I apprehending when I *understand* some one else's statement without knowing whether or not it states a fact?

As facts have logical form, so statements have grammatical form; and as facts have a matter or constituents in that form, so statements have a grammatical matter or grammatical constituents in that grammatical form. I mean that the sentence consists of words of various grammatical types, such as nouns, adjectives, prepositions, verbs, etc., but it isn't a mere random assortment of these, but an ordered system of them.

And as there are many facts of the same logical form, but of different constituents, of the same constituents but different forms, and of different constituents 'and different forms, so it is with the grammatical units we call sentences.

But there is an important difference: we can fabricate sentences but we cannot fabricate facts. Accordingly, there may be, and in fact there are, many sentences which do not state facts, while there are no facts which (in principle) could not be stated.

Next, the proper business of a statement is to state a fact. Prima facie we have to take any given statement as a statement of a fact since, in a question-begging phrase, we know that there is nothing else to state. The normal or standard (even if not the customary) employment of statement is in the expression of *knowledge*.

If Jones, for instance, says, 'The Earth is flat,' we say, 'He talks as if he knew or as if he thought he knew that the Earth was flat,' implying that it would be improper and abnormal (though not necessarily unusual) to employ statement in other mental conditions. As statements and names are symbols and symbols are tools, there is no harm in speaking of the normal, standard or proper employment of them. Accordingly we can say of a name that it ought only to be used when there really is something that has that name; and we can say of a statement that it ought only to be made when there really is a fact of which the statement is the statement.

Now when Sairey Gamp repeatedly propounded statements to Betsey Prig embodying the name 'Mrs Harris', Betsey Prig naturally, though wrongly, assumed that there was a person of whom 'Mrs Harris' was the name. And she was angry when she discovered that there wasn't. And when she discovered that there wasn't any such person, she discovered that the name 'Mrs Harris' was *meaningless* in the strict sense of not being the name of anything. Yet in another sense Sairey Gamp's sentences embodying the 'name' 'Mrs Harris' had not been meaningless and Betsey Prig had understood them perfectly.

What are the two senses of the word 'meaningless', in which in one way the sentences were and in the other were not meaningless?

The answer, I think, is fairly clear. The noise 'Mrs Harris' has all the linguistic properties of a name. It is just *as if* it were a name or, to put it *in extenso*, it has all the outward characteristics that it would have had if it had been the name of someone.

So Betsey Prig in understanding the sentences which embodied the noise was knowing this fact *about* the noise, that if it was what it simulated being, a genuine name, then there was a real person called Mrs Harris; or, what comes to the same thing, if and only if there really was such a person was the noise 'Mrs Harris' a genuine name. So in this sense it was *not* meaningless, for she knew quite clearly and precisely *what* it denoted *if* it denoted anything. There is no valid inference from the occurrence of a name-like noise to the existence of a thing having that noise for its name; but there is the genuine if–then fact about the noise that it is a standard name *if* there is a person of such and such a description. For linguistically the noise 'Mrs Harris' has all the properties that it needs to have to be a standard name. So 'Mrs Harris' is not a standard name, nor yet a mere noise. We can only call it a quasi-name.

A similar account holds of statements. In the strict sense, only those statements *mean* something which state a fact to some one who knows the fact. But there are many collocations of words which are *as if* they were standard statements. Grammatically there is nothing wrong or deficient in them. And these, though in the strict sense meaningless, are not meaningless in the way in which a haphazard collocation of words is meaningless. For we can see what they ought to mean, i.e. we can see what would have to be the case for them to be standard statements of fact, namely, that *if* so and so was the case, *then* this sentence would be the standard statement of it.

So a statement which does not state a fact known to us does not genuinely symbolize a reality and is therefore only a quasi-symbol. Its intelligibility consists in the fact that from simple inspection of it we can know that it is like what it would be *if* such and such were the fact and the fact were stated in a standard statement.

Again, certain sorts of markings on paper or cloth constitute maps. And a map is a map of some place. But if I come across a set of marks on paper more or less resembling some map that I have seen, though I *should* ask of it in the first instance, 'Is this a map?' in fact I accept its prima facies and ask 'What place is this a map of?' As if I had swiftly made the fallacious inference, 'This is like a map, therefore it is a map.' Now an 'imaginary map' can't be called a map of any place—for there is no *such* place, i.e. there is no place having such and such a coast-line, such and such towns and rivers. So strictly it is not a map at all. But (as the 'such' shows) if there was a place having a coast-line of a given description, and towns and rivers of a given description, then these markings would be a map of it. *Understanding* the map consists in seeing that it is *as if it were* a map of a place of such and such a description, without knowing whether there is such a place or not.

Now when a statement states a known fact about, say, Julius Cæsar, Julius Cæsar is a *constituent* in the fact; but the statement is *not* a constituent of the fact (save in the artificial cases of statements which state facts about themselves).

But in understanding a quasi-statement-of-fact I am knowing a fact *about* the statement, a fact, therefore, of which the statement is a constituent. *This* fact, however, is not anywhere *stated*, but only exhibited.

To recapitulate: understanding a statement embodies but does not consist in knowing the nature of the entities that the constituents of the statement, the words, mean, and knowing the form of fact which the grammatical form of the statement means. It goes beyond this knowledge and consists in knowing if *what* was the case would the statement state a fact. I understand a statement when I know what would make it a statement of fact. I know the peculiar constituents and structure of the statement, and further I know that having precisely that constitution it would be a normal or standard statement *if* so and so were the case (e.g. *if* the earth were flat and not round).

So that understanding the statement 'X is Y' is a case of knowing; not knowing that X really is Y, but knowing about the statement 'X is Y' that it is as if (it has the characters that it would have if) X is (or were) Y.

What is known is a hypothetical fact[1] or an if–then fact about the statement—and of course also about X.

THINKING OF ... AS

This brings us back to the original problem: *what* am I thinking when I am thinking of X as being Y?

The phrase 'to think of ... as' itself gives us the clue. It simply means to think of X as if it is (or were) Y, i.e. to think of X in the same way as one would think of it if it were Y and—we must add—one knew it.

Now if X were Y and I knew that X was Y, then in thinking of X what would be the sentence that I would think in? Surely in the sentence 'X is Y'. So, too, when I don't know that X is Y, in thinking of it as being Y, I shall be thinking of it in the statement 'X is Y'.

And here, too, as in the case of understanding another's statement, the statement is not *presentative* of a known fact, but it is a *constituent* of one, namely, the hypothetical fact about it that if, and only if, X is

---

[1] By a hypothetical fact I do not of course mean something of which it is a matter of conjecture whether it is a fact or not, but simply a fact the statement of which is of the form 'if X then Y'. I see no reason for denying that there are such facts and naturally I cannot accept the view of Meinong that 'if–then' statements state a relation between 'objectives' or propositions.

(or were) Y, the statement 'X is Y' does (would) state a fact. We may apply this to the thinking that is not in sentences but in images. (And it is just worth while to mention that the phrase 'to *imagine* X as Y' is not less common than 'to think of X as Y'.) I think of Smith as being taller than Jones in the visual image of Smith standing by Jones' side and towering over him. Now I cannot say that this image depicts the taller-ness of Smith than Jones, since for all I know Smith is not taller than Jones. But if Smith were taller than Jones and I knew it, then in thinking of the relative heights of Smith and Jones I would employ as a normal presentative the image of Smith towering over Jones. And as I can fabricate images in precisely the same way as I can fabricate sentences, I can, if I like, think of Smith in just the same way as I would if I knew him to be taller than Jones, namely, in the visual image of him towering over Jones.

The image does not present the fact that Smith is taller than Jones—there may be no such fact—but it is as if it did. It is therefore a *constituent* of the hypothetical fact that the image depicts their relative heights if and only if Smith is taller than Jones.

One qualification must be made. I have argued that 'to think of X as Y' means, when fully expressed, 'to think of X in the same way as one would think of it if X was Y and one knew it to be so'. And 'in the same way', I have suggested, means 'in the same sentence' or 'in the same image'. But it must be noticed that the sentence (or image) plays different roles in the case of knowledge and the case of mere thinking. In the one it does present a known fact, in the other it does not. So the phrase 'to think in . . .' must mean something different in the two cases. As of course it does. For in the one case it means to think in a symbol, in the other in only a quasi-symbol. The symbol proper—i.e. the statement of a known fact—symbolizes a fact in which it itself is not a constituent. The quasi-symbol *exhibits* but does not symbolize a fact which is in part *about itself*, namely, that it has such grammatical properties that it may state a fact and does so if there is such and such a fact.

I am afraid this sounds obscure enough. But, if it holds water, it will enable us to see in what sense several persons or one person on several occasions may 'think the same thing'. For we may all think of X as Y, since (*a*) X is a known reality (or we couldn't think about it); (*b*) Y is, e.g., a real and known quality, though not known to qualify X; and (*c*) we can all think of X as Y, for we can all think in the same sentence 'X is Y'. (I don't think there is any special difficulty in the notion of the same sentence having several occurrences. We play the same tune ten times over, yet it is still the same tune; we can all sing the same song and we can repeat the same gesture or moue. There is a special difficulty in the case of images; for we cannot *guarantee* that your image has the same design as mine.)

And so, if there is this sense in which several people can think alike of X as being Y, there is no further difficulty in allowing several people to *believe* the same thing. For the difference between believing that X is Y and thinking of X as Y is a difference of attitude and not of 'accusative'.

CONCLUSIONS

(1) There are not substantial propositions. There are facts, there are standard symbols, i.e. such as are statements of known facts, and there are non-standard or quasi-symbols which in grammatical structure, though not in presentative function, are like standard symbols. There is no grammatical difference between standard statements and non-standard ones such that from an inspection of the mere grammar of a sentence we can tell if it states a fact or not. But there is a relation between the grammatical structure of a statement and the logical structure of the fact that it states if it states one. So that we can know what is the logical structure of the fact *if such a fact there be* that the statement states.

Mutatis mutandis the same account will hold good of other sorts of symbols, such as images, maps, gestures, etc.

(2) The name 'proposition' then denotes, what grammarians have always used it to denote, the same as 'sentence' or 'statement'. Or it might be extended to cover all other symbols which do or might function as symbolic presentatives of facts. There would be no harm in calling maps, diagrams, pictures, images, etc., 'propositions' and reserving 'sentence' or 'statement' for *verbal* propositions.

'Proposition', then, is a name not for what I think but for what I think and talk *in*.

(3) I suggest that in the first instance, anyhow, that of which we say '*it* is true that . . .' or '*it* is false that . . .' is simply the statement or the sentence or the proposition. Only such things as sentences are properly to be described as true or false. A truth is just a true sentence, i.e. one which states a fact.

And I think the evidence of ordinary linguistic usage bears me out here. We *tell* the truth, we *say* truly, many a true *word* is *spoken* in jest. We don't ask 'Is it true to *think* that X is Y?' but 'Is it true to *say* that X is Y?'

Derivatively from this, we may without harm go on to label beliefs and opinions as true or false, though I think it is more usual to employ adjectives of another sort like 'right' and 'wrong', 'well-founded' and 'mistaken'.

Nor does it seem paradoxical to suggest (what follows from this) that the things which *contradict* one another are *dicta*. Of course contradiction is not a *grammatical* relation, and Logic, in studying such things as contradiction, incompatibility, etc., is not studying things first revealed by philology. Rather, in seeing that the statement 'X is Y' contradicts the statement 'X is not Y', the logician is seeing a logical relation between the apodoses of two hypothetical facts—namely, X is Y if 'X is Y' states a fact, and X is not Y if 'X is not Y' states a fact. Both hypothetical facts are facts together, but the apodoses *taken by themselves* cannot state coexistent facts.

(4) If this is so, then 'the problem of truth' is of extremely slight philosophical importance. There are important logical problems about the forms of facts, important epistemological problems about the nature of knowing, believing, opining, etc., and, anyhow, an interesting psychological problem as to what makes us believe what we do not know. But a study of the properties of sentences and markings on paper in virtue of which they state or do not state facts and are or are not maps seems a very departmental question.

Indeed this might have been anticipated. For we want to know the natures of realities, and questions about the natures of truths and falsehoods about the natures of realities are clearly subsidiary. For if they weren't subsidiary, we should have, I suppose, to say that, in order to know the nature of anything, we must first know something else, namely, a truth about the thing, and then come to know that it *is* true of the thing—which second stage, if possible, renders the first a detour and, if impossible, a blind alley.

3

SYSTEMATICALLY MISLEADING EXPRESSIONS

Reprinted from 'Proceedings of the Aristotelian Society', vol. XXXII, *1932, by permission of the editor*

Philosophical arguments have always largely, if not entirely, consisted in attempts to thrash out 'what it means to say so and so'. It is observed that men in their ordinary discourse, the discourse, that is, that they employ when they are not philosophizing, use certain expressions, and philosophers fasten on to certain more or less radical types or classes of such expressions and raise their question about all expressions of a certain type and ask what they really mean.

Sometimes philosophers say that they are analysing or clarifying the 'concepts' which are embodied in the 'judgments' of the plain man or of the scientist, historian, artist or who-not. But this seems to be only a gaseous way of saying that they are trying to discover what is meant by the general terms contained in the sentences which they pronounce or write. For, as we shall see, '*x* is a concept' and '*y* is a judgment' are themselves systematically misleading expressions.

But the whole procedure is very odd. For, if the expressions under consideration are intelligently used, their employers must already know what they mean and do not need the aid or admonition of philosophers before they can understand what they are saying. And if their hearers understand what they are being told, they too are in no such perplexity that they need to have this meaning philosophically 'analysed' or 'clarified' for them. And, at least, the philosopher himself must know what the expressions mean, since otherwise he could not know what it was that he was analysing.

Certainly it is often the case that expressions are not being intelligently used and to that extent their authors are just gabbling parrot-wise. But then it is obviously fruitless to ask what the expressions really mean. For there is no reason to suppose that they mean anything. It would not be mere gabbling if there was any such reason. And if the philosopher cares to ask what these expressions *would* mean *if* a rational man were using them, the only answer would be that they would mean what they would then mean. Understanding them would be enough, and that could be done by any reasonable listener. Philosophizing could not help him, and, in fact, the philosopher himself would not be able to begin unless he simply understood them in the ordinary way.

It seems, then, that if an expression can be understood, then it is already known in that understanding what the expression means. So there is no darkness present and no illumination required or possible.

And if it is suggested that the non-philosophical author of an expression (be he plain man, scientist, preacher or artist) does know but only knows dimly or foggily or confusedly what his expression means, but that the philosopher at the end of his exploration knows clearly, distinctly and definitely what it means, a twofold answer seems inevitable. First, that if a speaker only knows confusedly what his expression means, then he is in that respect and to that extent just gabbling. And it is not the role—nor the achievement—of the philosopher to provide a medicine against that form of flux. And next, the philosopher is not *ex officio* concerned with ravings and ramblings: he studies expressions for what they mean when intelligently and intelligibly employed, and not as noises emitted by this idiot or that parrot.

Certainly expressions do occur for which better substitutes could be found and should be or should have been employed. (1) An expression may be a breach of, e.g., English or Latin grammar. (2) A word may be a foreign word, or a rare word or a technical or trade term for which there exists a familiar synonym. (3) A phrase or sentence may be clumsy or unfamiliar in its structure. (4) A word or phrase may be equivocal and so be an instrument of possible puns. (5) A word or phrase may be ill-chosen as being general where it should be specific, or allusive where the allusion is not known or not obvious. (6) Or a word may be a malapropism or a misnomer. But the search for paraphrases which shall be more swiftly intelligible to a given audience or more idiomatic or stylish or more grammatically or etymologically correct is merely applied lexicography or philology —it is not philosophy.

We ought then to face the question: Is there such a thing as analysing or clarifying the meaning of the expressions which people use, except in the sense of substituting philologically better expressions for philologically worse ones? (We might have put the problem in the more misleading terminology of 'concepts' and asked: How can philosophizing so operate by analysis and clarification, upon the concepts used by the plain man, the scientist or the artist, that after this operation the concepts are illumined where before they were dark? The same difficulties arise. For there can be no such thing as a confused concept, since either a man is conceiving, i.e. knowing the nature of his subject-matter, or he is failing to do so. If he is succeeding, no clarification is required or possible; and if he is failing, he must find out more or think more about the subject-matter, the apprehension of the nature of which we call his 'concept'. But this will not be philosophizing about the concept, but exploring further the nature of the thing, and so will be economics, perhaps, or astronomy or history. But as I think that it can be shown that it is not true in any natural sense that 'there are concepts', I shall adhere to the other method of stating the problem.)

The object of this paper is not to show what philosophy in general is investigating, but to show that there remains an important sense in which philosophers can and must discover and state what is really meant by expressions of this or that radical type, and none the less that these discoveries do not in the least imply that the naïve users of such expressions are in any doubt or confusion about what their expressions mean or in any way need the results of the philosophical analysis for them to continue to use intelligently their ordinary modes of expression or to use them so that they are intelligible to others.

The gist of what I want to establish is this. There are many expressions[1] which occur in non-philosophical discourse which, though they are perfectly clearly understood by those who use them and those who hear or read them, are nevertheless couched in grammatical or syntactical forms which are in a demonstrable way *improper* to the states of affairs which they record (or the alleged states of affairs which they profess to record). Such expressions can

---

[1] I use 'expression' to cover single words, phrases and sentences. By 'statement' I mean a sentence in the indicative. When a statement is true, I say it 'records' a fact or state of affairs. False statements do not record. To know that a statement is true is to know that something is the case and that the statement records it. When I barely understand a statement I do not know that it records a fact, nor need I know the fact that it records, if it records one. But I know what state of affairs *would* obtain if the statement recorded a state of affairs.

Every significant statement is a quasi-record, for it has both the requisite structure and constituents to be a record. But knowing these, we don't yet know that it is a record of a fact. False statements are pseudo-records and are no more records than pseudo-antiquities are antiquities. So the question What do false statements state? is meaningless if 'state' means 'record'. If it means What *would* they record if they recorded something being the case? the question contains its own answer.

be reformulated and for philosophy but *not* for non-philosophical discourse must be reformulated into expressions of which the syntactical form is proper to the facts recorded (or the alleged facts alleged to be recorded).

When an expression is of such a syntactical form that it is improper to the fact recorded, it is systematically misleading in that it naturally suggests to some people—though not to 'ordinary' people—that the state of affairs recorded is quite a different sort of state of affairs from that which it in fact is.

I shall try to show what I am driving at by examples. I shall begin by considering a whole class of expressions of one type which occur and occur perfectly satisfactorily in ordinary discourse, but which are, I argue, *systematically misleading*, that is to say, that they are couched in a syntactical form improper to the facts recorded and proper to facts of quite another logical form than the facts recorded. (For simplicity's sake, I shall speak as if all the statements adduced as examples are true. For false statements are not formally different from true ones. Otherwise grammarians could become omniscient. And when I call a statement 'systematically misleading' I shall not mean that it is false, and certainly not that it is senseless. By 'systematically' I mean that all expressions of that grammatical form would be misleading in the same way and for the same reason.)

I. QUASI-ONTOLOGICAL STATEMENTS

Since Kant, we have, most of us, paid lip service to the doctrine that 'existence is not a quality' and so we have rejected the pseudo-implication of the ontological argument: 'God is perfect, being perfect entails being existent, ∴. God exists.' For if existence is not a quality, it is not the sort of thing that can be entailed by a quality.

But until fairly recently it was not noticed that if in 'God exists' 'exists' is not a predicate (save in grammar), then in the same statement 'God' cannot be (save in grammar) the subject of predication. The realization of this came from examining negative existential propositions like 'Satan does not exist' or 'unicorns are non-existent'. If there is no Satan, then the statement 'Satan does not exist' cannot be about Satan in the way in which 'I am sleepy' is about me. Despite appearances the word 'Satan' cannot be signifying a subject of attributes.

Philosophers have toyed with theories which would enable them to continue to say that 'Satan does not exist' is none the less still somehow about Satan, and that 'exists' still signifies some sort of attribute or character, although not a quality.

So some argued that the statement was about something described as 'the idea of Satan', others that it was about a subsistent but non-actual entity called 'Satan'. Both theories in effect try to show that something may *be* (whether as being 'merely mental' or as being in 'the realm of subsistents'), but not be in existence. But as we can say 'round squares do not exist', and 'real nonentities do not exist', this sort of interpretation of negative existentials is bound to fill either the realm of subsistents or the realm of ideas with walking self-contradictions. So the theories had to be dropped and a new analysis of existential propositions had to begin.

Suppose I assert of (apparently) the general subject 'carnivorous cows' that they 'do not exist', and my assertion is true, I cannot really be talking about carnivorous cows, for there are none. So it follows that the expression 'carnivorous cows' is not really being used, though the grammatical appearances are to the contrary, to denote the thing or things of which the predicate is being asserted. And in the same way as the verb 'exists' is not signifying the character asserted, although grammatically it looks as if it was, the real predicate must be looked for elsewhere.

So the clue of the grammar has to be rejected and the analysis has been suggested that 'carnivorous cows do not exist' means what is meant by 'no cows are carnivorous' or 'no carnivorous beasts are cows'. But a further improvement seems to be required.

'Unicorns do not exist' seems to mean what is meant by 'nothing is *both* a quadruped *and* herbivorous *and* the wearer of one horn' (or whatever the marks of being a unicorn are). And this does not seem to imply that there are some quadrupeds or herbivorous animals.

So 'carnivorous cows do not exist' ought to be rendered 'nothing is both a cow and carnivorous', which does not, as it stands, imply that anything is either.

Take now an apparently singular subject as in 'God exists' or 'Satan does not exist'. If the former analysis was right, then here too 'God' and 'Satan' are in fact, despite grammatical appearance, predicative expressions. That is to say, they are that element in the assertion that something has or lacks a specified character or set of characters which signifies the character or set of characters by which the subject is being asserted to be characterized. 'God exists' must mean what is meant by 'something, and one thing only, is omniscient, omnipotent and infinitely good' (or whatever else are the characters summed in the compound character of being a god and the only god). And 'Satan does not exist' must mean what is meant by 'nothing is both devilish and alone in being devilish', or perhaps 'nothing is both devilish and called "Satan",' or even '"Satan" is not the proper name of anything'. To put it roughly, 'x exists' and 'x does not exist' do not assert or deny that a given subject of attributes x has the attribute of existing, but assert or deny the attribute of being x-ish or being an x of something not named in the statement.

Now I can show my hand. I say that expressions such as 'carnivorous cows do not exist' are systematically misleading and that the expressions by which we paraphrased them are not or are not in the same way or to the same extent systematically misleading. But they are not false, nor are they senseless. They are true, and they really do mean what their less systematically misleading paraphrases mean. Nor (save in a special class of cases) is the non-philosophical author of such expressions ignorant or doubtful of the nature of the state of affairs which his expression records. He is not a whit misled. There is a trap, however, in the form of his expression, but a trap which only threatens the man who has begun to generalize about sorts or types of states of affairs and assumes that every statement gives in its syntax a clue to the logical form of the fact that it records. I refer here not merely nor even primarily to the philosopher, but to any man who embarks on abstraction.

But before developing this theme I want to generalize the results of our examination of what we must now describe as 'so-called existential statements'. It is the more necessary that, while most philosophers are now forewarned by Kant against the systematic misleadingness of 'God exists', few of them have observed that the same taint infects a whole host of other expressions.

If 'God exists' means what we have said it means, then patently 'God is an existent', 'God is an entity', 'God has being', or 'existence' require the same analysis. So '. . . is an existent', '. . . is an entity' are only bogus predicates, and that of which (in grammar) they are asserted are only bogus subjects.

And the same will be true of all the items in the following pair of lists.

None of these statements is really about Mr Pickwick. For if they are true, there is no such person for them to be about. Nor is any of them about Mr Baldwin. For if they were false, there would be no one for them to be about. Nor in any of them is the grammatical predicate that element in the statement which signifies the character that is being asserted to be characterizing or not to be characterizing something.

Mr Baldwin:	Mr Pickwick:
is a being	is a nonentity.
is real, or a reality.	is unreal or an unreality, or an appearance.
is a genuine entity.	is a bogus or sham entity.
is a substance.	is not a substance.
is an actual object or entity.	is an unreal object or entity.
is objective.	is not objective or is subjective.
is a concrete reality.	is a fiction or figment.
is an object.	is an imaginary object.
is.	is not.
	is a mere idea.
	is an abstraction.
	is a logical construction.

I formulate the conclusion in this rather clumsy way. There is a class of statements of which the grammatical predicate *appears* to signify not the having of a specified character but the having (or not having) of a specified *status*. But in all such statements the appearance is a purely grammatical one, and what the statements really record can be stated in statements embodying no such quasi-ontological predicates.

And, again, in all such quasi-ontological statements the grammatical subject-word or phrase *appears* to denote or refer to something as that of which the quasi-ontological predicate is being predicated; but in fact the apparent subject term is a concealed predicative expression, and what is really recorded in such statements can be re-stated in statements no part of which even appears to refer to any such subject.

In a word, all quasi-ontological statements are systematically misleading. (If I am right in this, then the conclusion follows, which I accept, that those metaphysical philosophers are the greatest sinners who, as if they were saying something of importance, make 'Reality' or 'Being' the subject of their propositions, or 'real' the predicate. For at best what they say is systematically misleading, which is the one thing which a philosopher's propositions have no right to be; and at worst it is meaningless.)

I must give warning again that the naïve employer of such quasi-ontological expressions is not necessarily and not even probably misled. He has said what he wanted to say, and anyone who knew English would understand what he was saying. Moreover, I would add, in the cases that I have listed, the statements are not merely significant but true. Each of them records a real state of affairs. Nor *need* they mislead the philosopher. We, for instance, I hope, are not misled. But the point is that anyone, the philosopher included, who abstracts and generalizes and so tries to consider what different facts of the same type (i.e. facts of the same type about different things) have in common, is compelled to use the common grammatical form of the statements of those facts as handles with which to grasp the common logical form of the facts themselves. For (what we shall see later) as the way in which a fact *ought* to be recorded in expressions *would* be a clue to the form of that fact, we jump to the assumption that the way in which a fact *is* recorded *is* such a clue. And very often the clue is misleading and suggests that the fact is of a different form from what really is its form. 'Satan is not a reality' from its grammatical form looks as if it recorded the same sort of fact as 'Capone is not a philosopher', and so was just as much denying a character of a somebody called 'Satan' as the latter does deny a character of a somebody called 'Capone'. But it turns out that the suggestion is a fraud; for the fact recorded would have been properly or less improperly recorded in the statement ' " Satan " is not a proper name' or 'No one is called "Satan"' or 'No one is both called "Satan" and is infinitely malevolent, etc.' or perhaps 'Some people believe that someone is both called "Satan" and infinitely malevolent, but their belief is false'. And none of these statements even pretend to be 'about Satan'. Instead, they are and are patently about the noise 'Satan' or else about people who misuse it.

In the same way, while it is significant, true and directly intelligible to say 'Mr Pickwick is a fiction', it is a systematically misleading expression (i.e. an expression misleading in virtue of a formal property which it does or might share with other expressions); for it does not really record, as it appears to record, a fact of the same sort as is recorded in 'Mr Baldwin is a statesman'. The world does not contain fictions in the way in which it contains statesmen. There is no subject of attributes of which we can say '*there* is a fiction'. What we can do is to say of Dickens '*there* is a story-teller', or of Pickwick Papers '*there* is a pack of lies'; or of a sentence in that novel, which contains the pseudo-name 'Mr Pickwick', '*there* is a fable'. And when we say things of this sort, we are recording just what we recorded when we said 'Mr Pickwick is a fiction', only our new expressions do not suggest what our old one did that some subject of attributes has the two attributes of being called 'Mr Pickwick' and of being a fiction, but instead that some subject of attributes has the attributes of being called Dickens and being a coiner of false propositions and pseudo-proper names, or, on the other analysis, of being a book or a sentence which could only be true or false *if* someone was called 'Mr Pickwick'. The proposition 'Mr Pickwick is a fiction' is really, despite its prima facies, about Dickens or else about Pickwick Papers. But the fact that it is so is concealed and not exhibited by the form of the expression in which it is said.

It must be noted that the sense in which such quasi-ontological statements are misleading is not that they are false and not even that any word in them is equivocal or vague, but only that they are formally improper to the facts of the logical form which they are employed to record and proper to facts of quite another logical form. What the implications are of these notions of formal propriety or formal impropriety we shall see later on.

II. STATEMENTS SEEMINGLY ABOUT UNIVERSALS, OR QUASI-PLATONIC STATEMENTS

We often and with great convenience use expressions such as 'unpunctuality is reprehensible' and 'virtue is its own reward'. And at first sight these seem to be on all fours with 'Jones merits reproof' and 'Smith has given himself the prize'. So philosophers, taking it that what is meant by such statements as the former is precisely analogous to what is meant by such statements as the latter, have accepted the consequence that the world contains at least two sorts of objects, namely, particular like Jones and Smith, and 'universals' like unpunctuality and virtue.

But absurdities soon crop up. It is obviously silly to speak of a universal meriting reproof. You can no more praise or blame a 'universal' than you can make holes in the Equator.

Nor when we say 'unpunctuality is reprehensible' do we really suppose that unpunctuality ought to be ashamed of itself.

What we do mean is what is also meant but better expressed by 'Whoever is unpunctual deserves that other people should reprove him for being unpunctual'. For it is unpunctual men and not unpunctuality who can and should be blamed, since they are, what it is not, moral agents. Now in the new expression 'whoever is unpunctual merits reproof' the word 'unpunctuality' has vanished in favour of the predicative expression '. . . is unpunctual'. So that while in the original expression 'unpunctuality' seemed to denote the subject of which an attribute was being asserted, it now turns out to signify the having of an attribute. And we are really saying that anyone who has that attribute has the other.

Again, it is not literally true that virtue is a recipient of rewards. What is true is that anyone who is virtuous is benefited thereby. Whoever is good, gains something by being good. So the original statement was not 'about virtue' but about good men, and the grammatical subject-word 'virtue' meant what is meant by '. . . is virtuous' and so was, what it pretended not to be, a predicative expression.

I need not amplify this much. It is not literally true that 'honesty compels me to state so and so', for 'honesty' is not the name of a coercive agency. What is true is more properly put: 'Because I am honest, or wish to be honest, I am bound to state so and so.' 'Colour involves extension' means what is meant by 'Whatever is coloured is extended'; 'hope deferred maketh the heart sick' means what is meant by 'whoever for a long time hopes for something without getting it becomes sick at heart'.

It is my own view that all statements which seem to be 'about universals' are analysable in the same way, and consequently that general terms are never really the names of subjects of attributes. So 'universals' are not objects in the way in which Mt Everest is one, and therefore the age-old question what *sort* of objects they are is a bogus question. For general nouns, adjectives, etc., are not proper names, so we cannot speak of 'the objects called "equality", "justice" and "progress"'.

Platonic and anti-Platonic assertions, such as that 'equality is, or is not, a real entity', are, accordingly, alike misleading, and misleading in two ways at once; for they are both quasi-ontological statements and quasi-Platonic ones.

However, I do not wish to defend this general position here, but only to show that in *some* cases statements which from their grammatical form seem to be saying that 'honesty does so and so' or 'equality is such and such', are really saying in a formally improper way (though one which is readily understandable and idiomatically correct) 'anything which is equal to *x* is such and such' or 'whoever is honest, is so and so'. These statements state overtly what the others stated covertly that something's having one attribute necessitates its having the other.

Of course, the plain man who uses such quasi-Platonic expressions is not making a philosophical mistake. He is not philosophizing at all. He is not misled by and does not even notice the fraudulent pretence contained in such propositions that they are 'about Honesty' or 'about Progress'. He knows what he means and will, very likely, accept our more formally proper restatement of what he means as a fair paraphrase, but he will not have any motive for desiring the more proper form of expression, nor even any grounds for holding that it is more proper. For he is not attending to the form of the fact in abstraction from the special subject matter that the fact is about. So for him the best way of expressing something is the way which is the most brief, the most elegant, or the most emphatic, whereas those who, like philosophers, must generalize about the *sorts* of statements that have to be made of *sorts* of facts about *sorts* of topics, cannot help treating as clues to the logical structures for which they are looking the grammatical forms of the common types of expressions in which these structures are recorded. And these clues are often misleading.

III. DESCRIPTIVE EXPRESSIONS AND QUASI-DESCRIPTIONS

We all constantly use expressions of the form 'the so and so' as 'the Vice-Chancellor of Oxford University'. Very often we refer by means of such expressions to some one uniquely described individual. The phrases 'the present Vice-Chancellor of Oxford University' and 'the highest mountain in the world' have such a reference in such propositions as 'the present Vice-Chancellor of Oxford University is a tall man' and 'I have not seen the highest mountain in the world'.

There is nothing intrinsically misleading in the use of 'the'-phrases as unique descriptions, though there is a sense in which they are highly condensed or abbreviated. And philosophers can and do make mistakes in the accounts they give of what such descriptive phrases mean. What are misleading are, as we shall see, 'the'-phrases which behave grammatically as if they were unique descriptions referring to individuals, when in fact they are not referential phrases at all. But this class of systematically misleading expressions cannot be examined until we have considered how genuine unique descriptions do refer.

A descriptive phrase is not a proper name, and the way in which the subject of attributes which it denotes is denoted by it is not in that subject's being *called* 'the so and so', but in its possessing and being *ipso facto* the sole possessor of the idiosyncratic attribute which is what the descriptive phrase signifies. If Tommy is the eldest son of Jones, then 'the eldest son of Jones' denotes Tommy, not because someone or other *calls* him 'the eldest son of Jones', but because he is and no one else can be both a son of Jones and older than all the other sons of Jones. The descriptive phrase, that is, is not a proper name but a predicative expression signifying the joint characters of being a son of Jones and older than the other sons of Jones. And it refers to Tommy only in the sense that Tommy and Tommy alone has those characters.

The phrase does not in any sense *mean* Tommy. Such a view would be, as we shall see, nonsensical. It means what is meant by the predicative expression '. . . is both a son of Jones and older than his other sons', and so it is itself only a predicative expression. By a 'predicative expression' I mean that fragment of a statement in virtue of which the having of a certain character or characters is expressed. And the having a certain character is not a subject of attributes but, so to speak, the tail end of the facts that some subject of attributes has it and some others lack it. By itself it neither names the subject which has the characters nor records the fact that any subject has it. It cannot indeed occur by itself, but only as an element, namely, a predicative element, in a full statement.

So the full statement 'the eldest son of Jones was married to-day' means what is meant by 'someone (namely, Tommy) (1) is a son of Jones, (2) is older than the other sons of Jones [this could be un-packed further] and (3) was married to-day'.

The whole statement could not be true unless the three or more component statements were true. But *that* there is someone of whom both (1) and (2) are true is not guaranteed by their being stated. (No statement can guarantee its own truth.) Consequently the characterizing expression '. . . is the eldest son of Jones' does not *mean* Tommy either in the sense of being his proper name or in the sense of being an expression the understanding of which involves the knowledge that Tommy has this idiosyncratic character. It only *refers* to Tommy in the sense that well-informed listeners will know already, that Tommy and Tommy only has in fact this idiosyncratic character. But this knowledge is not part of what must be known in order to understand the statement 'Jones' eldest son was married to-day'. For we could know what it meant without knowing that Tommy was that eldest son or was married to-day. All we must know is that someone or other must be so characterized for the whole statement to be true.

For understanding a statement or apprehending what a statement means is not knowing that this statement records this fact, but knowing what *would* be the case if the statement *were* a record of fact.

There is no understanding or apprehending the meaning of an isolated proper name or of an isolated unique description. For *either* we know that someone in particular is called by that name by certain persons or else has the idiosyncratic characters signified by the descriptive phrase, which require that we are acquainted both with the name or description and with the person named or described. *Or* we do not know these things, in which case we don't know that the quasi-name is a name at all or that the quasi-unique description describes anyone. But we can understand statements in which quasi-names or quasi-unique descriptions occur; for we can know what would be the case if someone were so called or so describable, and also had the other characters predicated in the predicates of the statements.

We see, then, that descriptive phrases are condensed predicative expressions and so that their function is to be that element or (more often) one of those elements in statements (which as a whole record that something has a certain character or characters) in which the having of this or that character is expressed.

And this can easily be seen by another approach.

Take any 'the'-phrase which is naturally used referentially as the grammatical subject of a sentence, as 'the Vice-Chancellor of Oxford University' in 'The Vice-Chancellor of Oxford University is busy'. We can now take the descriptive phrase, lock, stock and barrel, and use it non-referentially as the grammatical predicate in a series of statements and expressions, 'Who is the present Vice-Chancellor of Oxford University?', Mr So-and-So is the present Vice-Chancellor of Oxford University', 'Georges Carpentier is not the present Vice-Chancellor of Oxford University', 'Mr Such-and-Such is either the Vice-Chancellor of Oxford University or Senior Proctor', 'Whoever is Vice-Chancellor of Oxford University is overworked', etc. It is clear anyhow in the cases of the negative, hypothetical and disjunctive statements containing this common predicative expression that it is not implied or even suggested that anyone does hold the office of Vice-Chancellor. So the 'the'-phrase is here quite non-referential, and does not even pretend to denote someone. It signifies an idiosyncratic character, but does not involve that anyone has it. This leads us back to our original conclusion that a descriptive phrase does not in any sense *mean* this person or that thing; or, to put it in another way, that we can understand a statement containing a descriptive phrase and still not know of this subject of attributes or of that one that the description fits it. (Indeed, we hardly need to argue the position. For no one with a respect for sense would dream of pointing to someone or something and saying 'that is the meaning of such and such an expression' or 'the meaning of yonder phrase is suffering from influenza'. 'Socrates is a meaning' is a nonsensical sentence. The whole pother about denoting seems to arise from the supposition that we could significantly describe an object as 'the meaning of the expression x' or 'what the expression x means'. Certainly a descriptive phrase can be said to *refer* to or *fit* this man or that mountain, and this man or that mountain can be described as that to which the expression x refers. But this is only to say that this man or that mountain has and is alone in having the characters the having of which is expressed in the predicative sentence-fragment '. . . is the so-and-so'.

All this is only leading up to another class of systematically misleading expressions. But the 'the'-phrases which we have been studying, whether occurring as grammatical subjects or as predicates in statements, were not formally fraudulent. There was nothing in the grammatical form of the sentences adduced to suggest that the facts recorded were of a different logical form from that which they really had.

The previous argument was intended to be critical of certain actual or possible philosophical errors, but they were errors about descriptive expressions and not errors *due* to a trickiness in descriptive expressions as such. Roughly, the errors that I have been trying to dispel are the views (1) that descriptive phrases are proper names and (2) that the thing which a description describes is what the description means. I want now to come to my long-delayed muttons and discuss a further class of systematically misleading expressions.

SYSTEMATICALLY MISLEADING QUASI-REFERENTIAL 'THE'-PHRASES

(1) There frequently occur in ordinary discourse expressions which, though 'the'-phrases, are not unique descriptions at all, although from their grammatical form they look as if they are. The man who does not go in for abstraction and generalization uses them without peril or perplexity and knows quite well what he means by the sentences containing them. But the philosopher has to re-state them in a different and formally more proper arrangement of words if he is not to be trapped.

When a descriptive phrase is used as the grammatical subject of a sentence in a formally non-misleading way, as in 'the King went shooting to-day', we know that if the statement as a whole is true (or even false) then there must be in the world someone in particular to whom the description 'the King' refers or applies. And we could significantly ask 'Who is the King?' and 'Are the father of the Prince of Wales and the King one and the same person?'

But we shall see that there are in common use quasi-descriptive phrases of the form 'the so-and-so', in the cases of which there is in the world no one and nothing that could be described as that to which the phrase refers or applies, and thus that there is nothing and nobody about which or whom we could even ask 'Is it the so-and-so?' or 'Are he and the so-and-so one and the same person?'

It can happen in several ways. Take first the statement, which is true and clearly intelligible, 'Poincaré is not the King of France'. This at first sight looks formally analogous to 'Tommy Jones is not (i.e., is not identical with) the King of England'. But the difference soon shows itself. For whereas if the latter is true then its converse 'the King of England is not Tommy Jones' is true, it is neither true nor false to say 'The King of France is not Poincaré'. For there is no King of France and the phrase 'the King of France' does not fit anybody—nor did the plain man who said 'Poincaré is not the King of France' suppose the contrary. So 'the King of France' in this statement is not analogous to 'the King of England' in the others. It is not really being used referentially or as a unique description of somebody at all.

We can now redraft the contrasted propositions in forms of words which shall advertise the difference which the original propositions concealed between the forms of the facts recorded.

'Tommy Jones is not the same person as the King of England' means what is meant by (1) 'Somebody and—of an unspecified circle—one person only is called Tommy Jones; (2) Somebody, and one person only has royal power in England; and (3) No one both is called Tommy Jones and is King of England.' The original statement could not be true unless (1) and (2) were true.

Take now 'Poincaré is not the King of France'. This means what is meant by (1) Someone is called 'Poincaré' and (2) Poincaré has not got the rank, being King of France. And this does not imply that anyone has that rank.

Sometimes this twofold use, namely the referential and the non-referential use of 'the'-phrases troubles us in the mere practice of ordinary discourse. 'Smith is not the only man who has ever climbed Mont Blanc' might easily be taken by some people to mean what is meant by 'One man and one man only has climbed Mont Blanc, but Smith is not he', and by others, 'Smith has climbed Mont Blanc but at least one other man has done so too'. But I am not interested in the occasional ambiguity of such expressions, but in the fact that an expression of this sort which is really being used in the non-referential way is apt to be construed as if it *must* be referentially used, or as if any 'the'-phrase was referentially used. Philosophers and others who have to abstract and generalize tend to be misled by the verbal similarity of 'the'-phrases of the one sort with 'the'-phrases of the other into 'coining entities' in order to be able to show to what a given 'the'-phrase refers.

Let us first consider the phrase 'the top of that tree' or 'the centre of that bush' as they occur in such statements as 'an owl is perched on the top of that tree', 'my arrow flew through the centre of the bush'. These statements are quite unambiguous and convey clearly and correctly what they are intended to convey.

But as they are in syntax analogous to 'a man is sitting next to the Vice-Chancellor' and 'my arrow flew through the curtain', and as further an indefinite list could be drawn up of different statements having in common the 'the'-phrases 'the top of that tree' and 'the centre of that bush', it is hard for people who generalize to escape the temptation of supposing or even believing that these 'the'-phrases refer to objects in the way in which 'the Vice-Chancellor' and 'the curtain' refer to objects. And this is to suppose or believe that the top of that tree is a genuine subject of attributes in just the same way as the Vice-Chancellor is.

But (save in the case where the expression is being misused for the expression 'the topmost branch' or 'the topmost leaf of the tree') 'the top of the tree' at once turns out not to be referring to any object. There is nothing in the world of which it is true (or even false) to say 'that is the top of such and such a tree'. It does not, for instance, refer to a bit of the tree, or it could be cut down and burned or put in a vase. 'The top of the tree' does not refer to anything, but it signifies an attribute, namely, the having of a relative position, when it occurs in statements of the form 'x is at or near or above or below the top of the tree'. To put it crudely, it does not refer to a thing but signifies a thing's being in a certain place, or else signifies not a thing but the site or locus of a thing such as of the bough or leaf which is higher than any of the other boughs or leaves on the tree. Accordingly it makes sense to say that now one bough and now another is at the top of the tree. But 'at the top of the tree' means no more than what is meant by 'higher than any other part of the tree', which latter phrase no one could take for a referential phrase like 'the present Vice-Chancellor'.

The place of a thing, or the whereabouts of a thing is not a thing but the tail end of the fact that something is there. 'Where the bee sucks, there suck I,' but it is the clover flower that is there which holds the honey and not the whereabouts of the flower. All that this amounts to is that though we can use quasi-descriptive phrases to enable us to state where something is, that the thing is there is a relational character of the thing and not itself a subject of characters.

I suspect that a lot of Cartesian and perhaps Newtonian blunders about Space and Time originate from the systematically misleading character of the 'the'-phrases which we use to date and locate things, such as 'the region occupied by x', 'the path followed by y', 'the moment or date at which z happened'. It was not seen that these are but hamstrung predicative expressions and are not and are not even ordinarily taken to be referentially used descriptive expressions, any more than 'the King of France' in 'Poincaré is not the King of France' is ordinarily treated as if it was a referentially used 'the'-phrase.

Take another case. 'Jones hates the thought of going to hospital'; 'the idea of having a holiday has just occured to me.' These quasi-descriptive phrases suggest that there is one object in the world which is what is referred to by the phrase 'the thought of going to hospital' and another which is what is referred to by 'the idea of having a holiday'. And anyhow, partly through accepting the grammatical prima facies of such expressions, philosophers have believed as devoutly in the existence of 'ideas', 'conceptions' and 'thoughts' or 'judgments' as their predecessors did (from similar causes) in that of substantial forms or as children do (from similar causes) in that of the Equator, the sky and the North Pole.

But if we re-state them, the expressions turn out to be no evidence whatsoever in favour of the Lockean demonology. For 'Jones hates the thought of going to hospital' only means what is meant by 'Jones feels distressed when he thinks of what he will undergo if he goes to hospital.' The phrase 'the thought of . . .' is transmuted into 'whenever he thinks of . . .', which does not even seem to contain a reference to any other entity than Jones and, perhaps, the hospital. For it to be true, the world must contain a Jones who is sometimes thinking and sometimes, say, sleeping; but it need no more contain both Jones and 'the thought or idea of so and so' than it need contain both someone called 'Jones' and something called 'sleep'.

Similarly, the statement 'the idea of taking a holiday has just occurred to me' seems grammatically to be analogous to 'that dog has just bitten me'. And as, if the latter is true, the world must contain both me and the dog, so it would seem, if the former is true, the world must contain both me and the idea of taking a holiday. But the appearance is a delusion. For while I could not re-state my complaint against the dog in any sentence not containing a descriptive phrase referring to it, I can easily do so with the statement about 'the idea of taking a holiday,' e.g. in the statement 'I have just been thinking that I might take a holiday'.

A host of errors of the same sort has been generated in logic itself and epistemology by the omission to analyse the quasi-descriptive phrase 'the meaning of the expression x'. I suspect that all the mistaken doctrines of concepts, ideas, terms, judgments, objective propositions, contents, objectives and the like derive from the same fallacy, namely, that there must be *something* referred to by such expressions as 'the meaning of the word (phrase or sentence) x' on all fours with the policeman who really is referred to by the descriptive phrase in 'our village policeman is fond of football'. And the way out of the confusion is to see that some 'the'-phrases are only similar in grammar and not similar in function to referentially used descriptive phrases, e.g., in the case in point, 'the meaning of "x"' is like 'the King of France' in 'Poincaré is not the King of France', a predicative expression used non-referentially.

And, of course, the ordinary man does not pretend to himself or anyone else that when he makes statements containing such expressions as 'the meaning of x' he is referring to a queer new object: it does not cross his mind that his phrase might be misconstrued as a referentially used descriptive phrase. So he is not guilty of philosophical error or clumsiness. None the less his form of words is systematically misleading. For an important difference of logical form is disguised by the complete similarity of grammatical form between 'the village policeman is reliable' and 'the meaning of x is doubtful' or again between 'I have just met the village policeman' and 'I have just grasped the meaning of x'.

(Consequently, as there is no object describable as that which is referred to by the expression 'the meaning of x', questions about the status of such objects are meaningless. It is as pointless to discuss whether word-meanings (i.e., 'concepts' or 'universals') are subjective or objective, or whether sentence-meanings (i.e., 'judgments' or 'objectives') are subjective or objective, as it would be to discuss whether the Equator or the sky is subjective or objective. For the questions themselves are not about anything.)

All this does not of course in the least prevent us from using intelligently and intelligibly sentences containing the expression 'the meaning of x' where this can be re-drafted as 'what x means'. For here the 'the'-phrase is being predicatively used and not as a unique description. 'The meaning of x is the same as the meaning of y' is equivalent to 'x means what y means', and that can be understood without any temptation to multiply entities.

But this argument is, after all, only about a very special case of the systematic misleadingness of quasi-descriptions.

(2) There is another class of uses of 'the'-phrases which is also liable to engender philosophical misconstructions, though I am not sure that I can recall any good instances of actual mistakes which have occurred from this source.

Suppose I say 'the defeat of the Labour Party has surprised me', what I say could be correctly paraphrased by 'the fact that the Labour Party was defeated, was a surprise to me' or 'the Labour Party has been defeated and I am surprised that it has been defeated'. Here the 'the'-phrase does not refer to a thing but is a condensed record of something's being the case. And this is a common and handy idiom. We can always say, instead of 'because A is B, therefore C is D', 'the D-ness of C is due to the B-ness of A'. 'The severity of the winter is responsible for the high price of cabbages' means what is meant by 'cabbages are expensive because the winter was severe'.

But if I say 'the defeat of the Labour Party occurred in 1931', my 'the'-phrase is referentially used to describe an event and not as a condensed record of a fact. For events have dates, but facts do not. So the facts recorded in the grammatically similar statements 'the defeat of the Labour Party has surprised me' and 'the defeat of the Labour Party occurred in 1931' are in logical form quite different. And both sorts of facts are formally quite different from this third fact which is recorded in 'the victory of the Labour Party would have surprised me'. For this neither refers to an event nor records the fact that the Labour Party was victorious, but says 'if the Labour Party had won, I should have been surprised'. So here the 'the'-phrase is a protasis. And, once more, all these three uses of 'the'-phrases are different in their sort of significance from 'the defeat of the Conservative Party at the next election is probable', or 'possible', or 'impossible'. For these mean 'the available relevant data are in favour of' or 'not incompatible with', or 'incompatible with the Conservative Party being defeated at the next election'.

So there are at least these four different types of facts which can be and, in ordinary discourse, are conveniently and intelligibly recorded in statements containing grammatically indistinguishable 'the'-phrases. But they can be restated in forms of words which do exhibit in virtue of their special grammatical forms the several logical structures of the different sorts of facts recorded.

(3) Lastly, I must just mention one further class of systematically misleading 'the'-phrases. 'The whale is not a fish but a mammal' and 'the true Englishman detests foul play' record facts, we may take it. But they are not about this whale or that Englishman, and they might be true even if there were no whales or no true Englishmen. These are, probably, disguised hypothetical statements. But all I wish to point out is that they are obviously disguised.

I have chosen these three main types of systematically misleading expressions because all alike are misleading in a certain direction. They all suggest the existence of new sorts of objects or, to put it in another way, they are all temptations to us to 'multiply entities'. In each of them, the quasi-ontological, the quasi-Platonic and the quasi-descriptive expressions, an expression is misconstrued as a denoting expression which in fact does not denote, but only looks grammatically like expressions which are used to denote. Occam's prescription was, therefore, in my view: Do not treat all expressions which are grammatically like proper names or referentially used 'the'-phrases, as if they were therefore proper names or referentially used 'the'-phrases.

But there are other types of systematically misleading expressions, of which I shall just mention a few that occur to me.

'Jones is an alleged murderer', or 'a suspected murderer', 'Smith is a possible or probable Lord Mayor', 'Robinson is an ostensible or seeming or mock or sham or bogus hero', 'Brown is a future or a past Member of Parliament', etc. These suggest what they do not mean, that the subjects named are of a special kind of murderer, or Lord Mayor, or hero, or Member of Parliament. But being an alleged murderer does not entail being a murderer, nor does being a likely Lord Mayor entail being a Lord Mayor.

'Jones is popular' suggests that being popular is like being wise, a quality; but in fact it is a relational character, and one which does not directly characterize Jones, but the people who are fond of Jones, and so 'Jones is popular' means what is meant by 'Many people like Jones, and many more like him than either dislike him or are indifferent to him', or something of the sort.

But I have, I think, given enough instances to show in what sense expressions may seem to mean something quite different from what they are in fact used to mean; and therefore I have shown in what sense some expressions are systematically misleading.

So I am taking it as established (1) that what is expressed in one expression can often be expressed in expressions of quite different grammatical forms and (2) that of two expressions, each meaning what the other means, which are of different grammatical forms, one is often more systematically misleading than the other.

And this means that while a fact or state of affairs *can* be recorded in an indefinite number of statements of widely differing grammatical forms, it is stated better in some than in others. The ideal, which may never be realized, is that it should be stated in a completely non-misleading form of words.

Now, when we call one form of expression better than another, we do not mean that it is more elegant or brief or familiar or more swiftly intelligible to the ordinary listener, but that in virtue of its grammatical form it exhibits, in a way in which the others fail to exhibit, the logical form of the state of affairs or fact that is being recorded. But this interest in the best way of exhibiting the logical form of facts is not for every man, but only for the philosopher.

I wish now to raise, but not to solve, some consequential problems which arise.

(1) Given that an expression of a certain grammatical form is proper (or anyhow approximates to being proper) to facts of a certain logical form and to those facts only, is this relation of pro-priety of grammatical to logical form *natural* or *conventional*?

I cannot myself credit what seems to be the doctrine of Wittgenstein and the school of logical grammarians who owe allegiance to him, that what makes an expression formally proper to a fact is some real and non-conventional one–one picturing relation between the composition of the expression and that of the fact. For I do not see how, save in a small class of specially chosen cases, a fact or state of affairs can be deemed like or even unlike in structure a sentence, gesture or diagram. For a fact is not a collection—even an arranged collection—of bits in the way in which a sentence is an arranged collection of noises or a map an arranged collection of scratches. A fact is not a thing and so is not even an arranged thing. Certainly a map may be like a country or a railway system, and in a more general, or looser, sense a sentence, as an ordered series of noises might be a similar sort of series to a series of vehicles in a stream of traffic or the series of days in the week.

But in Socrates being angry or in the fact that either Socrates was wise or Plato was dishonest I can see no concatenation of bits such that a concatenation of parts of speech could be held to be of the same general architectural plan as it. But this difficulty may be just denseness on my part.

On the other hand, it is not easy to accept what seems to be the alternative that it is just by convention that a given grammatical form is specially dedicated to facts of a given logical form. For, in fact, customary usage is perfectly tolerant of systematically misleading expressions. And, moreover, it is hard to explain how in the genesis of languages our presumably non-philosophical forbears could have decided on or happened on the dedication of a given grammatical form to facts of a given logical form. For presumably the study of abstract logical form is later than the entry into common use of syntactical idioms.

It is, however, my present view that the propriety of grammatical to logical forms is more nearly conventional than natural: though I do not suppose it to be the effect of whim or of deliberate plan.

(2) The next question is: How are we to discover in particular cases whether an expression is systematically misleading or not? I suspect that the answer to this will be of this sort. We meet with and understand and even believe a certain expression such as 'Mr Pickwick is a fictitious person' and 'the Equator encircles the globe'. And we know that if these expressions are saying what they seem to be saying, certain other propositions will follow. But it turns out that the naturally consequential propositions 'Mr Pickwick was born in such and such a year' and 'the Equator is of such and such a thickness' are not merely false but, on analysis, in contradiction with something in that from which they seemed to be logical consequences. The only solution is to see that being a fictitious person is not to be a person of a certain sort, and that the sense in which the Equator girdles the earth is not that of being any sort of a ring or ribbon enveloping the earth. And this is to see that the original propositions were not saying what they seemed on first analysis to be saying. Paralogisms and antinomies are the evidence that an expression is systematically misleading.

None the less, the systematically misleading expressions as intended and as understood contain no contradictions. People do not really talk philosophical nonsense—unless they are philosophizing or, what is quite a different thing, unless they are being sententious. What they do is to use expressions which from whatever cause— generally the desire for brevity and simplicity of discourse—disguise instead of exhibiting the forms of the facts recorded. And it is to reveal these forms that we abstract and generalize. These processes of abstraction and generalization occur before philosophical analysis begins. It seems indeed that their results are the subject matter of philosophy. Pre-philosophical abstract thinking is always misled by systematically misleading expressions, and even philosophical abstract thinking, the proper function of which is to cure this disease, is actually one of its worst victims.

(3) I do not know any way of classifying or giving an exhaustive list of the possible types of systematically misleading expressions. I fancy that the number is in principle unlimited, but that the number of prevalent and obsessing types is fairly small.

(4) I do not know any way of proving that an expression contains no systematic misleadingness at all. The fact that antinomies have not yet been shown to arise is no proof that they never will arise. We can know that of two expressions x and y which record the same fact, x is less misleading than y; but not that x cannot itself be improved upon.

(5) Philosophy must then involve the exercise of systematic restatement. But this does not mean that it is a department of philology or literary criticism.

Its restatement is not the substitution of one noun for another or one verb for another. That is what lexicographers and translators excel in. Its restatements are transmutations of syntax, and transmutations of syntax controlled not by desire for elegance or stylistic correctness but by desire to exhibit the forms of the facts into which philosophy is the enquiry.

I conclude, then, that there is, after all, a sense in which we can properly enquire and even say 'what it really means to say so and so'. For we can ask what is the real form of the fact recorded when this is concealed or disguised and not duly exhibited by the expression in question. And we can often succeed in stating this fact in a new form of words which does exhibit what the other failed to exhibit. And I am for the present inclined to believe that this is what philosophical analysis is and that this is the sole and whole function of philosophy. But I do not want to argue this point now.

But, as confession is good for the soul, I must admit that I do not very much relish the conclusions towards which these conclusions point. I would rather allot to philosophy a sublimer task than the detection of the sources in linguistic idioms of recurrent misconstructions and absurd theories. But that it is at least this I cannot feel any serious doubt.

In this paper I have deliberately refrained from describing expressions as 'incomplete symbols' or quasi-things as 'logical constructions'. Partly I have abstained because I am fairly ignorant of the doctrines in which these are technical terms, though in so far as I do understand them, I think that I could re-state them in words which I like better without modifying the doctrines. But partly, also, I think that the terms themselves are rather ill-chosen and are apt to cause unnecessary perplexities. But I do think that I have been talking about what is talked about by those who use these terms, when they use them.

4

IMAGINARY OBJECTS

Reprinted from 'Proceedings of the Aristotelian Society', Suppl. vol. XII, *1933 by permission of the editor*

If we had given to the subject matter of this symposium the title 'What is the status of imaginary objects?' we should, I suspect, have advertised in a seemingly more illuminating way what our problem is. But it would in reality have been a very misleading title, for, as I hope to show in the course of my contribution, most of the difficulties in the problem arise out of the confused or false beliefs (*a*) that there are different kinds of status and (*b*) that imaginary objects are a species of object. What the correct way is of formulating the questions which I think need to be answered on this matter must be brought out at a later stage.

I take it that there is a natural sense in which we would say 'Mr Pickwick is an imaginary being' or 'Sea-serpents are fictitious monsters' and in which these propositions would be true. And by calling this sense 'natural', I think I mean that people who have no philosophical views would talk in this way and would understand what the propositions mean. And in a case of doubt they would know how to set to work to find out if the propositions were true or false.

And I take it, further, that these propositions, taken in this sense, would be recognized by everyone to be inconsistent with these other propositions (also understood in their 'natural' sense) 'Mr Pickwick is a real being', 'There really are sea-serpents' or 'Sea-serpents do exist'. So, still using these predicate-terms in this unsophisticated way, no one would accept the propositions 'Mr Pickwick exists and is imaginary' or 'Sea-serpents are fictitious and real'. These compound propositions contain contradictions of a sort which is patent even before logical and metaphysical enquiry begin, though, when they do begin, it is no easy matter to classify what sort of contradictions they are.

Nevertheless, as we saw, we do say and believe that Mr Pickwick is an imaginary being. So that, somehow (and it remains to show just how) the proposition 'Mr Pickwick is an imaginary being', taken in its natural sense, does not mean or entail what is meant by 'Mr Pickwick exists and is imaginary'. It is, indeed, incompatible with it. Consequently, despite linguistic appearances, 'Mr Pickwick is an imaginary being' is formally different from 'Mr Baldwin is an English statesman', in that while the latter does mean what is meant by 'Somebody who is called Mr Baldwin is both English and a statesman', the former does not mean what is meant by 'Somebody who is called Mr Pickwick is both imaginary and a being'.

So one thing which I want to show is what really is the logical form of the fact which the proposition 'Mr Pickwick is an imaginary being', taken in its natural sense, succeeds perfectly well in stating.

IMAGINARINESS NOT A PROPERTY

There is a class of predicates which philosophers have been wont to regard as signifying not any qualities, states, relations or kinds of things but as signifying the status of things. Such are 'exists', 'is real', 'is an object', 'is an entity', 'is', 'is non-existent', 'is unreal', 'is not an object', 'is a nonentity', etc. We might call them 'onto-logical' or, better, 'quasi-ontological predicates'. And when we say of something that it is real or existent or an entity, the grammar of the proposition suggests (falsely) that what is being said is formally analogous to what is said in propositions in which something is said to be red or hot or a tiger.

But existence is not a property. That is, it is not a quality or a state or a kind or a relation, such that it makes sense to say that there are two sorts of dachshund, real ones and unreal ones, or existent ones and non-existent ones, in the way in which there are black and brown ones. To put it very misleadingly, non-existent dachshunds are not dachshunds at all—for *ipso facto* they are not anything at all.

Nor is being real one among the attributes of anything. Rather, though this is again misleading, a thing's being real or being an entity or being an object just consists in the fact that it has attributes. And having attributes is not *another* attribute.

To say of something that it is an object or that it exists is to say nothing at all; we are *showing* that it is an object or that it exists when we say of it that it is green or a grandfather or irritated. And it cannot be necessary or significant to say of a determinate something that it is an object or that it exists. It can't be necessary, since to describe or name it is already to give it at least one determining attribute, namely that it has that name or description. And it can't be significant, since being a possessor of attributes is not an extra attribute, or even an attribute at all. Yet this is what we seem to be doing when we say of something that it is an entity, namely, we are saying of it that it is a possessor of attributes.

Conversely, to say of a named or described something that it is not real or is not an object or entity must be nonsensical. For its having that name or description is already a case of possessing an attribute, whereas the denial that it was real or was an entity was the denial that 'it' possessed any attributes. 'Jones is not an entity' must be nonsense. For if it is true of Jones, then there *is* Jones. And if there is not Jones, then there is nothing about which the denial is that it is an entity.

What then are we really saying when from the grammar we seem to be ascribing the quality, state, relation or kind, 'existence' or 'being real' to something? The analysis, which seems to me to be the correct one, is this. In the proposition 'x exists' or 'x does not exist' the term x which, from the grammar seems to be designating a subject of attributes, is really signifying an attribute. It is a concealed predicative expression. And the proposition is really saying 'something is x-ish' or 'nothing is x-ish'. So the proposition 'ether does not exist' is not 'about' something which has the name 'ether' or has the qualities which physicists used to list as constituting ether-ness. Instead it is denying that anything has just these qualities.

Now 'being imaginary', 'being a fiction' are predicate-expressions of the same quasi-ontological sort. There are not two species of elephant, real elephants and imaginary ones. The imaginary elephant has none of the attributes of an elephant or of anything else. For 'it' is not there to have any attributes—save in the special class of cases where I imagine something which is in fact a cow to be an elephant. Then it has all its cow-attributes.

Of course, there is a sense in which we can say that an imaginary cow may have all the qualities, states, relations, etc. of a 'real' cow, or a hundred imaginary dollars have those of a hundred 'real' ones. That is, we can imagine that something has such and such attributes. But being imagined by someone to have certain attributes is not the same thing as to have them; and as usually employed, the term 'imaginary' implies that the attributes imagined to characterize the thing do not really do so. And when we imagine that 'there is' something of a certain description, there need not be and usually there is not anything of that description.

I want to show, if I can, that as in the other cases of propositions with quasi-ontological predicates, so in the case of propositions of the type 'Mr Pickwick is an imaginary object' or 'Sea-serpents are imaginary objects', the apparent subject-term is, in fact, a concealed predicative expression, so that the propositions are not really, despite linguistic appearances, 'about' a Mr Pickwick or sea-serpents in the way in which 'Christ Church is a big college' is 'about' Christ Church. So that the question is not What sort of an object is Mr Pickwick? or What sort of being do sea-serpents enjoy? but, instead (since *ex hypothesi* there are no such objects), How do we *seem* to be able to make propositions 'about' a Mr Pickwick and 'about' sea-serpents?

There are three quite distinct classes of propositions which seem to be about Mr Pickwick, namely, those which Dickens makes in Pickwick Papers, those which readers make when discussing that romance, and those which philosophers make when they say, e.g., 'Mr Pickwick is an imaginary object.'

Their analysis is quite different, the sorts of truth or falsehood attaching to them are quite different, but their grammatical form tends to be the same. And I think that anyhow most of the questions which might be lumped together under the mis-title 'What is the status of Mr Pickwick?' can now be more correctly set in the form, What are those propositions really about which seem, grammatically, to be about a Mr Pickwick (*a*) when they are propositions in the Pickwick Papers, (*b*) when they are propositions about Pickwick Papers and (*c*) when they are philosophers' propositions? And the answers are (*a*) that Dickens' propositions are fiction just because they are not about anyone, though they pretend to be about someone; (*b*) that the reader's propositions are about the book or about the propositions in it; and (*c*) that the philosophers' propositions are about either the propositions of the sort (*a*) or the propositions of the sort (*b*).

'ABOUT'-NESS

But before I can deal with the question How can a proposition seem to be about an object of a certain description when there is no object of that description? I must prepare the ground by inquiring what it means to say of a proposition that it is or is not about a specified something. For as long as it is confusedly felt that the proposition 'Mr Pickwick visited Rochester,' and the philosophers' proposition 'Mr Pickwick is an imaginary entity' are 'about' a Mr Pickwick, so long will people continue to suppose that there is a Mr Pickwick somewhere—in Dickens' head, perhaps, or in a mysterious repository called an 'universe of discourse'.

If I say 'Ireland is bigger than the Isle of Wight', it would be natural, and I think correct, to say that my proposition is 'about' Ireland and the Isle of Wight, and it would not be natural or, I think, correct[1] to say that my proposition is 'about' being-bigger-than. And if I say 'Jones is gay', my proposition seems to be about Jones and not about 'gay', or 'is gay'. What is the nature of this assumption?

First of all, I suggest, without much confidence, that the way in which a proposition is naturally described as being 'about' something or several things is quite different from the way in which a conversation or a train of thought is said to be about something. As Cook Wilson points out (*Statement and Inference*, chap. IV), when in the course of a conversation I say 'this building is the Bodleian', the proposition may have been part *either* of a conversation the central topic of which was this building, in which case the assertion of its being the Bodleian is a new increment of information about the building that we had already been attending to *or* of a conversation the central topic of which was the Bodleian, in which case its being identical with the edifice pointed at is a new bit of information about the Bodleian. Very often the grammar of a sentence does not, and the stresses of the voice in the utterance of it do, indicate which term denotes the central topic and which the new information.

Now I think that when we say that something, say Mont Blanc, is the central topic of a conversation, we mean that all or most of the propositions and questions which constitute the conversation are 'about' Mont Blanc in the sense which I am investigating, and few of them are also about some other one subject. So it might be that each of the propositions in a conversation was about Mont Blanc and also about something else, different with each proposition. E.g., 'Mont Blanc is higher than Snowdon, Mont Blanc is lower than Everest, Mont Blanc is west of Vienna.' Each proposition is about two things, but the conversation is about Mont Blanc and not about the other things. The conversation is 'about' so and so in the sense of revolving around it.

This sense of 'about' presupposes the sense in which a single proposition is about something or several things, and it only throws light on it by contrast.

Analogous to and connected with the use of 'about', when we say that a proposition is 'about so and so', are the phrases 'true of' and

---

[1] Compare, however, Ramsey on Univerals in *The Foundations of Mathematics*.

'false of'. I suggest that whenever we would naturally say that a proposition is about a certain subject, we would also say that it is true or false of it. And again, we should feel, I think, that of the proposition 'Jones is gay' it would be natural and correct to say that it is true (or false) of Jones and not that it is true or false of 'gay' or 'is gay'.

The answer which I wish to give to this question What does it mean to say that a proposition is about something? is as follows. (I am not at all sure that it is an answer.) The proposition 'Mont Blanc is snow-capped' is about Mont Blanc in the sense that (1) it says that one mountain and one mountain only is called Mont Blanc and it is snow-capped, and (2) there *is* one mountain and one only which is called Mont Blanc. If there is such a mountain the proposition is true or false. If there is not such a mountain, the proposition is neither true nor false (although one of its ingredient propositions is false, namely, that there is a mountain called Mont Blanc).

When a proposition asserts that a something named or described in that proposition has a certain quality, is of a certain kind, is in a certain state, and when further something does, in fact, possess that name or answer to the description, then the proposition is about the thing with that name or with the properties compiled in the description. And when a proposition asserts that a something named or described in it is in a certain relation to another thing (or other things) named or described in it, and when further something answers to the first description and something else answers (or some other things answer) to the latter description (or descriptions), then the proposition is true or false of those things. Let us call that part of a proposition which names or describes that which the proposition is about, when the proposition *is* about something, the 'designation'.

A proper name, or a pronoun, or a descriptive phrase, may be a designation: e.g., in 'Mr Baldwin is a statesman', 'you are bored', 'the members of the Cabinet met to-day', 'Mr Baldwin', 'you', and 'the members of the Cabinet' are designations *if* (what I know or believe to be the case) someone really is called 'Mr Baldwin', *if* I really am addressing a person and *if* certain persons really are members of something which really is the Cabinet.

But some words and phrases look like designations when they are not, and are not taken to be designations. In 'no one will ever be the English Mussolini' and in 'she refused to become Mrs Smith', the propositions to be true or false do not require that anyone should in fact be the English Mussolini or Mrs Smith. 'The English Mussolini' and 'Mrs Smith' do not describe or name anyone and are not even supposed to do so by the ordinary reader of these sentences. They are used predicatively and not as designations.

But it is easy to coin propositions which *seem* to contain designations, and yet do not do so, owing to the fact that nothing in fact answers to the designation. When Dickens says 'Mr Pickwick wore knee-breeches', the proper name seems to designate someone; but if no one was called Mr Pickwick, then the proposition can't be true or false of the man called Mr Pickwick. For there was no one so called. And then the proposition is not really about someone. The same is the case with 'The first Atlantic swimmer dined with me yesterday'.

Let us call such seeming designations 'pseudo-designations'. Obviously there is no telling from the mere form of words of a proposition whether its words or phrases which profess to designate do in fact do so. But we can understand a proposition which contains what purports to be a designation, for we can know what would have to be the case for the proposition to be true or false of something, namely, that *if* something answers to the designation, then the proposition is true or false of that which does so answer.

That a proposition is about something is a matter of fact external to the meaning of the proposition. We cannot know merely by understanding a sentence that it is true of or false of something. To know this we have to know an extra matter of fact. Mere inspection of a sentence can only tell us what it *would* be about, namely that *if* there is a so and so, then the sentence is about it; and if not, then it is not about anything. Things are not meanings, that is, they are not elements in what we apprehend when we understand propositions.

And this enables us to say in a word what is the difference between an ordinary proposition in fiction and an ordinary lie. A lie is a proposition which is false of something. It contains a designation which does in fact apply to something, and it asserts of that something that it has a certain character which in fact it has not got. A proposition in fiction contains a pseudo-designation and professes to assert something of the thing designated. But as there is nothing answering to the designation, the proposition is not in fact true or false *of* anything. (In another sense it is false *of* everything. But it was not a proposition *about* everything.)

And of course as a fictitious story develops, the pseudo-designation becomes cumulatively more 'pseudo'. For while the first pseudo-designation was, say, 'the man called Mr Pickwick', the second is, say, 'the man called Mr Pickwick who presided over a philosophical society', and the third is 'the man who . . . and who quarrelled with so and so'. So that at the end of the book the pseudo-proper name 'Mr Pickwick' professes to designate someone to whom occurred all the events which the book as a whole purports to record.

We can now answer some of the earlier questions.

(1) How can we make propositions about Mr Pickwick or sea-serpents, given that they do not exist? We cannot. For a proposition is only about something when something in fact answers to the designation in it. And nothing answers to the pseudo-designation 'Mr Pickwick' or 'those sea-serpents'.

(2) How can we *seem* to make propositions about Mr Pickwick or sea-serpents? Easily: namely, just by coining pseudo-designations in the case of which it is false (though consequentially intelligible) to say that something answers to them.

(3) What or whom were Dickens' propositions about? No one. Nor did he believe that they were about anyone. But he pretended that they were about someone; that is, he fabricated propositions which were as if they were about a man called Mr Pickwick, who was testy, benevolent, obese, etc.

(4) What or whom are the propositions about which readers propound when they say 'Mr Pickwick did not visit Oxford'? Clearly their propositions are about the book, or the propositions printed on the pages of the book. They are saying, in a shorthand way, 'None of the sentences in the book says or implies that Mr Pickwick visited Oxford.' This is shown by the fact that in case of a dispute settlement would be looked for and reached by simple reading of the text. Registers of hotel visitors to Oxford would not be relevant. The readers are talking about what Dickens says. And what they say is true or false of the book.

(5) What or whom are *our* propositions about when we say 'Mr Pickwick is an imaginary entity'? Clearly we are just saying that the quasi-designations in the propositions which profess to be about a Mr Pickwick are pseudo-designations. We are saying 'there was no *such* person'; i.e., no one in fact had the name, qualities, chops and changes which someone would have had to have for Dickens' propositions to have been true or false of a person.

So to say 'Mr Pickwick is an imaginary entity' just *is* to say '"Mr Pickwick" is a pseudo-designation'. It is not ascribing a nebulous status to a man, but denying that a certain class of expressions which profess to apply to something do, in fact, apply to anything.

IMAGINING AND IMAGES

The same account holds good *mutatis mutandis* of the fictions which we depict to ourselves in pictures in the mind's eye. Here the place of names and descriptive phrases is taken by more or less complex images. These pretend to be *of* dragons, say, or knights, and we conjure up further images, etc. in which we seem to be representing these dragons or these knights as undergoing such and such adventures. But, of course, there are no such dragons or knights, so our pictures are not *of* dragons or knights, but only as if of dragons or knights. Only in this sense can I think about the dragon which I am picturing, namely, that I can understand what the pictures *would* be recording if they were recording and not merely pretending to record. The 'make-believe' is the same in this sort of imagining as in literary romancing. It is considering what is depicted as being the case or what is described as being the case, without, usually, much inclination to believe that the pictures or the descriptions are true.

IMAGINING

So far I have only tried to establish a point in logic, namely, that the proposition 'Mr Pickwick is an imaginary being' is not, as it seems to be, *about* a man called Mr Pickwick, and that it is not asserting, as it seems to be doing, that a man called Mr Pickwick has the joint attributes of being imaginary and being a being. In fact, the proposition is about a class of propositions, namely, those which by containing the seeming designation 'Mr Pickwick' seem to be about a man called Mr Pickwick. And it asserts of these propositions that their seeming designation does not really designate anything, so that the propositions containing it are not really about anything.

But I want now to raise the phenomenological question: What is the nature of the act of imagining, the occurrence of which is vouched for by the adjective 'imaginary' in the proposition 'Mr Pickwick is an imaginary being'? For while 'x is imaginary' entails 'x is unreal', its meaning contains something more, namely the existence and activity of an imaginer.

(1) All imagining is imagining *that* something is the case. The correct form of reply to the question What are you imagining? would be to state a complete proposition, prefaced by a 'that'. It would be incorrect to reply by naming or describing a thing. That is, imagining is in this respect analogous to knowing, believing,

71

opining and guessing, and not to seeing, fearing, hitting, making or begetting.

I believe that a lot of people are tempted to hold the erroneous belief that imaginary objects are objects with a special status because they suppose that an act of imagining has an object in the special sense of being correlated with a namable or describable *thing*, in the same sort of way as acts of seeing, fearing, hitting, making and begetting are correlated with namable or describable things. I state this quite dogmatically. Everyone will agree that *some* imagining is imagining that something is the case. And if I can show, as I have to do anyhow, that the cases which one would feel tempted to describe as imagining a person or imagining a thing are really cases of imagining that something is the case, I think I shall have done all that is required of me. I have, of course, already given the crucial reason why imagining cannot be correlative to an imaginary object —namely, that it is a tautology to say that imaginary objects do not exist. So there *could* be no such correlates.

(2) Imagining has nothing special to do with imaging. I may do my imagining in images, or in words, or in both together. But I can imagine some things being the case which I cannot possibly represent in mental pictures, e.g., that a pupil's slow-wittedness is the effect of certain hereditary factors. And much imaging occurs when I am not imagining, as in remembering. It is important to notice one fact about imaging. I may have an image and (in a sense to be explored) the image may be *of* Helvellyn, say. But the image is not itself a mountain. Now if I have an image, there is nothing in the image to guarantee that the world contains something such that the image is *of* it. It is not an internal property of an image to 'have an object', i.e., to be correlative to something else in the way required for us to be able to say that the image portrays or represents or is presentative of the thing.

Consequently, though I may say naturally and conveniently that I am having an image of a sea-serpent, this is loose. For it does not imply (nor is it in ordinary speech taken to imply) that there is a sea-serpent answering to the image.

The image is, thus, on all fours with a descriptive phrase, such as 'the first Atlantic swimmer'. As the phrase may describe no one, and so may not be a description *of* anyone, so an image may represent nothing, and so may not be a representation *of* anything.

All we can say of a given image is that if there is something which, and which alone, has the 'look' properties which the image signifies and if the image is used by the imager knowingly to serve as a designation of that thing, *then* we can call this thing 'the object of' the image. But in itself the image is only a collection of predicates, and there is no telling from the existence of the image alone whether it fits anything, in the sense that something has, and is alone in having, the characters signified by the elements of the image. I fancy that even more people are tricked by the fallacy 'I have a mental picture of Mr Pickwick and sea-serpents; therefore there must somehow be a Mr Pickwick and sea-serpents' than are tricked by the fallacy which I have already tried to expose, 'I can make propositions about Mr Pickwick and sea-serpents; therefore there must somehow *be* a Mr Pickwick and sea-serpents'.

(3) It is important to distinguish three different sorts of states of affairs which we may imagine to obtain. We may imagine something to be the case with a 'real' object, as when I imagine, for the purposes perhaps of an historical romance, Socrates as being a bachelor or a coward (supposing that there was and that I know that there was a Socrates). Or I may imagine something to be the case with an imaginary object, as when I imagine Mr Pickwick being tried for breach of promise. Or, thirdly, I can mix the two sorts and imagine Mr Pickwick (who did not exist) being locked up in the Fleet prison (which did exist). For brevity, I shall call them non-fabulous, fabulous and mixed imagining.

(4) In all sorts, it is possible to imagine something as being the case which we know not to be the case or to imagine something as being the case which we do not know to be the case but also do not know not to be the case. (I don't think that it would be consonant with ordinary usage to speak of imagining something's being the case which we do in fact know to be the case.) Thus I may imagine Napoleon to have visited Edinburgh either knowing that he did not, or not knowing that he did, if he did visit it.

And I may imagine that there is a burglar in my room, when in fact there is one in my room, although I do not know it. The long arm of coincidence *might* have secured that the Pickwick Papers was in fact an accurate record of fact, although Dickens knew none of the facts and was just making his story up out of his head. We shall see later that this possibility proves that even those cases of imagining which seem to be imagining things as distinct from imagining something to be the case are really of the form imagining that x is y.

(5) Lastly, it is useful to distinguish originative, constructive or creative imagining from derivative, reconstructive or loaned imagining. Dickens was imagining constructively when he first made up

the story of Mr Pickwick; we are imagining reconstructively when we read it.

But while it is correct enough to describe Dickens' activity as 'creative', when the *story* is considered as the product of his creation it is wholly erroneous to speak as if Dickens created a Mr Pickwick. For a created object is an object and exists. But, as we have seen, imaginary objects are not objects, and do not exist and so are not created. It remains to be seen what is the proper way of stating what we put improperly when we say (as we often do) that Dickens was the creator of such and such characters in fiction.

En route to trying to answer the general question what is the nature of acts of imagining something to be the case, I want to deal first with (*a*) reproductive imagining and (*b*) where this is imagining something to be the case with a 'real' object, that is, what I called non-fabulous imagining.

Someone has written, let us suppose, an historical romance about Socrates, in which he says, or says things which would imply, that Socrates was a coward. And we are supposing that I, the reader, know that there was a Socrates of such and such a description, so that I know the designations in the book which profess to designate a man of such and such a name and description do apply to one and only one man. So, in the strict sense, his propositions really are about someone.

I now read the proposition 'Socrates was a coward'; and I understand it, that is, I realize what character Socrates is being alleged to possess. I am seeing what would make the proposition true. If, and only if, the man called Socrates had been a coward, then 'Socrates was a coward' would have been true. I do not need to go further and believe that it is true—or that it isn't. I am already imagining Socrates as being a coward when I understand the proposition which says that he was. I am recognizing a fact which is conjointly about the proposition in the book and about Socrates. Reproductive imagining just is understanding a proposition that is given to one.

Of course one can only understand a proposition which is logically possible; that is, one can only realize what would have to be the case to make a given proposition true, if the proposition is not *formally* debarred from being true (or false). It must not be a logically non-sensical sentence. But that is not quite the same thing as to say that understanding a proposition is apprehending a possibility in the sense of apprehending the fact that something is not necessitated not to be the case by something or other. Understanding 'x is y' is realizing that x would be y if 'x is y' were true, and this entails that in some sense *x could* be *y*. But understanding '*x* is *y*' is not just realizing that *x* could be *y*. Doubtless, unless we knew that Socrates might have been a coward (for Socrates was a man and some men are cowards), we could not think of him as being a coward. But we express what we are imagining not by saying 'Socrates might have been a coward' but by saying 'Socrates was a coward'.

To put it loosely, to imagine something to be the case, it must be possible and I must know it to be possible for it to be the case. But the imagining is the imagining that which is possible and not its being possible. (Just as I can dwell in memory on something which is past without what I am dwelling on being the fact that the thing is past.) In other, though very crude, words, imaginary objects are possibles but not possibilities.

Given now that all that reproductive non-fabulous imagining is, in our case, understanding 'Socrates is a coward', let us ask the highly equivocal question What is the object of the imagining? It at once breaks up into a lot of questions.

(1) If it means 'Of *whom* am I imagining that he is a coward?' the answer is 'Socrates'. And he is a real object and not an imaginary one.

(2) If it means 'What is the character which I am imagining Socrates to possess?' the answer is 'cowardice'. And this is a real quality and not an imaginary one. (There couldn't be an imaginary quality.)

(3) If it means 'What is the fact about Socrates, the apprehension (i.e. knowing) of which is the imagining him to be a coward?' the answer is that there is no such fact. For imagining something to be the case is not knowing a fact, though it may and does involve the knowledge of some facts.

(4) If it means 'What facts must be known, without which knowledge I could not imagine Socrates being a coward?' the answer is that someone was called Socrates (perhaps that someone was a fifth century Athenian philosopher called Socrates, etc.), that there is such a thing as being cowardly, that some men are cowardly and Socrates was a man, etc. And that the terms of the sentence signify these characters, and that so and so would have to be the case for the proposition to be true.

(5) If it means 'What sort of an entity is Socrates' cowardice?' the answer is 'no sort'. For he was not a coward, or, if he was, imagining that he was a coward is not knowing the fact that he was.

(6) If it means 'What sort of an entity is Socrates' imagined cowardice?' the answer is that it is just the fact that someone, myself

or the historical novelist or both, imagined Socrates as being a coward. And this fact does not entail that Socrates was a coward. It simply is the fact that someone makes sense of the proposition which says that he was one, i.e., it is a fact about me, a proposition and Socrates. Nothing is left as a metaphysical residue to be housed in an ontological no-man's-land.

Now let us consider a case of reproductive fabulous imagining.

I read, 'Once upon a time there was a Welsh wizard called Rumtifoo, who lived on a cloud over the Sea of Syrup. One day Rumtifoo looked down and saw . . .' I can make sense of all this. There are those attributes, though I believe that no one and nothing has them. Being called Rumtifoo is a perfectly genuine property, for it is true (and not nonsensical) to assert that the present Prime Minister is *not* called Rumtifoo. No sea is in fact called the Sea of Syrup, but we can understand the falsehood that some sea is so called.

That is, I know if *what* was the case, would these propositions be true if somebody, namely if someone was Welsh, a wizard and called Rumtifoo. And I know further that, if this was the case and also if someone had besides this name and description the property of living on a cloud, etc., then the whole of the first compound proposition would be true of the wizard called Rumtifoo.

The only way in which this case differs from the Socrates case is that here there is no answer to the question Who are the propositions about, i.e. true or false of? 'Someone was Welsh and a wizard and called Rumtifoo' in a sense is false of everyone, but it is not (I think) *about* everyone. (I can't deal with this point here, but I doubt if general hypothetical propositions can be described as 'about' anything. For I fancy that only then is a proposition 'about' something when it makes sense to ask of it not merely '*what* is it about?' but '*which* of the so-and-so's is it about?')

But the Rumtifoo propositions *seem* to be about a person called Rumtifoo. Fabulous fiction consists in manufacturing this semblance.

So we can quickly run through the several questions which might be called the questions about the object of the imagining by saying (1) that these Rumtifoo propositions are not about anyone; (2) that they seem and are designed to seem to be about someone called Rumtifoo, but that no one was so called; (3) that the characters which are being imagined to characterize someone are Welshness, being a wizard, being called Rumtifoo, living on a cloud, etc.; (4) that imagining that these things are the case is not knowing the facts which would be recorded by the propositions which express what we are imagining, since there are no such facts; (5) that the knowledge required for the imagining is the knowledge that there are these characters, and that the terms of the propositions signify them; (6) that there is no fact or entity designated by the quasi-designation 'Rumtifoo's wizardry' or 'Rumtifoo's habitat on a cloud'; and (7) that the fact designated by 'Rumtifoo's imaginary existence, wizardry, etc.' is the fact that someone makes sense of the proposition 'once upon a time there was a Welsh wizard called Rumtifoo, etc.' Here again there is no namable or describable something left over of which we feel driven to say, 'Ah, but there still remains so and so, existing out of our time and our space and our world but existing in some fashion all the same.'

However, it will be felt that the kernel of the problem remains unnibbled. For the exciting question is not what are we doing who read or hear the fictions and fables of others, but what are the inventors of fictions and fables doing? For they aren't making sense of propositions which are given to them, but imagining things and *then* propounding what they imagine in propositions.

For the sake of brevity I am just going to be dogmatic and say that imagining is essentially done *in* symbols, images or words or what you will. We do not first imagine a state of affairs and then fix it in pictures or sentences; the thinking of something as being the case with something is already saying or picturing to oneself, together, of course, with the realization of what one is saying or picturing to be the case. We can then, if we choose, propound what we have imagined in other symbols, e.g., in written or spoken words, in gestures or oil paintings, and if we like we can publish our story to others. But from the start imagining is internal story-telling, and constructive imagining is from the start making a story up. (What makes us anxious or prone to do it and what it is, if we do it, which makes one fiction artistically better than another are not questions which I am called upon to settle.) Slight evidence for this sort of account of constructive imagining is afforded by language. The verbs 'imagine', 'represent to oneself', '*figurer*' and even 'say so and so is the case', are some testimony for my view that thinking of x as being y, or thinking of something as being z just is telling oneself 'x is y' or 'something is z', realizing what would be the case if one's tale were true.

However, I feel that there is something in constructive imagining which I have not done justice to. For in imagining we are not talking to ourselves at random and finding later, with surprise, that what we have said does in fact make sense. Our successive increments to our story have some affinities with each other and constitute

77

some sort of a consecutive narrative. Perhaps the extra elements are
(1) the consideration of certain highly general hypothetical propositions such as 'if x were a person he would have to have a face of
some sort or other and live somewhere or other and feed on some
diet or other' and (2) the decision to choose one out of such and such
a range of faces, one out of such and such a range of habitats and one
out of such and such a range of diets, in order that the combination
of them will seem to exemplify such and such quite specific personal
characteristics. I don't mean that in imagining we would usually say
all this to ourselves in so many words but that such general considerations are what give some sort of guidance to our successive
selections of adjectives. But if this or some analogous sort of
amplification is required, it will not affect the general account that I
have given of imagining, namely, that it consists in an activity of
fabricating what pretends to be a description or pictorial representation of something's being the case.

CREATING CHARACTERS

What then is Dickens doing when he is doing what we would find
it natural to describe as 'creating' one of his characters, say, Mr
Pickwick? He is telling himself, and later telling his public, that
once upon a time someone lived in London and was called Mr
Pickwick and was of independent means and had founded a club,
which was called the Pickwick Club, and he presided over it. And
then he tells himself, 'The man whom this description fits, did and
suffered so and so'. But of course his propositions contain only
pseudo-designations because the list of characteristics by which he
pretends to designate someone did not all—or even most of them—
belong to anyone. They might have done; for there is no *a priori*
proof that they could not have co-inhered. But we think, in fact,
that no such man ever existed. The word 'such' shows that what
Dickens did was to compound a highly complex predicate and
pretend that someone had the characters so signified.

Now suppose by sheer chance, without the knowledge of Dickens,
one person had existed, such that the Pickwick Papers were in fact
faithful biography. Then we could say that Dickens' propositions
were true of somebody. (Dickens would not, of course, have been
an historian, for he invented his propositions and did not found them
on evidence.) But it seems obvious that we could not say of the real
Mr Pickwick, 'Oh, he is not identical with the hero of the story.'
For his own life is *ex hypothesi* faithfully recorded there. We could

now understand the whole story as before and know as well that there was such a man. And we should not dream of saying that there were two heroes of the story, one real and one imaginary, and the real one was exactly similar to, though numerically different from, the imaginary one. On the contrary, we should say that while previously we had thought Pickwick Papers was only a *pretence* biography, we now find that, by coincidence, it is a real one.

And a more wild hypothesis will show still more clearly that the Pickwick Papers is one big composite predicate, the understanding of which does not involve knowing or believing that anyone was characterized by it. There *might* (logically) have existed two persons of each of whom the whole story was by chance true. (Unless Dickens anywhere says that the incidents in his story happened only once.)

In that case, just as 'is red-haired and has three sons' may, very probably, be truly predicated of several men and women, so the whole chain of propositions, from the first to the last, of Dickens' story would be with truth predicated of each of these two men. And Dickens' activity of fabricating the story and imagining it as a whole to characterize someone would not in the slightest degree alter its nature owing to the miraculous matter of fact that there were two persons of whom the whole story was true. It would only involve that Dickens' belief (which he nowhere expresses) that there never was such a person was false. Now clearly in this extravagant case Dickens did not create the two real Mr Pickwicks. Their parents did that. Dickens invented a composite description which was, in fact, true of them. But Dickens believing that it was true of no one, simply imagined or pretended or 'said' that it was true of someone. I suggest that this argument proves that what Dickens 'created' was not an individual with an odd status but a complex predicate such that there might have existed several instances of the compound character signified by it.

Before concluding, I must just mention one popular error about 'the imaginary', and clear out of the way one possible confusion.

The error that I refer to is that of supposing that 'imaginary objects' are 'ideas' or 'thoughts' or 'mental contents' or 'constructions', where these terms are taken to denote objects or entities of a special sort. The proper answer is that already given, namely, that imaginary objects are not objects, i.e., that Pickwick propositions and sea-serpent propositions are not really, as they seem, about a Mr Pickwick or about some sea-serpents.

But it is perhaps worth while to say a few words about this

specific type of theory. Mr Pickwick is clearly not an idea if 'idea' means image. If it means 'object of an image', then, as we have seen, images pretending to be *of* Mr Pickwick are not, in fact, *of* an object. There exists no sitter for the pseudo-portrait.

If Mr Pickwick is said to be an idea, whether as meaning an image or an act of thinking of any other sort, then this must be false. For the image or act exists and is not imaginary while Mr Pickwick is imaginary and does not exist. Moreover, mental acts cannot be wheeled in wheelbarrows.

If Mr Pickwick is described as the object or content or product of a mental act, then either the act really has an object or content or product or it has not. If it has, then Mr Pickwick is not imaginary but really exists. If it has not really an object, content or product (in the sense that it is true of something that it is correlative in one of these supposed ways to the act) then it does not advance matters to say that Mr Pickwick is one of these things. We shall still need to know how we can seem to talk about Mr Pickwick, given that he does not really exist.

Moreover, there is no empirical evidence for the existence of these supposed objects, contents or products, if they do exist. And no other sort of evidence should be admitted on a question of existence.

Of course, in another sense, Mr Pickwick is a mental construction —for the putting together the ingredients of the hugely compound predicate (that we call the Pickwick Papers) in the activity of imagining someone to have had these characters, is an activity and a constructive one. But no Mr Pickwick is constructed.

The possible confusion which I wished to mention is this. Dickens, or perhaps better, Meredith or Jane Austen, can show psychological or sociological insight in their novels, which can therefore somehow contain psychological or sociological truths. And it is sometimes said that, for this reason, propositions in fiction may be truths of a respectable sort. But it is clear that the way in which a novelist shows psychological insight is not (unless by way of digression or comment or by fathering general propositions upon his characters) by *stating* general propositions of the form 'anything that is x is y'; but by pretending to describe an instance of the law. The instance is imaginary, so the propositions professing to be about it are fictions. But the law may seem to find a very clear exemplification, and so the nature of the law may be made much more manifest in this way than in any other. The fact that the examples are faked tends to render them all the better as illustrations of the general principle in question. For irrelevant or conflicting characteristics can be omitted or left in the shade. But the trueness of the general proposition does not in the least degree modify the fictiousness of the story which purports to describe an instance of the general proposition.

The following are the main conclusions which I hope I have established or, at least, rendered plausible.

(1) Being imaginary is not an attribute.

(2) If it is true that Mr Pickwick is an imaginary being, it entails *not* that someone is both called Mr Pickwick and is imaginary and is a being, *but* that 'Mr Pickwick' designates no one and so when used in propositions as if it designated someone is only a pseudo-designation.

(3) Dickens' propositions are not true or false of a Mr Pickwick. They pretend to be true of a Mr Pickwick, but, as there was no such man, they are not true or even false of a man of that description.

(4) The propositions which readers of the Pickwick Papers make, which are of the form 'Mr Pickwick dined at Rochester' are not and are not naturally taken to be about a man called Mr Pickwick. They are about the novel and assert truly or falsely of that novel that it contains such and such propositions purporting to be about a Mr Pickwick.

(5) Dickens' propositions make sense, for all that no one exists of whom we can say 'he is described' or 'he is misdescribed by them'. We know what would be the case *if* someone had the characters by which Dickens pretends to be characterizing someone.

(6) Imagining is always imagining that something is the case.

(7) Where we seem to be imaginatively creating a thing or a person, we are in fact imagining that someone or something has a complex of characters.

(8) What is 'created' in an activity of imagining is the 'tale' that someone or something has such and such a complex of characters, that is, not a somebody but a seeming description-of-a-somebody.

(9) The phrase 'the object or content of an activity of imagining' is plurally ambiguous, but in none of its meanings does it designate or imply anything which designates an odd entity, e.g., a Mr Pickwick with a status of a queer sort.

(10) So there is no such question as 'What is the status of Mr Pickwick?' unless this means 'How do propositions *seem* to be about a Mr Pickwick, *if* there was no such person?'

5

'ABOUT'

Reprinted from 'Analysis', vol. 1, 1933, by permission of the editor

These remarks belong to terminology and partly only to English terminology. 'About' has many meanings and sometimes some of its ambiguities are dangerous to logicians. For the notions of the logical subject, subject of predicates, subject of attributes, substance, particular, term, constituent of a fact or proposition, denotation, description, incomplete symbol and logical construction are apt to be explicated in sentences which contain and hinge on the word 'about'.

I want to distinguish several senses in which a sentence is said to be 'about' something or, alternatively, in which the author of a sentence is said to be talking 'about' something.

(1) 'The sentence S is about Q' often means 'In the sentence S, Q is the grammatical subject or nominative to the verb (or main verb)'. Q will thus be any noun or pronoun or any phrase grammatically equivalent to a noun or pronoun. In this sense a sentence may be 'about' unicorns, the Equator, or living dangerously. I call this the 'about-nominative' or 'about (n)'.

(2) As a simple extension of this, 'The sentence S is about Q' often means 'The sentence S contains Q and Q is a noun or pronoun or a phrase equivalent to a noun or pronoun occurring in no matter what grammatical position in the sentence'. 'I climbed Helvellyn' is 'about (n)' me, but it is also 'about' Helvellyn. In this sense too a sentence can be 'about' the man in the moon, being-a-live-dog, or the average man. I call this the 'about-substantival' or 'about (s)'.

(3) Sometimes, a sentence contains two or more nouns or virtual nouns but of them one is naturally thought of as that which is being talked 'about' (in a third sense). This seems to mean that the sentence S is part of a conversation or discourse and that S and all or most of the other sentences in that conversation or discourse are alike in containing the noun or virtual noun Q and no other noun is common

to them. So Q signifies what is the central topic of the conversation or discourse, which is 'about' Q in the sense of revolving around it.

(Often, of course, Q will not actually occur in all or most of the sentences. But in some its place will be taken by some synonym or paraphrase of it and other sentences will allude or refer indirectly to Q, i.e. entail propositions which if put into words would contain Q or some synonym or paraphrase.)

To ask what a sentence is (in this sense) 'about' is to ask which of the nouns or virtual nouns in it signifies that which constitutes the central topic of the conversation or discourse of which it is a part. I call this the 'about-conversational' or 'about (c)'. Position in the sentence and vocal stress are often used to show which noun signifies the central topic. I think we must extend this use to cover parts of speech which are not nouns or virtual nouns. A conversation would be 'about' climbing, although the noun 'climbing' nowhere occurred, but verbs such as 'climbed' and adjectives like 'climbable' were common to all or most of the sentences. Yet, of course, all the sentences in a conversation could contain the word 'the' or 'was' or 'not' without our feeling that these words signified the central topic. I suppose we must say, rather vaguely, that any part of speech may be given special emphasis and so may be used to signify the central topic. Expressing things in noun-form is only one species of emphasis.

All these senses of 'about' are purely linguistic. Nothing of logical importance is said when a sentence is said to be 'about' something in one or other of these senses. I call them all species of the 'about-linguistic' or 'about (l)'.

(4) Sometimes (perhaps chiefly to philosophers) 'The sentence S is about Q' means 'S contains the logically proper name N or else the description D and Q *is* logically named N or else the characteristics signified by D do belong to Q and to nothing else'. I call this the 'about-referential' or 'about (r)'. It is neither a part of the wording or the speaking or the meaning of S that a part of it should in fact describe something. We could understand the sentence without knowing that its seeming description in fact applied to anything. (Perhaps this would not be so of sentences containing logically proper names, but I doubt if there are any.)

In this sense, a sentence cannot be 'about (r)' Mr Pickwick or the Equator even if it is 'about (n or s or c)' one or other of them.

Sometimes a sentence contains an ambiguous description which does in fact apply to both Q^1 and Q^2, but is intended by its author to refer to Q^1 and not to Q^2; we might then say, 'I was not talking "about" Q² but "about" Q¹.' But strictly we should say, 'I was not intending to talk about Q²; I was intending to talk about Q¹'; e.g. 'The Prime Minister visited America some years ago.'—'Yes, Baldwin did.'—'I was talking about Macdonald, not Baldwin.' But this is not an ambiguity in 'about (r)', but, I think, an ambiguity in 'talking'.

Note. There is always a presumption, often unwarranted, that if S is 'about (l)' Q, then S is 'about (r)' Q. Hence comes our reluctance to deny 'being' of a funny sort to unicorns, round squares, the Equator, Mr Pickwick and Justice. Indeed, often we are not content with the analysis of the meaning of a sentence which is 'about (l)' Q but not 'about (r)' it, until it is rendered into a sentence which is both 'about (n or s)' O and 'about (r)' O; e.g. 'The Equator is 2,500 miles from Oxford' means, roughly, 'x is on the Equator, if x is equidistant between the Poles. a, b, c, d . . . are towns, islands, lakes, etc. which are equidistant between the Poles and of them c is nearer to Oxford than any other of a, b, d . . . and c is 2,500 miles from Oxford'. Here we are, roughly, content because we get a sentence which is both 'about (n)' c and also 'about (r)' it. (Of course the analysis is crude, for the Poles are as bad as the Equator.)

I cannot explain the existence of this presumption. Many mistakes in logic and metaphysics come from it.

Facts about Q. It is not true or significant to say 'about (r)' anything that it is a fact, i.e. facts are not genuine entities. But it is often significant and true to say 'about (r)' a sentence S (1) that it is 'about (r)' Q and (2) that it states a fact about Q. I *think* that this means: 'S is "about (r)" Q and it says that Q is oblong (say) and Q *is* oblong'.

That is, we can say non-misleadingly that a sentence states a fact about Q, but only misleadingly can we speak 'about (n)' a fact or the fact about Q.

Thinking and Knowing about. I volunteer nothing about these 'abouts'.

I do not suppose that I have exhausted the senses in which a sentence is 'about' something.

6

INTERNAL RELATIONS

Reprinted from 'Proceedings of the Aristotelian Society', Suppl. vol. XIV, 1935, by permission of the editor

The question whether relations are internal or intrinsical to their terms is not univocal. For these adjectives are not merely metaphorical but are metaphors capable of several different non-metaphorical translations.

I do not think that it would serve the ends of a symposiastic discussion such as we are engaged in to probe too closely into the interpretation of Bradley's obscure utterances on the question, nor yet of the more or less dissimilar views of Bosanquet, Joachim, Royce and McTaggart. For I suppose we want to discuss philosophical and not historical or hermeneutic questions. A local piety does, however, induce me to make a brief prefatory remark or two about Bradley's views before coming on to the philosophical questions proper.

It is clear that both in his *Principles of Logic* and in his *Appearance and Reality* Bradley is partly expounding, partly expanding and partly criticizing theories of Herbart. I am not well acquainted with Herbart's rather odd form of Monadology, but I think that it was Bradley's interest in this metaphysic and in the logical views which underlie it which made it important for him (and for subsequent English philosophy) to argue, after Lotze, for the following points:

(1) Some relational propositions are true and are not analysable into complexes of attributive propositions—meaning by an attributive proposition a proposition stating that a certain particular has a certain quality. And things are related to one another just as 'really' as they have qualities (though this is not saying very much).

(2) Relations are not substances; or relations are only exemplified in such facts as that something is in a certain relation to something else.

(3) The fact that something is in a certain relation to something else is often and perhaps always a *sine qua non* of one or both of the somethings having at least one further character.

I think that these three propositions are true; and I think too that very often when Bradley calls relations 'internal' or denies that they are 'external', he only means that one or other of these propositions is true. So that when he says that relations are not external, he sometimes only means that Herbart's Monadology is false on one or other of these scores.

But sometimes he certainly has more in mind than this, and is maintaining one or two or all of three other theories which do not, I hope to show, follow from these innocent three propositions about relations. And when he and his followers argue to Monism or the Coherence Theory of Truth from the internality of relations, they are, I think, arguing from premisses about relational propositions which are false.

I come now to the philosophical questions themselves. And in what follows I shall frequently be using the substantive 'relation' or 'relations' when in strict accuracy I should speak rather of the fact that something is in a certain relation to something else; I shall not adopt Moore's distinction between relations and relational properties and should, if required, distinguish instead between determinable and determinate relational propositions or facts and between either of these and the *forms* of relational propositions or facts.

I am going to put forward and discuss one of the possible translations of the proposition that relations are internal to their terms, which can be made quite unambiguous. It is not the only possible translation, but it is one which it is important to have clear before we consider others. The pair of terms 'internal' and 'external' might be used as synonyms of the terms 'essential' and 'accidental', and these can be made to have a perfectly clear sense. For we can say that the having of one character is essential to the having of another, and we can say that the having of one character is accidental to having another. For example, when one character, such as being extended, is a logical *sine qua non* of another, say being square, then being extended is essential to being square. And as from something's being oblong it does not follow that it is green, we can say that being green is accidental to being oblong. In this use of the terms, it only makes sense to say that x is essential or accidental to y when x and y signify the having of characters. We cannot, in this use, say that Socrates is essential or accidental to anything, or that something is essential or accidental to Socrates, but only that Socrates' being a man is essential to his being a husband, or that the fact that Socrates is ugly is accidental to the fact that he is a philosopher.

Now there are lots of cases where the having of one character is in this way a *sine qua non* of the having of another, as well as lots of others where the having of one character is not a *sine qua non* of the having of another. Many relations are internal to other characters in this way, and many external to other characters. Being the husband of Xanthippe may be a *sine qua non* of being responsible for her debts and not be a *sine qua non* of being fond of her. But so may a quality be internal to a relation or a relation to a state or a dispositional property to a relation. Internality and externality (in this sense) to other characters is not the monopoly of relations.

Whenever it is true that unless something is so and so, it can't logically be such and such, being so and so is internal or essential to or a *sine qua non* of being such and such. And whenever it is true that a thing may be such and such whether or not it is so and so, being so and so is external or accidental to being such and such. Essentialness, in this sense, is the inverse of an incompatibility; for if the proposition 'this is red' is incompatible with the proposition 'this is not coloured' or 'not extended', then being coloured or extended is essential to being red. And if 'this is red' is compatible with 'this is not square', then being square is accidental to being red.

Well, then, on this interpretation 'relations are internal to their terms' means one of two things. Either it means (1) that if something is in a certain relation to something else, their being so related is a logical *sine qua non* of each of the things having *at least one* of its other characters; or it means (2) that if something is in a certain relation to something else, their being so related is a logical *sine qua non* of each of the things having *any* of its other characters.

Either it means (1) that if Socrates was not Xanthippe's husband, then *at least one* further proposition about Socrates would be false and at least one further proposition about Xanthippe would be false; or it means (2) that if Socrates was not Xanthippe's husband, then *none* of the other propositions which are in fact true about Socrates and Xanthippe could be true.

Let us consider the more economical interpretation first.

It is certainly very often the case that if two things which are in fact in a certain relation were not so related, each would then be without at least one further character. If I had never met Smith, I would not be fond of him or in the habit of thinking of him. If I were not smaller than Jones, I should not be frightened of him. And so on.

And it *may* be the case that for every character, relational or non-relational, that a thing possesses, there is some further character which it also possesses, which it could not possess but for the possession of the former. (It might, e.g., be the case that God knows or rejoices in every fact about everything and that his knowing or rejoicing that a given fact obtains entails that the fact does obtain. Then every fact would be internal to another fact.)

I cannot prove that every character is in this way internal to some other character. But even if it is so, the doctrine that every relation and in general every character is in this way internal to some further character would lead to no exciting consequences. It would still leave it open for this or that relation or, in general, this or that character to be external or accidental to some other character.

What would be of serious—even disastrous—logical and metaphysical importance would be a proof that relations are absolutely internal in the sense that if any two (or more) things whatsoever are in any relation whatsoever, their being in that relation is a logical *sine qua non* of their terms having *any* of their other characters. And sometimes it does seem that Bradley and his followers are interpreting in this way the proposition that relations are internal to their terms, since some of their conclusions about the universe do not seem to follow unless this is among their premises. (McTaggart's principle of Extrinsic Determination is something different, and sometimes Bradley seems to be half-consciously assuming the truth of something like McTaggart's principle and not that of the proposition that relations are absolutely internal in this sense.)

Now it seems to me to be demonstrably false that any relation is the logical *sine qua non* of all the other characters of its terms.

(1) Simple inspection of certain special cases shows us that the doctrine is false. For suppose two things A and B are similar in being both of the same shade of green. So far from its being the case that A's being green depends on or has for its logical *sine qua non* the fact that it is of the same colour as B, A and B would not be similar in colour unless A was, say, pea-green and B was pea-green.

The quality is here the *sine qua non* of the relation and not vice versa. And this is often the case. For Smith to be running faster than Jones, Smith must be running and Jones must be running.

(2) If one thing A was in a certain relation to another B, say that of being north of it, it would follow, on this doctrine, that any change of relative position would necessitate a wholesale change of all the other characters of both of them, colour, temperature, shape, size, elasticity, and solubility in sulphuric acid. For otherwise a character which survived the change of position would have belonged to its possessor whether or not it was north (or south) of the other, which is what we meant by calling a relation external to a character. But in fact there is no inference from the compass-bearings

of objects to their colours, shapes, sizes, etc. Moreover, the determinable character of being somewhere or other in space could not, on this doctrine, survive the change of place. So the universal proposition would have to be true that whatever is in space is north of B, which is absurd.

(3) It would follow, too, from the doctrine so rendered, that no universal could have more than one instance, or that no two things could be similar in any respect. For, if for any particular whatsoever there is at least one unique description, and if, as I think, for a description to be unique it must contain at least one relational predicate which is predicable of no other particular, then the fact that a given particular is and is alone in this relation would have to be a *sine qua non* of all its other qualities, states, dispositional properties, etc. So nothing else could have any of these qualities, states, dispositional properties, etc. Or, to put it the other way round, if two particulars were in any respect similar, then for the doctrine to be true it would have to be the case that every relation in which the one particular stood to everything else would have also to hold between the other particular and those terms. But as the one particular must stand to the other in at least one relation in which the latter cannot stand to itself (e.g., distance from it), the condition cannot be fulfilled. So, if the two are similar in a certain respect, there must be at least one relation which is external to their having the character in respect of which they are similar.

(4) There are plenty of cases in which two characters are essential to each other. If something has some shape or other, it has some size or other, and some position or other, and vice versa. Or if Smith is twice the height of Jones, Jones must be half the height of Smith and vice versa. But for the whole-hearted doctrine of the internality of relations (on this interpretation) to be true, *all* the relations in which a thing stands would have to be the *sine qua non*s of all. Otherwise some relations would be external to some other relations. But it is clear that most relations are not in this way the converses of most others. From the comparative sizes of two things nothing follows about their comparative temperatures or positions.

(5) It would follow, lastly, that no laws could hold of particulars nor even be thought to hold; nor could propositions of the form 'most A's are B', or 'many A's are B', be true or be thought to be true. For it is obvious that many rabbits (if there are rabbits) live in different places and at different dates and in different circumstances from many other rabbits. So these differences of relations should result in there being no propositions being true of all or even many

of them. For otherwise it will be true that many things, as being rabbits, have such and such characters whether or not they live on the Berkshire Downs, and this would be a case of a relation being in this sense external or accidental to some other characters.

These arguments seem to me to prove that relations are not in this sense internal to their terms; or that relations do not, in McTaggart's language, intrinsically determine all the other characters of their terms.

And I do not think that it is possible to escape this conclusion by either of two not unfashionable expedients. One is to say that if we only knew more or if we only knew everything we should then see that and how relations are the logical *sine qua non*s of all the other characters of their terms. Against this I am maintaining that we can and do now know that some relations are not essential to some of the other characters of these terms.

The other expedient is to say that relational propositions are 'in the end' not true or even, literally, false. What they say is the case cannot really be the case. I do not know what this means; but at least it cannot support the conclusion that relations are internal. For, on this interpretation, to call a relation internal is to say that if something were not in a certain relation to something else, neither of its terms could have any of their other characters. But if relational propositions cannot be 'really' true, this protasis cannot 'really' imply this or any other apodosis.

Before dropping this way of interpreting the internality theory, I want to show that exactly the same interpretation can be given to two other forms of words in which the doctrine is sometimes propounded.

(*a*) It is sometimes put by saying that the relations in which a thing is are parts of the 'nature' of the thing, or that a thing's nature would be different if it was not in a relation that it actually is in.

(*b*) And it is sometimes put by saying that the relations in which a thing is help to make it 'what it is'; or that a thing would not be what it is if it were not in a relation that it actually is in.

Now in either of these two forms the proposition 'relations are internal to their terms' *could* mean merely that if we had a complete list of a thing's predicates, its relational predicates would be items in the list. And this tautology was, perhaps, worth while for Bradley to voice, if Herbart's view was that the whole nature of a 'Real' was statable in attributive propositions (whether one or several makes no odds). But this proposition is to us innocuous and uninteresting.

Or, secondly, either of these ways of stating the internality theory might merely amount to saying that every relation is essential (in our sense) to at least one further character of each of its terms.

This might be true, though I know no proof of it. But it has no important consequences and is compatible with some or all relations being external or accidental to some other characters.

Or, thirdly, either of these ways of stating the internality theory might be another way of stating the absolute internality theory with which we have already dealt. For it might mean that if a thing is in a certain relation, that relation is in *such a way* part of the thing's nature that the thing's nature would be in *every* way different if it were not in that relation. And on the other formula the phrase 'what the thing is' may simply be a new name for 'all the thing's characters'; so to say that in a different relation the thing would not be what it is, could mean that all its other characters have this relation for their logical *sine qua non*.

And this we have seen is false.

But, incidentally, it seems to me improper to speak absolutely of the nature of a particular (unless we are referring to the complex of psychological dispositions in virtue of which, for example, we call Socrates good or ill-natured). We can properly speak of the nature of triangles or bicycles, or even, at a pinch, of the nature of this particular *as a triangle* or *as a bicycle*. In this sense we can sensibly ask whether a certain character belongs to the nature of bicycles, or to the nature of this as a bicycle. But it seems to me worse than a mistake in English diction to speak of the nature of Socrates or this pen absolutely, that is without the complementary reference to a character to be analysed, such as Socrates *qua* philosopher or this *qua* a pen. McTaggart, I know, does deliberately use the term 'nature' as the name for the sum of the qualities and relations of a particular, and I dare say Bradley and some of his followers do so too. But it seems to me not merely bad English, but a dangerous usage; for the fact that we can, in the other sense, discuss whether a certain character is part of the nature of a certain 'universal' (as whether having pneumatic tyres is part of the nature of a bicycle) does suggest that we can properly ask whether a certain character is a necessary part of the nature of Snowdon. And this gives a verbal plausibility to such theories as McTaggart's principle of Extrinsic Determination or the affiliated theory of the internality of relations with which I must next deal.

We must turn now to quite another sense in which relations are said to be internal to their terms. It said that if A is in a certain relation to B then A would not be what it is if it were not in that relation—and 'be what it is' means here, not, as before, have the characters that it has but be the thing that it is. Or, to put it another way, if A is in a certain relation to B, anything that is not in that relation to B is of logical necessity other than A—'other' meaning, not 'differing in some or all characters from A' but 'being numerically different from A'.

But I am at a loss with regard to this way of taking the theory that relations are internal to their terms not so much from failing to grasp the arguments for this conclusion but from failing to make sense of the conclusion itself. For I cannot satisfy myself that there *is* such a 'predicate' as 'being the particular that it is' or 'not being the particular that it is', and, consequently, I cannot understand what is being said when we are told that if something was not in a certain relation it would not be what it is.

First of all, there is no difficulty in having for the predicate of a proposition a definite description. I can certainly wonder if 'this is the face that launched a thousand ships', or assert it or deny it. But 'being the so and so' is just the having of a complex character, a character which is unsharable, indeed, for if anything has it only one thing can do so, but it is a character none the less. But for this interpretation 'being the thing that it is' must not be a descriptive phrase signifying a character. To take an example. This is above that and, for this doctrine to be true, if this were not above that, this would not be this. Or again, if Socrates were not Xanthippe's husband, Socrates would not be Socrates. Now 'being this' or 'being Socrates' (taking 'Socrates' to be a logically proper name) certainly does not signify the having a quality, the being in a state, the being of a kind, or the having a dispositional property. Is it plausible to say that it signifies the being in a relation? If so, 'this is this' must be an assertion of identity and so be the short for 'this is identical with this', and 'this is not or would not be this' must be short for 'this is or would be numerically other than this'. And, it may be asked, what is wrong with the ordinary doctrine that identity and otherness are *bona fide* relations?

I am not sure of this point, but I am not satisfied that 'this is (or is not) identical with this' is a significant proposition. To what question could it be the answer? Or if I am acquainted with *this* and with *that* what information could I require to give me an intellectual motive for asking, Is this other than that or not?

I am not, of course, suggesting that there are no uses for the terms 'same' and 'other'. I can want to know on hearing that my room has been visited twice in an afternoon whether the first visitor was the same person as the second or someone else. Knowing, that is, that someone visited my rooms at 3.0 p.m. and that someone visited my rooms at 4.0 p.m., I can wonder whether anyone both visited my rooms at 3.0 p.m. and visited them at 4.0 p.m. Or, to take a slightly different case, knowing that some face launched a thousand ships, I can wonder if this is or is not that face.

But it seems to me nonsense to ask if a particular is or is not something else than itself, and nonsense, consequently, to argue that a particular would be something else than itself if it were not in a certain relation.

But even if I am wrong about this, the doctrine turns out not to be in principle different from the doctrine that we have already discussed and I hope disposed of. For if 'this is identical with this' is a relational proposition (which I contest), then to say that if this were not in a certain other relation it would not be in this alleged relation of identity to this is simply to say that one relation is in our original sense internal or essential to another. And while there is no general objection to one relation being internal to another, there seems no way of proving in general that any sort of relation whatsoever must be internal to this (alleged) relation of self-identity, and most people who believe that self-identity is a relation would argue that it is patently internal to any of the other relations that its term may be in.

But there still remains to be considered the view that a particular in a certain relation would not be the particular that it is if it were not in that relation where the expression 'it would not be the particular that it is' is rendered not as a relational proposition but as some sort of attributive proposition. That is, the proposition 'if so and so, A would not be A' is interpreted as being, not of the form 'if so and so, A would not be identical with A', but simply '. . . , A would not be A'. 'Being A', and not 'being identical with A', is the alleged predicate. And the theory holds that relations are internal in the sense that A's being A depends on or entails its being in a given relation to something else. (I am taking 'A' to be the logically proper name or designation of a particular.)

Now, for this view to be true *or false*, it would have to be significant to predicate a logically proper name or designation of a logically proper name or designation; and it would have to be significant to assert or deny that *this* was *this*; and the question 'is anything this?' would have to mean something. But apart from the philosophical consideration that such alleged propositions and questions would contain no universals, it seems to me clear on inspection that they assert or ask just nothing at all. 'This' is not a predicate, and a sentence in which it pretends to function as one is meaningless. So there *could* be no such dispute as to whether this's being this does or does not depend on its being in one or other of its relations.

I should perhaps just point out that my belief that the question 'Is this this?' or 'Is that not that?' is nonsensical involves just the same scepticism about McTaggart's principle of Extrinsic Determination. And on this point I should say that I completely agree with Professor Broad's way of disposing of this alleged principle. For he shows that the principle amounts to this: A ('A' being a logically proper name) has a certain character C. If A were not C, A would not exist, since whatever was not C would be other than A. But Professor Broad properly points out that existence-propositions with logically proper names for their subjects are meaningless. So it is meaningless to say 'if so and so, A would not exist' or 'if so and so, A would exist'.

I shall wind up this part of my paper by a summary of the relevant things which I think are true.

(1) Some relational propositions state facts about their terms, i.e., are true, and are not analysable into attributive propositions. And I think that often Bradley was only trying to say this, as against Herbart, but, not being quite cured of the superstition that all propositions are attributives, fell back to stating it by saying that relations really do qualify or belong to their terms or are parts of their nature.

(2) Relations are not substances or, to put it loosely in another way, a relational proposition about Socrates and Xanthippe mentions two particulars and not three. Relations are only exemplified in the fact that terms are related.

(3) Relations are often and perhaps always internal to or logical *sine qua non*s of some of the other characters (relational or non-relational) of their terms; but they are often and I think always in the same way external to some of the characters of their terms. In particular, some non-relational character is generally if not always the logical *sine qua non* of a relation.

(4) Relations are not absolutely internal in the sense that if one thing is related to another, that relation is the logical *sine qua non* of all the other characters of both the terms.

(5) It is not the case or else it does not even make sense to say that a particular would not be the particular that it is if it were not in a relation that it actually is in.

But so far I have not said a word about causation or non-logical necessitation. And for several reasons I must not shirk at least opening a discussion on this matter, though I have myself no hope of closing it. For some people hold that causal laws do state logical implications or else assert 'connections' which contain logical implications or else assert 'connections' which are homogeneous with or a species of logical connections. And plenty of people, whatever their views on this matter, believe that everything in the world is causally conditioned by everything else, in such a way that nothing that exists or occurs could (causally) have been quite what it is had anything else in the world been different. So that whether or not all relations are internal, at least all things and events are internally related. (I think holders of the theory that all relations are internal sometimes confuse their theory with this one. They certainly use arguments which if valid would only establish that everything is causally conditioned by everything else.)

Now it does not seem to me to be a question proper for philosophers to discuss whether the universe is one big clock—whether, that is, everything that is or occurs is causally dependent for some or all of its characters on everything else that is or occurs. If we deem it to be the function of the experimental scientist to discover what is the cause or effect of what, we ought, I think, to leave it to him to discover whether some states of affairs in nature are causally *independent* of some others or not. It would be presumptuous for us to ostracize *a priori* this or that scientific hypothesis.

It should, however, be mentioned that the one-big-clock theory, so far from being in harmony with our ordinary beliefs, is in direct conflict with them. For we ordinarily believe in *special* laws, e.g., that unsupported bodies fall at such and such a rate of acceleration, which laws seem anyhow to exclude, not to include, reference to most of the states of most of the things in the world. Our belief in special laws may be, doubtless, so doctored as to become consistent with the other view that *the* cause of a given state of affairs can be nothing short of the whole state of the universe at the previous moment. But the doctoring is required.

But it is a philosophical task to enquire what sort of a fact, if any sort, is stated by those propositions which we call laws—what, for example, we mean by the 'if' in the proposition 'if water freezes, it expands', or what we mean by the 'involves' in 'a rise in temperature involves a quickening of the pulse', or, again, what we mean by the 'must' and 'cannot' in a 'shorter pendulum must swing faster than a longer one', or 'a longer pendulum cannot swing so fast as a shorter one'. And, to take another class of cases, it is a philosophical task to enquire what we mean when we say such things as 'the glass broke because a stone hit it', or 'this wind will make the clouds disperse'.

There are three types of analysis which are given to such causal propositions. Unfortunately, I cannot accept any of them. (1) There is the view that these propositions are or contain assertions of logical necessitation. (2) There is the view that these propositions are partly records of unbroken runs of observed concomitances in the past and partly announcements (or else symptoms) of the fact that their author feels sure that the concomitances will continue unbroken. (3) There is the view that as laws are neither propositions in formal logic nor yet compounds of singular propositions severally asserting established or establishable matters of fact, they are not propositions at all, and so are not true or false, but are only 'rules', i.e., imperatives or optatives to think, talk or behave in certain ways.

(1) Dr Ewing believes that causal laws are or contain logical entailments or else are or contain something homogeneous with logical entailments. And he puts his finger on the fact which makes many people anxious to adopt such a view when he shows that we 'argue' from one matter of fact to another. But the evidence is worthless. For if 'argue' means 'argue validly' in the sense of 'demonstrate', then it is not true that we can demonstrate either the general proposition that water expands when frozen or the particular prediction that this jug of water will burst if it freezes. It is surely notorious that the data of inductions are compatible with the falsity of the conclusions of those inductions. The sense in which the making of general hypotheses from empirical data or the making of particular causal inferences can be called 'arguing' is a different sense. In this new sense it does not contain the discerning of entailments. Even if Dr Ewing was right in suggesting that where we make good scientific inductions there lies an undiscerned entailment (so that, I suppose, an induction makes it probable that something entails something else), still the induction would not be that 'arguing' which, if it happened, would be the discerning of the entailment.

Now it is not, of course, unreasonable to say that there may be undiscerned entailments. Anyone who has ever failed to follow a valid demonstration is in the position of not discerning that something's being the case entails something else's being the case, although it in fact does so. But it does seem to me patent that nature is not just a theorem which happens to be too hard for us to reason out. For it seems to me that Hume proved that certain sorts of facts do not entail facts of certain sorts, namely, that particular matters of fact do not logically follow from different particular matters of fact. The three propositions 'this is water', 'this is freezing', and 'this is not expanding' are discernibly *not* incompatible. Or 'this water is expanding because it is freezing' is a synthetic proposition, and cannot be rendered into an analytic proposition whatever new information comes to be added to our store.

So until someone shows that there is another sort of 'argument' or demonstration which can establish that one proposition may 'involve' another and yet be compatible with its contradictory, I see no future for this way of analysing the 'ifs' and 'becauses' of causal laws or particular causal inferences.

(2) On the other hand, I cannot accept either the sort of analysis which Hume gives of such propositions as 'if water freezes, it expands'. Its analysis, according to him, would be, I take it, as follows: (*a*) on each occasion on which I have observed water freezing and on each occasion on which others, on whose testimony I rely, have observed it freezing, it has been observed to expand; and (*b*) I feel strongly disposed to expect water to expand when frozen on the next occasion or on all subsequent occasions.

For we think that some such expectations are somehow better justified than others, even though some of the latter are in fact held with greater confidence than some of the former. We think better of the expectations of the astronomer and even of the meteorologist than of the expectations of the superstitious, though the latter's beliefs are doubtless not less confident than the astronomer's and much more so than the meteorologist's.

And merely psychological accounts, like that of Hume, fail to explain how we can describe a belief as both confident and silly.

(3) Of the view that 'laws' are not true or false and so are not propositions at all, I follow the reasons given though I cannot accept them. But I do not understand the, I suppose, consequential doctrine that they are 'rules'.

Against the ordinary view that 'laws' are propositions, it is pointed out that they do not state particular matters of fact nor yet conjunctions of particular matters of fact. So no observation or set of observations can verify them. Nor are they propositions in formal logic or mathematics, so they are not necessary truths or 'tautologies', as these are rather misleadingly labelled nowadays. (I call the usage misleading because 'tautology' does not mean in its new use quite what it meant in the 'traditional' logic.)

Now I cannot accept the verification principle in its original simple form, if only because it leads to the consequence that almost if not quite all our ordinary propositions are not propositions at all. For propositions about the future, the past, and other people's experiences as well as all general propositions, whether universal or particular, have to be sacrificed or else violently misinterpreted. And we are only left with a vanishingly small class of genuine propositions, namely, genuinely singular propositions.

But, aside from this, I am unable to construe the conclusion that laws, not being propositions, are therefore 'rules'. For the understanding of a universal imperative or a universal optative seems to me to raise just the same problems as the understanding of a universal indicative statement. 'Never expect water to contract on being frozen' must be understood if it is to be obeyed, and if it can be understood the barriers seem to be removed which forbade us to understand 'water never freezes without expanding'.

But even if 'laws' ought to be or can be construed as 'rules', it remains the case that there are some such rules which we should be better advised to adopt than some others. In some way 'sunlight extinguishes fires' is a bad or unscientific rule. And we shall still need to know what makes one rule better than another and why the relative acceptability of a given rule varies with the amount of empirical data as well as with the degree of simplicity of the rule.

I have no answer of my own to the question which I put by asking what we mean by the 'if' of a natural law, given that we do not mean by it what we mean by the 'if' of a logical implication.

But there are one or two things that I should like to clear up in the question itself.

First, it is not clear to me that we are right to speak of causation as a relation, except in the loose way in which we say that 'if', 'and', 'either', 'or', signify 'relations' between facts or propositions. But what grammatical conjunctions signify are not homogeneous with what prepositions, comparative adjectives, and some transitive verbs signify. 'Either—or' does not signify a relation in the same sense of relation as 'above' or 'bigger than'.

Facts or propositions are not of the same logical type as things or particulars.

Next, it is a mistake to tie down the question to the special point of inference to the *future*. Induction, doubtless, starts from concomitances observed before or at the time of the induction; but the inferences may just as well be to past or contemporary as to future matters of fact. The matters of fact to which, e.g., geologists and doctors infer are very largely to matters of fact prior to or contemporary with the making of the inference. Prediction is only more dramatic than 'retrodiction' because we have one non-inferential way of knowing the past, namely, by memory, and no other way of knowing the future than by causal inference. Similarly, we can often observe the (roughly) contemporary, but not the future.

Next, the problem of causation and/or induction is often set in a question-begging way, namely, by means of verbs in the timeless present. Holders of regularity theories, for instance, tend to slide from saying 'thunder has regularly ensued upon lightning' to 'thunder regularly *ensues* upon lightning'. And Ramsey similarly slides from saying that certain sorts of opinions *have been* useful more often than harmful to saying that certain sorts of opinions *are* useful more often than harmful. But patently the transition from the past tense to the timeless present is that very transition from recording to generalizing the nature and warrant of which are in question.

Next, discussions of this sort of problems are apt to be unduly restricted in scope, by assuming that causality holds only between successive events, such as lightning and thunder or taking poison and dying. But laws are only *per accidens* laws of the *sequence* of events or states; they are not laws the less for stating (or seeming to state) the universal concomitance of quality with quality, or state with state, when the concomitants exist at the same time. A high temperature does not precede a rapid pulse, nor does the poker first get to a certain temperature and then become red. And roses are red and scented at the same time.

Last, while it is true that no set of observed concomitances can do more than give probability to a general hypothesis or else a particular prediction or retrodiction; and further, while I think it is true that sets of observations can in fact give such a probability, this does not, it seems to me, explain what our (probable) conclusions *mean*. If induction is sometimes in this sense rational, namely, that on such and such premisses such and such a conclusion is not indeed certain but more likely than not, yet still the conclusion is some sort of a synthetic proposition. It still asserts that something's having (or anything's having) one set of properties involves its having another set of properties, neither set entailing the other. And we are still left with our original question, What on earth is this 'involving'?

And, finally, I feel fairly sure that this question is not one the solution of which requires us to know more of what Locke calls the internal constitution of things. It is not that we need to know more physics or more chemistry before we can know what we mean when we say that water expands when it freezes.

These inconclusive reflections about causation should perhaps have been omitted. I have inserted them because I want to know what Mr Ayer and Professor Moore think about the question, and because I think that the dispute about the internality of relations in general is no longer an exciting one.

7

MR COLLINGWOOD AND THE
ONTOLOGICAL ARGUMENT

Reprinted from 'Mind', vol. XLVI, *1937*

Mr Collingwood, in his interesting *Essay on Philosophical Method*, is embarking on a set of enquiries which are of obvious importance. His aim is to find out what philosophy is and what is the right way of proceeding in that activity. And his enterprise has a special momentary interest, for of recent years the discussions of these questions have been the monopoly of one or two schools of thought which are poles asunder from the point of view which Mr Collingwood represents. For Mr Collingwood is presumably to be classified for what such labels are worth, as an Idealist, and it is high time that the questions which have been in the forefront of the debates of such thinkers as Russell, Moore, Broad, Wittgenstein, Carnap, Schlick, Stebbing, and again as the members of the school or schools of Husserl and Meinong, should be at least considered again in the quarters which protest (perhaps a little too much) allegiance to Plato, Kant, in his less Humean moods, and Hegel.

Now I think that Mr Collingwood's general views are wrong; but I want only to discuss, and if possible to refute, certain theories which he expounds in his chapter VI which is entitled 'Philosophy as Categorical Thinking'. And I confess at once that I intend to be destructive only. That is, I do not propose to say that philosophical propositions are all or mostly of this or that logical form, but only to show the mistakes which I believe Mr Collingwood makes when he tries to show that philosophical propositions are (in a certain sense of the term) categorical. The question is of cardinal importance; for he holds that philosophical propositions are in a peculiarly close way connected with what exists; in a way, indeed, in which the empirical sciences are remoter from what exists than philosophy is. And a part of his theory is that philosophy can by the Ontological Argument establish the existence of a very important somewhat, and that philosophy in general aims at discovering—and no other sort of enquiry can discover—the nature of the somewhat. So that, if Mr Collingwood is right, constructive metaphysics is the proper business of philosophy, and Hume and Kant were wrong in so far as they maintained that *a priori* arguments cannot establish particular matters of fact.

The chapter begins by elucidating the sense in which Mr Collingwood and logicians generally declare that the propositions of geometry and arithmetic are 'hypothetical', namely that though, in a sense, propositions may be 'about' triangles or circles, yet there do not have to exist any triangles or circles for the propositions to be true. They only say, 'if something had such and such properties, it would have such and such other properties'; and it is not said or implied that anything does so. At least, this is how I paraphrase Mr Collingwood's own statement. He himself says, 'In order to assert a proposition in mathematics it is not necessary to believe that the subject of discourse has any actual existence. We say that every square has its diagonals equal; but to say this we need not think that we have any acquaintance with actual squares. . . . What is necessary is not to believe that a square anywhere or in any sense exists, but to suppose it. . . . In mathematics, we frame a supposition and then see what follows from it; . . .' And this seems unexceptionable.

He then argues that not indeed the whole but the body of empirical science consists of propositions which are hypothetical in the same sense. I think he slightly obscures his position here by failing to distinguish the *generality* of the propositions which profess to state 'laws' from the innocent fictitiousness of certain sorts of scientific propositions which pretend to be about the 'standard cases' of roses, e.g., or tuberculosis. But I don't think it matters to the argument. (The way in which 'dogs are carnivorous' applies to Fido but does not depend for its truth on Fido's existing is different from the way in which 'the typical schoolboy likes cricket' applies to Tommy but neither states nor implies that he exists.) Mr Collingwood sees, of course, that empirical sciences must have propositions stating particular matters of fact among their premisses, and that they may (as in the Nautical Almanac, I suppose) embody others in the application of laws to the world. And these will be categorical. But he asserts (I am not clear why) that the body of scientific knowledge 'consists' of hypothetical propositions, and its categorical propositions are only 'necessary or fortuitous accompaniments of it'. But we need not quarrel over this, for it is clear that there are universal propositions in the findings of the empirical sciences and that these do differ in logical form from propositions asserting such particular matters of fact as that the patient's temperature has been this or that at such and such a time. Now Mr Collingwood wants to show that none or few of the propositions of philosophy are hypothetical in the sense in which the propositions of mathematics and the universal propositions of empirical science are hypothetical; but on the contrary that all or most philosophical propositions are categorical in the same sense (or anyhow an analogous sense) as the proposition about the patient's temperature was categorical.

But before we come to this I must, I fear, clarify one or two points in what I take to be Mr Collingwood's use of the term 'hypothetical'. First of all there are plenty of 'if-then' propositions which do imply the existence of their subjects. 'If Hitler lives for another year, he will be at loggerheads with Mussolini' cannot be true or false unless there exist a Hitler and a Mussolini. Mr Collingwood is obviously referring to the universality of general propositions rather than to their 'if-then'-ness; he is affirming, that is, that philosophical propositions differ from the propositions of mathematics and the general propositions of empirical science in the fact that philosophical propositions directly refer to something which exists in a way in which the others fail to do this. He is not making what would be the quite different point that philosophers never or seldom say that from something's being the case something else would follow.

At least I think that this is all that his argument about mathematical propositions and the universal propositions of the empirical sciences can be intended to establish. Yet in Section 4, where he appeals to the authority of Plato, Aristotle, Kant and Hegel, he does seem to confuse the two points. For in one breath he quotes Aristotle's definition of the subject-matter of metaphysics as reality or being, Hegel's declaration that 'the subject-matter of philosophy is no mere thought and no mere abstraction but *die Sache selbst*', as well as Plato's assertion that dialectic demands for itself a non-hypothetical starting-point, and Kant's dictum that 'in a critique of pure reason anything in the nature of a hypothesis must be treated as contraband'. But the Aristotle–Hegel point is quite different from the Plato–Kant point. Plato and Kant are saying that philosophy must not lay down propositions which depend for their truth upon premisses not known to be true. Philosophy does not consist in deducing consequences from assumptions. And this, though true and important, is not the same thing as to say that philosophical propositions state or entail particular matters of fact, i.e., that they are 'about' a designated entity. Some philosophers have, indeed, held that there are some general propositions which are known to be true *a priori*, and that philosophy starts from these. This theory (I don't think it is true) would secure what Plato and Kant are here demanding for philosophy without providing what Aristotle and Hegel require.

Let me try to restate the distinction between the two senses of 'hypothetical proposition' which seem to be confused in Mr Collingwood's treatment.

(1) Primarily Mr Collingwood means by 'hypothetical proposition' a general, indeed, a universal proposition of the form 'anything that is A is B' or 'if anything is A, it is B' or 'all A's are B'. Such propositions do not depend for their truth on this or that thing being an A and thus do not 'imply the existence of their subject-terms'.

(2) But sometimes he means by 'hypothetical proposition' a proposition which states that a certain consequent would follow if a certain protasis were true, when it is not known or said or implied that the protasis is true. The truth of the whole 'if-then' is independent of the truth or falsity of the protasis taken as an independent proposition. That is how we can make deductions from a mere assumption.

But (*a*) in *this* sense a hypothetical proposition may well depend for its truth on the existence of its subject-term: for it may, as we saw, be about Hitler or Julius Cæsar, and so depend for its being true or false on there existing a Hitler or a Julius Cæsar, though not, of course, on the protasis about Hitler, say, being true when taken as an independent proposition. The protasis of a hypothetical proposition may express the assumption that something not known to exist does exist; but it may equally well express the assumption that something known to exist has a character which it is not known to possess or is known not to possess, or the assumption that something known to exist does not exist. Not all assumptions are assumptions of the existence of a so and so.

And (*b*) the protasis of a *general* hypothetical proposition does not express the assumption that something of a certain description exists. 'Anyone found trespassing will be prosecuted' is a general hypothetical. But the protasis cannot be taken by itself. It is nonsense to say 'anyone is found trespassing'. There is no such animal as 'anyone'.

Now, as Mr Collingwood is concerned with such facts as that geometry is independent of the *existence* of squares, it is clear that his argument turns not on the general point that consequences can be deduced from protases which are assumed (i.e., not known to be true when taken as independent propositions), but on the special point that universal propositions do not depend for their truth on the existence of instances of the characters between which connection is asserted. For he is trying to prove not that philosophy requires self-evident premisses, but that it is about something which can be known to exist, for which purpose he has to show that its propositions are not *general* hypotheticals.

In Section 5 Mr Collingwood unfolds his main reason for thinking that philosophical propositions, or most of them, or the best of them, are not hypothetical but categorical. This we now see means that they refer to something which exists, or contain or rest on propositions which do so. And this must mean, to use language which is not Mr Collingwood's, that philosophical propositions are or contain or rest on propositions embodying either at least one logically proper name or else at least one definite description which does in fact describe something. In short, every philosophical proposition is or contains or rests on a genuine singular proposition. (Though on p. 136 Mr Collingwood distinguishes between the categorical singular judgements of history and the categorical universal (judgements) of philosophy. I cannot make head or tail of this. After the labours Mr Collingwood has taken to distinguish between (general) hypothetical propositions and categorical, it is upsetting to find that apparently after all some judgements may be universal and so (I suppose) expressible in purely general terms and yet categorical in the sense of referring to something actually existing. I fear that the principle of the overlap of Classes will be brought in to give us *carte blanche* to have it both ways when it suits our convenience!)

And his first argument for this conclusion is that the Ontological Argument is valid, and is presupposed by all other philosophical arguments, or the best of them. He paraphrases the goal of Anselm's arguments by saying that 'thought when it follows its own bent most completely and sets itself the task of thinking out the idea of an object that shall completely satisfy the demands of reason may appear to be constructing a mere *ens rationis*, but in fact is never devoid of objective or ontological reference'. (A caviller might want to know why the idea of an object *should* satisfy the demands of reason, or, more importantly, how reason can be dissatisfied with the idea of any object. And why should we suppose that it is in philosophy that thought is following its own bent most completely rather than in, say, astronomy or Antarctic exploration, in which we certainly discover things existing which we did not know of before?)

Mr Collingwood says, 'Anselm's argument that in conceiving a perfect being we are conceiving a subject possessed of all positive predicates, including that of existence, so that to think of this is already to think of it as existing, is an argument open to objection on the logical ground that existence is not a predicate; but the substance of his thought survives all such objections. . . .' But unfortunately this is precisely where I should have thought not only Hume and Kant but almost all recent logicians who have attended to the analysis of existential propositions would dig their heels in and say that the argument is an obvious fallacy *unless* existence is a 'predicate'; and that existence is not a 'predicate'. We can see how implications obtain between 'predicates', i.e., how *if* something is an A, it is B-ish. But how can the *existence* of an A or a B be implied? How can 'something is an A' follow from the proposition 'anything that is an A, is B-ish'? How can a particular matter of fact be deduced from *a priori* or non-empirical premises?

Mr Collingwood rather cavalierly dismisses Kant's refutation of the Ontological Argument as merely a result of 'that false subjectivism and consequent scepticism from which, in spite of heroic efforts, he never wholly freed himself'. 'With Hegel's rejection of subjective idealism, the Ontological Proof took its place once more among the accepted principles of modern philosophy, and it has never again been seriously criticised.' To my mind this dictum almost merits tears. One of the biggest advances in logic that have been made since Aristotle, namely Hume's and Kant's discovery that particular matters of fact cannot be the implicates of general propositions, and so cannot be demonstrated from *a priori* premises, is written off as a backsliding into an epistemological or psychological mistake, and all's to do again.

And we must swallow with regret the dismissal of the whole of the work in logic which can be loosely described as Russellian. Its criticisms, e.g., of the Ontological Argument must not be accounted serious criticism—because, I suppose, it has rejected that very subject-predicate logic which made it verbally plausible to argue from 'essence' to 'existence'. (Or perhaps because it happens to use Greek letters for some of its symbols instead of the canonised S, M and P.)

But to continue. Mr Collingwood, after showing that the Ontological Proof does not establish any particular *theological* truth, says, 'What it does prove is that essence involves existence, not always, but in one special case, the case of God in the metaphysical sense: the *Deus sive natura* of Spinoza, the Good of Plato, the Being of

Aristotle: the object of metaphysical thought. But this means the object of philosophical thought in general; for metaphysics, even if it is regarded as only one among the philosophical sciences, is not unique in its objective reference or in its logical structure; all philosophical thought is of the same kind, and every philosophical science partakes of the nature of metaphysics, which is not a separate philosophical science but a special study of the existential aspect of that same subject-matter whose aspect as truth is studied by logic and its aspect as goodness by ethics.' (But what is an 'existential aspect'? Is, after all, the existence of a thing just one among its other attributes or 'predicates'?)

'Reflection on the history of the Ontological Proof thus offers us a view of philosophy as a form of thought in which essence and existence, however clearly distinguished, are conceived as inseparable. On this view, unlike mathematics or empirical science, philosophy stands committed to maintaining that its subject-matter is no mere hypothesis, but something actually existing.'

But what is the cash value of this slogan 'Essence involves existence'? First of all, 'essence' is used only in relation; we speak of 'the essence of . . .' or so and so is 'essential to . . .' What sort of correlate is appropriate? We cannot speak (correctly) of the essence of this pipe or of Socrates, we can only speak (correctly) of the essence of some general character or description or 'predicate'. That is, we can say that it is part of the essence of Man, or of being a man, to be capable of inference. If x can't infer, then x is not a man.

There are cases, then, where we can correctly enough say that the essence of so and so involves so and so, namely where we can say that being of such and such a sort involves having such and such a property: or that if something has a certain character, it follows that it has such and such another.

Now there are some characters which are such that if anything has one of them, no other thing can have it; I think these are always complex; but for the present purpose that does not matter. 'Being the President of the United States on 19 August 1934' is a character which, I think, belongs to one man and could not belong to two or more. 'Being the oldest man now alive in Oxford' is another. We can call these, if we like, idiosyncratic or peculiar characters, or, if we prefer, call the phrases which symbolise them 'definite' or 'unique descriptions'. (The word 'the' is the customary English symbol for such non-sharable characters.) And in the case of these characters too we can say, though with a slight awkwardness, that being so and so is of the essence of having this or that idiosyncratic or peculiar character. It might, for example, be of the essence of being the senior member of a certain committee to be its chairman. But of course a definite description may not in fact apply to anyone, or a peculiar character need not characterise anyone. Oxford may have an exclusively feminine population and the United States may have no President. So, even in this special class of cases, 'being-*x* or being-the-*x* is essential to being-the-*y*' may be true, although nothing is the *x* or the *y*.

Now the Ontological Argument says that there is one case where a peculiar character C has as a part of its essence not, as elsewhere, a certain property P, but the fact-that-something-has-C.

It is part of the *analysis* of 'perfectness' that something is perfect. Part of the meaning of this one definite description is that the description fits something. Which is surely a glaring fallacy. Let us attempt to make it glare even more vividly.

It is maintained that in one case 'Essence involves existence'. What is this notion of 'involving'?

(1) Sometimes, perhaps, 'involves' means what is nowadays often meant by 'entails', namely the implication which holds between the having a certain specific character and the having the generic character of which the former is a species. Thus being green entails or 'involves' being coloured, and being square entails or 'involves' being shaped. But this is *not* the sense of 'involves' in which the Ontological Argument says that 'Essence involves existence'. For its champions would then have had to allow that the same argument would prove the existence of other things than God. But anyhow, as a question of history I doubt if any of them committed the absurdity of pretending that 'existence' is the name of a generic attribute.

(2) Sometimes 'involves' is used to express whatever it is that natural laws formulate; for example that a metal's being heated involves its expanding. But this sort of 'involving' (if, *pace* Hume, there is such a thing) is established only by induction. There is no contradiction in the negating of a natural law; whereas the Ontological Argument says that there is a contradiction in denying the existence of God or perfection.

(3) No; though I do not claim to have exhausted the various possible meanings of the word, the sense of 'involves' required for the Ontological Argument is 'includes' or 'contains as a part or constituent'. When I say that the essence of bicycles involves their having two wheels in tandem, I simply mean that the complex character of being a bicycle consists of the simpler characters *a*, *b*,

and c, and one of these simpler characters is that of having two wheels in tandem. So it is an analytic proposition to say that a bicycle has two wheels in tandem (unless it is a synthetic proposition about the English word 'bicycle', as is the case with dictionary definitions). And as this is precisely what was claimed by the Ontological Argument, namely that it is a contradiction to deny (i.e., an analytic proposition to affirm) that God exists, it is clear that 'involves' in 'Essence involves existence' means precisely 'contains as a part or constituent'.

But the parts of a complex of characters are characters. So unless existence is a character or 'predicate', it cannot be 'involved' (in this sense) in the essence of a complex character. Certainly, 'exists' is the grammatical predicate of heaps of English sentences; but it is precisely here that the fallacy of the Ontological Argument arises. For it assumes (what is false) that in every sentence which is of the noun-verb pattern or the noun-copula-adjective pattern, the noun is a genuine proper name and the verb or adjective ascribes a quality to the thing named by the grammatical subject. But even if Hume and Kant were too subjectivist for their treatment of existential propositions to be treated seriously, surely Russell's theory of descriptions and his consequential analysis of existential propositions as a species of general proposition has been before the philosophical public long enough for this ontological fallacy to merit immunity from any more exhumations.

Of course, there is a sense in which any character whatsoever involves existence. I mean that if it is true that something is green or square or north of London that something must exist. What has a quality or stands in a relation or is of a kind *ipso facto* exists. Being a Prime Minister involves existence; for if a man is Prime Minister he exists. (This is not a *significant* inference. But the object of the Ontological Argument was to show that there is one (peculiar) character of which we only know to start with that it *might* characterise something, from the analysis of the constitution of which we could discover that it *does* characterise something.)

But though it would be a contradiction to say 'this is a bicycle but it has not got two wheels in tandem' and nonsense to say 'this is a bicycle but it does not exist', it is not a contradiction or nonsense to say 'nothing has *deitas*'.

There is then no way of arguing validly to the existence of something of a certain description from non-empirical premises, namely from premises about the characters the combination of which is symbolised by the description. There is no way of demonstrating *a priori* particular matters of fact. Inferences to the existence of something, if there are any, must be causal inferences and inferences from the existence of something else. Nor are there any 'demands of reason' which can make us accept as proofs of existence combinations of propositions which contain an overt fallacy.

And if philosophy is or contains or rests on metaphysics and has no 'subject-matter' unless it has to do with a subject the existence of which is established only in this way, then there is no such philosophical science as metaphysics and no such thing as philosophy. But, as I see no force in the argument that philosophy would have no subject-matter unless it had access to a special entity, I do not find myself alarmed by this threat.

But this is not the end of the story. For in Section 7 Mr Collingwood goes on to a new line of argument, which he appears to think is merely an expansion or continuation of the previous one. To state briefly his new point, he argues that logicians enunciate principles of logic in propositions which themselves exemplify those principles. So their propositions exist. So the essence of the principles of logic involves the existence of examples of them.

The argument is so extraordinary that I must quote the relevant passages *in extenso*. After maintaining that logic has thought for its subject-matter and that it does not give a merely descriptive account of it, he says on page 129:

But neither is logic merely normative. A purely normative science would expound a norm or ideal of what its subject-matter ought to be, but would commit itself to no assertion that this ideal was anywhere realised. If logic were a science of this kind, it would resemble the exact sciences; it would in fact be, or be closely related to, mathematics. The reason why it can never conform to that pattern is that whereas in geometry, for example, the subject-matter is triangles, etc., and the body of the science consists of propositions about triangles, etc., in logic the subject-matter is propositions, and the body of the science consists of propositions about propositions. In geometry the body of the science is heterogeneous with its subject-matter; in logic they are homogeneous, and more than homogeneous, they are identical; for the propositions of which logic consists must conform to the rules which logic lays down, so that logic is actually about itself; not about itself exclusively, but at least incidentally about itself.

It follows that logic cannot be in substance merely hypothetical. Geometry can afford to be indifferent to the existence of its subject-matter; so long as it is free to suppose it, that is enough. But logic cannot share this indifference, because, by existing, it constitutes an actually existing subject-matter to itself. Thus, when we say 'all squares have their diagonals equal', we need not be either explicitly or implicitly asserting that any squares exist; but when we say 'all universal propositions distribute their subject', we are not only discussing universal propositions, we are also enunciating a universal proposition; we are producing an actual instance of the thing under discussion, and cannot discuss it without doing so. Consequently no such discussion can be indifferent to the existence of its own subject-matter; in other words, the propositions which constitute the body of logic cannot ever be in substance hypothetical. A logician who lays it down that all universal propositions are merely hypothetical is showing a true insight into the nature of science, but he is undermining the very possibility of logic; for his assertion cannot be true consistently with the fact of his maintaining it.

Similarly with inference. Logic not only discusses, it also contains reasoning; and if a logician could believe that no valid reasoning anywhere existed, he would merely be disbelieving his own logical theory. For logic has to provide not only a theory of its subject-matter, but in the same breath, a theory of itself; it is an essential part of its proper task that it should consider not only how other kinds of thought proceed, and on what principles, but how and on what principles logic proceeds. If it had only to consider other kinds of thought, it could afford to deal with its subject-matter in a way either merely normative or merely descriptive; but towards itself it can only stand in an attitude that is both at once. It is obliged to produce, as constituent parts of itself, actual instances of thought which realise its own ideal of what thought should be.

Logic, therefore, stands committed to the principle of the Ontological Proof. Its subject-matter, namely thought, affords an instance of something which cannot be conceived except as actual, something whose essence involves existence.

I shall find it hard to condense within reasonable limits my objections to this argument. But my main objects are to show first that this argument has nothing to do with the Ontological Argument, and second that it has no tendency to establish the general conclusion that the propositions of logic are not hypothetical. But I have one or two subsidiary bones to pick with Mr Collingwood as well.

The first of the subsidiary bones is this. Mr Collingwood is at pains to show that a logician who *denies* the existence of any instances of logically regular thinking must be wrong because he himself is producing an instance of that which he denies to exist. Now this might, *per accidens*, be so (though a man might, if he troubled, deny the occurrence of genuine singular propositions without producing one, or argue against the occurrence of syllogisms in Disamis by syllogisms in Baroco). But it has no bearing on the point. For (general) hypothetical propositions do not *deny* the existence of their subjects, they only do not affirm or imply their existence. So a man who maintained that all the propositions of logic are (general) hypotheticals would not be denying the existence of anything. So his exposure as himself a producer of propositions would no more disconcert him than a lecturer on canine diseases would be disconcerted by hearing the bark of a dog.

The second subsidiary bone is to point out that when Mr Collingwood argues that if logic was purely normative 'it would resemble the exact sciences: it would in fact either be, or be closely related to, mathematics', he does not seem to remember that this is precisely what is desired for logic by many logicians, past and present.

The third is this. It is not peculiar to logical propositions that they themselves (sometimes, not generally) belong to the subject-matter which they discuss. The English grammarian writes grammatically about grammar; the educationist lectures instructively about lecturing instructively; the signalling instructor may signal instructions about signalling to his pupils; Horace writes his *Ars Poetica* in poetry. Have *these* anything to do with the Ontological Argument?

I suppose Mr Collingwood would reply that it is accidental if the principles of grammar or elocution or poetry are conveyed in vehicles which themselves exemplify those principles, but it is necessary that logicians' propositions should instantiate the principles which they themselves propound.

But even this seems to me not to be so. For after all one can talk about singular propositions in general propositions, negative propositions in affirmative ones, relational in attributive and attributive in relational propositions. One can reason about the syllogism in non-syllogistic arguments and vice versa.

But let us suppose that sometimes logicians have to formulate logical principles or rules in propositions which are instances of them. Even so, the writer or reader might and usually would attend to what the propositions say without noticing that the propositions themselves were cases in point, just as he may study grammar without noticing that the grammarian is keeping the rules. And even if he noticed it he might still not use the instances as illustrations. It is indeed difficult to attend, so to speak, twice at once to a given proposition, namely once to what it says and once to the fact that it exemplifies the rule that it states.

So when Mr Collingwood says that 'no such discussion [as logic] can be indifferent to the existence of its own subject-matter', while it is not easy to see which of several things he means, it is easy to see that, in all the possible meanings of the expression, what he says is false.

(*a*) If he means that the reader of a logical text-book or the hearer of a logical lecture cannot understand the logical principles which are stated unless he uses the actual statements of them as illustrations, then this is false. For we very seldom find that this is the case, and when it is we very seldom do use the statement as an illustration; and generally we do not require an illustration at all.

(*b*) If he means that logical principles cannot be stated save in propositions which exemplify them, then this is in general false. How could, e.g., a singular proposition tell us what a singular proposition is? And how will Mr Collingwood state the principle of the syllogism in a syllogism?

(*c*) If he means that a given logical principle involves that a given logician should write or speak what he does write or speak about it, I challenge him to deduce from the principle of the syllogism the actual sentences which Mill or Russell propounds about it. The only thing of which we can say that it would of logical necessity be different from what it is if a given proposition of Mill or Russell had been omitted or worded differently is Mill's *System of Logic* or Russell's *Principia Mathematica*. And they are books and not logical principles. If a sheep exists its wool exists; and if Mill's *Logic* exists its 365th proposition exists; but its existence is involved not by the truth of the principle which it states but by the existence of the volume of which it is a part.

(*d*) But Mr Collingwood avers that when a general proposition is propounded by a logician which happens to be *about* general propositions, then it is incidentally about itself. And this suggests (I hope I am wrong in discerning this suggestion) that it is part of the *meaning* of this proposition that it should exist: i.e., that the truth of what the proposition states depends upon and so implies that this proposition should be written or spoken as and when and where it is.

Now, of course, the word 'about' is very ambiguous; but, in one sense of it, to say that a proposition is about itself is to commit the simplest of type-fallacies. But anyhow Mr Collingwood's own argument only entitles him to use the term 'about' in this other sense, namely that a proposition is 'about' *x* when it applies to *x*. So 'dogs are carnivorous' is 'about' Fido in the sense that Fido is a dog and so is carnivorous. But we have long since accepted with Mr Collingwood the view that (general) hypothetical propositions, while they may apply to this or that square or this or that case of tuberculosis, do not depend for their truth on this being a square or that being a case of tuberculosis. In the same way, then, if a logician's proposition is an instance of a logical principle, of which it is the statement, the principle will apply to the proposition, but it will not imply its existence. (How *could* a perfectly general truth like a logical principle imply a particular spoken or printed occurrence?) But of course we only need to ask the simple question How can we discover what propositions have been propounded by logicians? to see the position. For the answer is that we must read their books or hear their lectures, or infer from testimonies and traditions: that is, we can only discover this sort of fact empirically. We do not employ the Ontological Argument.

After all, Mr Collingwood did say that there was only one case where essence involves existence, namely, where the essence of God, or the Good, or Being implied its existence. But here what is being hailed as necessarily existing is not God or the Good or Being but this and that remark of this and that logician. So that even if logicians could not help uttering logically regular propositions (which alas! they *can* help), this supposed necessitation would be something quite different from the supposed analytic necessity of existing which the Ontological Argument ascribes to God or the Good or Being. All that Mr Collingwood's argument amounts to is that a man will be a bad logician unless he tells the truth and reasons validly or obeys the laws of logic which it is his professional business to expound. But there is, unfortunately, no logical contradiction in asserting that someone is a bad logician.

It is clear then that the fact that thousands of logicians' propositions exist or have existed has no tendency to show of what logical form the propositions of logic are or must be.

And it is clear too that the Ontological Argument is quite a different argument from this one of Mr Collingwood's which tries to establish the categorical nature of the propositions of logic from the fact that some logical principles are exemplified in the propositions which are employed to formulate them.

I hope Mr Collingwood will not find that my criticisms are vitiated by 'subjective idealism'.

8

BACK TO THE ONTOLOGICAL
ARGUMENT

Reprinted from 'Mind', vol. XLIV, *1937*

I am glad that Mr Harris challenges my attempted refutation of the Ontological Argument. It is a very important question about the nature of philosophical theories, whether philosophical arguments can establish the existence of anything. So it is encouraging to find someone who both believes in that possibility and produces arguments for it.

(1) I have no objection to the suggestion that the argument which I tried to show to be fallacious is not identical with the argument which Hegel, and perhaps also Professor Collingwood, champions. It is always possible that unsympathy may cause a critic to fail to read between the lines a doctrine which is clearly discerned to be there by more sympathetic spirits. And I have no desire to thrash out here hermeneutic questions, or adduce literary evidence that anyone does champion the Ontological Argument (as I represented it).

(2) The interesting question is whether the 'deeper truth' in the Ontological Argument, which Mr Harris thinks that I failed to discern, is a different argument from the one which I criticised, and if so, whether it is valid.

Now, as Mr Harris formulates this argument, it certainly is different in one very important respect from what I called 'the Ontological Argument'. And it is at first sight a much better argument. For it is a variant of the Cosmological Argument or the argument *a contingentia mundi*. It argues from the fact that our world of ordinary or finite experience is of a certain character. And this is certainly intended to be or to contain an empirical existence-proposition. 'We experience a world of such and such a sort' is an empirical or *a posteriori* premiss to his argument.

And as this is precisely what I demanded for any argument of which the conclusion is to be an existence-proposition, I might stop here, just expressing my contentment that Hegel and Mr Harris do admit by implication that arguments to existence from *a priori* premisses are invalid.

(3) Certainly arguments for the existence of fountain-pens or remote planets, or for the occurrence of past events, have very complex premisses, and may be described as resting upon certain systematic conceptions or notions of system. But this does not make those premisses non-empirical. The demands of mutual corroboration of perceptions must be satisfied, but they cannot be satisfied or unsatisfied unless perceptions occur. And of course such arguments can never constitute rigorous proofs. The pen's existence is never logically necessary, whatever empirical premisses we employ. (Any scientist can be baffled by a conjuror—for a time.)

However, we should be foolish not to accept the conclusions of hosts of such arguments. And if the argument for the Absolute is really of the same logical pattern, and if the premisses have the required empirical content plus systematic interlocking, we shall be foolish not to accept the conclusion that God or the Absolute exists. But is the doctrine really just a well-established hypothesis of Natural Science? Do the Fellows of the Royal Society support the views of Hegel in the same way as they vouch for spiral nebulae? Obviously they do not. So obviously the argument for the Absolute is not just a well-attested scientific hypothesis adduced to explain phenomena. What, then, is the difference?

(4) The difference is that the Cosmological Argument is not a scientists' argument but a philosophical argument. And, as Kant saw, it presupposes the Ontological Argument (in the form in which I tried to refute it). True, it covers its tracks by reassuringly introducing an empirical premiss about the whole world of fact or the world of finite experience. But this enters into the argument only in this way, that there is now alleged to be a contradiction not just in the denial of the existence of the Absolute but in the conjunction of this denial with the affirmation of the existence of our world of fact. The existence of our world of fact logically implies the existence of the Absolute. For the former is a part, or an aspect, or an appearance of the latter. (Incidentally, is it not high time that we were told which? For the alleged implication is different according to the relation adopted. On a matter of such importance we ought not to be left to pay our money and take our choice.) However, there are perfectly valid arguments of the various proposed forms.

(*a*) 'Here is the grin of a Cheshire cat' certainly entails that a Cheshire cat exists of which the grin is an aspect.

(*b*) 'Here is the tail of a cat' certainly entails that there is or has been a cat of which the tail is or was a part.

(*c*) 'Here is the smell of a cat' certainly entails that there is or was a cat of which the smell is or was an appearance. In each case the conclusion is certain—*if the premiss is known to be true*. And we can know empirically that a grin is a cat's grin, a tail a cat's tail, and a smell a cat's smell. But, of course, a similar grin, tail or smell might belong to quite a different animal. How do we, or Mr Harris, know that our world is an aspect, part or appearance of something else? From the *Proceedings of the Royal Society* or from philosophical considerations? empirically or *a priori*?

Apparently from philosophical considerations. And I want to show that these considerations are hollow unless the Ontological Argument is valid. But I must in fairness say that my interpretation of what these considerations are is largely conjectural. For I have got to read between the lines of Mr Harris's contribution.

The nerve of the argument lies in the significance of the adjective 'intelligible'. A certain conclusion must be accepted because without it the world of fact is philosophically unintelligible. But Mr Harris does not tell us what it is for something to be unintelligible or intelligible.

He does not mean, I think, by 'unintelligible' 'not yet subsumed under a causal law'. Else his paper would have been a defence of the methods of Newton, and not of an argument of Hegel. Moreover, he uses the phrase 'philosophically intelligible'.

I surmise that what he means is this. The existence of something or the occurrence of something is philosophically unintelligible when its existence or occurrence is a brute empirical fact, and not logically necessary; i.e., when the denial of it involves no contradiction. And the existence of something is philosophically intelligible when the assertion of it is the assertion of an analytic proposition or of a consequence analytically following from an analytic proposition or of a consequence analytically following from an analytic proposition. And this is the principle of the argument from Essence to existence, namely that there is something, the denial of the existence of which involves a contradiction.

Against this I shall only repeat the conclusion of my original argument; namely that existence propositions are synthetic, and are never logically necessary. So no existence-proposition is philosophically intelligible, if this is what it means to call something philosophically intelligible. But this does not imply that there is anything philosophically puzzling about the existence or occurrence of things and events in Nature, unless everything is puzzling which philosophers cannot demonstrate.

Now let us suppose that Mr Harris means something different from this by his phrase 'philosophically intelligible'. No matter what it is, it will have to be consistent with the admission that no existence-proposition can be logically necessary or demonstrable from *a priori* premises or such that its denial involves a contradiction.

So there will be no possibility of demonstrating that our world of fact couldn't exist unless there exists something else of which it is an aspect, part or appearance, unless we know *empirically* that our world of fact is an aspect of something, a part of something or an appearance of something. What sort of knowledge would this be?

I will not quarrel with the, to me, suspect noun of assemblage 'the world', except to say that I am not clear what it is supposed to be a totality of, or how, if it is a totality, it can be described as 'incomplete'.

Let us suppose that we are agreed as to what is denoted by 'our world of fact' or 'the world of finite experience', and concentrate on the question how we might discover empirically that it is an aspect, part or appearance of something else.

(*a*) '*x* is an aspect of *y*' is often true, e.g., 'that is the grin of a Cheshire cat'. But that there exists something which both grins and has such other properties as to rank as a cat of a certain sort is a complex synthetic proposition. There is no deducing those other properties from this one of grinning. Nor is there, strictly, an entailment between an occurrence of grinning and the existence of a grinner. Both are ways of expressing the single fact that something is grinning.

If it makes sense and is true to say that our world of fact is an aspect, then we are acquainted with the aspected something in being acquainted with the world. There is no place for an *argument* from the one to the other. Or if the argument was from that aspect which is our world to some other aspects, then the inference would not be logically necessary.

(*b*) '*x* is a part of *y*' is often true. But it is always a synthetic proposition. We have only inductive grounds for supposing that whenever things like cats' tails exist there are also things like cats that they are attached to. So it is a synthetic proposition to say that our world belongs to something else as part to whole. Its denial would contain no contradiction.

(*c*) '*x* is an appearance of *y*' is often true. But here, too, either the appearance is an abstraction from the thing appearing, in which case there is no inference from the existence of the one to that of the other. For only one existence is given. Or the inference is from one appearance to other appearances, properties, parts, etc. of the thing appearing, in which case the inference is not better than probable, and must rest on inductive grounds.

So the argument from intelligibility proves nothing, unless 'intelligible' means 'logically necessary'. The Cosmological Argument, then, if it is a philosophers' argument, embodies the principle of the old Ontological Argument, that there can be a logically necessary existence-proposition. And, as this is false, the Cosmological Argument is invalid. There can be no proof from *a priori* premisses that there exists something of which the world of finite experience is an aspect, part or appearance.

Nor will the argument be bettered by the substitution which Mr Harris recommends of some notion of being or being real in place of that of existing. For, apart from the suggestion, which I am sure Mr Harris did not intend to convey, that 'existing', 'being' and 'being real' signify different species of one (generic) attribute—the very error from which the old Ontological Argument drew its plausibility and its fallaciousness—, the arguments for the being or the being real of something of a certain description are of the same logical pattern as those for the existence of something. Indeed, I am at a loss to see any but a verbal difference between them.

Mr Harris must show that there is a contradiction in 'our world is not an aspect, part or appearance of anything else' or else that there are good empirical reasons for supposing that our world is an aspect, part or appearance of something else. And if he accepts the former task he must face the question: Can an existence-proposition be logically necessary?

I very much hope that Mr Harris will face this question. It is to me rather shocking that there should exist a large school of thought which treats as a well-established principle a doctrine which has been for a century and a half accused of formal fallaciousness. There may be an answer to the accusation—but it ought to be divulged, in order that it may be tested.

To summarize: A philosophical argument for the existence or reality of something must be of one of two forms.

(1) Either it argues that there is a contradiction in the denial of the existence or reality of such a thing, which is the Ontological Argument proper.

(2) Or it argues that something is empirically known to exist *but*

that it is logically impossible for anything to exist unless either its existence is logically necessary or its existence logically implies that something else exists of logical necessity.

Neither holds water if 'there exists a so and so' is a synthetic proposition or one the negation of which contains no contradiction and so is logically possible.

9

UNVERIFIABILITY-BY-ME

Reprinted from 'Analysis', vol. IV, *1936, by permission of the editor*

The notion of verifiability-in-principle, which is, I think, identical with Kant's notion of possible experience, is not yet puzzle-free. What does it mean to say that I could or could not have such sense-experiences or introspection-experiences as would verify or falsify the sentence 'something has property ϕ'? Or what does it mean to say that a certain experience or any experience of a certain sort is possible or impossible for me?

The verifiability-principle, in which I find puzzles, is sometimes formulated as 'the meaning of a proposition is the method of its verification'. This formulation is bad, for (1) propositions do not *have* meanings; (2) it is unclear what 'its' refers to; (3) 'method of verification' is vague.

I suggest the following: 'The whole meaning of a (non-tautologous) sentence is the fact that I could have certain specified experiences. I verify it when I have such experiences. I understand it when I realize that I could have them. A (non-tautologous) sentence is meaningless if, or in so far as, it does not signify the possibility of my having certain experiences.'

That there is a puzzle left unresolved is shown by the facts (1) that on a plausible interpretation of the principle it must be nonsensical to say that something took place at a time when I, being still unborn, could not have witnessed it and (2) that on the same or an affiliated interpretation of the principle it must be nonsensical for me to say that there are sense-experiences and introspection-experiences which are not mine. For example 'he feels anger like mine' would have to be nonsense. On this interpretation 'he is angry' has to mean 'he exhibits such and such anger-symptoms, which I do or could witness'. So, on this view, it would be a contradiction for me to say 'he is angry but does not exhibit anger-symptoms' or 'he exhibits anger-symptoms but is not angry'. Whereas 'I am angry' does not mean the same as 'I exhibit anger-symptoms', and if both are true the connection of the two truths is only synthetic. In other words 'angry' when applied to me stands for an introspectible emotion; when applied to other persons, it stands only for manifestations witnessable by me, like flushes, grimaces, quickened pulse and so on. Similarly 'a battle was fought in 1815' would have to mean 'I could find skeletons, records, memorials, etc'.

Now this view is a paradox, which does not prove that it is false, but warrants us in suspecting its soundness. As plain men we believe that 'he is angry' means the same sort of thing as 'I am angry'. A man, like a good actor, might simulate all or as many as you like of the symptoms of anger without being angry, or be angry and exhibit none of them. Or if he could not control his pulse-rate, this is only because a quick pulse stands to being angry as thunder to lightning. The connection is a causal and synthetic one, and not an analytic or semantic one. Similarly, as plain men we believe that 'an eclipse of the sun happened 1000 years before my birth' means the same sort of thing as 'an eclipse happened on my tenth birthday'.

Yet we have to admit that it would be absurd to say 'I remember events happening before I existed' or to say 'I find on introspection that someone not myself is angry'. And the unwitnessability-by-me both of pre-twentieth century events and of your anger is no mere question of practical difficulties of access (such as prevented Galileo from seeing things which we with improved telescopes see very well). No conceivable engineering or surgical dodge would make such witnessings possible. The supposition of my remembering happenings of dates earlier than the beginning of my existence is nonsensical, and so is that of my introspecting states of mind not my own. 'Some introspectibilia are not mine' seems to be in principle unverifiable by me, and yet we don't find self-evident the sort of solipsism that would result from admitting that it is meaningless to say it.

I suggest that the source of the trouble is a dual one. (1) The notion of 'could', 'might' or 'possible' which is contained in 'verifiable' and 'possible experience' has been left unconstrued. (2) The notions of 'I', 'mine', 'you', 'he', etc. have been left unconstrued.

It is notorious that 'possible' covers two quite different things, namely 'logically possible' and 'causally possible'. It is logically possible that I should see mountains on the far side of the moon, if there are any; but it is at present causally impossible. The task is impracticable but the supposition of it is not nonsensical. 'I cannot lift this rock' states an impracticability. But it would not even be this if it was nonsensical to suppose my doing so, as it would be to suppose my picking up a shadow. Otherwise causal laws would be analytic, tautological, knowable by pure reason, etc.

However, there is this important analogy between logical and causal possibilities (and impossibilities and necessities). A singular or particular assertion of possibility (impossibility or necessity) always entails a universal one. Indeed it is the joint assertion of a variable hypothetical and one or several instantial propositions.

For, I hold, to assert that so and so is logically possible is to say that something is compatible with something else, i.e. that x is ϕ does not entail that x is not ψ, or 'a ϕ can (logically) be a ψ', so that when I say 'this could (logically) be a ψ' I mean 'this *qua* a ϕ could be a ψ', i.e. 'from something's being a ϕ it does not follow that it is not a ψ *and* this is a ϕ'. And to say that something is causally possible is to say that 'whatever is ϕ is ψ' (where this states not an entailment but a law-proposition) is false. For instance 'a man may smile and smile and be a villain' denies the law-proposition 'villains never smile'. A singular or particular causal proposition like 'that dose of arsenic killed Jones' if true implies that men, or men of such and such constitutions who take such and such amounts of arsenic die; and adds to that law-proposition the instantial rider that Jones is such a man and took such a dose. (This is not the whole story.) Correspondingly a singular or particular causal-possibility statement is the joint assertion of the negative of a law-proposition and one or several instantial riders.

I can at present find no other account of possibility-propositions, and consequently, if only to clear the air, assert that a sentence of the pattern 'this may or could be so and so' is neither true nor false unless unpackable into 'this *qua* such and such may be so and so', where the phrase '*qua* such and such' indicates the protasis of the variable hypothetical involved. That is, to talk for the moment in the misguided language of 'logically proper names', if N is a logically proper name, 'so and so is possible or impossible for N' can only avoid being meaningless if some sort of description is surreptitiously or overtly tacked on to N (such as 'the chairman' or 'a bit of paper'). For we cannot say that N is compatible or incompatible with anything. We shall see that the very reason why I can say 'I can so and so' or 'so and so is impossible for me' is because 'I' and 'me' *in these uses* are not being used as naked, logically proper names. The pertinence of these considerations to the question of unverifiability-by-me is, I hope, obvious.

I now want to mention a class of cases where we get a conflation of logical and causal possibilities. 'That post could be knocked over by a skittle-ball' states, truly or falsely, a causal practicability. But 'that skittle-pin could be knocked over by a skittle-ball' states (or can do) an analytic proposition; for it would not be a skittle-pin if it could not be knocked over by a skittle-ball. The specific causal possibility or 'power' (as Locke calls it) is part of the concept of a skittle-pin. But, of course, that this stick is a skittle-pin, i.e. is, *inter alia*, upsettable by a skittle-ball is a synthetic proposition.

I want to show, if I can, that the logical impossibility of my verifying certain sorts of propositions is analogous to the logical impossibility of a skittle-pin being non-upsettable—namely that the logical impossibility derives from the fact that certain causal 'powers' are already part of the concept of that for which something is said to be logically impossible. Further, as 'skittle-pins are upsettable by skittle-balls' is an analytic proposition about things into the defini- tion of the sort of which there enters the notion of a causal power and as no causal proposition is itself analytic or logically necessary, the prior proposition 'there are or might be skittle-pins' *entails* that there might be posts which causally could not be upset by a skittle-ball.

I want to argue that by a partial parity of reasoning 'I can only find introspectively my own experiences' is an analytic proposition but one which indirectly *entails* that it is significant to say 'there are introspectible experiences which are not in me and so not intro- spectible by me'.

Take first the proposition 'I, who am blinded, cannot see'. This is an analytic proposition; but the notion of being blinded is a causal notion. 'I cannot see because I have cataract in both eyes' expresses a causal hypothesis. It would not be significant to say 'I am blinded' unless it meant something to say 'there is such a thing as sight and I am the sort of being to whom ability to see might (logically and causally) belong'. (We don't call the Equator blind; nor an oak-tree.) But of course both 'I have cataract' and 'I can not see' are synthetic propositions.

Take next 'I who was born in 1900 could not have witnessed the battle of Waterloo, which occurred in 1815'. Taking it, as against transmigrationists, that I did not exist before I was born, it is an analytic proposition that a person, e.g. I, could not have been born in 1900 and witnessed an event of 1815. But that I was born in 1900 and not in 1800 is a synthetic proposition. I might be a Rip van Winkle. It is a synthetic proposition also that the sight of an event cannot occur long after the event. (I can smell a fox long after it has departed, but probably not so long as a century afterwards.)

Well then, when someone says 'I could not have witnessed an event of a century ago' we must ask 'why not?' If he says 'why, you know I was only born thirty-six years ago', is the implication that he expected his being of that age to be part of what his personal pronoun 'I' signified? If so, then it is an analytic proposition that 'no one can be a witness of an event *and* not be a witness of anything until long after and I (born in 1900) postdate Waterloo (1815).'

(That a personal pronoun *can* signify important material facts is shown by 'he' and 'she', which signify sex, and the royal 'we', which signifies a unique rank.)

But if, what is more likely, he says, 'I couldn't have been at Waterloo because, as a matter of fact, I did not begin witnessing things until the twentieth century', there is nothing to stop me replying, 'Oh, but you have forgotten that you are a Rip van Winkle. You were at Waterloo.' He can say that it is historically false, but that entails that it is not nonsense. Or he can appeal to notorious facts about senescence, such as that if he had been there his hair would now be grey, or aver that he couldn't have forgotten the affair. But these are causal propositions which entail that the hypothesis is significant.

Suppose, what might easily have been the practice, that I modified with a new suffix the first personal pronoun with every birthday, so that between 19 August 1936 and 19 August 1937 I called myself 'I-bo' (meaning, 'I, who am now 36 years old'). Then it would be a contradiction to say 'I-bo could have witnessed events of 1815'. But then it would be a synthetic proposition to say that I-bo exist. So we can now put the issue thus. When I say 'I could not have witnessed the events of 1815', either this means 'I-bo could not have witnessed them' or it means 'I didn't witness them because as a matter of fact I was not, I believe, born in time'. Both entail that it is significant to say there were happenings which I could not have witnessed. For the one rests on the causal law that seeing is roughly synchronous with the events seen plus the two historical assertions that I began to see in 1900 and Waterloo was fought nearly a century before. The other is an analytic proposition in which relative recency of birth is part of what is signified by the pronoun 'I-bo'. But it is not an analytic proposition that I-bo exist, i.e. that I was born in 1900. (Cf. 'She couldn't be a headmaster.' This is an analytic proposition. But 'Jones is a woman' is synthetic. 'Jones is eligible for headmaster' is significant but not 'Jones, who is a woman, is eligible for headmaster'.) So I do not in historical fact satisfy and I-bo do not by definition satisfy the causal conditions of being a witness of Waterloo

(1815); and both these propositions entail that the supposition of these conditions being satisfied by an observer is a significant one.

To say that something existed or happened may very likely mean or imply that if anyone, having such and such sense-faculties and intellectual capacities, had been at a certain place at a certain time, he would have seen, heard, smelled and felt so and so. But the question Was I in fact such an observer? is an irrelevant question of historical fact. And the question Might I have been such an observer? is otiose anyhow and in some cases meaningless. It is otiose, for what such an observer would have witnessed he would have witnessed whether I or you were he. And it is in some cases a meaningless question, namely when the supposition of my being such an observer contains a contradiction. For example if the notion of being an ordinarily generated human being is part of what is understood by the pronoun 'I', then the supposition of my being a witness of the birth of my grandfather contains a contradiction, whereas the notion of your being a witness of the birth of my grandfather, if you are out of the family, contains none. Though it is still a matter of historical fact that you were born too late. But anyhow for it to be significant to say that I had a grandfather who was born on such and such a day, it is not required that anyone in particular should in fact have been a witness; but only that if a properly situated and equipped observer had existed he would have witnessed so and so. We might call this 'the principle of verifiability by any verifier you please'. I believe it to be the correct form, and that any reference to a particular person like me is a red herring or worse.

But we must turn to the thornier case of introspectibles. Is there a flaw in the deduction from the principle of verifiability by me of the solipsist doctrine that all introspectibles are experiences of mine? I think that there is. But of course it is not for me here to produce evidence that there *are* two or several persons having experiences in the sense in which I have experiences. It is only required to show that the supposition is not nonsensical.

Let me begin by allowing that it is an analytic proposition that all experiences that introspection reveals to me are my experiences. Also, what is either a kindred point or the same point, it is an analytic proposition that all the experiences which I can recall to memory are experiences of mine. So that emotions, thoughts, etc. which are not mine are logically incapable of being witnessed by me.

What do expressions like 'mine' or 'by me' mean? It is tempting but incorrect to say that to call an experience 'mine' is just another way of calling it 'introspectible' or 'rememberable' or both by me.

It is tempting, for then we could just say that it was a tautology to say that the experiences which I introspect or which I recall are mine, or vice versa. But it is incorrect. For Freud shows that I cannot (causally) introspect some of my experiences; and I cannot (causally) remember all my dreams. So 'mine' cannot mean 'introspected and/or recalled'. That what I introspect or recall are my experiences is an analytic proposition about introspection and memory and not about 'my'.

What then does make an experience 'mine' or a part of my life-history? (Cf. The analogous but more complex question, What makes an action mine in the sense that I am to blame for it?) What sort of a term is that which is signified by the pronoun 'I' in such sentences as 'I had a dream', 'I remember my dream', 'I cannot remember my dream', 'I find my motives are mixed', 'I first witnessed things thirty-six years ago', 'I am irritable', etc.

The first point that I want to make is that in this sort of use 'I' cannot be a logically proper name i.e. a demonstrative symbol lacking any descriptive elements. For, for one thing, if I am right about possibility-propositions, we could not say 'I can or cannot...' Nor could we say 'I am prone to...' As we saw, 'she' (in some non-nautical uses) already signifies the possession of a sex, i.e. exemplification of complex physiological and biological causal laws. In the same sort of way 'I' must already signify the possession of some very general attributes—so that there will be some sentences of the form 'I am not ϕ' which will be self-contradictory. But what? I suggest that in some quite ordinary uses 'I am a human being', 'I am either male or female', 'I can think' would be taken not merely as obvious and notorious truths about me, but as analytic ones. We may compare the alleged Chinese periphrasis for 'I', namely 'the person now speaking', where 'person' and 'ability to speak' are obviously complex concepts.

With qualms I am going to assume that it is a tautology to say 'I am a person', in some uses of 'I' and 'person'. What then does it mean to say 'There exists a person'? We want to have an outline answer to this if we are to make sense of the assertion 'That dream belonged to the same person as this fit of temper or this act of memory'. And of course I am not going to give the whole answer. I do not know it. But I want to suggest that the concept of a person must contain some very general causal 'powers', of the specification of most of which we are probably still ignorant. Nor can we deduce them from the fact that there is some law or other covering the phenomena. To illustrate the sort of thing I have in mind: We understand what it means to say 'Here is one piece of string and there is another and this knot is a part of the same piece of string as that knot'. But the tests of the alleged unity of (allegedly) one piece of string would be causal tests, such as seeing whether pulls were transmitted or not. If one knot stayed still however and whenever we pulled the other, we should be satisfied that they belonged to different pieces. If, conversely, it moved about a yard north when we pulled the other about a yard north, this would not satisfy us that they were bits of one piece of string. For two bits might be coupled together. But this means that by some operation other than cutting fibres we could secure that tugging one knot would not result in movement of the other. The notions of coupling and cutting fibres are again causal ones. Well, I want to suggest that the same sort of account must be given of 'belonging to one person'. Only the tests will not only be mechanical, but also physiological, biological, and psychological. How else do we break down an *alias*? Or establish that Sally Beauchamp's body was not 'possessed' by different 'shes' at different times?

The notion of 'mine', in the use we are discussing is or is partly a complex causal notion. It is that that makes biographical and autobiographical diagnosis possible. (Indeed I surmise, but am not sure, that there is no non-causal sense in which two things or events can be said to 'belong' to each other or to some third thing or event. For 'causation' is the name for any such connection between existences as allows of inferences from the one to the other. That flints do not dissipate and clouds do is a general causal fact about what flints are composed of and what clouds are made of. That there are persons existing through a longish stretch of time is partially analogous to the fact that there are such tough objects as flints.)

Now if some such outline account of personality is true, we can see how it might be an analytic proposition to say that one person cannot dream another person's dream, or that one person cannot recall or introspect another person's experiences, any more than a knot in one piece of string can be in another piece of string. Or any more than the Thames can flow between the banks of the Nile. But the very fact that the person who I am can't (logically) be a person who I am not, or have or recall or introspect the experiences of a person who I am not, entails that it is significant to say that there is a person other than I, having, recalling and introspecting experiences which are not mine. My experiences are private, certainly. That is a tautology. But privacy is a causal impossibility, though one which is partly constitutive of the concept of a person. But privacy being a causal notion, it must be significant to say that there are experiences which do not belong to me, just as the very fact that it is a tautology to say that skittle-pins are upsettable by skittle-balls entails that it is significant to say that there are some posts which could not (causally) be upset by a skittle-ball.

What then can I understand by the statement 'someone else is having a dream'? Assuming the truth of the principle of verifiability by any verifier you please, it would mean, 'Someone might wake up and recall having had a dream, or find on introspection a state of mind which could (causally) only be the after effect of a forgotten dream. Such an observer would have to be the dreamer of the dream. And I did not dream any such dream.'

This, of course, is no case of my having direct access to the dream, i.e. dreaming it or recalling dreaming it. For *ex hypothesi* I and the dreamer are different persons. The causal impracticability of the access is part of what is meant by the use of the two pronouns in the phrase 'you and I'. If I want to verify that someone else had a dream, I cannot (and would not, in fact, try to) do anything better than collect testimony and external symptoms. Nor can I do anything else about the battle of Waterloo. It would not be the me who I am if I could do any better. For the person who I am is a historically dated person.

For me to apprehend a synthetic proposition, assuming the generalized verifiability principle, I have only to consider certain general propositions about hypothetical observations and we must resist the temptation to tack on the proprietary label 'observations of mine', since this imports at the very least an unwanted existence-proposition about me: and in some cases the 'me' whose existence is imported is such that there is a contradiction in supposing that I could satisfy the causal conditions of making those observations.

I think that some philosophers feel a difficulty in the notion of a sentence conveying a meaning to me when what is conveyed is not a proposition directly or indirectly about me. How can I understand 'someone would see so and so' save by electing myself to be that someone?

(*a*) Certainly sentences don't convey anything unless they convey something to someone. They convey propositions only at those moments when someone is understanding them.

(*b*) But when we call sentences or quasi-sentences 'inconceivable', 'meaningless' or 'nonsensical' we do not mean that someone or a lot of people in fact fail to understand them, though they might if they were more intelligent understand them. We mean that no one could entertain what they profess to state, since they are self-contradictions or break some rule of formal logic.

(*c*) So the question is whether I find contradictions or other breaches of the rules of logic in what a sentence says. And in this sense it is not meaningless to speak of hypothetical observations without attaching the proprietary label 'of mine' to them.

(*d*) But there is the psychological difficulty of imagery. When I entertain the thought of someone seeing something, I do in fact illustrate with images of panoramas etc. in which of course the spectacle is my spectacle. That is why I cannot imagine the world after my death; for I continue to have visual images of rooms etc. which should be without me in them, but always have me in them as spectator. We have a similar difficulty when we think of the state of mind of someone who has been blind from birth. But this has nothing to do with the question of whether a sentence contains a contradiction or not.

CONCLUSION

There is no contradiction in saying, 'An observer with such and such faculties, opportunities etc. would witness so and so, but a person in my shoes could not (logically) be such an observer'.

The verifiability-principle can contain no reference to me.

The question What sorts of observation are logically possible for no-matter-what observer and what are logically impossible? requires elucidation. We do not yet know what 'verifiable in principle' means.

10

INDUCTION AND HYPOTHESIS

Reprinted from 'Proceedings of the Aristotelian Society', Suppl. vol. XVI, *1937, by permission of the editor*

I begin by mentioning some points in Miss MacDonald's contribution which are, I think, clearly enough true for it to be otiose for me to discuss them.

(1) Induction is not embryonic deduction. No contradiction is involved in the conjunction of the premisses of an induction with the negative of its conclusion.

(2) It does not follow nor is it true that it is proper to describe as 'accidental' or 'miraculous' the states of affairs to which we are or wish to be able to make causal inference. We apply these adjectives to what is unusual or irregular or to what is not explained by any or any known causal law and not to states of affairs for which a deductive metaphysician fails to find a demonstration. 'Contingent' is not synonymous with 'miraculous' or with 'fortuitous'.

(3) Scientists' general propositions are neither commands nor signals, statements or recommendations of habits. They are truths or falsehoods.

(4) In neither of the usual senses of 'hypothesis' is it true either that all the general propositions of science and ordinary experience or all their singular and general propositions are mere hypotheses.

For in some sense of 'established' some singular and general propositions are established. And there is a contradiction in describing a proposition as a hypothesis (i.e. conjectural proposition) but established. Some general propositions are established to be the explanations of others already known to be true. These are called 'laws' and not 'hypotheses'. And some non-general propositions are known to be true. These are called 'matters of fact' or 'facts' and not 'hypotheses'.

I might here do a little terminological sorting. In one sense of 'hypothesis' any proposition, singular or general, which is only conjectured to be true, is a hypothesis. In another sense, a proposition is a hypothesis which is such that if true it would be the explanation of some other accepted proposition or range of accepted propositions. A protasis or antecedent from which would follow certain apodoses or consequents, themselves taken to be true, is said to be a possible explanation of those consequents. It is said actually to be their explanation when it is itself taken to be true. And then we say, not 'if', but 'because'. In this sense a hypothesis is a conjectured protasis. Such a conjectured protasis is usually a more general proposition than the propositions which it explains or would explain, but this is not always the case, as for example in history and detection.

These two uses overlap. For a conjectured protasis is a case of a conjectured proposition and usually a conjectured proposition is conjectured as a possible explanation of something else which is not conjectural.

In neither use is 'hypothesis' equivalent to 'hypothetical proposition' where this is a title for an 'if-then' proposition. An 'if-then' proposition need not be conjectural and need not be as a whole a protasis to some further apodoses, though of course an 'if-then' proposition can be either or both. But in the second use a hypothesis is always a protasis in an 'if-then' proposition and in its first use it is usually so.

It is worth while to make these points. For a law-proposition, that is, a general proposition which explains or would explain a range of less general accepted propositions (1) is an if-then proposition, i.e. a variable or open hypothetical; (2) it is often itself conjectural and not established and (3) (by definition) it is an explanation or a possible explanation of a range of other propositions which are known or taken to be true.

On the other hand I have qualms about one of Miss MacDonald's professed detections of English idiom-nuance. To call a law-proposition 'established' and to call it 'known' do not seem to me to be the same thing: and though commonsense may say that we *know* certain law-propositions, I think that this is either false or else a boastful misuse of the word. What we do, perhaps, often know is that a law-proposition is so well established that it would be foolish to collect further evidence for it or to re-scrutinize our present evidence for it. We are often sure and warranted in being sure of a law-proposition. But to be sure is not the same as to know. There is no contradiction in saying that Newton was sure of so and so and was justified in being sure of it, and yet was mistaken; but there is a contradiction in saying that he knew it and was wrong.

However, even so, I agree with Miss MacDonald that we should be obliterating real and important distinctions if we followed the prescriptions of some logicians and called all propositions alike 'conjectural' or 'problematic', or all alike merely 'more or less probable'. There is a difference between the propositions which we should naturally express with 'is', 'was' and 'will be' and those which we should naturally express with 'may be' ,'might have been', 'probably' and 'very, very probably'. Namely, there is an important difference between the cases where the chances of subsequent correction are either nil or else genuinely inconsiderable and those where they are, however slight, still considerable. Physicists would be ill advised and not well advised to talk in the language of actuaries. Even if their conclusions differ, in the eyes of logicians, only in degree of probability, still big differences of degree ought to be and in ordinary parlance are in fact signalized by differences of idiom.

But when this is said, not very much is said. Let us accept, with some relief, Miss MacDonald's advice to us not to adopt certain over-Procrustean styles of diction which other philosophers have recommended, and let us resume with more confidence our workaday habit of talking with the vulgar. But *then* let us talk about induction. And here, I think, there remain certain thorny puzzles which cannot be removed by the mere knack of pricking up our ears for delicate differences of nuance between certain ordinary English words. The philosophical perspicacity required for the solution of these puzzles will be something more than nicety of stylistic taste, which is what, if I am not doing her an injustice, Miss MacDonald by her example recommends us to rely upon as our Open Sesame.

INDUCTION AND PREDICTION

Miss MacDonald unfortunately falls in with the tiresome fashion of tying up the problem of induction with that of prediction of the future. This is vexatious in two ways. First, it fails to formulate the problem in its most general form. Inductive generalizations claim to cover the unobserved, certainly, and future events and existents (if any) are indeed unobserved. But the converse is not true. There have existed and there exist now plenty of things and events which I am not observing and have not observed. We are looking for the rationale of inferences from the observed to the unobserved in all cases, and not merely in the case of the unobserved yet-to-be. Inferences from the present height of the tide to the present position of the moon, or inferences from present moraines to past glaciers, raise the same logical questions as to predictions of future eclipses.

Indeed even to tie the whole question down to the warrants, if any, for inferences from the observed to the unobserved is unduly to limit the question. For I may actually have observed both the lightning and the thunder, and come to think that the former caused the latter. And this thought equally raises the problem of induction.

So even if Miss MacDonald's short way with doubters about the yet-to-be is adequate, it fails to raise in its generality the problem of induction.

But, worse than this, there is a considerable difference between prediction on the one hand and inferences from the past or present observed to the past or present unobserved on the other. Namely, the founts of instances to which our laws are relied on to apply may now dry up. It may be true that all swans are either white or black and false that there are going to exist any more swans. It may be true that the height of the tide is functionally correlated with the position of the moon. But the tides and the moon may be near their end. For it is logically possible that a large scale cosmic catastrophe is impending, and that our physical universe will be thoroughly decomposed. And then there will be no swans or planets or trade-booms or arsenic-swallowers. So our predictions have an extra precariousness which does not attach to our retrodictions or to our inferences to the contemporary unobserved. For we know that a cosmic catastrophe has not occurred and is not now, in our vicinity, occurring. It does not matter that the danger is not great. The point is that we can contradict someone's prediction of an eclipse not only by denying the truth of his law-propositions or the truth of his observations of the contemporary heavens, but also by denying that there will exist a sun, moon and earth at the required date.

I suppose the modish preoccupation with prediction derives partly from the great practical utility of those sciences which do yield successful forecasts. For, unless clairvoyance about the future occurs, we have no ways of foreknowing save that of causal predictions, whereas memory and observation (and perhaps telepathy and clairvoyance) enable us to know much of the past and the contemporary. But there is, I suggest, another motive for the preoccupation. Whenever we infer to an unobserved matter-of-fact, the observations, if any, which verify those inferences are posterior to the making of the inferences. We first leap and then look.

It is tempting then to describe the inferences as predictions of those observations. 'There must have been a Roman villa here' is taken to mean 'When I dig I shall see such and such coins, mosaics, etc.'. If this is a motive, it should be dispelled, for it rests on a fallacy.

However, I am sure that Miss MacDonald would not deny this general point, so that in generalizing the scope of the problem of induction I am not controverting anything which she intended to assert.

INDUCTIVE ARGUMENT

We think that some law-propositions are established so fully that it would be foolish to desire further evidence for them or to re-scrutinize the present evidence for them. What we want to understand is how relatively slight stocks of empirical data endow law-propositions with so high a degree of trustworthiness. I call our stocks of empirical data relatively slight not merely in the sense that the laws may cover instances far more numerous than those we have inspected, but also in the sense that we with the time and opportunities available to us might often, had we wished, have increased those stocks very considerably.

That is, I want to canvass again certain questions concerning the nature of what I shall for a moment only and with apologies call 'inductive probabilities'.

When Hume showed us that the premisses of inductions are compatible with the negatives of their conclusions; and when it was seen, further, that his question What causes us to trust our inductions? yields no answer to the question What makes some inductions more trustworthy than others?, it was natural and partially correct for philosophers to say that inductive arguments are only a species of probable arguments. But the resultant enquiry into the nature of these arguments has, I think, been handicapped by a confusion, which is much more than a verbal confusion. Namely, philosophers have always tended to suppose that there is, if we could only put our fingers upon it, just one concept of probability. They have supposed that 'probable' is univocal.

I want, in a moment, to argue that there are at least three notions of probability, irreducible to each other, none being a species of any other and yet all being sufficiently affiliated for the joint name to be more than a mere pun. And, among other things, I want to show that in one *use* of 'probability' it is a tautology to say that all probabilities can be represented by fractions, while in other *uses* it would be a contradiction to say that any could. I shall try to isolate these three uses of 'probability', giving them for the purposes of this paper different titles. I must give a sketchy account of their main differences and affinities, but I shall chiefly concentrate on describing, so far as I can, the inter-actions between two of them. For my sole aim is to illuminate in part the notion of inductive probability.

But before I attempt this, it is relevant to my main purpose to quarrel with Miss MacDonald's way of justifying prediction. Her answer is this: 'What justifies prediction on the basis of a causal law is our past experience of regularities together with the application of accredited methods to determine the dependence of happenings upon each other.' But this begs all the questions. What run of con-comitances justifies us in treating the run as a regularity? And what accredits a method? I shall have a good deal to say about the former questions. On the latter, I should like to put a nail in the coffin of this fashionable notion that the problem of induction is resolved by the mere adulation of certain otherwise unspecified methods of enquiry.

Scientists, after all, win their titles, chairs, medals and obituary notices for all sorts of achievements. Some have supported or resisted a political régime, some have hailed from a favoured university or social stratum, some have invented or promised to invent instruments of war, while some have talked down to the readers of newspapers or talked up to the occupants of pulpits. Scientists get kudos in countless ways, but such successes cannot be what 'accredits' their methods of research.

The sole interpretation of the phrase 'accredited methods of science' which looks plausible is this. A method is accredited when exercises of it are very successful, that is, when particular researches conducted according to it have already resulted in numbers of true predictions or other causal inferences being made. And more (since random guessing on the racecourse often results in winners being picked)—the numbers of true predictions necessary to accredit the method by which they are arrived at must be considerably greater than random guessing would (probably) have provided. That is to say, to call a method 'accredited' is to say that researches conducted according to it have, up to date, opened otherwise improbably rich veins of true predictions.

But this criterion of what sorts of inferences are justified is patently a fraud. For the discovery that a certain method of research merits the title 'accredited' is itself a piece of induction. Accredited or discredited? What run of true predictions justifies us in accepting the general proposition that the method of the whole class of similar researches is 'good' or 'scientific' or 'accredited'? What run of white swans justifies us in generalizing that all swans are white? If this is not what the appeal to accredited methods means, it is to be feared that it will have to be taken instead as a simple appeal to authority. A law-proposition is properly established when the argument for it secures somebody's *imprimatur*. But no one could seriously defend such a criterion.

THREE CONCEPTS OF PROBABILITY

(1) *The plausibility of abstract theories.* People often describe theories such as those of philosophers as probable or improbable. This notion is different from both of the probability-concepts which are in normal employment in science, and I shall reserve for it the familiar and less misleading title 'plausibility'. An abstract theory or argument is plausible when, first, it purports to be demonstrative or probative, when, next, it is not obviously fallacious, and when, third, it has something of the same 'feel' as has attached to analogous arguments which have been probative.

It would be nonsense to describe a philosophical theory as 'probable' either in the sense of being statistically well supported or in the sense of being favoured by numerical odds. There is more to be said of the notion of plausibility, but not here.

(2) *Numerical odds.* If a certain proposition or set of propositions, such as the sum of our relevant information, is compatible with any one of a disjunctive set of other propositions being true but incompatible with more than one of them being true, then on the basis of that original proposition there is the chance that the first of the other propositions is true, the chance that the second is true, the chance that the third is true . . .

These chances can be counted, and the class of them all can be sub-divided into sub-classes in various ways. These sub-classes can be compared with each other and with the total class in respect of number of members.

If a normal die is lying flat there is one chance that the upper side is a six, and five that it is one of the other five faces; there are three chances of its being even-numbered to three of its being odd-numbered. There are twice as many chances of the upper face being three or more as of its being less than three. And so on.

Similarly the balance of chances against the top card in a normal pack being an ace is forty-eight against four. Simple arithmetic represents this by the fraction $\frac{12}{13}$ that it is not an ace, or $\frac{1}{13}$ that it is.

Let us call this sort of calculation 'the arithmetic of chances' and instead of speaking of 'probabilities' in this connection, speak of 'the numerical odds' or 'the balance of chances'. It is a tautology to say that the odds, in this sense, are numerable; or that the proportions obtaining between sub-classes of the same total class of chances can be represented by ordinary fractions. The mathematical operations involved are operations in simple arithmetic. (Numerical odds are sometimes confusingly called '*a priori* probabilities'.)

(3) *The reliability of inductions and the consequential inferences.* We think that other things being equal, a law-proposition based on many favourable instances is more reliable than one based on few; that one based on accurately measured instances is more reliable than one based on unmeasured or crudely measured instances; that a law-proposition which is relatively simple is more reliable than one which while explaining the same facts is relatively complicated. And, of course, we think that inferences deducted from more reliable law-propositions are more reliable than those deduced from less reliable law-propositions.

This sort of reliability cannot be defined in terms either of plausibility or of the balance of chances, though attempts have been made, by Jevons for instance, to define it in terms of the latter.

The three concepts have these affinities. All alike are concerned with relations between 'premisses' and 'conclusions' (though these words have different meanings in each case). In each case knowledge of the premisses does not suffice to enable us to know the truth of the conclusion. In each case knowledge of the premisses makes it more 'reasonable' to accept the conclusion than it would have been in the absence of that knowledge. (But 'reasonable' is not univocal either.) In each case the 'probability' that the premisses bestow on the conclusions is inherited by what propositions those conclusions entail. In each case the 'probability' bestowed by premisses on a conclusion is stronger than that bestowed by them upon the conjunction of that conclusion with some other proposition which is not entailed by it. And in each case the 'probability' bestowed by premisses upon the disjunction of two conclusions, neither of which entails the other, is as strong as or stronger than that bestowed on either taken by itself.

THE DIFFERENCES BETWEEN ODDS AND INDUCTIVE
RELIABILITIES

We need first to have clear two notions of statistical frequencies, which are often confused with each other. And both are often confused with the notion of numerical odds, for the simple reason that we can express all of them in fractions or percentages or with their aid. First, we may have made a number of observations, and recorded and classified them. We can then tabulate our findings in the form, say, that twenty-six of the two hundred boys in a school last year wore spectacles, i.e., that 13 per cent of them wore spectacles and 87 per cent did not. This is an actual frequency or a recorded percentage. No inference is involved except what is involved in the calculation that twenty-six out of two hundred $= \frac{13}{100}$ or 13 per cent.

We have not yet said anything about numerical odds or balances of chances. But we can if we like now do so and say that the proposition *Tommy was at that school last year* yields twenty-six chances that he wore spectacles and 174 that he did not, i.e. that the odds about his wearing spectacles are $\frac{13}{100}$.

But generically different from an actual frequency or a recorded percentage is an inferred frequency or an extrapolated percentage. If we argue that because in one school in one year 13 per cent of the boys wore spectacles, therefore 13 per cent of English schoolboys will wear spectacles next year or are doing so this year, then we are going beyond our data and making an inductive generalization. Indeed we are going beyond our data in two ways; for we are both inferring or conjecturing that there are or will be other English schoolboys and inferring or conjecturing that the same percentage will obtain among them as obtained among those examined.

As we have seen, an actual frequency or a recorded percentage can in principle be perfectly determinate and perfectly certain. Observing, recording, counting and reckoning are the only operations involved. But the extrapolated percentage is indeterminate in two dimensions. It is not certain that the same percentage will hold among the unregistered cases (if any) as held among the recorded cases. Other schools may well be better or worse lit, have more or less active oculists in attendance, draw from better or worse nourished classes of boys, and so forth.

But worse than this there is a flaw in the hypothesis that *any* determinate percentage will obtain among the unregistered cases. For the number of such cases is not determinate.

Take the figure of 48 per cent as representing the recorded percentage of female births among total births, and assume that this proportion will remain constant. What does this assumption mean? It cannot mean that out of *any* hundred births, 48 will be female, for we might be referring to 100 male births, or to 100 female births. Nor can it mean that out of the next or some otherwise randomly picked 100 or 1000 births, 48 or 480 will be female. For apart from the fact that if we chose instead the next 101 or 1001 births there could not be 48 per cent of females, there is nothing to prevent the next 100 or 1000 births from containing unusual runs of male or female births. And it will not do, either, to interpret the assumption as meaning that out of an infinite number of births, 48 per cent will be female. For it makes no sense to say that an infinite number of babies will be born.

No, what we mean is something like this, that the longer the list of births grows the nearer will the proportion of females approach to 48 per cent. It is unlikely to be exactly 48 per cent at any specified moment, and it could not be 48 per cent when the list contained any number which was not divisible by 25. But the longer the list grows, the smaller will be the gap, if any, between the actual percentage and 48 per cent. There are difficulties even in this interpretation, but even supposing them resolved, there remains this important difference between extrapolated percentages on the one hand and either numerical odds or recorded percentages on the other, that in the latter cases simple fractions represent what we are considering, while in the former only some such expression as 'tending towards 48 per cent' represents what we are considering. And this is additional to the other feature of the case, that we have only inductive warrant, if any, for relying on such an extrapolated percentage, whereas in the other two cases the fractions were known and not expected.

The next step to take in the isolation of numerical odds and inductive reliabilities is to refer to the notorious theorem of Bernouilli. He thought that under certain conditions a frequency or percentage proposition could be inferred not just by extrapolation from a recorded percentage but by mathematical deduction from an arithmetical odds proposition. Namely, under certain conditions, from the proposition that the chances against the top card being an ace are 12 to 1, he infers that the probability approaches to 1 that we shall have, in a very long (or long enough) series of draws, drawn twelve times as many non-aces as aces. Of course 'very long' is vague, and 'long enough' begs the question; and again when the number of drawings is not divisible by 13, the inferred percentage cannot coincide with the actual percentage. So again the notion of 'tending towards $\frac{1}{13}$' has to be employed. But for our questions the crux is contained in the reservation 'under certain conditions'. Under what conditions should we, and under what should we not, predict the proposed frequency? Clearly not if the shuffler rigs the deal with the intention and ability to get the ace to the top or away from the top of the pack to suit his own ends. And clearly not, again, if the ace cards are oddly shaped, so that they react to the shuffler's fingers in ways different from the reactions of the other cards. No, the condition under which the predicted frequency will tend towards the same fraction as that representing the numerical odds is that all of the several chances must be equiprobable. An ace card must be neither more nor less likely to be at the top of a pack after a shuffle than any other card. But what is *this* notion of probability in the words 'equiprobable' and (I coin it) 'unequiprobable'? If there is one chance of the coin lying head upwards and one of its lying tail upwards, what is meant by asserting or denying that those chances are equally probable? To jump at once to my conclusion, it can only mean 'equireliable'. It is a special case of the notion of inductive reliability. In the arithmetic of chances the notion has no place at all. It only has a place in propositions about the world, and so it may occur in propositions in which the arithmetic of chances is *applied* to things and events. But it is alien to arithmetic itself.

Certainly the arithmetic of chances employs the notion of the logical similarity or homogeneity of chances. The several chances, the classes of which we compare in respect of number of members, must be of the same type or level. We can calculate the chances of the top card being an ace against those of its being an even-numbered red card, but not against the chances of its being dirty or torn or combustible. Our fractions must represent slices out of one and the same disjunctive set. But that is all.

Suppose five horses are in for a race, of which four are brown and one is black. Then the numerical chances of the winner being brown are $\frac{4}{5}$; And this is true even if it is also known that the black horse is a Derby winner, while the rest are cart-horses. It would be prudent to wager almost anything on the black horse winning, for we have excellent inductive evidence that the chances are unequireliable, i.e. that the black horse can run much faster than any of the others. With this information it would be folly to offer a 4:1 bet against the black horse. But this does not affect the fact that there are four ways in which a competing horse might be both brown and the winner, while there is only one way in which a competing horse might be black and the winner. Again, whether the die is loaded or unloaded, there still exist six ways in which it (logically) could face the sky; so there are three ways in which an odd-numbered side could be uppermost. The chances of the upper side being of a value of 3 or more are still twice as numerous as its chances of being of a value of under 3. And so on. In the pure arithmetic of the chances there is no reference either to the loadedness or to the trueness of the die. But it is a tautology to say that if we know the die to be loaded in a certain way, we should be foolish to expect the 6 to crop up on average one time in six. Numerical odds are one thing, reasonable betting odds are quite another.

Yet of course there are cases where we ought to expect frequencies to tend to coincide with the fraction which represents the numerical odds. We ought to expect this in games of chance, in some insurance calculations and in some scientific theories, like the theory of the distribution of gas molecules. And just these cases prove the point that I am making. There only can exist games of chance because some people have found out enough about the slidings, runnings and balancings of physical objects like cards, roulette-balls and roulette-tables, and dice to be able to make them 'true'. And a die is 'true' when we are justified in expecting its fall-frequencies to tend towards coincidence with the numerical odds. Such justification is afforded by the inductive discoveries that bits of ivory of similar texture have similar weights and that things of similar weights and shapes have similar points of equilibrium; or again that bits of cardboard or wood of different colours but similar smoothness do not offer different frictions; or that different patterns on the faces of coins do not causally affect their balance, and so on. Equireliabilities and unequireliabilities are both experimentally discovered; and games of chance are necessarily restricted to operations with objects about which certain equireliabilities have been established—for they would not be games of chance under any other condition. A card-sharper is not playing a game of chance, for he secures that the positions of the cards are causally determined by some property of the cards, such as notches in their edges, which is causally connected with the cards having their individual conventional values. It is a game of chance when the position of a card is not the effect of anything to do with its conventional value. To call all of a set of homogeneous chances 'equireliable' is a shorthand way of saying that the anticipated percentages can be relied on to tend towards coincidence with the numerical odds-fraction.

So Bernouilli's theorem is, what it ought to be, a tautology. For it says that, for instance, if the chance of heads is equireliable with that of tails, in a long run of tosses the total number of heads can be relied on to approximate towards the fifty-fifty line—which is just what calling them equireliable means.

Similarly the converse, which is usually left unstated, is a tautology, namely that if the chances are unequireliable, the frequencies can be relied on to tend to deviate progressively away from the numerical odds-fraction. But these are not arithmeticians' tautologies. They are not a case of mathematical news about matters of fact, nor do they throw light on the notions of addition, subtraction, multiplication and division. They give part of the definition of the inductive notion of reliability.

What does it mean to say that a specific unequireliability has been established? (This is not the same as but preparatory to the question, What sort of evidence establishes it?) Consider two cases. Suppose, for simplicity, that people (logically) could only be either fat or medium or thin, and that they could only be irascible, mild and genial. This would yield two fields of chances; there would be two chances to one against Jones being fat, and two chances to one against his being genial. And on this basis, if Jones is fat, his chances of being genial are $\frac{1}{3}$, or if he is genial, his chances of being fat are $\frac{1}{3}$. The chances against a man being both fat and genial would be $\frac{1}{9}$.

Now suppose that in a long recorded frequency it was found that not one-third but two-thirds of the fat men were genial, and that not one-third but all of the genial men were fat, we should in fact say that there is some causal connexion between being fat and being genial, namely that fatness is a causal condition of geniality, and that geniality is the effect of fatness plus some other unidentified factor which is sometimes but not always present with fatness.

That is, the logically open chances of being genial and thin and of being genial and medium are (causally) ruled out; and the logically open chances of being fat and irascible or fat and mild are (causally) partly ruled out.

To believe in an unequireliability is to believe that a causal law is operative (which does not entail knowing or conjecturing what that law is). Conversely, if the proportion of blue-eyed men among the red-haired men in a long recorded frequency approximated towards either the numerical odds or, what is different, towards the recorded percentage of blue-eyed men among the total population, we should judge that there is no causal connection between red hair and blue eyes. Though if, as is the case, the recorded percentage of blue-eyed persons in the total population is grossly different from the numerical odds of (I invent it) $\frac{1}{7}$, we should judge again that there is some causal law about eye-colours.

Thus we discover that all of the logically possible swing-periods but one are ruled out for pendulums of a given length, while none of the logically possible colours or weights are ruled out. A pendulum can (causally) be of any colour or weight, but it can only enjoy one of all the logically possible swing-periods. There is a causal connexion between swing-period and length, and none between either of these and colour or weight.

The arithmetical balance of chances supplies, that is, a rule by the application of which we utilize our recorded frequencies as evidence for the causal dependence or the causal independence of those discriminable factors in recurrent situations which logically might vary independently. We don't usually bother to evaluate the relevant odds-fractions; we discern swiftly that the recorded percentage does or does not differ grossly from the odds-fraction without having to specify what this is. For we find a certain actual frequency surprisingly regular and the degree of our surprise is a rough index to the divergence of the actual percentage from the numerical odds. But Rhine, for example, deliberately uses such tests for clairvoyance as will exhibit in numerical form the divergence of the actual percentage of true 'guesses' from the numerical odds against a pure guess being true. He is of course presupposing the truth of the inductions made by designers and manufacturers of cards about the equireliability of the chances of particular cards being in particular positions.

The general nature of the argument is then this, that a big discrepancy between a recorded percentage and the numerical odds, when the number of cases registered is big enough, is good evidence that there is a causal law which explains the run, i.e. that the run is not merely a multiplied fortuitous coincidence. What is meant by 'fortuitous' and 'non-fortuitous'?

CHANCE, CHANCES AND CAUSAL INDEPENDENCE

It is obvious that no run, however long, of heads in coin spinning or sixes in dice throwing is logically impossible. Any recorded frequency is compatible with the assumption that the concomitances are in fact fortuitous or that the run has been merely a multiplied coincidence. No run *proves* unequireliability, i.e. *proves* that a causal law is operative. Yet quite short runs establish it beyond reasonable doubt.

What does it mean to describe a distribution or a run as 'chance' or 'fortuitous' or as 'mere coincidence'? What is the connexion of meaning between 'chances', as we have been speaking of them and 'chance' in the quite different sense of the 'fortuitous'?

As we have used the expression 'the chance of' or 'the chances of' it was a monosyllabic synonym for 'logical possibility'. To say that a certain proposition yields certain chances simply means that that proposition is compatible with the truth of any one out of a disjunctive set of other propositions. And this is quite different from the use of the word when we say that something came about by chance or that a conjunction of events or properties was a chance conjunction.

When given A, there is the chance or possibility of B, and the chance or possibility of C; and when, further, there is no causal law ruling out A-cum-B or A-cum-C, then we can call the actual conjunction of A and B or of A and C a chance conjunction. Thus Jones' being blue-eyed yields the chance that he has one Christian name, and the chance that he has two, and so on. And there is no causal inference from his being blue-eyed to his having or not having two Christian names. So if he is in fact both blue-eyed and the owner of one Christian name, this conjunction is a fortuitous or a chance conjunction. Similarly it is a chance conjunction if a salmon is dead and lying north and south. Of course there is a cause for its being dead and a cause for its lying in that direction; but there is no further causal law involved—or if there is then it is false and so not nonsensical to say that that conjunction was fortuitous. There is e.g. a cause for a compass needle lying north and south. Conversationally we seldom describe states of affairs as fortuitous unless there is some special motive (over and above the reasons) for denying it to be an example of one causal law, such as that it is *tempting* to describe it as due to one cause. We call an unprearranged meeting with a friend 'fortuitous' but not one with a stranger. For we expect to meet some stranger or other in most of the places we frequent, but usually when we meet friends we do so by appointment.

Conjunctions of events, properties, etc., when these are not to be explained by reference to one cause, are 'chance' or 'fortuitous' conjunctions. It should be noticed that single events or states of affairs cannot be and are not in fact ever described as fortuitous. Only concurrences are fortuitous—or non-fortuitous. For by ascribing something to chance, we are not denying that it was caused, or even that we know its cause; on the contrary we are ascribing it to a plurality of (causally and logically) independent causes. If we are wrong in thinking that the causes were independent, we are wrong in describing the composite state of affairs as fortuitous.

In a word, the concurrence of A and B is denied to be fortuitous when it is known or thought that A is the cause or effect of B or that both are effects of some one ulterior cause; it is asserted to be fortuitous when none of this is the case. We draw attention to the fortuitousness of a concurrence only when someone is inclined to believe that there is such a causal connexion, and so will be surprised to discover that there is none.

Some theorists delight to aver that nothing is causally independent of anything else. This is wrong. Causal dependences are enormously rarer than fortuitous conjunctions. This thunder is the effect of that lightning, but it is synchronous with countless other happenings, none of which are mentioned in the scientist's explanation of why it thundered. Law-propositions explaining specific sorts of states of affairs ignore all but a very few of the other things and happenings which are in fact cohabitants with those states of affairs in the one physical universe.

Every establishment of a law is also the tacit establishment of hosts of independences. Neap-tides are not the effects of elections, bird-migrations, foot-and-mouth disease, earthquakes ... but of such and such. So they are just as much or little to be expected tomorrow, whether there is or is not an election or an earthquake today. It is sometimes supposed that a scientific discovery is always the discovery of a law. This is false. Much more often it is the discovery of an independence. For each time a hypothesis is refuted, the truth of its contradictory is discovered. And to say that a suggested law-proposition is false is the same thing as to say that a suggested causal independence does not obtain, or that a certain causal independence does obtain. But these discoveries are not published, as a rule, in the text-books, for the number of them is so huge and the interest of each of them is so slight. (Similarly English dictionaries tell us what arrangements of letters make English words, but they do not tell us what arrangements of letters do *not* make words.)

People commonly confuse several different issues when considering the question of the justification of induction.

(1) Sometimes they pose the question What right have we to generalize from a finite number of observed cases to law-propositions which shall be true of an infinitely or indefinitely large number

of unobserved cases? But there is a muddle here. To infer to the existence of unobserved swans, say, be they past, present or future, is quite a different inference from the inference that a certain universal proposition is true for any swans. For this might be true, without it being true that many or any swans have escaped observation or will exist to be observed or unobserved.

A law is not an infinite conjunction of particular propositions and does not contain the prediction of the existence of instances of itself. Certainly we may often have good reasons for thinking that there have existed or do exist unobserved particulars or that some will exist. We may, for instance, find moraines where once there were glaciers, or see the tide rising when the sky is overcast. Or we may argue from a widespread distribution of specimens of fishes in certain explored parts of the sea to the probability of there existing other specimens in other parts of the sea; from the prevalence of sparrows in London in this decade to their prevalence in London (if any) in the next. But the inference to a certain population of specimens in other districts or periods is quite different from the inference to a causal dependence or independence of the properties of the specimens, if any, which exist in those districts and periods. The falsity or uncertainty of the former inference would have no tendency to vitiate the latter.

It is therefore a mistake to suppose that inductions are weak because the proportion of unexamined specimens to examined cases may be thousands or millions to one, or to suppose that they would be strong if the examined cases happened to exhaust or nearly to exhaust the list of actual cases.

(2) The problem What makes some sorts of inductions stronger than other sorts? is a genuine and soluble problem. There is an answer to the question Why do some inductions based on hosts of favourable instances achieve a level of reliability much more mediocre than some inductions which rest on only a few? But this question is often confused with the quite different one Do any inductions have any reliability at all? I doubt whether this is a genuine question—for they wouldn't be inductions if they had no reliability at all. An induction of zero reliability is, I think, as much an impossibility as a fallacious deduction. A fallacious deduction is not a deduction; an induction based on no empirical evidence *or* containing a contradiction is no induction.

Even one solitary conjunction of a with b is some evidence for there being a general causal connexion of a's and b's: and one case of a without b is some evidence for there being a general causal independence of a's and b's—of course it *proves* that there is not a simple causal connexion of a's with b's, but it does not prove that, for example, a's are not partial cause factors on which the existence of b's causally depends.

Any empirical proposition is evidence for a law, when, given the truth of the law plus that of some other empirical proposition, the truth of the first would logically follow; and any empirical proposition is evidence against a law when some proposition incompatible with it would follow in the same way. No further definition of 'evidence for' and 'evidence against' is required.

What is required is an analysis of the notions of 'stronger evidence' and 'sufficiently strong evidence'. That is, what in some sense requires 'justification' is not the thought that observation-propositions can be evidence for or against laws, but the thought that sets of such propositions can constitute evidence of greater or lesser strength.

The answer to this question is, I think, of the following pattern. One inductive argument is stronger than another (a) in the case of an argument *for* there being a causal dependence when the deviation of the recorded percentage from the numerical odds-fraction is wider and/or more stable and/or founded on more specimens; (b) in the case of an argument *against* there being a causal dependence when the coincidence of the recorded percentage with the numerical odds-fraction is closer and/or more stable and/or founded on more specimens. If, in the case of the former class, the recorded percentage is such that the assumption that there is a causal law operative, i.e. that a specific unequireliability exists, is now added to what had been our original premisses, so that a lot of the originally open chances are now assumed to be ruled out, and if the recorded percentage now tends stably towards coincidence with the new odds-fraction, then we have good evidence that this one causal law does obtain and no other relevant ones do.

I am suggesting indeed that this is what we mean when we describe inductive evidence as relatively good or strong, poor or weak.

Now suppose we have a variety of law-propositions graded according to the strength of their evidence, of which law-propositions one or a few outshine all the rest—and this condition does seem to exist—then it is natural to compare all the inferior hypotheses with these 'peak' hypotheses and to regard them as relatively frail and unsatisfactory. And in this use of 'frail' and 'unsatisfactory' it would be nonsense to describe the 'peak' ones so. If we take the tallest man as our standard we cannot describe him as 'rather puny'.

But we may still conceive of there being laws still better established than our 'peak' laws, just as it is conceivable that the tallest man should still be growing. I think that often when we have occasion to stigmatize certain hypotheses as only relatively probable, we are contrasting them against the standard of those which are at the moment best established. And we feel shocked at any description of these last as merely relatively probable—since it is these with relation to which the inferiority of the rest is assessed. However, we do also think that some of our 'peak' laws are so well established that it would be foolish to desire more confirmation. We think, that is, that they are not merely unexcelled by any of the other law-propositions which we consider, but that there is almost no room for them to be excelled. Their reliability seems to be *virtually* incapable of serious enhancement. I do not know if this belief is true. If it is true, there is a residual problem of justification which I cannot solve. But if so, it is quite a different problem from the problem of what constitutes one induction stronger or much stronger than others.

In what sorts of conditions do we think that inductions based on many instances are weaker than those based on few? Why was the (unjustly reprimanded) generalization 'All swans are white' weaker than 'the rate of oscillation of pendulums is a function of their length'? I suggest that anyhow part of the answer is this. The field of logically possible colour-variations of feathers is relatively small, perhaps only a dozen or two, but the field of possible variations in measurably discernible lengths or oscillation-periods is enormous. The range of logically possible swing-periods for any given swing of any given pendulum of any given length is so huge that the recording of a very stable and very wide deviation in a few cases from the almost unassessable odds-fraction rapidly multiplies the strength of the evidence of each observation.

The enormous difference in the magnitudes of the denominators of the odds-fractions in the two cases is the explanation for the relatively slow growth in reliability of our generalizations about swans compared to that of our generalizations about pendulums.

This point can be generalized. The advance in refinement of our methods of measurement is no mere concession to pedantry. Every step forward in precision strengthens and is designed to strengthen the force of the method of Concomitant Variations. When we progress from measuring to the nearest inch or second to measuring to the nearest tenth of an inch or second, we at once are in a position to enhance the reliability of those of our law-propositions which express functional dependence between magnitudes. For we at once multiply by 10, or by multiples of it, the denominators of our relevant odds-fractions.

I must record some provisos about this suggested account of inductive reliability. First, it is not quite the same thing as Jevons described as 'the inductive or inverse application of the theory of probability'. For this account of the reliability of inductions assumed the truth of Bernouilli's theorem without recognizing the non-arithmetical nature of the notions of equiprobability and unequi-probability. So it pretended that there was an argument from a recorded to an extrapolated frequency and thence back to an arithmetical odds-fraction, which implied that it was in principle possible to say, for example, that there exist odds of, say, a million to one in favour of the hypothesis of a certain causal law.

Any such theory seems to me to break down owing to the veiled confusion between inductive reliabilities and numerical odds.

I am suggesting that while odds-fractions, which can in principle be precisely determined, do enter into inductive arguments as the measure against which we determine the equireliabilities and unequireliabilities of the logically open chances, it does not follow and is not true that we can represent these reliabilities by fractions. Even an extrapolated percentage can only tend towards x per cent, and not only is this not a percentage, or a fraction, but it is no measure of the strength or reliability of that 'tending'. Two statisticians might assess the ratio of female births to male births as tending toward 50:50 or as tending towards 48:52 respectively. But nothing in these figures would show which of the statisticians was building on the better statistics.

Next, we must not confuse the nature of inductive arguments, as I have described this, with the argument for the increase in the odds against increasingly composite chances. If the odds about a coin lying head are even, the odds against it doing so twice in two spins are 3 to 1, and those against it doing so three times in succession are 7 to 1 and so on. Or the odds against all the members of a team having the same Christian name are much higher than those against one member or all of any specified section of that team doing so. It does not of course follow that a composite chance, against which the numerical odds are high, ought not to be expected to be realized. If in two consecutive races, the only racehorse competing was also the only black horse, while the numerical odds against a black 'double' would be high, the expectation of it being realized would be very good.

However it does at first sight look plausible to say that (if there are, say, 20 colours, then) the odds about a single swan being white are $\frac{1}{20}$, those about two consecutive swans being white are $\frac{1}{400}$, those about three conseuctive swans being white are $\frac{1}{8000}$ and so on, and thence to argue that the enormity of the numerical odds against even a short run of white swans is a measure of the probability conferred by such a run on the hypothesis of a causal law connecting whiteness of feathers with the other properties of swans.

But this will not do. For the odds against three white swans in succession are no higher than the odds against the sequence of a white swan, a black swan and a blue swan. *Any* composite chance has higher odds against it than has any sub-section of it. So any recorded runs of whatever regularity or irregularity would be in the same boat. But there is a further flaw in the argument. It makes sense to ask what the numerical odds are against a given object, such as a swan, being white. For we can draw up the disjunctive set of colours and count them. But it does not make sense to ask what the odds are against there *existing* a white swan or two white swans or three white swans. . . . Or we can assess the odds against three coins tossed consecutively lying in any specified arrangement of heads and tails, but we cannot assess the odds against there existing three coins or against three coins, given as existing, being tossed.

Given that an indeterminately described state of affairs obtains, we can count up the number of determinate shapes that it might take; but the obtaining or non-obtaining of a described state of affairs is not a shape that 'it' might take. For there is no 'it' if it does not obtain.

No, the form of the inductive argument, as I am trying to chart it, is this.

If the numerical odds about a given concurrence, say, of any given genial man being fat are $\frac{1}{3}$, and if in a recorded set of genial men 66 per cent are fat, then the longer the recorded list and the more stable the actual percentage and consequently the better attested the deviation of this percentage from the odds-fraction, the better is the evidence for the obtaining of some causal law or other connecting fatness and geniality. The prize cases would be those where 100 per cent of the recorded cases had a certain property and where the numerical odds against a single case having that property were very high. But cases of this sort are relatively rare.

Usually we are not registering the sheer presence or absence of a property when some other property is present or absent, but the presence of a certain magnitude when some other magnitude is present.

In such an argument the numerical odds-fraction is not a premiss in our inductions, such that from it plus our empirical data we deduce our law-propositions. Rather it is the measure we use, the yard-stick against which our empirical evidence makes it relatively 'probable' or 'improbable' that a causal law obtains. The arithmetic of chances gives us no more information about the world than geometry gives us information about the dimensions of St Paul's. But we use the arithmetic of chances in our inductions just as we use geometry in fixing the dimensions of St Paul's.

One last word on a point of etymology. It is likely to be felt that even if I am right in discerning heterogeneous uses of 'probability', still the *proper* use is that arithmeticians' use which I have paraphrased by such expressions as 'numerical odds' and 'balance of chances'.

Questions of propriety are questions of fashion, taste or history, and do not interest me much. But I suggest that in the original use of 'probable' it was a synonym for 'expectable' or 'bettable-on', and that the word was smuggled into arithmetic because the mathematicians were asked to provide a calculus to guide gamblers in games of chance and brokers in questions of insurance.

That the inductive notion of equireliability was already connoted by the very phrase 'games of chance' was unnoticed and it was vaguely supposed that arithmetic could give news about the fallings of dice, the rollings of roulette-balls and the sliding of cards, just because the arithmetic of permutations and combinations did apply so exactly to the runs of such games—*provided* that the boards, dice, coins, etc. were 'true' and that the players were not 'cheating', i.e. when the games were such that the arithmetic applied to them!

So I suggest that if any purloining was done, it was the arithmeticians who purloined the word from the gamblers and actuaries and not vice versa. But it does not matter so long as we, when we use the word, are clear whether we are referring to balance of chances, to reasonable expectations, to the plausibility of abstract theories or to something else.

I I

TAKING SIDES IN PHILOSOPHY

Reprinted from 'Philosophy', vol. XII, 1937, by permission of the editors

There is a certain emotion of repugnance which I, and I hope a good many would-be philosophers, feel when asked the conventional question, 'If you are a philosopher, to what school of thought do you belong? Are you an Idealist or a Realist, a Platonist or a Hobbist, a Monist or a Pluralist?'

We all habitually and conveniently employ these and dozens of other similar party-labels. And the standard histories of philosophy aid and abet us in treating the history of philosophy as a series of conflicts between opposing camps or election campaigns between rival factions. We even come to deem philosophers as worthy or unworthy of study according to the particular 'isms' of which they are alleged to be or confess themselves to be partisans. Sometimes quite well-meaning persons actually boast of being 'orthodox Hegelians' or 'orthodox Realists' as if the notion of orthodoxy in philosophy was a natural and appropriate one.

I fear, too, that in teaching the subject we are prone consciously or unconsciously to give our pupils the impression that they would be well advised not to inform themselves of the views or the arguments of philosophers belonging to this or that school.

Nevertheless, I dislike being asked how I cast my vote, and I want, if I can, to lay bare the sources of this dislike. But I should say at the very start that I am not arguing for eclecticism in philosophical thinking. To my mind eclecticism is only the most corrupt of all the 'isms'. It is our form of Coalitionism, a parasite on the party system.

The gist of my position is this.

There is no place for 'isms' in philosophy.

The alleged party issues are never the important philosophic questions, and to be affiliated to a recognizable party is to be the slave of a non-philosophic prejudice in favour of a (usually non-philosophic) article of belief. To be a 'so-and-so-ist' is to be philosophically frail. And while I am ready to confess or to be accused of such a frailty, I ought no more to boast of it than to boast of astigmatism or *mal de mer*. I am, that is, prepared to find myself classified and classified justly as a 'so-and-so-ist', only I think that that is something to be apologetic for. My 'ism' exists, doubtless, but it is not a banner so much as a susceptibility. So there ought to be nothing in philosophy corresponding to vote-casting. The question How do you vote between this 'ism' and that 'ism'? ought to be dropped in favour of the question Which way do your inclinations and biases pull you between this 'ism' and that?

(1) Part of my repugnance comes from this source. To be a member of such and such a school is to cleave to a certain tenet or set of tenets. And for the school to know itself, or be known by others, as a special school, the school, say, of Monists or Pragmatists, its tenets must be contestable. In fact, a set of tenets gets its label from being opposed. It is usually those who think it false who first call it 'Realism', or 'Rationalism' or 'Berkeleyanism'. In general 'isms' are unnamed until they are contested. They are also, as a rule, unchampioned until they are contested.

To cleave to an 'ism' is, then, to cleave to a disputable position. But what is it to cleave to a position? If it means to entertain no doubts of the truth of the theory, then this is an unforgivable irrationality, if the arguments against it have anything in them at all. And they will not be arguments if they haven't. It is sheer credulity to accept without question a theory which is in any part or degree logically fallacious or imperfect.

But sometimes a logically valid theory is disputed. Probably there still exist militant circle-squarers. So there would be nothing irrational in cleaving to an 'ism' the arguments for which were logically unassailable, although assailants in fact exist. But what would this 'cleaving' be? Just seeing that the arguments for the theory were valid and those against it were fallacious. On this showing, being a Realist, say, would just consist in seeing that Idealists reason very foolishly. And there would be no more reason for cherishing a school of Realism in philosophy than for fostering a school of non-circle-squarers in geometry. The party would contain everyone who could think straight in philosophical subjects. No philosophers would be outside it. So it would be no philosophic party at all.

Every 'ism' that can get to the point of acquiring a name is *philosophically* questionable, and is actually questioned by genuine philosophers. And that means that no philosopher has any excuse for cleaving to it. Any philosopher should see and welcome the logically valid part of its argument; and any philosopher should see and welcome the logically valid parts of the theory of its contestants. And there is nothing left which should convince anyone of the truth of the remainder of those theories—unless a philosopher is to be allowed to believe doctrines because he likes them.

Of course each of us is predisposed to swallow uncritically certain sorts of doctrines which happen to be congenial to him; and it is hygienic to recognize and confess these predispositions. But a fraternity of persons of kindred credulities could only constitute a school of 'misosophy'.

(2) Another consideration which I find underlying my distaste for party-labels in philosophy is this. The central issues between the self-announcing 'isms' turn out, when the fog of the early engagements is over, to be extremely refined and even academic differences. (I also think that they often turn out not to be genuine philosophical issues either. But I choose not to discuss this point here.) For example, it has been argued and not, I think, contested that the radical issue that splits Monists or Absolute Idealists from opposing 'schools' is the question whether relations are or are not internal to their terms. Now the question interests me, and is, I think, soluble. But if asked by a pupil what are the radical problems of philosophy, I could not with an easy mind tell him, 'Oh, such questions as whether relational propositions are analytic or not.' Or, to take another example, I should feel unhappy in saying that one of the major truths discovered by philosophers is the answer to the question that splits Platonists and anti-Platonists, namely, that general words are significant by being proper names of entities (or the negative, if it is preferred).

Yet the doctrines of principle (adherence to which, as we shall see, is what constitutes schools of thought) have to be fairly narrow and abstract propositions if the 'schools' are to be supposed to be standing for anything in particular. So they have to treat their single-plank election platforms as if they were the radical truths of philosophy. The radical topics that philosophy is about have to be represented as of these patterns—whether truths of fact can be deduced from *a priori* premises (the issue between Rationalism and Empiricism), whether 'I ought' is compatible with 'I had better not' (the issue between Utilitarianism and Intuitionism), whether the nature of what I know or think about entails that

I know or think about it (the issue between one form of Idealism and Realism). And so on.

Now doubtless such questions as these are watershed questions. As we vote on them, so we shall have to vote on many derivative questions. But to say that these are the central questions that face philosophers provokes the comment that they seem very technical specialists' questions. Indeed, they seem to be riddles which we need a lot of special training in philosophy to appreciate.

The chief fruits of the subject seem to be rather small potatoes. Now I am not complaining because these topics are unfit for the pulpit or the market-place; nor yet because they are abstract and logically fine-drawn. These are merits in a topic of philosophical inquiry. No, I am complaining, I think, because questions like these are *resultant* riddles and not *inaugurating* riddles. They are special posers which trip us up after we have travelled a good long way; they are not what set us travelling. To change the metaphor, there is the smell of sediment about them, as if they were what the tide has left behind it—after ebbing.

(3) However, these two grounds for girding at sectarian habits of thought and speech in philosophy are not yet at the root of the matter. The real root of my objection is, I think, the view that I take of the nature of philosophical inquiry. I am not going to expound it in full, but a part of the view is that it is a species of discovery. And it seems absurd for discoverers to split into Whigs and Tories. Could there be a pro-Tibet and an anti-Tibet party in the sphere of geography? Are there Captain Cook-ites and Nansenists?

But before developing this argument it will be useful to clear away some possible misinterpretations of the case for which I am arguing.

(a) I am as far as possible from deploring or ridiculing polemics in philosopical discussion. There could, in my view, be nothing more unwholesome than unanimity among philosophers. The unconvinced are the sharpest critics of an argument, and those who are also hostile are its warmest critics. And an argument which was not tested by sharp or warm critics would be at least half untested. I am only urging that the common motive for unconversion and hostility, namely, allegiance to an 'ism', is philosophically unjustifiable and ought to be discountenanced by philosophers. Arguments should be attacked because they are invalid, not because they are 'Monistic' or 'Pluralistic', 'Occamistic' or 'Spinozistic'.

Philosophy lives by dispute. For dispute is the testing of arguments. But debates under the eyes of Whips test nothing but solidarity.

(*b*) Nor, of course, am I defending the milk-and-water doctrine that all philosophers are really in the right and really seeing eye to eye with one another. All philosophers make mistakes, and even great philosophers commit howlers. And their mistakes often lie undetected for a long time, or, when detected, retain the credence of their disciples for woefully lengthy periods. It is often desirable that a philosopher should be refuted. What is improper is that he should be discredited for being a Left-Winger, say, or have his fallacies condoned because he is on the side of the angels in the party of the Right-Centre.

(*c*) There is one way of dividing philosophers into types which is perfectly legitimate, namely, the classification of them as Logicians, Moralists, Political Philosophers, Epistemologists, Metaphysicians (maybe), Jurisprudents, and so on. Certainly these compartments are not watertight, and a philosopher may justly be suspected of philosophic incompetence who ignores all philosophical questions save those in his one pet department. But a man may, like Butler, be predominantly excellent in the philosophy of conduct and motives, or, like Berkeley, in the philosophy of perception. There is nothing sectarian or schismatic about such preoccupations.

(*d*) And for certain ends, such as those of biography or the history of cultures (though not those of philosophy itself), it is often useful and correct to classify philosophers according to certain general casts of mind or temperaments. There are, we are told, the tender-minded and the tough-minded among philosophers; or again, there are those who are constitutionally Platonic and those who are constitutionally Aristotelian; there are the mystical and the matter-of-fact; the 'inflationists' and the 'deflationists'; those of the prophetic and those of the engineering casts of mind. The fact that we can get a fair measure of agreement between students of diverse sorts, how the major philosophic figures ought to be classified under such heads as these is good evidence that the contrast of psychological types is not altogether fictitious. To some extent the thoughts of the philosophers whom we study are congenial or uncongenial to us according to which of the two psychological baskets they are drawn from.

If we admit that there is some big difference of psychological types of this sort, we can take either of two attitudes towards it. We can say that one of the qualities of mind is a necessary part of excellence at philosophy, while the other is an insuperable disability. Or we can say that both are or can be assets—only assets which human beings can seldom, if ever, possess together. Neither view would justify the existence of philosophical sects. For suppose, on the one hand, that the 'prophetic' or tender-minded temperament is a *sine qua non* of philosophic excellence. Then it would follow that no one of the 'tough-minded' or 'engineering' temperament could be a philosopher. So the gulf would be one between philosophers and non-philosophers and not between one set of philosophers and another. (Astronomers do not boast a party of anti-Astrologists.) And, on the other hand, suppose that both temperaments are assets, so that some are excellent at philosophy because they are of the 'prophetic' type, while others are excellent at it because they are of the 'engineering' type. Then for the followers of those of one type to campaign against those of the other would be as stupid as it would be for a lover of poetry to declare war on the lovers of prose, or for a mountaineer to blackball from his club all maritime explorers.

Whether the 'prophetic' temperament, say, is analogous to blinkers or to long-sightedness there can be no grounds for a philosopher of the 'engineering' type to join a faction against the possessors of it. For either they are constitutionally impotent at philosophy, in which case they can be ignored as we ignore phrenologists and fortune-tellers; or else they have a special qualification for discovering certain sorts of philosophic truth which is denied to those of the more matter-of-fact type, who on their side will have a compensating ability to discover philosophic truths of another sort. And in this case, they are related as the physician to the surgeon, by difference of function and not by conflict of 'isms'.

But in any case this crude sort of psychological division can only serve to explain causally why some sorts of people are prone not to appreciate either some sorts or any sorts of philosophical arguments and questions, and not to feel either some or any sorts of philosophic qualms. It contributes nothing to the testing of such arguments, to the formulation or solution of such questions, or to the excitation or appeasing of such qualms. Again, it may explain causally why certain sorts of philosophers are congenial or uncongenial to me. It cannot explain what are the philosophical excellences or demerits of their work. (Incidentally, on a point of history, it seems to me that some of the best philosophers have enjoyed both temperaments. Plato, for example, 'engineers' in the *Theaetetus*, the *Sophist*, and the *Parmenides*. Kant is 'prophetic', perhaps, in his moral theory. Leibniz is both a formal logician and a 'heaven-sketcher'.)

Let us consider more closely than we have yet done what it is to be a member of a 'school of philosophy' or a champion of an 'ism' or a disciple of a philosophical teacher. For certainly there are people who have been with justice labelled, by others or by themselves, as Epicureans, Wolffians, Kantians, Spencerians, Bradleians, and the like. We speak familiarly and intelligibly of the schools of Aquinas, Duns Scotus, and Occam, and of the schools of Hegel, Brentano, and James. Are there not notoriously a Cambridge and a Vienna school? Was there not an Oxford tradition?

If there hadn't existed any such churches, claques, or cliques, there would have been no sectarian tradition for me to inveigh against. My whole case is that there is a schismatic tradition in philosophy, and that 'schismatic philosopher' is a contradiction in terms.

What then is a 'follower'? First, there is the deliberately abusive sense in which we sometimes use such descriptions, though it is not the use for which we are looking (namely, the use in which a man might say *with pride* that he 'followed' Hegel, or Wittgenstein). We can abusively describe someone as a follower or disciple of Nietzsche, say, who accepts because they are congenial to him those doctrines of Nietzsche which he understands and rejects by ignoring them the views of everyone else. A man who only attends to the views of one philosopher and takes them as gospel because they are to his taste is, of course, neither a philosopher nor a student of philosophy. In this sense of the word, to say 'I am a disciple of so-and-so' would mean: 'I prefer to shut my eyes to all doctrines and problems save those of so-and-so. I prefer also to shut my eyes to any defects there may be in so-and-so's theory. I swear *in verba magistri*.'

Next it might be suggested that what it means to say of someone that he is a follower of Epicurus, or a disciple of Kant, is that he believes all that Epicurus (or Kant) says, and nothing that any other philosopher says, save where he echoes Epicurus (or Kant). But this would be a silly definition of 'follower' or 'disciple'. For no one can remember all the dicta of any but the least copious of philosophers. And no philosophers are completely consistent. And all the best philosophers rebut views which they had themselves once believed. Nor can one disbelieve all the dicta of all other philosophers. For we cannot read, much less remember and much less still understand, all the dicta of all philosophers. And of those that we read and understand we cannot disbelieve all. For some are the direct contradictions of some others. And some are obviously true.

Even if by 'follower' we meant someone who is generally disposed to believe whatever he reads and remembers from Epicurus (or Kant), and is disposed in general to disbelieve what he reads and remembers from anyone else, we should have to say that such a man was a worshipper or a parrot, and no philosopher. For on such a definition a 'follower' would be one who never thought for himself. And there is no room for credence in philosophy. However, it is obvious that when philosophers or would-be philosophers are described as 'followers' or 'disciples', it is not ordinarily meant that they are just unthinking 'yes-men'. What else does it mean?

A third possible and more flattering definition of 'followers' would be this. To follow Aristotle, say, would be to see, after rational consideration, that Aristotle's conclusions are true because his arguments are valid, and also to see, after rational consideration, that no other philosophers argue validly for their conclusions.

But even in this sense no one but a fool could claim to be—and not even a fool could be—a follower of anybody. For neither Aristotle nor any other philosopher has failed to produce at least some defective and even fallacious arguments. Nor is Aristotle or any other philosopher the sole discoverer of valid arguments. And no human being could be so acquainted with all the arguments of all philosophers that he could dismiss all of them save some of those of, say, Aristotle as invalid.

A philosopher, or rather student of philosophy of this type, for whom 'following so-and-so' consists in seeing the validity of so-and-so's arguments, would have rather to describe himself in terms like this. 'I follow Aristotle in respect of arguments A, D, and F, but not of his arguments B, C, and E; I also follow Berkeley in respect of his arguments W, Y, and Z, but not of his arguments P...V, and X; I also follow Russell on such-and-such points, and Kant on such-and-such others ...' And then he would not be, in the ordinary sense of the word, for which we are still in search, anybody's 'disciple'. But he would be (almost) a philosopher. For the only bias or *parti pris* in his outlook would be one in favour not of persons or congenial doctrines but of valid arguments.

But even this is patently not the sense in which people actually claim with pride or thankfulness to be uncompromising Spinozists, sound Hegelians, unswerving Pragmatists, loyal Moderate Bradleians, or last-ditch Logical Positivists. To accept the philosophy of such-and-such a teacher (or group of teachers) is, it is rather vaguely felt, something more than merely to find his general temper of mind sympathetic, and something less than credulously to endorse every particular dictum or argument that he ever propounded. A philosophy, such as Hegelianism or Thomism, is something more definite than a mood, and less definite than a cento of propositions, or a sorites of special ratiocinations. It is in some way adoptable or discardible as a whole.

A philosophy, that is, is something which has a general trend; and it is or else it rests on some dominant structure of argument. So it can be in some important sense on the right track, for all that much of its detail may be faulty. Its terminology may be loose and confused; many of its special arguments may be fallacious or incomplete, and yet as a whole (or 'system', as it is dubbed in its testimonials) the philosophy of so-and-so may have the root of the matter in it. Conversely (so this vague theory would hold) the philosophy of such-and-such may be altogether on the wrong track, and its wrongness be not a whit compensated by the precision of its terminology or the cogency of its special arguments. The rottenness of the trunk is not excused by the fineness of its foliage.

Further, the rightness as a whole of a given philosophy does not derive from, though it is probably the source of the congeniality of the temperament of its author to us who appreciate it. Its rightness is something rational, and not merely temperamental or emotional. The rightness of, say, Rationalism or Critical Realism or Empirio-Criticism, is something for which the ability to think coherently plus the willingness to think honestly are the necessary and sufficient conditions. Monists, therefore, are radically good at philosophizing, and Pluralists radically bad at it (or vice versa). The members of the opposing school, championing as they do a philosophy which has the wrong general trend, are the victims of a mistake in principle, no matter what acumen they may exercise in questions of detail.

Accordingly every school of thought which is conscious of itself as such must and does maintain that the opposing school or schools of thought are in some way philosophically unprincipled. For they are blind to those principles which make its philosophy *a* philosophy and *the* philosophy.

Of course we are not often let into the secret of what these principles are. There is apt to be an almost Masonic reserve about them. Just as in politics Conservatives, Liberals, and Socialists would rather shed their blood to defend than court disaster by unpadlocking their Joanna Southcott's boxes of principles, so the militant advocates of the philosophical sects generally prefer to attack one another's derivative tenets rather than to win each other over by exhibiting those truths for the seeing of which rationality and honesty are supposed to be a sufficient condition.

And it must be confessed, in justification of this reserve, that when these principles are divulged, they are apt to bear a close resemblance either to undebatable platitudes or to dogmatic unplausibilities for neither of which could a man of sense and mettle fight with gusto.

But are there such principles? And if there are, are they the preserves of cliques? And, most important of all, how are they established, that is, what makes it reasonable to accept them and perversity or blindness to reject them?

It can hardly be maintained that they are self-evident axioms —else why does no one publish the first page of our Euclid for us? Moreover, they would have either to be self-evident because analytic, in which case no thinking man could fail to assent, with a yawn, to them; or they would have to be self-evident although synthetic. And the possibility of there existing such truths at all within philosophy can hardly be taken for granted in the face of Hume and Kant.

No, these doctrines of principle, which constitute (it is supposed) both the bedrock and the cement of any reputable 'ism', are established, and only established, by philosophical argument. (Or if no reasons can be given for them, they should be confessed by their adherents to be sheer dogmas, which philosophers are at liberty to accept or to reject at the dictates of their palates.)

So let us consider what it is to establish a doctrine by philosophical argument. What sort of an argument is a philosophical argument? Two answers can be dismissed without many words. Philosophical argument is not induction, and it is not demonstration *ordine geometrico*. It is not the latter. For we have no agreed or evident axioms to start with. In the sense of the word 'presupposition' in which philosophy is concerned with presuppositions, the goal of its labours is to reveal them. They are not the premisses of its arguments. And certainly philosophical argument is not induction. A philosopher is playing at science who culls statistics or experiments in laboratories. To suppose that a philosopher's propositions can be falsified or corroborated by a new empirical discovery is to annihilate the difference between philosophy and the special sciences.

Moreover, inductive arguments cannot yield better than probable conclusions, and (I say it dogmatically) no probable arguments are philosophical arguments. Certainly there is an important sense in which a philosopher's argument may be *plausible*, that is, not obviously invalid. Most philosophical arguments are too difficult for us to know that they are completely probative on first, or even fiftieth, examination. But we may see that they are plausible in a non-derogatory sense. Something (though we are not quite sure what) seems to be proved by certain steps (though we are not quite clear which) in the argument. But an argument which is plausible in this way is not a probable argument; it is an argument which probably (or not improbably) is probative. It has the prima facies of a probative argument.

No, a philosophical argument is neither a piece of induction nor a piece of Euclidean deduction. Its pattern may be labelled 'dialectical' if we like, though I am not clear that this means anything different from 'philosophical'. It is or aims at being logically rigorous, for self-contradiction is the promised penalty of default in it.

Now the ability to see that a philosophical argument is rigorous or has the prima facies of being rigorous is not the perquisite of any person or team of persons, though of course some people are more capable of philosophical thinking than others.

So the arguments which establish, or are supposed to establish, the 'principles' of a system of philosophy are inspectable by all. To accept (or reject) those principles on blind trust (or blind distrust) in the rigorousness of the arguments is partisanship of the irrational sort. If there are questions of principle in philosophy, there is one task primarily worthy of philosophers, namely, to examine the force of the arguments for and of the arguments against such principles without a *parti pris* for or against the truth of those principles. Any serious philosopher would be as grateful for rigorous arguments for as for rigorous arguments against the principles of 'Idealism' (say), or 'Thomism', or 'Logical Positivism'.

So if the opposition between rival 'isms' is, as both must claim, an opposition on a question of principle, the contestants ought to find in each other the keenest and most helpful coadjutors in the examination of the cogency of the arguments about that principle. A 'Thingummist' who is seriously concerned about the validity of the argument for 'Thingummism' should find the strongest arguments of the 'anti-Thingummists' the very test for which he craves of whether his own argument is rigorous or only plausible. And then they would not be rivals, but coadjutors in dispute. But the attitude of actual schools towards their rival schools seems to be something different. Content with the case for their own principles, they seem, as a rule, to ignore the case for the prosecution, as if presupposition of those sacred principles was a necessary condition of any argument being valid, including, it is to be feared, the very arguments by which those principles were established.

Of course this sort of attitude is not consciously or deliberately adopted, much less justified. There could be only two ways of justifying it, if justification was sought. One would be to say that there are private revelations of principles to selected and privileged people, so that the hapless majority of philosophers are to be pitied for being, through no fault or deficiency of their own, graceless. The other would be to admit that principles can be adopted according to personal predilection. But the intellectual conscience of the better philosophers would forbid them to immunize themselves from criticism by claiming that their principles are above or beneath argument. The only heresy in philosophy is the belief that there are philosophical orthodoxies.

So far I have spoken as if it was pretty clear what sort of a thing a 'principle' is. But in fact it is far from clear. The only account that I can give is this. A philosophical question is a question of principle when it is philosophically much more important than most other questions. And the relative importance of philosophical questions could be explained on these lines that when, given the answer to one question, it is at once clear what are the answers, or of what sort are the answers, to an expanding range of other questions, while the answers to any of the latter do not in the same way throw light on the former, then the former is a question of principle relative to the latter.

Or else, when in the case of a range of questions it is clear that none of them could be answered, or, perhaps, even be clearly formulated before some anterior question is answered, then this is a question of principle relative to them. The notion is simply that of one question being logically prior or cardinal to a range of other questions. It is tempting, but it would be too rash to say that there is one absolutely first question, or one set of absolutely first questions. Relations of logical precedence among questions are moderately easy to get fairly wide agreement about; but not so about absolute primacy.

A question of principle then is just an important or very important philosophical question. And that a question is important or very important is something for and against which there can be plausible and sometimes probative arguments. Often it is not contested that a question is important, though every suggested solution is hotly contested.

But there is no difference in kind between arguments on more and arguments on less important philosophical questions. The sort of logical rigour demanded is the same.

Nor must we say that the less important philosophical questions are not philosophical questions. This would be self-contradictory. Certainly there is room in philosophy for ingenuity on minor points. We need our deft joiners as well as our engineers and our prophets. Though at the present moment I am inclined to think that we are suffering from a spate of over-ingenuity. Indeed, of the two prevalent infections today, over-respectability and over-ingenuity, I am not sure which is the more enervating complaint.

DISCOVERY IN PHILOSOPHY

It is my opinion that there is an affirmative answer to the cynically meant question, 'Do philosophers ever discover anything?' The allegation that they do not is partly due to the fact that the champions of the 'isms' never acknowledge defeat. And indeed they are not often defeated. For their battles are usually sham battles. My view is simply this. Every rigorous philosophical argument is a discovery. And in a looser sense of the word 'discovery', even every plausible philosophical argument is a discovery. A valid philosophical argument is itself the revealing of something, and something of the sort of which philosophy is the search. Every philosopher who produces one new philosophical argument has made a philosophical advance. But it is not just the *conclusion* of his argument which is his discovery; it is the total argument for that conclusion. (Many histories of philosophy are worthless just because they think that, for example, Hume's philosophy can be presented, like pemmican, by cataloguing his conclusions. But if all we needed to learn from Hume's thinking could be propounded in the dozen odd sentences in which we would state Hume's conclusions, we should properly blame him for burying them in his ocean of other words. Whereas for his *argument* the Treatise errs in the direction of ellipse.)

When a philosopher or his commentator is asked to summarize what he has discovered, a bad mistake underlies the very posing of the question. It assumes that just as the astronomer's discoveries can be published to the world in a sentence or two, namely, sentences stating the new facts that he has discovered, so the philosophers ought to be able to tell us new facts. But philosophy does not discover, or look for, new matters of fact. In a sense, which I shall not try to elucidate, the philosopher throws new light, but he does not give new information. And the light that he throws is resident in the rigour of his arguments. Anthologies of the quotable dicta of the great philosophers pretend, sometimes, to be encyclopaedias of the 'results' of philosophy up to date. But they illuminate no one who has not himself followed the same lines of reasoning as they had done.

But if this, or something like this, is true, how can there be in philosophy 'isms' pitted against 'isms'? If, for example, we take Monism and Pluralism to be two accredited and antagonistic 'isms', then the Monist, if he is a philosopher at all, will be bound to say either that the case for Pluralism contains some plausible or probative philosophical arguments, so that the Pluralists will have discovered something which he had missed; or that Pluralism contains no philosophical arguments which are either plausible or probative, in which case it will not be a philosophical theory at all, and will not therefore be an antagonistic philosophical theory. Even if he alleges that the case for Monism is probative, while that for Pluralism is merely plausible and fallacious—and this would, I suppose, usually be the allegation of the one 'school' against its rival—he should confess that there must have been defects in the presentation of the case for Monism, else how could the case for Pluralism have looked plausible? How can an argument *seem* to refute a patently unanswerable case? The case for Monism, if really unanswerable, ought to be made patently unanswerable. So the existence of Pluralists will at least have done philosophy the service of advertising the fact that the case for Monism is either answerable or not patently unanswerable. In either case the Monist, if he is a serious philosopher, would give the Pluralist the credit for having made a philosophical discovery on a question of principle. And then the feud between the 'isms' is over, and we are left with a serious dispute on questions of philosophical importance. Instead of saying, 'I can't argue with Pluralists, for they are philosophically unprincipled,' the philosophically minded Monist will say, 'I can't argue profitably with anyone but a Pluralist. He is the only person who is keen to examine the rigorousness of the arguments on our questions of principle.' And the sect-labels would be dropped.

I have said that there is no philosophical information. Philosophers do not make known matters of fact which were unknown before. The sense in which they throw light is that they make clear what was unclear before, or make obvious things which were previously in a muddle. And the dawning of this desiderated obviousness occurs in the finding of a logically rigorous philosophical argument. Something that was obscure becomes obvious to me in the act of seeing the force of a particular philosophical argument. Nor can I make a short cut to that clarification by perusing the conclusions but skipping the reasoning of the argument.

Anyone who appreciates the argument *ipso facto* gets the clarification. Though, of course, it is often very hard to appreciate involved and abstract arguments, like that which constitutes the *Critique of Pure Reason*.

But if a philosopher does succeed in finding for himself and transmitting to his readers a new and valid philosophical argument, then he has made something obvious for mankind. The obscurity which he has overcome is, apart from collapses of cultures, dead from that time on. His arduously achieved discovery becomes a public truism, and, if it is of any importance, becomes crystallized in the diction and the thought of educated people, even though the great majority of them have never read a word of him. The historian who wants to find out what Aristotle or Locke 'discovered' must see what public truisms existed after the philosopher's work was done which were not even the topic of a clearly recognized question before he began it. Now when such a clarification has been effected and a previously unseen truism has become a part of the ordinary intellectual equipment of educated men, the discoverer of the truism will seem, on retrospect, to have been talking platitudes. And just that is his great achievement, so to emancipate men from an obscurity that they can regard as a platitude what their predecessors could not even contemplate clearly enough to regard as a paradox.

Those very parts of the work of Berkeley, say, or Hume to which we vouchsafe an unexcited 'Of course' are the discoveries of Berkeley and Hume.

But there can be, and are in fact, no faction-fights about the public truisms which are the real legacy of effective philosophizing. We do not marshal ourselves into Liberals and Conservatives about the points which a philosopher has made obvious. On the contrary, we contest about points which he has left contestable, points, namely, where he failed to make something obvious. We fight for or against some of his doctrines which are not truisms just because he has failed to establish them by probative or patently probative arguments. We enlist ourselves as his 'followers' on the points where he was unsuccessful in clarifying something. He is the leader of a party in those very paths where he is still blindfolded.

I conclude with a few concessions.

(1) Although, as I think, the motive of allegiance to a school or a leader is a non-philosophic and often an anti-philosophic motive, it may have some good results. Partisanship does generate zeal, combativeness, and team-spirit. And, when these impulses are by

chance canalized into the channels of a non-spurious philosophical dispute, the hostilities and militancies may aerate the waters and even drive useful turbines.

(2) Pedagogically, there is some utility in the superstition that philosophers are divided into Whigs and Tories. For we can work on the match-winning propensities of the young, and trick them into philosophizing by encouraging them to try to 'dish' the Rationalists, or 'scupper' the Hedonists. But this is a dodge for generating examination-philosophy rather than philosophy.

(3) The 'ism' labels remain, of course, applicable and handy, as terms of abuse, commiseration, or apologia. It is a neat and quick way of indicating the blinkers of a would-be philosopher to say, 'He does not consider such-and-such an argument or type of argument, but then, poor fellow, he is a die-hard Idealist (or a sound Realist, or a whole-hogging Pragmatist),' And we, too, shall be, with perfect justice, allocated to new or old-fangled 'isms'.

For, being human, we are, in philosophizing, as elsewhere, partial to views from irrational motives, such as vanity, personal devotions, local patriotisms, and race prejudices.

I am only urging that the employment of 'ism-labels' should be reserved for our intervals of gossip and confession. They should not occur in philosophical discussions.

(4) A big service that has been done to philosophy by the philosophical sects has been in respect of the technical terminology of philosophy. Philosophers no more dispense with technical terms than do plumbers. But language traps are the source of errors and confusions in philosophy. So a fairly copious supply of alternative and disparate founts of jargon is a considerable safeguard. And the occasional essays in inter-translation which occur when, for instance, a convinced anti-Thingummist tries to expound or criticize the views of a Thingummist are admirably fog-dispelling about the jargons of both, and not infrequently even about the philosophical problems themselves.

(5) An important part of philosophical thinking consists in the hypothetical trying-out of theories—seeing what would follow from the assumed theory, how far other theories would or would not be compatible with it, and so on.

Now much of the exploration can be done by a person who firmly believes the theory, although he has no good grounds for it. But whether he consciously adopts it as a not impossible theory, or is so irrationally imbued with it that it constitutes his inescapable 'point of view', he can follow out its consequences with profit to the subject.

Sometimes the added enthusiasm which comes from belief, however irrational, stimulates the exploration where it would have flagged in the absence of that credence. But none the less the disposition to be convinced of ill-founded or unfounded doctrines, or unconvinced of well-founded ones, is a 'misosophical' disposition.

(6) It is often claimed that the major 'lesson' that we ought to learn from a philosophical leader is not so much a doctrine or set of doctrines as a Method; and what unites a 'school' is not unanimity about conclusions, but agreement in the practice of the Method. We are to follow the example, not echo the pronouncements, of the founders. Now though it is not easy to say what we mean by a method of philosophizing, it seems to me clear that it does mean something. If there is more than one method of philosophy, or more than one strand in the method of philosophizing, the revealing of a new method or a new strand in the method is one of the biggest sorts of discovery that a philosopher can make.

However, that a proposed or exhibited method is a proper method or the proper method, or part of the proper method of philosophizing is not a truth of private revelation, or a matter of personal taste. It is a philosophical proposition, and one on a question of 'principle'. So a school which claimed to be, and alone to be, on the right track in virtue of its monopoly of the true Method would only be a special case of what we considered before, the pretended monopoly of philosophical principles. The rival sects would again be separated only by rival pretensions, unless they join in exploring the case for and the case against those pretensions. And then they are not rivals.

12

CATEGORIES

Reprinted from 'Proceedings of the Aristotelian Society', vol. XXXVIII, *1938, by permission of the editor*

Doctrines of categories and theories of types are explorations in the same field. And the field is still largely unexplored. Moreover the exploration of it is at present handicapped by certain vocabulary-differences between philosophers, which hinder them from reading one another's maps. My object in this paper is rather to remove certain obstacles to the exploration than to proffer surveys of my own.

The matter is of some importance, for not only is it the case that category-propositions (namely assertions that terms belong to certain categories or types) are always philosopher's propositions, but, I believe, the converse is also true. So we are in the dark about the nature of philosophical problems and methods if we are in the dark about types or categories.

I begin with some historical remarks, not in order to exhibit adeptness in philosophical palaeontology or even to make upstart doctrines respectable by discerning Norman blood in them, but as a convenient way of jointly opening up the philosophical questions and explaining some traditional terminologies of the topic.

ARISTOTLE'S CATEGORIES

What did Aristotle think that his list of Categories was a list of? The word 'category' meant what our word 'predicate' means and shared all the vagueness and ambiguity of this English substantive. But Aristotle's list of categories was not a glossary of all the predicates that there are. On at least a plausible interpretation of the doctrine, Aristotle's list is intended to be a list of the ultimate types of predicates. But what does this mean?

There are simple propositions, namely those which do not consist of more elementary propositions in junction with each other, that is to say there are propositions into the expression of which there cannot enter such conjunctions as 'and', 'or', 'if', 'although', 'because', etc. Of these simple propositions some are singular propositions, namely those each of which is about at least one named or directly indicated particular.

Collect a range of simple, singular propositions, all similar in being about the same particular or particulars, then the respects in which these propositions differ from one another will be their predicates. And these predicates are classified into a finite number of families or types, the differences between which types can be indicated, though not defined, in the following way.

Any simple proposition about Socrates, say, is an answer, probably a false one, to some question about Socrates. Any given question about Socrates will generate a range of possible answers, but not any proposition about Socrates will be an answer to this question about him. There are as many different types of predicates of Socrates as there are irreducibly different sorts of questions about him. Thus 'How big?' collects 'Six foot tall', 'five foot tall', 'ten stone', 'eleven stone', etc., and does not collect 'fair-haired', 'in the garden', or 'a stonemason'. 'Where?' collects predicates of location, 'What sort?' collects predicates of kind, 'What like?' collects qualities, and so on.

Any two predicates which satisfy the same interrogative are of the same category, and any two which do not satisfy the same interrogative are of different categories. In the main Aristotle seems to content himself with taking ordinary language as his clue to the list of heads of questions, and so of types of predicates.

This programme of cataloguing types was then expanded, either by Aristotle or by his followers. We can not only ask about a particular series of questions, each of which will yield in its answers a range of possible predicates of that particular; we can also ask with reference to any such predicate 'Who has it?' or 'What (in the sense of "which") has it?' The answers to these questions will name or indicate particulars, like 'Socrates', 'Fido', 'I' and 'the Queen'. Obviously these questions do not generate ranges of predicates, but ranges of subjects or possessors of predicates, that is, particular substances. So *Socrates* is in the category of Substance, whereas *snub-nosed* is in the category of Quality and *husband* in that of Relation. As a result of this expansion, 'category' no longer means 'type of predicate' merely, but 'type of term' where 'term' means 'abstractible factor in a range of simple, singular propositions'.

Aristotle's actual list of ten (or sometimes eight) types of terms is doubtless unsatisfactory. Certain of the alleged ultimate types are patently only subordinate branches of others, and the criteria used by Aristotle for determining whether a term is of this or that category are fairly loose, where they occur at all. But for his purposes this does not matter much. He chiefly required to be able to demarcate (*a*) qualities from relations, (*b*) both from substances, and (*c*) all three from sorts or kinds. And this he was now able in a rough and unprecise way to do. But we have other fish to fry, so we have to notice other defects in his scheme.

(1) It is not an easy matter to decide when a sentence expresses a simple proposition. For the fact that a sentence contains only one verb and no conjunctions does not prove that the proposition expressed by it is simple, i.e., that the sentence *could* not be paraphrased by a sentence containing conjunctions and a plurality of verbs. And in fact any sentence containing a description, or any sentence containing a dispositional adjective like 'brittle', or, again, any sentence containing a kind-name is thus paraphrasable or 'exponible'. Most grammatically simple sentences express non-simple propositions and so are exponible. (Modern logic largely consists in taking exponibility seriously.) And this involves that the isolation of terms is no simple matter either. Grammatically simple nominative-expressions and predicative-expressions do not necessarily or often stand for logically simple constituents or components of propositions. The classification of types of abstractible factors in simple propositions must be postponed to the classification of the varieties of propositional forms. We require first a docketing of what are expressed by form-words, namely 'syncategorematic' words like *all, some, a, the, any, not, if, or, and, than*, etc., together with what are expressed by grammatical constructions, before we can hope to pin down for indexing any irreducible categorematic words.

(2) Moreover, we need a method for exhibiting and, what is quite different, a method for establishing type-homogeneities and type-heterogeneities. Aristotle's method, so far as he had one, seems to have consisted in collecting the ordinary interrogatives of everyday speech. He then labels his more important types with nouns formed from these interrogative words. But no reason is given for supposing that the Greek stock of interrogative words is either as economical as possible or as rich as might be desired. However his clue, such as it was, was not a completely silly one. For after all 'propositional function' is only 'question' writ sophisticatedly. The propositional function '*x* is snub-nosed' differs only in practical associations from 'Who is snub-nosed?'; and 'Socrates is ϕ' exhibits no more or less than 'Where is Socrates?' or 'What-like (*qualis*) is

Socrates?' or 'How big is Socrates?' according to the *genre* selected for ϕ.[1]

In order to state more precisely where Aristotle was on the right track and where his enterprise is unsuccessful, and also because I shall need them later on in the course of this paper, I want here to introduce some technical idioms. It is patent that, in a certain sense, sentences contain parts; for two sentences can be partially similar and partially dissimilar. Let us call any partial expression which can enter into sentences otherwise dissimilar a 'sentence-factor'. Thus single words will be sentence-factors, but so will phrases of any degree of complexity as well as entire clauses. Thus, in the sentence 'I am the man who wrote this paper', 'I', 'the man who', 'who wrote this paper', 'wrote this paper' are all sentence-factors.

I call them 'factors', rather than 'parts', since 'parts' would suggest, what is false, that the elements so abstracted can exist outside any such combinations as constitute sentences and, what is worse, that they can occur indifferently anywhere in any such combination, i.e. that they are both independent and freely shuffleable counters. The word 'factor' is intended to suggest, what is true, that they can only occur as factors in complexes of certain sorts, and can only occur in them in certain determinate ways.

Now, though sentence-factors cannot be extracted from all combinations, they can be abstracted from any specified combination. If we take any sentence and substitute for any fragment of it a dotted line, or the phrase 'so and so', what is left is a sentence-factor with a signal (namely 'so and so' or the dotted line), to show that and how the sentence-factor requires completion. But the dotted line, though it requires some complement or other, would tolerate as its complements any out of an indefinite range of factors. Thus 'Socrates is...' or 'I am the man who so and so,' or 'Such and such implies that tomorrow is Saturday,' are not sentences but sentence-frames only, the gaps in which require to be completed by further sentence-factors. The required complements would, of course, have to be of different sorts in the three different frames. '... ugly' would complete one, '... visited Edinburgh yesterday' would complete the second, and 'Today's being Tuesday...' would complete the third, and none would complete either of the others.

But though not any factor is fit to be the complement of any gap, there is an indefinite range of possible factors of the same pattern which would complete any given gap. So we abstract a factor from

[1] Cf. Lewis and Langford, *Symbolic Logic*, pp. 332–4; and Carnap on 'W... questions' in *Logical Syntax of Language*, p. 296.

the other factor or factors in any concrete sentence by putting dotted lines or 'gap-signs' (like 'so and so' or 'x' or 'ϕ' or 'p') in the place or places of the other factor or factors. A gap-sign is not itself a word, or a phrase or a clause, nor is it the name or description of one; it is the name or index of a place for one or for any of a range of appropriate sentence-factors.

Now sentences and sentence-factors are English or German, pencilled or whispered or shouted, slangy or pedantic, and so on. What logic is concerned with is something which is indifferent to these differences—namely (it is convenient though often misleading to say), propositions and the parts or factors of propositions. When two sentences of different languages, idioms, authors or dates say the same thing, what they say can be considered in abstraction from the several sayings of it, which does not require us to suppose that it stands to them as a town stands to the several signposts which point to it. And, just as we distinguish propositions from the sentences which propound them, so we must distinguish proposition-factors from the sentence-factors which express them. But again we must not suppose that this means that the world contains cows and earthquakes *and* proposition-factors, any more than we are entitled by the fact that we can distinguish the two faces of a coin to infer that when I have a coin in my hand I have three things in my hand, the coin and its two faces.

Next, we have seen that the gap in a given sentence-frame can be completed by *some* but not by *any* alternative complements. But there are two sorts of 'can' here. 'So and so is in bed' grammatically requires for complements to the gap indicated by 'so and so' nouns, pronouns or substantival phrases such as descriptive phrases. So 'Saturday is in bed' breaks no rule of grammar. Yet the sentence is absurd. Consequently the possible complements must be not only of certain grammatical types, they must also express proposition-factors of certain logical types. The several factors in a non-absurd sentence are typically suited to each other; those in an absurd sentence or some of them are typically unsuitable to each other. To say that a given proposition-factor is of a certain category or type is to say that its expression could complete certain sentence-frames without absurdity.

If the interpretation that I have given of Aristotle's doctrine of categories is correct, we can say that in one important respect it was on the right track. For interrogative sentences, when considered in abstraction from their practical role as petitions or commands, are sentence-frames, and the interrogative words in them are gap-signs.

And by distinguishing varieties of sorts of questions, Aristotle is using a general method for exhibiting varieties of type of the factors which would be answers to those questions or complements to those gap-signs.

On the other hand his procedure is defective in the following ways. He only attempts to classify the types of a small sub-class of proposition-factors, namely the constituents and components of simple, singular propositions. Let us call these by their traditional (and typically ambiguous) title of 'terms'. All terms are factors but most factors are not terms. He proffers no test of when a sentence-factor does and when it does not stand for a term, and seems to assume that a grammatically simple word always stands for a constituent or component of a simple proposition. He relies, apparently, solely upon common sense and common parlance for evidence that a given factor is suited to fill a given gap. But worse than this, he does not recognize that the types of factors control and are controlled by the logical form of the propositions into which they can enter, except in the solitary case of particular substances which, he recognizes, cannot occupy the berths of qualities, relations, magnitudes, positions, kinds, etc. in what he takes to be simple propositions.

He, with the logicians of later ages, seems to have thought that while terms are coupled in propositions and while there are various types of terms, yet there is only one sort of coupling. For the very same term which occurs in one proposition as 'subject' can occur in another as 'predicate'.

As any letter of the alphabet may be juxtaposed with any other letter, without modifying the designs of those letters, so it seems to have been thought that there is no interaction between the form of a proposition and the types of the factors composing it. So no connexion was established between the formal properties of propositions which render inferences embodying them possible or impossible and the formal properties or types of the terms or other factors in them. The syllogistic rules which Aristotle discovered turn on the concepts expressed by such form-words as *all, some, this, not, and* and *implies*, but his treatment of them neither infects nor is infected by his classification of types of terms.

It is as though a grammarian were in his first chapter to give definitions of the types of parts of speech, such as nouns, prepositions, verbs, conjunctions, etc., and in a later chapter to give a quite independent discussion to the rules of syntax, when in truth just these rules must already be latent in the notions of noun, verb, conjunction, etc. It is to treat as freely shuffleable counters factors the determinate roles of which in the combination into which they can enter are just what constitute their types.

To know all about the logical form of a proposition and to know all about the logical types of its factors are to know one and the same thing.[1]

KANT'S JUDGMENT-FORMS AND CATEGORIES

Kant's doctrine of categories starts from quite a different quarter from that of Aristotle, and what he lists as categories are quite other than what Aristotle puts into his index. Kant quaintly avers that his purpose is the same as that of Aristotle, but in this he is, save in a very broad and vague sense, mistaken. Unfortunately Kant borrows for three out of his four heads of categories the same labels as Aristotle had used for three of his ten. As we shall see 'Quantity', 'Quality' and 'Relation' mean completely different sorts of things for the two philosophers.

Kant begins by giving a catalogue of judgment forms, a catalogue, that is to say, of the several ways in which one proposition may resemble or differ from another not in topic but in form. He makes no attempt to define the notion of form, or even to justify his catalogue, save by declaring, what is false, that it derived from the findings of traditional logic, which he assumes to be a completed body of ascertained truth. (1) All propositions are determined in respect of 'Quantity', i.e., in respect of the extension of their subjects, and so must be either universal, particular or singular, i.e., of the 'all', 'some' or 'this' form; (2) all propositions are either affirmative, negative or infinite, which are the three 'Qualities' of propositions; (3) all propositions are of one of the three 'Relation' patterns, 'S is P', 'if p then q', and 'p or q'; and (4) all propositions are of one of the three varieties of 'Modality', i.e., of the 'is' form, the 'may be' form or the 'must be' form. These judgment forms are not yet Kant's categories, but they are the source from which he, somewhat mysteriously, proposes to derive or deduce them.

Kant's line of approach was, in principle, much more enlightened than Aristotle's had been. Unfortunately his execution was hopelessly misguided. His sub-variety of 'infinite' judgments is a fraud;

---

[1] I apologize, not very humbly, for terminology which, here and elsewhere in this paper, I substitute for the terminology of 'propositional functions', 'variables', 'values' and the rest. I do so for the simple reason that this terminology has led to many confusions. Especially it failed to make obvious whether in talking of functions, variables, values, etc. we were talking of certain sorts of expressions or talking *with* certain expressions *of* certain sorts of things. Should we say that Socrates or 'Socrates' is a value of the variable in '*x* is snub-nosed'? The terminology which I use is meant to be overtly semantic. Its items, too, are meant to be reasonably self-explanatory.

there are several sorts of 'universal' judgment, but the sort which he was considering should come under the heading of hypothetical judgments; the division into assertoric, problematic and apodeictic is wrong-headed, the two last being special cases of hypotheticals; the division into categorical, hypothetical and disjunctive embodies a cross-division and contains one glaring omission, for (*a*) what he had in mind was the distinction between simple and compound propositions and (*b*) he omitted from this latter class conjunctive propositions of the 'p and q' form. Only of simple propositions is it true that they must be either affirmative or negative and either universal or particular or singular, since in a two-limbed conjunctive, disjunctive or hypothetical proposition, for instance, one of the conjoined propositions may be one while the second is one of the others. The distinction between the disjunctive and the hypothetical forms is false. No overt distinction is drawn between general and non-general propositions; no place is found for such propositions as 'seven cows are in the field', 'most men wear coats', 'John is probably dead'. And lastly in simple singular propositions no distinction is drawn between attributive and relational propositions; Aristotle's category of relational predicates is completely ignored. Indeed Kant fails to follow Aristotle's doctrine of categories at all, for he notices no type-differences inside subject-predicate propositions, and purloins the titles 'Quality', 'Quantity' and 'Relation' for his own quite different purposes, namely, in Aristotle's use 'green', 'sweet' and 'honest' signify qualities, but in Kant's use 'Quality' signifies a proposition's being affirmative or negative. 'Quantity' is, for Aristotle, the name of the family of predicates of magnitude or size; for Kant it is the name of the respect in which propositions are of the 'all . . .' or the 'some . . .' or the 'this . . .' form. Relations, lastly, are in Aristotle's use such predicates as 'cousin of', 'above', 'bigger than', but in Kant's they are what are expressed by such conjunctions as 'if', 'or' and (he should have added) 'and'.

But when all this is said, it has to be acknowledged that Kant was recognizing as cardinal in the search for categories or types facts which Aristotle had not noticed at all in this connection. Kant saw that there is a variety of respects in which propositions may be formally similar and dissimilar. As we saw, in Aristotle's doctrine of categories the roles of 'form-words' like *all, some, the, a, any, if, or, and, not* are unnoticed, and medieval followers relegated these words to limbo under the grudging appellation of 'syncategorematic'. Kant's doctrine (though he does not notice the point) restores them from the limbo of logic to its workshop.

Aristotle seems generally to suppose that while there is a moderate variety of types of factors, yet there is only one sort of coupling to which they are subject. (In his doctrine of Predicables he half sees that in general propositions there are different sorts of coupling, but this is not allowed to modify his theory of terms.) Kant sees that there is a galaxy of sorts of coupling and that these determine or are determined by the sorts of factors that can be coupled. Aristotle's is an 'alphabetic' theory of factors and a simple 'juxtaposition' theory of their combinations; Kant's is a 'syntactical' theory about the combinations of factors, and consequently a 'syntactical' theory about the types of those factors—or so I interpret his cryptic utterances about 'functions of unity'.

However, Kant's categories are not identical with his forms of judgment. They are, in some obscure way, the projections of these logical forms upon the field of natural things and events. Natural facts, facts, that is, that are establishable by observation or by memory of or induction from or causal inference from observations, all embody certain principles of structure, which somehow derive from the items in the table of judgment-forms. Nature consists of things possessing extensive and intensive magnitudes, being in states at particular moments of time and undergoing mutations or perpetuations of state according to causal laws. Everything empirical must and nothing non-empirical can embody these categories. So metaphysical propositions trespass against category-rules.

The mysterious Metapsychology, by means of which Kant tries to prove both that Nature must be so constituted and that we can know that it must be so constituted, need not be considered here. What would be relevant would be an exposition of the differences that Kant professes to find between his logical types and his categories or natural types. It looks as though he confusedly believed that there exist two sorts of facts or propositions, logicians' facts or propositions and scientists' facts or propositions, and that the forms of the latter are step-children of those of the former. But this would be an absurd view, for in fact the logicians' forms are simply what they abstract from ranges of partially similar and partially dissimilar propositions which hail, very likely, directly from the text-books of scientists, historians, explorers, mathematicians or theologians. So the alleged distinction is, I think, a bogus one.

Kant contributes nothing to the technical problem how to exhibit or symbolize type-homogeneities and heterogeneities in abstraction from the concrete factors which exemplify them. Nor does he explain how they are established, save by recommending us to read traditional logic.

Before leaving the history of the topic, we should notice one presupposition which Aristotle and Kant share, which is, I believe, unreflectively shared by a number of contemporary philosophers. Namely, it was supposed that there exists a finite catalogue of categories or types; for instance, that there exist just ten (or eight) types of terms, or that there exist just twelve judgment patterns, just as there exist just twenty-six letters in the English alphabet, just sixty-four squares on the chess-board and just six species of chessmen. This seems to be pure myth. There are various gambits at chess, but there is no finite roster of them; and there are various grammatical constructions of English sentences, but there can be no complete table of those varieties.

Scholasticism is the belief in some decalogue of categories, but I know of no grounds for this belief.

It follows that I do not think that we can ever say of a given code-symbolism in formal logic that its symbols are now adequate for the symbolization of all possible differences of type or form. It may, of course, be adequate for the exhibition of all the type-differences that concern us in the course of some particular enquiry.

GENERALIZATION OF THE TOPIC

When a sentence is (not true or false but) nonsensical or absurd, although its vocabulary is conventional and its grammatical construction is regular, we say that it is absurd because at least one ingredient expression in it is not of the right type to be coupled or to be coupled in that way with the other ingredient expression or expressions in it. Such sentences, we may say, commit type-trespasses or break type-rules. Latterly the attention of logicians has been focused on certain sorts of type-trespasses, like those which are committed by 'I am now lying' and '"heterological" is heterological'. These sorts are interesting, because their absurdities are not obvious but manifest themselves in the generation of contradictions or vicious circles, whereas 'Saturday is in bed' is obviously absurd before any contradictions are seen to result from the hypothesis that it is true.

Moreover, we can be actually led by seemingly valid arguments to propounding propositions of the former sorts, whereas only the deliberate intention to produce balderdash would get us to formulate sentences of the latter sort. That is, some type-trespasses are insidious and others are not. It is the insidious ones which force us to consider type-rules; the others we only attend to because we are already considering type-rules. But it would be a mistake to restrict the theory of types to the theory of certain special type-rules.

To ask the question To what type or category does so-and-so belong? is to ask In what sorts of true or false propositions and in what positions in them can so-and-so enter? Or, to put it semantically, it is to ask In what sorts of non-absurd sentences and in what positions in them can the expression 'so and so' enter? and, conversely, What sorts of sentences would be rendered absurd by the substitution for one of their sentence-factors of the expression 'so and so'? I adopt the word 'absurd' in preference to 'nonsensical' or 'meaningless' for the reason that both the two last words are sometimes used for noises like 'brillig' and 'abracadabra', and sometimes for collocations of words having no regular grammatical construction. Moreover, both have recently been adopted for polemical purposes in aid of a special theory. 'Absurd' has helpful associations with the *reductio ad absurdum,* and even its nuance of ridiculousness is useful rather than the reverse, for so many jokes are in fact type-pranks.

WHAT ARE TYPES TYPES OF?

Only expressions can be affirmed or denied to be absurd. Nature provides no absurdities; nor can we even say that thoughts such as beliefs or supposals or conceptions are or are not absurd. For what is absurd is unthinkable.

So it is, on the whole, prudent to talk logic in the semantic idiom and to formulate our theories and enquiries in such a way as to advertise all the time that we are considering whether such and such expressions may or may not be coupled in such and such ways with other expressions.

The danger is, of course, that we shall be taken and shall unwittingly take ourselves to be talking grammar, as if it was all part of one topic to say 'Plural nouns cannot have singular verbs' and 'The dotted line in ". . . is false" can be completed with "What you are now saying . . ." and cannot be completed with "What I am now saying . . ."'.

We try, then, to say that absurdities result from the improper coupling not of expressions but of what the expressions signify, though the coupling and mis-coupling of them is effected by operating upon their expressions.

But there is not and cannot be any univocal title for all the *significata* of expressions, since if there was such a title, all these *significata* would be of one and the same type. And just this is what was at bottom wrong with the Lockean terminology of 'ideas' and the Meinongian terminology of 'objects', words which were employed to perform exactly this impossible task.

Other commonly used titles have extra nuisances as well. 'Terms' retains some of its traditional associations and should be used, if at all, for particulars-or-qualities-or-relations, etc. 'Concepts' does not cover either particulars or entire propositions or even complexes of concepts. So I use 'proposition-factor' (intending it to have all possible type-ambiguities), to collect whatever is signified by any expression, simple or complex, which can be a complement to a gap-sign in some sentence-frame or other (or which can be a value of a variable in some propositional function or other). And, if asked such questions as Do proposition-factors exist? How many of them are there? Are they mental? What are they like?, my answer is, 'All such questions are ridiculous, since "factor" is and is meant to be the meeting-place of all type-ambiguities.'

Of course we could dispense with any such word. Its functions are purely stenographic. Questions about the types of factors are, in a way, just questions about the possibilities of co-significance of certain classes of expressions. But just as the 'factor' idiom (like the 'idea' idiom) is liable to entrap us in myth, so the semantic idiom is liable to entrap us in a confusion between logical and grammatical questions.

Two proposition-factors are of different categories or types, if there are sentence-frames such that when the expressions for those factors are imported as alternative complements to the same gap-signs, the resultant sentences are significant in the one case and absurd in the other. It is tempting but not quite correct to say, as the converse of this, that two factors are of the same type if there is any case where both can fill the same gap. For 'I' and 'the writer of this paper' can be alternative nominatives to hosts of significant sentences but both cannot fill the gap in '. . . never wrote a paper'. It follows that, though nearly, it is not quite, true to say that every gap-sign in its context in a determinate sentence-frame indicates the category of all its possible complements. But wherever a particular gap-sign is thus tolerant of typically dissimilar complements, that gap-sign has typical ambiguity which a better symbolism would escape. For the fact that a given gap in a sentence-frame *can* be filled by complements between which there are certain differences of form is itself a fact about the types of those different complements.

THE GENESIS OF TYPE-RIDDLES

How do we come to be exercised about the forms of propositions or the types of proposition-factors? Or, to put it in a less new-fangled way, what makes it urgent for us to find definitions or analyses of concepts? For we do not gratuitously rummage in dictionaries or encyclopaedias after notions on which to perform elucidations. Type-problems seem to be forced upon us in two main ways.

(1) There are concepts with which we are perfectly familiar and which we are perfectly competent to employ—incessantly occurring, for instance, in questions which we know quite well how to solve. Yet whole classes of ordinary propositions embodying one or more of such concepts, some of which propositions we have perfectly good reasons for accepting as true, are ruled out as false by other propositions, no less well authenticated, embodying other equally familiar concepts. In a word, we are confronted by antinomies. We are sure that some out of one family of propositions are true and that some out of another family are true, yet the truth of any from the one family seems flatly to contradict all out of the other. I see a bent stick and the stick is straight; I am to blame for an action, and the action issued from a character which my forebears bequeathed and my school moulded, and so on.

Now if the apparent contradictions or, rather, class of contradictions is resoluble, it can only be because the logical forms of the conflicting propositions are not what we had supposed, since it is only in virtue of the forms of propositions or the types of their factors that they do (or do not) imply (or imply the negatives of) one another.

(2) Then, when we have begun to explore the mechanics of some of our concepts and propositions, we find ourselves embarrassed by some purely technical perplexities. We are not quite sure how to use our own professional implements. But we only want to be sure of the designs of our trade-keys because we want to use them upon locks which were recalcitrant before we started our operations—unless we are carried away by virtuosity. Enquiries such as this one, into the nature of categories, or into the species of relations are in fact such technical questions. But *any* uncharted concept is liable to generate antinomies, for ignorance of its chart is ignorance of some of the implications and compatibilities of the propositions containing it. Concepts of common sense, of the sciences and of philosophy itself can and do all generate antinomies. The problem of the internality of relations arose out of antinomies resulting from the philosophers' technical concept of *relation*.

HOW ARE TYPES DETERMINED?

It has long been known that what a proposition implies, it implies in virtue of its form. The same is true of what it is compatible and incompatible with. Let us give the label 'liaisons' to all the logical relations of a proposition, namely what it implies, what it is implied by, what it is compatible with and what it is incompatible with. Now, any respect in which two propositions differ in form will be reflected in differences in their liaisons. So two propositions which are formally similar in all respects save that one factor in one is different in type from a partially corresponding factor in the other, will have liaisons which are correspondingly dissimilar. Indeed the liaisons of a proposition do not merely *reflect* the formal properties of the proposition and, what this involves, those of all its factors. In a certain sense, they are the same thing. To know all about its liaisons is to know all about the formal structure of the proposition, and vice versa—though I can obviously entertain or believe a proposition without having yet noticed all its liaisons. Indeed I must grasp it before I can consider them, otherwise I could not be the victim of antinomies.

The operation of extracting the type of a factor cannot exclude the operation of revealing the liaisons of propositions embodying it. In essence they are one operation. Of course, with the familiar sorts of propositions upon which logicians have worked for centuries or decades, we short-circuit the enquiry, by subsuming them direct under the appropriate formulae. But to be told that a proposition is of the form 'S a P' or of the form 'Ex. $\phi x. \sim \psi \chi$' is to be told nothing unless we are able to work with the code-symbols according to the rules of their use, which means unless we know how to read off the liaisons, the patterns of which are what these symbols prescribe.

Now the operation of formulating the liaisons of a proposition just is the activity of ratiocination or argumentation (in which of course there need not be, though there may be, a polemical purpose) And this is why philosophizing is arguing, and it is just this element of ratiocination which, as a rule, is left out of the latter-day definitions of philosophy as 'analysis'. For these generally suggest that analysing is some sort of paraphrasing. But some sorts of paraphrase throw no philosophical light, for they fail to exhibit just those features of propositions and their factors, obscurity about which involves us in antinomies, namely their liaisons which flow from or constitute their logical types and forms. Mere increase of prolixity is not enough. When an argument is a philosophical one and when not, are further questions the discussion of which would not here be in place.

THE TYPE OF CATEGORY-PROPOSITIONS

I call a proposition a 'category-proposition' which asserts something about the logical type of a factor or set of factors. Some types have been officially recognized and endowed with trade-names, like 'quality', 'state', 'substance', 'number', 'logical construction', 'category', etc. We could call these 'category-words'. Carnap mis-leadingly calls them 'universal words'. But propositions asserting that factors are of manned types differ only in brevity of expression from propositions asserting that factors are of described types.

All such propositions are philosophers' propositions (not neces-sarily, of course, of professional or paid philosophers), and the converse is also, I think, true.

Now assertions about the types of factors are, as we have seen, assertions about what sorts of combinations of them with other factors would and what would not produce absurdities. And as only collocations of symbols can be asserted to be absurd or, conse-quently, denied to be absurd, it follows that category-propositions are semantic propositions. This does not imply that they are of the same type as the propositions of philologists, grammarians or lexicographers. There are not English category-propositions as opposed to German ones, or Occidental as opposed to Oriental. Nor does it imply that they can say nothing about the 'nature of things'. If a child's perplexity why the Equator can be crossed but not seen, or why the Cheshire cat could not leave its grin behind it is perplexity about the 'nature of things', then certain category-propositions will give the required information about the nature of things. And the same will hold good of less frivolous type-perplexities. But what are the tests of absurdity?

13

CONSCIENCE AND MORAL CONVICTIONS

Reprinted from 'Analysis', vol. VII, *1940, by permission of the editor*

In discussing the conflict between Moral Sense theories of ethical knowledge (or conviction) and intellectual theories like those of Kant and Price, recently, I struck a point which was new to me. I had always vaguely supposed that 'Conscience' is ordinarily used to signify any sort of knowledge or conviction about what is right and wrong. So that *any* verdict about the rightness or wrongness either of a particular type of conduct or of a particular piece of conduct could be called a verdict of 'Conscience'. I had also supposed that 'conscience' was too vague and equivocal a word to enjoy any definite syntax.

But then I noticed that 'conscience' is *not* used in this way. We limit the verdicts of conscience to judgments about the rightness or wrongness of the acts only of the owner of that conscience. It is absurd to say, 'My conscience says that *you* ought to do this or ought not to have done that.' Judgments about the morality of other people's behaviour would not be called verdicts of conscience. If asked to advise someone else on a moral point, I could not without absurdity say that I must consult my conscience. Nor, if someone else misbehaves, can *my* conscience be said to disapprove. Conscience is a *private* monitor.

True, I can set myself to imagine moral problems. I can consider how my conscience would react if I were in your shoes, doing what you have done, or meditate doing. I can say, 'I could not do so and so with a clear conscience, so you ought not to do it.' But I can't say, '*My* conscience won't be clear if *you* do it.' What, then, is the difference between conscience and moral conviction which makes it absurd to regard the verdicts of my conscience as co-extensive with my moral convictions? Why can *my* conscience pass judgment only on *my* actions?

Originally, it appears, 'conscience' generally connoted 'self-knowledge' or 'self-consciousness'. Introspection would be an activity of 'conscientia', whether the objects of the introspection were or were not subjects of moral predicates. With the Reformation, if not earlier, self-inspection was supposed to be the direct discovery of the requirements of God. And 'Conscience' began to have the narrower meaning of the knowledge by self-inspection of *my* duties and faults. Butler links conscience very closely to 'reflection' (in Locke's sense), which is equivalent to introspection. But why should my moral convictions apply differently to me, just because direct inspection by me is restricted to *my* thoughts, motives and resolves?

Certainly, I can't know directly how you feel or what you think, but I can often know well enough by inference. And in reading a novel I can know all about the motives and desires of the characters, for the novelist tells me them. Yet, though I know all about you, or about the hero of the novel, I can't say that my conscience approves or disapproves either of your conduct or of his. Conversely, introspection and self-inspection are not sources of infallible knowledge. I can misdescribe to myself, without dishonesty, my own motives. I may, e.g., fail to find *Schadenfreude* in my 'serves him right' attitudes, though it is there.

So the difference cannot derive from that between my having *knowledge* of myself and only *opinions* about other people. If God is omniscient it would still be absurd to say that *his* conscience chided me for my behaviour.

At this point it looks tempting to go back and say (with the Moral Sensationalists) that, after all, my moral verdicts about myself do record special (moral) sense-perceptions, while my moral verdicts about others, involving as they do both generalisations of rules and inferential imputation of motives, dispositions, etc., are intellectual and rational. But this will not do. My particular verdicts of conscience are applications of general rules, imperatives or codes. My conscience says, 'You aren't being *honest*', and this involves understanding both what being honest is and that it is a general desideratum. (It is like one's prompt recognition that what one is saying is bad grammar, i.e., is a breach of a general rule. The facts that the recognition is prompt and may be unarticulated do not entail that we have a 'grammatical sense'.)

I suggest that the solution of the puzzle, which, I think, is a genuine one about the syntax of 'conscience' and of 'moral conviction', is in this direction. What is it to *have* a moral conviction? Or, what is it to *have* principles? At first, we begin by saying that it is to know or be convinced that some general proposition is true or that some universal imperative is right, or wise. But what are the public tests of whether a person really knows or is really convinced of so and so? They are, I think, the following:

(1) That he *utters* it regularly, relevantly and without hesitation.

(2) That other things which he says regularly, relevantly and unhesitatingly, presuppose it.

(3) That he is ready or eager to try to persuade other people of it and to dissuade them of what is inconsistent with it.

(4) That he regularly and readily behaves in accordance with it on occasions when it is relevant.

(5) That when he does not behave in accordance with it, he feels guilty, resolves to reform, etc.

We are inclined to say that (1) and (2) show that he intellectually accepts the principle; he thinks, e.g., that honesty is desirable: that (4) and (5) show that he is honest or pretty honest, and that (3) shows something between the two, namely, that he admires or respects honesty. And we should also be inclined to say that (1) and (2) taken *alone* show that he is not *really* convinced; the principle is a part of his intellectual furniture but not of his real nature. His acceptance of it is academic. It is not operative on his volitions, emotions and behaviour. But this is rather fishy. For it sets up a queer fence between thinking, feeling and willing; as if being a man of principle (say, being honest) differs from acknowledging honesty by the irruption of some new faculty, called will or feeling, which can accept principles, only not in the way in which thought does so. But thinking, e.g. believing, is an aspect of character or nature. The difference between not feeling qualms of doubt and not hesitating in bodily action is not a hard and fast line. *Saying* readily and *doing* readily seem to be related as species to genus, not as co-ordinate species of a higher genus. Talking to oneself or aloud is behaving. So there seems to be a sense in which *real* acceptance of a principle (does not lead to, but) *is* being disposed to behave in accordance with it. To 'know' a rule of conduct *is* to be regulated in one's conduct. To know *properly* the rules of grammar is to be able to talk correctly, to correct mistakes and to wince at those of others. A man's party manners show whether he 'knows' the rules of etiquette; his ability to *cite* 'Etiquette for Gentlemen' does not.

Supposing it conceded that sometimes appropriate behaviour is part of what we *mean* by certitude or acceptance of a proposition, let us label as 'operative' the knowledge or conviction which manifests itself in the disposition to behave—in *all* sorts of behaviour, including 'thinking'—in accordance with the principle which is said to be known or accepted. To be disposed to behave in a certain way in certain circumstances is to be prone or inclined to do so. Other things being equal, a person with a certain disposition will probably behave in the given way; that is what the word 'disposition' means.

Now if someone has operatively accepted a certain principle, but other things are not equal, i.e. he experiences some contrary impulse, there will not only exist a conflict between the temptation and the abstract principle; there will be actually experienced a conflict between the temptation and the disposition which is the operatively accepted principle. He will feel a tension because he *is* the two tendencies to act which are in conflict. 'It goes against the grain.' And these two tendencies, with their conflict, are visible on self-inspection or inferrible from what he can introspect. His knowledge or conviction of the principle is not an external censor but an internal competitor. His knowledge how he should behave does not *cause* but *is* a nisus to behaving in that way, but it is a *felt* nisus only when it is impeded.

But in passing verdicts on the conduct of others, our conviction, so to speak, cannot be more than academic. For me to believe that you should do so and so can be only to pronounce and perhaps to try to persuade; in the full sense of 'operative' my conviction about your duty cannot be operative, for it cannot issue in the required behaviour. (The desire to punish, rebuke and reform seems to be a response to the inoperativeness of merely finding fault.)

Or, alternatively, my application of a principle to you can take the form only of a verdict or of advice or exhortation, with perhaps subsequent reproof or punishment. But my application of my principle to me can take the form of doing what I should. In this sense conscience is never a merely verdict-passing faculty, it is a conduct regulating faculty. Its exercise is behaving or trying to behave and not describing or recommending. We credit conscience with *authority* as well as with knowledge. That is, we use the word 'conscience' for those moral convictions which issue not in verdicts but in behaving or trying to behave. So it is a tautology that my conscience cannot direct the behaviour of someone else.

This has analogies elsewhere. In a certain sense, I, having read the text-books and been a spectator, know how to swim; that is, I know what actions people must take to progress in a desired direction in the water, with the nostrils clear of the water. But no one would say that I really know how to swim or that I have swimming-skill, unless when I do it myself I usually succeed. And it would be absurd to say that I have skill or expertness in the swimming of others, though in the academic sense of the word 'know' I may know just what mistakes they are making. The proper manifestations of my skill are my performances and not mere directions to others. And the proper manifestations of my conscience are in my good conduct, or reluctance to behave ill or remorse afterwards and resolutions to reform. Conscience is not something other than, prior to or posterior to moral convictions; it is having those convictions in an operative degree, i.e. being disposed to behave accordingly. And it is active or calls for attention when this disposition is balked by some contrary inclination. Conscience has nothing to say when the really honest man is asked a question and when he has no temptation to deceive. He then tells the truth as he signs his name, without considering what to do or why he should do it or how to get himself to do it. Conscience is awake only when there is such a conflict. The test for the existence of such a conflict is the occurrence of attention to the problem of what is to be done. Pangs or qualms of conscience can occur only when I am both disposed to act in one way and disposed to act in another and when one of these dispositions is an operative moral principle. (And this 'can . . . only' is logical and not causal.) Wondering what to do is a manifestation of a balked disposition to act; if it was not balked I would act as I am disposed to act for that is what 'disposed' means. Consulting my conscience entails attending introspectively to my conflicting dispositions to act. Hence I cannot (logically) consult my conscience about what you are to do. Having a conscience to 'consult' is having a (partially) operative moral conviction.

Now there are convictions of rules of conduct other than moral ones. So they should in parallel circumstances engender naggings, commands, etc. parallel to those of conscience. Is this so?

(1) *Rules of Prudence.* I have learned from experience, doctors, hearsay, etc. that it is bad for me not to have a regular allowance of sleep each night. I know that I shall feel 'like death' tomorrow afternoon if I do not have at least seven hours of sleep. And I do habitually go to bed at 12, say, to be called at 8, without thinking of the effects of not doing so. 'Midnight is my bedtime' is the only thought that usually occurs to me if any thought occurs to me at all. Now, suppose, I am halfway through an exciting detective story at midnight. So I want to read on, and I am disposed to go to bed at 'my bedtime'. I do not feel guilty, but I find myself making excuses and promises for the future. Or, I tell myself that tomorrow afternoon is disengaged, so I can sleep then. So I do attend to factors in the situation similar to those which are considered in questions of

conscience. In certain of their uses, words like 'discretion' and 'caution' resemble 'conscience'. In the sense, e.g. in which my discretion guides my actions it cannot guide yours. To be cautious, provident, etc. is not just to acknowledge or enunciate certain propositions which may be true for everyone; it is to be disposed to live cautiously, providently, etc., which though it includes such acknowledging and enunciating does not reduce to them.

(2) *Rules of etiquette, fashion and social decorum.* 'We dress for dinner at Christ Church.' When we do this, the 'done' thing, we do not generally consider the utilities or aesthetic amenities of the practice. We just dress—i.e. it is a habit—but one which is actualised not only in dressing, but also in feeling surprised if a colleague dines in day clothes, in stopping teaching some time before dinner, etc. Our acceptance of the convention is manifested primarily by our behaving regularly and unquestioningly in accordance with it. Sometimes I am prevented from dressing. Then, while dining in mufti, I feel uncomfortable (though not guilty or imprudent). My sense of decorum, which is not, of course, a new mode of sense perception, nags gently. And in the sense in which I am punctilious about my own dinner uniform I cannot be punctilious about that of other people, I can be only noticing about them or critical of them.

(3) *Rules of arithmetic.* The accurate computer regularly observes the rules of addition, subtraction, multiplication and division. And his observance of them is not manifested in a special momentary act of acknowledging them, declaring them or teaching them, but in all his acts of accurate computation. His grasp of the rules is his ability and skill in working in accordance with them. He does not begin each morning's work by reciting an arithmetical creed. In a certain sense of 'think' he never thinks of the rules. In another sense of the word, however, he is thinking of the rules all the time; for he is continually applying them correctly and skilfully. The rules are now *habits* of operating. But his accuracy, flair or scrupulousness governs only his own computations. He cannot have a flair about the calculations of other people, though he knows the rules which they should keep and how these rules apply to their particular problems. But this knowledge is 'academic' while flair is practical. The former issues at most in behests and criticisms; the latter in accurate calculations. To know *operatively* the rules is to know how to calculate, i.e. to be able to calculate correctly, swiftly and without fatigue. The fact that many good mathematical teachers are bad mathematicians brings out these two opposed senses of 'knowing mathematics'. Is there anything in this field analogous to either the questions or commands

of conscience? I think there is. If a computer happens to know the answer which he expects to arrive at, e.g. from reading a pass book, he may through laziness or wishful thinking run too hastily through a column of figures and then, even though by accident his answer is correct, he feels a sense of guilt about his steps, and is inclined to go over them again more carefully. This is especially so when he gets to an answer which for some reason *must* be wrong. To locate and correct a mistake requires a special act of attention to what, say, certain figures do and do *not* add up to. His ordinary scrupulousness does not normally require the occurrence of actual scruples. But sometimes he has actually to feel scruples, which he would not feel unless he were dispositionally scrupulous, and on a given occasion has not been scrupulous enough. God would calculate (if at all) with 100% scrupulousness and 0% scruples. Similarly, he would always do the right thing and would never wonder what he ought to do. He would never consult his conscience and would never have pangs of conscience.

It might be said that having scruples, though they will be scruples of different sorts, is common to all cases where *real* acceptance of rules or principles is the being disposed to behave in a certain way, but where this disposition is balked of its normal actualisation by some special temptation or interruption. It is like trying to misspell one's own signature when writing one's own name has become an automatic habit. One *can* do it, but there is a resistance. One may compare also the practised cyclist trying to control a tricycle. His normal responses, e.g. in turning or in tilting, are balked by the abnormal situation. He knows (academically) what to do, but does not *really*, i.e. operatively, know how to do it. But as cycling well does not involve acknowledging or being able to cite laws of dynamics, one can scarcely speak of cycling scrupulously. Roughly, *this* sort of thing is a reflex and not an observance.

Conscience, then, is one species, among others, of scrupulousness; and scrupulousness is the operative acceptance of a rule or principle which consists in the disposition to behave, in all modes of behaviour, including saying to oneself and others, teaching, chiding, etc., in accordance with the rule. Scruples, whether of conscience or of any other species of scrupulousness, occur only when the normal actualisation of the disposition is impeded or balked. And they, too, are only a special way in which the disposition is actualised, viz. when it cannot be *normally* actualised. The reason why my conscience is not spoken of as either judging or commanding other people is the same as the reason why, in general, a man can be described as scrupulous only about his own acts, namely, that full operative acceptance of the rule can (logically) take the form only of conducting oneself in accordance with the rule. Your actions can't (logically) be exercises of or exhibit *my* skill, readiness, capacity, enthusiasm, etc.

This answer to the original puzzle will, of course, provoke the objection that it denies the hallowed distinctions between cognition, emotion and volition. For I am saying that in one sense, and a very important sense, of the word my being 'convinced' of something or my 'knowing' it do not *cause* but *consist* in my tending to feel certain feelings and to enact certain actions. It will be said that a thought may *engender* dispositions to feel and to act, but that these dispositions are not the causes of themselves.

I reply: (1) Then must it also be said that when I think in words, my saying so and so to myself is the *effect* of the thinking and not a constituent of it, that I first think and then tell myself what I have thought? But then I must think also what to tell myself and how to tell it, and this thinking must also have its own articulation which must in its turn be premeditated and so on. . . . Thinking *is* talking sensibly, but then why should it not equally be *behaving* sensibly?

(2) The present view, that among the criteria (*not* the symptoms) of belief and knowledge are dispositions to feel certain emotions and perform certain actions does not entail that 'thinking', 'feeling' and 'doing' are synonymous. It is still necessary to distinguish impulsive, reflex and automatic from intelligent, careful, purposive, deliberate and scrupulous actions; and silly from sensible, careless from careful, deliberate from unpremeditated, behaviour. Similarly, feeling indignant, shocked, awed, amused, thwarted, respectful differ from feeling uneasy, angry, or sleepy. Only rational beings in rational states of mind (i.e. not drunk, in a panic, or infantile) can (logically) feel the former, while animals and infants can feel the latter. Was Kant's obscure doctrine about 'Practical Reason' something like this view, and Aristotle's φρόνησις which manifests itself sometimes in *acting* from premises and which is internally connected with ἠθικὴ ἀρετή? What do we *mean* by 'judicious behaviour', 'scrupulous conduct', 'skilful or careful action'? It can't mean acting in consequence of certain 'sententious thinking'; for we can also say that the choice and control of the sentences in which we think, when we think 'sententiously', can be judicious and careful. Nor could the alleged causal connections between thinking and doing (or feeling) have been discovered by the people who speak of 'judicious behaviour' as an effect of 'sententious thinking', for whatever trained psychologists may do, the plain man cannot find the pure thinkings which are

to be inductively correlated with the supposedly resultant actions or feelings. So his use of phrases like 'judicious behaviour' do not signify instances of such correlations.

I have not tried to show what the differences are between conscience and other sorts of scrupulousness. That is not my present puzzle. Nor have I tried to list all the varieties of conduct which can be described as 'scrupulous'. There are plenty of others besides those mentioned; those, e.g. of good discipline in the Army and Navy, observance of Committee and Parliamentary procedure, keeping to the principles of good chess, bridge, grammar, strategy, style, prosody, and of the Judge adhering to the rules of admissible evidence. None of these adherences is 'mere' acknowledgment of general truths or imperatives. They are fully adopted in habitual observance and in feeling scruples about breaking the habits.

14

PHILOSOPHICAL ARGUMENTS

*Originally delivered as the Inaugural Lecture as Waynflete Professor of
Metaphysical Philosophy in 1945, and reprinted by permission of the
Clarendon Press, Oxford*

Robin George Collingwood held this Waynflete Chair for a lamen-
tably brief time. Yet his literary productivity during this short period
was immense. The time is not yet ripe for me to attempt to offer a
critical evaluation of these contributions to philosophy, nor, even
were I competent, should I on this occasion offer an appreciation of
his originality as an historian. He would himself, I think, have
desired recognition chiefly for his thoughts on the philosophy of
history. About these thoughts, therefore, I submit, with humility
and diffidence, a few reflections.

There are many branches of methodical inquiry into the different
departments of the world. There are the mathematical sciences, the
several natural sciences, and there are the humane or human studies
of anthropology, jurisprudence, philosophy, the linguistic and
literary studies, and history, which last embraces in one way or
another most of the others. There are also many disciplines which
teach not truths but arts and skills, such as agriculture, tactics, music,
architecture, painting, games, navigation, inference, and scientific
method. All theories apply their own several principles and canons
of inquiry and all disciplines apply their own several principles and
canons of practice. These principles were called by Professor
Collingwood their 'presuppositions'. In other words, all employ
their own standards or criteria by which their particular exercises are
judged successful or unsuccessful.

Now it is one thing intelligently to apply principles; it is quite
another thing to step back to consider them. A scientist who ceases
for a moment to try to solve his questions in order to inquire instead
why he poses them or whether they are the right questions to pose
ceases for the time to be a scientist and becomes a philosopher. This
duality of interests may, as history shows, make him both a good

philosopher and a better scientist. The best philosophical theories of mathematics have come from mathematicians who have been forced to try to resolve internal puzzles about the principles of their study, a philosophical exercise which has sometimes led to the origination of new mathematical methods and has often led to the origination of illuminating philosophical views. Every genius is the inventor of new methods and he must therefore be some sort of a critic of principles of method.

Professor Collingwood was an historian who was puzzled about the canons of historical research. He wanted not only to explain certain historical processes and events but also to elucidate what sort of a thing a good historical explanation would be. Nor was this a purely domestic or technological interest. For to see what is an historical explanation, is, among other things, to see how it differs from a chemical, mechanical, biological, anthropological, or psychological theory. The philosopher may, perhaps, begin by wondering about the categories constituting the framework of a single theory or discipline, but he cannot stop there. He must try to co-ordinate the categories of all theories and disciplines. The problem of 'Man's place in Nature' is, roughly, the problem of co-ordinating the questions which govern laboratory researches with the questions governing the researches prosecuted in libraries. And this co-ordination is done neither in libraries nor in laboratories but in the philosopher's head.

Professor Collingwood saw more clearly, I think, than did his most eminent predecessors in the philosophy of history that the appearance of a feud or antithesis between Nature and Spirit, that is to say, between the objectives of the natural sciences and those of the human studies, is an illusion. These branches of inquiry are not giving rival answers to the same questions about the same world; nor are they giving separate answers to the same questions about rival worlds; they are giving their own answers to different questions about the same world. Just as physics is neither the foe nor the handmaid of geometry, so history, jurisprudence and literary studies are neither hostile nor ancillary to the laboratory sciences. Their categories, that is, their questions, methods and canons are different. In my predecessor's word, they work with different presuppositions. To establish this point it is necessary to chart these differences. This task Professor Collingwood died too soon to complete but not too soon to begin. He had already made that great philosophic advance of reducing a puzzle to a problem.

Professor Collingwood kept himself aloof from the sparring and the shadow-boxing by which academic philosophers ordinarily strengthen their muscles and discharge their humours. What we lost by this abstention was compensated by the world's gain. For he wrote less for the eyes of his professional associates than for those of the intelligent citizens of the entire republic of letters. In consequence he achieved a style of philosophical writing and, I believe, diction, which at its frequent best is on a level with the higher ranges of English philosophic prose.

THE PROBLEM

Philosophers have in recent years given much consideration to the nature, objectives and methods of their own inquiry. This interest has been due partly to a certain professional hypochondria, since the conspicuous progress made by other studies has induced in philosophers some nervousness about the scale of their own successes. Partly, also, it has been due to the application of modern logical theory to the processes of the mathematical and the inductive sciences, which has automatically led to its application to philosophy. The exposition of the logical credentials of different sorts of scientific conclusions has posed in a bright if painful light the corresponding question about the foundations of philosophical doctrines.

My object is to exhibit the logical structure of a type of arguments which are proper to philosophical thinking. It makes no difference whether these arguments are used polemically in controversies between philosophers or peaceably in private philosophical reflection. For arguments are effective as weapons only if they are logically cogent, and if they are so they reveal connexions, the disclosure of which is not the less necessary to the discovery of truth for being also handy in the discomfiture of opponents. The love of truth is not incongruous with a passion for correcting the erring.

Philosophical arguments are not inductions. Both the premises and the conclusions of inductions can be doubted or denied without absurdity. Observed facts and plausible hypotheses have no more illustrative force in philosophy than is possessed by fictions or guesses. Nor have either facts or fancies any evidential force in the resolution of philosophical problems. The evidential force of matters of fact is only to increase or decrease the probability of general or particular hypotheses and it is absurd to describe philosophical propositions as relatively probable or improbable.

On the other hand philosophical arguments are not demonstrations of the Euclidean type, namely deductions of theorems from axioms or postulates. For philosophy has no axioms and it is debarred from taking its start from postulates. Otherwise there could be alternative philosophical doctrines as there are alternative geometries.

A pattern of argument which is proper and even proprietary to philosophy is the *reductio ad absurdum*. This argument moves by extracting contradictions or logical paradoxes from its material. It is the object of this discussion to show how this is possible and why it is necessary.

First it is expedient to distinguish the strong *reductio ad absurdum* from the weak *reductio*. The latter form is used in some of Euclid's demonstrations. He demonstrates the truth of a theorem by deducing from its contradictory consequences which conflict with the axioms of his system or with consequences drawn from them. It should be noticed that this argument proves only either that the required theorem is true if the axioms are true or that both are false, that is, that the contradictory of the required theorem is not compatible with the axioms. The strong reduction consists in deducing from a proposition or a complex of propositions consequences which are inconsistent with each other or with the original proposition. It shows (to express it in a fashion which will have to be amended later) that a proposition is illegitimate because it has logically absurd corollaries. The proposition under investigation is shown to be not merely false but nonsensical.

To prove that arguments of this type belong to philosophy it is enough to mention that it would be proper for a dissentient philosopher to try to demolish this or any other philosophical assertion by exhibiting contradictions latent in it. I am not trying to prove that no other types of argument are proper to philosophy.

On first consideration it will seem that arguments of the type *reductio ad absurdum* can have only a destructive effect. They may be effective in demolishing silly theories and thus possess, besides the pleasing property of defeating opponents, the useful one of clearing the site for subsequent constructive theory. But it will be felt that no demolitions can result in the erection of a new dwelling. I hope to disarm any such objection by showing that (to use another metaphor) *reductio ad absurdum* arguments are neither more nor less nihilist than are threshing operations. Or, to change the picture again, the position will be maintained that philosophical arguments of the type described have something in common with the destruction-tests by which engineers discover the strength of materials. Certainly engineers stretch, twist, compress, and batter bits of metal until they collapse, but it is just by such tests that they determine the strains which the metal will withstand. In somewhat the same way, philosophical arguments bring out the logical powers of the ideas under investigation, by fixing the precise forms of logical mishandling under which they refuse to work.

THE LOGICAL POWERS OF PROPOSITIONS

Every proposition has what will here be called certain 'logical powers'; that is to say, it is related to other propositions in various discoverable logical relationships. It follows from some as a consequence and it implies others. It is incompatible with some and merely compatible with others. It is evidence strengthening or weakening the probability of ulterior hypotheses. Further, for any logical powers possessed by a given proposition it is always possible to find or invent an indefinite range of other propositions which can be classed with it as having analogous logical powers or, as it is commonly put, as being of the same logical form.

For the rules of logic are general. Valid arguments exhibit patterns which can be manifested equally well by collocations of any other propositions of the same logical family. Formal logicians learn to extract the logical skeletons of propositions in virtue of which these and any other propositions embodying the same skeletons can function as premisses or conclusions of parallel valid arguments.

Now when people are using or considering a given proposition they cannot then and there be attending to all its logical powers. They cannot in one moment be considering it and all the valid arguments into which it might enter and all the fallacious arguments into which it might be improperly coerced. At best their grasp is adequate for them to be able to think out some of these logical powers if they have occasion to do so. Many of the logical powers of a proposition are not noticed at all in the routines of workaday thinking and of these a proportion baffles discovery even when the thinker is concentrating his whole intellectual strength upon the search for them. Thus people can correctly be said to have only a partial grasp of most of the propositions that they consider. They could usually be taken by surprise by certain of the remoter logical connexions of their most ordinary propositions.

None the less, though people's understanding of the propositions that they use is in this sense imperfect, there is another sense in which their understanding of some of them may be nearly or quite complete. For they may have learned from practice or instruction all their logical powers which govern the limited uses to which these propositions are ordinarily put. A boy learns quickly how to use such propositions as $3 \times 3 = 9$ or *London is due north of Brighton* without ever making the arithmetical or geographical mistakes which would be evidence of an imperfect grasp of such propositions. He does not know the rules governing the logical behaviour of these propositions but he knows by wont their logical course down a limited set of familiar tracks.

The fact that people, however intelligent, never achieve a complete appreciation of all the logical powers of the propositions that they use is one which will be seen to have important consequences. It should be noticed that even mastery of the techniques and the theory of formal logic does not in principle modify this situation. The extraction of the logical skeletons of propositions does not reveal the logical powers of those propositions by some trick which absolves the logician from thinking them out. At best it is merely a summary formulation of what his thinking has discovered.

When several different propositions are noticed having something in common (and when this common feature or factor is not itself a constituent proposition) it is convenient and idiomatic, though hazardous, to abstract this common factor and call it (with exceptions) an 'idea' or 'concept'. Thus men learn to fasten on the idea of mortality or the concept of price as that which is common to a range of propositions in which persons are affirmed or denied to be mortal or in which commodities are said to cost so much or to be exchangeable at such and such rates. Later they learn to isolate in the same manner more abstract ideas like those of existence, implication, duty, species, mind, and science.

In the early days of logical speculation these ideas or concepts were construed as being proper parts or substantial bits, an assemblage of two or more of which was supposed to constitute a proposition. They were often technically styled 'terms'. This erroneous theory has been the source of a multitude of damaging confusions. The truth is that what we label 'ideas' or 'concepts' are abstractions from the families of propositions of which they are common factors or features. To speak of a given idea is to speak summarily of the family of propositions resembling each other in respect of this common factor. Statements about ideas are general statements about families of propositions.

A natural but disastrous corollary drawn from the erroneous doctrine of terms was the assumption that the rules of logic govern the relations between propositions but have little or no bearing upon their factors. It was, indeed, early discerned that there are logically important differences of type or category between different classes of 'terms', 'ideas', or 'concepts', but the original and traditional classification of a few of these types lent nothing to and borrowed nothing from the study of the rules of inference. (True, certain rules of inference were seen to be interlocked with the concepts *all*, *some*, and *not*. But no niche was found even for these ideas in the table of categories of concepts.)

In fact the distinction between the logical types of ideas is identical with the discrimination between the logical forms of the propositions from which the ideas are abstractions. If one proposition has factors of different types from those of another proposition, those propositions are of different logical forms and have different sorts of logical powers. The rules governing the conjunctions of propositions in valid arguments reflect the logical constitutions of their various abstractible factors and features. There are as many types of terms as there are forms of propositions, just as there are as many uphill as downhill slopes.

It is therefore both proper and necessary to speak not only (at one level of abstraction) of the logical powers of propositions, but also (at a higher level of abstraction) of the logical powers of ideas or concepts. Of course, a description of the logical powers of a given idea is neither more nor less than a description of certain of the logical powers of all propositions similar to one another in having that idea as an abstractible common factor.

As people's understanding of the propositions that they use is always imperfect, in the sense that they never have realized and never could realize all the logical powers of those propositions, so their grasp of ideas or concepts is necessarily incomplete. The risk always exists that confusion or paradox will arise in the course of any hitherto untried operations with those ideas.

THE SOURCES OF LOGICAL PARADOXES

Concepts and propositions carry with them no signal to indicate the logical types to which they belong. Expressions of the same grammatical patterns are used to express thoughts of multifarious logical sorts. Men naturally, therefore, tend to be blind to the fact that different ideas have different logical powers or at least they tend to treat the varieties of logical types as being few in number. Even philosophers have assumed for over two thousand years that Aristotle's inventory of ten such types was exhaustive if not over-elaborate.

What happens when a person assumes an idea to be of one logical type when it really belongs to another?—when, for example, he assumes that the ideas *large* or *three* have logical powers similar to those of *green* or *merry*? The inevitable consequence is that naïve intellectual operations with those ideas lead directly to logically intolerable results. Concepts of different types cannot be coerced into similar logical conduct. Some sort of contradiction arises from the attempt and this, in fortunate cases, compels the thinker to turn back in his tracks and try to change his treatment of the outraged concept.

THE DIAGNOSIS AND CURE OF PARADOXES

Here there begins a new sort of inquiry, the deliberate attempt to discover the real (as distinct from the naïvely anticipated) logical powers of ideas. The logical absurdities which betray the original type-confusions give an intellectual shock and set a theoretical problem, the problem of determining with method and with definitive checks the rules governing the correct manipulation of concepts.

This task can be metaphorically described as the charting of the logical powers of ideas. The metaphor is helpful in a number of ways. People often know their way about a locality while quite unable to describe the distances or directions between different parts of it or between it and other familiar localities. They may know a district and still be perplexed when approaching it by an unaccustomed route or in a strange light. Again they may know the district and still give descriptions of it which entail that two different buildings are in one place or that one building lies in two different directions from a given object.

Our workaday knowledge of the geography of our ideas is in similar case—even of those ideas with which we can operate efficiently in the daily tasks in which we have been drilled. This workaday knowledge is knowledge but it is knowledge without system and without checks. It is knowledge by wont and not knowledge by rules.

There is another respect in which the metaphor of maps is useful. Surveyors do not map single objects like the village church. They put together in one map all the salient features of the area: the church, the bridge, the railway, the parish boundary, and perhaps the contours. Further, they indicate how this map joins the maps of the neighbouring areas, and how all are co-ordinated with the points of the compass, the lines of latitude and longitude and standards of measurement. Any error in surveying results in a cartographical contradiction.

The resolution of type-puzzles about the logical powers of ideas demands an analogous procedure. Here too the problem is not to pinpoint separately the locus of this or that single idea but to determine the cross-bearings of all of a galaxy of ideas belonging to the same or contiguous fields. The problem, that is, is not to anatomize the solitary concept, say, of liberty but to extract its logical powers as these bear on those of law, obedience, responsibility, loyalty, government and the rest. Like a geographical survey a philosophical survey is necessarily synoptic. Philosophical problems cannot be posed or solved piecemeal.

This description of the inquiry into the logical powers of ideas as being analogous in some respects to a geographical survey is, of course, of illustrative utility only within narrow limits. In one important respect among many others the analogy breaks down. The correctness of a geographical survey is established by two major sorts of checks; the presence of a cartographical contradiction proves that the survey is erroneous but visual observations are positive evidence of its veracity. In the extraction of the logical powers of ideas there is no process directly corresponding to visual observation. Hence the primacy in philosophical reasoning of the *reductio ad absurdum* argument. The object to which this philosophical destruction-test is applied is the practice of operating with an idea as if it belonged to a certain category, that is, as if it had powers corresponding to those of an accepted model. Initially this practice is naïve and unpremeditated. Sometimes it is deliberately recommended and adopted. In this case the destruction-test is being applied to a philosopher's theory.

The earliest philosophical problems are set by contradictions inadvertently encountered in the course of non-philosophical thinking. As every new theory begins certain new concepts come into currency, concepts which are cardinal not merely to its conclusions but even to its questions. Being new, their logical powers are still unexplored, and, being new, they are unthinkingly credited with logical powers similar to those of ideas the discipline of which is familiar. Paradoxical consequences flowing from conventional operations upon them reveal that they have characters of their own. So must horses have startled their first masters by their non-bovine shape and behaviour.

When the deliberate attempt is made to find the harness which will fit refractory concepts, the method is adopted of consciously looking for further logical paradoxes and contradictions. The rules governing the logical conduct of an idea are imperfectly grasped so long as there remain unexamined chances that it is still being mishandled. Absurdities are the original goad to philosophical thinking; they continue to be its scalpel.

This process can without injustice to the genealogy of the word be called 'dialectical', though there seems no reason to constrict the process within the symmetrical confines of the hallowed double-entry method often associated with its employment. It is also the procedure followed, though not explicitly prescribed, by those who prefer to describe philosophy as being the clarification of ideas, the analysis of concepts, the study of universals and even the search for definitions.

AN OBJECTION

At this point it is necessary to face and resolve a difficulty—indeed a contradiction—which threatens to make nonsense of everything that I have said. Its emergence and its resolution may serve as an illustration of my general position.

It has been said that philosophical problems arise from a tendency of propositions (as we inadvertently handle them) to generate absurd consequences. But if the consequences of a proposition are absurd that proposition is absurd and then there can be no such proposition. It is absurd to say that there are absurd propositions. It is logically impossible for there to be a proposition of such a type that there could be no propositions of that type. It seems to follow that the *reductio ad absurdum* can never be applied, though the argument establishing this point itself exemplifies that pattern.

The solution is that expressions and only expressions can be absurd. Only of a given expression such as a sentence, therefore, can it be said that it cannot be construed as expressing a proposition of a certain logical constitution or, perhaps, a proposition of any logical constitution. This is what the *reductio ad absurdum* does. It discloses that a given expression cannot be expressing a proposition of such and such a content with such and such a logical skeleton, since a proposition with certain of these properties would conflict with one with certain of the others. The operation by which this is established is in a certain fashion experimental or hypothetical. *If* the expression is expressing a proposition at all, it cannot be expressing one analogous in these respects to certain familiar propositions and in those respects to others, since the corollaries of part of the hypothesis are at variance with those of another part. It is a hypothetical argument of the pattern known as *ponendo tollens*. In extreme cases it may establish that the expression cannot be expressing a proposition of any pattern; in milder cases it proves only that it cannot be expressing a proposition of certain specified patterns.

For examples, take the two statements 'Numbers are eternal'

and 'Time began a million years ago'. Both are linguistically regular statements but the latter sentence expresses no proposition. It tries to say what cannot be significantly said, viz. that there was a moment before which there was no possibility of anything being before anything else, which contains a patent contradiction. The former sentence is nonsensical if construed as expressing a proposition of one type but not if construed in another way. If it is construed as a terse way of saying that numbers are not temporal things or events or, better, that numerical expressions cannot enter into significant expressions as subjects to verbs with tenses, then what it says is true and important. But if it is construed, as childlike people have construed it, as saying that numbers, like tortoises, live a very long time—and in fact, however old they get, they cannot die—then it could be shown to be absurd. It is nonsense when construed as an item of biology but true when interpreted as an application of the theory of logical types to arithmetical ideas.

Reductio ad absurdum arguments, therefore, apply to the employment and misemployment of expressions. So it is necessary to recast what was said earlier. Statements about the misreading of the logical powers of propositions and ideas should be reformulated somewhat as follows.

Certain classes of expressions when functioning in certain classes of contexts either have or are unthinkingly supposed to have a certain logical force. And when I speak of an expression as having or being credited with a certain logical force I mean no more than that it expresses or is assumed to express an idea or proposition with certain logical powers, in the sense adumbrated above. It is therefore always possible to inquire what consequential propositions would be true if the expression under investigation expressed or helped to express a proposition the logical powers of which were analogous to those of a known model. It is always initially possible that this logical experiment will reveal that some of the consequences of the assumption conflict with some of its other consequences and thus reveal that the attribution of this logical force to this expression in this use was a false one. The genuine logical force of the expression (if it has a force at all), must therefore be such that the propositions which it helps to express have constitutions which are insured against these and other contradictions.

THE FUNCTION OF THE 'REDUCTIO AD ABSURDUM'

The discovery of the logical type to which a puzzle-generating idea belongs is the discovery of the rules governing the valid arguments in which propositions embodying that idea (or any other idea of the same type) can enter as premisses or conclusions. It is also the discovery of the general reasons why specific fallacies result from misattributions of it to specific types. In general the former discovery is only approached through the several stages of the latter. The idea is (deliberately or blindly) hypothetically treated as homogeneous with one familiar model after another and its own logical structure emerges from the consecutive elimination of supposed logical properties by the absurdities resulting from the supposals.

This programme appears vexatiously circuitous and one is tempted to dream of some direct way of fixing the logical powers of puzzle-generating ideas, which shall share with the method of progressive *reductio* the merit of being rigorous while improving on it by dispensing with trial and error. But, whatever other methods of search may be used, there remains this important fact about its object, that to find or understand a rule it is necessary to appreciate not only what it enforces but also what it permits and what it forbids. People are not fully seized of a logical rule if they have not considered the absurdities against which it prescribes. The boundaries of a right of way are also boundaries of forbidden ground. So no method of discovering the legitimate employments of a concept can dispense with the method of forecasting the logical disasters consequent upon illegitimate operations with it. Before the argument comes to its close, it is necessary to clear up three subsidiary points.

SYSTEMATIC AMBIGUITY

It is commonly supposed that a particular concept is precisely indicated by reference to a particular expression, as if, for example, the idea of equality were unmistakably identified by being described as that for which the word 'equality' stands.

There are, of course, in all languages some words which happen to have two or more different meanings. That is how puns are possible. But these ambiguities are of no theoretical interest. They are random in their occurrence, they can be circumvented by simple translation or paraphrases and the different ideas expressed by a pun-word have generally so little connexion with one another that the context in which the word is used normally suffices to specify which idea is intended to be conveyed. But there is another sort of elasticity of signification which characterizes the use not of a few but of most or of all expressions and which is such that the paraphrases and translations of an expression with a certain elasticity of significance will normally have a precisely similar elasticity. This sort of ambiguity is systematic in further respects. The various ideas expressed by an expression in its different uses are intimately connected with each other. They are in one way or another different inflections of the same root.

A given word will, in different sorts of context, express ideas of an indefinite range of differing logical types and, therefore, with different logical powers. And what is true of single words is also true of complex expressions and of grammatical constructions.

Consider the adjective 'punctual'. It can be used to characterize a person's arrival at a place, the person who arrives there, his character and even the average character of a class of persons. It would be absurd to compare the punctuality of a man on a particular occasion with that of his arrival on that occasion; it would be absurd to compare the punctuality of his character with that of his arrival on a particular occasion; and it would be absurd to compare the punctuality of Naval officers as a class with that of a particular Naval officer. These and similar absurdities show that the word 'punctual' undergoes inflections of significance when applied to different types of subjects. There would be the same inflections of significance in French or German and parallel inflections with other words of the same sort, like 'tidy' and 'industrious'. So, where precision is wanted, it is wrong to speak of 'the idea' of punctuality, although the word 'punctual' does not become a pun-word by having a different logical force for each different type of context in which it is used.

A philosophically more interesting example is afforded by the verb to 'exist'. It may be true that there exists a cathedral in Oxford, a three-engined bomber, and a square number between 9 and 25. But the naïve passage to the conclusion that there are three existents, a building, a brand of aircraft and a number, soon leads to trouble. The senses of 'exists' in which the three subjects are said to exist are different and their logical behaviours are different. The discovery of different logical inflections in the forces of expressions is made by the impact upon us of the absurdities resulting from ignoring them; the determination of those differences is done by pressing the search for further such absurdities. Unnoticed systematic ambiguities are a common source of type-confusions and philosophic problems. Philosophers are sometimes found lamenting this readiness of languages to give to one expression the power of expressing an indefinite variety of ideas; some of them even recommend reforms of usage which will pin single meanings to single expressions. But, in fact, the capacity of familiar dictions to acquire new inflections of logical forces is one of the chief factors making original thought possible. A new thought cannot find a new vehicle ready-made for it, nor can the discrimination of the logical powers of new ideas precede the birth of the knowledge (by wont) of how to think with them. As some spanners are designed to be adjustable, so as to fit bolts of the same shape but different sizes, so, though undesigned, those linguistic instruments of thought are found to be most handy which are the most readily adjustable. The suggestion that men should coin a different diction to correspond with every difference in the logical powers of ideas assumes, absurdly, that they could be aware of these differences before being taken aback by the paradoxes arising from their naïvely attributed similarities. It is like suggesting that drill should precede the formation of habits or that children should be taught the rules of grammar before learning to talk.

ABSTRACTION

I have been speaking so far as if all ideas alike generate philosophical puzzles. But this needs correction. To put it roughly, concrete ideas do not generate such puzzles, abstract ideas do. But this distinction between concrete and abstract as well as that between lower and higher abstractions requires a clarification, of which no more than a sketch can be given here. By a 'concrete idea' is meant one the original use of which is to serve as an element in propositions about what exists or occurs in the real world. It could be introduced or explained to an inquirer by confronting him with one or several specimens from the real world, or else by presenting him with physical models, pictures or mental images of specimens. Propositions containing such ideas can be called first-order propositions. Questions about their truth and falsehood can in favourable cases be settled by observation or sets of observations.

Ideas like *spaniel, dog, ache, thunder* in their original use are instances of concrete concepts. In this use they generate no philosophical puzzles, since one learns from the routines of daily experience the scope and the limits of their application. Their 'logical geography' is taught by one's daily walks. Such concepts are formed from noticing similarities in the real world.

Quite different from these are what are often called 'abstract ideas'. It is a negative mark of these that a person cannot be introduced to such concepts by being presented with corresponding realities. Nothing in the world exemplifies *the economic man, the Spaniel* (as this idea occurs e.g. in *the Spaniel is a descendant of the Wolf*), or *2* (as this occurs e.g. in *2 is a prime number*). It is a positive mark of some abstract ideas that they can be expressed by abstract nouns, like 'justice', 'circularity' and 'wickedness'; but this is the exception rather than the rule. The proposition *the economic man buys in the cheapest and sells in the dearest market* is an abstract proposition, though nothing in the vocabulary of the sentence indicates that the proposition is of a different logical type from *the old man buys his tobacco in the neighbouring tobacconist's shop*.

Abstract propositions do not directly describe the real world but nor do they directly describe any other world. They apply indirectly to the real world, though there are various types of such indirect application. Arithmetic is not about inventories, but inventories satisfy arithmetical propositions; geometry does not describe Asia, but the geography of Asia is an application of geometry, and so on. To form abstract ideas it is necessary to notice, not similarities between things in nature, but similarities between propositions about things in nature or, later on, between propositions about propositions about things in nature. . . . But this conclusion has an air of mystery, deriving from the fact that propositions are themselves abstractions. The world does not contain propositions. It contains people believing, supposing and arguing propositions. This amounts (nearly enough) to saying that the world contains linguistic and other expressions, used or usable by no-matter-whom, which expressions, when used, express truths or falsehoods. To talk about a given proposition is therefore to talk about what is expressed by any expression (of no matter what linguistic structure) having the same logical force as some given expression, as such expressions are or might be intelligently used by persons (no matter whom).

This doctrine, that to speak of a specified proposition is to speak of persons (no matter who) using expressions (no matter of what sorts) having the same logical force as that of a given expression, can be proved. In any particular instance, it is always significant to suggest that there is no such proposition, since the given sentence is absurd, having, perhaps, parts which have correct uses in other contexts but cannot be combined in this way to form a sentence with an integral logical force.

With these safeguards it is correct to say that some propositions are about other propositions and are therefore second- or higher-order propositions. Some higher-order propositions, which form, perhaps, the most numerous class, are only about other propositions in the special sense that they are about partial similarities between otherwise different propositions. For any given proposition there may be found a range of different propositions sharing with it and with each other some one common factor. 'Socrates is wise' expresses a proposition having something in common with what is expressed by 'Plato sapiens est'. This common factor can be expressed by a skeleton sentence of the pattern 'so and so is wise' (where 'so and so' announces the gap in the skeleton sentence). Similarly the skeleton sentence 'if p then q' expresses what is common to a range of hypothetical propositions.

Propositions about such factors of propositions, with certain exceptions, are ordinarily said to be propositions about abstractions or abstract ideas. They are higher-order propositions about isolable features of ranges of lower-order propositions and describe the logical force of skeleton sentences equipollent with a given skeleton sentence. Thus, a proposition about wisdom does not mention Socrates or Plato; facts about Socrates and Plato are irrelevant to its truth. Yet the general fact that there are or might be subjects of whom it could be true that they were wise is not irrelevant to the logical force of the word 'wisdom' and it is consequently relevant to the truth of propositions about wisdom. This illustrates the sense in which it has been said that abstract propositions do not describe the world, or any other world, but do indirectly apply to the world. It is always possible to accuse a submitted abstract idea of absurdity or rather to accuse an expression purporting to express an abstract idea of being an absurd expression. Naturally enough language does not provide many nonsensical single words but there frequently occur absurd complex expressions, purporting to express complex concepts, when such a complex is illegitimate. The fact that such accusations are always significant proves that abstract propositions always embody overt or covert inverted commas. (Indeed any abstract proposition if expressed with maximum logical candour would be seen to be describing a tenuous morsel of the real world, namely an expression in inverted commas. But of course it only mentions such an expression as a means of specifying the idea or proposition which is the logical force of that and any equipollent expression.)

There is, of course, an unlimited variety of types and orders of abstract ideas, but all alike can generate philosophical puzzles, just because experience of the real world gives us no drill in their correct use. Mistaken views about abstractions are not rebutted by a bruised shin or a parched throat. Nor does the language used to express abstract ideas vary with their different varieties. The charting of their logical powers consists therefore in the checking of their logical behaviour against logical rules, which is the operation described in this lecture, i.e. the elimination by *reductio ad absurdum* of logical powers incorrectly ascribed or ascribable to them.

Another general point can now be established. For any abstract proposition there must be a range of propositions of a lower level, since the abstract proposition describes factors common to them. This implies that corresponding to any abstraction there is at a lower proposition-level an idea being actually used (and not described). There must be at this lower level knowledge by wont of some powers of this idea before there can begin the higher-level research into the rules governing those powers. We must know in practice how to decide whether Socrates is wise or clever before we can debate the abstract question of the relations between wisdom and cleverness. (Hence philosophy is sometimes said to tell us only what we knew before. This is as true as the corresponding statement about M. Jourdain's knowledge of prose before his introduction to grammar.)

This indicates what was missing in my prefatory account of the method and effects of philosophical reasoning. This was likened to threshing, which separates the grain from the chaff, discards the chaff and collects the grain. Philosophical reasoning separates the genuine from the erroneously assumed logical powers of abstract ideas by using the *reductio ad absurdum* argument as its flail and winnowing fan, but knowledge by wont of the use of concreter ideas is also necessary as its floor.

CRUCIAL AND CARDINAL IDEAS

Though all abstract ideas alike are liable to generate philosophical puzzles, some demand priority in philosophical examination. Of these one class consists largely of the new theory-shaping ideas which are struck out from time to time in the fields of science, criticism, statesmanship, and philosophy by men of genius. Genius shows itself not so much in the discovery of new answers as in the discovery of new questions. It influences its age not by solving its problems but by opening its eyes to previously unconsidered problems. So the new ideas released by genius are those which give a new direction to inquiry, often amounting to a new method of thinking.

Such crucial ideas, being new, are at the start unco-ordinated with the old. Their potency is quickly recognized but their logical powers have still to be determined, as, correspondingly have those logical powers of the old ideas which have yet to be correlated with the new. The task of assimilating the new crucial ideas into the unfevered bloodstream of workaday thought is rendered both more urgent and more difficult by the fact that these ideas necessarily begin by being exciting. They shock the settled who execrate them as superstition, and they spell-bind the young who consecrate them into myth. That cloud and this rainbow are not dispelled until philosophers settle the true logical perspectives of the ideas.

Quite distinct from these, though often integral to them, are what may be described as philosophically cardinal ideas, those, namely, the logical unravelling of which leads directly to the unravelling of some complex tangle of interconnected ideas. Once these key-ideas are charted, the geography of a whole region is, at least in outline, fixed. No general clue can be given for predicting which ideas will turn out to have this catalytic power. To discern this is the privilege of philosophic genius.

15

KNOWING HOW AND
KNOWING THAT

Reprinted from 'Proceedings of the Aristotelian Society', vol. XLVI,
1946, by permission of the editor

Preamble

In this paper, I try to exhibit part of the logical behaviour of the
several concepts of intelligence, as these occur when we characterise
either practical or theoretical activities as clever, wise, prudent,
skilful, etc.

The prevailing doctrine (deriving perhaps from Plato's account of
the tripartite soul) holds: (1) that Intelligence is a special faculty, the
exercises of which are those specific internal acts which are called
acts of thinking, namely, the operations of considering propositions;
(2) that practical activities merit their titles 'intelligent', 'clever', and
the rest only because they are accompanied by some such internal
acts of considering propositions (and particularly 'regulative'
propositions). That is to say, doing things is never itself an exercise
of intelligence, but is, at best, a process introduced and somehow
steered by some ulterior act of theorising. (It is also assumed that
theorising is not a sort of doing, as if 'internal doing' contained some
contradiction.)

To explain how thinking affects the course of practice, one or more
go-between faculties are postulated which are, by definition, incapable of considering regulative propositions, yet are, by definition,
competent correctly to execute them.

In opposition to this doctrine, I try to show that intelligence is
directly exercised as well in some practical performances as in some
theoretical performances and that an intelligent performance need
incorporate no 'shadow-act' of contemplating regulative propositions.

Hence there is no gap between intelligence and practice corresponding to the familiar gap between theory and practice. There is no

need, therefore, to postulate any Janus-headed go-between faculty, which shall be both amenable to theory and influential over practice.

That thinking-operations can themselves be stupidly or intelligently performed is a notorious truth which by itself upsets the assumed equation of 'exercising intelligence' with 'thinking'. Else 'stupid thinking' would be a self-contradictory expression and 'intelligent thinking' would be a tautology. It also helps to upset the assumed type-difference between thinking and doing, since only subjects belonging to the same type can share predicates. But thinking and doing do share lots of predicates, such as 'clever', 'stupid', 'careful', 'strenuous', 'attentive', etc.

To bring out these points I rely largely on variations of one argument. I argue that the prevailing doctrine leads to vicious regresses, and these in two directions. (1) If the intelligence exhibited in any act, practical or theoretical, is to be credited to the occurrence of some ulterior act of intelligently considering regulative propositions, no intelligent act, practical or theoretical, could ever begin. If no one possessed any money, no one could get any money on loan. This is the turn of the argument that I chiefly use. (2) If a deed, to be intelligent, has to be guided by the consideration of a regulative proposition, the gap between that consideration and the practical application of the regulation has to be bridged by some go-between process which cannot by the pre-supposed definition itself be an exercise of intelligence and cannot, by definition, be the resultant deed. This go-between application-process has somehow to marry observance of a contemplated maxim with the enforcement of behaviour. So it has to unite in itself the allegedly incompatible properties of being kith to theory and kin to practice, else it could not be the applying of the one in the other. For, unlike theory, it must be able to influence action, and, unlike impulses, it must be amenable to regulative propositions. Consistency requires, therefore, that this schizophrenic broker must again be subdivided into one bit which contemplates but does not execute, one which executes but does not contemplate and a third which reconciles these irreconcilables. And so on for ever.

(Some philosophers postulate a special class of acts, known as 'volitions', to perform this desperate task. Others postulate some special impulses which can both motivate action and lend docile ears to regulative propositions.) In fact, of course, whatever 'applying' may be, it *is* a proper exercise of intelligence and it is *not* a process of considering propositions.

Regresses of this pattern show, I suggest, not only that the pre-

213

vailing doctrine is mistaken in equating exercises of intelligence with acts of theorising, but also what sort of a mistake it is. It is that radical sort of mistake which can be labelled a 'type-mistake'. I shall here content myself with stating summarily what this mistake is. I do not develop this logicians' moral in the remainder of this paper.

Adverbs expressing intelligence-concepts (such as 'shrewdly', 'wittily', 'methodically', 'scrupulously', etc.) have hitherto been construed in the wrong logical type or category, namely, as signal-ising the occurrence of special internal acts of that proprietary brand which we call 'thought' or 'theory'.

But in fact they signalise not that a performance incorporates extra acts, whether of this brand or of any other brand, but that the performance itself possesses a certain style, method or *modus operandi*. Intelligently to do something (whether internally or externally) is not to do two things, one 'in our heads' and the other perhaps in the outside world; it is to do one thing in a certain manner. It is some-what like dancing gracefully, which differs from St. Vitus' dance, not by its incorporation of any extra motions (internal or external) but by the way in which the motions are executed. There need be no more moves in a job efficiently performed than in one inefficiently performed, though it is patent that they are performed in very different ways. Nor need a tidy room contain an extra article of furniture to be the *real* nominee of the adjective 'tidy'.

Phrases such as 'technical skill', 'scrupulous conduct' and even 'practical reason' denote capacities to execute not tandem operations but single operations with special procedures.

This is why ordinary language does not provide specific verbs corresponding to our specific intelligence-adverbs and adjectives.

(This is not quite true of the adverb 'voluntarily', since here philosophers have coined the specific verb 'to will'. But this verb has no ingenuous employment. If it was ever employed, it would be a proper question to ask, 'When we will, do we always, sometimes or ever will voluntarily?' Attempts to answer this question would quickly get the verb relegated to its proper place, on the shelf tenanted by 'phlogiston'.)

To put it in Aristotelian terms, intelligence-concepts belong to the category not of ποιεῖν or of πάσχειν but of πῶς. This is why we, like Aristotle, squirm when we hear intelligence-criteria addressed as 'Values' or 'The Good'. For these locutions and associated cour-tesies suggest that they are superior but occult substances, which is an even worse type-mistake than treating them as superior but occult activities or occurrences.

Philosophers have not done justice to the distinction which is quite familiar to all of us between knowing that something is the case and knowing how to do things. In their theories of knowledge they concentrate on the discovery of truths or facts, and they either ignore the discovery of ways and methods of doing things or else they try to reduce it to the discovery of facts. They assume that intelligence equates with the contemplation of propositions and is exhausted in this contemplation.

I want to turn the tables and to prove that knowledge-how cannot be defined in terms of knowledge-that and further, that knowledge-how is a concept logically prior to the concept of knowledge-that. I hope to show that a number of notorious cruces and paradoxes remain insoluble if knowing-that is taken as the ideal model of all operations of intelligence. They are resolved if we see that a man's intelligence or stupidity is as directly exhibited in some of his doings as it is in some of his thinking.

Consider, first, our use of the various intelligence-predicates, namely, 'wise', 'logical', 'sensible', 'prudent', 'cunning', 'skilful', 'scrupulous', 'tasteful', 'witty', etc., with their converses 'unwise', 'illogical', 'silly', 'stupid', 'dull', 'unscrupulous', 'without taste', 'humourless', etc. What facts or what sorts of facts are known to the sensible which are not known to the silly? For example, what truths does the clever chess-player know which would be news to his stupid opponent? Obviously there is no truth or set of truths of which we could say, 'If only the stupid player had been informed of them, he would be a clever player,' or 'When once he had been apprised of these truths he would play well.' We can imagine a clever player generously imparting to his stupid opponent so many rules, tactical maxims, 'wrinkles', etc. that he could think of no more to tell him; his opponent might accept and memorise all of them, and be able and ready to recite them correctly on demand. Yet he might still play chess stupidly, that is, be unable intelligently to apply the maxims, etc.

The intellectualist (as I shall call him) might defend his case by objecting that the stupid player did not 'really' or 'fully' know these truths. He had them by heart; but this was perhaps just a set of verbal habits, like the schoolboy's rote-knowledge of the multiplication table. If he seriously and attentively considered these truths he would then be or become a clever player. Or, to modify the suggestion to avert an obvious rejoinder, if he seriously and attentively considered these truths not just while in bed or while in church but while playing chess, and especially if he considered the maxim relevant to a tactical predicament at the moment when he was involved in that predicament, then he would make the intelligent move. But, unfortunately, if he was stupid (*a*) he would be unlikely to tell himself the appropriate maxim at the moment when it was needed and (*b*) even if by luck this maxim did occur to him at the moment when it was needed, he might be too stupid to follow it. For he might not see that it was the appropriate maxim or if he did, he might not see how to apply it. In other words it requires intelligence not only to discover truths, but also to apply them, and knowing how to apply truths cannot, without setting up an infinite process, be reduced to knowledge of some extra bridge-truths. The application of maxims, etc., is certainly not any mere contemplation of them. Equally certainly it can be intelligently or stupidly done. (This is the point where Aristotle's attempted solution of Socrates' puzzle broke down. 'How can the back-slider know moral and prudential maxims and still fail to behave properly?' This is only a special case of the general problem. 'How can a man be as well-informed as you please and still be a fool?' 'Why is a fool not necessarily an ignoramus?')

To switch over to a different example. A pupil fails to follow an argument. He understands the premisses and he understands the conclusion. But he fails to see that the conclusion follows from the premisses. The teacher thinks him rather dull but tries to help. So he tells him that there is an ulterior proposition which he has not considered, namely, that *if these premisses are true, the conclusion is true*. The pupil understands this and dutifully recites it alongside the premisses, and still fails to see that the conclusion follows from the premisses even when accompanied by the assertion that these premisses entail this conclusion. So a second hypothetical proposition is added to his store; namely, that the conclusion is true if the premisses are true as well as the first hypothetical proposition that if the premisses are true the conclusion is true. And still the pupil fails to see. And so on for ever. He accepts rules in theory but this does not *force* him to apply them in practice. He considers reasons, but he fails to reason. (This is Lewis Carroll's puzzle in 'What the Tortoise said to Achilles'. I have met no successful attempt to solve it.)

What has gone wrong? Just this, that knowing how to reason was assumed to be analysable into the knowledge or supposal of some propositions, namely, (1) the special premisses, (2) the conclusion, plus (3) some extra propositions about the implication of the conclusion by the premisses, etc., etc., *ad infinitum*.

'Well but surely the intelligent reasoner *is* knowing rules of inference whenever he reasons intelligently.' Yes, of course he is, but knowing such a rule is not a case of knowing an extra fact or truth; it is knowing how to move from acknowledging some facts to acknowledging others. Knowing a rule of inference is not possessing a bit of extra information but being able to perform an intelligent operation. Knowing a rule is knowing how. It is realised in performances which conform to the rule, not in theoretical citations of it.

It is, of course, true that when people can reason intelligently, logicians can then extract the nerve of a range of similar inferences and exhibit this nerve in a logicians' formula. And they can teach it in lessons to novices who first learn the formula by heart and later find out how to detect the presence of a common nerve in a variety of formally similar but materially different arguments. But arguing intelligently did not before Aristotle and does not after Aristotle require the separate acknowledgment of the truth or 'validity' of the formula. 'God hath not . . . left it to Aristotle to make (men) rational.' Principles of inference are not extra premisses and knowing these principles exhibits itself not in the recitation of formulae but in the execution of valid inferences and in the avoidance, detection and correction of fallacies, etc. The dull reasoner is not ignorant; he is inefficient. A silly pupil may know by heart a great number of logicians' formulae without being good at arguing. The sharp pupil may argue well who has never heard of formal logic.

There is a not unfashionable shuffle which tries to circumvent these considerations by saying that the intelligent reasoner who has not been taught logic knows the logicians' formulae 'implicitly' but not 'explicitly'; or that the ordinary virtuous person has 'implicit' but not 'explicit' knowledge of the rules of right conduct; the skilful but untheoretical chess-player 'implicitly' acknowledges a lot of strategic and tactical maxims, though he never formulates them and might not recognise them if they were imparted to him by some Clausewitz of the game. This shuffle assumes that knowledge-how must be reducible to knowledge-that, while conceding that no operations of acknowledging-that need be actually found occurring. It fails to explain how, even if such acknowledgements did occur, their maker might still be a fool in his performance.

All this intellectualist legend must be rejected, not merely because it tells psychological myths but because the myths are not of the right type to account for the facts which they are invented to explain. However many strata of knowledge-that are postulated, the same crux always recurs that a fool might have all that knowledge without knowing how to perform, and a sensible or cunning person might know how to perform who had not been introduced to those postulated facts; that is, there still remains the same gulf, as wide as ever, between having the postulated knowledge of those facts and knowing how to use or apply it; between acknowledging principles in thought and intelligently applying them in action.

I must now try to speak more positively about what it is like to know-how. (*a*) When a person knows how to do things of a certain sort (e.g., make good jokes, conduct battles or behave at funerals), his knowledge is actualised or exercised in what he does. It is not exercised (save *per accidens*) in the propounding of propositions or in saying 'Yes' to those propounded by others. His intelligence is exhibited by deeds, not by internal or external dicta. A good experimentalist exercises his skill not in reciting maxims of technology but in making experiments. It is a ruinous but popular mistake to suppose that intelligence operates only in the production and manipulation of propositions, i.e., that only in ratiocinating are we rational. (*b*) When a person knows how to do things of a certain sort (e.g., cook omelettes, design dresses or persuade juries), his performance is in some way governed by principles, rules, canons, standards or criteria. (For most purposes it does not matter which we say.) It is always possible in principle, if not in practice, to explain why he tends to succeed, that is, to state the reasons for his actions. It is tautology to say that there is a method in his cleverness. But his observance of rules, principles, etc. must, if it is there at all, be realised in his performance of his tasks. It need not (though it can) be also advertised in an extra performance of paying some internal or external lip-service to those rules or principles. He *must* work judiciously; he *may* also propound judgments. For propounding judgments is just another special activity, which can itself be judiciously or injudiciously performed. Judging (or propositional thinking) is one (but only one) way of exercising judiciousness or betraying silliness; it has its own rules, principles and criteria, but again the intelligent application of these does not pre-require yet another lower stratum of judgments on how to think correctly.

In short the propositional acknowledgement of rules, reasons or principles is not the parent of the intelligent application of them; it is a step-child of that application.

In some ways the observance of rules and the using of criteria resemble the employment of spectacles. We look through them but not at them. And as a person who looks much at his spectacles betrays that he has difficulties in looking through them, so people who appeal much to principles show that they do not know how to act.

There is a point to be expounded here. I have been arguing in effect that ratiocination is not the general condition of rational behaviour but only one species of it. Yet the traditional associations of the word 'rational' are such that it is commonly assumed that behaviour can only be rational if the overt actions taken are escorted by internal operations of considering and acknowledging the reasons for taking them, i.e., if we preach to ourselves before we practise. 'How else [it would be urged] could principles, rules, reasons, criteria, etc. govern performances, unless the agent thought of them while or before acting?' People equate rational behaviour with premeditated or reasoned behaviour, i.e., behaviour in which the agent internally persuades himself by arguments to do what he does. Among the premisses of these postulated internal arguments will be the formulae expressing the principles, rules, criteria or reasons which govern the resultant intelligent actions. This whole story now seems to me false in fact and refutable in logic. We do not find in fact that we persuade ourselves by arguments to make or appreciate jokes. What sorts of arguments should we use? Yet it certainly requires intelligence or rationality to make and see jokes. But worse than this, when we do, as often happens, go through the process of persuading ourselves to do things, this process is itself one which can be intelligently or stupidly executed. So, if the assumption were correct, it would be necessary for us to start one stage further back and to persuade ourselves with second-order arguments to employ first-order persuasions of a cogent and not of a silly type. And so on *ad infinitum*. The assumption, that is, credits the rationality of any given performance to the rational execution of some anterior performance, which would in its turn require exactly the same treatment. So no rational performance could ever be begun. Aristotle's Practical Syllogism fails to explain intelligent conduct, since its explanation is circular. For the postulated syllogising would itself need to be intelligently conducted.

What has happened once again is that intellectualists have tried to explain prudence, say, or skill by reference to a piece of acknowledging-that, leaving unexplained the fact that this internal operation would itself have to be cannily executed. They have tried to explain, e.g., practical flair by reference to an intellectual process which, unfortunately for their theory, again requires flair.

We should, before leaving this side of the matter, notice one variant of the doctrine that knowing-how is reducible to a set of knowings-that. It could be argued that as knowing-how always involves the knowing of a rule (in some broad sense of 'rule'), this could be equated with the knowing not of *any* sort of truth, but of the truth of a general hypothetical of the pattern 'whenever so and so, then such and such'. For much, though not all, intelligent behaviour does consist in taking the steps likely to lead to desired results. The knowledge involved might therefore be knowing that when actions of a certain sort are taken in certain situations, results of a certain sort tend to occur.

The answer to this is twofold: (1) a man might accept any set of such hypothetical propositions and still not know how to cook or drive a car. He might even know them well enough to be a good teacher and still be stupid in his own performances. Conversely a girl might be a clever cook who had never considered any such general hypothetical propositions. If she had the knack or flair, she could do without news of the inductive generalisation.

(2) The suggested general hypotheticals are inductive generalisations. But making sound, as distinct from rash inductions is itself an intelligent performance. Knowing how to make inductions cannot await news of this higher-order induction, that when people assemble certain quantities of evidence in certain ways and produce conclusions of certain sorts, those conclusions tend to be true. Else induction could never begin; nor could the suggested higher-order induction have any data.

There is another difficulty. Sometimes we do go through the internal operation of persuading ourselves to do things, just as we often go through the external operation of persuading other people to do things. Let us suppose that the persuasion is cogent, i.e., that the recipient is convinced by it. What happens then? Does he necessarily do what he has been persuaded to do? Does he necessarily practise what he preaches? Notoriously not. I frequently persuade myself to smoke less, filling and lighting my pipe at the very moment when I am saying 'yes' to the conclusion of the argument. Like Medea, I listen and am convinced, but I do not obey. You say, 'Ah, but you weren't "really" or "effectively" convinced. You said "yes" in some theoretical or academic way, but you were not wise enough to say "yes" in the practical way of putting your pipe back in your pocket.' Certainly. This proves that unwisdom in conduct cannot be defined in terms of the omission of any ratiocinations and consequently that wisdom in conduct cannot be defined solely in terms of the performance of any ratiocinations. The intelligent application in practice of principles, reasons, standards, etc. is not a legatee of the consideration of them in theory; it can and normally does occur without any such consideration. Indeed we could not consider principles of method in theory unless we or others already intelligently applied them in practice. Acknowledging the maxims of a practice presupposes knowing how to perform it. Rules, like birds, must live before they can be stuffed.

(c) We certainly can, in respect of many practices, like fishing, cooking and reasoning, extract principles from their applications by people who know how to fish, cook and reason. Hence Izaak Walton, Mrs Beeton and Aristotle. But when we try to express these principles we find that they cannot easily be put in the indicative mood. They fall automatically into the imperative mood. Hence comes the awkwardness for the intellectualist theories of stating what are the truths or facts which we acknowledge when we acknowledge a rule or maxim. We cannot call an imperative a truth or falsehood. The Moral Law refuses to behave like a fact. You cannot affirm or deny Mrs Beeton's recipes. So, in the hope of having it both ways, they tend to speak guardedly of the 'validity' rather than the 'truth' of such regulative propositions, an idiom which itself betrays qualms about the reduction of knowing-how to knowing-that.

What is the use of such formulae if the acknowledgement of them is not a condition of knowing how to act but a derivative product of theorising about the nerves of such knowledge? The answer is simple. They are useful pedagogically, namely, in lessons to those who are still learning how to act. They belong to manuals for novices. They are not quasi-premisses in the postulated self-persuasions of those who know how to act; for no such self-persuasions occur. They are imperative because they are disciplinary, because they are in the idiom of the mentor. They are banisters for toddlers, i.e., they belong to the methodology and not to the methods of intelligent practices. What logicians have long half-realised about the *venue* and functions of their rule-formulae has yet to be learned by moral philosophers about their imperatives and ought-statements. When they have learned this they will cease to ask such questions as whether conscience is an intuitive or discursive faculty. For knowing how to behave is not a sort of knowing-that, so it is neither an intuitive nor a discursive sort of knowing-that. The question itself is as nonsensical as would be the corresponding question about the sense of humour or the ability to infer. Other bogus ethico-episte-mological questions also vanish, like the question whether impera-tives or ought-statements are synthetic or analytic, *a priori* or *a posteriori* truths. How should we deal with such questions if posed about Mrs Beeton's recipes?

Another ethical muddle is also cleared up. Philosophers sometimes say that conscience issues imperatives or dictates. Now 'conscience' is an old-fashioned faculty-word, but if the assertion means that the conscientious man exercises his consciousness by issuing propositions or prescriptions, then this is false. Knowing how to behave is exhibited by correct behaviour, just as knowing how to cook is exhibited by palatable dishes. True, the conscientious man may be asked to instruct other agents how to behave, and then he will, if he knows how, publish maxims or specific prescriptions exemplifying maxims. But a man might know how to behave without knowing how to give good advice.

Sometimes a man might give good advice who did not know how to behave. Knowing how to advise about behaviour is not the same thing as knowing how to behave. It requires at least three extra techniques: ability to abstract, ability to express and ability to impress. In another class of cases, a generally conscientious man might, in certain interference-conditions, not know how to behave, but be puzzled and worried about his line of action. He might then remind himself of maxims or prescriptions, i.e., he might resume, for the moment, the adolescent's task of learning how to behave. He would be issuing imperatives or ought-propositions to himself, but he would be doing so just because he did not know how to behave. He would be patching up a gap in his knowledge-how. And he might be bad at self-counsel without being a bad man. He might have a correct 'hunch' that his self-suasions were invalid, though he could detect no fallacy in them. There would be a circle in the attempted description of conscience as a faculty which issues imperatives; for an imperative is a formula which gives a description or partial definition of what is known when some one knows how to behave. You couldn't define a good chef as one who cites Mrs Beeton's recipes, for these recipes describe how good chefs cook, and anyhow the excellence of a chef is not in his citing but in his cooking. Similarly skill at arguing is not a readiness to quote Aristotle but the ability to argue validly, and it is just this ability some of the principles applied in which were extracted by Aristotle. Moral imperatives and ought-statements have no place in the lives of saints or complete sinners. For saints are not still learning how to behave and complete sinners have not yet begun to learn. So neither experiences scruples. Neither considers maxims.

Logical rules, tactical maxims and technical canons are in the same way helpful only to the half-trained. When a person knows how to do things of a certain sort, we call him 'acute', 'shrewd', 'scrupulous', 'ingenious', 'discerning', 'inventive', 'an expert cook', 'a good general', or 'a good examiner', etc. In doing so we are describing a part of his character, or crediting him with a certain dispositional excellence. Correspondingly when we describe some particular action as clever, witty or wise, we are imputing to the agent the appropriate dispositional excellence. The way in which rules, standards, techniques, criteria, etc. govern his particular performances is one with the way in which his dispositional excellences are actualised in those performances. It is second nature in him to behave thus and the rules etc. are the living nerves of that second nature. To be acute and consistent in reasoning is certainly to apply rules of inference to the propositions considered. But the reasoner does not have both to consider propositions and to cast sidelong glances at a formula; he just considers the propositions efficiently. The rules are the rails of his thinking, not extra termini of it. The good chess-player observes rules and tactical principles, but he does not think of them; he just plays according to them. We observe rules of grammar, style and etiquette in the same way. Socrates was puzzled why the knowledge which constitutes human excellence cannot be imparted. We can now reply. Learning-how differs from learning-that. We can be instructed in truths, we can only be disciplined in methods. Appropriate exercises (corrected by criticisms and inspired by examples and precepts) can inculcate second natures. But knowledge-how cannot be built up by accumulation of pieces of knowledge-that.

An explanatory word is necessary here. 'Discipline' covers two widely disparate processes, namely, habituation and education, or drill and training. A circus seal can be drilled or 'conditioned' into the performance of complicated tricks, much as the recruit is drilled to march and slope arms. Drill results in the production of automatisms, i.e. performances which can be done perfectly without exercising intelligence. This is habituation, the formation of blind habits. But education or training produces not blind habits but intelligent powers. In inculcating a skill I am not training a pupil to do something blindly but to do something intelligently. Drill dispenses with intelligence, training enlarges it. (It is a pity that Aristotle's sensible account of the formation of wise characters has been vitiated by the translator's rendering of ἐθισμός as 'habituation'. Aristotle was talking about how people learn to behave wisely, not how they are drilled into acting mechanically.) When the recruit reaches the stage of learning to shoot and read maps, he is not drilled but taught. He is taught to perform in the right way, i.e., to shoot and to use maps with 'his head'. Unlike the seal he becomes a judge of his own performance—he learns what mistakes are and how to avoid or correct them. He learns how to teach himself and so to better his instructions. He acquires not a habit but a skill (though naturally skills contain habits). (Neglect of this distinction between conditioning and training is what vitiates Hume's account of Induction.) The fact that mathematics, philosophy, tactics, scientific method and literary style cannot be imparted but only inculcated reveals that these too are not bodies of information but branches of knowledge-how. They are not sciences but (in the old sense) disciplines. The experts in them cannot tell us what they know, they can only show what they know by operating with cleverness, skill, elegance or taste. The advance of knowledge does not consist only in the accumulation of discovered truths, but also and chiefly in the cumulative mastery of methods.

One last point. I have, I hope, proved that knowing-how is not reducible to any sandwich of knowing-that, and that our intelligence-predicates are definable in terms of knowing-how. I now want to prove that knowing-that presupposes knowing-how.

(1) To know a truth, I must have discovered or established it. But discovering and establishing are intelligent operations, requiring rules of method, checks, tests, criteria, etc. A scientist or an historian is primarily a man who knows how to decide certain sorts of questions. Only secondarily is he a man who has discovered a lot of facts, i.e., has achieved successes in his application of these rules etc. (though of course he only learns how to discover through exercises in discovery; he does not begin by perfecting his method and only later go on to have successes in applying it). A scientist, that is, is primarily a knower-how and only secondarily a knower-that. He couldn't discover any particular truths unless he knew how to discover. He could know how to discover, without making this or that particular discovery.

(2) But when I have found out something, even then irrespective of the intelligence exercised in finding it out, I can't be said to have knowledge of the fact unless I can intelligently exploit it. I mean this. I might once have satisfied myself of something, say the distance between Oxford and Henley; and I might have enshrined this in a list of road distances, such that I could on demand reel off the whole list, as I can reel off the multiplication table. So in this sense I have not forgotten what I once found out. But if, when told that

Nettlebed is so far out from Henley, I cannot tell you how far Nettlebed is from Oxford, or if, when shown a local map, I can see that Oxford to Banbury is about as far as Oxford to Henley but still cannot tell you how far Oxford is from Banbury or criticise false estimates given by others, you would say that I don't know the distance any longer, i.e., that I have forgotten it or that I have stowed it away in a corner where it is not available.

Effective possession of a piece of knowledge-that involves knowing how to use that knowledge, when required, for the solution of other theoretical or practical problems. There is a distinction between the museum-possession and the workshop-possession of knowledge. A silly person can be stocked with information, yet never know how to answer particular questions.

The uneducated public erroneously equates education with the imparting of knowing-that. Philosophers have not hitherto made it very clear what its error is. I hope I have provided part of the correction.

16

WHY ARE THE CALCULUSES OF LOGIC AND ARITHMETIC APPLICABLE TO REALITY?

Reprinted from 'Proceedings of the Aristotelian Society', Suppl. vol. xx, 1946, by permission of the editor

In this unavoidably perfunctory paper I volunteer nothing about mathematics. I restrict myself to some opinions about the application of rules of logic. My object is to make definite some issues suitable for a general discussion.

I

The writings of formal logicians consist mainly of two kinds of pronouncements. One kind is composed of explanatory observations and these are expressed chiefly in ordinary prose. The other kind is composed of formulae, which are ordinarily expressed in a code. What do these formulae declare? They are formulations of rules of inference or consistency-rules. They express what fallacies are breaches of. They are the results of operations of a certain sort, the operations namely which constitute the professional craft of formal logicians. In these operations some rules are established as deriving from others, so, at least in intention, the rules are presented not merely in assemblages, but in systematic arrangements, themselves subject to logical rules.

For my purposes, what matters is not how logical rules are established but what they 'say'. We are inclined to explain that what they 'say' is, in a special sense of 'why', why it is correct or legitimate to draw certain conclusions from certain premises and why it is incorrect or illegitimate to draw others.

It is often convenient to express rules of inference in sentences of the pattern 'if . . . then, . . .', for example, *if p implies q, then not-q implies not-p*. But we need to distinguish two sorts of logicians' 'if-then' declarations. If we compare (*a*) *if p implies q, then not-q implies not-p* with (*b*) *if given that today is Monday, tomorrow is Tuesday, then given that tomorrow is not Tuesday, today is not Monday,* we notice that the first is catholic while the second is particularised, the first is formal while the second has determinate filling or the first is a skeleton while the second has meat on its bones. Let us call the first an 'open hypothetical' and the second a 'closed hypothetical'. (We can of course think of hypotheticals which are meatier than the first but bonier than the second.)

Clearly the closed hypothetical is not a *consequence* of the open hypothetical. Actual syllogisms are not deduced from Barbara; they are (if of the same figure) all alike valid as being specimens of syllogisms in Barbara. A logician's closed hypothetical stands to the corresponding open inference-rule not as an implication of it but as an application of it—but only in one sense of 'application'. One of our objects being to clear up the relevant notions of application, let us instead call a logician's closed hypothetical a 'specification' of the corresponding open hypothetical.

In constrast with this sense in which a meaty hypothetical is an application of a bony hypothetical there is the quite different but very important sense in which we say that a person who, on hearing that tomorrow is not Tuesday, concludes that today is not Monday, is conjointly applying both the open hypothetical *if p implies q, then not-q implies not-p* and the closed hypothetical *if given that today is Monday tomorrow is Tuesday, then given that tomorrow is not Tuesday today is not Monday.* He is moving from actually accepting a premiss to actually accepting a conclusion in accordance with the specification of the general rule. He performs an intellectual operation and if challenged to justify it he could cite first the closed hypothetical and then, if required, the open hypothetical.

In this sense of 'apply' in which a person who executes an operation in accordance with a rule is said to be applying the rule, a rule is applied only in performances or operations. Let us say that performances or operations conducted in accordance with rules are 'observances' of those rules, and distinguish from them performances or operations which are 'breaches' of those rules. A breach of a rule of logic is a fallacy; an observance of it is a valid inference. To speak of an inference as an observance or as a breach of a rule of logic is only a condensed way of saying that the author of the inference has made his inference in conformity with or in breach of a rule of inference.

It should be noticed that a closed hypothetical can be a specification of an open hypothetical, but it cannot be an observance or breach of it. A person's passage from a premiss to a conclusion can be an observance or breach of a rule of logic, but it cannot be a specification of it.

This distinction between these two senses of 'application' is not peculiar to logic. The rule of grammar that plural nouns govern plural verbs is applied (specified) in: A sentence in which the subject is 'Frenchmen' and the verb is a modification of the verb 'to be' has the verb 'are' (or 'were', etc.). But it is applied (observed) in the statement by *The Times* leader-writer 'Frenchmen are . . .' In an inferior journal it might have been contravened by the statement 'Frenchmen is . . .'.

Rules of inference, like the rules of grammar, chess, etiquette and military funerals are performance-rules. References to them are references to criteria according to which performances are characterised as legitimate or illegitimate, correct or incorrect, suitable or unsuitable, etc. The point deserves emphasis for this reason. There is a *third* sense of 'application' in which a police-description of a wanted man may apply or partially apply to me. All or some of the attributes ascribed to him may belong to me. If the description fits me it applies to me (though in a fourth derivative sense it may not be intended to apply to me).

Confusing 'apply' (= 'fit') with 'apply' (= 'observe') and perhaps also with 'apply' (= 'specify') some people have worried themselves by speculating how or why the rules of inference apply to the world; they have tried to imagine what an illogical world would be like. But the puzzle is an unreal one. We know already what an illogical man is like; he is the sort of man who commits fallacies, fails to detect the fallacies of others, and so on. The reason why we cannot imagine what an illogical world would be like is that a tendency to flout performance-rules can only be attributed to performers. The world neither observes nor flouts the rules of inference any more than it observes or flouts the rules of bridge, prosody or viticulture. The stars in their courses do not commit or avoid fallacies any more than they revoke or follow suit.

The inclination to suppose that rules of logic are police-descriptions of wanted facts is strengthened by some analogies between our ways of talking about rules and our ways of talking about laws of nature. Some man-made rules are called 'laws', such as those which are made by legislators; and rules of inference are sometimes called 'laws of thought'. These usages suggest that logical rules come from the same basket as laws of nature. Moreover some performance-rules, like rules of inference and rules of skill, are not results of convention or legislation as rules of games and rules of the road are. There is no M.C.C. which can amend the rules of inference or the canons of style. It is vaguely felt, therefore, that these rules which are not man-made are found by men in the ways in which laws of nature are found. Further, it is convenient to express laws of nature in formulae of the open 'if . . . then' pattern as well as to express specifications of those laws in formulae of the closed 'if . . . then' pattern, syntax-usages which remind us of the formulae of logic. Finally, somewhat as particular operations of drawing conclusions can be said to be 'governed' by rules of inference, so particular happenings and states of affairs are said to be 'governed' by laws of nature.

But of course the way in which rules of inference rule out certain performances is not that they debar their happening; they show only why they are incorrect if they do happen. Laws of nature rule out certain imaginable conjunctions of happenings or states of affairs in quite a different way. Hence while there can and do occur breaches of logical rules, there cannot and do not occur breaches of laws of nature. It makes sense to speak of someone obeying or disobeying a performance-rule, none to speak of things disobeying or obeying laws of nature.

Certainly there are important differences between rules of inference and such other kinds of performance-rules as those of golf, prosody and infantry-drill. The big difference pertinent to our problem is that it is partly by inferences that we come to know the world. The sciences of things are theories and theories are the official locus of rules of logic.

A theory which is logically faulty is a bad theory. If a scientist or historian who has produced an inconsistent or inconsequent theory later repairs the inconsistencies and strengthens the weak links, his grasp of his subject has improved. Finding out about the world is hampered by bad logic just as success at chess is hampered by bad strategy and the feeding of an army is hampered by bad arithmetic. But the avoidance and correction of logical faults are not the discovery of new facts about the world. Efficient romancing also requires logical acumen, but the exercises of this acumen do not dilute the resultant romances with veracious reports about the real nature of things.

In fine; there are two main senses, different from one another, in which a rule of inference is said to be applied, but in neither sense is it significant to say that the rule applies to the world in the sort of way in which a police-description of a wanted man applied to me or to him.

II

So far I have spoken as if all logical rules are of the same type, but this is not so. Doubtless there are many different types of logical rules, but I want here to distinguish only two types.

Performance-rules in general seem to fall into two main classes which I shall, for brevity, label 'Procrustean rules' and 'canons'. Procrustean rules are those which enable us to grade a given performance as correct or incorrect, legitimate or illegitimate. The rules of grammar and spelling are, with a few exceptions, Procrustean; so are the rules of the road, of chess, cricket, syllogistic reasoning and rifle-range practice.

Quite different from these are the rules or canons of style, strategy, prudence, skill and taste. A good chess player does not only not break the rules of chess, he observes a number of tactical and strategical principles as well. He is not playing chess at all if he does not observe its Procrustean rules; he is not playing efficiently unless he also applies maxims of generalship. Similarly Gibbon did not just write correctly, he wrote with power and elegance. He observed canons of style as well as rules of grammar.

Procrustean rules can generally be expressed in brief formulae or terse orders. These can be memorised and breaches of them can be promptly detected. Observance of them can be inculcated by sheer drill and so become, at least in normal circumstances, automatic or habitual. We do not now have to wonder how to spell correctly or talk grammatically.

Canonical rules, on the other hand, commonly resist codification. They cannot be memorised nor can observance of them become an habitual routine. We learn them by practice, but not by sheer drill. They are taught by criticism rather than by rote, and we have never finished learning them. All methods, techniques, crafts, skills, etc. are subject to canonical rules. The faults we find with performances are for breaches of such canons just as much as for breaches of Procrustean rules.

There are canons of experimental method. A good experimentalist has to be careful, accurate, neat, ingenious, patient, self-critical, self-confident, exploratory and so on. There are also canons of purely theoretic method. A good mathematician does not merely avoid misreckonings and fallacious demonstrations, he also has a sense of direction, a nose for elegance and a capacity for recognising the fertility or infertility of new theorems, and the relative powerfulness or powerlessness of new methods of proof. The formal logician himself in selecting, ordering and proving his Procrustean rules of inference is guided by similar non-Procrustean canons.

Now the principles of induction seem to resemble canons rather than Procrustean rules. They are akin rather to the tactical and strategic maxims than to the rules of chess. Experts find fault with indifferent researchers, not on the score that any of their operations have been incorrect but, for example, on the score that they were rather aimless, or that they were rather rash or rather over-cautious or that they were muddled or unoriginal. There is no decalogue of Inductive Fallacies and no Code Napoleon of the Rules of Induction. So some rules of logic are not Procrustean legitimacy-rules.

However this makes no difference to my earlier assertion that it is nonsense to ask how or why rules of logic apply to the world. Both the Procrustean and the canonical rules of logic are performance-rules. Only performances can be or fail to be in accordance with them. If they are applied, that is a fact about the efficiency and intelligence of theorists, not a fact about any radical docility of the world.

III

What is it like for someone to operate in accordance with a per-formance-rule? It is sometimes supposed that he has to go through three or four stages: (1) to consider and/or accept an open-rule formula; (2) to consider and/or accept that specification of this rule-formula which is appropriate to his situation; (3) to construct in theory a plan of operation conforming to the rule and to its specifi-cation; (4) to put this plan into operation. (These stages are some-times quaintly assimilated to the steps of a syllogism. Doing some-thing according to a rule is then described as going through a Practical Syllogism. But drawing a conclusion in Barbara is a special case of operating in accordance with a rule. Operating in accordance with a rule cannot therefore be described as a special case of drawing a peculiar conclusion in Barbara.)

Now it is easy to show that this four-stage process is a myth. For to go through these four stages would itself be a process with a *correct* procedure, and so be subject to a higher-order rule. Moreover of the first two supposed stages the agent would have to pick on the appropriate rule and the appropriate specification of it, yet his application of the required criteria of appropriateness would be just another piece of operating according to a rule.

On the other hand we should not say that a parrot had argued correctly or even argued at all if, having been drilled to say 'Socrates is mortal', it said this immediately after someone had pronounced a pair of premisses from which this truth followed. A novice at chess might by luck make a move that upset his opponent's entire plan of campaign; but we should not describe him as applying this or that maxim of defensive strategy.

We say that a performance is an application of a rule, if and only if the performer knows what he is doing, and this not in the way in which I may know that I am breathing or blinking, but in some other way. The performance must be such that the agent would not or would probably not have done it if he had not known how to tackle such situations.

A person or parrot would be said not to know how to draw conclusions if *inter alia* he asserted the same conclusion after hearing quite different premisses, failed to protest if someone else accepted the original premisses but denied that Socrates was mortal etc., etc. To apply a rule is to do something knowing how to do what situations of that sort require. What constitutes a person's possession of this knowledge is not the fact that on any particular occasion he actually does anything extra, but the fact that he is ready, competent or inclined to do certain suitable things on occasions more or less like this. He does not merely say 'Socrates is mortal' or merely move his knight to a certain square; a parrot or a novice might do this. He does it alertly, cautiously, critically, resolutely, etc., he would not (probably) make a slip without at once noticing and correcting it; he would, if asked, explain why this was the only correct or the most expedient thing to do; he would not repeat it if the circumstances were not quite the same; he would appreciate why someone else acted in the same way in similar circumstances and so on. There need be nothing in the performance of a *solitary* operation to show witnesses or even the agent himself whether the performance was an exercise of skill, prudence, taste, logical acumen or any other brand of intelligence, but this does not prevent a *series* of performances from showing beyond question that the agent knows how to do things of that sort. One bull's-eye does not prove the possession, nor one 'outer' the lack of markmanship, but the records of a few target-practices show whether or not a man knows how to shoot. Ways of operating are displayed not by single operations but by arrays of operations and to have a method is to operate in certain ways. Of course, to have a blind habit is also to operate in certain ways, namely in certain stereotyped ways. What distinguishes habitual actions from actions done with method is the adaptation of the latter to differences in the problems, situations, etc. We might say that it is the irregularity of some classes of performances which shows that their author is applying rules. (This is more manifest in the application of canons than in the application of Procrustean rules.)

There were reasoners before Aristotle and strategists before Clausewitz. The application of rules of reasoning and strategy did not have to await the work of their codifiers. Aristotle and Clausewitz were, in fact, only able to extract these rules because they were already being applied. The crystallisation of performance-rules in rule-formulae is, in some cases, not the condition of their being applied but a product of studies in the methodology of the practices in which they have already been applied. People who construe logicians' rule-formulae as descriptions of the spine and ribs of the world are committing only a more ambitious form of the same error as that committed by those who construe these rule-formulae as premisses requiring to be intellectually acknowledged before intelligent performances can begin. Both assume that a logician's rule-formula 'says' something informative. The mistake is not peculiar to them. Other people think that such a rule-formula 'says' something uninformative.

17

'IF', 'SO', AND 'BECAUSE'

Reprinted from 'Philosophical Analysis', edited by Max Black, 1950, Cornell University Press, by permission of the book's editor

Logicians say oddly little about inferences. They prefer to change the subject and talk instead about hypothetical statements. For instance, they shy off discussing what we do with such dicta as 'Today is Monday, so tomorrow is Tuesday' and discuss instead such dicta as 'If today is Monday, tomorrow is Tuesday'. In consequence they are apt to misdescribe or ignore the actual employments that we give to 'if-then' statements. A good deal of light would be thrown upon the theoretical uses of 'if-then' statements by an enquiry into some of the nontheoretical uses to which we put other sorts of 'if-then' sentences, such as conditional promises, threats, injunctions, wagers, requests, and counsels. In particular, the regulation of our practical conduct by accepted rules, like the rules of games, etiquette, morals, style, grammar, and technology, has much in common with the regulation of our theorising conduct by our acceptance of variable hypothetical statements (or 'laws'). In this paper, however, I try to bring out at least part of the force of some 'if-then' sentences in another way, and shall accordingly be limiting the discussion to hypothetical statements proper, namely, those which can or must appear in the exposition of true or false theories. I try to exhibit the major differences between our theoretical uses of 'if-then' sentences and our theoretical uses of 'so' or 'therefore' sentences, as well as the connections between them. (But the distinction between theory and practice is not hard-edged. Are we being theoretically active or practically active when we converse? Or when we give verbal swimming-instructions? Or when we make requests and bets?)

There is a third class of theory-constituting sentences which also needs to be considered, namely, those of the pattern '. . ., because . . .'. For these are different as well from inferences as from hypothetical statements and yet are closely related to both. I shall call statements of this class 'explanations'.

234

In using 'if-then' sentences and in using 'because' sentences we are stating or asserting. 'If today is Monday, tomorrow is Tuesday' is a true statement; 'Tomorrow is Tuesday, because today is Monday' is another statement which may be true. But 'Today is Monday, so tomorrow is Tuesday' is not a statement. It is an argument, of which we can ask whether it is valid or fallacious; it is not an assertion or doctrine or announcement of which we can ask whether it is true or false.

We can, indeed, ask whether its premiss is true, and whether its conclusion is true; but there is not the third question 'Is it true that today is Monday so tomorrow is Tuesday?' An argument is not the expression of a proposition, though it embodies the expressions of two propositions.

By what criteria do we decide whether an expression is a statement or not? We cannot rest with the grammatical criterion that the verb is, or the verbs are, in the indicative mood and that the sentence ends with a full stop and not a question mark. For in some hypothetical statements, both verbs may be in the subjunctive mood; and conversely in arguments, both verbs are in the indicative mood. Neither of them is a question, but only one of them is a statement.

Another criterion would be this. Usually we should call a sentence a 'statement' if by shifting its verb and replacing its full stop by a question mark a recognisable question resulted. 'All men are mortal' is a statement, for 'Are all men mortal?' is a question; 'It is Tuesday tomorrow because it is Monday today' is a statement, for 'Is the reason why it is Tuesday tomorrow that it is Monday today?' is a proper if not very natural question. Using this criterion we are helped to see that arguments are not statements, since there is no way of producing a question out of 'Today is Monday, so tomorrow is Tuesday' by shifting verbs and replacing the full stop by a question mark. But then we should notice that there is no very natural way of converting an 'if-then' statement into a question either. Indeed, where it is easy to formulate natural questions to which 'because' statements are answers, e.g., by asking 'Why is it Tuesday tomorrow?' or 'Why do you say that it is Tuesday tomorrow?' it is not easy, though it is not impossible, to formulate any natural questions to which 'If it is Monday today, it is Tuesday tomorrow' would be an answer. In this respect hypothetical statements seem to behave more like arguments than like explanations.

Next, when a person makes a statement to the effect that something is the case, it is always or usually appropriate to ask whether he knows, believes, or supposes that it is the case; we can ask whether he is lying or mistaken and so question the truth of what he has told us; we can contradict him; we can consider the evidence for and against what he has said; and we can thank him for the information that he has given us. But when he produces an argument, none of these responses is appropriate. We may consider whether he is right to draw that conclusion 'q' from that premiss 'p', but we cannot ask whether he knows, believes, or merely supposes that p, *so* q. Indeed 'p, *so* q' cannot be the filling of any 'that' clause. We may rebut his argument, but we cannot contradict it; we can contradict his premiss and his conclusion, but we cannot rebut them. We may describe his premiss and his conclusion as pieces of information; but his argument from the one to the other is not an extra piece of information. We can examine his evidence for his conclusion, but we cannot ask for evidence for or against his move from his evidence to his conclusion.

Finally, it is an important, if not the important, feature of our use of words like 'statement', 'proposition', and 'judgment' that any statement, proposition, or judgment can function as a premiss or a conclusion in arguments. Suitability for what may be summarily called the 'premissory job' is one of the main things that make us reserve the title of 'statement' for some sentences in distinction from all the rest. Commands, reproaches, questions, laments, exhortations, and plaudits are not constructed for incorporation as they stand into arguments, either as premisses or conclusions. By 'a statement' we mean, at least *inter alia*, a sentence that is constructed for such incorporation. And then it is patent that arguments themselves are not statements. The conclusion of one argument may be the premiss of another argument, but an argument itself cannot be the premiss or conclusion of an argument. Nothing follows from 'p, *so* q', nor does 'p, *so* q' follow from anything. 'p, *so* q' cannot perform the premissory job. Hypothetical statements and 'because' statements, on the other hand, can be premisses and conclusions in arguments (though only in relatively high-level arguments).

We might say, provisionally, that an argument is no more a statement than a piece of multiplication is a number. An argument is an operation with statements, somewhat as a pass is an operation with a football. Since an argument is not a statement, it is neither a categorical nor an hypothetical statement; nor is it any third sort of statement, like a 'because' statement, which, though not classifiable as categorical or hypothetical, must certainly rank as a statement.

But there is an important connection between the argument 'Today is Monday, so tomorrow is Tuesday' and what is told in the hypothetical statement 'If today is Monday, tomorrow is Tuesday'.

For, in considering the argument, we can enquire not only whether the premiss is true and the conclusion is true, but also whether the conclusion is legitimately drawn from the premiss. And to ask whether the conclusion is legitimately drawn from the premiss is to raise the question whether it is true that, if today is Monday, to-morrow is Tuesday. In some way the validity of the argument requires the truth of the hypothetical statement and to concede the truth of the hypothetical statement is to concede the argument. This already shows part of the point of making hypothetical statements. But just how does the validity of the argument require the truth of the hypothetical statement?

(*a*) It might erroneously be suggested that an argument requires the truth of the corresponding hypothetical statement in the way in which 'That creature is a fox' requires the truth of 'That creature is a mammal', namely, that the hypothetical statement follows from or is entailed by the argument. But this will not do. For an argument, not being a statement, is not the sort of thing that can be described as entailing or not entailing statements. Certainly 'If today is Monday, tomorrow is Tuesday' follows from the statement 'The argument "Today is Monday, so tomorrow is Tuesday" is a valid one'; but it neither follows nor does not follow from the argument 'Today is Monday, so tomorrow is Tuesday'. An argument is not a statement about its own merits, and it cannot do what a statement about its merits can do.

(*b*) It might erroneously be suggested that an argument '*p, so q*' is nothing more or less than a stylistically veiled conjunctive state-ment, the candid expression of which would be '*p, and (if p, then q) and q*'. So the argument requires the truth of the hypothetical state-ment in the way in which 'Jack and Jill fell down the hill' requires the truth of 'Jill fell down the hill'. But this will not do. For con-junctive statements are true or false statements, not valid or invalid arguments. They can, *en bloc*, be premisses or conclusions of argu-ments; they can be asserted, questioned, and contradicted, known, believed, or guessed. A man with a good memory might remember that '*p, and (if p, then q) and q*' without having drawn a conclusion or followed the drawing of a conclusion by anyone else. If the hypo-thetical statement were false, its conjunction with '*p*' and '*q*' would render the conjunctive statement false, but it would not render it a fallacy; and a person who asserted such a statement would show that he was in error but not that he was illogical.

(*c*) It might, conversely, but equally erroneously, be suggested that '*p, so q*' requires the truth of '*if p, then q*' because the hypothetical sentence is just the argument '*p, so q*', misleadingly worded; so that '*p, so q*' requires '*if p, then q*', since that is simply to say that '*p, so q*' is equivalent to '*p, so q*'. But this will not do. In '*if p, then q*' no premiss is asserted and no conclusion is drawn. A person might say '*if p, then q*' and then accept '*but not-p*' and '*not-q*' without withdrawing what he had said. Moreover a hypothetical statement can function in the premissory way and in the conclusion way, which an argument cannot do. It can also with a change of style be contradicted or questioned. 'It could be Monday today, without its being Tuesday tomorrow' (e.g., on the occasion of a calendar reform) contradicts 'If it is Monday today, it is Tuesday tomorrow'; and 'Can it be Monday today and not Tuesday tomorrow?' is the corresponding query.

(*d*) More plausibly but still erroneously, it might be suggested that an argument requires the truth of the corresponding hypothetical statement in this way. An argument '*p, so q*' is always invalid unless the premiss from which '*q*' is drawn incorporates not only '*p*' but also '*if p, then q*'. '*q*' follows neither from '*if p, then q*' by itself, nor from '*p*' by itself, but only from the conjunction '*p and (if p, then q)*'. But this notoriously will not do. For, suppose it did. Then a critic might ask to be satisfied that '*q*' was legitimately drawn from '*p and (if p, then q)*'; and, to be satisfied, he would have to be assured that '*if (p and [if p, then q]), then q*'. So this new hypothetical would have to be incorporated as a third component of the conjunctive premiss, and so on forever—as the Tortoise proved to Achilles. The principle of an inference cannot be one of its premisses or part of its premiss. Conclusions are drawn from premisses in accordance with principles, not from premisses that embody those principles. The rules of evidence do not have to be testified to by the witnesses.

It is not merely that the officially recognised Rules of Inference cannot be given the role of premiss components in all the specific inferences that are made in accordance with them. The same thing is true of the most 'meaty' and determinate hypothetical statements, like 'If today is Monday, tomorrow is Tuesday'. This equally is not a premiss from which, together with 'today is Monday' the conclusion 'so tomorrow is Tuesday' is drawn. The argument 'Today is Monday, so tomorrow is Tuesday' is an application of 'if today is Monday, tomorrow is Tuesday'; and it is in this notion of application that lies the answer to our question 'How does a valid argument require the truth of the corresponding hypothetical statement?'

Part of this last positive point may be brought out in this way. If we ask, 'What is the point of learning cooking recipes, bridge conventions, or rules of the road?', the obvious beginning of the answer is 'In order to be able to cook dishes properly, play bridge properly, and drive vehicles properly'. Correspondingly, if we ask for evidence that someone knows these things, an obvious beginning of the answer is that he does cook properly, play bridge properly, and drive vehicles properly. But we may, though we need not, expect more than this. We may expect the learner not only to be able and ready to operate properly in the kitchen, at the bridge table, and on the road, but also to be able and ready to *tell* the recipes, the conventions, and the rules of the road; to tell them, for example, when someone else needs tuition, or to tell them when he has to justify his own operations, or to tell them when a debate is in progress about possible improvements in the methods of cooking, playing bridge, or using roads.

In the same sort of way, if we ask what is the point of learning '*if p, then q*', or what is the evidence that someone has learned it, part of the answer would be a reference to the learner's ability and readiness to infer from '*p*' to '*q*' and from '*not-q*' to '*not-p*', to acquiesce in the corresponding arguments of others, to reject affiliated invalid arguments, and so on. But we should also expect him on certain, perhaps rare, occasions to *tell* his hearers or readers '*if p, then q*'. He would be expected to be able and ready to make the hypothetical statement when someone else required to be taught, when he himself was under challenge to justify his inference operations, and so on.

The question 'What is the point of learning "*if p, then q*"?' is quite different from the question 'What is the point of making the statement "*if p, then q*"?' When we learn something, we cannot be learning *only* how to teach it—else there would be no 'it'. When we teach a lesson, we cannot be teaching *only* how to teach that same lesson, else there would be no lesson. Thus, making a hypothetical statement is sometimes giving an inference precept; and the first object of giving this precept is that the recipient shall make appropriate inferences. A posterior object of giving him this precept is, perhaps, that he shall in his turn give this inference precept to others, again with the same primary object, that they shall learn to perform the appropriate inferential operations.

Knowing '*if p, then q*' is, then, rather like being in possession of a railway ticket. It is having a licence or warrant to make a journey from London to Oxford. (Knowing a variable hypothetical or 'law' is like having a season ticket.) As a person can have a ticket without actually travelling with it and without ever being in London or getting to Oxford, so a person can have an inference warrant without actually making any inferences and even without ever acquiring the premisses from which to make them. The question 'What is the point of getting or keeping a railway ticket?' is quite different from the question 'What is the point of showing or handing over a ticket?' We get and keep tickets in order to be equipped to travel from London to Oxford (on occasions when we are in London and wish to travel to Oxford). But we show tickets in order to satisfy officials that we have the right to travel, and we hand tickets over to other people in order to give them both the right to travel and the opportunity to satisfy officials that they have that right.

Neither buying a ticket, nor owning a ticket, nor showing or transferring a ticket is travelling. Nor are we making or following the inference '*p, so q*' when we get or retain the knowledge that '*if p, then q*', or when we utter or write the statement '*if p, then q*'. But what we have learned, when we have learned it, and what we have taught, when we have taught it, is, in the first instance, to argue '*p, so q*', or else '*not-q so not-p*', etc., and to accept such arguments from others. And as travel warrants can be invalid in various ways, so 'if-then' statements can be false. Uncovenanted journeys can be made from London to Oxford, and from 'Today is the 28th of February' to 'Tomorrow is the 1st of March'.

It must be realised that asserting '*if p, then q*' is not making a report of any inference or a comment on any inference. Nor is it recommending, exhorting, confessing, requesting, or commanding anything. It is not talking about inferring any more than showing up a ticket or transferring a ticket is talking about a railway journey.

We should now turn to consider briefly the force of dicta like 'It is Tuesday tomorrow, because it is Monday today', i.e., answers to questions of the type 'Why so-and-so?'. Explanations are not arguments but statements. They are true or false; they are answers to questions; they can express what someone knows, believes, guesses, or queries; and they can be premisses or conclusions of arguments. (But it should be noticed that there is a didactic use of 'because' sentences, in which they function much more like arguments than like statements, namely when a teacher wishes to lead his pupils by the hand from the premiss to the conclusion of an argument familiar to him but new to them. He may say 'Because this and that, therefore so-and-so'. He is then synchronously leading them along the path and showing them the signposts.)

Now the statement '*q, because p*' cannot be true unless '*q*' and '*p*' are true. It also cannot be true unless '*if p, then q*' is true. In these respects, that it requires the truth of '*p*', '*q*', and '*if p, then q*', it has obvious analogies to the argument '*p, so q*'. But the sense of 're-quires' is different, since explanations are true or false, but not valid or invalid, while arguments are valid or invalid but not true or false. If a person accepts '*p, so q*' as not only valid but also correct, in the sense both that its premiss and conclusion are true and that the argument from the one to the other is legitimate, then he is com-mitted to accepting '*q, because p*' as true, and vice versa; yet '*q, because p*' is not a paraphrase of '*p, so q*', any more than surrendering one's ticket to the ticket collector at one's destination is making a legitimate train journey. To say '*q, because p*' is not to say, in other words, '*p, so q*'. But nor is it to say, '*p, and q, and (p, so q)*'. For, '*p, so q*', not being a statement, cannot be a component of a conjunctive statement. Nor is '*q, because p*' equivalent to '*p, and (if p, then q) and q*'; for a person who said this would not have given the explanation of '*q*', though he would have provided material out of which such an explanation could be constructed. He would have mentioned what was in fact the (or a) reason for '*q*', but he would not yet have given it as the reason for '*q*'. (Nor, in real life, do we form conjunctive statements out of component statements of such different constitu-tions as '*p*' and '*if p, then q*'.) No, in saying, '*q, because p*', we are not just asserting but *using* what is expressed by '*if p, then q*'; we are putting it to work or applying it; we are attaching '*q*' to '*p*' in accordance with the licence conveyed by '*if p, then q*'. For the question 'Why "*q*"?' is the question 'From what premiss is "*q*" legitimately drawn?'; and the answer to this question has to give not just the true premiss '*p*', but, therewith, the title to infer from '*p*' to '*q*'.

In other words, just as the inference '*p, so q*' does not embody '*if p, then q*' as a component of its premiss, but rather applies it in being an operation with '*p*' and '*q*' executed in conformity with it, so '*q, because p*' does not embody '*if p, then q*' as a component of its 'because' clause but applies it in another way.

Should we class explanations as categorical or as hypothetical statements? The answer must be: 'They are neither—nor are they conflations of categorical with hypothetical statements.' The dichotomy 'either categorical or hypothetical', though initially clarifying, is finally muddling. Is the umpire a player or a spectator? He is neither a player nor a spectator nor both a player and a spectator.

The still somewhat nebulous notion of application may now be clarified by a new consideration. There is an important respect in which at any rate some hypothetical statements differ both from inferences and from explanations; namely there can be what are called 'variable hypotheticals', but there could not be variable inferences or variable explanations. We can say 'If anyone is a man, he is mortal', but we cannot say either 'Anyone is a man, so he is mortal' or 'Because anyone is a man, he is mortal' or 'Anyone is mortal, because he is a man'. The premiss and conclusion of an inference are propositions, not propositional functions, statements and not statement skeletons; and the same thing is true of the clauses of a 'because' statement. True, the premiss and the conclusion of an inference may be entire variable hypothetical statements. From 'Whoever reads Plato in the original reads Greek' it follows that 'Whoever reads Plato in the original reads a language other than Latin'. But in the way in which the clauses of a variable hypothetical statement are themselves not statements but statement indents, inferences and explanations cannot have statement indents for their terminals.

Much as some railway tickets are season tickets, licensing their holders to make a given journey on any day during a stated period, so some hypothetical statements are, so to speak, seasonal inference warrants. And just as no journey can be a seasonal journey, so no inference or explanation can be a variable inference or a variable explanation. Permits can be open, but permitted actions cannot be open.

Now it is just this fact that such hypothetical statements are open that makes other statements, like premisses and conclusions, eligible as fillings for them. That something is an eligible filling for (or satisfies) an open specification is part of what is meant by saying that the statement, rule, or warrant (etc.) incorporating the specification 'applies' to that something. A certain local parking regulation applies to me and my car in this way. For though it does not mention us, it tells what any private car owner may or may not do about parking his car (no matter what its age, make, colour, or price). But I and my car do not then, in our turn, 'apply' to anything further. What I do on a particular occasion with my car may comply with or be a breach of this regulation; but it makes no sense to suggest that there is something else that, in a similar way, complies with or is a breach of what I do with my car on this occasion. Or there may be exceptions to a rule, law, or maxim, but such an exception cannot, in its turn, be something to which there could be, in the same way, exceptions. 'Save for . . .' can be tacked on to a variable hypothetical statement, but not on to an inference or an explanation. I shall try shortly to show that some kind of openness, variableness, or satisfiability characterises all hypothetical statements alike, whether they are recognised 'variable hypotheticals' like 'For all x, if x is a man, x is mortal' or are highly determinate hypotheticals like 'If today is Monday, tomorrow is Tuesday'.

Let me, however, first take stock. Part of what I have been trying to do is to show that the activities of asserting and following both hypothetical statements and explanations are more sophisticated than the activities of wielding and following arguments. A person must learn to use arguments before he can learn to use hypothetical statements and explanations. In arguing (and following arguments) a person is operating with a technique or method, i.e., he is exercising a skill; but in making or considering hypothetical statements and explanations he is, for example, giving or taking instruction in that technique or operation. Roughly and provisionally, he is not cooking, but writing or reading a cookery book, not practising an art but teaching it or receiving tuition in it.

Another, though connected, object has been this. Fascinated by the model of simple, singular, affirmative, attributive, or relational statements, theorists are apt to ask 'What exactly do hypothetical statements assert to characterise what?' or 'What exactly do "because" statements assert to be in what relation to what?' or, more generally, 'What do such statements describe?' or 'What matters of fact do they report?' And they are apt to toy with verbally accommodating replies about Necessary Connections between Facts, or Internal Relations between Universals, and the like. But if such statements are, as I have argued, sophistications upon inferences, the corresponding re-wording of their question shows clearly what has gone wrong. For if I ask 'What exactly do arguments assert to characterise what?' or 'What exactly do inferences state to be in what relation to what?' the reply is easy. Arguments are not assertions or statements at all and so are not attributive or relational statements. Hume might be doctored into saying: 'Causality is not a relation; for "p, so q" is an inference and not a statement, and so is not the statement of a relation. "So" is not a relation word, or a relational predicate, or a predicate of any sort. For "p, so q" is not a subject-predicate statement since it is not a statement at all. Predicting an event from another event is not describing a bond, for it is not describing.' But this point has been generally overlooked, partly owing to the habit of ignoring inferences (which are not statements) and concentrating instead on hypothetical statements and explanations (which are), and partly owing to the tacit and false assumption that such statements belong to pre-inferential levels of discourse, instead of to post-inferential levels.

243

It is time now to harden the edges of the notion of application from another side. When I learn '*if p, then q*', I am learning that I am authorised to argue '*p, so q*', *provided that I get my premiss* '*p*'. But the hypothetical statement does not tell me '*p*', any more than getting a ticket puts me on to the train. The statement '*if p, then q*' does not incorporate the statements '*p*' and '*q*', as these statements certainly are incorporated in such dicta as '*p and q*', '*q, because p*', '*p, so q*', and '*p, although q*'. In saying '*if p*, then *q*', I am not stating '*p*' or '*q*' or in any way committing myself to the truth of '*p*' or '*q*'; I am stating or asserting something, but I am not stating or asserting them. Neither the statement '*p*' nor the statement '*q*' enters into the statement '*if p*, then *q*'. Yet, especially when so encoded, the hypothetical statement does very much look like a statement incorporating the two component statements '*p*' and '*q*'. If it does not incorporate them, then the coding must be highly misleading. I am going to argue for just this conclusion.

In ordinary English we very often so word our hypothetical statements, that the protasis expression after the word 'if', and the apodosis expression after the word 'then' (if this occurs) have both the vocabulary and the syntax of statements. The protasis and apodosis expressions in 'If it is Monday today, (then) it is Tuesday tomorrow' look and sound exactly like the statements 'today is Monday' and 'tomorrow is Tuesday' as these might appear either by themselves or as components of a conjunctive statement, or as premiss and conclusion of an inference, or as *explicandum* and *explicans* in an explanation. But sometimes in ordinary English, often in old-fashioned English and commonly in languages like Latin, the protasis clause and the apodosis clause are worded subjunctively. And to say that they are worded subjunctively is to say that they are not worded as statements are worded. In 'If it be Monday today, it is Tuesday tomorrow', one of the clauses does not look or sound like a statement. In 'If it were Monday today, it would be Tuesday tomorrow', neither clause looks or sounds like a statement.

We have another familiar way of wording hypothetical statements. Although the standard textbooks discuss 'modal propositions' in a different chapter from that in which they discuss hypotheticals, the differences between modal and hypothetical statements are in fact purely stylistic. There is only one colloquial way of correctly negating the superstitious hypothetical statement 'If a person walks under a ladder, he comes to grief before the day is out', namely, by saying, 'No, a person may (might or could) walk under a ladder and not come to grief.' And the only colloquial way of putting a question to which an 'if-then' statement is the required affirmative answer is to ask, for example, 'Can an Oxford Vice-Chancellor not be (or Need he be) a Head of a College?'

But if we reword, as we always can reword, an 'if-then' statement as a statement of the pattern 'It cannot be Monday today and not be Tuesday tomorrow', we see at once that what follows 'cannot' and 'and' has none of the appearances of a statement. The statement-like appearance of the clauses of those 'if-then' statements which are not subjunctively worded is a deceptive appearance and one which always can be and often is obviated in stylistically different paraphrases. But if so, the logicians' code style (which I have myself been using) 'if p, then q' is deceptive. For the letters 'p' and 'q' as they occur here look and sound just like the 'p' and 'q' that occur in conjunctive statements, inferences, and explanations. But if the clauses of a hypothetical statement are not statements, then logicians ought not to flag them so. The practice tempts their users and their pupils to assume the truth of such falsities as these: hypothetical statements assert connections between statements or between judgments or between propositions or between facts or between aspects or features of the Real; they are truth functions of atomic statements; and so on.

Cook Wilson was much more nearly right when he said that hypothetical statements assert relations between questions. This still will not do, for just as nothing is stated or asserted, so nothing is asked in the protasis or in the apodosis; and if no one is being asked anything, no question is occurring. But he was right in seeing that no statement is made by either clause and so that the hypothetical statement as a whole is not telling us anything about any such incorporated statements. Nor is it a resultant, product, or truth function of any incorporated statements. But he was on the right track, too, in a further and more positive respect. What the hypothetical statement does embody is not statements but statement specifications or statement indents—bills for statements that statements could fill. Similarly, what the parking regulations embody is not cars or drivers but specifications that cars and their drivers can satisfy. It is because hypothetical statements embody statement specifications that an inference from one statement to another can be described as being 'in accordance with' or being 'an application of' the hypothetical. The premiss fills the protasis bill; the conclusion fills the apodosis bill. They 'fulfil the conditions'. Now this notion of statement indents, or statement specifications is indeed very close to the notion of a question. For a question does contain a specification of what is required, and what is required is a statement, for an answer to a question is a statement. Of course, asking a question does not consist merely in voicing a statement specification. Asking a question is doing a specific conversational job with such a specification. Uttering a hypothetical statement is doing another specific job with a couple of statement specifications, with either of which by itself, or with both of which conjointly, a person with a different interest could have made a request for a specified piece of information. There are, I suppose, plenty of other conversational, administrative, and theoretical things which are done with statement specifications.

Now just as 'Who . . . ?' can be answered by 'Socrates . . .' and the variable 'x' in 'x . . .' can have 'Socrates' for one of its values, so 'Is today Monday?' can be answered by 'Today is Monday', and '. . . today be Monday' can have 'Today is Monday' for one of its values. This is the sense in which I said earlier that all hypotheticals are variable hypotheticals. 'Variable' and 'hypothetical' are related as genus to species. (But this is not the sense in which logicians have separated some hypotheticals as 'variable hypotheticals' from the rest.)

If a consignment of bicycles fills the bill in an export licence, the bill that it fills is not itself that consignment of bicycles or a consignment of anything else; it is only the verbal specification of such a consignment. Similarly if a statement fills a bill, the bill that it fills is not that statement nor any other statement. Putting an export licence into an envelope does not involve putting a consignment of bicycles into that envelope; it involves putting into the envelope that part of the flimsy which carries the specification of the consignment. Putting the words 'today is Monday' and 'tomorrow is Tuesday' into a hypothetical statement does not involve putting a premiss or a conclusion into that statement; it is only putting in the specifications of such a premiss and conclusion. And as export licences can be drafted, though no bicycles are manufactured, so hypothetical statements can be made though no premiss statement or conclusion statement is ever made.

Sometimes it is suggested that the difference between the occurrence of 'it is Monday today' and 'it is Tuesday tomorrow' in a hypothetical statement and their occurrence as answers to questions or as premiss and conclusion in an inference is merely this: In the hypothetical statement, 'today is Monday' and 'tomorrow is Tuesday' occur in an 'unasserted' way, whereas in the other contexts they occur in an 'asserted' way. The suggestion is that to be asserted is a luxury extra, like italicisation. But this will not do. If nothing is asserted, or no statement is made, then no question is answered, nothing is contradicted, no premiss is used, no conclusion is drawn, no information or misinformation is given. A statement bereft of its employments is not a statement and an expression debarred from doing any of the jobs of a statement has either no job or else a different job.

What tempts people to say this sort of thing, as well as to say such things as that hypothetical statements assert relations between statements, propositions, or facts is the patent similarity between protasis expressions and apodosis expressions (as commonly worded) on the one hand and statements on the other. There need not be, though there can be, a vocabulary flag or syntax flag to show that they are not statements. The standard code symbolisation '*if p, then q*' reinforces this temptation. For surely logicians, of all people, would not symbolise completely disparate things by identical symbols. Or have they too assumed that indistinguishable styles prove identity of function?

In many ordinary cases there is no similarity whatsoever between bills and what fills them. The specification of a consignment of bicycles in an export licence is not in the slightest degree like a consignment of bicycles. The specification is a bit of paper covered with typewritten letters; the bicycles are bits of iron, steel, rubber, and aluminium. A railway ticket from London to Oxford has nothing on it resembling London or Oxford.

But some specifications are very similar to the things that satisfy them. A cooking instructor may teach cookery not in words or diagrams, but in dumb show. He goes through the motions that his pupil is to go through. He is not telling her what to do, but showing her what to do. If she is inattentive or clumsy, he may complain that her actions do not comply with the requirements he had made of her. Yet he imparted these requirements to her only by making motions. It must be noticed that he is not cooking. He does with an empty spoon what she is to do with a full spoon; he does with a cold oven what she is to do with a hot oven. The difference between their operations is not to be described by saying that she is concocting edible ('asserted') puddings, where he had been concocting not-to-be-eaten ('unasserted') puddings. For he had not been concocting a pudding at all, but only showing her how to do it *when she had got the ingredients and the hot oven.*

Much as no concocting is done in the movements staged by the demonstrator, so no premisses are used or conclusions drawn by a person making a hypothetical statement. But also, much as the operations to be done with ingredients are specified by the very similar but empty-handed operations of the demonstrator, so the inferential operations to be done with statements are specified by the very similar but empty-handed verbal operations of the author of a hypothetical statement. We might say that delivering a hypothetical statement is teaching in dumb show what to do with statements— save that in this case the demonstration cannot be in dumb show since the operation that is being taught is itself a talking (or writing) operation. In somewhat the same way, an actor manager may instruct his actors how to deliver their words, not by telling them, but by showing them what to do. He too cannot do this in dumb show.

The cooking demonstrator is neither handling ingredients and utensils nor talking about them. His activity is not one either of using or of mentioning flour, sugar, spoons, or ovens. The actor manager is similarly not mentioning or (strictly) using the utterances that he is showing his actors how to deliver. For he is not acting to an audience, but teaching his actors to do so. But even the actors in speaking their parts before the audience are not, strictly, using their words. They are not being defiant, remorseful, loving, or desperate, but only pretending to be so. Their utterances cannot be classified as either 'use' or 'mention'. *A fortiori*, the actor manager's actions of teaching (by showing) how convincingly to seem defiant, remorseful, etc. are not classifiable as either 'using' or 'mentioning'. In the same way, the author of a hypothetical statement is neither using nor mentioning any premiss statements or conclusion statements. He is showing, empty-handed, how to use them. We might say that he is making a dummy inference, with a didactic purpose. It may be noticed that showing what to do is a more sophisticated performance than doing it ingenuously, though a less sophisticated one than telling what to do.

Before concluding, I must mention some points which need to be borne in mind.

(1) 'If' sometimes means 'even if', or 'although'; such an 'if' clause functions not as a premiss indent, but as an indent for a 'but' statement.

(2) The author of an unfulfilled conditional like 'If Hannibal had marched on Rome, he would have taken it' does not work empty-handed. He commits himself to the falsity of 'he marched on Rome' and 'he took it'. His assertion is, in consequence, not far removed from being an explanation why Hannibal did not take Rome. However, I do not think that 'If he had marched on Rome, he would have

taken it' is a paraphrase of 'The reason why he did not take it is that he did not march on it'. It would not naturally be proffered as the answer to a 'why' question or a 'why not' question, though I think that its truth would entail and be entailed by the truth of the 'because' answer to such a 'why not' question.

(3) I have said nothing about different varieties of inferences, hypothetical statements, and explanations. (*a*) For all three, we can find sets of specimens which are logically truistic, arguments 'valid in virtue of their form alone' and hypothetical statements and explanations which are 'true in virtue of their form alone'. e.g., 'Jack and Jill fell down the hill, so Jill fell down the hill'; 'If Jack and Jill fell down the hill, Jill fell down the hill'; and 'Jill fell down the hill, for both Jack and Jill fell down the hill'. (*b*) For all three, again, we can find specimens which are valid or else true in virtue of some tight convention or arrangement, like those which yield inferences, inference warrants, and explanations about matters of calendar fact or matters of chess fact. (*c*) For all three, again, we can find sets of specimens the validity or truth of which requires to be vouched for by observation and experiment.

(4) I have said nothing about statements of the kind '"*p*" entails "*q*" or "*q*" does (or does not) follow from "*p*"'. Such locutions are used (roughly) not by the players in the field but by the spectators, critics, and selectors in the grandstand. They belong to the talk of logicians, cross-examiners, and reviewers. It should be noticed here too that the codification '"*p*" entails "*q*"' is uncandid where '"*p*" would entail "*q*"' would be candid. For '"*p*" entails "*q*"' could be, and in real life ordinarily would be construed to mean that the true conclusion '*q*' is legitimately drawn from the true premiss '*p*'; and to say this is quite different from saying that 'if there were a true statement satisfying the protasis, there would be legitimately deducible from it a true statement satisfying the apodosis'.

18

HETEROLOGICALITY

Reprinted from 'Analysis', vol. XI, 1950, by permission of the editor

In *Analysis* (N.S. no. 16, March 1950) Mr Lawrence ably criticises Russell's use of an alleged paradox (that of 'heterological' being homological, if heterological, and vice versa) as a proof of the thesis of language-hierarchies. I agree with his conclusions, but I do not think he brings out the main reason why it is an improper question even to ask whether 'heterological' is heterological or homological.

Some people introduce themselves on meeting strangers. Others do not do this. They might be distinguished as 'self-nominators' and 'non-self-nominators'. If Dr John Jones on meeting a stranger begins by saying 'Dr John Jones', he acts as a self-nominator. So, too, if he says 'Captain Tom Smith', save that now he gives a pseudonym. If he says 'it's a fine day', 'I'm a doctor' or 'I'm a self-nominator (or a non-self-nominator)', then he has given a true or false description of the weather, his profession or his practice of announcing or withholding his name; and in the last case his action belies or bears out his remark. But he has not given his surname, Christian name, nickname or pseudonym. '. . . a self-nominator' and '. . . a non-self-nominator' are the tail ends of character descriptions. Such descriptions require that the person described has a name to give, though this is only referred to, not given. Epithets are not names, even when they carry references to names.

A perverse parent might name his child 'Non-self-nominator', as there was once a club named 'The Innominate Club'. The son might then correctly give his name as 'Master Non-self-nominator Brown'. But he would no more have belied his announcement than a big man does by introducing himself as 'Alderman Little'. Names are not epithets, even though the same vocables constitute an epithet in some language or other.

To say 'I am a self-nominator (or non-self-nominator)' not only is not to give one's name; it is not even to describe one's name, as I might describe my name by saying that it rhymes with 'smile'.

Unfortunately the term of art 'description' is often used to cover idioms which, in ordinary life, would not be called 'descriptions' at all. No policeman would accept as a description the phrase 'my name' (in 'I never volunteer my name'). What I refer to with such expressions can, in principle, be specified or particularised. But ways of referring to things are not ways of answering consequential requests for information about those things. Very often we employ referring expressions which also have a descriptive force, e.g. 'she' and 'yonder lame horse', and a hearer may get the reference while contesting the attribution of femininity or lameness.

For it to be true that I do or do not give my name, there must be a 'namely-rider' of the pattern '. . ., namely John Jones'. Nor could it be true that a person had a profession or a disease without there being a namely-rider of the pattern '. . ., namely the Law' or '. . ., namely asthma'. The namely-riders need not be known to the persons who make or understand the statements that have them. I know that there is a day of the week on which I shall die, but I do not know what it is. The day of my death could not be *just* the day of my death, but no particular day of the week.

Like anything else, linguistic expressions can be described or mis-described by appropriate epithets. An epitaph, a peroration, a son-net, a phrase, or a word may be English, mispronounced, vernacular, full of sibilants or obscene. The vocabulary of philologists is neces-sarily full of epithets appropriate to linguistic expressions, as the vocabulary of botanists is of those appropriate to plants. The methods of finding out what epithets can be truly applied to particu-lar expressions are (crude or refined) philological methods. The properties of expressions established by these methods are philo-logical properties. Thus 'disyllabic', 'of Latin origin', 'rhymes with *fever*', 'solecism' and 'guttural' are philological epithets, standing for philological properties.

Most epithets, like astronomical, pharmaceutical and botanical epithets, are not appropriate to linguistic expressions. Cottages, but not phrases, may be thatched or unthatched, tiled or untiled. Reptiles do or do not hibernate; adverbs neither do nor do not. When an epithet is not a philological epithet, the question whether or not it applies to a given expression is an improper question.

Philological epithets do not constitute a proper genus. There are widely different interests that amateur or professional philologists may take in expressions, and widely different questions that they can raise about them. Phonetic epithets are not congeners of stylistic, orthographic, grammatical or etymological epithets.

It is no accident that a philological epithet may stand for a property of expressions and itself be one of the expressions that have that property. 'English', like 'cow', is an English word, 'polysyllable', like 'Saturday', is a polysyllable. Conversely, a philological epithet may stand for a property the possession of which can be truly denied of that epithet. 'French' is not a French word; 'monosyllable' is not a monosyllable; 'obsolete' is not obsolete. The question whether the property for which a philological epithet stands does or does not belong to that epithet itself is a proper question, e.g. whether 'dactyl' is or is not a dactyl and whether 'mispelt' is or is not misspelt.

One may then construct two artificial parcels: one of those philological epithets which have the philological properties for which they stand; the other of those which lack the properties for which they stand. The first might be called 'self-epithets'; the second 'non-self-epithets'. 'Deutsch' is a self-epithet, 'obscene' a non-self-epithet. 'Written', here, is a non-self-epithet; in manuscript it was a self-epithet.

Now the question is supposed to arise, 'Are "self-epithets" and "non-self-epithets" themselves self-epithets or non-self-epithets? In particular, is "non-self-epithet" a non-self-epithet or a self-epithet?'

But before starting to wriggle between the horns of this dilemma, we must consider whether the question itself is a proper question; i.e. whether 'self-epithet' and 'non-self-epithet' belong to the class of philological epithets at all. As we have seen, most epithets do not belong to this class, so we cannot assume that these two (invented) classificatory expressions do so either. Certainly at first sight they look as if they do belong to it, since we can ask whether 'monosyllabic' is a self-epithet or not, and decide that it is a non-self-epithet. The predicate end of the sentence '"monosyllabic" is a non-self-epithet' does look like a philological epithet of 'monosyllabic'. It's a predicate of a quoted expression, isn't it?

But, if we recollect that 'self-nominator' and 'non-self-nominator' were not names but epithets carrying references to unmentioned names, we may suspect that 'self-epithet' and 'non-self-epithet' are not philological epithets, but expressions carrying references to unmentioned philological epithets. And this suspicion can be confirmed.

How do we decide (*a*) whether words (including 'English' and 'polysyllabic') are English or polysyllabic, etc. and (*b*) whether words like 'English' and 'polysyllabic' are or are not self-epithets? We decide questions of the former sort by (elementary or advanced) philological methods. We consult dictionaries, count syllables, use stop watches, and listen to linguaphone records. But we do not decide whether words are self-epithets or not by examining them by further philological methods. There is no visible, audible, grammatical, etymological or orthographical feature shared by 'French', 'monosyllabic', 'obscene' and 'misspelt'. On the contrary, we call them 'non-self-epithets' because we find by various philological methods that 'French' is not a French word, 'obscene' is not an obscene word, 'misspelt' is not misspelt; and we have decided to list as 'non-self-epithets' all those philological epithets which lack the philological properties for which they stand. We find by philological methods that these and other quite different philological epithets stand severally for, perhaps, not even generically kindred philological properties, and that the epithets lack the properties for which they stand; we then collect them together as 'non-self-epithets' not in virtue of any common philological properties that they all stand for but in virtue of their being alike in lacking the philological properties for which they severally stand. So 'non-self-epithet' and 'self-epithet' do not stand for any philological properties of expressions. Their use is to assert or deny the possession of ordinary philological properties by the epithets which stand for them. Their use *presupposes* the ordinary use of philological epithets in the description of expressions of all sorts (including philological epithets); it is not, therefore, a part of that ordinary use. 'Orthographic' is a self-epithet only *because* 'orthographic' both has and stands for a certain philological property, namely that of being correctly spelled. Unless there was an opening for this namely-rider, there would be no job for the expression 'self-epithet', just as there would be no job for the expression 'self-nominator' if there were no opening for such a namely-rider as '... namely, John Jones'. As 'self-nominator' carries a reference to a name which it is not and does not mention, so 'self-epithet' carries a reference to an ordinary philological property which it does not itself stand for.

At first sight, however, the statement that 'English' is a self-epithet does seem not merely to refer to but to mention the philological property of being in the English tongue. For we English-speakers are all so familiar with the use of the word 'English', that we are tempted to suppose that to be told that 'English' is a self-epithet is to be told that 'English' is an English word. But this is not so. A person who knew no German but had been told the use of 'self-epithet' and 'non-self-epithet' could understand and believe the statement that the German adjective 'lateinisch' is a non-self-epithet. He would be believing that 'lateinisch' stands for some specific philological property or other (he would not know which) and that 'lateinisch' lacks that property. He knows that it is now proper to ask the rider-question 'Namely, which philological property?' since if this question had no answer, then 'lateinisch' could not be either a self-epithet or a non-self-epithet. For 'lateinisch' to be a non-self-epithet, it must be false that 'lateinisch' is *lateinisch*, whatever being *lateinisch* is. 'Lateinisch' could no more be *just* a non-self-epithet, without there being a specific, but as yet unmentioned, philological property which it lacked, than a person could be *just* christened, without being christened 'John' or 'James' or '. . .'.

'Self-epithet' and 'non-self-epithet' do not stand for any of the specific philological properties which could be mentioned in the namely-riders for which they leave openings, any more than 'christened . . .' is a Christian name. Logicians' category-words are not among the words listed under those category-words. 'Fiction' is not the name of one of the novels catalogued under the librarian's heading of 'Fiction'. 'Self-epithet' and 'non-self-epithet' are not philologists' epithets, but logicians' ways of dividing philologists' epithets into two artificial parcels, which, naturally, are not among the contents of those parcels.

In this connection I adopt and adapt an important argument of Mr Lawrence (p. 78). 'English' is a self-epithet, because 'English' is an English word. But 'self-epithet' does not *mean* '. . . is an English word'—else '"Deutsch" is a self-epithet' would be false, instead of being true. Or if '"English" is a self-epithet' could be paraphrased by '"English" is an English word', then since German words are not English and 'Deutsch' is a German word, '"Deutsch" is a non-self-epithet' would have to be true, when in fact it is false. Of itself, 'self-epithet' tells us nothing about the tongues to which 'English' and 'Deutsch' belong, any more than about the tongue to which 'polysyllabic' belongs, which is also a self-epithet. 'Either English or German or Lithuanian or a self-epithet' would be an absurd disjunction. So would any disjunction be absurd in which ordinary philological epithets were coupled by 'or' with 'self-epithet' or 'non-self-epithet'. 'Self-epithet' and 'non-self-epithet' convey no philological information about words. They are specially fabricated instruments for talking *en bloc* about the possession or non-possession by philological epithets of whatever may be the philological properties for which they stand. Such instruments are not among the philological epithets that they help logicians to discuss.

To put all this in the official terminology of 'heterological' and 'homological': we can say 'obsolete' is heterological, because 'obsolete' has not gone out of fashion and 'obsolete' *means* 'gone out of fashion'; we can say 'polysyllabic' is homological, because 'polysyllabic' *is* a word of many syllables and *means* 'of many syllables'.

Now the words 'heterological' and 'homological' have and lack a number of ordinary philological properties. They are adjectives, polysyllabic, English (perhaps), cacophonous, aspirated and neologistic; they are *not* prepositions, slang, or of Latin origin. But what we are asked to decide is whether 'heterological' and 'homological' are themselves heterological or homological, i.e. whether among the philological properties which 'heterological' and 'homological' have and lack, they have or lack the philological properties of homologicality and heterologicality. But to ask this is to suppose that 'heterological' and 'homological' *do* stand for philological properties, i.e., that there could be words which were *just* heterological or *just* homological and not heterological or homological *because* lacking or possessing such and such ordinary philological properties. And this supposition is false. For to say that a word is heterological or homological is to refer to, without mentioning, some philological property (*not* heterologicality or homologicality) for which that word stands and which does or does not belong to that word. In using 'heterological' and 'homological' we are not mentioning word-properties, but referring to unmentioned word-properties. And references to unmentioned word-properties are not mentions of those or of extra word-properties, any more than references to unspecified diseases are themselves the specifications of those or of extra diseases. If unpacked, the assertion that 'heterological' is heterological would run: 'Heterological' lacks the property for which it stands, namely that of lacking the property for which it stands, namely that of lacking the property . . . No property is ever mentioned, so the seeming reference to such a property is spurious.

This seeming paradox arises from treating certain umbrella-words coined for the purpose of collecting epithets into two families as if they were themselves members of those families. To ask whether 'heterological' and 'homological' are heterological or homological is rather like asking whether Man is a tall man or a short man. We do not need statute-hierarchies to save us from deciding whether Man is a tall or a short man; or language-hierarchies to save us from deciding whether 'heterological' is heterological or homological. It is not even, save *per accidens*, a matter of minding our inverted commas but a matter of minding our grammar. Minding our inverted commas, in the required ways, *is* minding our grammar.

The same inattention to grammar is the source of such paradoxes as 'the Liar', 'the Class of Classes . . .' and 'Impredicability'. When we ordinarily say 'That statement is false', what we say promises a namely-rider, e.g. '. . ., namely that today is Tuesday'. When we say 'The current statement is false' we are pretending *either* that no namely-rider is to be asked for *or* that the namely-rider is '. . ., namely that the present statement is false'. If no namely-rider is to be asked for, then 'The current statement' does not refer to any statement. It is like saying 'He is asthmatic' while disallowing the question 'Who?' If, alternatively, it is pretended that there is indeed the namely-rider, '. . ., namely, that the current statement is false', the promise is met by an echo of that promise. If unpacked, our pre-tended assertion would run 'The current statement {namely, that the current statement [namely that the current statement (namely that the current statement . . .'. The brackets are never closed; no verb is ever reached; no statement of which we can even ask whether it is true or false is ever adduced.

Certainly there exist genuine hierarchies. My Omnibus *Short Stories of O. Henry* is not a short story by O. Henry; nor is my batch of (five or six) Omnibus books a sixth or seventh Omnibus book. But 'I possess a batch of Omnibus books' has the namely-rider '. . ., namely *The Short Stories of O. Henry, The Short Stories of W. W. Jacobs*, etc., etc.'; just as 'I possess the Omnibus *Short Stories of O. Henry*' has the namely-rider '. . ., namely "The Third Ingredient", etc., etc.'. Obviously, we could go on to talk of the set of batches of Omnibus books in the possession of Oxford professors, and so on indefinitely. But at no stage can the mention of a set, or batch, or Omnibus *be* the mention of what it carries a reference to, but is not a mention of, namely what would be mentioned in their promised namely-riders, if these were actually provided.

In ordinary life, we commonly have different words with which we make our different references, such as 'Centre Forward', 'team', 'Division', 'League'. This prevents there being any linguistic temptation to talk as if a team might sprain its left ankle, or as if the League might win or lose the Cup. If we stick to one such word the whole way up the ladder (like 'class' and 'number') we are so tempted. Having failed to prevent such confusions arising, we have to seek remedies for them after they have arisen.

There are genuine hierarchies, so there exist (efficient and in-efficient) ways of talking about them. But our (quite efficient) way of talking about footballers, teams, Divisions and Leagues is not itself to be described as a hierarchy of languages or ways of talking.

Talking about the Berkshire League is not talking about talking about talking about the individuals who play, e.g. for a given village. Certainly the talk about the League is on a high rung of generality; a whole echelon of namely-riders goes unstated. But no inverted commas are improvidently omitted. The relation of referring expressions to their namely-riders is not to be elucidated in terms of the relation of comments on expressions to the expressions on which they are comments. On the contrary, the relation of a comment to the expression on which it is a comment is (when it refers to this without citing it) just another case of the relation of a referring expression to the content of its namely-rider.

Many of the Paradoxes have to do with such things as statements about statements and epithets of epithets. So quotation-marks have to be employed. But the mishandling which generates the apparent antinomies consists not in mishandling quotation-marks but in treating referring expressions as fillings of their own namely-riders.

A team neither does nor does not sprain its left ankle. It is not one of its eleven possessors of left ankles, though a mention of the team carries a reference to these possessors of ankles. 'Heterological' neither has nor lacks any philological property for which it stands. It is not one of the philological epithets to which it and its opposite number are special ways of referring.

19

THINKING AND LANGUAGE

Reprinted from 'Proceedings of the Aristotelian Society', Suppl. vol.
xxv, 1951, by permission of the editor

To say that a person thinks or considers that something is the case
is not at all the same sort of thing as to say that he is now thinking or
considering. And neither is it at all the same sort of thing as to say
that he is now stating what he thinks is the case. He is thinking if,
for example, he is at this moment trying to decide something. But
what he now thinks is what he has already decided. He may ponder,
as he can scramble, hard, methodically, wearily or unavailingly. But
he cannot believe something, or be at his destination, hard, methodically, wearily or unavailingly.

Our concern is with such activities as pondering, musing and
calculating and so only indirectly with such states as being of an
opinion or having one's mind made up; and so only indirectly,
again, with such activities as declaring one's opinion or telling what
one has found out.

The title 'thinking' is not reserved for the labours of trying to
decide things. I am thinking if I am going over, in my head, the
fortunes of the heroine of a novel that I have been reading; or if I
am re-savouring a well turned argument, though I have long since
accepted its conclusion. Or if I am drifting in idle reverie from one
topic to another. Only some thinking is excogitation; only some
thinking is work; only some thinking has a topic or a problem.

Nor do we limit the work of pondering, deliberating or considering to activities of trying to arrive at truths. Composing, translating,
planning, organising and designing involve deliberating, but what is
achieved when the deliberations are successful is not a contribution
to theory or to general knowledge. Something has been thought out
but no new information has been got. A problem has been solved,
but no question has been answered. Not all problems are questions.
Not all knowing is knowing what to say.

Lastly, we do not reserve the title 'thinking' for inner processes.

The child, told to think again, is not disobeying if he mutters audibly, 'Seven times seven is forty-nine, nine and carry four; seven times two is fourteen; four plus four is eight; one hundred and eighty-nine.' The architect is thinking out his design for his war-memorial while studiously arranging and rearranging toy bricks on the carpet; and the composer is not taking a holiday from the labours of composition while his fingers move over the keys, so long as they move in a burdened, searching, tentative and critical manner.

The chief problem set us by Miss Murdoch is to give a philosophical account of the ways in which in real life we report stretches of our ponderings and musings. I accept her problem and am, I hope, only widening its scope, if I pose it as well for those deliberations which are not, as for those which are, done in our heads. As she says, we have lots of idioms for describing these workings and these driftings; and we employed and understood them long before we had heard of psychology and epistemology. But there is usually an ostentatious picturesqueness in these idioms. They work because they are graphic; but for the same reason they cannot be construed literally. And we seem unable to find unpicturesque paraphrases for them. So I can, indeed, *tell* you what my musings were like, but I can tell you only what they were *like*. I can say, for instance, that I was going round and round in circles, though actually I was sitting in a chair; or that what I was after just eluded my grasp, though in fact my hand was filling my pipe. What I was doing was, in fact, unlike the activities to which I liken it, in respect of those very concrete details of which 'go round in circles' and 'grasp' remind us. Yet it really was like those activities in the respects required. The thinker 'in a fog' and the walker in a fog are both laboriously getting nowhere; in growing despondency, both are repeating moves already made, without knowing how to stop these repetitions. Or the thinker and the fruit-picker are in the same plight. Success seems very close, yet their capacities are not quite sufficient; they know what they are after and what is needed in order to get it, yet what is needed is not forthcoming. The recipient of the metaphor is expected to discount the very concrete details of ladders, branches, right arms and apples, without which there could be no apple-picking. Some other frustration-story, like that of just not catching a fish, might have done just as well, though its concrete detail was quite different. What is meant to be discerned is community of plot, not similarity of incident. But, of course, there is no plot where there do not exist some incidents or other.

I may effectively describe a wind as brutal, fierce, sportive or drowsy. But I could also describe it as a 30 m.p.h. wind, coming from the NNE., of such and such a temperature and humidity, with such and such intervals between gusts and lulls. But when I want to tell you of a stretch of my thinking, I seem to be without an Air Ministry vocabulary with which to replace my picturesque idioms. Attempts have indeed been made to provide such a vocabulary. But when we have learned the lingoes of impressions, ideas, concepts, associations, gentle forces, vivacities, cognitions, judgements and propositions, we find that we cannot couch our reminiscences in such terms. We cleave instead to such expressions as 'bogged down', 'losing the thread', 'casting around', 'seeing daylight', 'germinating', 'dawning', 'floundering', 'consolidating' and a thousand others. So what stops us describing what has been going on in non-graphic terms? If the concrete incidents of fruit-picking and fishing can be unpicturesquely reported, why do the concrete incidents of a stretch of thinking appear to be so shy? I shall suggest an answer to this query different from Miss Murdoch's and Mr Lloyd's.

When we start to theorise about thinking, we naturally hanker to follow the chemist's example, namely, to say what thinking consists of and how the ingredients of which it consists are combined. Processes like perspiring, digesting, counting and apple-picking can be broken down into ingredient processes, coordinated in certain ways. So it seems reasonable to expect thinking to yield to the same treatment. But this is a mistake. There is no general answer to the question 'What does thinking consist of?'

If asked 'What does working consist of?' we should quickly object that there was no general answer. Some sorts of work are done with some sorts of tools, others with other sorts. But sometimes the same work might be done with alternative tools. Some work does not require tools at all. The dancer uses her limbs, but her limbs are not implements. A headmaster might do his work though deprived of the use of his arms, or his legs or his eyes. Some sorts of work are done with special materials, like string or Carrara marble. But the work might be done with different materials, and some work does not require materials at all. An artist's model need not even be attending to her work. She might be paid for sleeping or playing patience in the studio. There need be no action, inner or overt, performed by the policeman on his beat, which he may not also perform when strolling round the same streets when his work is over. Not all work is for pay; not all work is unpleasant; not all work is tiring. Nothing need be done, thought, or felt by the professional footballer at work that might not be done, thought or felt by the amateur at play. *Work* is a polymorphous concept. There is nothing which must be going on in one piece of work which need be going on in another. Nothing answers to the general description 'what work consists of'. None the less, each specific job is describable. The workman can be told what he is to do. The concepts of *fighting, trading, playing, housekeeping* and *farming* are also polymorphous concepts, where the concepts of *boxing* and *apple-picking* are nearly enough non-polymorphous.

The concept of *thinking* is polymorphous. There is no general answer to the question 'What does thinking consist of?' There are hosts of widely different sorts of toilings and idlings, engaging in any one of which is thinking. Yet there need be nothing going on in one of them such that something else of the same species or genus must be going on in another of them. Where certain specific sorts of incidents must be going on for someone to be counting, any of a wide variety of heterogeneous incidents can be going on when he is thinking. Just as there are hundreds of widely differing operations, including apple-picking, to be occupied in any one of which is to be doing farm-work; so there are lots of widely differing operations, including multiplying, all of which are proper specimens of thinking.

Consider the dictum that in thinking the soul is talking to itself. It is clearly both too wide and too narrow. An actor's part may be running through his head while he eats and walks, even though he wishes it would stop. If he is not deliberately rehearsing his part or even considering the merits and demerits of his words, he can deny that he is thinking, while allowing that he is saying significant things to himself. Conversely, a poet, essayist or philosopher may be trying hard to find the word, phrase or argument that he needs, but the time when he is thinking what to say is the time when he still has nothing to say. In some thinking, the soul is only stammering to itself.

But we should also, sometimes, describe a person as pondering who was neither saying nor struggling to say anything to himself or aloud. The architect might try to think out his design for the war-memorial by arranging and re-arranging toy bricks on the carpet; the sculptor might plan a statue in marble by modelling and re-modelling a piece of plasticine. The motorist might weigh the pros and cons of different roads, poring over a map or seeing stretches of the alternative roads in his mind's eye. The guide might be planning tomorrow's climb, methodically scanning through a telescope the slopes, precipices and water-courses of the mountain from his hotel. He might eventually decide his route, but when asked to describe it, have to go through some additional labours in order to put his plan into words or on a sketch-map. He might even be unequal to these additional labours. Having thought out a route does not entail being ready or even able to tell it in words or sketch it on a map.

A musician, asked how a piece of music goes, might try hard to run over it in his head or hum it aloud. Even if he succeeds in thinking out how it goes, he need not be expected to be able to tell, but only to show how it goes. So, sometimes, in thinking, the soul is humming or merely struggling to hum to itself, or aloud; though a person might be humming to himself or aloud who was not and had not been trying to think out how the piece went.

We philosophers need to be doubly suspicious of the dictum that in thinking the soul is talking to itself. For, on the one hand, our own professional brand of thinking is taught in books, articles, lectures and debates and is intended to get its results deployed in these same prosaic mediums. And, on the other hand, we, like philologists, lawyers and political controversialists, have *ex officio* to examine the dicta of other people and of ourselves. We have to think *about* bits of prose and we are trained to direct our thinking towards the production of bits of prose. But the tricks of one trade need not be the Tricks of Trade.

Even when a person has been thinking in English or French, he may not have said anything to himself in completed prose. Perhaps his ponderings moved in detached words, tentative and broken phrases and mere promissory jottings of sentences. When his ponderings are over we may expect him to tell in ordered prose what he has decided; but we have no right to demand that his ponderings themselves had the continuity of a lecture or the fluency of an ordinary remark. Conversely, he might have been conducting a glib internal monologue without having been thinking hard or even at all.

Some theorists, in partial recognition of the polymorphousness of the concept of thinking, have allowed that the equation of think-ing with monologue is too narrow. They have suggested instead a more tolerant equation, a more general answer to the question 'What does thinking consist of?' Thinking, they say, is operating with symbols, where 'symbol' is taken to stand for a genus of which verbal expressions are only one species. The motorist's visual images, the geometrician's diagrams, the architect's toy bricks, the musician's hummed notes and the guide's glimpses of the mountain-side would belong to other species of this hospitable genus. On this view, thinking consists of occurrences of symbols, manipulated in certain ways. Moreover, since symbols are thought of as tokens, deputies or proxies, this account of thinking seems to satisfy a felt need to say that thinking is unlike perceiving and handling in that the thinker somehow gets on terms with absentee realities. He can grasp them without having contact with them, since he has contact with their delegates instead. He negotiates through envoys. Thought is free because it can manage with only vicarious interviews. Thinking, perhaps, just *is* having vicarious interviews. It is acquaintance at a distance.

I think that I am agreeing with Miss Murdoch in holding that this is the wrong sort of account to give of thinking. We want to describe our descriptions of the thinking that we do, not to produce hypotheses to explain how some supposed gulfs are bridged. But I am disagreeing with her and with Mr Lloyd on another matter. For it is false or else highly misleading to say that thinking consists of symbols, handled in certain ways. Apart from my previous point that there is nothing of which we can say quite generally 'thinking consists of that', there is a special reason for denying that it consists of symbols in particular. For, in the most familiar use of 'symbol', words and, *a fortiori*, phrases, sentences and arguments are not symbols at all.

'XII' and '12' are symbols; so are 'x', 'y' and ' = '; so are contour-lines, the Union Jack, a club tie, and the items of the Morse Code. When we call them 'symbols' we think of them as signs doing duty for other expressions. The sign ' + ' on a map does duty for the word 'church' or '*église*', since these take up too much room. The sign ' + ' in mathematics does duty for the expression 'plus' or 'added to', which takes up too much room. 'XII' and '12' do duty for the word 'twelve', and wearing a club tie is a way of announcing, without words, that the wearer is a member of the club. Symbols, in this use, are indeed proxies. They are proxies for other expressions, which are not themselves, in their turn, substitutes for still other expressions. The symbol ' + ' in a map is a substitute for the word 'church' or '*église*'; but it is not a substitute for a church. A chapel might be an alternative place of worship, but a mark on a map could not be this. The words 'church' and '*église*' themselves are not proxies *either* for a church *or* for any other expression for a church. 'R.N.' stands for, or does duty for the title 'the Royal Navy'; but it is not a deputy for the Royal Navy. Only, perhaps, the United States Navy could deputise for the Royal Navy. Nor is the title 'the Royal Navy' a substitute or *locum tenens* for any other title for the

Royal Navy. A flint or a boot-heel can do duty for a hammer. But a hammer does not do duty for anything else. It does its own job. If it had no job of its own, there could be no question of the flint or the boot-heel doing its duty for it. To know what is the job of the hammer is not to know what it is a *locum tenens* for. But to know how, in this situation, the flint and the boot-heel are being used *is* to know what they are in lieu of. In this familiar use of 'symbol', an ordinarily literate man, told that a new book was written in symbols, would infer that it was not for him, but only for mathematicians, say, or Freemasons. If told that it was written in vernacular symbols, he would not know what to infer. If his map carried a key to the symbols used, he would consult the key in order to find out what '—' stands for; but he would not consult the key again in order to find what 'church' signifies. So far from words and phrases being symbols, symbols are ordinarily thought of as being precisely *not* words or phrases, but designed proxies for them.

I do not say that this use of 'symbol' is the only allowable use. But as it is a stock use, there are obvious risks in saying that the English and French languages are systems of symbols, or that all thinking is operating with symbols. For we continue to think of symbols as proxies, and are therefore encouraged to suppose that each English and French expression is a substitute or deputy for something or other, and that to know what it means or signifies is to know that it is a proxy for such and such a specifiable something. We are then liable to equate 'signify' with 'stand for', and 'stand for' with 'do duty for' or 'represent'.

It needs, I hope, no further argument to establish that in this stock use of 'symbol', pictures in the mind's eye, hummed notes, glimpses of a mountain-side and the sculptor's plasticine are not symbols either. Nor is any clarity got by saying that they constitute private languages. It is just another way of seeming to give a general answer to the question 'What does thinking consist of?'

Miss Murdoch and Mr Lloyd are both properly chary of equating thinking with using ordinary language. It is worth while collecting some of the main reasons for rejecting the equation. First, to say that someone has been thinking does not entail that he has been saying or trying to say anything aloud or to himself. Next, to say that he has succeeded in thinking something out does not entail that he is ready or even able to tell in words what he has thought out. Next, even when he reports having been thinking in English or French, this, as Miss Murdoch rightly says, does not mean that some English or French expressions have just cropped up in his head or been just 'cast upon a screen'. He was not just *having* words, but, perhaps, rummaging for and finding them. They met a need. It is tempting to put this point by saying that he was not just *having* words but *using* them—the difference being like that between finding a hammer in one's hand and hammering a nail with it. But even this is not quite right. Expressions can occur without merely cropping up and also without being put to work. There are ways of being purposefully busy about ladders other than scaling heights with them. One can, for example, be designing, constructing or repairing ladders. One can be moving them or erecting them. One can be hunting for them or bargaining for them. One can be giving oneself practice in erecting and climbing them. Similarly, a person who is thinking in English, may be trying to construct or improve a rejoinder for some later occasion. He is not using it yet. He may be giving himself practice in putting his case, in preparation for his trial. He is not putting it yet. Or, like a man who sets a gingerly foot on a rung of a ladder, not to climb it but to see whether it will bear his weight tomorrow, so a thinker might be tentatively handselling a formula, an argument, an aphorism or a rhyme, to see whether he will be able to put it to its intended job at a later stage. What a thinker is doing with (or about or to) the expressions that occur makes all the difference; and there are scores of widely different things that he may be doing with (or about or to) them. Until we have heard his economic story, his technical story, his tactical story, or his artistic story, we do not know what he was trying to do or what he accomplished or failed to accomplish. And if we have not got its plot, we have not got any part of the story but only a welter of, so far, pointless details. A pure chronicle of the occurrence of expressions (or of images, hummed notes, glimpses or fingerings of plasticine) would not yet be even the beginning of a history of the thinker's pondering.

We can now begin to see why our ordinary ways of describing our ponderings and musings tend to be graphic and not literal. It is because we want them to be histories and we want them not to be chronicles. We want the plot to be told in abstraction from the actual but substitutable details. To tell the plot without the detailed incidents requires the employment either of idioms so general as to be lifeless or of graphic idioms which show the point by illustrating it. The concept of thinking being polymorphous, the chronicles of two stretches of thinking need not contain any homogeneous episodes; and the episodes assembled in the chronicles of one stretch of thinking can also be as heterogeneous as you please. One architect may design his war-memorial in toy bricks, another in diagrams on a drawing-board. Who cares? But we care a lot what were the architects' problems, their obstacles, their tastes, their prejudices, their ingenuities, their reasons, their negligences, their disappointments and their results. Certainly there would be nothing to give the history of, if nothing chronicleable had taken place. Historians do not narrate extra events, over and above those narrated by chroniclers. They tell us different sorts of things—interesting things—about those same events that the chroniclers report uninterestingly. Naturally, too, most of what is or might be chronicled goes unmentioned by the historian. For it might have been different in myriad ways from what it was without affecting the plot.

If we ask a soldier to tell us about a battle, we do not expect to be told all or many of the myriad details of which the battle and the battlefield happened to consist. We do not care which of his boots he wore, when he had a cigarette, over what tussocks of grass he walked or what he said to the sergeant during a lull in the fighting. We want to know how the battle went, and why it went that way. We want the tactical and strategic plot of the story of the battle, and the telling of this requires careful neglect of its negligible detail. Detail is negligible when it could have been widely different from what it was without making any difference to the story of the course of the battle. The narrator can, of course, injudiciously neglect pertinent details or injudiciously mention negligible details.

The course of a game of cricket or bridge cannot be told without referees' expressions pertaining directly or indirectly to the score, but it can be and usually is told without mention of most of the countless incidents in it which did not have or look like having any influence on the score. To tell what needs to be told about a business deal, references must be made to profits, losses, risks and precautions, but not, ordinarily, to telephone numbers, office furniture or brands of notepaper. To catalogue these appurtenances—and there could be no deals without some appurtenances or other—would be to change the subject. There is, of course, nothing ineffable, private or gossamery about these appurtenances. They are merely beside the point. They could have been quite different without the course of the deal having been different.

In talking about particular instances of polymorphous concepts like *trade, farming, housekeeping* or *thinking,* the opposition between relating what counts and mentioning the details and appurtenances is necessarily a strong one. When we want to compare the policies of traders in quite different lines of trade, the techniques of housekeepers with quite different ménages, or the clumsinesses of athletes in quite dissimilar sports, we need—and find—idioms which, while neutral between the disparate details of the activities, are appropriate to the similarities and differences between the policies, techniques and clumsinesses of the agents. One of our ways of designing such idioms, is to borrow some of the non-polymorphous expressions for specific proceedings (like 'baiting the hook' or 'taking two bites at the cherry') the concrete detail of which is meant to be discounted.

Take a case of pondering. A chess-player may be considering what move to make. Perhaps he tentatively moves his queen to a new square, keeping his fingers on her; then he takes her back, and tries an alternative move, and retracts that. Or perhaps he sits with his hands in his pockets, and merely switches his gaze from one square to another, and back again. Or perhaps he shuts his eyes and visualises the board as it would look if he made this move, or that move. Or perhaps he is saying to himself or aloud, in Polish or English, 'If I move her to square so and so, she will be threatened by his bishop; but if I move her to square such and such, she will be boxed in by her own pawns.' Or perhaps there occurs a patchwork of bits and pieces of incidents, of all these and other sorts. But when invited to tell what he had been doing, he will construe the invitation not as a request to give a chronicle of these details but as a request to tell us what his predicament was, what reasons weighed with him for and against alternative solutions to it, what decision he came to and how it contributed to his victory or defeat. It is not that he has no literal way of describing the details; he just wants to tell us what matters and not to tell us what does not matter, i.e., to talk chess, and to spare us and himself pointless reminiscences. When he does give us a bit of chess history, he is likely, but not bound to use graphic idioms, like 'threat' and 'boxed in'.

I repeat that though the idioms in which a piece of economic, strategic, domestic or athletic history is told come from quite different founts from those in which the corresponding chronicles would be told, they do not chronicle different sequences of happenings. They do not, therefore, chronicle some extra happenings which possess the odd property of baffling literal description. A plantation of larches may be heart-shaped (which none of the larches are); but the surveyor who discovers that the plantation is heart-shaped has not come across anything which the forester has not come across who has been cataloguing the larches in the plantation. Yet the surveyor need not notice that the plantation is a plantation of larches, but only that it is a plantation of some trees or other; and the forester need not notice that the plantation is heart-shaped, though he realises that it is some shape or other. Nor need the findings of the one be deducible from the findings of the other. They are answering different and independent questions about the same trees. We shall be disappointed if we search the surveyor's reports for botanical information, or the forester's reports for topographical information. We shall be in error if we construe the surveyor's reports as giving botanical information in metaphors. We shall be in even worse error if we think that botanical information has the queer property that it can be given only in metaphors. What, sometimes, induces the surveyor to give topographical information in graphic terms, like 'heart-shaped', is that they convey what needs to be conveyed more swiftly or more vividly than would the highly general idioms of Euclidean geometry.

Mr Lloyd tells us that there are three distinguishable sorts of levels of thinking. But he says that it is doubtful if the first sort would really be called 'thinking' unless the second supervened. He says that what distinguishes this second sort of activity is that it is not thinking, but thinking *about*. And the third, being publicly intelligible, is in fact language and therefore, like the first could not properly be called 'thinking'. If this third sort is what he describes as 'being wise after the event', then it certainly could not be called 'thinking'. A sleeper may be a wise man, but he is not thinking. Mr Lloyd winds up this rather mystifying catalogue of three things which are not thinking by saying that each kind affects the other; and each is necessary to the other in order to have a game of thinking at all. It is the combination of them that is called 'thinking'. Some of the time, it looks as if Mr Lloyd is putting forward this stratification theory as a psychological hypothesis, or else as an established psychological generalisation. But some of the time he talks as if he gleaned it by a logical analysis of the concept of thinking. He says, 'They are logical distinctions, rather; but they are, I think, also stages or processes which do occur (though rapidly) one after another.' Later he says, 'Let us abandon the mixture of observation and speculation.' But he also recommends his view by arguments of the philosophical kind. Certain processes would not properly be called 'thinking' unless certain auxiliary processes went with them. And he says, too sweepingly, 'So, unless he can now state some proposition (which he need not have believed), we hesitate to agree with a man that he *has* been thinking.' Moreover, he discusses, I think illuminatingly, what is logically required for a description to be the description of a game of football. The course of a game cannot—logically cannot—be told without referees' expressions for scores, penalties, tactics, victories and the like.

If Mr Lloyd's stratification theory were just an empirical generalisation, it would be open for a man to say that he, for his part, found four or twelve levels in his thinking, or else, only two or one. To rule out such a possibility on the score that then what he found could not properly be called 'thinking' would be to swing over from an empirical to a philosophical stratification theory. And a very odd philosophical theory this would be. If the number of planets may not be decided on purely logical grounds, why should the number of distinguishable and rapidly successive processes that commonly go with one another be decidable by logic? Could logic also decide precisely how rapidly they chase one another, after the thinker has taken coffee or rum?

I believe that what Mr Lloyd half-meant to distinguish was not three sorts of separately recordable processes but three sorts of things that can be significantly said about stretches of thinking.

When a person has been engaged in a piece of pondering, (1) there has been going on a welter of incidents, which he might subsequently recollect, if he troubled to do so, all or any of which might have taken place without his having done the pondering that he did do, and all or any of which could have been replaced by some quite dissimilar incidents without making much or any difference to the pondering that he did. The narration of these incidents would be a bit of pure chronicling. (2) The thinker has, perhaps, been trying to solve a certain problem, using certain methods, meeting with certain obstacles, having certain bits of good or bad luck, exercising much or little care and achieving or failing to achieve certain desiderated results. The narration of these features of the situation would be a bit of history and it would have to use a lot of what I may call, too largely, 'tactical idioms' or 'referees' idioms'. Such a history would cover, without according much particular mention to the incidents chronicled under (1). The contents of the historical narrative are not extra chronicleable incidents, any more than the plot of a play is an extra scene or action in the play. (3) In some, but not all, cases the accomplishment of the task—if it is accomplished—involves the thinker's being equipped to declare his policy, scheme or theory. Having made up his mind what is the case or what is the thing to do, he is ready to notify us what he has decided. Readiness to do this is, sometimes, part of the result aimed at. The business of actually telling us what he has decided is, of course, no part of the activity of trying to decide it, any more than eating is any part of the activity

269

of preparing a meal. In telling us what he has decided, the thinker is, if Mr Lloyd wishes, using his 'wisdom after the event'. But he is not describing or retroactively monitoring his ponderings, any more than eating a meal is describing or retroactively controlling the cooking of it. True, the thinker's resultant theory or plan (if the thinking was a piece of theorising or planning) has, *inter alia*, logical merits and demerits; and the tactical account of his pondering will necessarily contain expressions pertaining to these intended merits and feared demerits, much as an account of a game must contain expressions pertaining to intended scores and feared penalties. This threefold distinction is not a distinction between sorts or levels of thinking. It is a distinction between sorts of accounts of thinking. The first and second are different sorts of accounts of the course of the thinker's deliberations, namely the chronicler's and the historian's accounts. The chronicler's account does not tell us what we usually want to be told. It mentions the things that went on in the course of the game, fight or work, without saying anything about how the game, fight or work went. The historian's account tells us how the undertaking went but, often by using graphic idioms, spares us mention of all or most of what did happen to go on, but might very well not have gone on, in the course of it. The third sort of account is the scorer's account. It tells us about a certain kind of result of certain kinds of deliberations. It tells us not what went on in the course of the deliberating, but what came out of it; not what the year's workings consisted of, but what dividends were declared at the end of them. I agree with Mr Lloyd that our interest is usually the shareholder's interest.

I have tried to show that there can be thinking where there is no talking and no attempt to talk; that a person can have thought something out but not be ready or even able to tell what he has decided; that there can be thinking in which verbal expressions though worked upon or worked for, are not worked *with*; that thinking can embody the occurrences of hosts of things other than linguistic expressions and also other than symbols. Thinking cannot be defined as monologue or as operations with symbols. So I am likely to be asked, 'What then of the pre-occupation of latter-day philosophers with linguistic questions? Has it all been a mistake? If you deny the equation of thinking with talking to oneself or, more generally with operations with symbols, must you not deny the doctrine, based on this assumed equation, that philosophy is some sort of talk about talk?' But this question issues from a mis-apprehension. The view that philosophy has *ex officio* to do with language did not derive from a theory about what pondering consists of, i.e., from a psychological or epistemological premiss. It derived, mainly, from Russell's distinction between the true-or-false and the nonsensical. Certain logical paradoxes had to be resolved by showing that certain classes of seemingly well formed sentences could not state either truths or falsehoods. Wittgenstein, as I construe him, saw in this distinction, as Russell did not, the wanted differentia between saying scientific things and saying philosophical things; between being informative or misinformative about the world and telling or showing the logic of what we say about the world.

Only of expressions can we ask whether they make sense or not, or why they do or do not make sense. Only of formulated arguments can we ask whether they are valid or not. Only to the statements of theories, policies or schemes (etc.) can the litmus-papers of logicians be applied—to the results, that is, not to the processes of excogitation. Dicta are intelligible or unintelligible; bits of pondering, *pace* Mr Lloyd, cannot be either. Houses can be divided into those which are habitable and those which are uninhabitable; but building operations neither meet not fail to meet these requirements of the housing inspector.

I wish I had room to discuss the points with which Mr Lloyd is chiefly concerned, namely (1) the unformalisability of natural languages, (2) the deliquescence of the distinction between analytic and synthetic statements in natural languages, and (3) the replacement of the notion of descriptions tallying with facts by the notion of persons trying to describe things as effectively as they can. But, important though these points are, they do not seem to me to lead very directly towards the solution of Miss Murdoch's central problem.

20

FEELINGS

Reprinted from 'The Philosophical Quarterly', vol. 1, 1951, by permission of the editor

We talk of ourselves and other people 'feeling' things very multifariously.

(1) There is the perceptual use, in which we say that someone felt how hot the water was or felt the rope round his neck or felt that the spoon was sticky. Feeling, in this use, is one of our ways of detecting or discerning things. We feel with our fingers or our tongues, as we see with our eyes, and we can be good or bad at detecting different sorts of things in this way and we can improve or deteriorate at it. We can try to feel things and either fail or succeed, and we can feel things indistinctly or distinctly.

If my teeth were chattering, I might detect the fact by hearing them or by seeing them in a mirror. Or I might feel them chattering with my tongue or lips. But ordinarily I feel them chattering without using instruments, fingers, tongue or lips; just as while I might find out that my feet were cold with my hand or with a thermometer, ordinarily I find it out without employing either instruments or other bodily organs. Should I say that I feel that they are cold in or with my feet themselves? In real life I do not say this. I just say that they are cold. But if my feet were very numb, and I were asked whether they were cold, I might have to reply, 'Wait a minute. I must feel them with my hands, since, for the moment, I cannot feel whether they are warm or cold in or with my feet themselves.' The fact that I do not know which preposition, 'in' or 'with', we should use to make this contrast, shows how unnatural the usage is.

(2) Connected with the perceptual use of the verb 'to feel', there is its exploratory use. I feel for the matches in my pocket or feel my horse's legs. This exploratory use of the verb stands to its perceptual use as 'peer' and 'look' stand to 'see' and as 'listen' stands to 'hear'. Feeling, in this use, can be successful or unsuccessful and can be continued for a period, intermitted and resumed. It can be careful,

skilful, and methodical, or haphazard and unsystematic. A doctor may carefully feel my pulse, yet fail to feel it, just as he may peer but fail to see.

(3) Also connected with the perceptual use of the verb, there is what I may call the mock-use of it. The condemned man already 'feels' the rope round his neck, though there is not yet any rope round his neck, just as he 'hears' the tolling bell, though it is not yet tolling, and he 'sees' the gallows, though they are not yet erected. Sometimes we say 'feels as if', 'seems to feel', or 'imagines he feels', to avoid having to produce the ironical tone of voice or the quotation marks which indicate the mock-use of the verb. (All words are capable of mock-use. 'Your "lion" was only a donkey' is not a self-contradiction.)

(4) Different from any of these is the use of 'feel' in connection with such complements as aches, tickles, and other local or pervasive discomforts. To feel a tickle and to have a tickle seem to be the same thing. The spoon may be sticky or my teeth may be chattering, without my feeling it (or seeing or hearing it). But there could not be an unfelt tickle. And whereas, if numbed, I might only indistinctly feel my teeth chattering, there is no question of indistinctness or distinctness in my feeling a tickle but only, what is quite different, a question of the tickle being violent or faint, or, which is different again, a question of the tickle having much, little, or no attention paid to it. In this use of 'feel', one cannot try to feel an ache or tickle, and one cannot be or become good or bad at feeling such things. Feeling, in this sense of having, is not a sort of discerning, detecting or finding, or, of course, any sort of searching or rummaging. Pickpockets may become adept at feeling coins and watches in other people's pockets. No one can be good or bad at feeling itches.

Conversely, while we are ready to classify the tickle or ache that one has as a special sort of feeling or sensation, we certainly will not classify as a special sort of feeling or sensation what one feels, in the perceptual use of the verb. What one feels, in the perceptual use, is the heat of the bath water or the chattering of one's teeth, or a watch in someone's pocket.

(5) Quite different, again, is the use of the verb 'feel' when followed by an adjective of what I shall vaguely call 'general condition', for example 'to feel sleepy, ill, wide-awake, slack, fidgety, vigorous, startled, uneasy, depressed, cross', and so on. There is no sharp line between the general conditions which one would call 'bodily' and the general conditions which one would call 'mental'. One would report feeling out of sorts to a doctor and report feeling

depressed, perhaps, to a psychiatrist. But both practitioners might be interested to hear that one felt languid, fidgety or vigorous. Startling world news might stop one feeling sleepy, while something out of a bottle might dispel one's depression. No argument is needed to show that this use of the verb is not its perceptual use or its exploratory or its mock-perceptual use.

On the other hand there is a strong tendency to assimilate it to the use of 'feel' in 'feel a tickle'. As a certain sort of distressing feeling or sensation is *had* when one has a tickle; so it is often supposed, there must be some feeling or sensation, perhaps of a rarefied or complex kind, which is had by a person who feels unfit or wide-awake or anxious. But the trouble is that for any specific feeling that can be mentioned as capable of being had, it is always possible for a person to say that he feels unfit, wide-awake or anxious though he has not got that specific sensation. Certainly when I am anxious, I often do have a sort of heavy and coldly burning sensation in the pit of my stomach. But I should never say, 'Oh no, I don't feel at all anxious, for I have not had that sensation in the pit of my stomach once today.' Or I may feel angry and not have the tense feeling in my jaw muscles or the hot feeling in my neck, even though very often I do have these or other sensations when I am angry.

Conversely, for any such specific feeling that you like to mention, it is possible for a person to have that sensation and not to feel unfit, say, or depressed or angry. The tense feeling in my jaw might go with cracking nuts or watching a trapeze artist, and the hot feeling in my neck might go with standing on my head or holding my breath. So there is at least a prima facie case for the view that to feel out of sorts or vigorous or sorry does not entail that any specifiable feelings are had, in the way in which aches are had.

There is one important difference inside this use of 'feel'. If I feel unfit or tired or worried or cross, I can always significantly and sometimes truthfully say that I feel *acutely* or *intensely* so. But if I feel fit or fresh or tranquil or good-tempered, there is no question of my condition being intense or acute. But here I can say instead that I feel *completely* well or *perfectly* contented, as I cannot say that I feel completely cross or perfectly worried. The point is this. Just as when I say 'I met nobody', I am not reporting a meeting, but the absence of one, so when I say 'I felt absolutely calm or perfectly at my ease or quite well' I am not reporting that I was upset in any way, but that I was not upset at all. Epistemologists sometimes talk of the feelings of familiarity and sureness. Now I can feel acutely strange or faintly dubious. But when I do not feel at all strange or dubious, then to say 'I felt quite at home or confident' is just to say that I did not feel at all strange or dubious. Our word 'sure' derives from the Latin 'securus', '*free* from anxiety'.

(6) There is the very common usage in which we speak of feeling that something is the case. I can feel that there is a flaw in your argument, or that a thunderstorm is brewing or that she has something on her mind. If someone feels that something is the case, he does not *think* that it is the case. He is inclined to think so, but has not yet taken sides. It is like the difference between mistrust and accusation.

If a person thinks that something is the case, which is not so, then he is in error. But if he merely feels that something is the case, which is not so, then, though he is attracted by error, he is not wedded to it. He is tempted to hold a certain view, but he has not yet succumbed to the temptation. His mind is not yet closed; it is still ajar. This use of 'feel' is obviously not the perceptual, the mock-perceptual, or the exploratory use. But nor does it seem to have much to do with the use in which people say that they feel aches and therefore have more or less distressing feelings or sensations. For no special sensation is had when I feel that there is a flaw in your argument. The questions 'Where do you feel it? Would an aspirin allay it? Have you got it now? Does it come and go, or is it there all the time?' are not pertinent questions. My feeling that there is a flaw in your argument can be strong, but not intense or acute, continuous or intermittent. I am in no distress. (The edges of the distinction between 'feel that' and 'think that' are not hard. Feeling that something is the case slides into thinking that it is the case; and we often use 'feel that' instead of 'think' as a sort of polite hypocrisy.)

(7) Lastly there is an interesting idiom, which I daresay is a purely English idiom, in which we speak of feeling like doing something. I may say that during the funeral service I felt like laughing, or that in the train I felt like taking a nap. It is a near paraphrase of this idiom to say that I was tempted to laugh or to take a nap; but it does not always do. For we speak of temptation only when there exists some scruple against yielding to it. Thus I was tempted to laugh at the funeral, in a way in which I was not tempted to take a nap in the train, since there was no objection to my sleeping. Perhaps a garrulous neighbour kept me awake, but scruples did not do so. There is, however, a special point about feeling like doing something. If the clown at the circus says or does something funny, I laugh straightaway, and I do not then say that I had felt like laughing. I reserve the expression 'I felt like laughing' for occasions in which I

was inclined to laugh, but was, at least for a short period, inhibited or prohibited from doing so. It is only when there has been time for the idea of doing something to occur to me, and to occur seductively, that I want to say in retrospect that I felt like doing it. It is when the action to which one is inclined is delayed or impeded or prevented or when its consummation is relatively slow or only partial that one wants to speak of having felt like doing it. My toes tingle to kick the intruder downstairs only when I do not instantaneously do so. I feel like having a smoke only when I am not smoking.

Here again, there seems to be little connection between feeling like doing something and having a sensation. A man may feel like writing a letter to *The Times* protesting at the unfair incidence of Death Duties; but we do not think that there is a peculiar feeling (or covey of feelings) associated with writing to *The Times* on this subject; and if there were, we should not know what sort of feeling this was, since we have never done the thing. So the fact that we understand perfectly what is meant when a man tells us that he felt like writing such a letter to *The Times*, shows that we do not construe his statement as a description of some special feelings that he has had.

On the other hand, there is an important connection between, for example, feeling tired and feeling like sitting down, or between feeling indignant and feeling like writing a protesting letter to *The Times*. That he should, from time to time, feel like doing certain sorts of concrete things is one of the things that we expect of a person who is in this or that mood or general condition. He is in the mood, *inter alia*, to have such ideas not only occur to him but occur seductively. We expect the angry person not only to talk gruffly, scowl, and slam the door, but also to entertain fancies of doing all sorts of hostile things—most of which, of course, he cannot do and would not permit himself to do, even if he could.

Here, then, are seven different uses of the verb 'to feel'. I expect there are plenty more. I have, for instance, said nothing of feeling pleased, soothed, relieved, triumphant or exhilarated. But seven are enough. Consideration of them is liable to set up in us two opposing theoretical tendencies. To begin with, we have a strong craving to assimilate all the other uses to one of them. Perhaps in emulation of chemists, we hanker to reduce to a minimum the number of kinds of elements or constituents of which minds are made, and accordingly we hanker to make the word 'feeling' stand for a homogeneous something. Legends about the soul being tripartite foment (and sometimes derive from) this emulation.

We are like the child who cannot help supposing that all the MacTavishes in the world must belong to the family of MacTavishes who live next door. It is a family surname, isn't it? So it must be the name of a family. When subject to this craving, we are particularly liable to assimilate all the uses of 'feel' to its use in 'feel a pain or tickle'. Or sometimes we try to assimilate even feeling pains and tickles to that perceptual use in which we feel certain anatomically internal things like palpitations, cramps and creakings in the joints. But later, when we have attended to even a few of the grosser differences that there are between, for example, feeling for a box of matches and feeling that there is a flaw in an argument, or between feeling homesick and feeling a shooting pain in one's right eye, we tend to suppose that it is a chapter of sheer linguistic accidents that the one verb 'feel' is used in all these disparate ways; and that English would have been a better language if it had provided seven (or more) quite different verbs. Having realised that not all Mac-Tavishes need be members of the family next door, we incline to scout the idea that there might even be a common clan-origin for them, and to reproach Somerset House for permitting people from different families to have the same surname. In resistance to both of these two tendencies, I now want to suggest that though the seven cited uses of 'feel' are not members of one family, still they do have some traceable genealogical connections.

In discussing the perceptual use of 'feel', I pointed out that when I detect my teeth chattering, this detection need not take the form of seeing or hearing or feeling with finger, tongue or lips. That they are chattering might be perceived, to use the unnatural expressions, in or with the teeth themselves. With some anatomically internal things, this is even more conspicuous. If one of my joints creaks, neither you nor I may be able to hear or feel the creaking with our fingers. But I (unless anaesthetised) can do what you cannot; for I can feel it creaking in or with the joint itself. So I can perceive some things that you could not easily, if at all, perceive in any way, unless perhaps you had me on the operating table. For my knee joint is mine and not yours, so you cannot feel things in it, as I can do. Compare the following cases. When I frown slightly you are, usually, in a much better position than I for detecting it, since you can see it, while I cannot see it or, ordinarily, feel it. When my right fist clenches, you are in only a slightly worse position than I, for we can both see it, and we can both feel it, you with any of your fingers, and I with the fingers of my left hand. But besides this, I can also, unless numbed or recently hit on the right funny bone, feel it clenched in my right fist itself. But when my throat is constricted or my heart thumps you are in a very much worse position than I, for you can detect this only if you take rather elaborate steps; whereas I can detect it without taking any steps at all. So for some (not all) such facts about my body, you may find it highly convenient and sometimes quite necessary to ask me what I feel. We have here a sort of (graduatedly) privileged access to such things as palpitations of the heart, cramps, and creaks in the joints.

If a cobweb brushes my cheek, I may or may not detect it; but if I do detect it, I may detect it not by sight, but by feeling it in the cheek that is brushed. But, further, if a cobweb brushes my cheek, I may feel a tickle, and as we have seen, feeling or having a tickle is not the same sort of thing as distinctly or indistinctly perceiving something brushing my cheek. It would be just a poor joke to say that I have felt two things, namely something brushing my cheek, and also a tickle. I have a tickle, perhaps, *because* something lightly brushed my cheek; but this could be the case without my having detected anything brushing my cheek.

Now the place that I want to rub or scratch is the part of the cheek that the cobweb brushed; and the part of the cheek that the cobweb brushed, is, if I detected it in this way at all, the part of the cheek in which I felt it brushing me. In this sort of case I find where to scratch *pari passu* with finding where something brushed me; and this I may detect with the part of me that is brushed. The transition from saying 'I felt something brush my cheek' to saying 'I felt something tickling my cheek' and from there to 'I felt a tickle on my cheek' is an easy and natural one. But it certainly is a transition. The adverbs 'clearly' and 'distinctly' can qualify the verb in its first use, but not in its third use. The second use, 'I felt something tickling my cheek', is a bridge between the two.

What sort of a thing is a tickle?, or rather, What sort of a state of affairs am I reporting when I say that I have or feel a tickle? It is all right, but it gets us no further, to say that a tickle is a 'sensation'. It actually impedes progress if we recall what the standard theories tell us about sensations. Indeed what I want, among other things, to know is what we mean by this word 'sensation'.

Let us consider first the derivative use of 'tickled', in which to say that a person is or feels tickled is to say that he is amused. What is the connection between feeling tickled and laughing? Clearly it is not a necessary connection, since a person who feels tickled may repress his laughter, or be so weak in lungs or throat or so busy singing that he cannot laugh.

We might try to maintain that since feeling tickled involves wanting to laugh, we want to laugh in order to banish the tickle. Having the tickle is a cause or condition of wanting to laugh. But this certainly will not do. I do not first feel tickled and then decide that laughter would be a good remedy and then, if permitted, produce the remedial laughter. To feel tickled seems logically and not merely causally to involve having an impulse to laugh—or rather having an impulse to laugh when one must not laugh or cannot laugh or cannot laugh enough. To feel tickled either is or involves wanting to laugh, in the sense of 'want' in which a dog wants to scratch when prevented from doing so. It is not a cause of which wanting to laugh is an effect. Nor even is my laughing, if I do laugh, an effect of which my feeling tickled was the cause. For I *felt* tickled only because I could not or would not laugh. I was amused enough to laugh, but there was an obstruction to my laughing, or to my laughing enough. My feeling tickled was, more nearly, an effect of the existence of an impediment to laughing. It was amusement under duress.

To return now to the tickle that the cobweb gives me. Having or feeling the tickle, I have an impulse to scratch or rub the part of my cheek that was brushed by the cobweb. But feeling the tickle is surely not the cause of which the impulse to scratch is an effect. If I have an intolerable tickle, I have an irresistible impulse to scratch; but I am not the victim of *two* compulsions. I have elsewhere argued for the idea that a tickle just *is* a thwarted impulse to scratch, and that it is localised in my cheek, say, only in the sense that that is where I have an impulse to scratch myself. But I do not think now that this will do. The connection between having a tickle and wanting to scratch seems to me neither a cause-effect connection between events, nor a paraphrase-relation between expressions.

It will be noticed that, on very different levels, there is a close parallel between feeling a tickle and feeling like writing to *The Times*. Both are bound up with not-yet-satisfied inclinations to do certain things. The big difference is that the one is a primitive, unsophisticated or merely 'animal' inclination; the other is a sophisticated and acquired inclination. The former is localisable, the latter is not (save in the far-fetched sense that the indignant man's fingers may itch for the fountain-pen). It is easy to think of intermediate cases. Thirst, as the baby is thirsty, is quite unsophisticated. Thirst for a cup of hot, sweet tea demands more sophistication. The transition from feeling thirsty to feeling like drinking some hot, sweet tea and from this to feeling like going out for a country walk or feeling like writing to *The Times* seems to be a fairly smooth transition, though of course the gap between its terminals is very wide indeed. One way in which this

gap develops is worth mentioning. When I feel a very unsophisticated or purely 'animal' distress, like feeling a tickle or feeling leg-
weary, the things I have an impulse to do are very restricted. I have
an impulse *either* to scratch *or* to rub my cheek—and that is all. Or I
have an impulse *either* to dawdle *or* to sit down *or* to lie down—and
that is all. But when I feel like protesting about the unfair incidence
of Death Duties, either fountain-pen, or pencil or typewriter will do;
and such and such phrases will do either here or there; and I might
employ either this adjective or that adverb. Moreover there are other
papers than *The Times* and other ways of making protests than
writing to the papers.

In a word, the behaviour of a thirsty infant or a dog with a tickle is
easier to predict than that of an indignant, literate man; correspondingly, distresses of the primitive sort commonly have a local
seat; while the sophisticated distresses tend not to do so. Both rank
as feelings, but only the former are ordinarily called 'sensations'.

Of a battery of unsolved conceptual questions about sensations, I
want here to raise one. We say that a man with a parched throat, an
aching head, or an itching rash can, in certain circumstances, *forget*
his discomfort. A competing excitement may totally absorb him; or
by an effort of will he may concentrate his whole mind upon some
other matter. The more acute his discomfort, the less likely is he to
get or keep his mind on other things; his effort of will has to be the
more strenuous or the countervailing excitement has to be the
greater. It seems to be a tautology to say that, as his discomfort
approaches torture, the difficulty of distracting his mind from it
approaches impossibility.

Now if he does for a time forget his headache, should we say that
his headache has stopped? Or that it has continued, but been for a
time unfelt? Or that it has been felt all along, but has not for that
time distressed him?

We hardly want to say that the burning house across the road was
an anodyne—indeed if we did want to say this, we should not want
to say that it caused the man to 'forget' his pain. In this use of
'forget', we can only forget discomforts that are still there. Nor
could we well speak of the *difficulty* of distracting a person from his
itches, if we did not think that in some way the itches were in
competition with the jokes or anecdotes by which we try to distract
him. On the other hand we are reluctant to speak either of unfelt
pains, or of felt but unnoticed pains, or of pains being both felt and
noticed but (in this use) completely forgotten. So what ought we
to say?

I find it harder to suggest a natural transition from 'feeling a tickle' or 'feeling like taking a nap' to the use of 'feel' followed by an adjective of general condition, like 'unfit', 'uneasy' or 'cross'. For what one is said to feel, in this use, is something so generic and, as a rule, so non-momentary that it is in sharp contrast with, for instance, tickles which are highly specific, well localised, and exist only for well-defined and short periods. But I suppose the thing might develop in this way. First, there are some kinds of bodily distresses, which are not narrowly localisable or clockable. An ache has a spread, both lateral and in depth, that a prick or a scald has not, and one may have the sensation of exhaustion or chilliness all over and all through one's body. There need be no other answer to the question 'Where do you feel slack, shivery or sore?' than 'Everywhere'. Similarly, a lot of such sensations are more or less lingering. A shooting pain is felt at a moment and for a moment, but an ache or nausea is not like that. We should not call a short, sharp pain an 'ache'.

Next, having learned to talk and understand talk about feeling particular tickles, the child can generalise this, and speak of feeling tickles all over his body or of his keeping on feeling tickles in different places. He learns to use 'feel' in ways to which the questions When? and Where? are inappropriate, since 'here, there and everywhere' and 'most of the time' are already connoted by its generalised use. When he says 'I feel uncomfortable', he knows that this covers a lot of different momentary and lingering, pin-pointed and spread discomforts. He might begin by 'my head is too hot, and the sheets are rumpled and a moment ago my nose wanted blowing', but he would soon give up the idea of presenting an inventory. It was a matter of all sorts of discomforts crowding in on one another and overlapping one another ever since he went to bed.

From this sort of generalised reference to lots of particular felt distresses, it is not a difficult transition to generalised references to distresses of the unlocalisable because sophisticated kinds. There are quite enough analogies between feeling uncomfortable in bed yesterday evening and feeling uncomfortable during a conversation about the peccadilloes of one's friends, to make the use of 'feel' natural for both situations—even though in the latter situation one might be unable to specify any momentary or lingering, localisable or spread distresses that one had felt. Feeling irritated is, in lots of ways, like feeling irritations all over, even though it is unlike it in the one way that no itches or anything like itches need be felt when one feels irritated.

What, lastly, is to be said of the expression 'to feel that something is the case'? We speak of feeling strongly that there is a flaw in the argument, but not of feeling it acutely or of feeling it distinctly or of feeling it carefully. No sort of perception or perceptual exploration is suggested, nor any sort of tolerable or intolerable distress or even freedom from distress. We can, perhaps, suggest paraphrasing the expression by 'I am (or feel) strongly inclined to say that there is a flaw in the argument' and this reminds us of the expression 'to feel like doing so and so'. But 'I feel that there is a flaw in the argument' is not quite the same thing as 'I feel like saying that there is a flaw in it'. For one thing, if I feel like taking a nap, and do take it, then, to put it crudely, the situation is restored. I do not, ordinarily, then feel like taking another nap. But if I feel that there is a flaw in the argument, and come out with the flat assertion that there *is* a flaw there, the situation is not restored. So I was not just hankering to say something; and if I do just say that there is a flaw in the argument, I still continue merely to feel that there is a flaw in it. Just saying so does not satisfy me. So perhaps we should say that to feel that something is the case is to hanker not to *say* but to believe that it is the case. But now the difficulty is that believing that something is the case is not something that we can execute or, therefore, hanker to execute. A person can be ordered to say something, but not to believe it. (This is not because believing that something is the case is an insuperably difficult task, like jumping over the moon, but because there is no such task. It is not difficult or easy to believe things.) Nor can feeling that something is the case be equated with wanting to believe that it is the case, for I can feel that the international situation has not improved, though I should like to believe that it has improved. Feeling that something is the case is, in fact, not a sort of hankering at all. There is no question of it being relieved or gratified. It is more like being on a slope or having a momentum, nisus, or slide in a certain direction.

Part of the contrast between feeling that there is a flaw in your argument and thinking so seems to be this. If a person thinks so, then he can give some sort of an answer to the question why he thinks it, what sort of a flaw it is, and even perhaps whereabouts in the argument it is. But if he merely feels that it has a flaw, then of course he has no answer to such questions. He is just dissatisfied or reluctant or uneasy or suspicious. He cannot think what to say.

Most of us can never do better than feel that a joke was in bad taste, or that the shape of a Chinese bowl is exactly right. We have not got the vocabulary with which to answer questions; much less have we got the competence to make the right use of such a vocabulary. In other cases we possess the vocabulary and some of the requisite competence in using it, but have not yet mobilised it, or not adequately. At the moment I only feel that there is a flaw in your argument; but if you will hold your peace for a little while, I hope to be able to tell you, if not the flaw in the argument, at least some reason for thinking that it has one. My objections are not yet at the tip of my tongue, but they are moving in that direction. I can't yet think what to say, but it's coming.

I have said that to feel that there is something wrong is to be just dissatisfied, reluctant, uneasy, or suspicious. Now these adjectives belong to the class of adjectives of general condition. In some circumstances we should use these same adjectives in order to tell in what mood or frame of mind a person was. But here they are used in a special way for a special context; for they have what I may call 'propositional attachments'. It is one sort of thing to feel suspicious of a bridge; it is not quite the same sort of thing to feel suspicious of an argument. Reluctance to commit his weight to a bridge may characterise an elephant; reluctance to commit himself to the conclusion of an argument can characterise only an educated human being. It is, if you like, an attitude (blessed word!) not towards things in general (as depression is), nor towards a particular thing or person (as covetousness and indignation are), but towards intellectual articles such as theories, arguments, hypotheses and the like.

The transition from feeling satisfied or dissatisfied after a meal, to feeling satisfied or dissatisfied with one's treatment by the hotel servants, and from there to feeling satisfied or dissatisfied with a theory, a proof, or a piece of calculation, is, I think, though long, still a natural one, even though there is nothing corresponding to gnawing feelings in the stomach when one feels dissatisfied with, say, the Lamarckian theory of evolution.

To feel that something is the case is not the same as to feel sure that it is the case. Feeling sure is *not* feeling any qualms. Hence one can feel quite or perfectly sure, i.e. feel absolutely no qualms at all. But one feels strongly (or fairly strongly or not very strongly) that something is the case; and what has some strength may always not be strong enough. I may yet find out by examination that the argument is valid after all.

There exist in English the picturesque idioms 'I feel in my bones that so and so' and 'I feel in my heart of hearts that such and such'. These idioms suggest that when we speak of feeling that something is the case, we are, sometimes, influenced by the perceptual use of 'feel', and particularly by this use in connection with anatomically internal happenings and conditions. The analogy works, apparently, in two or three distinct ways. (*a*) What I detect when I feel my heart palpitating is something which you cannot detect in my way, and not easily or conveniently in any other way. My report is that of a solitary uncorroborated reporter. (*b*) But it is also a virtually incontrovertible report. My way of detecting the palpitations does not involve steps or apparatus or clues or indications. The palpitations are not diagnosed or inferred but felt—and that is good enough, because it is as good as anything could be. (*c*) But detection by feeling also has something unsatisfactory about it, namely that feeling is constitutionally imprecise—imprecise as judged by the standards officially set by sight. If, in the dark, I have to tell the time by feeling the hands of the clock with my fingers, I cannot determine the exact time, as I can when I can see the clock. And my position is much worse if I can feel the hands of the clock only with my elbow or my toes. Anatomically internal things, though detected, sometimes, with the highest reliability, are also detected with gross nebulousness. We cannot say in our ordinarily fairly precise terms what we detect by feeling, because what we detect in that way is itself incurably blurred. It is like trying to catch a jelly-fish on a fish-hook. Now when we report that we feel that so and so is the case, our reports are, in a somewhat similar way, also solitary, uncorroborated, incontrovertible, and too blurred to be made articulate. When I feel that there is something amiss with an argument, I do not yet *see* what is wrong with it. If I did see what was wrong with it, then of course I could say what was wrong with it, and if I could say this, then 'feel' would no longer be the verb to use. 'Feel' goes with 'can't quite say'. Note that it is not a case of something being too delicate to be caught by our gross linguistic tools, but of its being too amorphous to be caught by our over-delicate linguistic tools. (Sometimes we say that an argument *smells* bad or that a promise *rings* untrue. Smelling and hearing are also inferior ways of perceiving. They warn us vaguely of things which we would prefer to have a good look at if only we could.)

One further point. For a person to feel that there is something wrong with an argument, he must have heard or read the argument and understood or misunderstood it. An infant could not feel that there was a flaw in an argument or that the orator was being insincere. We need training to be capable of feeling that something is the case. But feeling that something is the case is not something that we execute or perform or accomplish. It is not a piece of trying (like considering), or an achievement (like finding or solving). Now some theorists who enjoy multiplying faculties, speak of Sense, Reason and Intuition as different faculties, and part of what they have in mind when they speak of Intuition is such facts as that husbands sometimes feel that their wives are worried, connoisseurs feel that the shape of a Chinese bowl is just right, and generals feel that the moment for the counter-attack has arrived.

The inarticulateness of such feelings is, of course, just what is wanted to set apart the elevated and inscrutable findings of Intuition from the mundane and scrutinisable findings of Reason. Now this sort of talk is obviously silly. But it is true that some people's 'noses' can be relied on in some sorts of matters, namely when they are intelligent people, with a good deal of practice in matters of this sort. The directions in which they are inclined to move, though they cannot say why, tend to turn out to have been the right directions. If a schoolgirl feels that 'Eclipse' will win the Derby, we should not be influenced; if a shepherd, of ripe years, feels that there will be a storm, we should take our raincoats with us; if a wife feels that her husband is out of sorts, he probably is, unless she is very newly married or very silly; and if the dealer feels that the picture is genuine, while the collector feels that it is a fake, we had better look up their records before taking sides.

Feeling, in this use, is not a magical way of getting the answers to questions, alternative to calculating, cross-examining, weighing pros and cons, and so on. It is not a way of getting answers at all. It is not something that can be done cautiously or recklessly, skilfully or clumsily, for it is not something that is done. None the less, the hunches of a person who is experienced and judicious in the right matters are generally, not always, the right hunches to ride. And if he and we did not ride hunches, we should never move at all; though equally, if we merely rode hunches without doing any careful work as well, we should seldom get to a destination and never get our hunches educated. In every move we make, theoretical, or practical (or aesthetic etc.), we are putting some trust in our 'noses'. What matters is whether our 'noses' have become or been made trust-worthy.

It is not even always requisite or desirable that a person should try to move on from feeling that something is the case to producing an articulate case for it being so. It is the business of the judge, but it is not the business of the members of the jury to give reasons for a verdict. Their business is to give the right verdict, not to satisfy a Court of Appeal that it was the right verdict to give. Nor, necessarily, should the general prepare himself to satisfy critics that he chose the right moment for the counter-attack. He might be a good general but a bad lecturer at the Staff College; there is no contradiction in saying that he had good reasons for ordering the counter-attack at that moment, though he could not then or subsequently tell himself or anyone else what they were. We are all pretty much in his position in the business of sizing up people's characters. Our goodness or badness at making such estimates need not and does not vary concomitantly with our goodness or badness at producing justifications for them.

It is a philosophical misfortune that, partly under the influence of tripartitionism, many theorists have assimilated 'feeling-that' to emotion, as though the possession of strategic flair or a cultivated taste in ceramics were akin to being a chronic worrier or being easily vexed or scared. The hapless artist seems to have suffered the worst from this muddle. He is sometimes alleged to be having some emotion or other (other than that of being thoroughly interested in his job) whenever he is doing his work; or at least to be in some unexplained way reviving or recalling some emotion that he has previously had. And if he is any good, then the effect of his work on those who listen to his music, read his stories, or look at his pictures or dining-room chairs, is that they too are induced to have this emotion. Which particular emotions these are, is usually left unspecified; presumably because we should only have to mention such emotions as boredom, jealousy, restlessness, irritation and hilarity in order to make the whole story sound as ridiculous as it is. (Nameless aesthetic emotions are sometimes called in at this point to save the theory's face.)

We do properly use the phrase 'feel that' in reporting exercises of taste, and we do properly use the verb 'feel' in reporting such things as agitations and tranquillities. But to say that a person feels that something is the case is not to give any answer at all to the questions 'How does he feel?' and 'In what mood is he?', though answers to these questions are often required to explain why judgements in matters of taste or elsewhere are perverted.

21

THE VERIFICATION PRINCIPLE

Reprinted, in English translation, from the original French in 'Revue Internationale de Philosophie', vol V, 1951, by permission of the editors

When, towards the close of the nineteenth century, Mach launched his campaign against metaphysics, he had, apparently, quite a limited objective. His purpose was not that of ridding philosophy of a nuisance or of putting philosophy on the secure path of a methodical discipline. His purpose was to rid science of an interloper. He seems to have found that, in many regions of physical, biological and psychological theory, doctrines were current and seriously regarded which claimed to settle some of the more general problems of the scientists, despite the fact that they had been thought out not in the laboratory but in the philosopher's study. Sometimes the philosopher was a philosophically corrupted scientist. In particular, it seems, many such *a priori* doctrines were presented as universal statements about things in nature, competing for general acceptance with certain statements of laws at which scientists had arrived by their *a posteriori* methods. In a word, the object of Mach's offensive was not philosophy but philosophy in the wrong place—philosophy pretending to decide general questions in physical, biological or psychological theory.

It would be an interesting problem for the historian of ideas to find out to what extent academic philosophers and philosophically minded scientists in the German-speaking world did actually try to dictate conclusions to the scientists, and to what extent such dictations were an actual menace or nuisance. We may conjecture, with some evidence to support us, that the prestige of philosophy in German and Austrian universities, and its general presence in the curricula even of scientific students did have a considerable and perhaps distorting influence upon scientific theorising—an influence to which, outside the special field of psychology, there were few parallels in the English-speaking academic world. There were here, certainly, challenges to the authority of the sciences from theologians and philosophers, like the attacks upon the geologists, the Darwinians and, more recently, upon Einstein. But these were pretty quickly laughed out of court. No War of Independence needed to be declared. In the German-speaking world, at least, the situation appears to have been, and still to be very different. There seem to have been good pedagogic reasons, as well as some nationalistic motives, for the vehemence of the Machians against philosophy in the wrong place. And contemporary academic philosophers in Germany continue blandly to ignore the rebellion, as if they had not learned that there is such a thing as philosophy in the wrong place, much less that they are in any danger of doing it.

When Mach condemned as 'pseudo-problems' certain sorts of metaphysicians' questions, he had in mind chiefly those questions their answers to which purported to be contributions to physical, biological or psychological theory, contributions which, mimicking the law-statements of science, made claim to hold good for things and happenings in this world. Save for making several strictures upon the Kantian notion of things-in-themselves, he did not concern himself much with metaphysical statements purporting to give news of particular existences or occurrences in another world. It was bogus laws of nature that he wished to exorcise from science; and it was with this end in view that he tried to work out an account of genuine laws of nature which would separate these from the bogus general hypotheses excogitated in the philosopher's armchair.

His own attempts to analyse the differences between genuine and sham scientific hypotheses were more vigorous than successful. He was inclined to burke the problem of induction by characterising a genuine hypothesis as a merely economical compendium, summary or résumé of observed matters of fact, though he realised that, somehow, it also possessed the important power to generate predictions of matters of fact not yet observed. He tended to stress the brevity at the expense of the fertility of scientific formulae. By contrast, the sham law-statements of the metaphysician are neither inventories of observations made, since he makes none, nor yet founts of predictions of observations still to be made, since he will make none. Such sham law-statements are factually vacant, for all that they purport to cover all the facts. They result from no investments and they yield no dividends. Mach saw that there was some intrinsic or logical connection between genuine statements of laws (or hypotheses) and statements of particular matters of fact, such that, lacking this connection, a general statement was not merely a false hypothesis, but a sham one. But his own account of this connection was wrong. It ruled out, certainly, the sham law-statements of the meddling philosopher; but it also, by implication, ruled out the genuine universal statements or laws of the scientist.

Study of *Principia Mathematica*, the *Tractatus Logico-Philosophicus*, Keynes' *Treatise on Probability* and kindred works in formal and inductive logic encouraged the members of the Vienna Circle to strengthen their master's logically naïve discrimination between genuine and sham hypotheses. In particular, Russell's distinction between the true-or-false, on the one side, and the meaningless or nonsensical, on the other, was used to rigorise Mach's notions of 'pseudo-problem' and 'meaningless question'. General propositions were (in the early days) construed as truth-functions (*not* epitomes) of atomic propositions. Laws (or hypotheses) were, not quite consistently with this, held to be true-or-false if and only if the facts predicted in accordance with them were-or-were-not as predicted. A law-statement was significant if it could conceivably be (no matter whether it actually was) borne out by observation of the appropriate facts. A would-be law-statement for which no programme of verification or falsification could be suggested, was senseless. So metaphysicians' general hypotheses were senseless, and senseless hypotheses were metaphysical.

Mach's limited requirements would, perhaps, have been satisfied by a principle which accorded or refused significance to an ostensible law-statement according as it met or failed to meet this criterion of inductive verifiability or falsifiability. For he was not interested in the credentials of singular statements, most general statements, of ethical, political, aesthetic, legal or religious statements; or in the credentials of most questions or any commands, requests, verdicts or promises. He was interested only or chiefly in the credentials of the would-be scientific universal statements that we call 'laws' or 'hypotheses'. But the members of the Vienna Circle were more ambitious. They wanted to win not a local campaign but a many-fronted war. They wanted to prove not only that certain ostensible law-statements, fathered by philosophers on to particular scientific theories, were meaningless; but that all metaphysical assertions were meaningless and even that all non-scientific utterances were metaphysical. They generalised what was nearly (though not quite) the right thing to say about the connections between law-statements and statements of observational fact into a general criterion of significance. In the epigram 'the meaning of a proposition is the method of its verification', the word 'proposition' was made to cover not just statements of natural law but statements of every kind.

This generalisation felt all the more natural because of an ambiguity in the word 'hypothesis'. 'Hypothesis' is sometimes used to denote any true or false law-statement, i.e. any variable hypothetical statement of the pattern 'Whenever . . ., then . . .'. But it is also sometimes used to denote any conjectural statement whatsoever. The statement 'my neighbour is in pain' would not be a hypothesis in the former use; it would be a hypothesis in the latter. Moreover, at least on some theories of induction, all law-statements are eternally condemned to some degree of conjecturalness. So it was linguistically easy to assimilate the description of the theoretical work promised by an ostensible law-statement to the description of the procedures of settling conjectures, and then, in reverse, to assimilate all the procedures of settling conjectures to the special procedures of inductively establishing or refuting conjectural law-statements.

The notions of verification and falsification are naturally attached very closely to the notion of conjecture. Only conjectures need to be or can be verified or falsified. Established truths, whether particular or general, need no further verification and are not open to falsification. Established falsehoods need no further falsification and are not open to verification. Questions, commands, rebukes, promises and prayers need neither and are open to neither. Moreover the framing and testing of conjectural law-statements is not indeed the whole, but the cardinal part of scientific research. Observations ancillary to no hypotheses are as unrewarding as hypotheses admitting of no observational tests. (Both may in fact, in their different ways, be suggestive, but it is accidental, and therefore exceptional, if they turn out to be so.) Scientific discussions are, in consequence, rich in considerations of what does or might verify or falsify still conjectural hypotheses.

But this fact that scientific discussions are and ought to be full of considerations of what does or might verify or falsify still conjectural hypotheses does not quite justify the epigram that the meaning of a proposition is the method of its verification, even when this is given a restricted application to ostensible law-statements. Or perhaps we might say that it justifies the epigram but does not justify the definition into which it was beatified. To say of a statement that what it tells us is how we should establish whether what it tells us is true or false leaves the 'it' suspended. On the other hand there certainly is an intrinsic connection between a law-statement and the less general or particular statements which it licenses us to infer from other less general or particular statements established by observation. There is no such thing as learning a conjuring-trick while remaining ignorant of how to perform the trick on particular occasions. There is no such thing as learning the rules of the road while remaining ignorant of what to do in particular traffic-junctures (save in the sense that one can learn the words by heart without understanding them). Nor is there any such thing as discovering or mastering a general hypothesis, while remaining incapable of inferring particular conclusions—which may or may not be in the future tense—from premisses satisfying the protasis of the law and found out, directly or indirectly, by observation. An ostensible law-statement which we cannot conceive how to apply in any concrete inferences is indeed a sham hypothesis.

But this point needs to be hedged with some precautions. First, it is not true to say, what is sometimes said, that a law-statement is itself a prediction or a budget of predictions. It itself reports no particular matters of fact, and therefore provides no premisses from which particular matters of fact can be inferred. It authorises us to move from certain sorts of factual statements, *if and when we get them*, to others. Laws of heredity do not tell us who has had or who will have haemophilia. Nor does inventing or mastering a recipe for a cake give us either the ingredients of any cakes or any cakes.

Next, though entertaining a hypothesis temporally precedes the making of some of the concrete inferences by whose fate we test the virtues of the hypothesis, it does not follow that all these inferences are predictions, inferences, that is, to states of affairs obtaining at dates later than those of the states of affairs from which we infer them. The dermatologist may infer a wound from a scar, or a scar from a wound, or streptococci from a swelling. Successful predictions are dramatically satisfactory, since their makers could not possibly have cheated. But that is all.

Third, and most important, while it is certainly true that we test hypotheses by taking account of the fate of the concrete inferences which we make in accordance with them, it is not true that we make inferences in accordance with them solely in order to test them. We test a recipe by seeing whether cakes made in accordance with it are good or bad, but this is not the whole point of the recipe. The normal reason for following a recipe is that we want to have cakes to eat. Not all cooking is experimenting. We could say that understanding a recipe is knowing how to make cakes of a certain sort; we could not say that understanding a recipe is knowing how to tell from the cakes made according to it whether it is a good or bad recipe—though this is, of course, the way to find out whether it is a good or bad recipe. Similarly we could say that understanding a law-statement is knowing what concrete inferences to draw from certain concrete premises, but not that it is knowing how to tell from the fates of such inferences whether the statement is true or false—though, again, this is, of course, the way to test the statement.

Perhaps, then, we should correct the epigram and say that the meaning of a law-statement is the method of its application, i.e. the pattern of the concrete inferences that it authorises. This would un-tether the epigram from its restrictive connection with the special experimental purpose of testing the hypothesis, without affecting the important truths that conjectural law-statements do indeed require to be tested and that the way of testing them is to notice the fate of some of their applications in concrete inferences. In this revised form, the slogan would say no more than that understanding a law-statement is knowing what concrete inferences could be made from certain premises; i.e. that an ostensible law-statement tells us nothing, and so is not a true or false law-statement, unless it tells, truly or falsely, what concrete inferences may be made from certain premises. This would provide what Mach wanted, without playing havoc with all sorts of other statements which do not function as inference-licences. It would conserve the required intrinsic con-nection between law-statements and statements of observable matters of fact, since these are just the premises and the conclusions of the concrete inferences which the law-statement licenses. But would it be subject to the charge of the suspended 'it' which holds against the epigram in its original form?

Compare the three following assertions. (1) 'What a cake-recipe tells us is what to do in the kitchen in order to find out whether it is a good or a bad recipe.' (2) 'What a cake-recipe tells us is what to do in the kitchen in order to make cakes of a certain sort.' (3) 'To find out whether a cake-recipe is a good or a bad one, it is necessary to make some cakes according to the recipe and see if they are palatable and digestible.' The second and third assertions are obvious truths. The first, having the suspended 'it', is patently unsatisfactory, for all that it has much of the ring of the obviously true third assertion. This third assertion is derivative from the second, in the sense that a person who failed to grasp what a recipe tells him to do in the kitchen is disqualified from making the investigation prescribed in the third assertion.

The reason why the first assertion, with the suspended 'it', is unsatisfactory is that it purports to say that what an utterance of a certain sort, namely a recipe, tells us is the way to find out whether what it tells us is acceptable or unacceptable—and this is just a variant of 'The Liar'.

The needle's eye of the generalised Verification Principle was so narrow that it excluded not only a few Teutonic camels, but nearly all domestic animals as well. But we must not be ungrateful to it. The question 'What sort of evidence or reasons, if any, would establish or refute an assertion of this or that sort?' has proved to be a philosophically fertile question—fertile, not because it has done what was intended, namely, segregated just one class of legitimate statements from a huge congeries of illegitimate statements; but because it has done what was not intended, namely, brought out a great variety of differences between lots of classes of legitimate utterances. What was bought as a lens has worked as a prism. It has helped to reveal the important fact that we talk sense in lots of different ways, and we can talk nonsense in lots of different ways. And if this discovery has made us forget the sham contributions to scientific theories made by some trespassing metaphysicians, perhaps this does not matter very greatly. In the English-speaking world the scientists do not read such contributions at all; and the philosophers not conspicuously much. The miscreants who threaten Princess Science do not seem to be very burly or strenuous ruffians; nor does that undistressed lady herself betray much anxiety for the services volunteered by her Don Quixotes. But certainly it is wise to be on the look-out for ruffians—if only because it reminds us not to let ruffianly traits develop in ourselves.

22

THINKING

Reprinted from 'Acta Psychologica', vol IX, 1953, by permission of North-Holland Publishing Company

I want to ask two questions. The first question is Why has so little emerged from the painstaking investigations of psychologists in the theory of thinking? The second question, which undercuts the first, is What have these investigators supposed that they were looking for?

(1) Consideration of the problems tackled, e.g., by the Würzburg School and its successors makes a philosopher like myself feel qualms of professional guilt. Again and again we find psychologists trying to observe, measure and describe just those ingredients or basic components of thinking operations which logicians and epistemologists have solemnly assured them must, on *a priori* grounds, be there. For example, some of our philosophical great-grandfathers declared that thoughts consist of ideas, variously originated and variously concocted. These ideas were then identified (since nothing else could be found with which to identify them), with mental images. Dutifully the experimental psychologists began to enquire how these ideas or images constitute thinking, or, when doubts arose, what their roles in thinking are if they do not entirely constitute it, and what other ingredients can be detected filling in the gaps.

Our philosophical grandfathers, for excellent philosophical reasons, switched the brunt of their reflections from terms to propositions, from ideas to judgements; and dutifully the experimental psychologists laboured to observe, measure and describe the mental acts or processes of judging. Logicians and epistemologists have debated the notions of abstraction and generalisation; and the researchers dutifully set to work to isolate, under laboratory conditions, these officially sponsored acts or processes of abstracting and generalising. The unpalatable truth is that we philosophers have told epistemological fables, and the experimental psychologist has dutifully essayed the natural history of our fabulous monsters. What seems to have happened is this. The logicians and epistemologists were in fact trying to give functional descriptions of the various kinds of elements into which constructed theories were analysable. Their eyes were on the terms, the connectives, the phrases, the propositions and the arguments of which published theories consist. But the descriptive apparatus that they employed for this end was, for some 300 years, a predominantly Cartesian or Lockean apparatus. They were trying to describe the functions of bits of theoretical discourse; but their descriptions were couched as narratives of introspectible mental processes. Thus they decoyed the experimental psychologists into the profitless enterprise of trying to provide systematised information about these mythical introspectibles—or, later on, the equally mythical unintrospectibles.

(2) An odd feature of the situation is this. Naturally the psychologist knows as well as the schoolboy knows, what thinking is. He couldn't *not* know, any more than the footballer couldn't *not* know what football is. He has practised it all his life, he got a lot of training in it at school, he has taught and examined other people, he has communicated his thoughts and followed the thoughts of others. He knows what it is like to be stumped, befogged, weary, puzzled and successful; what it is like to keep or lose the thread, to go round in circles, to give problems a rest and so on and so on. What, then, does he *not* know that he still wants to find out? For example, Watt and his subjects knew, before the experiments began, that trying to think out the answer to a question is not of a piece with saying 'Tweedledee' after someone else has said 'Tweedledum'. For saying 'Tweedledee' in this way is not giving the answer to a question; nor does saying it issue from wondering what is the right thing to say. In short, association is notoriously not pondering, just as slithering is notoriously not marching. Yet a long series of patient experiments was supposed to be required to show that thinking cannot be dissected into associations.

Again some experimentalists claim to have established on a firm experimental basis the generalisation that thinking is intimately connected with tasks or problems. But how did they conduct their experiments? By setting to their subjects tasks or problems which the experimenters already knew could be solved by thinking and could not be answered without thinking. It is as if someone should claim to have established inductively that footballers try to score goals, and to have established this by getting them to play some games of football. If they did not know what football was, how could they set their subjects to engage in specimen games of it? It should be noticed that these experimentalists took care not to ask their subjects to tell how many chimney-pots there are in London, or whether Shakespeare ever had mumps. They and their subjects were too well aware that such questions cannot be answered just by thinking. They did not discover the problem-solving nature of thinking by experimental questioning; they selected soluble questions for their subjects because they already knew that trying to solve such problems is thinking. To put it over crudely, it is a fact not of psychology but of grammar that the verbs 'wonder' and 'consider' are followed by indirect questions. Why then pretend to have to establish it experimentally—and by a method of interrogation which shows that it was known from the start anyway? Why confuse conceptual with empirical questions?

(3) I think that part, but only part of the tendency of logicians and epistemologists, and, after them, of psychologists to assume that there must exist some isolable and describable ingredients of thinking comes from this origin. If you ask me of what basic movements rowing or jumping consists, I can give you the answer, or at least I know how to find out the right answer to give. It is natural to suppose, then, that 'thinking' stands also for a specific process or activity, composed in various ways out of some common, recurrent, elements. Such a supposition is encouraged by the age-old dogma that our mental life is subdivided into three distinguishable strands or strata, Cognition, Conation and Feeling. This tripartite dogma itself suggests analogies from Chemistry. But if I asked you to tell me the basic elements of which *working* consists, or of which *gardening* consists, or of which *housekeeping* consists, you would be quick to see the trap I was laying for you. You would say, quite rightly, that words like 'gardening', 'working' and 'housekeeping' cover a great number of widely different things. Two men may both spend their leisure hours in gardening without one of them doing any of the things that the other does. Conversely, the professional footballer at work does a great number of things very similar to things done by the amateur footballer who is not working but playing. There are no ingredient activities common and peculiar to gardening or to working—or to thinking.

Now if someone was under the impression that there did exist some such ingredient activities common and peculiar to gardening or working, he would be forced to allow that they were extremely difficult to isolate. I suggest that part of the difficulty that the experimental psychologists have had in isolating any ingredient acts or

states common and peculiar to thinking is just this same difficulty—
that of isolating something which is not there to isolate.

Let us just briefly notice a very few of the many different things
that we class as thinking. I am thinking if I am going over in my head
the courses that I had at last night's banquet. Here there is no
problem to solve, no decision to reach. I am thinking, but I am not
trying to think anything out. It is more like reverie than like excogitation. On the other hand, if I am doing a piece of multiplication, I
am trying to think something out. Yet here there is no room for
inventiveness, cleverness or inspiration. There is just a piece of drill,
which I can get right or else bungle, and which I can do swiftly and
easily or only slowly and laboriously. I am not in any degree puzzled
or befogged, and I know all the time exactly what I have got to do
and how to do it. There is here no struggling for the right word or
phrase, no question of trying to capture the half-formed thought, no
place for the bright idea, no room for flair. Compare with this my
thinking when trying to translate a Latin poem into an English one.
Here there is no question of trying to excogitate an unknown truth.
I have a task, but no question, and the solution of my task, if I get it,
is not a proposition but an English poem. My problem is how most
faithfully and effectively to say something, when I already know, in
Latin, what it is that I want to say in English. Here there is plenty of
room for inventiveness, inspiration, and flair but little or no room
for anything like ratiocination. There is no passage from premisses to
conclusion. Suppose, lastly, that yesterday I was set a complicated
puzzle, and either thought out the answer or was given it by someone
else. Today I go over the solution in my head, moving along the
steps which lead to the answer. Here I have no live problem, for I
got the answer yesterday. I am not even unsure of the steps. I made
sure of them yesterday. But I am attentively re-tracing an argument,
in somewhat the same way as I may go over in my head the courses
at yesterday's banquet. Am I thinking or not? Of course, I am thinking, just as I am walking, though not exploring, if I repeat today a
walk that I took for the first time yesterday.

We see then that the word 'thinking' covers some activities which
are attempts to reach the answers to questions, as well as others
which are not; some activities in which there is scope for originality
and insight, as well as others where there is not; some activities
which incorporate ratiocination, as well as others which do not;
some activities, like multiplication and translation, which require
special training, as well as others, like reverie, which do not. To look
for some common and peculiar ingredients of all thinking is like

looking for an ingredient common and peculiar to cat's-cradle, hide-and-seek, billiards, snap and all the other things which we call 'games'.

(4) But now for a point of quite a different sort. People breathe, digest, and grow arthritic, however little or much they know about respiration, digestion and arthritis. But people do not play cricket without knowing a lot about cricket—and this is not because they first find themselves playing cricket and then start investigating what they are doing. To play cricket is to do a variety of things all of which one has to learn to do. Cricket is a complex of knacks and techniques, or of drills and skills. It is a truism that a man cannot play cricket who does not know how to play cricket, and what he knows is all that cricketing consists of. There are no hidden ingredients of cricket, though there are all sorts of inevitable and fortuitous concomitants of playing cricket, like panting and perspiring.

Now some, but not all of the things that come under the heading of 'thinking' are in partly the same way complexes of drills and skills. I once had to learn the drills of multiplication and division, and without this training I would not have been even an inefficient multiplier or divider. I should not have multiplied or divided at all. Again, I had to learn how to translate from English into Latin and Greek, and from Latin and Greek into English. This schooling imposed a lot of sheer drills upon me, but it also developed some skills as well.

Consequently the thinking which I do in multiplying and translating is something which I could not conceivably do without having learned and not forgotten how to do it. I cannot *not* know the knacks, drills and techniques of the computing and translating that I do (though it does not follow that I am as competent to tell other people what they are as my schoolmasters had to be). Knowing these is knowing what computing and translating consist of. There are no further, concealed ingredients to look for. In some sorts of thinking, like philosophising and composing, the place of drills, wrinkles and prescribable techniques is much smaller than in computation and translation. To teach a student to philosophise, one cannot do much save philosophise with him. The notion of a welltrained philosopher or poet has something ludicrous in it. But philosophising and composing are largely without prescribable techniques not because, like panting, perspiring and digesting, they go on so automatically as to be below the level even of being easy; but because to be successful in them is to advance ahead of all the beaten tracks. They require not manuals but practice, stimulation, hard work and flair. There are, patently, lots of kinds of thinking which have something but not everything in common with computing, something else in common with composing, something else in common with philosophising and so on and so on. The judge may have a very complex problem to solve involving interpretation of law, elucidation of technicalities, unravelling skeins of variegated testimony, and keeping the essentials of the issue steadily before the jury. He may be varyingly good or bad at each of these (and lots of other) more or less dissimilar kinds of thinking. But he is occupied in all of them at once. Similarly the bridge-player's ponderings are, as the snap-player's are not, an amalgam of highly diverse kinds of considering, at some of which he may be relatively good while he is relatively bad at others. I daresay most of the stretches of thinking which occupy us are mixtures in this general way.

The point is this. To put it for the moment much too bluntly, thinking is an art, like cricket, and not just a natural process, like digesting. Or, to put it less bluntly, the word 'thinking' covers a wide variety of things, some, but not all of which embody, in differing degrees and respects, such things as drills, acquired knacks, techniques and flairs. It is just in so far as they do embody such things that we can describe someone's thinking as careless or careful, strenuous or lazy, rigorous or loose, efficient or inefficient, wooden or elastic, successful or unsuccessful. Epithets like these belong to the vocabularies of coaches and umpires, and are inapplicable to such natural processes as digesting. We cannot be clever or stupid at digesting, nor yet conservative or independent. (It would be interesting to consider how far epistemologists and psychologists have, unwittingly, yearned to describe thought after the model of digestion.)

Notice that I am not saying that stretches of thinking and games of cricket are not processes. Of course they are. Nor am I saying that thinking and cricketing are unnatural, in any frightening sense of the word. It is quite natural for people to multiply, translate, and theorise, just as it is quite natural for them to play cricket. All that I am saying is, that people, like dogs and lizards can digest without knowing anything about digestion; they can digest whether awake or asleep, infantile or adult, lunatic or sane; but multiplying, translating and theorising, like cricket, have to be learned, and practised; people have to acquire a liking for doing them, and to attend to what they are doing when doing them. To be able to do them is to know what they consist of. Notice, too, that not all the things we class as thinking are subject to the epithets of coaches or umpires. A man in a daydream is thinking, but he is not daydreaming hard, efficiently, rigorously or successfully; nor yet is he daydreaming inefficiently, loosely, carelessly or unsuccessfully. He is not navigating well or badly; he is just drifting.

Notice, lastly, that I am not arguing that there is nothing in thinking that needs to be explored by psychological and physiological methods. The researches of Galton, Henry Head, Freud and Sherrington have led to new knowledge and will lead to more. It is the search for some ingredients or mechanism, whether introspectible or unconscious, common and peculiar to all that goes by the name of 'thinking' which seems to me to be a search for a will-o'-the-wisp. My conclusion is that the experimental investigation of thinking has been, on the whole, unproductive, because the researchers have had confused or erroneous notions of what they were looking for. Their notions of what they were looking for were confused or erroneous partly because they were borrowed from the official philosophical doctrines of the day. They were the heirs of conceptual disorders. To get the conceptual disorders out of one's system what is needed is not hard experimental work but hard conceptual work.

23

ORDINARY LANGUAGE

Reprinted from 'The Philosophical Review', vol. LXII, *1953, by permission of the editors*

Philosophers' arguments have frequently turned on references to what we do and do not say or, more strongly, on what we can and cannot say. Such arguments are present in the writings of Plato and are common in those of Aristotle.

In recent years, some philosophers, having become feverishly exercised about the nature and methodology of their calling, have made much of arguments of this kind. Other philosophers have repudiated them. Their disputes on the merits of these arguments have not been edifying, since both sides have been apt to garble the question. I want to ungarble it.

'ORDINARY'

There is one phrase which recurs in this dispute, the phrase 'the use of ordinary language'. It is often, quite erroneously, taken to be paraphrased by 'ordinary linguistic usage'. Some of the partisans assert that all philosophical questions are questions about the use of ordinary language, or that all philosophical questions are solved or are about to be solved by considering ordinary linguistic usage.

Postponing the examination of the notion of *linguistic usage*, I want to begin by contrasting the phrase 'the use of ordinary language' with the similar-seeming but totally different phrase 'the ordinary use of the expression "..."'. When people speak of the use of ordinary language, the word 'ordinary' is in implicit or explicit contrast with 'out-of-the-way', 'esoteric', 'technical', 'poetical', 'notational' or, sometimes, 'archaic'. 'Ordinary' means 'common', 'current', 'colloquial', 'vernacular', 'natural', 'prosaic', 'non-notational', 'on the tongue of Everyman', and is usually in contrast with dictions which only a few people know how to use, such as the technical terms or artificial symbolisms of lawyers, theologians, economists, philosophers, cartographers, mathematicians, symbolic

logicians and players of Royal Tennis. There is no sharp boundary
between 'common' and 'uncommon', 'technical' and 'untechnical'
or 'old-fashioned' and 'current'. Is 'carburettor' a word in common
use or only in rather uncommon use? Is 'purl' on the lips of Everyman, or on the lips only of Everywoman? What of 'manslaughter',
'inflation', 'quotient' and 'off-side'? On the other hand, no one
would hesitate on which side of this no-man's-land to locate 'iso-
tope' or 'bread', 'material implication' or 'if', 'transfinite cardinal'
or 'eleven', 'ween' or 'suppose'. The edges of 'ordinary' are blurred,
but usually we are in no doubt whether a diction does or does not
belong to ordinary parlance.

But in the other phrase, 'the ordinary use of the expression
"..."', 'ordinary' is not in contrast with 'esoteric', 'archaic' or
'specialist', etc. It is in contrast with 'non-stock' or 'non-standard'.
We can contrast the stock or standard use of a fish-knife or sphygmomanometer with some non-regulation use of it. The stock use
of a fish-knife is to cut up fish with; but it might be used for cutting
seed-potatoes or as a heliograph. A sphygmomanometer might, for
all I know, be used for checking tyre pressures; but this is not its
standard use. Whether an implement or instrument is a common
or a specialist one, there remains the distinction between its stock
use and non-stock uses of it. If a term is a highly technical term, or
a non-technical term, there remains the distinction between its stock
use and non-stock uses of it. If a term is a highly technical term,
most people will not know its stock use or, *a fortiori*, any non stock
uses of it either, if it has any. If it is a vernacular term, then nearly
everyone will know its stock use, and most people will also know
some non-stock uses of it, if it has any. There are lots of words,
like 'of', 'have' and 'object', which have no one stock use, any more
than string, paper, brass and pocket-knives have just one stock use.
Lots of words have not got any non-stock uses. 'Sixteen' has, I
think, none; nor has 'daffodil'. Nor, maybe, have collar-studs. Non-
stock uses of a word are, e.g., metaphorical, hyperbolical, poetical,
stretched and deliberately restricted uses of it. Besides contrasting
the stock use with certain non-stock uses, we often want to contrast
the stock use of an expression with certain alleged, suggested, or
recommended uses of it. This is a contrast not between the regular
use and irregular uses, but between the regular use and what the
regular use is alleged to be or what it is recommended that it should
be.

When we speak of the ordinary or stock use of a word we need
not be characterising it in any further way, e.g., applauding or

recommending it or giving it any testimonial. We need not be appealing to or basing anything on its stock-ness. The words 'ordinary', 'standard' and 'stock' can serve merely to refer to a use, without describing it. They are philosophically colourless and can be easily dispensed with. When we speak of the regular night-watchman, we are merely indicating the night-watchman whom we know independently to be the one usually on the job; we are not yet giving any information about him or paying any tribute to his regularity. When we speak of the standard spelling of a word or the standard gauge of British railway tracks, we are not describing or recommending or countenancing this spelling or this gauge; we are giving a reference to it which we expect out hearers to get without hesitation. Sometimes, naturally, this indication does not work. Sometimes the stock use in one place is different from its stock use in another, as with 'suspenders'. Sometimes, its stock use at one period differs from its stock use at another, as with 'nice'. A dispute about which of two or five uses is the stock use is not a philosophical dispute about any one of those uses. It is therefore philosophically uninteresting, though settlement of it is sometimes requisite for communication between philosophers.

If I want to talk about a non-stock use of a word or fish-knife, it is not enough to try to refer to it by the phrase 'the non-stock use of it', for there may be any number of such non-stock uses. To call my hearer's attention to a particular non-stock use of it, I have to give some description of it, for example, to cite a special context in which the word is known to be used in a non-stock way.

This, though always possible, is not often necessary for the stock use of an expression, although in philosophical debates one is sometimes required to do it, since one's fellow-philosophers are at such pains to pretend that they cannot think what its stock use is—a difficulty which, of course, they forget all about when they are teaching children or foreigners how to use it, and when they are consulting dictionaries.

It is easy now to see that learning or teaching the ordinary or stock use of an expression need not be, though it may be, learning or teaching the use of an ordinary or vernacular expression, just as learning or teaching the standard use of an instrument need not be, though it can be, learning or teaching the use of a household utensil. Most words and instruments, whether out-of-the-way or common, have their stock uses and may or may not also have non-stock uses as well.

A philosopher who maintained that certain philosophical questions are questions about the ordinary or stock uses of certain expressions would not therefore be committing himself to the view that they are questions about the uses of ordinary or colloquial expressions. He could admit that the noun 'infinitesimals' is not on the lips of Everyman and still maintain that Berkeley was examining the ordinary or stock use of 'infinitesimals', namely the standard way, if not the only way, in which this word was employed by mathematical specialists. Berkeley was not examining the use of a colloquial word; he was examining the regular or standard use of a relatively esoteric word. We are not contradicting ourselves if we say that he was examining the ordinary use of an unordinary expression.

Clearly a lot of philosophical discussions are of this type. In the philosophy of law, biology, physics, mathematics, formal logic, theology, psychology and grammar, technical concepts have to be examined, and these concepts are what are expressed by more or less recherché dictions. Doubtless this examination embodies attempts to elucidate in untechnical terms the technical terms of this or that specialist theory, but this very attempt involves discussing the ordinary or stock uses of these technical terms.

Doubtless, too, study by philosophers of the stock uses of expressions which we all employ has a certain primacy over their study of the stock uses of expressions which only, e.g., scientific or legal specialists employ. These specialists explain to novices the stock uses of their terms of art partly by talking to them in non-esoteric terms; they do not also have to explain to them the stock uses of these non-esoteric terms. Untechnical terminology is, in this way, basic to technical terminologies. Hard cash has this sort of primacy over cheques and bills of exchange—as well as the same inconveniences when large and complex transactions are afoot.

Doubtless, finally, some of the cardinal problems of philosophy are set by the existence of logical tangles not in this as opposed to that branch of specialist theory, but in the thought and the discourse of everyone, specialists and non-specialists alike. The concepts of *cause, evidence, knowledge, mistake, ought, can,* etc. are not the perquisites of any particular groups of people. We employ them before we begin to develop or follow specialist theories; and we could not follow or develop such theories unless we could already employ these concepts. They belong to the rudiments of all thinking, including specialist thinking. But it does not follow from this that all philosophical questions are questions about such rudimentary concepts. The architect must indeed be careful about the materials of his building; but it is not only about these that he must be careful.

'USE'

But now for a further point. The phrase 'the ordinary (i.e. stock) use of the expression "..."' is often so spoken that the stress is made to fall on the word 'expression' or else on the word 'ordinary' and the word 'use' is slurred over. The reverse ought to be the case. The operative word is '*use*'.

Hume's question was not about the word 'cause'; it was about the *use* of 'cause'. It was just as much about the *use* of 'Ursache'. For the use of 'cause' is the same as the use of 'Ursache', though 'cause' is not the same word as 'Ursache'. Hume's question was not a question about a bit of the English language in any way in which it was not a question about a bit of the German language. The job done with the English word 'cause' is not an English job, or a continental job. What I do with my Nottingham-made boots— namely walk in them—is not Nottingham-made; but nor is it Leicester-made or Derby-made. The transactions I perform with a sixpenny-bit have neither milled nor unmilled edges; they have no edges at all. We might discuss what I can and cannot do with a sixpenny-bit, namely what I can and cannot buy with it, what change I should and should not give or take for it, and so on; but such a discussion would not be a discussion about the date, ingredients, shape, colour or provenance of the coin. It is a discussion about the purchasing power of this coin, or of any other coin of the same value, and not about *this coin*. It is not a numismatic discussion, but a commercial or financial discussion. Putting the stress on the word 'use' helps to bring out the important fact that the enquiry is an enquiry not into the other features or properties of the word or coin or pair of boots, but only into what is done with it, or with anything else with which we do the same thing. That is why it is so misleading to classify philosophical questions as linguistic questions—or as non-linguistic questions.

It is, I think, only in fairly recent years that philosophers have picked up the trick of talking about the use of expressions, and even made a virtue of so talking. Our forefathers, at one time, talked instead of the *concepts* or *ideas* corresponding to expressions. This was in many ways a very convenient idiom, and one which in most situations we do well to retain. It had the drawback, though, that it encouraged people to start Platonic or Lockean hares about the status and provenance of these concepts or ideas. The impression was given that a philosopher who wanted to discuss, say, the concept of *cause* or *infinitesimal* or *remorse* was under some obligation to start by deciding whether concepts have a supra-mundane or only a psychological existence; whether they are transcendent intuitables or only private introspectibles.

Later on, when philosophers were in revolt against psychologism in logic, there was a vogue for another idiom, the idiom of talking about the *meanings* of expressions, and the phrase 'the concept of cause' was replaced by the phrase 'the meaning of the word "cause" or of any other with the same meaning'. This new idiom was also subject to anti-Platonic and anti-Lockean cavils; but its biggest drawback was a different one. Philosophers and logicians were at that time the victims of a special and erroneous theory about meaning. They construed the verb 'to mean' as standing for a relation between an expression and some other entity. The meaning of an expression was taken to be an entity which had that expression for its name. So studying the meaning of the phrase 'the solar system' was supposed or half-supposed to be the same thing as studying the solar system. It was partly in reaction against this erroneous view that philosophers came to prefer the idiom 'the use of the expressions ". . . caused . . ." and ". . . the solar system"'. We are accustomed to talking of the use of safety-pins, banisters, table-knives, badges and gestures; and this familar idiom neither connotes nor seems to connote any queer relations to any queer entities. It draws our attention to the teachable procedures and techniques of handling or employing things, without suggesting unwanted correlates. Learning how to manage a canoe-paddle, a traveller's cheque or a postage-stamp is not being introduced to an extra entity. Nor is learning how to manage the words 'if', 'ought' and 'limit'.

There is another merit in this idiom. Where we can speak of managing, handling and employing we can speak of mismanaging, mishandling and misemploying. There are rules to keep or break, codes to observe or flout. Learning to use expressions, like learning to use coins, stamps, cheques and hockey-sticks, involves learning to do certain things with them and not others; when to do certain things with them, and when not to do them. Among the things that we learn in the process of learning to use linguistic expressions are what we may vaguely call 'rules of logic'; for example, that though Mother and Father can both be tall, they cannot both be taller than one another; or that though uncles can be rich or poor, fat or thin, they cannot be male or female, but only male. Where it would sound unplausible to say that concepts or ideas or meanings might be meaningless or absurd, there is no such unplausibility in asserting that someone might use a certain expression absurdly. An attempted or suggested way of operating with an expression may be logically illegitimate or impossible, but a universal or a state of consciousness or a meaning cannot be logically legitimate or illegitimate.

'USE' AND 'UTILITY'

On the other hand there are inconveniences in talking much of the *uses* of expressions. People are liable to construe 'use' in one of the ways which English certainly does permit, namely as a synonym of 'utility' or 'usefulness'. They then suppose that to discuss the use of an expression is to discuss what it is useful for or how useful it is. Sometimes such considerations are philosophically profitable. But it is easy to see that discussing the use (versus uselessness) of something is quite different from discussing the use (versus misuse) of it, i.e., the way, method or manner of using it. The female driver may learn what is the utility of a sparking-plug, but learning this is not learning how to operate with a sparking-plug. She does not have or lack skills or competences with sparking-plugs, as she does with steering-wheels, coins, words and knives. Her sparking-plugs manage themselves; or, rather, they are not managed at all. They just function automatically, until they cease to function. They are useful, even indispensable to her. But she does not manage or mismanage them.

Conversely, a person who has learned how to whistle tunes may not find the whistling of tunes at all useful or even pleasant to others or to himself. He manages, or sometimes mismanages his lips, tongue and breath; and, more indirectly, manages or mismanages the notes he produces. He has got the trick of it; he can show us and perhaps even tell us how the trick is performed. But it is a useless trick. The question How do you use your breath or your lips in whistling? has a positive and complicated answer. The question What is the use, or utility of whistling? has a negative and simple one. The former is a request for the details of a technique; the latter is not. Questions about the use of an expression are often, though not always, questions about the way to operate with it; not questions about what the employer of it needs it for. They are How questions, not What-for questions. This latter sort of question can be asked, but it is seldom necessary to ask it, since the answer is usually obvious. In a foreign country, I do not ask what a centime or a peseta is for; what I do ask is how many of them I have to give for a certain article, or how many of them I am to expect to get in exchange for a half-crown. I want to know what its purchasing power is; not that it is for making purchases with.

'USE' AND 'USAGE'

Much more insidious than this confusion between the way of operating with something and its usefulness, is the confusion between a 'use', i.e. a way of operating with something, and a 'usage'. Lots of philosophers, whose dominant good resolution is to discern logico-linguistic differences, talk without qualms as if 'use' and 'usage' were synonyms. This is just a howler; for which there is little excuse except that, in the archaic phrase 'use and wont', 'use' could, perhaps, be replaced by 'usage'; that 'used to' does mean 'accustomed to'; and that to be hardly used is to suffer hard usage.

A usage is a custom, practice, fashion or vogue. It can be local or widespread, obsolete or current, rural or urban, vulgar or academic. There cannot be a misusage any more than there can be a miscustom or a misvogue. The methods of discovering linguistic usages are the methods of philologists.

By contrast, a way of operating with a razor blade, a word, a traveller's cheque or a canoe-paddle is a technique, knack or method. Learning it is learning how to do the thing; it is not finding out sociological generalities, not even sociological generalities about other people who do similar or different things with razor blades, words, travellers' cheques or canoe-paddles. Robinson Crusoe might find out for himself how to make and how to throw boomerangs; but this discovery would tell him nothing about those Australian aborigines who do in fact make and use them in the same way. The description of a conjuring-trick is not the description of all the conjurers who perform or have performed that trick. On the contrary, in order to describe the possessors of the trick, we should have already to be able to give some sort of description of the trick itself. Mrs Beeton tells us how to make omelets; but she gives us no information about Parisian chefs. Baedeker might tell us about Parisian chefs, and tell us which of them make omelets; but if he wanted to tell us how they make omelets, he would have to describe their techniques in the way that Mrs Beeton describes the technique of making omelets. Descriptions of usages presuppose descriptions of uses, i.e., ways or techniques of doing the thing, the more or less widely prevailing practice of doing which constitutes the usage.

There is an important difference between the employment of boomerangs, bows and arrows, and canoe-paddles on the one hand and the employment of tennis rackets, tug-of-war ropes, coins, stamps and words on the other hand. The latter are instruments of inter-personal, i.e., concerted or competitive, actions. Robinson

Crusoe might play some games of patience; but he could not play tennis or cricket. So a person who learns to use a tennis racket, a stroke-side oar, a coin or a word is inevitably in a position to notice other people using these things. He cannot master the tricks of such inter-personal transactions without at the same time finding out facts about some other people's employment and misemployment of them; and normally he will learn a good many of the tricks from noticing other people employing them. Even so, learning the knacks is not and does not require making a sociological study. A child may learn in the home and the village shop how to use pennies, shillings and pound notes; and his mastery of these slightly complex knacks is not improved by hearing how many people in other places and years have managed and now manage or mismanage their pennies, shillings and pound notes. Perfectly mastering a use is not getting to know everything, or even much, about a usage, even when mastering that use does causally involve finding out a bit about a few other people's practices. We were taught in the nursery how to handle a lot of words; but we were not being taught any historical or sociological generalities about employers of these words. That came later, if it came at all.

Before passing on we should notice one big difference between using canoe-paddles or tennis rackets on the one hand and using postage stamps, safety-pins, coins and words on the other. Tennis rackets are wielded with greater or less skill; even the tennis-champion studies to improve. But, with some unimportant reservations, it is true to say that coins, cheques, stamps, separate words, buttons and shoelaces offer no scope for talent. Either a person knows or he does not know how to use and how not to misuse them. Of course literary composition and argumentation can be more or less skilful; but the essayist or lawyer does not know the meaning of 'rabbit' or 'and' better than Everyman. There is no room here for 'better'. Similarly, the champion chess-player manoeuvres more skilfully than the amateur; but he does not know the permitted moves of the pieces better. They both know them perfectly, or rather they just know them.

Certainly, the cultured chess-player may describe the permitted moves better than does the uncultured chess-player. But he does not make these moves any better. I give change for a half-crown no better than you do. We both just give the correct change. Yet I may describe such transactions more effectively than you can describe them. Knowing how to operate is not knowing how to tell how to operate. This point becomes important when we are discussing, say, the stock way (supposing there is one) of employing the word 'cause'. The doctor knows how to make this use of it as well as anyone, but he may not be able to answer any of the philosopher's enquiries about this way of using it.

In order to avoid these two big confusions, the confusion of 'use' with 'usefulness' and the confusion of 'use' with 'usage', I try nowadays to use, *inter alia*, 'employ' and 'employment' instead of the verb and noun 'use'. So I say this. Philosophers often have to try to describe the stock (or, more rarely, some non-stock) manner or way of employing an expression. Sometimes such an expression belongs to the vernacular; sometimes to some technical vocabulary; sometimes it is betwixt and between. Describing the mode of employment of an expression does not require and is not usually helped by information about the prevalence or unprevalence of this way of employing it. For the philosopher, like other folk, has long since learned how to employ or handle it, and what he is trying to describe is what he himself has learned.

Techniques are not vogues—but they may have vogues. Some of them must have vogues or be current in some other way. For it is no accident that ways of employing words, as of employing coins, stamps and chessmen, *tend* to be identical through a whole community and over a long stretch of time. We want to understand and be understood; and we learn our native tongue from our elders. Even without the pressure of legislation and dictionaries, our vocabularies tend towards uniformity. Fads and idiosyncrasies in these matters impair communication. Fads and idiosyncrasies in matters of postage stamps, coins and the moves of chessmen are ruled out by explicit legislation, and partly analogous conformities are imposed upon many technical vocabularies by such things as drill-manuals and text-books. Notoriously these tendencies towards uniformity have their exceptions. However, as there naturally do exist many pretty widespread and pretty long-enduring vocabulary usages, it is sometimes condonable for a philosopher to remind his readers of a mode of employing an expression by alluding to 'what everyone says' or 'what no one says'. The reader considers the mode of employment that he has long since learned and feels strengthened when told that big battalions are on his side. In fact, of course, this appeal to prevalence is philosophically pointless, besides being philologically risky. What is wanted is, perhaps, the extraction of the logical rules implicitly governing a concept, i.e., a way of operating with an expression (or any other expression that does the same work). It is probable that the use of this expression, to perform this job, is widely current; but whether it is so or not is of no philosophical interest. Job-analysis is not Mass Observation. Nor is it helped by Mass Observation. But Mass Observation sometimes needs the aid of job-analysis.

Before terminating this discussion of the use of the expression 'the use of the expression "..."', I want to draw attention to an interesting point. We can ask whether a person knows how to use and how not misuse a certain word. But we cannot ask whether he knows how to use a certain *sentence*. When a block of words has congealed into a phrase we can ask whether he knows how to use the phrase. But when a sequence of words has not yet congealed into a phrase, while we can ask whether he knows how to use its ingredient words, we cannot easily ask whether he knows how to use that sequence. Why can we not even ask whether he knows how to use a certain sentence? For we talk about the meanings of sentences, seemingly just as we talk of the meanings of the words in it; so, if knowing the meaning of a word is knowing how to use it, we might have expected that knowing the meaning of a sentence was knowing how to use the sentence. Yet this glaringly does not go.

A cook uses salt, sugar, flour, beans and bacon in making a pie. She uses, and perhaps misuses, the ingredients. But she does not, in this way, use the pie. Her pie is not an ingredient. In a somewhat different way, the cook uses, and perhaps misuses, a rolling-pin, a fork, a frying-pan and an oven. These are the utensils with which she makes her pie. But the pie is not another utensil. The pie is (well or badly) composed out of the ingredients, by means of the utensils. It is what she used them for; but it cannot be listed in either class of them. Somewhat, but only somewhat, similarly a sentence is (well or badly) constructed out of words. It is what the speaker or writer uses them for. He composes it out of them. His sentence is not itself something which, in this way, he either uses or misuses, either uses or does not use. His composition is not a component of his composition. We can tell a person to say something (e.g. ask a question, give a command or narrate an anecdote), using a specified word or phrase; and he will know what he is being told to do. But if we just tell him to pronounce or write down, by itself, that specified word or phrase, he will see the difference between this order and the other one. For he is not now being told to use, i.e. *incorporate* the word or phrase, but only to pronounce it or write it down. Sentences are things that we say. Words and phrases are what we say things *with*.

There can be dictionaries of words and dictionaries of phrases.

But there cannot be dictionaries of sentences. This is not because such dictionaries would have to be infinitely and therefore impracticably long. On the contrary, it is because they could not even begin. Words and phrases are there, in the bin, for people to avail themselves of when they want to say things. But the sayings of these things are not some more things which are there in the bin for people to avail themselves of, when they want to say these things. This fact that words and phrases can, while sentences cannot, be misused, since sentences cannot be, in this way, used at all is quite consistent with the important fact that sentences can be well or ill constructed. We can say things awkwardly or ungrammatically and we can say things which are grammatically proper but do not make sense.

It follows that there are some radical differences between what is meant by 'the meaning of a word or phrase' and what is meant by 'the meaning of a sentence'. Understanding a word or phrase is knowing how to use it, i.e., make it perform its role in a wide range of sentences. But understanding a sentence is not knowing how to make it perform its role. The play has not got a role.

We are tempted to suppose that the question How are word-meanings related to sentence-meanings? is a tricky but genuine question, a question, perhaps, rather like How is the purchasing power of my shilling related to the purchasing power of the contents of my pay-envelope? But this model puts things awry from the start.

If I know the meaning of a word or phrase I know something like a body of unwritten rules, or something like an unwritten code or general recipe. I have learned to use the word correctly in an unlimited variety of different settings. What I know is, in this respect, somewhat like what I know when I know how to use a knight or a pawn at chess. I have learned to put it to its work anywhen and anywhere if there is work for it to do. But the idea of putting a sentence to its work anywhen and anywhere is fantastic. It has not got a role which it can perform again and again in different plays. It has not got a role at all, any more than a play has a role. Knowing what it means is not knowing anything like a code or a body of rules, though it requires knowing the codes or rules governing the use of the words or phrases that make it up. There are general rules and recipes for constructing sentences of certain kinds; but not general rules or recipes for constructing the particular sentence 'Today is Monday'. Knowing the meaning of 'Today is Monday' is not knowing general rules, codes or recipes governing the use of this sentence, since there is no such thing as the utilisation or, therefore, the re-utilisation of this sentence. I expect that this ties up with the fact that sentences and clauses make sense or make no sense, where words neither do nor do not make sense, but only have meanings; and that pretence-sentences can be absurd or nonsensical, where pretence-words are neither absurd nor nonsensical, but only meaningless. I can say stupid things, but words can be neither stupid nor not stupid.

PHILOSOPHY AND ORDINARY LANGUAGE

The vogue of the phrase 'the use of ordinary language' seems to suggest to some people the idea that there exists a philosophical doctrine according to which (*a*) all philosophical enquiries are concerned with vernacular, as opposed to more or less technical, academic or esoteric terms; and (*b*), in consequence, all philosophical discussions ought themselves to be couched entirely in vernacular dictions. The inference is fallacious, though its conclusion has some truth in it. Even if it were true, which it is not, that all philosophical problems are concerned with non-technical concepts, i.e. with the mode of employment of vernacular expressions, it would not follow from this (false) premiss that the discussions of these problems must or had better be in jurymen's English, French or German.

From the fact that a philologist studies those English words which stem from Celtic roots, it does not follow that he must or had better say what he has to say about them in words of Celtic origin. From the fact that a psychologist is discussing the psychology of witticisms, it does not follow that he ought to write wittily all or any of the time. Clearly he ought not to write wittily most of the time.

Most philosophers have in fact employed a good number of the technical terms of past or contemporary logical theory. We may sometimes wish that they had taken a few more pinches of salt, but we do not reproach them for availing themselves of these technical expedients; we should have deplored their long-windedness if they had tried to do without them.

But enslavement to jargon, whether inherited or invented, is, certainly, a bad quality in any writer, whether he be a philosopher or not. It curtails the number of people who can understand and criticise his writings; so it tends to make his own thinking run in a private groove. The use of avoidable jargons is bad literary manners and bad pedagogic policy, as well as being detrimental to the thinker's own wits.

But this is not peculiar to philosophy. Bureaucrats, judges, theologians, literary critics, bankers and, perhaps above all, psychologists and sociologists would all be well advised to try very hard to write in plain and blunt words. None the less, Hobbes, who had this virtue of writing plainly and bluntly, was a lesser philosopher than Kant, who lacked it; and Plato's later dialogues, though harder to translate, have powers which his early dialogues are without. Nor is the simplicity of his diction in Mill's account of mathematics enough to make us prefer it to the account given by Frege, whose diction is more esoteric.

In short, there is no *a priori* or peculiar obligation laid upon philosophers to refrain from talking esoterically; but there is a general obligation upon all thinkers and writers to try to think and write both as powerfully and as plainly as possible. But plainness of diction and power of thought can vary independently, though it is not common for them to do so.

Incidentally it would be silly to require the language of professional journals to be as exoteric as the language of books. Colleagues can be expected to use and understand one another's terms of art. But books are not written only for colleagues. Their judge should not address the jury in the language in which he may address his brother judges. Sometimes, but only sometimes, he may be well advised to address even his brother judges, and himself, in the language in which he should address the jury. It all depends on whether his technical terms are proving to be a help or a hindrance. They are likely to be a hindrance when they are legacies from a period in which today's questions were not even envisaged. This is what justifies the regular and salutary rebellions of philosophers against the philosophical jargons of their fathers.

There is another reason why philosophers ought sometimes to eschew other people's technical terms. Even when a philosopher is interesting himself in some of the cardinal concepts of, say, physical theory, he is usually partly concerned to state the logical cross-bearings between the concepts of this theory and the concepts of mathematical, theological, biological or psychological theory. Very often his radical puzzle is that of determining these cross-bearings. When trying to solve puzzles of this sort, he cannot naïvely employ the dictions of either theory. He has to stand back from both theories, and discuss the concepts of both in terms which are proprietary to neither. He may coin neutral dictions of his own, but for ease of understanding he may prefer the dictions of Everyman. These have this required neutrality, even if they lack that semi-codification which disciplines the terms of art of professionalised thought. Barter-terms are not as well regimented as the terms of the counting-house; but when we have to determine rates of exchange between different currencies, it is to barter-terms that we may have to turn. Inter-theory negotiations can be and may have to be conducted in pre-theory dictions.

So far I have, I hope, been mollifying rather than provoking. I now want to say two philosophically contentious things.

(*a*) There is a special reason why philosophers, unlike other professionals and specialists, are constantly jettisoning *in toto* all the technical terms of their own predecessors (save some of the technical terms of formal logic); i.e., why the jargon words of epistemology, ethics, aesthetics, etc. seem to be half-hardy annuals rather than hardy perennials. The reason is this. The experts who use the technical terms of bridge, law, chemistry and plumbing learn to employ these terms partly from official instructions but largely by directly engaging in the special techniques and by directly dealing with the special materials or objects of their specialism. They familiarise themselves with the harness by having to drive their (to us unfamiliar) horses.

But the terms of art of philosophy itself (save for those of formal logic), are not like this. There is no peculiar field of knowledge or adeptness in which philosophers *ex officio* make themselves the experts—except of course the business of philosophising itself. We know by what special sorts of work mastery is acquired of the concepts of *finesse, tort, sulphanilamide* and *valve-seating*. But by what corresponding special sorts of work do philosophers get their supposed corresponding mastery of the concepts of *Cognition, Sensation, Secondary Qualities* and *Essences*? What exercises and predicaments have forced them to learn just how to use and how not to misuse these terms?

Philosophers' arguments which turn on these terms are apt, sooner or later, to start to rotate idly. There is nothing to make them point north rather than nor'-nor'-east. The bridge-player cannot play fast and loose with the concepts of *finesse* and *revoke*. If he tries to make them work in a way palatable to him, they jib. The unofficial terms of everyday discourse are like the official terms of specialisms in this important respect. They too jib if maltreated. It is no more possible to say that someone knows something to be the case which is not so than it is possible to say that the player of the first card in a game of bridge has revoked. We have had to learn in the hard school of daily life how to deploy the verb 'know'; and we have had to learn at the bridge-table how to deploy the verb 'revoke'. There is no such hard school in which to learn how to deploy the verbs 'cognise' and 'sense'. These go through what motions we care to require of them, which means that they have acquired no discipline of their own at all. So the philosophical arguments which are supposed to deploy these units win and lose no fights, since these units have no fight in them. Hence, the appeal from philosophical jargon to the expressions which we have all had to learn to use properly (as the chess-player has had to learn the moves of his pieces) is often one well worth making; where a corresponding appeal to the vocabulary of Everyman from the official parlance of a science, of a game or of law would often, not always, be ridiculous. One contrast of 'ordinary' (in the phrase 'ordinary language') is with 'philosophers' jargon'.

(b) But now for quite a different point and one of considerable contemporary importance. The appeal to what we do and do not say, or can and cannot say, is often stoutly resisted by the protagonists of one special doctrine, and stoutly pressed by its antagonists. This doctrine is the doctrine that philosophical disputes can and should be settled by formalising the warring theses. A theory is formalised when it is translated out of the natural language (untechnical, technical or semi-technical), in which it was originally excogitated, into a deliberately constructed notation, the notation, perhaps of *Principia Mathematica*. The logic of a theoretical position can, it is claimed, be regularised by stretching its non-formal concepts between the topic-neutral logical constants whose conduct in inferences is regulated by set drills. Formalisation will replace logical perplexities by logical problems amenable to known and teachable procedures of calculation. Thus one contrast of 'ordinary' (in the phrase 'ordinary language') is with 'notational'.

Of those to whom this, the formaliser's dream, appears a mere dream (I am one of them), some maintain that the logic of everyday statements and even the logic of the statements of scientists, lawyers, historians and bridge-players cannot in principle be adequately represented by the formulae of formal logic. The so-called logical constants do indeed have, partly by deliberate prescription, their scheduled logical powers; but the non-formal expressions both of everyday discourse and of technical discourse have their own unscheduled logical powers, and these are not reducible without remainder to those of the carefully wired marionettes of formal logic. The title of a novel by A. E. W. Mason, *They Wouldn't Be Chessmen*, applies well to both the technical and the untechnical expressions of professional and daily life. This is not to say that the examination of the logical behaviour of the terms of non-notational discourse is not assisted by studies in formal logic. Of course it is. So may chess-playing assist generals, though waging campaigns cannot be replaced by playing games of chess.

I do not want here to thrash out this important issue. I want only to show that resistance to one sort of appeal to ordinary language ought to involve championing the programme of formalisation. 'Back to ordinary language' can be (but often is not) the slogan of those who have awoken from the formaliser's dream. This slogan, so used, should be repudiated only by those who hope to replace philosophising by reckoning.

VERDICT

Well, then, has philosophy got something to do with the use of expressions or hasn't it? To ask this is simply to ask whether conceptual discussions, i.e., discussions about the concepts of, say, *voluntariness*, *infinitesimals*, *number* or *cause* come under the heading of philosophical discussions. Of course they do. They always have done, and they have not stopped doing so now.

Whether we gain more than we lose by sedulously advertising the fact that what we are investigating is the stock way of operating with, say, the word 'cause', depends a good deal on the context of the discussions and the intellectual habits of the people with whom we are discussing it. It is certainly a long-winded way of announcing what we are doing; and inverted commas are certainly vexatious to the eye. But, more important than these nuisances, preoccupation with questions about methods tends to distract us from prosecuting the methods themselves. We run, as a rule, worse, not better, if we think a lot about our feet. So let us, at least on alternate days, speak instead of investigating the concept of *causation*. Or, better still, let us, on those days, not speak of it at all but just do it.

But the more long-winded idiom has some big compensating advantages. If we are enquiring into problems of perception, i.e. discussing questions about the concepts of seeing, hearing and smelling, we may be taken to be tackling the questions of opticians, neuro-physiologists or psychologists, and even fall into this mistake ourselves. It is then salutary to keep on reminding ourselves and one another that what we are after is accounts of how certain words work, namely words like 'see', 'look', 'overlook', 'blind', 'visual-ise' and lots of other affiliated expressions.

One last point. I have talked in general terms about learning and describing the modes of employment of expressions. But there are many different dimensions of these modes, only some of which are

317

of interest to philosophers. Differences of stylistic elegance, rhetorical persuasiveness, and social propriety need to be considered, but not, save *per accidens*, by philosophers. Churchill would have made a rhetorical blunder if he had said, instead of 'We shall fight them on the beaches . . .', 'We shall fight them on the sands . . .'. 'Sands' would have raised thoughts of children's holidays at Skegness. But this kind of misemployment of 'sands' is not the kind of mishandling that interests us. We are interested in the informal logic of the employment of expressions, the nature of the logical howlers that people do or might commit if they strung their words together in certain ways, or, more positively, in the logical force that expressions have as components of theories and as pivots of concrete arguments. That is why, in our discussions, we argue *with* expressions and *about* those expressions in one and the same breath. We are trying to register what we are exhibiting; to codify the very logical codes which we are then and there observing.

24

PROOFS IN PHILOSOPHY

Reprinted in English translation from the original French in 'Revue Internationale de Philosophie', vol. VIII, *1954, by permission of the editors*

Philosophers do not provide proofs any more than tennis-players score goals. Tennis-players do not try in vain to score goals. Nor do philosophers try in vain to provide proofs; they are not inefficient or tentative provers. Goals do not belong to tennis, nor proofs to philosophy.

Certainly some philosophers are also mathematicians, like Descartes, Leibniz and Frege. Some philosophers are also Formal Logicians, like Aristotle, Frege and Russell. Philosophers may prove theorems in mathematics and Formal Logic, just as tennis-players may score goals in the winter. But the strengths and weaknesses of Aristotle or Frege in discussing philosophical points are distinct from their strengths and weaknesses in proving theorems in Formal Logic or in mathematics. There could be persons, who were superior to Aristotle in proving theorems in Formal Logic, whom we should still rank below Aristotle as philosophers.

But to say that philosophers do not prove or even try to prove things sounds over-violent in two ways. (1) First, some philosophers, like Spinoza, have deliberately tried to do for certain philosophical matters what Euclid did for geometrical matters. Attempted proofs of the existence of God and the immortality of the soul bespatter the chronicles of philosophy from Plato to 1953. I do not want to waste your time in debating whether such attempts should be listed as a peculiar variety of philosophising or as bad philosophising or as non-philosophical enterprises undertaken by men who, in other parts of their work, were genuine philosophers. So let me say, more guardedly, that anyhow some of the characteristically philosophical products of anyhow some of the best philosophers have not been proofs, quasi-proofs, pseudo-proofs or even would-be proofs.

(2) But for another reason also it sounds over-violent to say that anyhow some characteristic and excellent specimens of philosophising are not either good or bad attempts at proving. For it sounds like saying that some good philosophising is like most poetry or like much preaching, namely, that it is not argumentative or not ratiocinatory. I maintain, on the contrary, that the best products of the best philosophers are argumentative, indeed that they are not merely argued, but are themselves arguments. It is for the powerfulness and originality of his arguments that a philosopher merits the respect of his colleagues.

Yet these powerful arguments of his are not rigorous proofs, and they are not unrigorous proofs either. Frege, for example, uses some powerful arguments in his philosophical discussions of the concept of number, yet these arguments are neither inferior nor superior to his proofs of his theorems in the body of his *Grundgesetze*. They are not exercises in the same genre; they are not candidates for the same honours.

When I say that a philosophical argument employed by Frege, say, or Plato is powerful, I do not mean that it is rhetorically persuasive. On the whole, Plato is rhetorically more efficient than Aristotle, but we can distinguish the question whether a certain argument of Aristotle is more or less powerful than a corresponding argument of Plato from the question whether the presentation of the one is more or less persuasive than the other. Philosophical arguments can be or fail to be logically powerful in a sense of 'logically' closely related to the sense in which a proof may be or fail to be logically rigorous. Why do I say that anyhow some characteristically philosophical arguments are not proofs?

Theorems can be learned, understood and used in abstraction from their proofs. Sometimes a proposition of which there does not yet exist a proof may be intuitively obvious, so that the discovery of its proof is posterior to the discovery of the truth of that proposition. The corresponding things do not hold of philosophical arguments. It would be absurd to try to tell a student the results of Plato's ratiocinations about the concepts of knowledge and false belief, without introducing him to those ratiocinations themselves; or to make him learn by heart and use Frege's elucidation of the concept of number while exempting him from appreciating the argumentation which gave that elucidation. There could not be a list of Aristotle's or Kant's findings. There are no philosophical theorems, not even slippery or foggy theorems.

Sometimes, I think, this absence of a list of philosophical theorems is mis-diagnosed. It is supposed that while ideally there would exist such listable theorems, in fact they do not exist because the philosopher, unfortunately, has to operate with the soft and vaporous concepts of everyday untechnical discourse, where the mathematician operates with hard and chiselled, technical concepts. But this sort of apology is mistaken. The concept of number for which Frege gave his philosophical elucidation was that hard and chiselled concept which is used in counting and calculating—yet still his philosophical arguings were totally unlike his establishings of logistical theorems. The concepts of *infinitesimal* and *point* which exercised philosophers like Zeno, Aristotle, Berkeley and Whitehead were the non-vernacular concepts which were actually and efficiently employed by mathematicians in the course of their far from vaporous work.

Next, where proofs exist, premisses exist. A proof is unsatisfactory if, among other things, it is left unclear just what premisses have been used and if it is doubtful whether they are true. Philosophers' arguments are not laid out in this way—or when, in pious imitation of Euclid's Elements or *Principia Mathematica*, philosophers do pretend to display sets of necessary and sufficient premisses, the debate instantly moves back a step. The philosophical point at issue is seen to be lodged not in the use to which these premisses were put by their employer, but in those pretended premisses themselves. Cartesians like to trumpet '*cogito, ergo sum*' as a premiss to some promised philosophical theorems. Moore, I think, has sometimes thought of Common Sense as a budget of premisses for philosophers. The reaction of philosophers has always been the critical one, 'We don't want to build anything on these premisses'. Their reaction, I suggest, ought to be, 'We don't want premisses at all, because we don't want theorems'. Only we have been shy of saying anything of the sort, because we have inadvertently assumed that any argument with any degree of logical powerfulness must have the shape of a premiss-theorem proof.

Well, then, what can be positively said about the arguments which we expect to find in the debates of good philosophers and to produce in our own debates? I am not going to lay down any wide generalisation or suggest any piece of legislation. I want to consider just one thing which we sometimes have to do by argument in the course of some philosophical discussions. Whether it is typical or not, I do not want to debate.

Let me begin by reminding you of the familiar distinction between techniques and technologies, or methods and methodologies, between, say, music and musicology. It is one thing to have learned to do a thing correctly or well; it is quite another thing to be able to tell how to do it correctly or well. A surgeon who has learned or invented a trick can perform it, but he may lack the quite different skill of formulating verbal instructions telling other surgeons what to do and what to avoid when essaying the trick.

Between the naïve performance of his trick and the sophisticated business of giving verbal instructions about its performance, there is an intermediate activity, less naïve than the first and less sophisticated than the second, namely that of demonstrating or showing the trick—rehearsing its operations one by one, in a conspicuous manner, and at a deliberately reduced speed.

Now suppose that the surgeon himself tries to formulate the verbal instructions or recipe for the performance of this trick. How does the surgeon test these proposed instructions—how does he satisfy himself that the suggested recipe does or does not answer to the operations that he knows how to perform? He must go through his trick, as he has learned to do it, yet rehearse it with one eye on the corresponding items of the suggested recipe. He must show off the ingredient operations of his trick in order to match them against the ingredient prescriptions of the recipe; and this is not easy—especially since the first verbal recipe or instruction-formula to be suggested will certainly be only a very schematic, outline affair.

Now to apply this to our concern.

It is one thing to be able to count, add, subtract and multiply, i.e. to operate with numbers. Schoolboys can do these things. It is quite another thing to formulate verbal recipes or instructions for correct operations with numbers. Schoolboys do not have to try to do this new, sophisticated thing, but, for certain purposes, certain adults do have to try to do this. They have, so to speak, to try to codify the operation-rules for numerical expressions, as primitive tribal legislators have to try to codify the conduct-rules which the tribe observes but does not propound. What is true of numerical expressions is true of nearly all expressions, whether non-technical, technical or semi-technical. We learn how to operate with them consistently and systematically before we can consider verbal instructions for operating with them. We first have to learn how to operate with them properly, e.g. in asking answerable questions, in giving obeyable orders, in making checkable statements, and so on. Later on we may have also to consider codifications of these previously uncodified, yet still rule-governed practices of ours. As it is sometimes not very happily put, we have to make explicit the previously implicit 'logic' of their employment. This means that we have a matching-problem just like that of my surgeon, namely the problem of matching already well-mastered operations with these expressions, against suggested and more or less schematic instructions for those operations. In particular, we have to rehearse arguments pivoting on these expressions in order to match these arguments against the more or less roughly outlined argument-patterns which the suggested instructions codify. Notice that here, unlike the case of the surgeon, the procedure under examination is itself a batch of operations with expressions. We are trying to codify in words of one level the rules observed in the employment of words of another level. I shall give two examples. Plato needed to discuss the place in human life of *pleasure*; he needed, therefore, to put it crudely, to be able to say what sort of a thing pleasure is. He noticed that among things that we enjoy are such things as eating when we are hungry and drinking when we are thirsty. Eating and drinking are processes, namely transitions from emptiness to repletion. They are processes of replenishment. He then suggested that the pleasures of eating and drinking, the enjoyment we get from them, are in the same manner processes or, more specifically, transitions from one state to another. Against this, Aristotle argued in effect as follows. If enjoying something were a process from state to state, it would follow that a person could have begun to enjoy something but been prevented from finishing, as a person can begin his dinner but be prevented from completing it. But, though a person may enjoy something for a short time or for a long time, he cannot have half an enjoyment. Enjoyments can be great or small, but not fractional. This demolishes Plato's assimilation of the concept of pleasure to the general type of concepts of process or transition. Aristotle has shown that a batch of elementary argumentative operations which are legitimately made with process-expressions, like 'dine', cannot be made with expressions like 'enjoy'. But in doing this he has not merely done something destructive; he has done something constructive. He has added a new item to the formulation of the needed recipe. He has found a specific fault in a suggested codification; he has thereby fixed a specific positive element in the required codification. To correct is to rectify.

Next, consider one of the things that Frege had to do and did. Certain thinkers, who were as competent at simple arithmetic as Frege, suggested that adjectives such as 'one', 'two' and 'three' stood, like the adjectives 'green', 'square' and 'honest', for qualities of things—somewhat mysterious qualities, perhaps, but still qualities.

Frege demolished this matching-suggestion by, so far as I recall, such arguments as this. If the men in this room are honest then I, who am in this room, am honest. But if the men in this room number thirty-five, it does not follow that I number thirty-five. Moreover, not merely do I not number 35, but I do not even number 1, or any other number. The Oxford Professors in this room number 1, and I am an Oxford Professor in this room and no one else is. But 'numbering 1' is not, as 'honest' is, the sort of predicate which can characterise me. It can characterise only such subjects as 'the Oxford Professors in this room'. Numerical expressions will not go through all the same inference-hoops as quality-expressions. The suggested matching of those with these collapses. But with this collapse, something positive arises; we can now say one positive thing about the logical behaviour of numerical expressions—a positive thing which is akin to an important feature of existence-expressions.

Notice that in these two examples the suggested verbal recipes were worded with the aid of logicians' classificatory words such as 'process' and 'quality'. But there are lots of other ways in which one may formulate our codifications of the inference-métiers of concepts.

I suggest now that we can see the reason why anyhow some characteristically philosophical arguments are not of the premiss-theorem pattern. For they are operations not *with* premisses and conclusions, but operations *upon* operations with premisses and conclusions. In proving something, we are putting propositions through inference-hoops. In some philosophical arguments we are matching the hoops through which certain batches of propositions will go against a worded recipe declaring what hoops they should go through. Proving is a one-level business; philosophical arguing is, anyhow sometimes, an inter-level business.

Moreover, to prove something, we must have true premisses. For the philosopher's business what matters is not whether a concrete proposition incorporating (non-vacuously) the concept, say, of *pleasure* is true, but only what *would* confirm it, what *would* refute it, etc. He is, so to speak, not making real inferences, but rehearsing them for his own matching-purposes. Similarly the surgeon who is trying to teach his tricks to others by showing them off, step by step, in a conspicuous manner and at a reduced speed is not then and there trying to extract an invalid's appendix. Still less is he trying to do this when he is matching his procedure against some suggested verbal instructions in this procedure. He is only *rehearsing* his trick for his new non-clinical purpose.

One last word. Philosophers' problems do not in general, if ever, arise out of troubles about single concepts, like that, say, of *pleasure* or that of *number*. They arise, rather, as the traffic-policeman's problems arise, when crowds of conceptual vehicles, of different sorts and moving in different directions meet at some conceptual cross-roads. All or a lot of them have to be got under control conjointly. This is why, in its early stages, a philosophical dispute strikes scientists and mathematicians as so messy an affair. It *is* messy, for it is a traffic-block—a traffic-block which cannot be tidied up by the individual drivers driving their individual cars efficiently.

25

PLEASURE

Reprinted from 'Proceedings of the Aristotelian Society', suppl. vol. XXVII, 1954, by permission of the editor

What sort of a difference is the difference between taking a walk which one enjoys and taking a walk to which one is indifferent?

(1) It might be suggested that it is, in genus if not in species, the sort of difference that there is between walking with a headache and walking without one; and that somewhat as one walker may recollect afterwards not only the ordinary acts and incidents of his walk, but also the steady or intermittent pains that he had had in his head while walking, so another walker who has enjoyed his walk might recall both the ordinary acts and incidents of his walk and also the steady pleasure or the intermittent pleasures that had been concomitant with the walk. It might even be suggested that as one walker may recollect that his headache had become specially acute just as he reached the canal, so another might recollect that his pleasure had become specially acute just as he reached the canal.

A person who made such a suggestion need not hold that to enjoy a walk is itself to have a special bodily sensation or series of bodily sensations concurrent with the walking. He might admit that while we can ask in which arm an agreeable or disagreeable tingle had been felt, we could not ask in which arm the agreeableness or disagreeableness of it had been felt. He might admit, too, that in the way in which pains yield to local or general anaesthetics, enjoyment and distaste are not the sorts of states or conditions for which anaesthetics are appropriate. But he might still suggest that pleasure is a non-bodily feeling, in supposedly the same generic sense of 'feeling' as pain is a bodily feeling. If sophisticated enough, he might suggest that pleasure is a specific, introspectible *Erlebnis*, where a headache is a specific bodily *Erlebnis*. Now a sensation or *Erlebnis*, like a tingle, may be agreeable, disagreeable or neutral. If enjoying and disliking were correctly co-classified with such *Erlebnisse* or feelings, one would expect, by analogy, that one could similarly ask whether a person who had had the supposed pleasure-feeling or dislike-*Erlebnis* had liked or disliked having it. Enjoying or disliking a tingle would be, on this showing, having one bodily feeling plus one non-bodily feeling. Either, then, this non-bodily feeling is, in its turn, something that can be pleasant or unpleasant, which would require yet another, non-bodily feeling, . . . ; or the way or sense, if any, in which pleasure and distress are feelings is not in analogy with the way or sense in which tingles are feelings.

There are other places where the suggested analogy between pleasure and tingles collapses. If you report having a tingle in your arm, I can ask you to describe it. Is it rather like having an electric shock? Does it mount and subside like waves? Is it going on at this moment? But when you tell how much you are enjoying the smell of peat smoke in my room, you cannot even construe the parallel questions about your enjoyment. Nor is your inability to answer due merely to the very important fact that in order to attend to my questions you have to stop attending to the smell, and so cannot still be enjoying it. You cannot answer my questions even in retrospect. There is no phenomenon to describe, except the smell of the peat smoke.

(2) The enjoyment of a walk might, however, be co-classified by some, not with feelings like tingles, but with feelings like wrath, amusement, alarm and disappointment—which is a very different use of 'feeling'. It could be urged that though the walker would not naturally say that he had felt pleased all the time or had kept on feeling pleased, still he could quite naturally say such things as that he had felt as if he were walking on air, or that he had felt that he could go on for ever. These dicta, which would certainly suggest that he had enjoyed his walk, should, on this second view, be construed as reporting a passion or emotion, in that sense of those words in which a person who is scared, thrilled, tickled or surprised is in the grip of a more or less violent passion or emotion.

This second assimilation too collapses. The walker may enjoy his walk very much, but he is not, thereby, assailed or overcome by anything. A man may be too angry or surprised to think straight, but he cannot enjoy his walk too much to think straight. He can be perfectly calm while enjoying himself very much.

Panic, fury and mirth can be transports, convulsions or fits, but the enjoyment of the smell of peat smoke is not a paroxysm like these—not because it is very mild, where they are violent, but because it is not the sort of thing that can be resisted, whether successfully or unsuccessfully. It cannot be given way to, either.

It is not a gale or a squall, but nor is it even a capful of wind. There is no conquering it or being conquered by it, though there is certainly such a thing as conquering or being conquered by the habit of indulging in something or the temptation to indulge in it.

(3) There is the third, though surely not the last, use of 'feeling' in which moods or frames of mind like depression, cheerfulness, irritability and *insouciance* are often called 'feelings'. Typically, though not universally, a mood lasts some hours or even a day or two, like the weather. But the mood of irritability is unlike the emotion or passion of anger, not only in its typical duration and not only in being more like squally weather than like a squall, but also in not having a particular object. A man is angry with his dog or his tie, but his irritability has no particular object, except, what comes to the same thing, the Scheme of Things in General. To be irritable is to be predisposed to lose one's temper with no matter which particular object. A person in a cheerful or energetic mood is predisposed to enjoy, *inter alia*, any walk that he may take; but what he enjoys is this particular walk. His enjoyment of it is not the fact that he is predisposed to enjoy any occupations or activities. Moreover, he enjoys his walk only while taking it, but he had felt cheerful or energetic, perhaps, ever since he got out of bed. So enjoying something is not the same sort of thing as being or feeling cheerful. On the contrary, the notion of being cheerful has to be explained in terms of the notion of pleasure, since to be cheerful is to be easy to please.

Sensations, emotional states and moods can, in principle, all be clocked. We can often say roughly how long a tingle or a headache lasted, very roughly how long a fit of rage or amusement lasted, and extremely roughly how long a mood of depression or cheerfulness lasted. But pleasure does not lend itself to such clockings. The walker can, indeed, say that he enjoyed his walk until it began to rain, two hours after he started out; or the diner can say that he enjoyed, though decreasingly, every bite of Stilton cheese that he took until satiety set in with the penultimate bite, and that this series of bites took about six minutes. But he cannot clock the duration of his enjoyment *against* the duration of the thing he enjoyed. He can, at best, divide the duration of the walk or meal into the parts which he enjoyed and the parts which he did not enjoy. The enjoyment of a walk is not a concomitant, e.g. an introspectible effect of the walking, such that there might be two histories, one the history of the walk, the other the history of its agreeableness to the walker. In particular there would be a glaring absurdity in the suggestion that the enjoyment of a walk might outlast the walk—unless all that was intended was that the walker enjoyed the walk and then enjoyed some after-effects or memories of the walk; or that the walk had made him cheerful for some time afterwards.

Psychologists nowadays often avoid idioms which suggest that enjoying a walk is having a special feeling while one walks, by speaking instead of the 'hedonic tone' of the walker. This new idiom, apart from performing its one antiseptic function, does not by itself advance very much our conceptual enquiry. It does not make clear what sort of a thing pleasure is. Is the hedonic tone the sort of thing that could, conceivably, be induced by drugs or hypnosis—as Dutch courage and somnolence can be induced? Could a person be qualified by hedonic tone, without his doing or having anything in particular to enjoy doing or having? So let us try to make a more positive move of our own.

Sometimes I enjoy a smell, sometimes I dislike it, and very often I am quite indifferent to it. But I could not enjoy it, dislike it or be indifferent to it if I were totally oblivious or unaware of it. I cannot say, in retrospect, that I liked the smell but did not notice it. I could, of course, enjoy a complex of smells, views, cool air and running water without paying special heed to any one of them. But I could not have enjoyed just that complex while being totally oblivious of any one of those components of it. This 'could not' is not a causal 'could not'. To say that a person had enjoyed the music, though too preoccupied to listen to it even as a background noise, would be to say something silly, not to report a *lusus naturae*. Unnoticed things, like ozone in the air, may certainly cause us to feel vigorous or cheerful. There may well be such an unnoticed cause of our being predisposed to enjoy, *inter alia*, the food and the music. But then we do not enjoy the ozone, but the food and the music; and of these we cannot be both oblivious and appreciative.

Similarly, when a person temporarily forgets his headache or tickle, he must cease, for that period, to be distressed by it. Being distressed by it entails not being oblivious of it. But just what is this connection between enjoying and attending, or between being oblivious and being undistressed? What, to begin with, is there to be said about the notions of attention and oblivion themselves?

When we consider the notion of attending, a subject which we consider far too seldom, we are apt to fancy that we have to do with some nuclear, one-piece notion; as if, for example, all attending were comparable with just switching on and aiming a torch in

order to see what is there whether we see it or not. But in real life
we use a wide variety of idioms for attending, most of which will
not quite or even nearly do duty for one another. Some of these
idioms correspond not too badly with the model of the torch-beam;
others do not correspond with it at all.

For example, if at the prompting of someone else I come to
notice a previously unnoticed smell, the way I become alive to the
smell has some kinship with the way the hedgehog comes to be
seen when the torch-beam is directed upon it. But then the way in
which a strong smell so forces itself on my attention that I cannot
not notice it is much more like a piece of barbed wire catching me
than like an object being picked out by my exploring torch-beam.

When we describe someone as writing or driving carefully, we
are describing him as attending to his task. But he is not, save *per
accidens*, taking note of the things he is doing, since he is playing
not an observer's part but an agent's part. He is taking pains to
avoid, among other things, ambiguities or collisions, where noticing
a strong smell does not involve taking pains at all.

Consider some other differences between the functions of such
idioms as those of noticing, heed, being careful, being vigilant,
concentrating, taking interest, being absorbed, giving one's mind
to something, and thinking what one is doing. When excited or
bored, I may not think what I am saying; but to say this is to say
less than that I am talking recklessly. I may be interested in something when it would be too severe to say that I am concentrating
on it; and I may concentrate on something which fails to capture
my interest. Attention is sometimes attracted, sometimes lent, sometimes paid and sometimes exacted.

Philosophers and psychologists sometimes speak of 'acts' of
attention. This idiom too is partially appropriate to certain contexts
and quite inappropriate to others. When a person is actually bidden
by someone else or by himself to attend, there is something which
with some effort or reluctance he *does*. Where his attention had been
wandering, it now settles; where he had been half-asleep, he is now
wide awake; and this change he may bring about with a wrench.
But the spectator at an exciting football match does not have to
try to fasten or canalise his attention. To the question 'How many
acts of attention did you perform?' his proper answer would be
'None'. For no wrenches had occurred. His attention was fixed on
the game but he went through no operations of fixing it. The
same man, listening to a lecture, might perform a hundred operations of fixing his attention and still fail to keep his mind on what

was being said. Acts of attending occur when attending is difficult. But sometimes attending is easy; and sometimes it is difficult, sometimes impossible not to attend.

Even where it is appropriate to speak of acts of attention, the word 'act' carries very little of its ordinary luggage. In ordinary contexts we apply very multifarious criteria in determining what constitutes one act. Perhaps making one move in chess is performing one act; perhaps doing enough to warrant prosecution is performing one act; and perhaps getting from the beginning to the end of a speech without being side-tracked is one act. But a person who has, say, hummed a tune from beginning to end, not absent-mindedly but on purpose and with some application, has not performed two acts or accomplished two tasks, one of humming plus one of giving his mind to reproducing the tune; or, at any rate, he has not performed two acts in that sense of 'two acts' in which it would make sense to say that he might have done the second but omitted the first. Giving his mind to reproducing the tune is not doing something else, in the way in which a person sawing wood while humming is doing something else besides humming. We should say, rather, that a person who hums a tune with some concentration is humming in a different way from the way in which he hums automatically, for all that the difference might make no audible difference. It makes his humming a different sort of action, not a concomitance of separately performable actions.

I suggest that explicit talk about such things as heed, concentration, paying attention, care and so on occurs most commonly in instruction-situations and in accusation-situations, both of which are relatively small, though important, sections of discourse. Elsewhere, even when talking about human beings, we tend to make relatively few explicit mentions of these things, not because it would be irrelevant, but because it would be redundant to do so. The notions are already built into the meanings of lots of the biographical and critical expressions which we use in talking to people and about them. In partly the same way we do not often need to make explicit mention of the special functions of particular utensils and instruments; not because they have not got functions, but because the names of these utensils and instruments themselves generally tell us their functions. The gunsmith does not advertise 'Guns to shoot with'.

When, in our philosophising, we do remember how notions of care, vigilance, interest and the like are built into the meanings of lots of our biographical and critical expressions, we may still be tempted to assimilate all of these notions to the two special notions that are cardinal for pedagogues and disciplinarians, of *studying* and *conforming*. We then find that our resultant account of the spectator's interest in an exciting game has a smell of unreality about it. For he is not taking pains to improve his wits, or dutifully abiding by any rules. He is attending, but not in either of these special modes of attention. Being excited or interested is not being sedulous; it is, more nearly, not-having-to-be-sedulous.

The general point that I am trying to make is that the notion of *attending* or *giving one's mind to* is a polymorphous notion. The special point that I am trying to make is that the notion of *enjoying* is one variety in this genus, or one member of this clan, i.e. that the reason why I cannot, in logic, enjoy what I am oblivious of is the same as the reason why I cannot, in logic, spray my currant-bushes without gardening.

Let us consider again the moderately specific notion of *interest*. To be, at a particular moment, interested in something is certainly to be giving one's mind to it, though one can give one's mind to a task, without being interested in it. The notions of *being fascinated, carried away, being wrapped up in, excited, absorbed, puzzled, intrigued*, and many congeners, clearly tie up closely, though in different ways, with the notion of interest. Now to say that someone has been enjoying a smell or a walk at least suggests and maybe even implies that he has been interested in the smell or in the exercise and the incidents of the walk—not that he gave his mind to them in e.g., the sedulous way, but rather that his mind was taken up by them in a spontaneous way. This is, of course, not enough. Alarming, disgusting and surprising things capture my attention without my having to fix my attention on them. So do pains and tickles.

I should like, at this stage, to be able to answer these questions: What is it, in general, to give one's mind to something? What, more specifically, is it to give one's mind to something in the mode of being interested in it? What, finally, is it to give one's mind to something in that special dimension of interest which constitutes enjoyment? I cannot do this, but will throw out a few unscholastic remarks.

It will not, I think, be suggested that interest is either a separable process or activity or a peculiar feeling. Even if there are acts of attention, there are not acts of interest, or pangs of it either. *En passant*, it is just worth mentioning that a person might be, for a spell, wholly taken up with something, like a smell or a taste, though he would not claim that the smell or taste had been interesting—or of course boring either. We tend to reserve the adjective 'interesting' for what provokes hypotheses or even for what would provoke hypotheses in the best people. A connoisseur might find a wine interesting; the ordinary diner might describe it as piquant or attractive or just nice.

Think of the partly metaphorical force of the expressions 'absorbed' and 'occupied'. When the blotting-paper absorbs the ink, we picture the ink as unresisting and the blotting-paper as having the power. It thirstily imbibes every drop of the docile ink and will not give it up again. Somewhat similarly, when a child is absorbed in his game, he—every drop of him—is sucked up into the business of manipulating his clockwork trains. All his thoughts, all his talk, all his controllable muscular actions are those of his engine-drivers, signalmen and station-masters. His game is, for the moment, his whole world. He does not coerce or marshal himself into playing, as, maybe, his conscripted father does. Else there would be some drop of him which was recalcitrant to the blotting-paper. Yet when we say that he is wholly absorbed in his game, we do not accept the entire parallel of the ink and the blotting-paper. For the blotting-paper had been one thing and the ink-blot another. But the game which absorbs the child is nothing but the child himself, playing trains. He, the player, has, for the moment, sucked up, without resistance, every drop of himself that might have been on other businesses, or on no business at all.

Or think of the notion of occupation. Victorious troops occupy a city; its police, administration, communications and commerce are managed according to the policy or the whims of the victors. The citizens' public and private doings are subject to the permission and perhaps to the direction of their new masters. Yet there are different kinds of occupation. The city may be managed tyrannically, stiffly, amicably, paternally or fraternally; and while the citizens may feel like slaves or helots or infants, they might feel like adolescents who are being shown how to be free; how to manage themselves. Somewhat so a person who is occupied in reading may feel oppressed; but he may feel merely shepherded, or advised, or partnered, or trusted, or left to his own devices. But here again the parallel is only fragmentary, since here both the citizens and the occupying troops are the reader himself. He is under the control and he is the controller. It is his policy or his whim that directs and permits those doings of his own which, if he were unoccupied would otherwise be without these directions and permissions—and therefore be quite different doings.

There is an important objection which could be made against both of these attempted illustrations. It could be said that I have in fact been sketching an elucidation of the notions of absorption and occupation which fails for the reasons for which a *circulus in definiendo* ruins an attempted definition. To say that the child who is totally absorbed in a game has all his thoughts, conversation and controllable muscular movements sucked up into the one activity of playing trains would be simply to say that being absorbed in A involves not being absorbed in B, C or D. To say that a person who is occupied in reading brings and keeps all his doings under a unified control is only a long-winded way of saying that while he is engaged in reading, he is not engaged in bicycling or conversing; and these are truisms. I hope that I mean something less nugatory than this. A man who is not employed by one employer may not be employed by any other. He may be employable, but unemployed. Or he may be unemployable. Somewhat similarly, a person who is not taking an interest in A, need not be taking an interest in anything else. He may be inert, i.e. asleep or half-asleep. But he may not be inert and yet not be taking an interest in anything at all. He may be the victim of *ennui*, in which case he actively yawns, fidgets, wriggles, scratches, paces up and down and whistles; yet he may do all of these things absent-mindedly or mechanically. He is restless but not employed; energetic but not occupied. He does plenty of things, but not on purpose, carefully with zeal or enjoyment. He is accomplishing nothing, for he is essaying nothing. He is merely responding to stimuli. The right thing to say would perhaps be that the child's game sucks up not all his thoughts, conversation and controllable muscular movements but rather all his energies. These energies, when so sucked up, become the thinking, conversing and manipulating that constitute his playing. But this notion of energies seems a rather suspicious character.

What is the point of pressing analogies or even plays upon words like these? One point is this. Where, as here, unpicturesque discourse still eludes us, the harm done by subjugation to one picture is partly repaired by deliberately ringing the changes on two or three. If they are appropriate at all, they are likely to be appropriate in different ways and therefore to keep us reminded of features which otherwise we might forget. The analogy of the blotting-paper may remind us of what the analogy of the torch-beam would, by itself, shut out of our heads, namely the facts—the conceptual facts—that there can be attending where there is no switching on of attention, and that there can be attending where there is no question of exploring or discerning. The analogy of the military occupation of a city may keep us in mind of the conceptual facts, which the other analogies do not bring out, that giving one's mind to something may, but need not involve mutinousness, reluctance or even dull acquiescence. One's mind may be given readily and it may be given with zest. Not all control is oppression. Sometimes it is release. Both the analogy of the blotting-paper and the analogy of the fraternal military occupation are meant to indicate, in a very unprofessional way, the conceptual region in which pleasure is located. But, at best, the real work remains to do.

26

SENSATION

*Reprinted from 'Contemporary British Philosophy, Third Series'
edited by H. D. Lewis, 1956, by permission of George Allen &
Unwin Ltd.*

One of the things that worry me most is the notion of sensations or sense-impressions. It seems, on the one hand, very hard to avoid saying that hearing, seeing, and tasting could not happen unless appropriate sense-impressions were received; and yet also very hard to give a coherent account of what such sense-impressions are, or how the having of sense-impressions is connected with, say, our hearing a conversation or our seeing a tree.

There seem to be some very good reasons for saying that sense-impressions can occur in abnormal situations, when no perceiving occurs. For example, after looking at a bright light I have an after-image; or if I knock my head I seem to see stars or lightning flashes; or when I have a bad cold I have a singing noise in my head. One seems bound to say that in these situations I have optical or acoustic sensations or sense-impressions, and that it is just in the presence of these that the similarity consists between merely having an after-image and genuinely seeing a tree, or between merely having a singing in my head and genuinely hearing the choir singing in the concert-hall. In cases of genuine perception, we are inclined to say, we both have sense-impressions, produced or stimulated in the normal ways, and also contribute something of our own, namely, to put it too picturesquely, the interpretation or significance, without which we should not have perceived, say, an oak-tree. Yet the moment we start to press this tempting idea we are landed in familiar difficulties. Colours as we see them and sounds as we hear them seem at once to collapse into internal reactions or states of ourselves. The oak-tree is not really green and the tenor's voice is not literally shrill. The sense-impressions which were supposed to make perception of trees and choirs possible finish by becoming screens between ourselves and trees or choirs.

The sensible qualities of things in the world cease to be qualities of those things and become, instead, momentary states of our own minds or nervous systems. They come to have the status of stomach-aches, caused, indeed, fairly indirectly by mechanical and chemical properties of external things, of the intervening medium, and of our own nervous systems, but no more to be equated with attributes of external things than my stomach-ache is an attribute of the uncooked beans which indirectly caused my stomach to ache.

There are further difficulties. First, the notion of sense-impression seems to be a technical or specialist notion. People without special theories or technical knowledge of physiology, optics, chemistry or psychology know well how to use the concepts of seeing, hearing and smelling, though not the concept of *sense-impression*. They have to be introduced to this notion by being introduced to the outlines of special theories about the physics and physiology of perception. Only after having heard a bit about the propagation of waves and the like, and then about the trans-mission of impulses up the nerves, and then perhaps also something about the psychology of stimuli and responses—only then can they begin to use the notion of *sense-impressions*. Consequently, in the ordinary contexts in which we talk about seeing, hearing and the rest, no mention is made of sense-impressions, any more than in ordinary contexts in which meat, vegetables, and fruit are discussed, any mention is made of calories or vitamins. As I might put it, the concept of *perception* is on a more elementary or less technical level than that of *sense-impression*. We can know all that is a part of common knowledge about seeing and hearing, without knowing anything about these impressions. But from this it follows directly that the concept of sense-impression is not any sort of component of the concept of perception, any more than the concept of *vitamin* is any sort of component of the concept of *dinner*.

Unfortunately, however, the logical situation is a confused one. For we are perfectly familiar with not one, but at least two quite different non-technical notions of *sensation*—and philosophers and psychologists have nearly always tried to equate their technical notion of *sense-impression* with one, or more often with both, of these non-technical notions of *sensation*. They pass without apology from saying that without optical or auditory sense-impressions there is no seeing or hearing, to saying that seeing and hearing involve the having of sensations, as if the one assertion were a mere paraphrase of the other.

To get this point a bit clearer, let me examine in some detail the two non-technical notions of sensation.

First, there is the sense of the word 'sensation' or the word 'feeling', in which sensations or feelings are such things as pains, tickles, feelings of nausea, suffocation, thirst, and the like. A pain is what anodynes and anaesthetics exist to relieve or prevent. Sensations of this sort can be more or less acute or intense; they can be short-lived or protracted, and they are, in general, localisable in particular parts of the body. Most sensations, in this sense of the word, if not all of them, are in some degree distressing. Some philosophers, like Bishop Berkeley, have argued, quite fallaciously it seems to me, that the family which includes such things as pains, tickles and feelings of suffocation also includes such things as our sensations of temperature. When I bring my hand nearer and nearer to the fire, I begin by feeling increases in the heat, but at a certain point the heat is intense enough to hurt. Berkeley argues that therefore a feeling of warmth differs only in degree from the feeling of pain. So the feeling of warmth is a state of myself in the way in which a pain is.

But this will not do at all. For one thing, some weight must be attached to the fact that no one does suppose that painfulness characterises the fire, in the way in which they do suppose that warmth does. A child will say that the fire is so hot that it hurts his hand, and thus is already distinguishing between an effect which the fire has upon him from a property which the fire has, without which it would not hurt him. Moreover, feeling, say with one's hand, that the fire is hotter than it was, is finding the answer to a question. The owner of the hand is discriminating something, finding out a difference. In some cases he would admit to having made a mistake. He had not been careful enough. But in having a pain there is no finding anything out, no discerning of similarities or differences, no place, even, for mistakes and so no room for carelessness or lack of carefulness. Feeling, in the sense of finding out or discerning, the warmth of things is a kind of perception, and a kind at which some people, like bakers and laundry-girls, become better than other people; it is the product of an acquired skill; but feeling, in the sense of suffering pains, is not a kind of perception, and there is no question of one victim being better or worse than another at feeling toothaches. In this sense of 'feeling' or 'sensation', pains are not things the feeling of which is the product of an acquired skill. So far from the feeling of warmth being merely a lower degree of the feeling of pain, the two things are 'felt' only in quite different senses of the word. They are not even species of one genus, as perhaps seeing and tasting are species of the one genus, perception. They belong to different categories from one another. The attempt to classify felt temperatures with felt pains, and so to show that felt warmth is a state or reaction in ourselves, as pain in some way is, was a logical mistake.

We need, therefore, to distinguish the sense of 'feeling' or 'sensation' in which we call pains and tickles 'feelings' or 'sensations' from the entirely different sense in which we say that we perceive some things not by seeing, hearing, smelling, or tasting, but by feeling—the sense in which we say that a person whose feet or fingers are numb with cold has lost sensation or the power of feeling things with his fingers and toes. Let me just remind you of some of the properties of external things which are perceived by feeling, as opposed to seeing, hearing, smelling or tasting. First, to detect how hot or cold something is, we have to feel it with the hands, or lips, or tongue, or, less efficiently, with other parts of our bodies. We cannot see, hear or smell how cold things are. Next, to detect the roughness, smoothness, slipperiness or stickiness of the surfaces of things, we normally have to handle them or finger them. Next, to detect whether something is vibrating, stiff, resilient, loose in its socket and so on, we usually have to touch it, and very likely also muscularly to manipulate it. Some people are much better than others at discrimination-tasks of these kinds. Doctors can feel the pulses of patients which are too faint for you or me to detect and the trained driver can feel the car going into a skid long before the novice could have done so.

We should notice that tactual and kinaesthetic detection is unlike seeing, hearing, tasting, and smelling in one important respect. What I detect by seeing, hearing, tasting, and smelling are, with extremely few exceptions, properties or features of things and happenings outside me. What I detect tactually and kinaesthetically *may* be properties or features of external though contiguous things and events; but they may be and quite often are properties or features of anatomically internal things and events. I can detect, sometimes, the beating of my own heart, the distension of my own stomach, the straining or relaxing of my own muscles, the creaking of my own joints, and the fishbone in my own throat. A doctor, I imagine, learns to detect by feeling the congestion of his own lungs.

In this sense of 'feeling', feeling is a species of perception or perceptual discrimination. We have to learn to do it; we may be better or worse than other people at doing it. There is room for care and carelessness in doing it; and there is always the possibility of making mistakes. To be able to feel things, in this sense, is to have got a certain amount of a specific skill or family of skills, just as to be able to detect and discriminate things by seeing, hearing, tasting, and smelling is to have got a certain amount of a specific skill or family of skills. In all cases alike there can be trained or untrained observers. To detect or discriminate something, whether by sight or touch, is to achieve something, namely, to find something out by the exercise of an acquired and perhaps deliberately trained skill. This shows how enormously different is the sense of the verb 'feel' when used to denote detection by touch from the sense of the verb 'feel' when used to denote the suffering of a pain or other discomfort.

But different though these two concepts of 'feeling' or 'sensation' are, still both are quite untechnical concepts. The child has learned to use both long before he has heard of any physiological, neurological or psychological theories.

So now we can ask whether it is true that all perceiving involves the having of sensations or the feeling of anything, in either of these senses. Well, to begin with, it is perfectly clear that usually when I see, hear, taste or smell anything, or detect something by touch, I do not suffer any discomfort or pain in my eyes, ears, tongue, nose or fingertips. Seeing a tree does not hurt my eyes; and hearing a bird singing does not set up the slightest sort of tickling feeling in my ears. Sometimes, certainly, looking at things, like the headlights of motor cars, or listening to things, like the whistle of a railway-engine a few yards away, does hurt my eyes and ears. But not only is this exceptional but, still more important, these disagreeable sensations do not help, they hinder perception. I see much better when I am not being dazzled than when I am. Sensations, in this sense, are not usually present when perception occurs; and when they are present, they tend to impair perception. They are not *sine qua non*s of perception.

But nor is it true that when I see, hear or smell things I feel anything with my eyes, ears and nose, in the sense of detecting something tactually or kinaesthetically. When I see a green tree, I do not concomitantly detect, with my eyes, the warmth or coldness, the smoothness or roughness, the vibrations or the resilience of anything. My eyes are very inferior organs with which to detect things tactually and kinaesthetically. My ears and nose are even worse. But whether they are good or bad, when I see things with my eyes, I do not therewith have to detect something else tactually or kinaesthetically with those eyes of mine, and usually I do not; and similarly with my ears and nose. With my tongue the situation is slightly different. Usually when I taste things, I do also detect with my tongue the temperature and some of the tactually and kinaesthetically discoverable properties of the food or the drink in my mouth. But even this is a case of concomitance and not dependence. I can taste the taste of onions when there is no longer anything in my mouth with a temperature of its own or with any shape or consistency of its own. In tasting, I often do in fact, but I do not in logic, have also to feel anything with my tongue, in the sense of 'feel' in which I feel the roughness of the nutshell or the smoothness of the eggshell with my fingers or, sometimes, with my tongue. My tongue is, so to speak, a double sense-organ. I can both feel things with it and taste things with it. But I can feel the shape and surfaces of things like spoons without tasting anything; and I can taste e.g. onions or pepper without feeling anything.

So when philosophers and psychologists assert that all perceiving involves the having of sensations or the feeling of something, either they are dead wrong, or else they are using a third, quite different notion of feeling or sensation. In particular, the notion of sensing or having sense-impressions, which, they assert, is a component of the notion of perceiving, must be a notion quite different both from the notion of feelings like pains and tickles, and from the notion of tactual and kinaesthetic detection or discrimination.

But at this point there arises something of a crux. When a person has a pain we think that he must, in some sense of the word, be conscious or aware of the pain; and when a person detects or discriminates something by touch, his perceiving what he perceives must also be, in some sense of the word, conscious. A person cannot require to be told by someone else that he is in pain or that he has just perceived something. Well then, what of the sense-impressions which, we are told, enter into perceiving? Are we conscious of them or do we have to be told of their existence by others, or, perhaps, infer to them ourselves in accordance with some more or less technical theory of optics or neurology or psychology? It is generally maintained that our sense-impressions are certainly and necessarily things that we are conscious of and cannot be unconscious of, as we cannot, with certain reservations, be unconscious of our pains and tickles and as we cannot see, hear or taste things unconsciously. Indeed it is apt to be maintained that if sense-impressions were things of which we were unconscious, then they could not do their proper business, namely, that of providing the basic *given* elements in seeing, hearing and the rest. Well then, are we conscious of having sense-impressions? Do people ever say whether to themselves or to anyone else, 'I am having' or 'I have just had a sense-impression of such and such a description'? Or rather, since the actual term 'sense-impression' is obviously a somewhat technical, classificatory term, do people ever say, to themselves or others, 'I am having', or 'I have just had a so and so', where the concrete filling of the vacancy 'so and so' would be something which properly fell under the technical, classificatory term 'sense-impression'? Certainly people say that they see trees or have just heard some birds singing; but these verbs of perception carry too much luggage to be what is wanted. Certainly too, people sometimes say, more non-comittally, 'I see something green', or 'I have just heard a twittering noise'. But these expressions also carry too much luggage. A person who said 'I see something green' might then learn that there was a tree in front of him, and say 'Then what I saw was a green tree, though I did not at the time know that the green thing I saw was a tree'. What is wanted, apparently, is some family of expressions, in constant and familiar use by everyone, in which they report, without inference or external information, the occurrence of a conscious experience unencumbered, as yet, with any beliefs or knowledge about the existence or properties of any external object.

Sometimes it is suggested that we do report such basic experiences in such utterances as 'I seem to smell onions' or 'I thought I heard birds singing' or 'It looks as if there is a green tree over there'. In reporting mere appearances, without committing ourselves to their veracity, we are, it is suggested, reporting the having of sense-impressions without the addition of any perceptual claims about the external world. But this will not do. We use such tentative, guarded or non-committal expressions in all sorts of fields or departments, in most of which there is no question of there being any appropriate sense-impressions to isolate. I can say, after a rapid piece of calculation in my head, '15 × 16 appears to make 220'; I can say, after a cursory glance, 'It looks as if the river here is about twice the width of the road in front of my house'; I can say 'She appeared to be half-angry and half-amused'; and I can say 'The period of general inflation seems to be coming to an end'.

Now all these are guarded statements of what I am tempted or inclined to judge to be the case, though I do not yet commit myself to their being the case. Yet no one supposes that in saying such things I am reporting the occurrence of any sense-impressions. Statements of the form 'it looks as if', 'there seems to be', 'apparently, . . .' are not *ex officio* dedicated to the wanted reports of the experiences alleged to be basic ingredients in sense-perception. So we cannot, unless provided with some extra restrictions which are not in fact provided, adduce idioms of these patterns as being the untutored, uninferential deliverances of our consciousness of the postulated sense-impressions. We have, in fact, no special way of reporting the occurrence of these postulated impressions; we are, therefore, without the needed marks of our being conscious of such things at all. For there is surely something absurd in maintaining that we are constantly conscious of some things in the way in which we are conscious of pains, and yet have no way of telling ourselves or other people anything whatsoever about them.

We must acknowledge, therefore, that the view of some epistemologists and psychologists that there are sense-impressions is not arrived at at all in the way in which everyone comes to know that pains and tickles occur, or in the way in which everyone comes to know that we sometimes detect things by sight, hearing, taste, and touch. The view that sense-impressions occur is arrived at as a deduction from a theory, or perhaps from two or more seemingly interlocking theories.

I want to separate out two quite different theoretical allegiances which, in their different ways, drive people to postulate sense-impressions.

(1) If a child and a man are looking at the first word of the first line of a page, the man may say that he sees the word 'Edinburgh' misprinted, where the child may not detect the misprint but say only that he sees the word 'Edinburgh'. The child's eyesight is as good as the man's, but because he is worse at spelling, he fails to see the misprint that the man sees. If now an illiterate Esquimau looks at the same part of the page, though his eyesight is excellent, he will not see a word at all, but only some black marks.

Or if a countryman and a townsman, with equally good sight, are looking at the same field, the one may say that he sees a field of young wheat, while the other may say only that he sees a field of green stuff. In these and countless other such cases, the one observer claims to discern much more than the other, though admitting that their eyesight is equally good. It is natural and tempting to say that the observer whose eyes, somehow, tell him more is putting more into his report of what he sees or that he is giving to it a fuller 'interpretation' than the other can do. He has learned more spelling or more agriculture than the other, so he includes in his report of what he sees the extra information which his previous experience and education had equipped him with. His report of what he sees is inflated with knowledge or beliefs which the other man does not possess; in short it carries a mass of ideas or thoughts which are absent from the other observer's report of what *he* sees. In detecting a misprint or a field of young wheat he seems, therefore, to be combining the piece of seeing, which, presumably, contains only what the townsman's seeing contains, with a piece of thinking, which the townsman is unable to supply. What is more, this extra thought-luggage may be right or wrong. The countryman may have misidentified the green crop.

Now there exists a view, which is accepted almost as an axiom, that all thinking, or anyhow all thinking which is intended to result in the discovery or establishment of truths, is inferring; and therewith that all errors and mistakes issue from fallacious reasoning. Accordingly, when philosophers and psychologists consider things like the detection of misprints or the identification of the green crop with young wheat, they automatically describe the thinking-element in this detection and identification with reasoning. The question at once arises, Whence then do we get the initial premisses of our perceptual conclusions? On this view, the premisses must be ascertained at a level prior to any thinking, and prior therefore to any exploitation of knowledge or beliefs previously acquired. There must be a totally non-cogitative acceptance of some basic premisses for us to be able to move from these initial data to our correct or incorrect perceptual conclusions about misprints or young wheat. It is, I think, with this idea in mind that many thinkers use the expression 'sense-data' for the postulated sense-impressions which must be there to inaugurate our perceptual inferrings. For 'datum' ordinarily has the force of 'evidence' or 'reasons'. A datum is something that we reason from and does not itself have to be reasoned to.

This reason for postulating the existence of sense-impressions seems to me a bad reason, and bad on two scores. First, if it is not true that all thinking is inferring, then it need not be true that the thinking which enters into perceptual recognition, identification, comparison, etc., is inferring, and if it is not, then the search for its fund of premisses is a search for nothing. In multiplying we think out the answers to questions, but our results are not conclusions and our mistakes are not fallacies. This thinking does not start from any data or premisses; and the same might be true of the thinking that is supposed to go on in perceptual recognition, identification, etc. But, second, it seems to me false or at least highly misleading to say that a man who detects a misprint or a farmer who identifies the green crop with growing wheat is necessarily *thinking* at all.

For one thing, the misprint and the nature of the crop might be discerned at sight or in a flash. As soon as his eye falls on the misprinted word, the man might start to pencil in the correction. There might be no moment, however short, in which he could be described as pondering, reflecting or putting two and two together. He might say, quite truly, that he saw the misprint the moment his eye fell on the word, and that he did not have time to think or even that he did not need to think.

To meet this sort of objection, epistemologists and psychologists sometimes say that though he does not remember doing any thinking, and though the time available for thinking seemed to be wanting, still he must have thought, and so his thinking must have been done at lightning speed—and this might be the reason why he cannot remember doing any thinking afterwards. But we should mistrust these 'musts'. Why must he have done any pondering, considering or putting two and two together? All that the argument up to date has shown is that if he had not previously learned to spell, he could not now recognise misprints at sight. But why must the exploitation of knowledge previously acquired take the form of pondering? We ponder when things are not obvious to us. But when previous training results in things being obvious at sight, which would not have been obvious without that training, why should we have to postulate a present piece of pondering to explain the immediate obviousness of the misprint? Ordinarily we account for someone needing to stop to think by showing how something was, at the start, unobvious to him. But here, apparently, the fact that the misprint is immediately obvious to him is supposed to need to be explained not just by reference to his prior education, but also by the postulation of the performance by him of a piece of thinking, with the queer property of not requiring any time for its performance.

So I maintain not only that perceptual recognition, identification, etc. need not embody any inferential thinking, but that they need not embody any thinking at all. They involve the possession and exploitation of knowledge previously acquired. But this exploitation is not thinking. So the argument for the occurrence of sense-impressions to be the data or premisses for the inferential thinking embodied is doubly broken-backed.

(2) There is another theoretical allegiance which helps to drive philosophers, psychologists, physiologists, and physicists into postulating the existence of sense-impressions. This is their natural and up to a point proper allegiance to causal theories of perception. We learn from optics and acoustics about the transmission of light and sound; we learn from physiology the structure of the eye and ear; we are learning from neurophysiology about the transmission of impulses along the nerve-fibres. When we ask what makes seeing and hearing possible, and what makes them impossible or inefficient, we derive our answers, quite properly, from the relevant stretches of these scientific theories.

We trace the propagation of light from a light-giving source to the surface of a light-reflecting object and thence to the lens and the retina of the human eye; we then trace the nervous impulses set up at the retina to the right place in the brain. Some further transformation may then be supposed such that the terminal neural impulse sets up, somehow, a psychic or mental reaction, and thus seeing takes place—or rather, since seeing a misprint requires a special education and maybe also, as is often supposed, a special act of lightning-speed thinking, we should perhaps say that the last neural impulse sets up a mental reaction which is the necessary spur or stimulus to seeing, though seeing consists not only in this stimulus but also in some part of our immediate response to it. This sort of account of perception operates naturally with the notions of propagation, transmission, impulse, stimulus and response, rather than with the notions of *data*, premisses, evidence, and conclusions. Sense-impressions are now thought of not as steps in a lightning-swift argument but as links in a causal chain. They are indeed often spoken of as 'given', but they are 'given', now, in the sense in which electric shocks are given, not in the sense in which Euclid's axioms are given, i.e. are the uninferred premisses for inferred consequences. 'Given' now means 'inflicted', not, as before, 'accepted without argument'. Sense-impressions are now thought of as things impressed on us, impulses transmitted through us, not as things found by us by some sort of pre-cogitative finding.

Now there can be no quarrelling with this sort of account, whether we are thinking of the stages covered by optics and acoustics, or whether we are thinking of the stages covered by physiology and neurophysiology. The final stage, covering a supposed jump from neural impulses in the body to mental experiences, or sense-impressions is, however, quite a different matter.

It presupposes the Cartesian body-mind view which I have found fault with at some length in my book. But, apart from this general objection, there remains the specific objection that the existence of these sense-impressions is something postulated; they are not things which anyone reports who has not been convinced by the whole story of the chain of physical, neural and psychic impulses. Even if the Cartesian view were true, yet still we should be without the Cartesian grounds for asserting the existence of sense-impressions which we possess for pains and tickles.

What has gone wrong? It seems to me that this is what has gone wrong. The perfectly proper and necessary research into the physics of light and sound, and into the physiology of seeing and hearing, came to be misrepresented as an enquiry which when completed would 'explain' seeing and hearing—explain it, that is to say, in the sense of 'explain' in which an earthquake is explained by seismological theory or diabetes is explained by a certain branch of pathology. The idea, then, is that what we need to know about seeing and hearing is the various physical and physiological conditions from modifications in which we could infer to the cessation or alteration of our seeing and hearing; in short, that our questions about perception are merely causal questions.

Now of course we have causal questions to ask about perception, and the sciences of optics and acoustics, ophthalmology and neurology have either already provided us with the answers to these causal questions or can confidently be expected to provide them in the fairly near future. But not all our questions about perception are causal questions; and the proffering of causal answers to non-causal questions leads to inevitable dissatisfaction, which cannot be relieved by promises of yet more advanced causal answers still to be discovered.

Perceiving, as I have pointed out earlier, is exercising an acquired skill; or rather it embodies the exercise of an acquired skill. Seeing a misprint is an impossibility for someone who has not learned to spell. Now about the exercises of any acquired skills there are, of course, causal questions to be asked. If a tightrope-walker succeeds in walking along the stretched wire, we can, of course, ask and fairly easily find out the answers to all sorts of causal questions about his performance—mechanical questions about his equilibrium, physiological questions about his muscles and nerves, and pedagogic questions about the training he had received, and so on. But quite different from these causal questions are technical questions, questions, that is, about the nature of the task of tightrope-walking, about the various kinds of mistakes that are to be avoided, and the various kinds of attentiveness, courage and ingenuity which make for success—all the things which the tightrope-walker must either have been taught by his trainers or have found out for himself. Lessons of this sort need not include much, if any, of the information which might be provided by the physicist, the physiologist or the psychologist. Nor does the chess-player need to know anything about the physiology of his muscular system, despite the fact that he could not be good or even bad at chess if he could not move his fingers and hands where he wished.

In the same sort of way, I am arguing that some questions about perceiving, and particularly those which are of interest in epistemology, are not causal questions—though there are such questions, and many of them have been answered—but questions about, so to speak, the *crafts* or *arts* of finding things out by seeing and hearing, including questions about the nature of mistakes and failures in perception and their relations with mistakes and failures in thinking, spelling, counting, and the like.

It is not that hearing and smelling are queer happenings which are exempt from causal conditions, but that not all questions about hearing and smelling are questions about these causal conditions. Checkmating an opponent at chess is certainly a happening, and a happening conditioned by all sorts of known and unknown causes. But the chess-player's interest is not in these causes, but in the tactics or strategy or sometimes just the luck of which the checkmating was the outcome. It is not the dull physical fact of the arrival of the Queen at a particular square, it is the fact that this arrival constituted the success or victory of the player, which is what is significant for the players and spectators of the game. Similarly, finding out something by seeing or hearing is, so to speak, a success or victory in the game of exploring the world. This seeing or hearing is of course susceptible of a complete and very complex causal explanation, given in terms of optics or acoustics, physiology, neurology and the rest; but the player's interest is not primarily in the contents of this explanation, but in the exploratory task itself and its accomplishment.

In other words, verbs like 'see' and 'hear' do not merely denote special experiences or mental happenings, with special causal antecedents; they denote achievements of tasks, or successes in undertakings. There are questions of technique to be asked about them as well as questions of causal conditioning, and questions of technique are not answerable by any multiplication of answers to questions of causal conditioning; they are questions of quite different types.

So I want to suggest that the postulation of sense-impressions as causal antecedent of seeing and hearing, only an antecedent not of a physical or physiological, but of a psychological kind arose from two sources, (1) a proper realisation of the fact that physical and physiological causal accounts of perception cannot answer technical questions about perceptual successes and failures; (2) an improper non-realisation of the fact that what was lacking to such causal accounts was not that they needed an extra, psychological link in the causal chain; but that they were answers to causal questions and not to questions of technique. When we want to describe the differences between hearing, mishearing, and non-hearing, no discovery or postulation of causal links can give us what we want. Sense-impressions were postulated as the missing causal links which would solve a problem which was not a causal problem.

However, after all this has been said, I confess to a residual embarrassment. There is something in common between having an after-image and seeing a misprint. Both are visual affairs. How ought we to describe their affinity with one another without falling back on to some account very much like a part of the orthodox theories of sense-impressions? To this I am stumped for an answer.

27

THE THEORY OF MEANING

Reprinted from 'British Philosophy in Mid-Century', edited by C. A. Mace, 1957, by permission of George Allen & Unwin Ltd.

We can all use the notion of *meaning*. From the moment we begin to learn to translate English into French and French into English, we realize that one expression does or does not mean the same as another. But we use the notion of meaning even earlier than that. When we read or hear something in our own language which we do not understand, we wonder what it means and ask to have its meaning explained to us. The ideas of understanding, misunderstanding and failing to understand what is said already contain the notion of expressions having and lacking specifiable meanings.

It is, however, one thing to ask, as a child might ask, What, if anything, is meant by 'vitamin', or 'abracadabra' or '$(a+b)^2 = a^2 + b^2 + 2ab$'? It is quite another sort of thing to ask What are meanings? It is, in the same way, one thing to ask, as a child might ask, What can I buy for this shilling?, and quite another sort of thing to ask What is purchasing-power? or What are exchange-values?

Now answers to this highly abstract question, What are meanings? have, in recent decades, bulked large in philosophical and logical discussions. Preoccupation with the theory of meaning could be described as the occupational disease of twentieth-century Anglo-Saxon and Austrian philosophy. We need not worry whether or not it is a disease. But it might be useful to survey the motives and the major results of this preoccupation.

Incidentally it is worth noticing that many of these issues were explicitly canvassed—and some of them conclusively settled—in certain of Plato's later Dialogues, and in the logical and other works of Aristotle. Some of them, again, were dominant issues in the late Middle Ages and later still with Hobbes; and some of them, thickly or thinly veiled in the psychological terminology of 'ideas', stirred uneasily inside British epistemology between Locke and John Stuart Mill. But I shall not, save for one or two back-references, discuss the early history of these issues.

The shopkeeper, the customer, the banker and the merchant are ordinarily under no intellectual pressure to answer or even ask the abstract questions What is purchasing-power? and What are exchange-values? They are interested in the prices of things, but not yet in the abstract question What is the real nature of that which is common to two articles of the same price? Similarly, the child who tries to follow a conversation on an unfamiliar topic, and the translator who tries to render Thucydides into English are interested in what certain expressions mean. But they are not necessarily interested in the abstract questions What is it for an expression to have a meaning? and What is the nature and status of that for which an expression and its translation or paraphrase are both the vehicles? From what sort of interests, then, do we come to ask this sort of question? Doubtless there are many answers. I shall concentrate on two of them which I shall call 'the Theory of Logic' and 'the Theory of Philosophy'. I shall spend a good long time on the first; not so long on the second.

(1) *The Theory of Logic.* The logician, in studying the rules of inference, has to talk of the components of arguments, namely their premisses and conclusions and to talk of them in perfectly general terms. Even when he adduces concrete premisses and conclusions, he does so only to illustrate the generalities which are his proper concern. In the same way, he has to discuss the types of separable components or the types of distinguishable features of these premiss-types and conclusion-types, since it is sometimes on such components or features of premisses and conclusions that the inferences from and to them pivot.

Now the same argument may be expressed in English or in French or in any other language; and if it is expressed in English, there may still be hosts of different ways of wording it. What the logician is exploring is intended to be different to these differences of wording. He is concerned with what is said by a premiss-sentence or a conclusion-sentence, not with how it is worded.

So, if not in the prosecution of his inquiry, at least in his explanations of what he is doing, he has to declare that his subject-matter consist not of the sentences and their ingredient words in which arguments are expressed, but of the propositions or judgments and their constituent terms, ideas or concepts of which the sentences and words are the vehicles. Sometimes he may say that his subject matter consists of sentence-meanings and their constituent word-meanings or phrase-meanings, though this idiom is interestingly repellent. Why it is repellent we shall, I hope, see later on. So in giving this sort of explanation of his business, he is talking *about* meanings, where in the prosecution of that business he is just operating *upon* them.

For our purposes it is near enough true to say that the first influential discussion of the notion of meaning given by a modern logician was that with which John Stuart Mill opens his *System of Logic* (1843). He acknowledges debts both to Hobbes and to the Schoolmen, but we need not trace these borrowings in detail.

Mill's contributions to Formal or Symbolic Logic were negligible. It was not he but his exact contemporaries, Boole and de Morgan, and his immediate successors, Jevons, Venn, Carroll, McColl and Peirce who, in the English-speaking world, paved the way for Russell. On the other hand, it is difficult to exaggerate the influence which he exercised, for good and for ill, upon British and Continental philosophers; and we must include among these philosophers the Symbolic Logicians as well, in so far as they have philosophized about their technical business. In particular, Mill's theory of meaning set the questions, and in large measure, determined their answers for thinkers as different as Brentano, in Austria; Meinong and Husserl, who were pupils of Brentano; Bradley, Jevons, Venn, Frege, James, Peirce, Moore and Russell. This extraordinary achievement was due chiefly to the fact that Mill was original in producing a doctrine of meaning at all. The doctrine that he produced was immediately influential, partly because a doctrine was needed and partly because its inconsistencies were transparent. Nearly all of the thinkers whom I have listed were in vehement opposition to certain parts of Mill's doctrine, and it was the other parts of it from which they often drew their most effective weapons.

Mill, following Hobbes's lead, starts off his account of the notion of meaning by considering single words. As we have to learn the alphabet before we can begin to spell, so it seemed natural to suppose that the meanings of sentences are compounds of the components, which are the meanings of their ingredient words. Word-meanings are atoms, sentence-meanings are molecules. I say that it seemed natural, but I hope soon to satisfy you that it was a tragically false start. Next Mill, again following Hobbes's lead, takes it for granted that all words, or nearly all words, are names, and this, at first, sounds very tempting. We know what it is for 'Fido' to be the name of a particular dog, and for 'London' to be the name of a particular town. There, in front of us, is the dog or the town which has the name, so here, one feels, there is no mystery. We have just the familiar relation between a thing and its name. The assimilation of all or most other single words to names gives us, accordingly, a cosy feeling. We fancy that we know where we are. The dog in front of us is what the word 'Fido' stands for, the town we visited yesterday is what the word 'London' stands for. So the classification of all or most single words as names makes us feel that what a word means is in all cases some manageable thing that that word is the name of. Meanings, at least word-meanings, are nothing abstruse or remote, they are, prima facie, ordinary things and happenings like dogs and towns and battles.

Mill goes further. Sometimes the grammatical subject of a sentence is not a single word but a many-worded phrase, like 'the present Prime Minister' or 'the first man to stand on the summit of Mt Everest'. Mill has no qualms in classifying complex expressions like these also as names, what he calls 'many-worded names'. There do not exist proper names for everything we want to talk about; and sometimes we want to talk about something or somebody whose proper name, though it exists, is unknown to us. So descriptive phrases are coined by us to do duty for proper names. But they are still, according to Mill, names, though the tempting and in fact prevailing interpretation of this assertion differs importantly from what Mill usually wanted to convey. For, when Mill calls a word or phrase a 'name', he is using 'name' not, or not always, quite in the ordinary way. Sometimes he says that for an expression to be a name it must be able to be used as the subject or the predicate of a subject-predicate sentence—which lets in, e.g. adjectives as names. Sometimes his requirements are more stringent. A name is an expression which can be the subject of a subject-predicate sentence—which leaves only nouns, pronouns and substantival phrases. 'Name', for him, does not mean merely 'proper name'. He often resisted temptations to which he subjected his successors.

Before going any further, I want to make you at least suspect that this initially congenial equation of words and descriptive phrases with names is from the outset a monstrous howler—if, like some of Mill's successors, though unlike Mill himself, we do systematically construe 'name' on the model of 'proper name'. The assumption of the truth of this equation has been responsible for a large number of radical absurdities in philosophy in general and the philosophy of logic in particular. It was a fetter round the ankles of Meinong, from which he never freed himself. It was a fetter round the ankles of Frege, Moore and Russell, who all, sooner or later, saw that without some big emendations the assumption led inevitably to fatal impasses. It was, as he himself says in his new book, a fetter round the ankles of Wittgenstein in the *Tractatus*, though in that same book he had found not only the need but the way to cut himself partially loose from it.

I am still not quite sure why it seems so natural to assume that all words are names, and even that every possible grammatical subject of a sentence, one-worded or many-worded, stands to something as the proper name 'Fido' stands to the dog Fido, and, what is a further point, that the thing it stands for is what the expression means. Even Plato had had to fight his way out of the same assumption. But he at least had a special excuse. The Greek language had only the one word ὄνομα where we have the three words 'word', 'name' and 'noun'. It was hard in Greek even to say that the Greek counterpart to our verb 'is' was a word but not a noun. Greek provided Plato with no label for verbs, or for adverbs, conjunctions etc. That 'is' is a word, but is not a name or even a noun was a tricky thing to say in Greek where ὄνομα did duty both for our word 'word', for our word 'name' and, eventually, for our word 'noun'. But even without this excuse people still find it natural to assimilate all words to names, and the meanings of words to the bearers of those alleged names. Yet the assumption is easy to demolish.

First, if every single word were a name, then a sentence composed of five words, say 'three is a prime number', would be a list of the five objects named by those five words. But a list, like 'Plato, Aristotle, Aquinas, Locke, Berkeley' is not a sentence. It says nothing, true or false. A sentence, on the contrary, may say something—some one thing—which is true or false. So the words combined into a sentence at least do something jointly which is different from their severally naming the several things that they name if they do name any things. What a sentence means is not decomposable into the set of things which the words in it stand for, if they do stand for things. So the notion of *having meaning* is at least partly different from the notion of *standing for*.

More than this. I can use the two descriptive phrases 'the Morning Star' and 'the Evening Star', as different ways of referring to Venus. But it is quite clear that the two phrases are different in meaning. It would be incorrect to translate into French the phrase 'the Morning Star' by *l'Étoile du Soir*. But if the two phrases have different meanings, then Venus, the planet which we describe by these two different descriptions, cannot be what these descriptive phrases mean. For she, Venus, is one and the same, but what the two phrases signify are different. As we shall see in a moment Mill candidly acknowledges this point and makes an important allowance for it.

Moreover, it is easy to coin descriptive phrases to which nothing at all answers. The phrase 'the third man to stand on the top of Mount Everest' cannot, at present, be used to refer to anybody. There exists as yet no one whom it fits and perhaps there never will. Yet it is certainly a significant phrase, and could be translated into French or German. We know, we have to know, what it means when we say that it fits no living mountaineer. It means *something*, but it does not designate *somebody*. What it means cannot, therefore, be equated with a particular mountaineer. Nor can the meaning conveyed by the phrase 'the first person to stand on the top of Mount Everest' be equated with Hillary, though, we gather, it fits him and does not fit anyone else. We can understand the question, and even entertain Nepalese doubts about the answer to the question 'Is Hillary the first person to conquer Mount Everest?' where we could not understand the question 'Is Hillary Hillary?'

We could reach the same conclusion even more directly. If Hillary was, *per impossibile*, identified with what is meant by the phrase 'the first man to stand on the top of Mount Everest', it would follow that the meaning of at least one phrase was born in New Zealand, has breathed through an oxygen-mask and has been decorated by Her Majesty. But this is patent nonsense. Meanings of phrases are not New Zealand citizens; what is expressed by a particular English phrase, as well as by any paraphrase or translation of it, is not something with lungs, a surname, long legs and a sunburnt face. People are born and die and sometimes wear boots; meanings are not born and do not die and they never wear boots— or go barefoot either. The Queen does not decorate meanings. The phrase 'the first man to stand on the top of Mount Everest' will not lose its meaning when Hillary dies. Nor was it meaningless before he reached the summit.

Finally, we should notice that most words are not nouns; they are, e.g. adverbs, or verbs, or adjectives or prepositions or conjunctions or pronouns. But to classify as a name a word which is not even a noun strikes one as intolerable the moment one considers the point. How could 'ran' or 'often' or 'and' or 'pretty' be the name of anything? It could not even be the grammatical subject of a sentence. I may ask what a certain economic condition, moral quality or day of the week is called and get the answer 'inflation', 'punctiliousness' or 'Saturday'. We do use the word 'name' for what something is called, whether it be what a person or river is called, or what a species, a quality, an action or a condition is called. But the answer to the question 'What is it called?' must be a noun or have the grammar of a noun. No such question could be answered by giving the tense of a verb, an adverb, a conjunction or an adjective.

Mill himself allowed that some words like 'is', 'often', 'not', 'of', and 'the' are not names, even in his hospitable use of 'name'. They cannot by themselves function as the grammatical subjects of sentences. Their function, as he erroneously described it, is to subserve, in one way or another, the construction of many-worded names. They do not name extra things but are ancillaries to the multi-verbal naming of things. Yet they certainly have meanings. 'And' and 'or' have different meanings, and 'or' and the Latin *aut* have the same meaning. Mill realized that it is not always the case that for a word to mean something, it must denote somebody or something. But most of his successors did not notice how important this point was.

Even more to Mill's credit was the fact that he noticed and did partial justice to the point, which I made a little while back, that two different descriptive phrases may both fit the same thing or person, so that the thing or person which they both fit or which, in his unhappy parlance, they both name is not to be equated with either (or of course both) of the significations of the two descriptions. The two phrases 'the previous Prime Minister' and 'the father of Randolph Churchill' both fit Sir Winston Churchill, and fit only him; but they do not have the same meaning. A French translation of the one would not be a translation of the other. One might know or believe that the one description fitted Sir Winston Churchill while still questioning whether the other did so too. From just knowing that Sir Winston was Prime Minister one could not infer that Randolph Churchill is his son, or vice versa. Either might have been true without the other being true. The two phrases cannot, therefore, carry the same information.

Mill, in effect, met this point with his famous theory of denotation and connotation. Most words and descriptive phrases, according to him, do two things at once. They *denote* the things or persons that they are, as he unhappily puts it, all the names of. But they also *connote* or signify the simple or complex attributes by possessing which the thing or person denoted is fitted by the description.

Mill's word 'connote' was a very unhappily chosen word and has misled not only Mill's successors but Mill himself. His word 'denote' was used by him in a far from uniform way, which left him uncommitted to consequences from which some of his successors, who used it less equivocally, could not extricate themselves. For Mill, proper names denote their bearers, but predicate-expressions also denote what they are truly predicable of. Fido is denoted by 'Fido' and by 'dog' and by 'four-legged'.

So to ask for the function of an expression is, on Mill's showing, to ask a double question. It is to ask Which person or persons, thing or things, does the expression denote? in one or other of Mill's uses of this verb—Sir Winston Churchill, perhaps—; but it is also to ask What are the properties or characteristics by which the thing or person is described?—say that of having begotten Randolph Churchill. As a thing or person can be described in various ways, the various descriptions given will differ in connotation, while still being identical in denotation. They characterize in different ways, even though their denotation is identical. They carry different bits of information or misinformation about the same thing, person or event.

Mill himself virtually says that according to our ordinary natural notion of meaning, it would not be proper to say that, e.g., Sir Winston Churchill is the meaning of a word or phrase. We ordinarily understand by 'meaning' not the thing denoted but only what is connoted. That is, Mill virtually reaches the correct conclusions that the meaning of an expression is never the thing or person referred to by means of it and that descriptive phrases and, with one exception, single words are never names, in the sense of 'proper names'. The exception is just those relatively few words which really are proper names, i.e. words like 'Fido' and 'London', the words which do not appear in dictionaries.

Mill got a further important point right about these genuine proper names. He said that while most words and descriptive phrases both denote or name and connote, proper names only denote and do not connote. A dog may be called 'Fido', but the word 'Fido' conveys no information or misinformation about the dog's qualities, career or whereabouts, etc. There is, to enlarge this point, no question of the word 'Fido' being paraphrased, or correctly or incorrectly translated into French. Dictionaries do not tell us what proper names mean—for the simple reason that they do not mean anything. The word 'Fido' names or denotes a particular dog, since it is what he is called. But there is no room for

357

anyone who hears the word 'Fido' to understand it or misunderstand it or fail to understand it. There is nothing for which he can require an elucidation or a definition. From the information that Sir Winston Churchill was Prime Minister, a number of consequences follow, such as that he was the leader of the majority party in Parliament. But from the fact that yonder dog is Fido, no other truth about him follows at all. No information is provided for anything to follow from. Using a proper name is not committing oneself to any further assertions whatsoever. Proper names are appellations and not descriptions; and descriptions are descriptions and not appellations. Sir Winston Churchill *is* the father of Randolph Churchill. He is not *called* and was not christened 'the father of Randolph Churchill'. He is called 'Winston Churchill'. The Lady Mayoress of Liverpool can give the name *Mauretania* to a ship which thenceforward has that name. But if she called Sir Winston Churchill 'the father of Sir Herbert Morrison' this would be a funny sort of christening, but it would not make it true that Morrison is the son of Sir Winston Churchill. Descriptions carry truths or falsehoods and are not just arbitrary bestowals. Proper names are arbitrary bestowals, and convey nothing true and nothing false, for they convey nothing at all.

Chinese astronomers give the planets, stars and constellations names quite different from those we give. But it does not follow that a single proposition of Western astronomy is rejected by them, or that a single astronomical proposition rejected by us is accepted by them. Stellar nomenclature carries with it no astronomical truths or falsehoods. Calling a star by a certain name is not saying anything about it, and saying something true or false about a star is not naming it. Saying is not naming and naming is not saying.

This brings out a most important fact. Considering the meaning (or Mill's 'connotation') of an expression is considering what can be said with it, i.e. said truly or said falsely, as well as asked, commanded, advised or any other sort of saying. In this, which is the normal sense of 'meaning', the meaning of a sub-expression like a word or phrase, is a functional factor of a range of possible assertions, questions, commands and the rest. It is tributary to sayings. It is a distinguishable common locus of a range of possible tellings, askings, advisings, etc. This precisely inverts the natural assumption with which, as I said earlier, Mill and most of us start, the assumption namely that the meanings of words and phrases can be learned, discussed and classified before consideration begins of entire sayings, such as sentences. Word-meanings do not stand to sentence-meanings as atoms to molecules or as letters of the alphabet to the spellings of words, but more nearly as the tennis-racket stands to the strokes which are or may be made with it. This point, which Mill's successors and predecessors half-recognized to hold for such little words as 'if', 'or', 'all', 'the' and 'not', holds good for all significant words alike. Their significances are their roles inside actual and possible sayings. Mill's two-way doctrine, that nearly all words and phrases both denote, or are names, and connote, i.e. have significance, was therefore, in effect, though unwittingly, a coalition between an atomistic and a functionalist view of words. By the irony of fate, it was his atomistic view which was, in most quarters, accepted as gospel truth for the next fifty or seventy years. Indeed, it was more than accepted, it was accepted without the important safeguard which Mill himself provided when he said that the thing or person denoted by a name was not to be identified with what that name meant. Mill said that to mean is to connote. His successors said that to mean is to denote, or, more rarely, both to denote and to connote. Frege was for a long time alone in seeing the crucial importance of Mill's argument that two or more descriptive phrases with different senses may apply to the same planet or person. This person or planet is not, therefore, what those phrases mean. Their different senses are not their common denotation. Russell early realized the point which Mill did not very explicitly make, though Plato had made it, that a sentence is not a list. It says one thing; it is not just an inventory of a lot of things. But only much later, if at all, did Russell see the full implications of this.

I surmise that the reasons why Mill's doctrine of denotation, without its safeguards, caught on, while his truths about connotation failed to do so, were two. First, the word 'connote' naturally suggests what we express by 'imply', which is not what is wanted. What the phrase 'the previous Prime Minister of the United Kingdom' signifies is not to be equated with any or all of the consequences which can be inferred from the statement that Churchill is the previous Prime Minister. Deducing is not translating. But more important was the fact that Mill himself rapidly diluted his doctrine of connotation with such a mass of irrelevant and false sensationalist and associationist psychology that his successors felt forced to ignore the doctrine in order to keep clear of its accretions.

Let me briefly mention some of the consequences which successors of Mill actually drew from the view, which was not Mill's, that to mean is to denote, in the toughest sense, namely that all significant expressions are proper names, and what they are the names of are what the expressions signify.

First, it is obvious that the vast majority of words are unlike the words 'Fido' and 'London' in this respect, namely, that they are general. 'Fido' stands for a particular dog, but the noun 'dog' covers this dog Fido, and all other dogs past, present and future, dogs in novels, dogs in dog-breeders' plans for the future, and so on indefinitely. So the word 'dog', if assumed to denote in the way in which 'Fido' denotes Fido, must denote something which we do not hear barking, namely either the set or class of all actual and imaginable dogs, or the set of canine properties which they all share. Either would be a very out-of-the-way sort of entity. Next, most words are not even nouns, but adjectives, verbs, prepositions, conjunctions and so on. If these are assumed to denote in the way in which 'Fido' denotes Fido, we shall have a still larger and queerer set of nominees or *denotata* on our hands, namely nominees whose names could not even function as the grammatical subjects of sentences. (Incidentally it is not true even that all ordinary general nouns can function by themselves as subjects of sentences. I can talk about *this* dog, or *a* dog, or *the* dog which . . .; or about *dogs*, *all* dogs, or *most* dogs, and so on. But I cannot make the singular noun 'dog' by itself the grammatical subject of a sentence, save inside quotes, though I can do this with nouns like 'grass', 'hydrogen' and 'Man'.) Finally, since complexes of words, like descriptive and other phrases, and entire clauses and sentences have unitary meanings, then these too will have to be construed as denoting complex entities of very surprising sorts. Now Meinong in Austria and Frege in Germany, as well as Moore and Russell in this country, in their early days, accepted some or most of these consequences. Consistently with the assumed equation of signifying with naming, they maintained the objective existence or being of all sorts of abstract and fictional *entia rationis*.

Whenever we construct a sentence in which we can distinguish a grammatical subject and a verb, the grammatical subject, be it a single word or a more or less complex phrase, must be significant if the sentence is to say something true or false. But if this nominative word or phrase is significant, it must, according to the assumption, denote something which is there to be named. So not only Fido and London, but also centaurs, round squares, the present King of France, the class of albino Cypriots, the first moment of time, and the non-existence of a first moment of time must all be credited with some sort of reality. They must *be*, else we could not say true or false things of them. We could not truly say that round squares do not exist, unless in some sense of 'exist' there exist round squares for us, in another sense, to deny existence of. Sentences can begin with abstract nouns like 'equality' or 'justice' or 'murder', so all Plato's Forms or Universals must be accepted as entities. Sentences can contain mentions of creatures of fiction, like centaurs and Mr Pickwick, so all conceivable creatures of fiction must be genuine entities too. Next, we can say that propositions are true or false, or that they entail or are incompatible with other propositions, so any significant 'that'-clause, like 'that three is a prime number' or 'that four is a prime number', must also denote existent or subsistent objects. It was accordingly, for a time, supposed that if I know or believe that three is a prime number, my knowing or believing this is a special relation holding between me on the one hand and the truth or fact, on the other, denoted by the sentence 'three is a prime number'. If I weave or follow a romance, my imagining centaurs or Mr Pickwick is a special relation holding between me and these centaurs or that portly old gentleman. I could not imagine him unless he had enough being to stand as the correlate-term in this postulated relation of being imagined by me.

Lastly, to consider briefly what turned out, unexpectedly, to be a crucial case, there must exist or subsist classes, namely appropriate *denotata*, for such collectively employed plural descriptive phrases as 'the elephants in Burma' or 'the men in the moon'. It is just of such classes or sets that we say that they number 3000, say, in the one case, and o in the other. For the results of counting to be true or false, there must be entities submitting to numerical predicates; and for the propositions of arithmetic to be true or false there must exist or subsist an infinite range of such classes.

At the very beginning of this century Russell was detecting some local unplausibilities in the full-fledged doctrine that to every significant grammatical subject there must correspond an appropriate *denotatum* in the way in which Fido answers to the name 'Fido'. The true proposition 'round squares do not exist' surely cannot require us to assert that there really do subsist round squares. The proposition that it is false that four is a prime number is a true one, but its truth surely cannot force us to fill the Universe up with an endless population of objectively existing falsehoods.

But it was classes that first engendered not mere unplausibilities but seemingly disastrous logical contradictions—not merely peripheral logical contradictions but contradictions at the heart of the very principles on which Russell and Frege had taken mathematics to depend. We can collect into classes not only ordinary objects like playing-cards and bachelors, but also such things as classes themselves. I can ask how many shoes there are in a room and also how many pairs of shoes, and a pair of shoes is already a class. So now suppose I construct a class of all the classes that are not, as anyhow most classes are not, members of themselves. Will this class be one of its own members or not? If it embraces itself, this disqualifies it from being one of the things it is characterized as embracing; if it is not one of the things it embraces, this is just what qualifies it to be one among its own members.

So simple logic itself forbids certain ostensibly denoting expressions to denote. It is at least unplausible to say that there exist objects denoted by the phrase 'round squares'; there is self-contradiction in saying that there exists a class which is a member of itself on condition that it is not, and vice versa.

Russell had already found himself forced to say of some expressions which had previously been supposed to name or denote, that they had to be given exceptional treatment. They were not names but what he called 'incomplete symbols', expressions, that is, which have no meaning, in the sense of denotation, by themselves; their business was to be auxiliary to expressions which do, as a whole, denote. (This was what Mill had said of the syncategorematic words.) The very treatment which had since the Middle Ages been given to such little words as 'and', 'not', 'the', 'some' and 'is' was now given to some other kinds of expressions as well. In effect, though not explicitly, Russell was saying that, e.g., descriptive phrases were as syncategorematic as 'not', 'and' and 'is' had always been allowed to be. Here Russell was on the brink of allowing that the meanings or significations of many kinds of expressions are matters not of *naming* things but of *saying* things. But he was, I think, still held up by the idea that saying is itself just another variety of naming, i.e. naming a complex or an 'objective' or a proposition or a fact—some sort of postulated *Fido rationis*.

He took a new and most important further step to cope with the paradoxes, like that of the class of classes that are not members of themselves. For he now wielded a distinction, which Mill had seen but left inert, the distinction between sentences which are either true or false, on the one hand, and on the other hand sentences which, though proper in vocabulary and syntax, are none the less nonsensical, meaningless or absurd; and therefore neither true nor false. To assert them and to deny them are to assert and deny nothing. For reasons of a sort which are the proper concern of logic, certain sorts of concatenations of words and phrases into sentences produce things which cannot be significantly said. For example, the very question Is the class of all classes which are not members of themselves a member of itself or not? has no answer. Russell's famous 'Theory of Types' was an attempt to formulate the reasons of logic which make it an improper question. We need not consider whether he was successful. What matters for us, and what made the big difference to subsequent philosophy, is the fact that at long last the notion of meaning was realized to be, at least in certain crucial contexts, the obverse of the notion of the nonsensical —what can be said, truly or falsely, is at last contrasted with what cannot be significantly said. The notion of meaning had been, at long last, partly detached from the notion of naming and re-attached to the notion of saying. It was recognized to belong to, or even to constitute, the domain which had always been the province of logic; and as it is at least part of the official business of logic to establish and codify rules, the notion of meaning came now to be seen as somehow compact of rules. To know what an expression means involves knowing what can (logically) be said with it and what cannot (logically) be said with it. It involves knowing a set of bans, fiats and obligations, or, in a word, it is to know the rules of the employment of that expression.

It was, however, not Russell but Wittgenstein who first generalized or half-generalized this crucial point. In the *Tractatus Logico-Philosophicus*, which could be described as the first book to be written on the philosophy of logic, Wittgenstein still had one foot in the denotationist camp, but his other foot was already free. He saw and said, not only what had been said before, that the little words, the so-called logical constants, 'not', 'is', 'and' and the rest, do not stand for objects, but also, what Plato had also said before, that sentences are not names. Saying is not naming. He realized, as Frege had done, that logicians' questions are not questions about the properties or relations of the *denotata*, if any, of the expressions which enter into the sentences whose logic is under examination. He saw, too, that all the words and phrases that can enter into sentences are governed by the rules of what he called, slightly metaphorically, 'logical syntax' or 'logical grammar'. These rules are what are broken by such concatenations of words and phrases as result in nonsense. Logic is or includes the study of these rules. Husserl had at the beginning of the century employed much the same notion of 'logical grammar'.

It was only later still that Wittgenstein consciously and deliberately withdrew his remaining foot from the denotationist camp. When he said 'Don't ask for the meaning, ask for the use', he was imparting a lesson which he had had to teach to himself after he had finished with the *Tractatus*. The use of an expression, or the concept it expresses, is the role it is employed to perform, not any thing or person or event for which it might be supposed to stand. Nor is the purchasing power of a coin to be equated with this book or that car-ride which might be bought with it. The purchasing power of a coin has not got pages or a terminus. Even more instructive is the analogy which Wittgenstein now came to draw between significant expressions and the pieces with which are played games like chess. The significance of an expression and the powers or functions in chess of a pawn, a knight or the queen have much in common. To know what the knight can and cannot do, one must know the rules of chess, as well as be familiar with various kinds of chess-situations which may arise. What the knight may do cannot be read out of the material or shape of the piece of ivory or boxwood or tin of which this knight may be made. Similarly to know what an expression means is to know how it may and may not be employed, and the rules governing its employment can be the same for expressions of very different physical compositions. The word 'horse' is not a bit like the word 'cheval'; but the way of wielding them is the same. They have the same role, the same sense. Each is a translation of the other. Certainly the rules of the uses of expressions are unlike the rules of games in some important respects. We can be taught the rules of chess up to a point before we begin to play. There are manuals of chess, where there are not manuals of significance. The rules of chess, again, are completely definite and inelastic. Questions of whether a rule has been broken or not are decidable without debate. Moreover we opt to play chess and can stop when we like, where we do not opt to talk and think and cannot opt to break off. Chess is a diversion. Speech and thought are not only diversions. But still the partial assimilation of the meanings of expressions to the powers or the values of the pieces with which a game is played is enormously revealing. There is no temptation to suppose that a knight is proxy for anything, or that learning what a knight may or may not do is learning that it is a deputy for some ulterior entity. We could not learn to play the knight correctly without having learned to play the other pieces, nor can we learn to play a word by itself, but only in combination with other words and phrases.

364

Besides this, there is a further point which the assimilation brings out. There are six different kinds of chess-pieces, with their six different kinds of roles in the game. We can imagine more complex games involving twenty or two hundred kinds of pieces. So it is with languages. In contrast with the denotationist assumption that almost all words, all phrases and even all sentences are alike in having the one role of naming, the assimilation of language to chess reminds us of what we knew *ambulando* all along, the fact that there are indefinitely many kinds of words, kinds of phrases, and kinds of sentences—that there is an indefinitely large variety of kinds of roles performed by the expressions we use in saying things. Adjectives do not do what adverbs do, nor do all adjectives do the same sort of thing as one another. Some nouns are proper names, but most are not. The sorts of things that we do with sentences are different from the sorts of things that we do with most single words—and some sorts of things that we can significantly do with some sorts of sentences, we cannot significantly do with others. And so on.

There is not one basic mould, such as the 'Fido'-Fido mould, into which all significant expressions are to be forced. On the contrary, there is an endless variety of categories of sense or meaning. Even the *prima facie* simple notion of naming or denoting itself turns out on examination to be full of internal variegations. Pronouns are used to denote people and things, but not in the way in which proper names do so. No one is *called* 'he' or 'she'. 'Saturday' is a proper name, but not in the same way as 'Fido' is a proper name—and neither is used in the way in which the fictional proper name 'Mr Pickwick' is used. The notion of denotation, so far from providing the final explanation of the notion of meaning, turns out itself to be just one special branch or twig on the tree of signification. Expressions do not mean because they denote things; some expressions denote things, in one or another of several different manners, because they are significant. Meanings are not things, not even very queer things. Learning the meaning of an expression is more like learning a piece of drill than like coming across a previously unencountered object. It is learning to operate correctly with an expression and with any other expression equivalent to it.

(2) *The Theory of Philosophy.* I now want to trace, rather more cursorily, the other main motive from which thinkers have posed the abstract question What are meanings? or What is it for an expression to have a certain sense?

Until fairly recently philosophers have not often stepped back from their easels to consider what philosophy is, or how doing philosophy differs from doing science, or doing theology, or doing mathematics. Kant was the first modern thinker to see or try to answer this question—and a very good beginning of an answer he gave; but I shall not expound his answer here.

This question did not begin seriously to worry the general run of philosophers until maybe sixty years ago. It began to become obsessive only after the publication of the *Tractatus*. Why did the philosophy of philosophy start so late, and how did it come to start when and as it did?

It is often not realized that the words 'philosophy' and 'philosopher' and their equivalents in French and German had for a long time much less specific meanings than they now possess. During the seventeenth, the eighteenth and most of the nineteenth centuries a 'philosopher' was almost any sort of a *savant*. Astronomers, chemists and botanists were called 'philosophers' just as much as were Locke, Berkeley or Hume. Descartes's philosophy covered his contributions to optics just as much as his contributions to epistemology. In English there existed for a long time no special word for the people we now call 'scientists'. This noun was deliberately coined only in 1840, and even then it took some time to catch on. His contemporaries could not call Newton a 'scientist', since there was no such word. When a distinction had to be made, it was made by distinguishing 'natural philosophy' from 'moral' and 'metaphysical philosophy'. As late as 1887, Conan Doyle, within two or three pages of one story, describes Sherlock Holmes as being totally ignorant of philosophy, as we use the word now, and yet as having his room full of philosophical, i.e. scientific, instruments, like test-tubes, retorts and balances. A not very ancient Oxford Chair of Physics still retains its old label, the Chair of Experimental Philosophy.

Different from this quite important piece of etymological history is the fact that both in Scotland and in England there existed from perhaps the time of Hartley to that of Sidgwick and Bradley a strong tendency to suppose that the distinction between natural philosophy, i.e. physical and biological science on the one hand and metaphysical and moral philosophy, perhaps including logic, on the other, was that the latter were concerned with internal, mental phenomena, where the former were concerned with external, physical phenomena. Much of what we now label 'philosophy', *sans phrase*, was for a long time and by many thinkers confidently, but quite wrongly, equated with what we now call 'psychology'.

John Stuart Mill sometimes, but not always, uses even the grand word 'metaphysics' for the empirical study of the workings of men's minds. Protests were made against this equation particularly on behalf of philosophical theology, but for a long time the anti-theologians had it their own way. A philosopher, *sans phrase*, was a Mental and Moral Scientist—a scientist who was exempted from working in the laboratory or the observatory only because his specimens were collected at home by introspection. Even Mansel, himself a philosophical theologian with a good Kantian equipment, maintained that the science of mental phenomena, what we call 'psychology', was the real basis of even ontological or theological speculations.

So not only did the wide coverage of the word 'philosophy' encourage people not to look for any important differences between what scientists, as we now call them, do and what philosophers, as we now call them, do; but even when such differences were looked for, they were apt to be found in the differences between the investigation of physical phenomena by the laboratory scientist and the investigation of psychological phenomena by the introspecting psychologist.

As I see it, three influences were chiefly responsible for the collapse of the assumption that doing philosophy, in our sense, is of a piece with doing natural science or at least of a piece with doing mental science or psychology.

First, champions of mathematics like Frege, Husserl and Russell had to save mathematics from the combined empiricism and psychologism of the school of John Stuart Mill. Mathematical truths are not mere psychological generalizations; equations are not mere records of deeply rutted associations of ideas; the objects of geometry are not of the stuff of which mental images are made. Pure mathematics is a non-inductive and a non-introspective science. Its proofs are rigorous, its terms are exact, and its theorems are universal and not merely highly general truths. The proofs and the theorems of Formal or Symbolic Logic share these dignities with the proofs and theorems of mathematics. So, as logic was certainly a part of philosophy, not all of philosophy could be ranked as 'mental science'. There must, then, be a field or realm besides those of the material and the mental; and at least part of philosophy is concerned with this third realm, the realm of non-material and also non-mental 'logical objects'—such objects as concepts, truths, falsehoods, classes, numbers and implications.

Next, armchair mental science or introspective psychology itself began to yield ground to experimental, laboratory psychology. Psychologists like James began to put themselves to school under the physiologists and the statisticians. Scientific psychology began first to rival and then to oust both *a priori* and introspective psychology, and the tacit claim of epistemologists, moral philosophers and logicians to be mental scientists had to be surrendered to those who used the methods and the tools of the reputable sciences. So the question raised its head What then were the objects of the inquiries of epistemologists, moral philosophers and logicians, if they were not, as had been supposed, psychological states and processes? It is only in our own days that, anyhow in most British Universities, psychologists have established a Faculty of their own separate from the Faculty of Philosophy.

Thirdly, Brentano, reinforcing from medieval sources a point made and swiftly forgotten by Mill, maintained as an *a priori* principle of psychology itself, that it is of the essence of mental states and processes that they are *of* objects or contents. Somewhat as in grammar a transitive verb requires an accusative, so in the field of ideas, thoughts and feelings, acts of consciousness are directed upon their own metaphorical accusatives. To see is to see something, to regret is to regret something, to conclude or suppose is to conclude or suppose that something is the case. Imagining is one thing, the thing imagined, a centaur, say, is another. The centaur has the body of a horse and does not exist. An act of imagining a centaur does exist and does not have the body of a horse. Your act of supposing that Napoleon defeated Wellington is different from my act of supposing it; but what we suppose is the same and is what is expressed by our common expression 'that Napoleon defeated Wellington'. What is true of mental acts is, in general, false of their accusatives or 'intentional objects', and vice versa.

Brentano's two pupils, Meinong and Husserl, happened, for different reasons, to be especially, though not exclusively, interested in applying this principle of intentionality or transitivity to the intellectual, as distinct from the sensitive, volitional or affective acts of consciousness. They set out, that is, to rectify the Locke–Hume–Mill accounts of abstraction, conception, memory, judgment, supposal, inference and the rest, by distinguishing in each case, the various private, momentary and repeatable acts of conceiving, remembering, judging, supposing and inferring from their public, non-momentary accusatives, namely, the concepts, the propositions and the implications which constituted their objective correlates.

Where Frege attacked psychologistic accounts of thinking from the outside, they attacked them from the inside. Where Frege argued, for instance, that numbers have nothing psychological or, of course, physical about them, Husserl and Meinong argued that for the mental processes of counting and calculating to be what they are, they must have accusatives or objects numerically and qualitatively other than those processes themselves. Frege said that Mill's account of mathematical entities was false because psychological; Husserl and Meinong, in effect, said that the psychology itself was false because non-'intentional' psychology. The upshot, however, was much the same. With different axes to grind, all three came to what I may crudely dub 'Platonistic' conclusions. All three maintained the doctrine of a third realm of non-physical, non-psychological entities, in which realm dwelled such things as concepts, numbers, classes and propositions.

Husserl and Meinong were both ready to lump together all these accusatives of thinking alike under the comprehensive title of Meanings (*Bedeutungen*), since what I think is what is conveyed by the words, phrases or sentences in which I express what I think. The 'accusatives' of my ideas and my judgings are the meanings of my words and my sentences. It easily followed from this that both Husserl and Meinong, proud of their newly segregated third realm, found that it was this realm which provided a desiderated subject-matter peculiar to logic and philosophy and necessarily ignored by the natural sciences, physical and psychological. Mental acts and states are the subject-matter of psychology. Physical objects and events are the subject-matter of the physical and biological sciences. It is left to philosophy to be the science of this third domain which consists largely, though not entirely, of thought-objects or Meanings—the novel and impressive entities which had been newly isolated for separate investigation by the application of Brentano's principle of intentionality to the specifically intellectual or cognitive acts of consciousness.

Thus, by the first decade of this century it was dawning upon philosophers and logicians that their business was not that of one science among others, e.g. that of psychology; and even that it was not an inductive, experimental or observational business of any sort. It was intimately concerned with, among other things, the fundamental concepts and principles of mathematics; and it seemed to have to do with a special domain which was not bespoken by any other discipline, namely the so-called third realm of logical objects or Meanings. At the same time, and in some degree affected by these influences, Moore consistently and Russell spasmodically were prosecuting their obviously philosophical and logical inquiries with a special *modus operandi*. They, and not they alone, were deliberately and explicitly trying to give analyses of concepts and propositions—asking What does it really mean to say, for example, that this is good? or that that is true? or that centaurs do not exist? or that I see an inkpot? or What are the differences between the distinguishable senses of the verb 'to know' and the verb 'to be'? Moore's regular practice and Russell's frequent practice seemed to exemplify beautifully what, for example, Husserl and Meinong had declared in general terms to be the peculiar business of philosophy and logic, namely to explore the third realm of Meanings. Thus philosophy had acquired a right to live its own life, neither as a discredited pretender to the status of the science of mind, nor yet as a superannuated handmaiden of *démodé* theology. It was responsible for a special field of facts, facts of impressively Platonized kinds.

Before the first world war discussions of the status and role of philosophy *vis-à-vis* the mathematical and empirical sciences were generally cursory and incidental to discussions of other matters. Wittgenstein's *Tractatus* was a complete treatise dedicated to fixing the position mainly of Formal Logic but also, as a necessary corollary, the position of general philosophy. It was this book which made dominant issues of the theory of logic and the theory of philosophy. In Vienna some of its teachings were applied polemically, namely to demolishing the pretensions of philosophy to be the science of transcendent realities. In England, on the whole, others of its teachings were applied more constructively, namely to stating the positive functions which philosophical propositions perform, and scientific propositions do not perform. In England, on the whole, interest was concentrated on Wittgenstein's description of philosophy as an activity of clarifying or elucidating the meanings of the expressions used, e.g. by scientists; that is, on the medicinal virtues of his account of the nonsensical. In Vienna, on the whole, interest was concentrated on the lethal potentialities of Wittgenstein's account of nonsense. In both places, it was realized that the criteria between the significant and the nonsensical needed to be systematically surveyed, and that it was for the philosopher and not the scientist to survey them.

At this point, the collapse of the denotationist theory of meaning began to influence the theory of philosophy as the science of Platonized Meanings. If the meaning of an expression is not an entity denoted by it, but a style of operation performed with it, not a nominee but a role, then it is not only repellent but positively misleading to speak as if there existed a Third Realm whose denizens are Meanings. We can distinguish this knight, as a piece of ivory, from the part it or any proxy for it may play in a game of chess; but the part it may play is not an extra entity, made of some mysterious non-ivory. There is not one box housing the ivory chessmen and another queerer box housing their functions in chess games. Similarly we can distinguish an expression as a set of syllables from its employment. A quite different set of syllables may have the same employment. But its use or sense is not an additional substance or subject of predication. It is not a non-physical, non-mental object—but not because it is either a physical or a mental object, but because it is not an object. As it is not an object, it is not a denizen of a Platonic realm of objects. To say, therefore, that philosophy is the science of Meanings, though not altogether wrong, is liable to mislead in the same way as it might mislead to say that economics is the science of exchange-values. This, too, is true enough, but to word this truth in this way is liable to make people suppose that the Universe houses, under different roofs, commodities and coins here and exchange-values over there.

Hence, following Wittgenstein's lead, it has become customary to say, instead, that philosophical problems are linguistic problems —only linguistic problems quite unlike any of the problems of philology, grammar, phonetics, rhetoric, prosody, etc., since they are problems about the logic of the functionings of expressions. Such problems are so widely different from, e.g. philological problems, that speaking of them as linguistic problems is, at the moment, as Wittgenstein foresaw, misleading people as far in one direction as speaking of them as problems about Meanings or Concepts or Propositions had been misleading in the other direction. The difficulty is to steer between the Scylla of a Platonistic and the Charybdis of a lexicographical account of the business of philosophy and logic.

There has been and perhaps still is something of a vogue for saying that doing philosophy consists in analysing meanings, or analysing the employments of expressions. Indeed, from trans-atlantic journals I gather that at this very moment British philosophy is dominated by some people called 'linguistic analysts'. The word 'analysis' has, indeed, a good laboratory or Scotland Yard ring about it; it contrasts well with such expressions as 'speculation', 'hypothesis', 'system-building' and even 'preaching' and 'writing poetry'. On the other hand it is a hopelessly misleading word in some important respects. It falsely suggests, for one thing, that any sort of careful elucidation of any sorts of complex or subtle ideas will be a piece of philosophizing; as if the judge, in explaining to the members of the jury the differences between manslaughter and murder, was helping them out of a philosophical quandary. But, even worse, it suggests that philosophical problems are like the chemist's or the detective's problems in this respect, namely that they can and should be tackled piecemeal. Finish problem A this morning, file the answer, and go on to problem B this afternoon. This suggestion does violence to the vital fact that philosophical problems inevitably interlock in all sorts of ways. It would be patently absurd to tell someone to finish the problem of the nature of truth this morning, file the answer and go on this afternoon to solve the problem of the relations between naming and saying, holding over until tomorrow problems about the concepts of existence and non-existence. This is, I think, why at the present moment philosophers are far more inclined to liken their task to that of the cartographer than to that of the chemist or the detective. It is the foreign relations, not the domestic constitutions, of sayables that engender logical troubles and demand logical arbitration.

28

PREDICTING AND INFERRING

*Reprinted from 'Proceedings of the Colston Research Society', vol. IX,
in 'Observation and Interpretation in the Philosophy of Physics', 1957,
by the University of Bristol, by permission of the Society*

To predict is to assert that something will happen or will be the
case at a time later than the making of the prediction. It is to assert
something in the future tense. A person who makes a prediction
may be just guessing, or asserting something that he believes on
mere hearsay, or prophesying from what he believes to be inspiration. He may even predict what he believes or knows will not be
the case, like a sharepusher in order to deceive or like a doctor in
order to encourage. But sometimes a prediction is a reasoned
prediction. The author expects something to happen because he
has evidence that it will do so. Some predictions, but not all, are
the conclusions of good or bad inferences. The fact that these are
nowadays the most highly respected predictions must not lead us
to suppose that a prediction is, *ex vi termini*, the conclusion of an
inference. To predict is not itself to infer; it is not necessarily
even to declare a conclusion of an inference. Old Moore's Almanac
is full of predictions which are not conclusions of inferences, even
bad ones. Conversely, it is not necessarily the case that the conclusion of an inference is a prediction. The inferences of a detective,
an historian, a geologist, a palaeontologist and a cosmologist are
very often inferences to past events or states of affairs. The inferences of a doctor, a general and a bridge-player are very often
inferences to contemporary states of affairs. Not all inferred
conclusions are in the future tense. This point is worth making
since there is at present something of a vogue for tying up problems
about induction with the special notion of inference to the future.
But inferences to the unobserved has-been and inferences to the
unobserved is-now are just as respectable as inferences to the unobserved is-to-be. The only difference of importance is that the
future is inevitably unobserved now, whereas the what-has-been

and what-is-now *might* have been observed or be being observed, instead of having to be inferred.

The vogue of concentrating on scientists' predictions has had another damaging effect on popular views about science. Many people speak as if the forecasting work of astronomers and meteorologists was typical of all scientific investigation—as if, that is to say, the chemist, the nuclear physicist and the endocrinologist all had their advance information to give us about things to come about next Wednesday week in something like the way in which the Nautical Almanac gives us advance news about the positions of the stars and the time of high and low tide days or years ahead, or like the way in which meteorologists give 24 or 48 hour forecasts of the weather. But it is clear that the provision of forecasts of these kinds is no part of the business of most sciences, not even of astronomy or meteorology save when these are *applied*. Ask the biochemist for information about anything that will be happening tomorrow week, and he will laugh and tell you that prophecy is not his business. No, the way in which reasoned predictions do belong essentially to the business of any scientist is quite different. He predicts not what will be going on in the world at large, but, for example, what will be the result of the experiment he has himself set up inside his own laboratory. What occurs there, if all goes well, is something which he himself had deliberately and carefully tried to get to occur; and usually, save when he is giving a demonstration or exhibition, he tries to get it to occur in order to test his still tentative theory that in such and such specified and controlled conditions just such a happening or state of affairs does ensue. His predictions are conditional experimental predictions—experimental both in the sense of being tentative and in the sense of being made for the sake of testing a theory.

They are not forecasts of a future state of the public world, but tentative inferences to a future state of the object under experiment in his own laboratory, under conditions designed and created by himself. Since the actual outcome of the experiment is meant to verify or falsify the theory which generated the inference to it, that inference was in some degree tentative. If the theory was already known to be true, or else to be false, there would be no point in setting up an experiment to show whether it was true or false—save, again, for demonstration to pupils, i.e. for didactic ends. Whereas the forecasts in the Nautical Almanac or weather forecasts are meant to inform the public and not to test theories or to teach them.

Certainly, when the researcher's theory has been definitely or adequately established, it can then, very often, be turned to practical account, i.e. applied to the world outside the laboratory to generate inferences to past, present or future happenings *not* under control conditions, as well as to generate techniques for bringing about or preventing the happening of such things. Part, though not the whole of the *application* of a theory consists in inferences to happenings or states of affairs in the world, i.e. to happenings or states of affairs the occurrence of which is not due to the intentions of the theorist and the labours of his technical assistants. Notice that the theory which generates, *inter alia*, inferences to the future, present and past states of affairs is not itself an inference or a budget of inferences to future, present, or past states of affairs. The theory itself is stated in tenseless terms, or rather in terms which are tense-neutral, as the terms of an algebraical formula are number-neutral. It does not itself assert that anything in particular has happened, is happening or is going to happen. I mention this obvious point because we sometimes hear theories described as predictive theories or as explanatory theories, phrases which might be misconstrued to mean that the theories themselves are or contain predictions or explanations of particular matters of fact. (I am not here talking about the theories of detectives or historians. These are, normally, hypotheses about particular happenings. Even if definitively or adequately established, they will not rank as laws. This is not their business.)

From now on I want to concentrate on what I have called 'experimental inferences', including experimental inferences whose conclusions are predictions, that is those inferences which a person testing a theory or hypothesis makes more or less tentatively, in order to confirm or else upset the theory that generates the inference. If the theory *works* then, *inter alia*, the particular inferences made on the basis of it, if validly drawn from true observational premises, will be successful, i.e. their conclusions will turn out to be true. This is part of what we mean by saying that the theory works. But we must notice that there can be theories or hypotheses which are experimentally empty, since they do not empower us to make any particular inferences, or, therefore, to test the theory by the successes or failures of any experimental inferences. For example, a person may have the theory that whatever happens anywhere is due to Fate. But from this theory he can derive no specific inferences to anything that is going to happen or has happened. It is an inferentially hollow theory. Some theories, like some doughnuts, are partly hollow and partly not. I want to concentrate on the testing of non-hollow theories by the successes and failures of the particular inferences generated by them. Notice first, a point I have already made, that the fact that someone *asserts* something in, say, the future or the past tense does not by itself involve that he has inferred. He might just be guessing, or making things up or repeating something that he had been told. Notice, second, that even when his assertion is both the conclusion of an inference and turns out to be true, this is not enough for us to grade his inference as a good one. He might have inferred a true conclusion from premises some or all of which were false, or he might have inferred invalidly. In either case his arriving at a true conclusion would be a matter of lucky coincidence. For example, a seismologist might come to the true conclusion that there had been an earthquake at a certain time and in a certain place, though he was arguing from false newspaper reports of tidal waves reaching the shores of the ocean at certain times. Or he might argue from good seismographic data, but make a howler or two in his calculations, and yet, by luck, arrive at a true conclusion about the locus and the time of the earthquake. In neither case would we allow or he continue to claim that his inference showed that his seismological theory had worked. For it was not his theory but mere luck which had got him to the right answer. No marks are bestowed upon his inference by the mere truth of its conclusion. Consequently no credit or discredit is reflected back on to his theory. Though he intended to test his theory, what he actually performed did not test it.

While a mere prediction, i.e. an assertion in the future tense, may be called successful simply if it turns out true, an *inference* to a conclusion in the future tense can be said to have succeeded or come off only if (1) the conclusion turns out true, (2) the observational premises were true, and (3) the drawing of this conclusion from those premises is valid, i.e. does not embody a sheer miscalculation or logical howler.

As the epithet 'successful' is equivocal, let us call a prediction which comes out right merely a 'happy' prediction, however arrived at or even if merely guessed. And let us call an inference a 'scoring' inference if its conclusion is both true and correctly drawn from true premises. I will say that a theory scores, or makes a score, if a factual inference based on it is a scoring inference. Now if I have conceived a non-hollow theory or hypothesis, and if I want to establish it to the satisfaction of myself and my colleagues, I shall certainly try to make inference-scores with it. But—and here we are getting a look at the old problem of induction from what is, I hope, a slightly new angle—I shall not be required by you or by my own conscience to assemble masses and masses of parallel inference-scores. It is not a matter of drowning surviving doubts under a Niagara of repetitions.

In an important way, I have shown you that my theory works, up to a point, if I have shown it generating just one inference-score; I have shown that it works rather well if I have shown you a fair variety of non-parallel inferences scoring. But there is, I think, no likelihood of your being discontented with these inference-scores merely on the ground that there have not yet been quite enough of them—as if it were a case of statistical inference being objected to on the ground that the sample extrapolated from was too small a fraction of the population extrapolated to.

Indeed, I might say, subject to a *démenti* to be made in a moment, that the problem of induction is not a problem about the legality of arguments from samples to populations, whether closed or 'open' populations; it is rather a problem about the legality of arguments from inference-scores to the truth and adequacy of the theories or hypotheses that generate those inferences. But now I want to withdraw this phrase 'the *legality of arguments* from inference-scores to the truth of theories'. For the maker of the theory or hypothesis does not *argue* from the scoring of the grounded inferences to the conclusion that the theory that generated them works. He *shows* that it works by showing it working, and he shows it working by showing inference-scores being made. Or, in other cases, the critic shows that the theory does *not* work by showing it not working, i.e. by showing inference-scores being attempted but not made. For example, someone had the theory that bats avoid bumping into obstacles when flying about a dark room not by seeing but by hearing where the obstacles are, and that they hear where they are by picking up echoes of noises emitted by themselves. This theory generated, *inter alia*, the concrete factual inferences (a) that this bat Sally (let's call her) will avoid the wires stretched across the room even when her eyes are sealed over; (b) that this bat William will hit wires if his ears are sealed down, and will continue to blunder into some wires when one ear is sealed down and the other not; (c) that this bat Charlie will hit wires if his squeaking apparatus is put out of action though his ears are not interfered with. These three concrete inferences all scored; and so showed that, anyhow up to a point, the theory worked. But the experimenter did not, I suppose, formulate a premiss-conclusion argument of the queer

377

pattern '*Because* the factual inference about Sally scored and the factual inference about William scored and the factual inference about Charlie scored, *therefore*, the theory works'. He had *shown* it working, not *inferred to* its working.

So if by 'inductive inference' or 'inductive argument' we mean to be referring to a special kind of inference or argument from scoring-inferences to the truth of the theory generating them, then I think that there is no such special kind of inference or argument—not merely that it is not an inference of the, in itself, quite reputable pattern of inference from sample to population, but that it is not a kind of inference at all.

We do indeed discover laws; we do indeed establish or upset hypotheses by making experimental inferences and seeing whether they score or not; and we do indeed teach pupils and satisfy critics by showing them these inferences scoring. But not all discovering is inferring; not all establishing is proving; not all instructing is arguing.

So far I have been speaking vaguely of a theory 'generating' the particular factual inferences, which are, so to speak, the encashments of it. I want to say a bit more about this. When I say that my bat-expert's theory *generated*, among others, the particular factual inference that because William's ears were sealed down therefore he would blunder into the wires, I do not mean that this factual inference was *deduced* from the theory. For an inference or argument is not a proposition, and so cannot be something that follows or does not follow from a proposition.

For the same reason, the driver who argues 'I have seven gallons of petrol left in my tank, and two in the can, so I have nine gallons of petrol altogether' does not *deduce* this argument from the equation $2 + 7 = 9$ or from the conjunction of this equation with factual propositions about the amounts of petrol in the containers. He deduces the factual conclusion that he has nine gallons left from the factual premiss that he has seven gallons in the tank and two in the can. But the deduction of this quantitative conclusion from this quantitative premiss is not itself a conclusion deduced from anything else. For *it* is not true or false but only valid or fallacious, and so is not the sort of thing that could be deduced. But still knowledge that $7 + 2 = 9$ *is* necessary for the deduction—only necessary not as knowledge of the truth of a premiss may be necessary if a conclusion is to be known to be true, but in quite another way. A child who has learned that $7 + 2 = 9$ has already learned that 7 somethings plus 2 somethings make 9 somethings, and so has, in a way, learned that 7 gallons of petrol plus 2 gallons of petrol make

9 gallons of petrol. And having learned this, then on finding that there are 7 gallons in the tank and 2 in the can, he knows what conclusion to draw—or rather he just draws it, in full knowledge of what his title is to draw it, namely the arithmetical truth that $7+2 = 9$.

However, though there is an important analogy, there is also an important difference between this sort of case, and the cases that we are considering. The child knows, and everyone knows, that $7+2 = 9$. Its truth is not in question and is not up for testing. It is not an empirical law or hypothesis. But we are dealing with inference-generating theories which are not truisms and are up for testing. Even if the formulation of the theory incorporates some general equations, still these are not algebraical truisms but candidates for the status of laws of nature, or bye-laws of nature. They are an essential part of what is up for testing. Still, the way in which they generate tentative, experimental inferences is, for what concerns us, the same as the way in which the arithmetical truism $7+2 = 9$ generates the untentative factual inference 'there are 7 gallons in the tank and 2 in the can, so there are 9 gallons all told'. In either case a piece of sheer miscalculation will result in the generated inferences not necessarily being false conclusions, but being invalid arguments.

In our cases, unlike the case of the gallons of petrol, the scoring or the non-scoring of the generated experimental inferences is what goes to show that the theory generating them does or does not work well, or fairly well or very well. (There is, I suppose, no question of a theory ever being claimed to work perfectly well for all conceivable applications. There is always room for further amendments.)

I want to stress the point made before that it is not just the fact that the *conclusions* of these experimental inferences turn out right that renders them scoring inferences. Rather it is the fact that these true conclusions are legitimately derived from true observational premisses. The specific mode or route of derivation is of crucial importance. For this is the place where the structure of the theory exhibits itself. It exposes its nervous system in the nerves of the concrete inferences that it generates.

The only important thing that I have tried to do is this. (1) I italicized the too commonly ignored distinction between predicting and inferring, or between statements in the future tense and arguments the conclusions of which may be, but may not be, in the future tense. (2) I then tried to switch the centre of gravity of disputes about induction, verification, confirmation, infirmation, etc. from the happiness or unhappiness of predictions on to the scoring or non-scoring of concrete inferences and in particular of concrete experimental inferences. I argued (or perhaps I only declared) that the relation between a theory and the experimental inferences that it generates is such that these do indeed *show* that the theory works or does not work, since they show it working or failing; but there is no question of there having to exist a special sort of argument, to be called 'an inductive argument', *from* the successes and failures of the inferences *to* the truth of the theory. *A fortiori* there is no question of there having to exist a sort of inductive argument the cogency of which increases with the sheer multiplication of favourable instances, in the way in which the evidential value of a sample really does, in certain conditions, increase, up to a point, with increases in the ratio between its size and the size, if it has one, of the population of which it is a sample.

29

ON FORGETTING THE DIFFERENCE
BETWEEN RIGHT AND WRONG

Reprinted from 'Essays in Moral Philosophy' edited by A. I. Melden, 1958, by permission of the University of Washington Press

'*Don't you know the difference between right and wrong?*' '*Well, I did learn it once, but I have forgotten it.*' This is a ridiculous thing to say. But why is it ridiculous? We forget lots of things, including lots of important things, that we used to know. So what is the absurdity in the idea of a person's forgetting the difference between right and wrong?

I think the question worthy of discussion, if only because the epistemological wheels on which ethical theories are made to run are apt to be wooden and uncircular.

Only one philosopher, so far as I know, has discussed my question. Aristotle does so very briefly in the *Nicomachean Ethics* 1100b 17 and 1140b 29.

First, let us get rid of two possible misconstructions of my question.

In speaking of a person's knowing or not knowing the difference between right and wrong, I shall not be speaking of him as knowing or not knowing the solutions to philosophers' conceptual questions like 'What are the definitions of Rightness and Wrongness, respectively?' A properly brought-up child knows the difference between right and wrong, for all that he has never heard an argument from Kant or Thrasymachus and would not have understood their definitions if he had. Anyhow, there is no absurdity in the idea of a philosophy student's having forgotten some ethical definitions or analyses that he had once known. He would not thereby cease to know the difference between right and wrong.

Next, the assertion that it is absurd to say that a person might forget the difference between right and wrong could be misconstrued as the ascription to our knowledge of right and wrong of an inspiring kind of indelibility, perhaps a Heaven-hinting innateness

381

or a trailing cloud of glory. No such edifying moral can be looked for. If it is absurd to say that one has forgotten the difference, it is also absurd to say that one recollects it. If it is absurd to say that one's knowledge of the difference between right and wrong might, like one's Latin, get rusty, then it is also absurd to say that it actually remains, like one's English, unrusty.

(1) It might be suggested that there is a quite simple reason why we cannot forget the difference between right and wrong, namely, that daily life gives us constant reminders of it. Somewhat as, throughout December, Christmas carols, Christmas cards, and butchers' shops constantly remind us of the imminence of Christmas Day, so the daily procession of duties to be done and derelictions to be apologized for keeps us constantly in mind of the difference between right and wrong. But this explanation will not do. A very forgetful person remains unreminded in the midst of reminders. Even the knot in his handkerchief does not remind him of anything. Moreover, a man might happen to sojourn in a part of the world where there were no reminders of Christmas. If this were all, then the maker of the paradoxical remark might just be in the rare position of being unusually forgetful or unusually unexposed to obligations; and then his remark would be not ridiculous but only hard to credit. Forgetting the difference between right and wrong would then be merely a rare thing, like forgetting one's own name.

This suggested explanation is a causal hypothesis. It offers to tell what makes people very unlikely to forget the difference between right and wrong. It therefore assumes that there is such a thing as forgetting this difference. But our question is, rather, 'Why is there no such thing? Why will "forget" and "be reminded of" not go with "the difference between right and wrong"?'

(2) A better, though still inadequate, explanation would be this. Knowing the difference between right and wrong is of a piece not with remembering particular matters of fact, like names, dates, and engagements, but with knowing how to do things, knowing the way from place to place, knowing Latin, and knowing the rules of the road in one's own country. Such things do not slip our memories, nor are knots tied in our handkerchiefs to keep us in mind of them. Knowledge here is mastery of techniques rather than mere possession of information; it is a capacity that can improve or decline, but cannot just come in and go out. We acquire such knowledge not just from being told things but from being trained to do things. The knowledge is not imparted but inculcated. It is a second nature, and therefore not evanescent. Now our knowledge

of the difference between right and wrong certainly is in many important respects much more like a mastery than like the retention of a piece of information. It is, for instance, inculcated by up-bringing rather than imparted by dictation. It is not a set of things memorized and is not, consequently, the sort of knowledge of which shortness of memory is the natural enemy.

Nonetheless, there is such a thing as forgetting much or all of one's Latin. With desuetude, one does become rustier and rustier, until one has totally forgotten it. We know what we have to do to keep up our Latin, our geometry, or our tennis, namely, to give ourselves regular practice. Just here is one place where the analogy breaks down between knowing the difference between right and wrong and having mastery of a science or a craft. One's knowledge of the difference between right and wrong does not get rusty; we do not keep up our honesty by giving ourselves regular exercises in it. Nor do we excuse a malicious action by saying that we have recently been short of practice in fair-mindedness and generosity. Virtues are not proficiencies. The notion of being out of practice, which is appropriate to skills, is inappropriate to virtues.

Aristotle's explanation of the fact that there is no such thing as forgetting the difference between right and wrong seems to be that moral dispositions are, from constant exercise, much more abiding things than even our masteries of sciences and crafts. In the latter there is forgetting, though only gradual forgetting; in the former there happens to be none. But the difference does not seem to be just a difference in degree, or even just a difference between a small magnitude and zero. Nor is it just a matter of anthropological fact that our knowledge of the difference between right and wrong never decays. The notion of decay does not fit.

En passant, when I argue that we do not impose moral exercises upon ourselves in order to prevent our knowledge of the difference between right and wrong from rusting, since the notion of rusting does not belong, I am not denying that we can or should drill ourselves into good habits and out of bad ones. I am only denying that such self-disciplining is to be assimilated to the exercises by which we prevent our Latin or our tennis from getting rusty. The object of moral drills is not to save us from forgetting the difference between right and wrong, but to stiffen us against doing what we know to be wrong.

Neither, to make the obverse point, am I denying that moral deterioration occurs. People often do get more callous, less public-spirited, meaner, lazier, and shiftier. What I am denying is that such deteriorations are to be assimilated to declines in expertness, i.e. to getting rusty.

(3) A third explanation would be this. Since virtues are not skills, that is, since to be unselfish or patient is not to be good *at* doing anything, perhaps virtues should be classed rather with tastes and preferences, and particularly with educated tastes and cultivated preferences. As the music-lover had once to learn to appreciate music, and the bridge-player had to learn both to play and to enjoy playing bridge, so the honest man had to be taught or trained to dislike deception, and the charitable man had to be taught or trained to want to relieve distress. Doubtless, as some people take to music from the start as a duck takes to water, so some people are naturally more prone than others to be frank and sympathetic. But to be honest or charitable on principle, even against the impulses of the moment, involves knowing the difference between right and wrong—much as, unlike the mere relishing of one piece of music more than another, appreciating the superiority of the one piece over the other involves knowing their relative merits and demerits. Taste is educated preference, preference for recognized superiorities. To be able to recognize superiorities is to know the difference between good and bad.

Now likings, whether natural or cultivated, can be lost. Most grown-ups have lost the enthusiasm for playing hide-and-seek, and some cease to enjoy tobacco and poetry. There can also be deteriorations in taste. A person who once had appreciated the excellences of Jane Austen might become so coarsened in palate as to cease to recognize or relish them.

It is relevant to my problem that we do not call such losses or deteriorations 'forgetting'. Perhaps the absurdity in speaking of someone's forgetting the difference between right and wrong is of a piece with the absurdity in speaking of someone who has lost the taste for poetry as having forgotten the difference between good and bad poetry.

When a person has an educated taste, he can speak of himself as having learned or been taught not only to recognize the differences between, say, good and bad singing or good and bad tennis strokes, but also to appreciate, i.e., to like, admire, and try for the good and to dislike, despise, and avoid the bad. Knowing, in this region, goes hand in hand with approving and disapproving, relishing and disrelishing, admiring and despising, pursuing and avoiding. Indeed, their connection seems even closer than mere hand-in-hand concomitance. There seems to be a sort of incongruity in the idea of a person's knowing the difference between good and bad wine or poetry, while not caring a whit more for the one than for the other; of his appreciating without being appreciative of excellences. When we read, 'We needs must love the highest when we see it', we incline to say, 'Of course. We should not be seeing it if we were not loving it. The "needs must" is a conceptual one. At least in this field, the partitions are down between the Faculties of Cognition, Conation, and Feeling.'

Now whether this inclination is justified or not, it exists just as much in our thinking about the knowledge of right and wrong. Here, too, there seems to be an incongruity in the idea of a person's knowing that something wrong had been done, but still not disapproving of it or being ashamed of it; of his knowing that something would be the wrong thing for him to do, but still not scrupling to do it. We hanker to say that, if he has no scruples at all in doing the thing, then he cannot know that it is wrong, but only, perhaps, that it is 'wrong', i.e., what other people call 'wrong'.

Socrates used to ask the important question, 'Can Virtue be taught?' It puzzled him, very properly, that if virtue can be taught there exist no pundits in courage, abstinence, or justice. If we, too, think that knowledge of the difference between right and wrong is knowledge, ought we not to be puzzled that universities and technical colleges do not give courses in industriousness, fair-mindedness, and loyalty? But the moment such a suggestion is made, we realize that the non-existence of pundits and colleges of the virtues is not a lamentable lacuna in our society. It would be silly to try to provide such instruction; silly, since knowledge of the difference between right and wrong is not the sort of thing that such instruction could bestow. We continue to think that children have to be taught the difference between right and wrong, but we know in our bones that this teaching is not a species of either factual or technical instruction. What sort of teaching, then, is the teaching of the difference between right and wrong? What sort of learning is the learning of this difference? What kind of knowing is the knowing of it? Maybe we can approach an answer to these questions by considering the teaching and learning of tastes.

A person who has received technical instruction in tennis, music, or landscape gardening may, but may not, owe to his instructor a second debt of gratitude for having taught him also to enjoy these things. A person who has learned from a geographer and a botanist the special features of the Lake District may have been inspired by

Wordsworth also to love this district for these features. As one gets to know a person better, one may learn to respect or admire him. Learning to enjoy, to love, or to admire is not acquiring a skill or a parcel of information. Nonetheless it *is* learning. There is a difference between a mere change-over from disliking rice pudding to liking it, and learning to appreciate wines, poems, or people for their excellences. Learning to appreciate requires some studiousness, judiciousness, and acuteness. The judge has reasons to give for his likings, his verdicts, and his choices.

True, the special notions of *lessons, instruction, coaching, examinations, laboratories, courses, manuals,* and the like are no part of the idea of learning to enjoy or learning to admire. Even if Wordsworth really does teach us to love the Lake District, he does not merit or need a professor's chair. But this is only to say again that admiring, enjoying, and loving are not efficiencies or equipments. The notions of *learning, studying, teaching,* and *knowing* are ampler notions than our academic epistemologies have acknowledged. They are hospitable enough to house under their roofs notions like those of *inspiring, kindling,* and *infecting.*

It will be objected, I expect, that what is called 'learning to enjoy' or 'being taught to admire' is really always two processes, namely, (1) coming to know some things, and (2), as an effect of coming to know them, coming to like or admire. An emotional condition, disposition, or attitude is caused by a cognitive act or disposition. As the rolling of the ship makes me feel sick, so discovering a person's characteristics makes me experience feelings of admiration toward him. So, presumably, as certain nostrums save me from feeling sick when the ship rolls, certain other nostrums might save me from admiring a person when I have discovered what a staunch friend he is. Alternatively, if this sounds too ridiculous, then a peculiarly intimate kind of causal connection has to be invoked in order to represent the connection between knowing and admiring as still a causal one, and yet as one that is exempt from preventions.

If we ask what the supposedly antecedent process of coming to know consists in, we are likely to be told that it consists in coming to be equipped with some information or/and coming to be relatively efficient at doing certain sorts of things, *plus*, perhaps, coming to be able and ready to explain, instruct, criticize, and so forth. These are not effects of coming to know; they are concrete examples of what coming to know is coming to. But why not add that sometimes coming to know *is*, also, *inter alia*, coming to admire or enjoy? If making a skilful tennis stroke or a skilful translation is doing something that one has learned to do, i.e., is an exercise and not an effect of knowledge, why may not admiring a person for his stanchness be, in a partly similar way, an example and not an after-effect of what our study of his character has taught us? The reply that what is learned must be either a piece of information or a technique begs the question, since the question is, in part, 'Why must it be either one or the other?'

How does all this apply to our knowledge of the difference between right and wrong? We are unwilling to allow that a person has learned this difference who does not, for instance, care a bit whether he breaks a promise or keeps it, and is quite indifferent whether someone else is cruel or kind. This *caring* is not a special feeling; it covers a variety of feelings, like those that go with being shocked, ashamed, indignant, admiring, emulous, disgusted, and enthusiastic; but it also covers a variety of actions, as well as readinesses and pronenesses to do things, like apologizing, recompensing, scolding, praising, persevering, praying, confessing, and making good resolutions. Now, if we consider what in detail a person who has learned the difference between right and wrong has learned, we do not naturally draw a line between some things, namely, what he has learned to say and do, and other things, namely, what he has learned to feel, and relegate the latter to the class of mere after-effects of his learning to say and do the proper things. In thinking about his conscience or his sense of duty, we do not naturally fence off his qualms from his acts of reparation; his pangs from his confessings or his resolvings; his prickings from his perseverings. *Because* he has learned the difference between right and wrong, he both makes reparations and feels contrite; and the 'because' is the same noncausal 'because'. Certainly his feeling contrite is not an exercise of a technique or the giving of a piece of information; but the same is true, though for different reasons, of his making reparations, persevering, reproaching, resolving, and keeping appointments. All are marks, though different sorts of marks, of his knowing the difference between right and wrong; all show, though in different ways, that he has principles, and what these principles are; any one of them is one of the many sorts of things that we have in mind when we say of him that he has a sense of duty.

Now we can begin to see why it is ridiculous to say that one has forgotten the difference between right and wrong. To have been taught the difference is to have been brought to appreciate the difference, and this appreciation is not just a competence to label correctly or just a capacity to do things efficiently. It includes an inculcated caring, a habit of taking certain sorts of things seriously.

A person who used to care may, indeed, cease to care or to care so much. But ceasing to care is not forgetting, any more than ceasing to believe something or to mistrust someone is forgetting. 'Forget' is reserved, apparently, mainly for the nonretention of information and the loss of skills through desuetude, though it is also used for ceasing to notice things, e.g., for the oblivion brought by sleep or distractions.

This use of 'forget' for the loss of information and technical abilities, and its nonuse for cessations of caring, may go with another difference. If I have ceased to enjoy bridge, or come to admire Picasso, then *I* have changed. But, if I have forgotten a date or become rusty in my Latin, I do not think of this as a change in *me*, but rather as a diminution of my equipment. In the same way, a person who becomes less or more conscientious is a somewhat changed person, not a person with an enlarged or diminished stock of anything. In a testimonial both personal qualities and equipment need to be mentioned, but the equipment is not mentioned among the personal qualities.

So far I have been pressing some analogies between things like tastes and pastimes on the one hand and virtues on the other; I have concentrated on ways in which the notions of *learning, teaching,* and *knowing* lock in with notions of *caring,* i.e. *enjoying, admiring, despising, trying, avoiding,* and so forth; and I have tried to show how, in these connections, they detach themselves from the notion of *forgetting.* But we must not push assimilation to the point of identification.

The man who knows the difference between good and bad tennis strokes, and applauds or tries for the good ones and pities or avoids the bad ones, is something of a specialist. The man who appreciates wines is something of a connoisseur. They have acquired special technical abilities and, therewith, special enjoyments. We others may envy them for both. But knowledge of the difference between right and wrong is common knowledge, and it is not mastery of a technique. There is nothing in particular that the honest man knows, *ex officio,* how to do. He is not, *ex officio,* even a bit of an expert at anything. Nor is his life enriched by some extra relishes. He possesses nothing for us to envy.

Often, though not always, we study to become relatively good at things, e.g. games, fine arts, and recreations, because we either enjoy them from the start or anyhow expect to get pleasure from them in the end. Our elders coerce us into learning to swim, largely because they think that we shall miss a lot of pleasure afterward if we do not learn to swim, or to swim well. But this is nothing like the reason or reasons for which elders train the young to be honest. The truth-lover has no treats to match against those of the music-lover. A sense of duty is not an esthetic sensibility; nor is the passion for righteousness indulged as the passion for bridge or birdwatching is indulged. It is not addiction to a sport or hobby. Certainly there are activities, like most work, in which, although technical excellence pleases and bad craftsmanship displeases, still the jobs are not done or even done well only for pleasure's sake. But the honest or charitable man has not, *ex officio*, any particular job to do, much less to be proud of doing well rather than botching. Knowing the difference between right and wrong is not identical with knowing the difference between good and bad work, even though they resemble one another in the fact that ceasing to care how one does one's job, like ceasing to care what one does, is not a case of forgetting.

One more reinsurance. I have claimed to detect an incongruity, and the same sort of incongruity, in the idea of a man's knowing the difference between right and wrong but not caring a bit whether he lies, say, or tells the truth; in the idea of a man's recognizing, without being appreciative of, the excellences of Jane Austen; and in the idea of a craftsman's knowing the difference between good and bad workmanship without taking any pride in his own good work or feeling any contempt for the bad work of others. I may seem to have equated this knowing with having learned to take seriously. But there is a trap here.

I may be a bit shocked and indignant at an exhibition of unfairness, while you are much shocked and highly indignant. I care a bit about it, and you care much more. But this does not involve that you know more differences between right and wrong than I do, if this makes any sense, or that you know the difference better, if this makes any sense. Similarly, a specimen of Shakespeare's literary genius may please me while it thrills you. We appreciate the same excellence, though we are unequally appreciative of it. So even if, in some domains, to teach is, *inter alia*, to kindle, still we do not think of what is taught as varying in magnitude with the heat of the fire. The match is the same, but the fuels are different.

One last point. In most fields instructors can misinstruct. I may be taught that the Battle of Hastings was fought in 1077, and I may be taught to grip fiercely my billiard cue and my steering wheel. While I retain faith in my instructor, I shall still claim to know the date of the battle and to know how to control the cue and the steering wheel; but, when I have learned better, I shall agree that I had not formerly known the date of the battle or how to control the cue or the wheel. I have to unlearn what I was originally taught.

There is no difficulty in conceiving of misinstruction in the particular articles of codes of etiquette. A boy might well be trained to remain respectfully hatted in a lady's drawing-room and punctiliously to end his letters to tradesmen with 'Yours sincerely'. Nor is there much difficulty in conceiving of mis-instruction in some of the bylaws of morality. Some people used scrupulously to pay all their gambling debts before paying off any of their debts to servants and tradesmen. Their consciences had been educated to insist on this priority.

But there is a difficulty in conceiving of a person's being taught to be selfish, deceitful, cruel, and lazy on principle; to be morally shocked at exhibitions of fair-mindedness; or scrupulously to make reparations for his backslidings into unselfishness. The notion of moral non-education is familiar enough, but the notion of moral miseducation has a smell of absurdity. There is a whiff of the same smell of absurdity in the notion of the would-be connoisseur of wines or engravings being mis-taught, taught, that is, to relish wines for their immaturity or to admire engravings for their smudginesses. However, the smell of absurdity is less strong here. The Albert Memorial does seem to have been admired for its architectural badnesses.

The oddness, if it exists, in the idea of moral miseducation might be one source of the strength of the notion of the Moral Law. But to follow up this train of thought would seduce me into talking Ethics.

30

A PUZZLING ELEMENT IN THE NOTION OF THINKING

Reprinted from 'Proceedings of the British Academy', vol. XLIV, *1958, Oxford University Press, by permission of the British Academy*

Usually when we philosophers discuss questions about thinking, we concentrate, for very good reasons, upon what people do or might think; that is, on the opinions that they form, the beliefs that they have, the theories that they construct, the conclusions that they reach and the premisses from which they reach them. In a word, our usual questions are questions about the truths or falsehoods that people do or might accept. Their thoughts, of which we discuss the structures, the implications and the evidential backings, are the results in which their former ponderings and calculations have terminated. For when a person knows or believes that something is the case, his knowledge or belief is something that he now has or possesses, and the pondering which got him there is now over. While he is still wondering and pondering, he is still short of his destination. When he has settled his problem, his task of trying to settle it is finished.

It should not be forgotten that some of the problems that we have to try to settle are not theoretical problems but practical problems. We have to try to decide what to do, as well as try to decide what is the case. The solution of a problem is not always a truth or a falsehood.

We should not assume, either, that all thinking is trying to settle problems, whether theoretical or practical. This would be too restrictive. A person is certainly thinking when he is going over a poem that he knows perfectly, or dwelling on the incidents of yesterday's football match. He has, or need have, no problems to solve or results to aim at. Not all of our walks are journeys.

Lastly, we should not assume that all or even most of the truths or falsehoods that are ours are the fruits of our own ponderings. Fortunately and unfortunately, a great part of what we believe and know we have taken over from other people. Most of the things that we know we have not discovered for ourselves, but have been taught. Most of the things that we believe we believe simply because we have been told them. As with worldly goods, so with truths and falsehoods, much of what we possess is inherited or donated.

It is a vexatious fact about the English language that we use the verb 'to think' both for the beliefs or opinions that a man has, and for the pondering and reflecting that a man does; and that we use the noun 'thought' both for the truth or falsehood that he accepts, and for the activity of reflecting which, perhaps, preceded his acceptance of it. To think, in the sense of 'believe', is not to think, in the sense of 'ponder'. There is only the verbal appearance of a contradiction in saying that while a person is still thinking, he does not yet know what to think; and that when he does know what to think, he has no more thinking to do.

The problems which I wish to discuss are questions not about the propositions that a person does or might believe, but about his activities of pondering, perpending, musing, reflecting, calculating, meditating, and so on. I shall be talking about the thinking which is the travelling and not the being at one's destination; the winnowing and not the grain; the bargaining and not the goods; the work and not the repose.

A person does not have to be advanced in age or highly schooled in order to be able to give satisfactory answers to ordinary interrogations about his thinking. A child who has never heard a word of psychological or philosophical discourse is not in the least embarrassed at being asked what he had been thinking about while sitting in the swing. Indeed, if asked not very long afterwards, he is likely to be quite ready to give a moderately detailed account of the thoughts that he had had, and even perhaps of the rough sequence in which he had had them. The task does not feel to him hugely different from the task of recounting what he had been doing so quietly or so noisily in the nursery or what he had seen and whom he had met during his afternoon walk.

Nonetheless, familiar though we are with the task of recounting our thoughts, we are embarrassed by a quite different task, set to us by the psychologist or the philosopher, the task, namely, of saying what the having of these thoughts had consisted in. I mean this. If during a certain period I had been, say, singing or mending a gate or writing a testimonial, then when recounting afterwards what I had been doing, I could, if required, mention the concrete ingredients of my activity, namely the noises that I had uttered, the hammer-blows that I had struck, and the ink-marks that I had made on the paper. Of course, a mere catalogue of these concrete happenings would not yet amount to an account of what I had been doing. Singing a song is not just uttering one noise after another; the sequence of noises must be a directed sequence. Still, if no noises are made, no song is sung; and if no ink-marks are produced, no testimonial is written. If I recollect singing or writing a testimonial, then I recollect that I made some noises or some ink-marks.

But when I recollect, however clearly, a stretch, however recent, of my musing or pondering, I do not seem to be, in the same way, automatically primed with answers to questions about the concrete ingredients of the thoughts the having of which I have no difficulty in recounting. I tell you, for example, '. . . and then the idea occurred to me that, since it was Sunday, I might not be able to get petrol at the next village.' If now you ask me to say what concrete shape the occurring of this slightly complex idea had taken, I may well be stumped for an answer, so stumped, even, as half to resent the putting of the question.

You might press your irksome question in this way. You say, 'Well, you have just recounted to us in a dozen or more English words the idea that had occurred to you. Did the idea itself occur to you in English words? Does your recollection of the idea occurring to you incorporate the recollection of your saying something to yourself in a dozen or more English words, whether in your head or *sotto voce*? Or, having recently returned from France, did you perhaps say something to the same effect to yourself in a dozen or more French words?' To this very specific question my answer might be, 'Yes; I do now recall saying something to myself in my head, in English words, to the effect that as it was Sunday there might be no petrol available in the next village.' But my answer might be, 'No; I don't recall saying anything to myself at all.' Or my answer might be, 'Well, I'm not absolutely sure that I did not just say "Sunday" in my head, but I'm sure that I did not say anything more.'

Your pertinacity is irritating, since I want to say that it does not really matter whether I said anything to myself or not. Having the idea in question did not require my saying anything to myself, in the way in which singing does require uttering noises and repairing a gate does require *either* hammering *or* wire-tying *or* bolt-tightening *or* something of the same concrete sort.

Ignoring my irritation you now press me with another batch of specific queries. You say, 'If when you had that idea you did not say anything to yourself in your head or *sotto voce*, then was it that instead you saw some things in your mind's eye? Was it that you had mental pictures blurred or sharp, well coloured or ill coloured, maybe of villagers entering a village church, and of a garage with its doors closed; so that it was in this concrete shape, or something like it, that the idea came to you that since it was Sunday you might not be able to get petrol?' Again I might answer, 'Yes, I did visualize scenes like this.' But I might answer, 'No, I am sure that I did not visualize anything.' Or I might answer, 'Well, I do remember seeing in my mind's eye the duck-pond of the village in question: I usually do when I think of that village. But this had nothing to do with the special idea that the garage there might be closed for Sunday.' Once again I might be irked at the question being pressed at all. Why should my thinking the thought have gone with either the saying of something to myself or with the seeing of something in my mind's eye or with any other proprietary happenings?

There are, however, certain special thinking-activities which certainly do seem to require our saying things in our heads or *sotto voce* or aloud, and we need to examine what there is about these special activities which requires the inward or outward production of words and phrases.

(*a*) If I have been trying to compose a poem or an after-dinner speech, then I must indeed have been producing to myself words and phrases, examining them, cancelling or improving them, assembling them and rehearsing assemblages of them. That is, if my thinking happens to be a piece of thinking what to say and how to say it, then it must incorporate the tentative, exploratory, and critical saying of things to myself; and then, if asked to recount in retrospect whether I had been saying things to myself in English or in French, I should answer without hesitation. There is here no question of my first thinking out my poem or my speech, and only then, in reply to posthumous interrogations, putting my composition into words. The thinking was itself a piece of word-hunting, phrase-concocting, and sentence-mending. It was thinking *up* words, phrases and sentences.

(*b*) If I have been doing a slightly complex piece of computation, whether in my head or on paper, like multiplying £13 12*s*. 4*d*. by 7, then not only must my answer, if I obtain one, be a numerical or worded formula, £95 6*s*. 4*d*., perhaps, but also the results of the interim multiplying-operations, dividing-operations, and adding-operations will be numbers. What I say to myself in my head, if I do the sum in my head, will parallel the things that I should write down one after another if I worked the sum out on paper, and these will be numbers of pounds, shillings, or pence. If asked afterwards whether I had, at a certain stage, said to myself 'Seven twelves are eighty-four, plus two, makes eighty-six' or whether I had in my mind's eye seen the corresponding numerals, or both together, I might recollect just which I had done; and I should not feel irked at the suggestion that I must have done one or the other. Certainly, multiplying does not consist merely in saying numbers aloud or in our heads; but we are ready to allow that it requires this, or some alternative, in the same sort of way as singing a song requires, though it does not reduce to, the uttering of noises. Trying to get the correct answer, unlike just making a guess at it, involves trying to establish checkable intermediate steps, in order to make the correct moves from those steps to the right answer; and these steps, to be checkable, must be formulated.

(c) Some kinds of problems, like those of advocates, debaters, and philosophers, have something in common with the task of composition and something in common with the task of computation. The thinker has, all the time, both to be trying to find out what to say and how to say it, and also to be trying to establish as true what he says. He wants his hearers—including himself—not only to understand what he says but also to accept it, and to accept it perforce. As his task is, in two dimensions, a forensic task, his thinking involves him in producing and canvassing, in however sketchy a manner, words, phrases, and sentences, conclusions, reasons, and rebuttals of objections.

Now if, improvidently, we pick on one of these three special varieties of thinking as our universal model, we shall be tempted to say, as Plato said, that 'in thinking the soul is conversing [or perhaps 'debating'] with herself', and so postulate that any piece of meditating or pondering whatsoever has got, so to speak, to run on the wheels of words, phrases, and sentences.

Or, if forced by our own reminiscences to allow that sometimes we have thoughts when no wording of these thoughts takes place, we may then be tempted simply to give to the model one extension and postulate that in thinking the soul is *either* conversing with itself *or else* performing some one specific alternative to conversing, such as visualizing things. In either case we are presupposing that thinking, of whatever sort, must, so to speak, employ a concrete apparatus of some specifiable kind or other, linguistic or pictorial or something else. This general presupposition is sometimes formulated in the following way. Just as an Englishman who has become perfectly familiar with the French language may say that he can now think in French, so, and in the same sense of 'in', he must always think either 'in' his native English or else 'in' some alternative apparatus, like French or visual imagery or algebraical symbols or gestures or something else that he can produce, on demand, from his own resources. The generic term 'symbol' is sometimes used to cover all the postulated vehicles of thinking. It is a psychological necessity, or perhaps even a part of the very concept of thinking, that when thinking occurs, there occur, internally or externally, things or symbols that the thinker thinks in.

It is if we make this presupposition that we are especially embarrassed at being required to tell in retrospect in what symbols (in this awkwardly distended use of the word) we had, for example, the idea that as it was Sunday there might be no petrol available at the next village. For often we cannot recollect any such vehicles being present on the occasion when, as we clearly do recollect, we had that thought.

I want to attack this presupposition. I want to deny that it even makes sense to ask, in the general case, what special sort or sorts of things we think *in*. The very collocation of 'think' with 'in so and so' seems to me factitious, save in our very special case of the Englishman who describes himself as now being able to think in French. So let us clear his case out of the way. Only "think about"

The primary thing that he means when he says that he now thinks in French is that when he has to talk to Frenchmen, he does not any longer have to think out how to say in French what he wants to say. He no longer, for example, has first to say to himself in English what he wants to say, and then to struggle to translate from English into French for the benefit of his French audience. The composition of French remarks is no longer any more difficult for him than the composition of English remarks, that is, it is not difficult at all. But to say that he no longer has to think out how to say things in French has not the slightest tendency to show that all or most of the thoughts that he thinks are now accompanied or 'carried' by the production of French words. It is only to say that *when he is conversing with Frenchmen* he does not have to think about the vehicles of this conversing. When he does have to compose in French he does not have to think *up* French words. But most of the things he thinks about are not matters of French composition, just as most of the things we think about are not matters of English composition. Roughly, he thinks in French when he says what he wants to say in French without any groping or fumbling.

Secondarily, when he says that he now thinks in French, he may also mean that *when* he debates matters with himself he conducts these debates in French without wondering how to put his points in French; and, more generally, that *when* he converses with himself in internal monologue he does this in French without having to consider how to say in French what he wants to say. Even so, to describe him as thinking in French, because what he says to himself he says effortlessly in French, is to put a new strain on the phrase 'thinking in', under which it did not labour in our primary use of the phrase 'to think in French'. One never does ask it, but *could* one ask a friend who has been deliberating what to do whether he had been deliberating in English? If we did ask him this, I suspect that he would reply that while he had said or half-said a lot of things to himself in English, this had not been any part of his deliberating. He had not deliberated *by means* of saying things to himself, any more than the proof-corrector searches for misprints *by means of* putting marks in the margins of the galley-proof.

But anyhow, what is true of his debatings and conversings, whether with Frenchmen or with himself, need not be true of his thinkings which are done when no debating or conversing is done. The phrases 'in French' and 'in English' do attach natively to verbs of saying; it does not follow that they attach to verbs of thinking, unless the thinking happens to be thinking what to say or how to say it.

Strained though it may be, save in the one special context, to speak of a person thinking in French or in English, it is worse than strained to speak of him as thinking in, say, mental pictures. Certainly it is true, not of all people, but of many, when thinking about certain sorts of matters, though not of all, that they see things in their mind's eyes, and even that their ability to solve some of their problems is tied up, somehow, with their ability to visualize clearly. Doubtless, some chess-players can think out chess problems in their heads, if and only if they can visualize chess situations clearly and steadily.

Consider this case of the would-be solver of a chess problem. First let us provide him with a chess-board and the requisite chessmen. He disposes the pieces in their proper places and then, with his eyes fixed on the board and his fingers moving piece after piece, he tries to think out the solution to his problem. Are we to say that the thinking that he is doing is done 'in' pieces of ivory or 'in' the experimental moves that he makes with these pieces of ivory? Clearly, there is no place for the word 'in' here. He is thinking *about* the pieces; he is thinking out what they could and could not do or suffer if he moved elsewhere or if kept where they are.

But now suppose that we refuse to provide him with a chess-board, so that he has to tackle his task entirely in his head. The chess problem itself that he has to solve is exactly the same as before; but he is now confronted with an extra set of tasks which he had not had to cope with before. He has, among other things, to remember, at each given moment, exactly where each of the pieces is, whereas previously he just looked and saw where it was. He is like the hostess who can see which of her guests is sitting next to which until the light fails; then she has to remember their positions. This remembering may be preceded by the labour of trying to remember; or she may not have to try. She may just remember. Now if the chess-player has to struggle to remember the positions of his pieces, this struggling could obviously not be described as involving the employment of mental pictures of their positions. He struggles because he cannot yet remember and therefore cannot yet see in his mind's eye how the pieces had been disposed. If in the course of this struggling alternative possible dispositions are pictured, still these, if wrong, have to be scrapped. They are not the vehicles but the boss-shots of the thinking. Conversely, when, after struggling to remember the positions of the pieces, the chess-player does remember, then his seeing them in his mind's eye, if he does do this, is not something by means of which he gets himself to remember. It is the goal, not a vehicle of his struggle to remember. *A fortiori*, if he remembers without having to try to remember, then his mental picture of the positions of the pieces is not something that he thought *in* or *with* or *on*, since he did not have to think at all.

Certainly this chess-player has to *use his memory* in trying to solve the chess problem in his head, where he had not had to use his memory when he had had the board in front of him. But this is not at all the same thing as to say that he *uses his memory images* in trying to solve the problem in his head. If we hanker still to reserve some special sense for the phrase 'using images', this will be very different from the sense of the verb in which we speak of someone using such and such French words when speaking to

Frenchmen. That we cannot talk French without using French words is a dull truism; that some people cannot solve chess problems in their heads without, in some sense, using mental pictures may be true, but it is not a logicians' truism.

So now we seem to be farther off than ever from achieving what we thought that we wanted, namely to nominate some reasonably concrete stuff to be the peculiar apparatus of all of our thinkings.

No singing without noises, no testimonial-writing without ink-marks, no thinking without . . ., but we can nominate no proprietary things or sets of things to fill this gap. Indeed, we have, I hope, become suspicious of the very attempt to assimilate in this way thinking with these other special activities, which do possess their own proprietary implements or materials.

We may be tempted to postpone the evil day by suggesting that thinking differs from singing and testimonial-writing just because its proprietary stuff is a very peculiar stuff, more transparent and more shapeless than jelly-fishes, more scentless than the most scentless gases, and more uncapturable than rainbows. Perhaps its stuff is the stuff that dreams are made of, mental or spiritual stuff, and that is why it slips through our retrospective sieves. But we are soon brought to our senses if we remind ourselves that our own neighbours' very ordinary children, Tommy and Clara, make no more bones about recounting the thoughts that they have had than in recounting the games that they have played or the incidents that they have witnessed. They seem to need no esoteric instructions in order to be able to tell us of the ideas that have come to them or the thinking that they have done. In a way these are the most domestic and everyday sorts of things that there could be. The seeming mysteriousness of thinking derives from some sophisticated theoretical presuppositions, presuppositions which induce us, though only when theorizing, to try to squeeze out of our reminiscences or our introspections some evasive but pervasive drop of something, some psychic trace-element the presence of which, in bafflingly minute doses, is required if thinking is to occur. Yet Tommy and Clara, who were never told of any such psychic trace-element, describe their thinkings in ways which we understand perfectly; nor, when we tell them of the thoughts that crossed Cinderella's mind as she sat among the ashes, do we employ a strange para-chemical vocabulary.

Now let us drop, for the time being, the attempt to find a filling or a set of alternative fillings for the gap in the slogan 'No thinking without such and such' and consider a different, though connected, problem.

When a person who has been for a short or a long time musing or pondering is asked what he had been thinking about, he can usually, though not quite always, give a seemingly complete and definite answer. All sorts of answers are allowable; for example, that he had been thinking about his father, or about the next General Election, or about the possibility of getting his annual holiday early, or about yesterday's football match, or how to answer a letter. What he has been thinking about may or may not be, or contain, a problem. We can ask him whether he had decided how to answer the letter and if so what his decision was. But his thoughts about yesterday's football match may have been entirely uninterrogative. He was thinking it over, but not trying to think anything out. His thinking terminated in no results; it aimed at none. Now though, normally, the thinker can give a seemingly complete and definite answer to the question What had he been thinking about?, he can very often be brought to acknowledge that he had had in mind things which, at the start, it had not occurred to him to mention. To take a simple instance. A rowing enthusiast says that he had been thinking about the Oxford University crew; and if asked bluntly, would deny that he had at that moment been thinking about the Cambridge crew. Yet it might transpire that his thought about the Oxford crew was, or included, the thought that, though it was progressing, it was not progressing fast enough. 'Not fast enough for what?' we ask. 'Not fast enough to beat Cambridge next Saturday.' So he had been thinking about the Cambridge crew, only thinking about it in a sort of threshold way. Or I ask a tired visitor from London what he has been thinking about. He says, 'Just about the extraordinary peacefulness of your garden.' If asked, 'Than what do you find it so much more peaceful?' he replies, 'Oh, London, of course.' So in a way he was thinking not only of my garden but of London, though he would not, without special prompting, have said for himself that he had had London in mind at all. Or my visitor says, 'How lovely your roses are,' and then sighs. Why does he sigh? May he not, in a marginal way, be thinking of his dead wife who had been particularly fond of roses?—though he himself would have said, if asked, that he was only thinking about my roses. He does not say to me or to himself, 'Roses—her favourite flower.' But roses are, for him, her favourite flower. The thought of them is an incipient thought of her.

Take one more case. I ask the schoolboy what he is thinking about, and he says that he had been trying to think what 8×17 makes. On further questioning it turns out that his total task is to multiply £9 17s. 4d. by 8, and that at that particular moment he had got to the 17s. So I ask him whether he had forgotten the 2s. 8d. that he had got when multiplying the 4d. by 8; and now he says that he had not forgotten this; indeed he was keeping the 2s. in mind ready to add to his shillings column. So, in a way, his thought was not totally filled by the problem of multiplying 17×8. The thought of the total multiplication task was, in a controlling though background way, built into his interim but foreground task of multiplying 17×8. For it was not just 17, but the seventeen shillings of the £9 17s. 4d. that he was then engaged in multiplying by 8. He would have gone on from the shillings to the pounds if I had not interrupted.

It was not that my widowed visitor just *forgot* and had to be reminded that he had been thinking about his wife as well as about the roses, but that his task of telling just what he had had in mind was in some important ways totally unlike the task of trying to recall, say, just how many telephone calls he had made during the morning. The difference between merely thinking how fine these roses are and thinking how she would have admired them is not like the difference between having made eleven and having made twelve telephone calls, namely a difference in the number of happenings to be recorded. Recounting one's thoughts is not like turning back to an earlier page and trying to give an exhaustive inventory of the items one rediscovers there. The question whether or not the Cambridge crew had been in the rowing-enthusiast's mind was not one that he could settle by racking his brains to recollect a bygone fleeting something. In our example it was settled in quite a different way, namely by asking him what the rate of progress of the Oxford crew had seemed to him inadequate for. When he acknowledges that he had been, in a threshold way, thinking of the Cambridge crew, one thing that he does not say is, 'Ah yes, your question *reminds* me that the Cambridge crew was in my thoughts after all.' He had not been reminded of a forgotten item but shown how his account of his thought had been an incomplete account. He had failed to indicate part of its internal tenor.

Reporting one's thoughts is not a matter of merely chronicling the items of a procession of quick-fading internal phenomena. If we can pick out any such phenomena and record them, our record of them is not yet a statement of the drift or content of a piece of thinking. The way in which the widower's thinking of the roses was, in a way, thinking about his wife is not that during the time that he was thinking about the roses there occurred one or two very fleeting wafts of recollections of his wife. Such wafts do occur, but it was not them that he was acknowledging when he acknowledged that in thinking of the roses he had been incipiently thinking of his wife. Rather, he had thought of the roses *as* her favourite flower; in the way in which the rowing-enthusiast had thought of the progress of the Oxford crew *as* insufficient to beat Cambridge; or in the way in which the schoolboy had thought of the 17 that he was multiplying by 8 *as* the 17*s*. to be dealt with after the 4*d*. and before the £9.

What, then, is the virtue of this 'as', which makes a young man's thought of next Thursday *as* his 21st birthday different from his mother's thought of next Thursday *as* early-closing day for Oxford shops?

We can approach at least a part of the answer in this way. Sometimes we deliberately advise people to think of something *as* so and so. For instance, when giving a child his very first explanation of what a map is, we might tell him to think of the map of Berkshire *as* a photograph taken from an aeroplane very high up over the middle of Berkshire. This may already lead him to expect to find big things showing on the map, like towns, rivers, highroads, and railways, but not very small things like people, motor-cars, or bushes. A little later he enquires, in perplexity, what the contour-lines are which wriggle so conspicuously along and around the Berkshire Downs. We tell him to think of them *as* high-water marks left by the sea, which had risen to drown even the highest parts of the county. This flood, he is to suppose, subsided exactly fifty feet every night, leaving a high-water mark each time. So a person walking along one high-water mark would remain all the time at the same height above the normal level of the sea; and he would all the time be 100 feet higher than someone else who was following the next high-water mark but one below him. Quite likely the child could now work out for himself why the contour-lines are closely packed on the side of a steep hill and widely separated on a gradual incline.

Getting him to think of the map as a photograph taken from very high up, and of the contour-lines as high-water marks makes it natural or at least quite easy for him to think further thoughts for himself. It is to implant the germs of these further thoughts into his initially sterile thoughts about the map. If there was no follow-up, however embryonic and whether in the desired direction or any other, then he had not thought of the map as a photograph or of the contours as high-water marks. To describe someone as thinking of something as so and so is to say of him, at least *inter alia*, that it would be natural or easy for him to follow up this thought in some particular direction. His thinking had those prospects, that trend in it. It should be noticed that what thinking of something as so and so leads naturally or easily into may be subsequent thinkings, but it may equally well be subsequent doings. The golf professional who tells me to think of my driver not as sledge-hammer but as a rope with a weight on the end expects me to cease to bang at the ball and to begin to sweep smoothly through the ball. The parent who gets his child to think of policemen not as enemies but as friends gets him not only to think certain conse-quential thoughts but also to go to policemen for help when lost.

A person who thinks of something as something is, *ipso facto*, primed to think and do some particular further things; and this particular possible future that his thinking paves the way for needs to be mentioned in the description of the particular content of that thinking—somewhat as the mention of where the canal goes to has to be incorporated in our account of what this adjacent canal-stretch is. Roughly, a thought comprises what it is incipiently, namely what it is the natural vanguard of. Its burthen embodies its natural or easy sequel.

There are other things as well which are, in partly similar ways, constitutionally inceptive. To lather one's chin is to prepare to wield one's razor. Here the vanguard act is an intentional or even deliberate preparation for the future act. We had to learn thus to pave the way for shaving. To brace oneself is to get ready to jump or resist at the next moment; but this inceptive movement is not normally intentional or the result of training; it is instinctive. The tenors that our thoughts possess are similarly sometimes the products of training; but often not. In all cases alike, however, the description of an inceptive act requires the prospective specification of its due or natural sequel. Notice that its due or natural sequel may not actually come about. Having lathered my chin, I may be called to the telephone; and the dog, having braced himself, may be reassured or shot. We must employ the future tense in our description of the inceptive act, but we must hedge this future tense with some 'unlesses'.

At first sight we may suspect the presence of a circularity in

the description of something as essentially the foreshadowing of
its own succession. But this feature, without any air of circularity,
belongs also to our descriptions of promises, precautions, threats
and betrothals, and even of nightfalls, thaws and germinations.
There could be no complete description of such things which
was not proleptic. However, our special case seems to be in a
worse plight since I am saying that a piece of thinking of something as something is natively inceptive of, *inter alia*, subsequent
thinkings in a way in which a thaw is not the inception of another
thaw, or a nightfall the beginning of another nightfall.

So here we are reminded, if not of circles, at least of the verse:

> Big fleas have little fleas upon their backs to bite 'em,
> Little fleas have lesser fleas and so *ad infinitum*.

But is this reminder disconcerting? Were we not already aware
in our bones of just such a feature of thinking, namely that any
attempt to catch a particular thought tends to develop into an
attempt to catch up with something further? Our story of a particular piece of thinking seems in the nature of the case to terminate
in nothing stronger than a semi-colon. It is not incidental to
thoughts that they belong to trains of thought.

Now maybe we can begin to see the shape of the answers to both
of our two dominant questions. We can begin to see why it is that
the narrative of a piece of my thinking cannot be merely the
chronicling of actual, monitored happenings 'in my head'. For the
content of the thinking comprised its tenor and to describe its
particular tenor is prospectively to mention its natural or easy
sequels.

But also we can begin to see why we cannot, and do not in our
heart of hearts wish to reserve for our thinkings any peculiar
concrete stuff, apparatus, or medium, X, such that we can say,
'As no singing without noises, so no thinking without X.' For
adverting to anything whatsoever can be what puts a person, at
a particular moment, in mind of something or other. The motorist
in the last village but one before home may think of the petrol-
station alongside of him *as* being possibly the last place for buying
petrol on a Sunday. The widower thinks of my roses that he is
gazing at as being of the sort of which she was so fond. The schoolboy thinks of the number 17 that his eye is on as the 17*s*. in the
total of £9 17*s*. 4*d*. that he has to multiply by eight. The poet thinks
of the word 'annihilating' that crops up in a conversation as a

candidate for the gap in his half-composed couplet. The housewife thinks of next Thursday as the day when she will not be able to shop in Oxford after lunch, while her son thinks of it as the day when he comes of age. We could stretch our slogan, if we hanker for a slogan, to read 'No thinking without adverting to something or other, no matter what', but then it would be as empty as the slogans 'no eating without food', 'no building without materials' and 'no purchases without commodities'.

However, the very vacuousness of our new slogan 'no thinking without adverting to something or other, no matter what' has a certain tension-relieving effect. From the start we felt, I hope, a gnawing uneasiness at the very programme of treating thinking as a special, indeed a very special activity, special in the way in which singing is one special activity and gardening is a battery of other special activities. For while there certainly are lots of special kinds or brands of thinking, such as computing, sonnet-composing, anagram-solving, philosophizing, and translating, still thinking is not an activity in which we are engaged only when we are *not* singing, writing testimonials, gardening, and so on. Thinking is not a rival occupation to these special occupations, in the sense that our time has to be parcelled out between them and thinking, in the way in which our time does have to be parcelled out between golf and gardening, between testimonial-writing and lecturing, between anagram-solving and chess-playing, and so on. For we have to be thinking if we are to be singing well, writing a just testimonial, or gardening efficiently. Certainly, we had better not be doing sums or anagrams in our heads while singing or lecturing; but this is because we had better be thinking how to perform our present task of singing or lecturing. We had unwittingly sold the central fort from the start, when we asked ourselves, in effect, 'Given that noise-making, of a certain sort, is what goes to make singing the proprietary occupation that it is, what is it that, analogously, makes thinking the proprietary occupation that it is?' The verbal noun 'thinking' does not, as we knew in our bones all along, denote a special or proprietary activity in the way in which 'singing' does. Thinking is not one department in a department-store, such that we can ask What line of goods does it provide, and what lines of goods does it, *ex officio*, *not* provide? Its proper place is in all the departments—that is, there is no particular place which is its proper place, and there are no particular places which are not its proper place.

If we had worded our original programme by asking 'What

department and what proprietary apparatus are reserved for *the using of our wits*?' we should have seen through this question straightaway. We do not, notoriously, use our wits wherever and whenever we should use them, but there is no field or department of human activity or experience of which we can say, 'Here people can use their fingers, their noses, their vocal chords or their golf-clubs, but not their wits.' Or if we had worded our early question by asking 'In what special medium or with what special instruments is our use of our wits conducted?', we should have seen through this question too. We swim in water, we sing in noises, we hammer with hammers, but using our wits is not a co-ordinate special operation with its own counterpart medium, material, or implements. For one can use one's wits in swimming, singing, hammering, or in anything else whatsoever. I do not suggest that the idiom of *using one's wits* is a pure substitute for the idiom of *thinking*. There is an element of congratulation in our description of someone as having used his wits, an element which would be out of place, for example, in talking of my widower's thinking of roses as his wife's favourite flower. None the less, if we realize why it would be absurd to try to isolate out a proprietary activity of using one's wits and a reserved field for it, we realize why it actually was absurd to try to isolate out a proprietary activity of thinking and a reserved field for it.

Why do we not require our schools to give separate lessons in thinking, as they do give separate lessons in computing, translating, swimming, and cricket? The answer is obvious. It is because all the lessons that they give are lessons in thinking. Yet they are not lessons in two subjects at the same time.

31

USE, USAGE AND MEANING

Reprinted from 'Proceedings of the Aristotelian Society', Suppl. vol.
xxxv, 1961, by permission of the editor

In 1932 Mr. (now Sir) Alan H. Gardiner published *The Theory of Speech and Language* (Clarendon Press). A central theme of his book was what, with some acknowledged verbal artificiality, he labelled the distinction between 'Language' and 'Speech'. I shall draw, develop and apply this distinction in my own way.

A Language, such as the French language, is a stock, fund or deposit of words, constructions, intonations, *cliché* phrases and so on. 'Speech', on the other hand, or 'discourse' can be conscripted to denote the activity or rather the clan of activities of saying things, saying them in French, it may be, or English or some other language. A stock of language-pieces is not a lot of activities, but the fairly lasting wherewithal to conduct them; somewhat as a stock of coins is not a momentary transaction or set of momentary transactions of buying, lending, investing, etc., but is the lasting wherewithal to conduct such transactions. Roughly, as Capital stands to Trade, so Language stands to Speech.

A Language is something to be known, and we get to know it by learning it. We learn it partly by being taught it, and partly by picking it up. For any given part of a language, a learner may not yet have learned that part; or he may have learned it and not forgotten it, or he may have learned it and forgotten it, or he may have half-learned it; or he may have half-forgotten it. A Language is a corpus of teachable things. It is not, of course, a static corpus until it is a dead language. Nor would two teachers of it always agree whether something should be taught as a part of that language. Is French literary style to be taught by teachers of the French Language or by teachers of French Literature? Just when does an acceptable turn of phrase become an idiom? How old can a neologism be? What about slang?

Saying something in a language involves but does not reduce to knowing the requisite pieces of that language. The speaker is here and now employing what he had previously acquired and still possesses. He is now in the act of operating with things of which he has, perhaps for years, been the possessor. The words, constructions, intonations, etc. that he employs in saying what he says in these words, constructions, etc. is not another part of that language. It is a momentary operation *with* parts of that language, just as the buying or lending that I do with part of my capital is not itself a part of that capital, but a momentary operation with a part of it. That, indeed, is what my capital is for, namely, to enable me to make purchases, benefactions, loans, etc., with parts of it whenever I wish to do so. It is a set of moderately permanent possibilities of making particular momentary transactions.

If I say something in French, then, even though what I say has never been said before, I do not thereby enlarge the French language, i.e., increase the amount to be learned by a student of the French language. The fact that he does not know what I said does not entail that there is a bit of the French language that he has still to learn. Dicta made in French are not parts of the French language. They are things done with parts of the French language. You might utilise the same parts in saying something identical with or quite different from what I said. Your act of saying it is not mine, and neither is a part of the fund on which we both draw. But dicta can notoriously fossilise into clichés. '*Je ne sais quoi*' can now be used as a noun; and '*Rest and be Thankful*' can be a proper name.

We are tempted to treat the relation between sentences and words as akin to the relation between faggots and sticks. But this is entirely wrong. Words, constructions, etc. are the atoms of a Language; sentences are the units of Speech. Words, constructions, etc. are what we have to learn in mastering a language; sentences are what we produce when we say things. Words have histories; sentences do not, though their authors do. I must have learned the words that I utter when I say something with them. I need not, and, with reservations, cannot have learned the sentence that I come out with when I say something. It is something that I compose, not something that I have acquired. I am its author, not its employer. Sentences are not things of which I have a stock or fund. Nor are my buyings and lendings things of which I have a hoard or purseful.

In daily life we do not often mention as such the sentences that people produce. We speak instead of their allegations, complaints, promises, verdicts, requests, witticisms, confessions and commands. It is, in the main, people like grammarians, compositors, translators, amanuenses and editors who need to refer to the things that people say as 'sentences', since they are *ex officio* concerned with such matters as page-space, punctuation, syntax, plagiarisation, and so on. None the less, what they are interested in are instances of someone, actual or imagined, alleging, complaining, warning, joking, etc., though their special concern is with the punctuation of them and not with their humourousness; with their length and not with their truth; with their moods and tenses and not with their relevance or rudeness.

When Caesar said '*veni; vidi; vici*', he said three things, though he used only three Latin words. Then is '*vici*' a word or a sentence? The queerness of this disjunctive question is revealing. What Caesar produced, orally or in writing, on a certain day, was a laconic sentence, if a sentence is an instance of someone saying something. In this instance Caesar said something which was true. But he said it using only one Latin word, a word which had long been there for anyone to use anywhen in saying all sorts of considerably different things. The word was not true, or, of course, false either. Caesar boasted '*vici*', but the dictionary's explanation of the verb '*vici*' need say nothing about Caesar boasting. What it describes was, perhaps, also used by, *inter alios*, some concussed gladiator asking anxiously '*vici?*' The boast '*vici*' was a different sentence from the question '*vici?*', though the authors of both used the same Latin word, of which neither was the inventor. The word '*vici*' was there, in their common fund, to be employed, misemployed or left unemployed by anyone anywhen. The boast '*vici*' and the query '*vici?*' were two momentary speech-acts in which this one word was utilised for saying different things. Our question 'Is "*vici*" a word or a sentence?' was queer because its subject was ambiguous. Was it about a speech-episode, like a boast or a query, or was it about an inflected Latin verb? It was queer also because '. . . a word or a sentence?' was a disjunction between predicates of quite different categories, on a par with '. . . a bat or a stroke?'

Is the interrogative sentence '*vici?*' a part of the Latin language? Well, would a student still have some Latin to learn who had never met it? Surely not. What he had learned is enough to enable him to construe it if he should ever need it. What he construes are employments of Latin words, constructions, etc.; what he must know in order to construe or understand these employments, are the Latin words, inflections, constructions, etc. He must know the word in order to understand the one-word boast or question; but that knowing is not this understanding; what he had long since known is not what he has just understood or misunderstood. As we employ coins to make loans, but do not employ lendings, so we employ words, etc. in order to say things, but we do not employ the sayings of things—or misemploy them or leave them unemployed either. Dictions and dicta belong to different categories. So do roads and journeys; so do gallows and executions.

Sometimes a person tries to say something and fails through ignorance of the language. Perhaps he stops short because he does not know or cannot think of the required words or constructions. Perhaps he does not stop, but produces the wrong word or construction, thinking it to be the right one, and so commits a solecism. Perhaps his failure is of lesser magnitude; he says something unidiomatically or ungrammatically; or he gets the wrong intonation or he mispronounces. Such failures show that he has not completely mastered, say, the French language. In the extended sense of 'rule' in which a rule is anything against which faults are adjudged to be at fault, solecisms, mispronunciations, malapropisms, and unidiomatic and ungrammatical constructions are breaches of the rules of, e.g., the French language. For our purposes we do not need to consider the sources or the status of rules of this kind, or the authorities whose censures our French instructor dreads. Solecisms are in general philosophically uninteresting. Nor, for obvious reasons, do we often commit solecisms, save when young, ill-schooled, abroad or out of our intellectual depth.

The reproof 'You cannot say that and speak good French' is generically different from the reproof 'You cannot say that without absurdity'. The latter is not a comment on the quality of the speaker's French, since it could be true though the speaker had spoken in flawless French, or had not been speaking in French at all, but in English or Greek instead. The comment, if true, would be true of what was said whatever language it was said in, and whether it was said in barbarous or impeccable French or English. A mispronunciation or a wrong gender may be a bit of faulty French, but a self-contradiction is not a fault-in-French. Cicero's *non sequitur*s were not lapses from good Latin into bad Latin. His carelessness or incompetence was not linguistic carelessness or incompetence, if we tether the adjective 'linguistic' to the noun 'Language' as this is here being contrasted with 'Speech'.

There is an enormous variety of disparate kinds of faults that we can find or claim to find with things that people say. I can complain, justly or else unjustly, that what you said was tactless, irrelevant, repetitious, false, inaccurate, insubordinate, trite, fallacious, ill-timed, blasphemous, malicious, vapid, uninformative, over-informative, prejudiced, pedantic, obscure, prudish, provocative, self-contradictory, tautologous, circular or nonsensical and so on indefinitely. Some of these epithets can be appropriate also to behaviour which is not speech-behaviour; some of them cannot. Not one of them could be asserted or denied of any item in an English or French dictionary or Grammar. I can stigmatise what you said with any one of these epithets without even hinting that what you said was faulty in its French or whatever other language you said it in. I grumble at your dictum but not at your mastery of the language that it was made in. There are countless hetero-geneous disciplines and corrections which are meant to train people not to commit these Speech-faults. Not one of them belongs to the relatively homogeneous discipline of teaching, say, the French language. Speech-faults are not to be equated with Language-faults. Nothing need be wrong with the paints, brushes and canvas with which a portrait is bungled. Painting bady is not a pot of bad paint.

Logicians and philosophers are, *ex officio*, much concerned with kinds of things that people say or might be tempted to say. Only where there can be fallacies can there be valid inferences, namely in arguments; and only where there can be absurdities can there be non-absurdities, namely in dicta. We are presented with *aporiai* not by the telescope or the trawling-net, but by passages in books or by ripostes in debates. A fallacy or an impossible consequence may indeed have to be presented to us in French or English, etc. But it does not follow from this that what is wrong with it is anything faulty in the French or English in which it is presented. It was no part of the business of our French or English instructors to teach us that if most men wear coats and most men wear waist-coats it does not follow that most men wear both. This is a different sort of lesson and one which we cannot begin until we have already learned to use without solecism 'most', 'and', 'if', etc. There are no French implications or non-implications, so though 'p' may be said in French and 'q' may be said in French, it is nonsense to say 'q does not follow from p in the best French'. Similarly, what is impossible in 'The Cheshire Cat vanished, leaving only her grin behind her' is not any piece of intolerably barbarous English. Carroll's wording of the impossible story could not be improved, and the impossibility of his narrated incident survives translation into any language into which it can be translated. Something was amusingly wrong with what he said, but not with what he said it in.

I have a special reason for harking on this point that what someone says may be fallacious or absurd without being in any measure solecistic; i.e., that some Speech-faults, including some of those which matter to logicians and philosophers, are not and do not carry with them any Language-faults. Some philosophers, oblivious of the distinction between Language and Speech, or between having words, etc. to say things with and saying things with them, give to sentences the kind of treatment that they give to words, and, in particular, assimilate their accounts of what a sentence means to their accounts of what a word means. Equating the notion of the meaning of a word with the notion of the use of that word, they go on without apparent qualms to talking as if the meaning of a sentence could equally well be spoken of as the use of that sentence. We hear, for example, that nonsensical English sentences are sentences that have no use in English; as if sentences could *be* solecisms. Should we expect to hear that a certain argument is henceforth to contain an Undistributed Middle in B.B.C. English?

My last sentence but three, say, is not something with which I once learned how to say things. It *is* my saying something. Nor is an execution something erected to hang people on. It *is* the hanging of somebody. Part of what we learn, in learning the words of a language, is indeed how to employ them. But the act of exercising this acquired competence, i.e., the saying something with them is not in its turn an acquired wherewithal to say things. It neither has nor lacks a use, or, therefore, a use in English.

The famous saying 'Don't ask for the meaning; ask for the use' might have been, and I hope was, a piece of advice to philosophers, and not to lexicographers or translators. It advised philosophers, I hope, when wrestling with some *aporia*, to switch their attention from the trouble-giving words in their dormancy as language-pieces or dictionary-items to their utilisations in the actual sayings of things; from their general promises when on the shelf to their particular performances when at work; from their permanent purchasing-power while in the bank to the concrete marketing done yesterday morning with them; in short, from these words *qua* units of a Language to live sentences in which they are being actively employed.

More than this; the famous saying, in association with the idea of Rules of Use, could and I think should have been intended to advise philosophers, when surveying the kinds of live dicta that are or might be made with these trouble-giving words, to consider especially some of the kinds of non-solecistic Speech-faults against which the producer of such live dicta ought to take precautions, e.g., what sorts of dicta could not be significantly made with them, and why; what patterns of argument pivoting on these live dicta would be fallacious, and why; what kinds of verification-procedures would be impertinent, and why; to what kinds of questions such live dicta would be irrelevant, and why; and so on. To be clear about the 'how' of the employment of something we need to be clear also about its 'how not to', and about the reasons for both.

Early in this century Husserl and later Wittgenstein used the illuminating metaphors of 'logical syntax' and 'logical grammar'. Somewhat as, say, indicative verbs used instead of subjunctive verbs render some would-be Latin sentences bad Latin, so certain category-skids and logical howlers render dicta, said in no matter which tongue, nonsensical or absurd. A so-called Rule of Logical Syntax is what a nonsensical dictum is in breach of. But the analogy must not be pressed very far. The rules of Latin syntax are part of what we must learn if we are to be able to produce or construe Latin dicta. They are parts of the equipment to be employed by someone if he is to say either sensible or silly things in decent Latin. The Rules of Logical Syntax, on the other hand, belong not to a Language or to Languages, but to Speech. A person who says something senseless or illogical betrays not ignorance but silliness, muddleheadedness or, in some of the interesting cases, over-cleverness. We find fault not with his schooling in years gone by but with his thinking here and now. He has not forgotten or mis-remembered any of his lessons; he has operated unwarily or over-ingeniously in his execution of his momentary task. In retrospect he will reproach not his teachers, but himself; and he will reproach himself not for never having known something but for not having been thinking what he was saying yesterday.

The vogue of using 'Language' and 'linguistic' ambivalently both for dictions and for dicta, i.e., both for the words, etc. that we say things in and for what we say in them, helps to blind us to the wholesale inappropriateness of the epithets which fit pieces of language to the sayings of things with those pieces; and to the wholesale and heterogeneous inappropriatenesses of the variegated epithets which fit things said to the language-pieces and language-patterns that they are said in.

It remains true that philosophers and logicians do have to talk about talk or, to put it in a more Victorian way, to discourse about discourse. But it is not true that they are *ex officio* concerned with what language-teachers are *ex officio* concerned with.

32

A RATIONAL ANIMAL

Originally delivered as the Auguste Comte Memorial Lecture, published 1962 by the Athlone Press, and now reprinted by permission of the London School of Economics and Political Science

The respected dictum 'Man is a rational animal' has by now acquired an old-fashioned air. For one thing we are no longer such pious Aristotelians as to suppose that one species of animal or vegetable is distinguished from all the other species of the genus by some single and simple differentiating property. Nature does not kowtow to the canons of definition *per genus et differentiam*.

For another thing we are accustomed to think of rationality as an excellence, as farsightedness, strength and loyalty are excellences. So just as it would strike us as absurd to say that all men are far-sighted or all men are strong or loyal, it strikes us as absurd to say that all men are rational. All men cannot excel. For some men to be picked out as tall or witty, they must be picked out from the ruck of men who are not tall or witty; and if being rational is being exceptionally good at something or other, then not all men or even most men can be exceptionally good at this, any more than all men or even most men can be giants or dwarfs or champion boxers. A scale must have a middle and a foot, else it cannot have a top. Moreover, for quite other reasons, we have lost optimism about the prevalence in the world and the influence of this special excellence of rationality. Apart from the fact that it could not be deserved by all of us, the testimonial seems to be undeserved by any of us.

Of course, when we half-assented to the dictum 'Man is a rational animal', we were not or should not have been using this notion of rationality as a testimonial-notion. What we had or should have had in mind is that there is a special task or craft or calling, or more likely a family of tasks, crafts or callings at which men, unlike other animals, can be *either* good *or* bad *or* moderate. It is a peculiarity of men that they can sometimes succeed, but it is also their peculiarity that they can sometimes fail in certain undertakings in which other animals not only cannot succeed, but cannot even fail. They cannot compete at all, and therefore not even unsuccessfully. A lion not only cannot be good, he cannot even be bad, at reasoning, and an infant or an idiot not only cannot argue logically, he cannot even argue illogically. He cannot argue at all, and so gets neither good nor bad marks for his arguments, since these do not exist. We might inject a hygienic astringency into the original respected dictum by saying that there are certain important stupidities and sillinesses of which only men can ever be found guilty, and therefore of which only men can ever be found not guilty. The only animal that is *either* irrational *or* rational is man.

So now let us turn to the question what the thing is or, more circumspectly, what the things are at which it is peculiar to men to be either good or bad or indifferent, the peculiarity, indeed, which even men do not possess when they are infantile or senile, when out of their minds or asleep or fuddled or in a panic.

Inheritance of the Academy's veneration for geometry may lead some of us to reply to this question that what is peculiar to us rational animals is that we can ratiocinate, in the very special sense that we can construct proofs of theorems or at least follow and concur in other people's proofs of them; we are all, though in embarrassingly different degrees, village Euclids. If we do put forward this very specific answer, most of us do so, probably, with somewhat uneasy consciences, because rigorous demonstrations have been outside our ken since our schooldays. We never produce them and we never meet them, unless we reverently consult the authorized repositories of them. So probably we would wish to liberalize our answer and say, less exactly, that it is peculiar to human beings to be able, in some degree, to give and to recognize reasons, good or bad, for propositions, to think, that is, the pros and cons of thoughts; or that we are able, in low or high degree, to do this and also to advance, legitimately or illegitimately, from accepted or considered propositions to new propositions, that is, to make good or bad inferences.

At this point, however, we feel or should feel the rumblings of an internal mutiny. However pivotal it may be to the notion of a proper human being that he has some capacity, however slight, to produce and follow proofs of propositions; or to give and accept reasons for propositions; or to draw and concur in inferences from propositions to propositions; still surely it is not only for his puny, modest or glorious accomplishments in this dry and chilly propositional arena that we grade his life as a man's life as distinct from a brute's life, an infant's life or an idiot's life. We feel dimly, but deeply, and surely correctly, that human beings merit their bad, medium or good marks for other things than only those in which schoolmasters are professionally interested. The human nature that we have so far demarcated from sub-human nature seems to be a one-sidedly Academic human nature. Surely men differ from lions and infants in being liable to sillinesses, stupidities and wrong-headednesses other than scholastic ones, and in being capable of being judicious in other ways than judicial ways. It is in his actions as well as in his calculations and ratiocinations that a man, unlike a lion or an infant, can be rash or circumspect, original or hackneyed, careless or careful. In his feelings and reactions also, he, but not the lion, may be or avoid being petty, impatient and malicious. It may by now be unidiomatic to stigmatize someone as 'irrational' for being peevish, obstinate or sentimental, but epithets like 'foolish', 'silly' and 'stupid' come quite naturally to our lips. Nor do we await the results of any examinations or intelligence tests before coming out with such verdicts. We can esteem a man highly for his fair-mindedness or calmness without wanting to know anything at all about his powers of ratiocination, just as, in the other direction, we can think highly of his theorizing or his forensic powers, while still reserving judgement about his tact, his temper or his sportingness.

At this point we feel some temptation to say, with august precedents to give us the courage to say it, that the Reason which distinguishes us who possess it from the brutes, infants and idiots that lack it is a dual Faculty. There is Theoretical Reason and there is Practical Reason. Theoretical Reason is our capacity, small or great, to think thoughts, that is, to operate from and with propositions. Practical Reason is our capacity, small or great, to conduct ourselves according to moral principles in the warm world of action, and, therewith, our capacity also to feel the proper feelings towards the inhabitants and the furniture of this world. Only a creature possessed of Practical Reason can either cheat or play fair, either desert or keep the ranks; but also only a creature with Practical Reason can feel contemptuous or emulous, proud or ashamed, guilty or guiltless. Whether this Faculty of Practical Reason is to be thought of as the brother-officer of Theoretical Reason or as its sergeant-major is a question the interest of which has, by our demythologizing time, somewhat dwindled, without altogether disappearing. For we are now nearly, though not quite, immune from the temptation to picture our different abilities and liabilities as internal agencies or therefore as superior or subordinate agencies. My sense of humour is my capacity to make jokes; it is not an agent in my insides which makes my jokes for me. It is not, therefore, an agent which takes orders from or gives orders to my Reason or my Sense of Decorum.

But before embarking on what survives of this mythological question about the relative army-ranks of Theoretical and Practical Reason, we need to ask ourselves whether we have yet been open-handed enough. Is it enough to say that man is, *in posse*, not merely something of a village Euclid, but also something of a village Hampden? a weak or strong candidate not only for intellectual, but also for moral honours? For there are plenty of human talents other than theoretical talents, which can be educated, miseducated and neglected; and there are plenty of tastes and scruples other than moral tastes and scruples into which the human adolescent can be growing up. For example, unlike a lion or an infant, a man can have a good or a poor sense of humour; yet a poor sense of humour is neither a moral vice or weakness nor yet an intellectual failing. A lion, unlike a man, neither respects nor flouts technical standards of craftsmanship; it is neither an artist nor a philistine; it is neither tactless nor tactful, courteous nor brusque; it has neither a good nor a bad head for business; it is neither a good nor a bad player of tennis or chess or hide-and-seek; it is neither sentimental nor unsentimental nor cynical. There are hosts of kinds of faults and failings other than intellectual *or* moral faults and failings, of which only human beings can be accused or acquitted. Merely to split Reason into Theoretical and Practical Reason is to leave unattached lots and lots of our familiar and interesting contributions to daily life which are peculiar to us rational animals. Ought we not, in order to reinforce Theoretical and Practical Reason, also to invoke artistic Reason, conversational Reason, commercial Reason, strategic Reason and sporting Reason?

A little while ago we felt mutinous against the traditional dictum which seemed to identify what is peculiar to human nature with too narrow a range of qualities, namely, with certain academic qualities. But now, I expect, we begin to feel uneasy with the opposite idea which seems to identify it with too wide a range. It then seemed over-stingy to say that man is an animal that can cope with propositions. Now, I expect, it seems unpromisingly hospitable to say just that man is an animal that can do and feel all the things that man can, and the other animals cannot. So we should try now to see whether there is not some common thread that runs through all the various actions, efforts, reactions and feelings which need to be classified as peculiar to human nature, irrespective of whether these are to be sub-classified as intellectual or moral or artistic or conversational or commercial or sporting, and so on indefinitely. Let us try this approach. We might say, not without risk of grave misunderstanding, that, in the most hospitable possible sense of the word, it is Thought that is peculiar to the human animal, and that it is only because he can and does think that he can and does play competitive games, see jokes, act parts, make music, strike bargains, curb his irritation or impatience, play fairly, behave decorously, and so on. That he acts or reacts in any of these ways entails that he thinks. We can fight off the old menace of describing human nature in unwarrantably academic terms by saying that the thinking that is involved in these actions and reactions need not be scholastically trained thinking, perhaps need not even be propositional thinking. The child who can find fault with the singing of a song or can resent an undeserved scolding need not be able to formulate his protests, much less be able to defend them against objections. Still he apprehends that the song has been mis-sung or that he has been scolded for doing something which he did not do, and this apprehending must be classified as belonging to thinking. For it could be misapprehension, and misapprehension is thinking something to be the case which is not the case. A creature which cannot think cannot misapprehend or, therefore, correctly apprehend either. The thinking of the child when he invents a new stratagem in hide-and-seek, or when he chuckles at a practical joke, may well be quite unarticulated and unschooled thinking, but 'thinking' it must be called if we are to be able to say that the stratagem was a stupid one or that what he chuckled at was not the practical joke that he took it to be, but a hostile or careless act.

How must we suppose that the thinking of such unschooled, pre-propositional thoughts enters into the performance of even such nursery actions and into the having of even such nursery feelings? When we say, as we must say, that a creature or an infant that cannot think cannot do such things as resent an undeserved scolding or test a new stratagem in hide-and-seek, what kind of dependence have we in mind?

One answer comes all too quickly to our lips, namely the 'cause-effect' answer. The resenting or the inventing depends on the thinking as the freezing of a pond depends on the falling of the temperature of the water. The thinking is a causal condition and presumably a causal precursor or inaugurator of the resenting or the experimenting. Our inference from the child's experiment or resentment to his thinking the requisite thought is a diagnostic inference. 'Here are the symptoms, so *there* there must have been the cause.' The child must first have been thinking a thought and then—and therefore—gone on to feel the resentment or to test his new stratagem. 'First came the flash of lightning and then—and therefore—there occurred the rumble of thunder.'

Unfortunately, or rather fortunately, this captivating cause-effect answer leads to immediate troubles. By what systematic or unsystematic sequences of observations and experiments did we discover, or could we have discovered, that human beings never or hardly ever resent things, find things funny, test things, or even come out with significant and pertinent remarks save when they have, very very shortly beforehand, or even at the same time, been entertaining the requisite thought? By what experiments did we establish the causal law that lions, infants and idiots never do the antecedent or concomitant thinking of thoughts, without which their behaviour cannot rank as either prudent *or* imprudent, careful *or* careless, conceited *or* modest, non-conformist *or* conformist? Did we first find them not thinking these thoughts, and therefore conclude that their conduct did not qualify for these epithets? How did we find them not thinking these thoughts? How, indeed, did we find the child, or our own selves, thinking them? Worse still. The doctor can describe in its own right and in observational terms that haemorrhage or that sprain to which he infers from these visible or palpable external symptoms, just as we can give its own description in observational terms to that lightning-flash of which this rumble of thunder is the effect. But in what sort of terms, even, are we to describe those postulated prefatory or concomitant thinkings of apparently unformulated thoughts which are supposed to trigger off all our specifically human actions and reactions? In real life we have no general difficulty in recognizing another person's utterance as a legitimate complaint or as a pertinent query, and this recognition does not in real life await the confirmation of any diagnostic hypothesis. Yet according to the cause-effect theory, we ought to remain quite unsure what, if anything, the utterance was an expression of until we had tracked its causation back to a prior or collateral cogitative occurrence, to which, unfortunately, we outsiders are forbidden access, and for the characterization of which we and he lack even a vocabulary.

In our own case we are, in normal circumstances, perfectly

ready to tell others or ourselves what we did, why we did it and what was the situation, actual or supposed, in which we did it; or we are perfectly ready to tell how we felt, about what and with what justification or seeming justification. The action or feeling so readily described was indeed that of a thinking being. An action or feeling of that description could not have been a passage in the life of a lion, an infant or an idiot, or even, sometimes, in the life of a man who had been without our special training, history or interests. But still the mention of the postulated previous or synchronous occurrence of a separate act or process of thinking a thought seems to be no natural, necessary or even possible ingredient in what we so readily and usually satisfactorily divulge about what we did or felt and why we did or felt it. I have no difficulty in telling you what amused me, but in telling you this I do not recount a story of the pattern 'I began by having the thought that so and so, and then a tickled feeling came over me and then a chuckle issued from me'. Rather, in telling you what I was amused at or what I chuckled at, I am already telling you the thought without which I should not have been amused. My thought or apprehension of the ridiculous incident was not the cause of my being amused. It was partly constitutive of it, somewhat as the headside of a penny is indeed part of what makes it the penny that it is, and yet is obviously not a separately existing agency that causes the penny to be the penny that it is.

To describe someone as laughing at a ridiculous incident is, of course, to say more than just that he made a laughing noise. It is to say that he laughed in appreciation, or perhaps misappreciation of the quality of the incident. But this does not require, indeed it does not permit us to say that there took place in him, first, an emotionless, spectator's appreciation of a situation and, second, somehow triggered off by this detached and contemplative appreciation, a spasm of a feeling and the expulsion of a laughing noise. More nearly it is to say just that he appreciated—gleefully appreciated—the ridiculous incident; or just that he found the incident funny. Certainly he could not have found it funny if he had not got adequately developed wits; and he would not have found it funny if, owing to panic, absence of mind, preoccupation, inebriation or sleep, he had not been using those wits. His being intelligently alive to the ridiculous incident, his feeling of amusement and his laughter, though not independent parts, are indeed distinguishable features of that single momentary passage in his life. For particular purposes they can be given separate mentions or emphases, as can the profile, complexion and expression of his face. But just as the separately mentionable characteristics of his face are not parts of it, or therefore separable parts of it, so his intelligent appreciation of the ridiculous incident, his feeling tickled and his laughing are not parts or therefore separately occurring parts of his amusement at the incident.

Nor does the anxious mother first dispassionately consider an unformulated truth about her child's illness and then go on to have a feeling of anxiety and then go on to wring her hands. She thinks anxiously, and she is anxious enough to keep on thinking about her child, and to think little of other things, unless as things connected with and coloured by her child's danger.

It must be confessed that we do sometimes picture a person's waking life as a description-baffling procession of passionless and unexecutive acknowledgements of unarticulated truths or falsehoods triggering off actions, emotions, gestures, smiles, shudders and losses of appetite. We picture his life so when we look at it through the blinkers of certain epistemologies. So much the worse for those blinkers. But what is it that not only persuades us to put on these blinkers but even gets us to feel at home in them? It is, I think, this. Besides and in sharp contrast with this very hospitable notion of thinking, as that using or misusing of our wits which is internal to or constitutive of all our specifically human actions and reactions, we have another very specific, almost professional, notion of thinking, namely as the reflecting that is done by the Thinker as distinct from the Agent, the thinking that deservedly ranks as, in high or low degree, theoretical thinking. Here we can speak, intelligibly enough, of the thinking of thoughts in some detachment from the momentary practical tasks or concerns of the thinker. This reflecting can be very crudely described as operating from and with propositions; and the thinking of these thoughts has indeed a certain chilly disengagement from the urgencies of the moment, as well as a certain impersonality. My theoretical problem or answer today might be your theoretical problem or answer tomorrow or last year. Human rationality has here separate and, if you like, genuinely academic objectives and chores of its own, objectives and chores in which the Greeks could with justice say that barbarians, being totally unschooled, could not participate. To put an edge on this contrast: on the one hand we should certainly wish to say that the tennis-player is, in the hospitable sense of the verb, thinking, since he is attending to the game, and applying or misapplying to fresh contingencies lessons that he has learned. Not only his long-term strategies but also his momentary movements can be politic and cunning or stupid and ill-judged. All the time he is estimating and mis-estimating things. His using his wits and his playing the game are one single occupation, not two rival occupations, or even two allied occupations. On the other hand, in the special, semi-professional sense of the verb, he must stop playing if he wants to think, i.e. to reflect, and he must stop reflecting if he wants to play tennis. If he is reflecting about some intellectual problem, even a problem about tennis, he is not then and there giving his mind to his game. If he is engaged in the one activity, then he is wholly or partly disengaged from the other. They are rival occupations. It is by this special family of distinctively intellectual operations that the notion of Reason has traditionally been monopolized.

This, I suggest, is why, when we find it necessary to say that, for example, tennis-playing involves thinking, namely thinking what to do and how to do it, we feel ourselves forced to say, what in our hearts we know to be false, that the activity of playing tennis has got to be a rapid procession of momentary and unrecorded intellectual or theorizing operations triggering off the several muscular movements. For unwittingly we have identified all exercises of our wits with a very special class of them, namely with certain special exercises of our academically trained and academically motived wits; so we have had to postulate the occurrence of unrecorded quasi-propositional operations to explain, in a cause-effect way, what it was that enabled, say, the tennis-player to anticipate his opponent's return; or enabled the child to appreciate a joke or try out a new stratagem in hide-and-seek. For we argue with apparent but unreal cogency that since he was thinking, he must have done, with fearsome celerity, a bit of what the theorist does, namely reflecting. Finding ourselves under pressure to pick out that feature of a person's actions and reactions which constitutes his giving his mind to them, we naturally but unprofitably skidded into identifying this feature with some accredited variety of intellectual operation, some recordable, though unrecorded, stroke of theorizing. We assumed, quite wrongly, that what takes a bit of intelligence must incorporate a bit of intellectual work; that for an act or feeling to be that of a more or less reasonable man it would have to trot in tandem behind an unacknowledged act of ratiocination; or that to think what one is doing or saying, one must perform, like lightning, a bit of thinking and then pass on to a bit of doing or saying.

So now we need to confront, face to face, this distinction between, on the one hand, the perfectly general notion of thought, as what is partly constitutive of all specifically human actions and reactions, and, on the other hand, the quite special and almost professional notion of thought, as a separate, self-moving and self-piloting activity of reflection, requiring some specialist training and governed by standards of its own. What are the differences and what are the connections between intelligent conduct in general and intellectual operations in particular? Between being a bit intelligent and doing a bit of reflecting or theorizing? In asking this question I am, I think, asking—but not asking only—how are Theoretical Reason and Practical Reason related?

Before tackling this problem directly, we need to make a perfectly general preliminary clarification. Whether we are considering the case of a child momentarily perplexed by a practical joke, or the case of a tennis-player momentarily hesitating between one movement and another, or the case of a historian at a loss for an explanation of some historical event, in describing him as thinking we are describing him as wondering, as *trying* to solve his practical or theoretical problem. He is pondering, undecided, unsettled. He is in a state of search, and very often, though not always, in a state of bafflement, that is, of not yet knowing what to do in order to solve his problem. For example, when conversing with a foreigner in his own language, I may be frequently trying, and sometimes trying in vain, to make out what he means; and trying also, and perhaps in vain, to put into words of his language the things that I want to say to him. Often, too, I may have to try, maybe in vain, to frame a reply which will not offend or embarrass a person of his nationality. Now contrast with this my normal situation in conversing with my own friends. Here, most of the time, though not quite all of the time, I have not merely no great difficulties, but no difficulties at all in understanding what they say or in making myself understood by them; and I have to take not merely no great pains, but no pains at all to avoid wounding their susceptibilities. Certainly I am attending to what they say, and my replies are appropriate and unmechanical. I am alert and not absent-minded, asleep or *distrait*. But I do not, most of the time, wonder at all what they mean or what I am to say. I am not in a state of search or bafflement. I am using, but I am not taxing, my conversational wits. I am conversing adequately, perhaps even well, but I am not trying to do so, and *a fortiori* I am not trying in vain to do so.

Naturally such unhesitant, unobstructed, fluent conversing pre-supposes a prior mastery of conversational English and a prior familiarity with my interlocutors. Once I did have to study English, and to study the ways and foibles of my friends. But now that I have learned, I can converse with them, most of the time, not merely with very little effort but with no effort at all. I succeed in exchanging ideas with them without any present studying. Of course this agreeable and untaxing situation ceases to obtain the moment the conversation turns towards embarrassing topics, or the moment the circle is joined by a hot-gospeller or by an acquaintance in deep mourning.

To generalize this point. Not all successes are preceded by attempts; not all findings are preceded by searches; not all gettings are preceded by labours. In all fields, from the nursery to the laboratory, more or less painfully acquired capacities can develop into absolute facilities, so that the exercises of these capacities are at last, though only in normally propitious circumstances, totally unhesitant, totally unperplexed and totally unlaborious. Some things which earlier had been slightly or very difficult are now so completely easy that we do not trouble to describe them as even easy. Some things which earlier had been obscure or strange are now so completely obvious that we do not trouble to describe them as even obvious, any more than I would ordinarily trouble to describe as 'quite light' the match or the pin that I pick up from the floor. Of course, the fact that something, say walking down familiar stairs, is now completely easy does not involve that we never stumble; the fact that its meaning is or seems perfectly obvious does not involve that we never misunderstand a friend's remark. Total unlaboriousness does not entail impeccability. Theorists who enjoy inventing Faculties sometimes use the grand word 'intuition' to cover certain of our totally unlaborious gettings. They are then troubled by the occurrence of the occasional stumbles and mis-understandings against which their fine new Faculty ought to be proof.

Certainly, I should not yet have acquired complete facility in anything if the risk of going wrong was still a serious one. A thing cannot yet be or seem quite obvious to me if repeated sad experiences have forced me to continue to be on my guard against being mistaken about such things. If, for example, from my hardness of hearing or from the similarity of their voices, I could not safely distinguish the voice of one of my friends from that of another, then it would not be or seem obvious to me that a heard voice belonged to one and not to the other. On the other hand, the fact that I tell one friend from another by his voice, without any effort or dubiety, does not exclude the possibility that very occasionally I get them wrong. Facility involves predominant but not exceptionless success.

Thinking, wondering, pondering, puzzlement, bafflement and effort belong to the level below that of perfect facility. I am thinking when I am trying to make out whose voice it is; but I am not thinking or wondering when I unhesitatingly recognize or, very occasionally, misrecognize it, any more than I am searching for the moon when I see it shining in the sky above my head. None the less, just as I am using my eyes when I see the moon, though I did not have to peer or scan with them first, so I am using my wits when I recognize a friend's voice, though I did not have to start by doing any wondering, surmising or speculating with them. If I had been deranged or panic-stricken or *distrait* or fuddled, I should not have recognized the voice.

The man who sees a joke straight off is using, but not exerting his wits. He does not try to see it, since he does not need to try. The man who has to try, and perhaps tries in vain to see a joke is thinking or wondering. Both seeing the joke without hesitation or effort, and trying to see it, i.e. thinking it over, exemplify intelligence or, if you like, rationality, in the most hospitable sense of the words. But it is the former, not the latter, which exemplifies it at its best. For to ponder is to be still unsuccessful, and to have to ponder is to fall short of complete facility. But still, effortless gettings and accomplishings presuppose the prior occurrence of effortful gettings and effortful accomplishings. Facility now is the harvest of difficulty then. The qualities of a man's wits are shown both by his effortless gettings and accomplishings and by his effortful gettings or missings, accomplishings or failures. But it is the latter which have made the former possible. If I can now very often detect misprints at a glance, it is only because in childhood I industriously and interestedly struggled with the recalcitrant mysteries of spelling.

In short, if a person has, without the slightest difficulty or hesitation, seen a joke or a misprint, then it is true of him that he has used his wits, yet false that he has been wondering or pondering. He has found something without having to rummage for it.

Now we can return to our big residual problem. How is the way in which all specifically human actions and reactions require thought or rationality, i.e. the use or misuse of at least partially trained wits, related to the way in which certain, rather special and even specialist activities of reflecting belong to some men at some times only, namely at the times when we describe them as occupied in thinking as contrasted with doing? Is there a smooth line of development from the child who chuckles at a practical joke, or from the tennis-player who anticipates his opponent's return to the historian, say, who tries, perhaps successfully, to find the explanation of a historical incident, or to the scientist who tries, perhaps successfully, to rigorize the Mendelian genetic theory? Is theorizing just a much more highly advanced stage of that of which, say, resenting an undeserved scolding is a very primitive stage? Is the child who tries out a new stratagem in hide-and-seek already a nursery-Newton?

I am going to argue that the line is not a smooth line, and so that there is more than a mere increase in complexity between the problems which we solve or try to solve, say, in the nursery or on the football-field, and those which we solve or try to solve in our capacity of scientists, historians, economists, scholars, philosophers, etc.; or even those which we solve or try to solve in our capacity of schoolboys studying arithmetic, translation, geography or essay-writing. But I shall not, of course, be maintaining that there was a day in everyone's life, or even that it makes sense to say that there was such a day, when he was promoted, or promoted himself from the ranks of those who just have intelligence and use it to the rank of those who have and use their Intellect or their Faculty of Theoretical Reason.

The entirely general notion of thought that we have been considering is that of, for example, the thinking what to do or how to do it of the person who is trying to win his game of tennis, or trying to converse with a foreigner. His problem is, in a wide sense, a practical though not a moral problem, and his successful solution of it is his success in the game or the conversation. His thinking is, as we have seen, not a precursor of or a preparatory step towards his doing what he wants to do; it is an element, and an essential element, in his trying to do it. It is not a separately reportable stretch of an autonomous activity; it is a constitutive feature of his successful or unsuccessful tennis-playing or conversing. It just *is* the fact that he is trying intelligently, or, quite often, succeeding without having to try. He does not have one motive for thinking what to do and another motive for doing the thing; nor is he the victim of a division between two occupations, one the playing or the conversing and the other the thinking how to play or converse. He has, at this stage, no interest in the problem *how* to think how to play or converse. His playing may be judicious or ill-judged, but his thinking how to play is not yet itself judicious or ill-judged thinking. It may be quick or slow thinking, and efficient or inefficient thinking; but he is not yet trying to think efficiently how to play, but only trying to play efficiently. In retrospect he may find fault with the way he played, but not, as yet, with the way in which he considered how to play. He may accuse himself of playing carelessly, but not yet of thinking carelessly how to play.

In strong contrast with this, the thinking or the reflecting which we are ready to classify as intellectual work, no matter whether of low or of high level, is thinking in which the thinker is necessarily at least slightly concerned to think properly. His thinking has standards of its own, such that in retrospect the thinker may find fault with the way in which he had thought, and he may accuse himself of thinking carelessly in this or that specific respect. Now we are considering the thinking which it is the business of schools and universities to train and to stimulate. Students there are being deliberately trained and stimulated to think like good mathematicians or good historians or good philosophers or good biochemists or good composers of Latin verse or good grammarians. This is in some degree specialist thinking, and it is thinking that has achieved a sort of autonomy, since it now moves under its own steam, carries cargoes of its own and is steered by compasses of its own. It is a separate occupation. The question 'What is he doing?' can be answered by 'He is thinking'. Moreover it has a weak or strong self-correcting factor built into it. Behind, and not at all far behind the examiner's question 'What do you think about so and so?' there lies in wait the question 'Why do you think so?, i.e. with what justification do you think so?' To impart propositions without giving their justification is to try to persuade, not to try to teach; and to have accepted such propositions is to believe, not to know.

I illustrate this crucial point by a partial parallel. If a wanderer is lost, he wants to find out how to reach his destination. He looks around him, moves off in one direction, then circles round, and so on. Yet we should not yet rank him as an explorer, and *a fortiori* not as a geographer. For, first, he is not scanning the countryside or scrambling round it in order to advance his, or mankind's, geographical knowledge. All he wants is to get home. He is searching, but he is not *re*searching. Second, his scannings and his rovings have, I am supposing, no method or technique in them. He does not know how so to organize them as to make it probable or certain that he will in the end reach the river or the railway-track. He does not, for example, consistently follow the stream downhill, or he does not systematically quarter the ground, or mark off the paths that he has already tried and abandoned. He has a good reason for hunting, namely that he needs to get home before nightfall. But he has, I am supposing, no general reasons, good or even bad, for the particular hunting-moves that he makes. If his search is successful, it may succeed only by luck, or by half-memory, or by unschooled hunch or by native sense of direction; it does not succeed by being efficiently conducted.

In contrast with him, the explorer also roves and also scans, but he roves and scans methodically, and the methods are learned methods of finding out the lie of the land, whatever land it may be. Whether or not he also happens to want to arrive at a personal destination, his actions now have an independent objective of their own, namely to ascertain the geography of the area. What he discovers about the terrain may, or may not, subsequently prove useful for the particular practical purposes of people, including himself, who want to get home, want to picnic, want to find bog-flowers or transport timber and so on. But what he discovers about the terrain, being indifferently useful for all these practical purposes, is neutral between them. The geographical knowledge that he acquires is qualified to become anybody's property, and therefore not the personal property of anyone in particular. The formulability of this knowledge in words or in cartographical symbols is part and parcel of its being, in principle, at once public property and neutral as between the different momentary concerns of different individuals. The explorer's findings are, as such, disengaged from any particular urgencies. Moreover, exploration is, as such, subject to canons of procedure. It has a discipline, a gradually developing discipline of its own. There are correct versus incorrect, economical versus uneconomical ways of making surveys, of describing terri-torial features, of recording observations, and of checking estimates and measurements. The explorer, to be an explorer, must have learned from others or found out for himself some of these pro-cedures if he is today to be putting them into practice. He can reproach himself or be reproached by others for carelessness, precipitancy, inaccuracy or muddle-headedness, as distinct from inexpertness, only if he fails to work in ways in which he already knows how to work.

If he is an explorer at all, then, though he may be surprised to hear it, he already has something of an explorer's conscience, that is, some contempt for shoddy work and some self-recrimination for mistakes and omissions. Even without the prospects of fame or remuneration he has at least a slight inclination to do the job properly. Indeed, other things being equal, he now likes exploring for its own sake. At least a corner of his heart is in it. Exploring is, in some measure, an autonomous occupation. It can be a sufficient answer to the question 'What is he engaged in at the moment?' to say 'He is exploring such and such a bit of country', as it would not have been a sufficient answer to the question about the lost wanderer 'What is he engaged in at the moment?' to say 'He is roving around and scanning such and such a bit of the country'.

I hope it is obvious where I want to go from this half-way house. Thought in the near-professional or near-academic sense of the word stands to thinking in the general sense of the word as exploring and surveying stand to procedureless searching for the way home. Theoretical thinking is, in some degree, self-motivated, and it is subject to its own canons of 'correct' versus 'incorrect', 'economical' versus 'uneconomical', i.e. it has a discipline. The theorist as such has some special equipment and some special standards, a special conscience, special tastes and a special hobby. In a word, we can now credit him with that famous Faculty, an Intellect.

It does not matter in the least, for my purposes, whether our specimen thinker's intellectual pursuit is that of an historian, a mathematician, a philosopher, a literary critic, a philatelist, a grammarian or a bird-watcher; and it does not matter in the least, for my purposes, whether he is proficient, moderate or poor at it; whether he is whole-hearted or half-hearted in it; whether he is a professional or an amateur; or whether he is an adult or an adolescent. If he can do intellectual work at all, he knows what it is to get something wrong, and he knows what it is to be in a muddle; and knowing this, he also cares, however slightly, about getting things right and getting things sorted out. He would prefer to be out of the muddle, and he apologizes for the mistake. He may sulk under adverse criticism, but he can still distinguish just from unjust criticism.

Part of what I am saying is that, in its specialist sense, thought, i.e. intellectual work, has a discipline or rather a battery of disciplines of its own. But this assertion is liable to be misconstrued in two quite different ways.

(1) First, it is, I think, sometimes assumed that there is just one type of intellectual fault against which the thinker must have been trained and must now be wary, namely breach of the rules of Logic. Doubtless fallaciousness in reasoning is, in some important way, the most radical thing that can be wrong with a person's theoretical thinking. But in one scientist's criticism of the theory of another scientist, or in one historian's criticism of the work of another historian, accusations of formal fallacy are pretty rare. The faults that are actually found there belong to a wide range of different types, with most of which the formal logician has no official concern. A first-rate mathematician and a first-rate literary critic might share the one intellectual virtue of arguing impeccably, while their other intellectual virtues could be so disparate that neither could cope even puerilely with the problems of the other. Each thinks scrupulously inside his own field, but most of their scruples are of entirely different kinds. Though equally vigilant against fallacy, they also take quite different sorts of precautions against quite different sorts of mistakes, muddles and omissions. Perhaps our inherited tendency to equate rationality with the capacity to prove theorems or to deduce conclusions from premises is connected with this assumption that fallaciousness, because, maybe the most radical, is in the last resort the only, fault that a theorist can be guilty of, an assumption as far-fetched as the idea that head-on collisions are the sole penalties of bad driving on the highway.

(2) There is a second way in which it would be quite natural to misconstrue my military metaphor of the 'disciplines' of intellectual work. It might be taken to imply or suggest that the thinking of the really high-grade theorist moves—distressingly unlike our own thinking—as soldiers move on the barrack-square. One evolution is smartly succeeded by another evolution, one controlled pace forward is smoothly succeeded by one controlled step to the right, and so on. There is indeed some thinking which does go like this, namely what we do when adding, subtracting, multiplying and dividing. Here we can make controlled step after controlled step without hesitancy or loss of direction. Cash registers are better than we are at these operations. But most thinking is not and could not be like this. 'Disciplined' does not mean the same as 'regimented' or 'drilled'. A person's thinking is subject to disciplines if, for example, he systematically takes precautions against personal bias, tries to improve the orderliness or clarity of his theory, checks his references, his dates or his calculations, listens attentively to his critics, hunts industriously for exceptions to his generalizations,

deletes ambiguous, vague or metaphorical expressions from the sinews of his arguments, and so on indefinitely. His thinking is controlled, in high or low degree, by a wide range of quite specific scruples; and this is very different from the way in which his multiplying and dividing are regimented by those few stereotyped drills that were inculcated in him in his schooldays.

Moreover, the excogitation of a theory, or of a comprehensive and explanatory historical narrative, is not a morning's task, like laying two hundred bricks, or a five minutes' task, like a piece of long division. It can be a month's task or a decade's task, like constructing a garden. Its development is a gradual, fitful and intermittent affair. Hypotheses have to be left to germinate, grow, flower and seed themselves, or, still more often, to wither and to die. Ideas have to be weeded out, or pruned back or transplanted; the soil has to be left fallow; pests have to be poisoned, and so on.

Now, at last, we can begin to see more clearly than before how the ideas of rationality, reasonableness and reasons are internal to the notion of the thinking that needs to be graded as intellectual work. For this thinking essentially embodies the element of self-correction. Hunch, native sense of direction, following good examples, though indispensable, are no longer enough. The thinker cares, at least a little bit, whether he gets things right or wrong; he is at least slightly concerned to think properly. This involves that the question of justification is always a live question. For any hypothesis or suggestion that is made, for any question that is asked, for any argument that is constructed or even sketched, for any example that is adduced, for any word or phrase or even comma that is used, the challenge is there in the foreground or in the background, 'Why?', 'With what right?', 'For what reason?' In this respect, the ever-present justification-demand is like the justification-demand that can always be made for any action that we perform and even for any of our reactions or feelings that are to rank as being specifically human. But the difference that matters to us is that the reasons given in justification of intellectual or theoretical operations or efforts are necessarily themselves intellectual or theoretical reasons. They are *ex officio* propositional considerations. They are not *ex officio* moral or prudential or aesthetic reasons, any more than they are reasons of courtesy, fashion, competitive prowess or good business.

Naturally, though unfortunately, the preoccupation of philosophers with theoretical reasons or justifications has often induced them to treat practical reasons and justifications as mere varieties

or off-shoots of theoretical reasons, as if all scruples and all carefulness reduced, somehow, to theorists' scruples and theorists' carefulness. The genus has been reduced to a variety of one of its own
species, just because this species has, and deserves, so special a
cachet. Remembering too well that the historian must reply to the
question 'With what justification?' by citing his documentary or
archaeological evidence; or remembering too well that a Euclid
must reply to the question 'With what justification?' by adducing
a derivation from axioms, philosophers have sometimes yielded
to the temptation of supposing that the question 'With what
justification?' when asked about an action, or an emotion, or a
literary innovation should also be replied to by adducing a proof,
or at least something colourably like a proof, or by adducing a
corpus of bits of evidence, or at least of things colourably like bits
of evidence. 'How else,' we can hear them muttering, 'how else
could a reason be a justification of something, unless in the way in
which a premiss is a reason for a conclusion? How could there be
practical successes or failures save as repercussions of successes or
failures in theorizing? How could a person do the right thing or
do a wrong thing, save as the after-effect of doing the right theoretical thing or a wrong theoretical thing? How could a person be a
backslider in his conduct, save as the after-effect of a bit of backsliding in his theoretical reflections about how he should behave?'
To ask such questions as these surely is to ask, in effect, 'How
could a person learn anything in the nursery, unless he had already
learned in the university how to learn nursery lessons?' or 'How
could M. Jourdain talk prose before he had mastered some prose-
formulated propositions about the conditions of significant prose?'
How could the unmanufactured horse possibly get and remain in
front of the manufactured cart?

If we enjoy the egotistical pastime of giving to mankind testimonials which we withhold from other creatures; or if, more
sensibly but still platitudinously, we like to give to civilized man
testimonials which we withhold from uncivilized man, and to
civilized man at his highest, which we half-withhold from civilized
man at his decent but unglorious mean, we shall certainly lay great,
though not exclusive, emphasis on his past performances and his
future promises as a theorist, that is, as an advancer of knowledge,
no matter whether this be knowledge of nature, mathematical
knowledge or knowledge of human ways and human callings.
What we must not do is to confuse testimonials with explanations.
Yet this is just what we do when we treat special and specially

inculcated proficiencies as elemental agencies or forces; for example, when we treat Theoretical Reason as the cause of human nature's being human nature; or when we treat all our doings as the effects of some of our propositional doings, and all our faults as visible footprints left in the mud by the privy commission of inarticulate fallacies.

33

ABSTRACTIONS

*Reprinted from 'Dialogue' (Canadian Philosophical Review), vol. 1,
1962, by permission of the editors*

St Augustine said, 'When you do not ask me what Time is, I
know perfectly well; but when you do ask me, I cannot think what
to say.' What, then, was it that he knew perfectly well, and what
was it that he did not know? Obviously he knew perfectly well
such things as these, that what happened yesterday is more recent
than what happened a month ago; that a traveller who walks four
miles in an hour goes twice as fast as a traveller who takes two
hours over the same journey. He knew how to say things and how
to understand things said to him which specified dates, durations
and times of day; epochs, seasons and moments. He knew when it
was midday and he could use the calendar. He could cope efficiently
and easily with concrete chronological and chronometrical tasks.
He could use and understand tensed verbs. What he could not do
is to give any reply at all to such abstract questions as these: what
is it that there is twice as much of in a fortnight as in a week? Why
could Time, unlike a battle, never have started, and why can Time,
unlike a concert, never come to a stop? Does Time flow on at an
uniform or an irregular speed, and, in either case, is its speed
measured in a second sort of Time? In short, what is Time—
is it a Thing or a Process or a Relation? Is it a sort of cosmic
river, only one without any tangible water between its non-existing
banks? One which flows out of no spring and pours out into no
ocean?

We might say that Augustine, like anyone else, could answer
concrete factual questions about times; but that, like everyone
else, he could not answer abstract questions about the concept
of Time. But what is this difference between concrete or factual
questions and abstract or conceptual questions?

Take another example. Hume, like any other sensible person,
knew perfectly well how to distinguish between one occasion when

he met a friend by appointment and another occasion when he
met a friend by chance; or between one game of cards when the
dealer dealt himself all the aces by trickery and another when
the dealer dealt himself all the aces by sheer luck. None the less,
when Hume, as a philosopher, asks himself What is Chance? he
actually gives an answer which we can swiftly prove to be wrong.
He says that since whatever comes about is due to some cause,
and since chance is not a cause, therefore, to say that something,
like a meeting between friends, has come about by chance can only
mean that it has come about from some cause of which we are
ignorant. But this answer must be wrong, for though we are
ignorant of the cause of cancer, we should never say that cancer
comes about by chance. The phrase 'by chance' cannot therefore
be equivalent to the phrase 'from an unknown cause'. Hume tried
but failed to answer his abstract question about the concept of
chance, though in everyday life he knew perfectly well how to
distinguish fortuitous coincidence from non-fortuitous conjunctions
of affairs. We are tempted to say that he did not know the meaning
of the abstract noun 'Chance', despite the fact that he knew perfectly
well the meaning of the adverbial phrase 'by chance'. Yet how
could he possibly know the one without knowing the other?

To change the example once more, you yourselves would find
it difficult to tell me what Knowledge is and how it differs from
True Belief, yet your difficulty, whatever it is, does not continue
to embarrass you when asked such concrete questions as these:
Do you still know the date of the Battle of Waterloo? At what
age did you learn or come to know Pythagoras' theorem? Why
are memorised gibberish syllables easier to forget, i.e. cease to
know, than significant sentences, and sentences in prose easier
to forget than sentences in verse?

Notice that in this case, while my abstract epistemological
question employed the abstract noun 'knowledge', in my concrete
questions this abstract noun did not occur, but only the active
verbs 'know', 'learn' and 'forget'. So we are tempted to say that
we do not know the meaning of the abstract noun, though we are
perfectly at home with the meanings of the active verbs. Yet this
cannot be right, for if a person understands perfectly well the
active verbs 'know', 'learn', and 'forget' he knows all that he
needs in order to understand the abstract noun 'knowledge'. If a
child has learned what it is for someone to conquer or protect
someone else, he needs no further lessons in order to understand
the abstract nouns 'conquest' and 'protection'.

Similarly with adjectives. A person who is quite familiar with the idea of things being probable or improbable is fully equipped to understand the abstract noun 'probability'—yet is not thereby equipped to answer the abstract, conceptual question 'What is probability?' or 'Is probability a property of happenings, though only some future ones, or is it a property of some of our thoughts about happenings?' Questions like those that perplexed Augustine and defeated Hume, namely the abstract questions about Time and Chance, can be classified as conceptual questions. They are questions *about* Concepts. But a question such as 'How long did the battle last?' or 'Did the friends meet by chance or by design?' is a question *about* a battle or a meeting. Here the ideas of temporal duration and of fortuitousness are being operated *with*; but they are not here being operated *upon*. Somewhat similarly, the sculptor operates with a chisel, but it is the stone that he is operating upon. It would be the business of the mechanic, not the sculptor, to operate upon the chisel itself.

With some exaggeration we might try saying that a conceptual question or conceptual statement typically has for its grammatical subject an abstract noun, like 'Time' or 'Chance' or 'Probability', where a factual question about a battle, or a meeting, or the weather would incorporate the corresponding concrete ideas only by means of its verbs or adjectives or adverbs. The weather forecast that tells us that in a certain region there will probably be snowstorms tomorrow has for its subject the weather in a certain place, and not the concept of probability. This idea comes in only adverbially, as a qualification of the expectations about the weather. But to say this would be too violent. For the weather forecast might just as well be worded in this way: 'There is the probability' or 'There is a high probability of snowstorms in such and such a region'. This forecast employs the abstract noun 'probability', though its author would certainly tell us, if asked, that he was not talking about the concept of probability, but only talking about the weather. The presence of the abstract noun 'probability' or 'time' does not prove that the sentence incorporating it expressed a proposition about the concept of Probability or the concept of Time. It can do so, but it need not. Correspondingly, a philosopher or logician might be discussing the concept of Knowledge, Time, Chance or Probability, although he abstained from employing those abstract nouns or any others.

How is an abstract assertion, however it is worded, about the concept of Time, or Probability or Knowledge related to the concrete assertions in which, perhaps, a battle is said to have lasted for three days, snowstorms are asserted to be probable, or the schoolboy is said no longer to know Pythagoras' theorem? (1) Clearly the abstract assertion about the concept is, in an important way, more sophisticated than the concrete assertions. A child who had not yet progressed far enough to understand that snow would probably be falling tomorrow, would *a fortiori* not yet be equipped to understand assertions about the concepts of Probability and Time. (2) But more than this. Abstract assertions about the concepts of Probability and Knowledge are parasitic upon concrete assertions expressed, perhaps, with the adverb 'probably' and the verb 'know', 'learn' or 'forget'—parasitic in this way, that the maker of an assertion about Probability or Time or Knowledge is saying in perfectly general terms something *about* what is said when, for example, it is said that snow will probably be falling tomorrow, or that the schoolboy has forgotten what he had once learned, namely, Pythagoras' theorem. What functioned as predicate or a part of the predicate of the concrete assertion is itself the subject matter that is being talked about in the abstract assertion. Statements about Probability are, in an important way, statements *about* what it is that is stated when we state that something will probably happen or what it is that is asked when someone asks whether it is more likely to snow than to rain. To put it over-grammatically, the abstract noun 'probability' is parasitic upon, *inter alia*, the adverb 'probably', and the abstract noun 'Time' is parasitic upon, *inter alia*, the tenses of ordinary tensed verbs. The chisel with which, this morning, the sculptor was carving the stone, is, this afternoon, the object upon which the mechanic is working. But he is always working upon the chisel *as* the tool with which stone-carving has been done and is to be done again, though stone-carving is not being done with it this afternoon.

Maybe we can now begin to see part of what it was that perplexed Augustine. It puzzled him that, so to speak, in the morning he could, without error or confusion, produce and follow ordinary remarks containing tensed verbs and specifications of dates, hours and epochs, and yet, so to speak, in the afternoon he could not answer questions about the concept of Time. The morning task and the afternoon task belong to different levels; and the afternoon task requires reconsidering, in a special way, features of what had been done, perfectly efficiently perhaps, but still naïvely, in the morning. In the morning he had talked good sense about everyday topics in, *inter alia*, temporal dictions; but in the afternoon he had to try to talk good sense about the good sense that, in the morning, he had talked in those temporal dictions.

But now for a further point. The persons responsible for publishing weather forecasts are constantly having to tell their hearers that, for example, snowstorms are likely in certain regions, while in other regions, though snowstorms are possible, rainy weather is much more probable; and so on. From what intellectual motive can they or anyone else raise what I am calling the 'afternoon'-conceptual questions, namely the questions about what had been contributed to their morning forecasts by their expressions 'probably', 'possible, but less likely' and so on? If, in the morning, they knew quite well what they were saying, why do they or other people need, in the afternoon, to try to say things about the well-understood things that they had said in the morning? How are any conceptual problems left requiring a solution, if the meteorologist had, in the morning, said with truth, consistency and clarity all that he meant to say about tomorrow's weather? What light is there for a conceptual discussion in the afternoon to throw on themes in which the meteorologist had in the morning been in no darkness at all? He and his hearers knew what he meant, so how can he need to be given an autopsy on what he meant? What questions about Time are left to perplex Augustine, after he has said and understood all the chronological and chrono-metrical things about the everyday world that he had needed to say and understand before lunch?

Let us take a new example. We are all, in everyday life, constantly having to consider concrete questions of existence and non-existence. How long ago did mammoths exist and how long have they been extinct or non-existent? Does there exist a prime number between 23 and 29? Is this island uninhabited or do there exist some human beings on it? Even when we speak of people constructing or demolishing bridges or houses we are speaking of them as bringing bridges or houses into existence, and as rendering them no longer existent. When theists and atheists dispute about the existence of God, they may not come to an agreement on their problem; but they do not differ in their employment of the notions of existence or non-existence.

None the less, there do arise, so to speak, in the afternoon, well-known problems about the concepts of existence and non-existence. How can non-existence be ascribed to anything, say a prime number between 23 and 29, or to a 20th century mammoth, if there *is*, i.e. if there *exists* nothing of which this or any other

439

predicate can be predicated? Just how do 100 imaginary dollars differ from 100 real or existent dollars, if I can imagine my 100 imaginary dollars as having all the properties of the real dollars, including that of being real? Once again we have to ask how it is that we are, in the morning, perfectly at home with the idea of things existing or being extinct or non-existent, and yet, in the afternoon, find ourselves challenged to describe what it was that we had earlier been at home with. Yet we do, somehow, need to be able to describe it. What sort of a need is this? To ask this is to ask what sorts of problems are specifically philosophical problems. Why do we need to philosophise?

Let us try out this suggested answer. A man at the dinner-table may know very well the difference between an onion and a beetroot. He knows their names, he knows how they taste, he can tell them apart from their looks and smells; maybe he even knows how to cultivate and cook them. But he cannot classify them; he cannot say to what different botanical *sorts* onions and beetroots belong. So perhaps we are in a similar position. We can, in concrete cases, tell existence from non-existence, knowledge from ignorance, a month from a minute; but we cannot say what sort of a thing it is for something to exist, what sort of a thing knowing is, or what sort of a thing a minute is a short stretch of. Perhaps problems about concepts are classificatory problems. I daresay that this is how Socrates thought of his philosophical problems, namely as problems the solution to which, if he could ever find them, would be of the pattern 'Virtue is a species of Knowledge, differing from other species of Knowledge in such and such respects'.

I do not think that this suggested answer is right, and for this reason. The philosophically interesting and crucial problems are problems about concepts which are, typically, too pervasive or too catholic to be treated as mere species of higher genera. The concepts of Time, Knowledge, Probability, Cause, Chance, Existence, Negation, and so on, are not departmental notions, and *a fortiori* not sub-departmental notions; they are inter-departmental. They belong, to put it metaphorically, not to this or that special vocabulary but to the topic-neutral syntax of our thoughts about the world.

So now let us consider another suggestion. Instead of thinking of a man who knows onions from beetroots but cannot tell us to what botanical sorts they belong, let us now think instead of the inhabitant of a village who knows well every house, field, stream, road and pathway in the neighbourhood and is, for the first time, asked to draw or consult a map of his village—a map which shall join on properly to the maps of adjacent districts and in the end to the map of his country and even of his continent. He is being asked to think about his own familiar terrain in a way that is at the start entirely strange, despite the fact that every item that he is to inscribe or identify in his map is to be something that he is entirely familiar with. In the morning he can walk from the church to the railway station without ever losing his way. But now, in the afternoon, he has to put down with compass bearings and distances in kilometres and metres the church, the railway station and the paths and roads between. In the morning he can show us the route from anywhere to anywhere; but it still puzzles him in the afternoon to describe those routes—describe them not just in words but in such cartographical terms that his local map will fit in with the maps of his entire region and country. He has, so to speak, to *translate* and therefore to re-think his local topographical knowledge into universal cartographical terms. Now he has to survey even his own dear home as if through the transparent pages of an international atlas.

I think you will agree that Augustine's puzzlement about the concept of Time has a good deal in common with the puzzlement of our villager who is asked to think about his home-village in cartographical terms.

We should notice that part of what perplexes the villager when for the first time asked to draw or to read a map of a place in which he is entirely at home is that he has to describe it in perfectly general, cartographical terms—terms, that is, which are shared by all other places. Where he normally thinks of *his* home, *his* church and *his* railway station in personal terms, now he has to think of them in impersonal, neutral terms. For him his village is unlike every other village in being the centre of his own life; but the map is neutral as between his village and any other. It represents them all by different arrangements of the same dots, lines and colours. All their distances, compass bearings and heights above sea level are given in the same unemphatic, impartial, impersonal code. The map is not a local snapshot; or an album of local snapshots; it is a slice out of an universal diagram. When he is out of the country, a snapshot of his home may make him feel homesick; but the map-reference of his home will not do this.

None the less the map is a store of knowledge about his district, for which his own personal familiarity with it can never deputise. Besides being personally intimate with his neighbourhood, he does also need to know its geography. He has learned something valuable when he has made the, at first, perplexing transition from thinking of his neighbourhood in only personal and practical terms, to thinking of it also in neutral, public, cartographical terms. Unlike Augustine, he can now say, 'When, in the morning, you do not ask me questions, I can guide you on foot from anywhere in the district to anywhere else; but, when in the afternoon, you do ask me questions, I can now *also* tell you the distances in kilometres and the compass bearings between anywhere in the district and anywhere else in the district, or anywhere else in the country or even anywhere else in the whole wide world.' Not only can he cope with the familiar morning tasks, but he can now also cope with the sophisticated afternoon tasks. Both are territorial tasks about one and the same region; but they are tasks of different levels. The 'afternoon' or cartographical task is more sophisticated than the 'morning' task of merely guiding someone from the church to the station. But this 'afternoon' task is also in an important way parasitic upon tasks of the 'morning' type, since the 'cash value', so to speak, of what the code-symbols in the map represent consists wholly in such things as the fields, bridges, paths, rivers and railway-stations with which the local inhabitants and visitors and even the Ordnance Surveyors themselves became familiar not by studying maps but *ambulando*.

How should we apply this analogy of the two levels of topo-graphical knowledge to the difference on which we have been concentrating, namely the difference between concrete and abstract, morning and afternoon, factual and conceptual considerations? In this way. In making my everyday unphilosophical statements, in asking my ordinary factual questions or in giving my concrete, practical advice, I say what I have to say with a variety of familiar words and phrases. These may be quite untechnical expressions or they may be technical or semi-technical expressions. Some of them may be unfamiliar to some people, but if I myself am not familiar with them, either I avoid trying to use them, or I am in doubt whether I have said what I wished to say.

Now every word or phrase that I so employ—with a few exceptions, such as expletives—so contributes to my statement, question or advice that it would have been a different statement, etc., had I used a different non-synonymous word or phrase instead. It would have been a different statement, different in having different implications, in requiring different tests for truth or falsehood, in being compatible and incompatible with different affiliated statements, in being evidence for or against different corollaries, and so on. Let us label these for brevity its 'implication threads'. If I am familiar with a word or phrase, then I know, *ambulando*, the particular differences, of these sorts, that it contributes to the particular statements etc. in which I employ it. Having said something sensible with it, I know how to go on saying particular things that contribute to make co-sense with what I said. So far I am like the villager who, on leaving the church, turns right in order to walk home and never has to nullify his first steps by turning back in his tracks. He is continuously on the correct route all the way—unless he is absent-minded or distracted; and this reservation applies to my talking and thinking too.

But now we have to notice a new point. The things that we say often, indeed usually, contain a mixture or plurality of words or phrases. We have to marry the contribution made by one to the contributions made by all the others; and sometimes the implication threads generated by one of them pull or seem to pull across or away from the implication threads generated by another. For example, I might truly and intelligibly describe a weary sailor in a storm as having toiled voluntarily, although reluctantly; and then I find myself in a perplexity. For I seem to be saying that he toiled not under compulsion but because he volunteered to do it, despite the fact that he did not want to do it. The natural implication threads of 'voluntarily' seem to pull away from the natural implication threads of 'reluctantly'. So now it is not enough to be familiar with the separate contributions of the two adverbs. I need to be able to *say* how their apparent conflict is an unreal one, as it must be if my original statement was intelligible and true. I am now confronted by a conceptual problem, though doubtless a fairly elementary and local one. But still it is a problem the solution of which requires consideration in perfectly general terms of the notions of *action, motive, preference, strength of desires, choice* and so on, with no particular reference to this sailor or this storm. I have, so to speak, now to place on the same regional map the ideas of 'voluntarily' and 'reluctantly' with each of which by itself I am quite at home. I have to orientate them together with one another, and also orientate them together with the other familiar ideas with which they must or may come into conjunction. I have to fix what I may call their 'logical bearings' *vis-à-vis* one another and *vis-à-vis* all their other normal or possible neighbours. Of course the big philosophical issues are not those which, like my specimen about the sailor, just happen more or less accidentally to crop up now and then, but those which inevitably present themselves over and over again. When we speak, as we constantly have to speak, in the very same breath, of a responsible human agent acting in a world which is, as he himself also is, a field of chemical, mechanical and biological causes and effects, we are not merely liable, but bound, to find ourselves perplexed by the seeming interferences between the implication threads belonging to our causal ideas and the implication threads belonging to our moral ideas. Men *must*, we feel, be free; yet they *must*, we also feel, be amenable to prediction and explanation. Their actions cannot be mechanical. Yet also they cannot be unmechanical.

But how? And now we can see, I hope, that the answer to this question 'But how?' is not one the answer to which can be provided either out of our morning familiarity with the ideas of culpability and merit; or out of our morning familiarity with the ideas of impact, attraction, pressure and tension, stimulus and response. We have now, instead, suspiciously to trace and test in their own right the implication threads which ordinarily we naïvely rely upon. We have now to operate *upon* what we ordinarily operate readily and unquestioningly *with*. We now need the theory of our daily practice, the geography of our daily walks. When two or twenty familiar implication threads seem to pull across and against one another, it is no longer enough to be able unperplexedly to follow along each one by itself. We need to be able to state their directions, their limits and their interlockings; to think systematically *about* what normally we merely think competently and even dexterously *with*. Our familiarities are now at seeming loggerheads with themselves; so an afternoon discipline and method have to be superimposed upon our morning habits. However forcibly a man may, in the morning, argue on this or that concrete topic, he may still need to learn a quite new kind of lesson, namely how, in the afternoon, to assess the forces of those arguments and how to compare and correlate them with the forces of seemingly interfering or cooperating arguments.

It follows *first* that the philosophical examination of a concept, like that, say, of Time or Probability or Voluntariness, can never be the examination of that concept by itself, but only the examination of it *vis-à-vis* its numerous neighbour-concepts, and then *vis-à-vis* their innumerable neighbours too. Even the cartographer cannot produce a map that is the map just of one boulder by itself, or one stretch of water by itself. It follows *second* that the procedure of the philosophical examination of a concept is necessarily an argumentative or, if you prefer, a dialectical procedure. The philosopher has done nothing at all until he has shown the directions and the limits of the implication threads that a concept contributes to the statements in which it occurs; and to show this he has, so to speak, to tug these threads through their neighbouring threads, which, in their turn, he must simultaneously be tugging.

What cross-bearings are to the cartographer, crossing implication threads are for the philosopher. Augustine's after-breakfast ability to say things in temporal terms and to understand things said in temporal terms was not enough by itself to enable him, after lunch, to co-ordinate the contributions to statements of these temporal terms with the contributions made to them by associated terms of different sorts. He was like the sailor, who, though perfectly at home in his own ship, is asked about the disposition and organisation of the fleet to which his ship belongs. This is not just a new question of an old sort. It is a question of a new sort.

34

THINKING THOUGHTS AND
HAVING CONCEPTS

*Reprinted, in English translation, from the original French in
'Logique et Analyse', no. 20, 1962, by permission of
Editions Nauwelaerts s.a.*

There are many philosophical contexts in which we need to
determine the structures, the types and the levels of truths and
falsehoods; to consider, for example, what makes it legitimate or
illegitimate to infer one from another or to support one by another.
In the course of such enquiries we often need to consider the
affiliations, types and levels of the concepts into which these truths
and falsehoods are analysable. Thus we may need to determine
that one concept differs from another as genus from species, as
species from fellow-species, as relation from quality, and so on.
We could crudely label such problems as *logical* or *near-logical*
problems.

There are also many philosophical contexts in which we need to
consider problems about the thinking that people are, from time
to time, actually engaged in—their wonderings, doubtings, dis-
coverings and concludings; their being surprised or unsurprised,
perplexed or unperplexed, careful or careless, inventive or conservative, and so on. We could label such problems as *epistemological*
or *phenomenological* problems.

At certain places these *epistemological* or *phenomenological* questions
necessarily interlock with those logical and near-logical questions,
and then we find ourselves somewhat embarrassed to describe
how the truths and falsehoods and their component concepts that
were under investigation in the former contexts enter into our
epistemological accounts of the live thinking that people really do.

For example, the concepts of *planet* and *orbit* are concepts of
different types, both of which enter, in different ways, into certain
ranges of astronomical truths. Or the concepts of *square root of* and
seven are concepts of different types, and both may enter, in different

446

ways, into arithmetical truths. So, in some way, the astronomer engaged in comparing the orbit of one planet with the orbit of another planet is operating with the concepts of *orbit* and *planet*; and the student of arithmetic who, at a particular moment, is trying to find out the number of which 7 is the square root, is operating with the concepts of *square root of* and *seven*. But what is involved in this vague notion of 'operating with concepts'? Have we to say, for example, that at a certain moment of their morning's work the astronomer and the student were in process of *having in mind* the concepts of *orbit* and *square root of*? What would it be like to be just having in mind a concept? Is there a particular, recollectable experience of having in mind the concept of *square root of*? Can it occur by itself? If not, why not? Can you obey me if I tell you to dismiss all else from your mind and just conceive the concept of *square root of*? Why not?

It might be suggested that at the moments when the astronomer says to himself, in his head, ' . . . orbit . . .', then, at that moment, he is actively having in mind what the word 'orbit' means—provided, of course, that he is thinking what he is saying to himself, and not just absent-mindedly parroting the word. But, for one thing, this suggestion does nothing but raise the same question over again. Is there a particular, recollectable experience of actively having in mind what is signified by the word that is currently coming off one's tongue? We are reminded of the unprosperous attempts made by Locke, Berkeley and Hume to locate 'ideas' among the recollectable experiences of a person who has just been thinking about something in particular.

A more important objection to this suggestion is this. Suppose you are asked to find the smallest prime number after 1300. You begin, perhaps, by selecting the first dozen or two dozen odd numbers that run up from 1301, since obviously no even number will be a candidate. You then eliminate those ending in ' . . . 5 ', since these will be multiples of 5. You then eliminate those the digits of which and up to 3 or multiples of 3, since these will all be divisible by 3, and so on. Now in an important way, all these operations of yours, being directed towards the discovery of a number greater than 1300 which is divisible only by itself and 1 are somehow operations with the concept of *prime number*. You are working *with* the concept during the whole five-minute search, though the *phrase* 'prime number' comes off your lips, if at all, only once or twice during those five minutes. Similarly, the concept *if* somehow governs the whole of a, perhaps lengthy, hypothetical

447

proposition, though the word 'if' is over and done with by the time the second word in the sentence is produced. In short, the temptation to postulate the existence of special intellectual acts or experiences of 'concept-conceiving' or 'idea-having' needs to be resisted *ab initio*. It is not in this sort of way that the concept of *orbit* enters into the live thinking of the astronomer while he is working out the differences between the orbits of Venus and Mars. A stretch of thinking is not a procession of ephemeral incidents of having-concepts-in-mind. There are no such incidents, and if there were, a mere procession of them would not amount to thinking. So now let us approach the problem from a new angle.

There was a time before which I had not got the concept of *square root of*; there was a later time since when I have had it; and there was an interim period, short or long, during which it was not yet quite mine, though no longer not mine at all. Whatever it is that I possess when I have got the concept of *square root of*, the acquiring it is a case of learning something.

But there are no separate lessons in say, legal or arithmetical concepts, separate, that is, from lessons in law or arithmetic themselves—save that a teacher might tell his students to learn by heart a battery of definitions of legal or arithmetical terms, in the silly expectation that retention of these definitions would constitute possession of the corresponding legal or arithmetical concepts.

Instead of asking the Lockean question How did we form the abstract idea or acquire the concept of *square root of*? let us ask instead What were we unable to do until we had acquired it? It is at once clear that the answer to this question is interestingly general. We were unable, *inter alia*, to understand the question What is the square root of 16? or of any other number. We were unable to try to decide between two rival answers to this question. We were unable even to wonder whether all numbers have square roots. We were unable to infer from the information that 81 is the square of 9, that 9 is the square root of 81. We were unable to see the joke, such as it is, in 'Some vegetables have round roots and some numbers have square roots'. We were unable to paraphrase sentences containing 'square root' into sentences not containing it. And so on.

To acquire the concept is to become able to cope with that indefinite range of intellectual and even merely conversational tasks which share with one another this common feature of having something or other to do with a number's being what a square number is the square of. What has been learned is being actively applied when, for example, the joke is being appreciated, the calculation is being made or attempted, the question is understood or posed, and so on, indefinitely.

To try to find out what is the square root of 289, and to appreciate the joke, such as it is, about round roots and square roots are two bits of very different kinds of thinking. They have, certainly, something quite specific in common. But to point to what they have in common is not to point to a separately recollectable experience or a separately performable act. To borrow an analogy from Plato, when you pronounce the monosyllable 'top' and I pronounce the monosyllable 'but', what you have pronounced has indeed something in common with what I have pronounced, namely the consonant 't'. But there was no separate pronouncing of a separately audible 't'-noise.

As nothing less than an integral syllable can be pronounced, yet two otherwise different syllables can still have something, e.g. a consonant in common, somewhat similarly nothing less than an integral joke can be appreciated, an integral equation be challenged or an integral arithmetical problem be tackled, yet these otherwise very different integral intellectual acts can still have something in common, e.g. the concept *square root of*.

We could have reached the same negative phenomenological conclusion from the other end, namely from the logical or near-logical end. For we could have asked this question: Given a sentence which conveys a truth or a falsehood, say the sentence If John is the uncle of Sarah, then at least one of Sarah's parents was not an only child, how is the truth that the sentence as a whole conveys related to what is signified by the particular words in it? For example, is the meaning of 'if' or of 'uncle' or of 'not' a genuine part of this integral truth? Is the truth just an assemblage of the several meanings of the several words in the sentence?

Familiar considerations show that this could not be the case. For the same words in a different order might have produced a falsehood, or a different truth, or a piece of nonsense. The meanings of the words in a sentence are functionally interlocking. Concepts are not bricks out of which truths and falsehoods are built, any more than vowels and consonants are components out of which syllables are composed. Rather a concept, say the concept *if* or *uncle of*, is what can be common to an indefinite range of otherwise different integral truths, falsehoods, questions, commands, entreaties, etc. It is abstracted from them, not extracted out of them. It is not itself an integral *significatum*, any more than a consonant is itself an integral *pronunciatum*. It is a factor, not a slice.

I have one last point which I want to make because it has, I think, been too little discussed. A boy who has learned to count and is now beginning arithmetic is told that numbers divide up into odd numbers and even numbers. He asks which are which and is told, *first*, that 2, 4, 6, 8 and 10 are even numbers, while 1, 3, 5, 7, 9 are odd numbers; *second*, that the number of the left-hand page of any book is an even number; *third*, that any number is an even number which is next-door-neighbour to 1, 3, 5, 7 or 9, or to any number ending in one of these; *fourth*, that any number which is 2 or a multiple of 2 is an even number. After his first lesson he can tell us correctly which of the numbers under 11 are even and which are odd.

After his second lesson he can tell which of the numbers up to, may be, 500 or 600 are even—when he has access to a book.

After his third lesson he can tell us, for *any* number, whether it is even or odd.

After his fourth lesson he can tell us not only what numbers are even but also, so to speak, what *makes* them even.

And now we ask, at which stage has he 'got the concept of *even number*'? For at each stage there is some task which he can perform, which he could not do before, and by the third stage he can answer correctly all questions of the form 'Is . . . an even number?' Yet we are inclined to say that so long as he has not yet realised that even numbers are divisible by 2, he has not really got the concept of *even number*; or else that he has not yet got the whole of it. Having been told what a prime number is, he might still seriously and methodically search for that logical impossibility, an even prime number between 30 and 50.

I suggest that the question Has he really got the concept or has he got the whole of the concept *so and so*? is like the question Has he really learned the art or has he learned the whole art of skating?

35

TEACHING AND TRAINING

*Reprinted from 'The Concept of Education', edited by R. S. Peters,
published 1967, by permission of Routledge & Kegan Paul Ltd. and
Humanities Press Inc.*

I have no teaching tricks or pedagogic maxims to impart to you, and
I should not impart them to you if I had any. What I want to do is
to sort out and locate a notion which is cardinal to the notions of
teaching, training, education, etc. about which too little is ordinarily
said. This notion is that of *teaching oneself* which goes hand in glove
with the notion of *thinking for oneself.* You will all agree, I think,
that teaching fails, that is, either the teacher is a failure or the pupil
is a failure if the pupil does not sooner or later become able and
apt to arrive at his own solutions to problems. But how, in logic,
can anyone be taught to do untaught things? I repeat, how, in
logic, can anyone be taught to do untaught things?

To clear the air, let me begin by quickly putting on one side an
unimportant but familiar notion, that of the self-taught man.
Normally when we describe someone as a self-taught man we think
of a man who, having been deprived of tuition from other teachers,
tries to make himself an historian, say, or a linguist or an astronomer, without criticism, advice or stimulation from anyone else,
save from the authors of such textbooks, encyclopaedia articles and
linguaphone records as he may happen to hit on. He hits on these,
of course, randomly, without having anyone or anything to tell
him whether they are good ones, silly ones, old-fashioned ones
or cranky ones. We admire the devotion with which he studies,
but, save for the rare exception, we pity him for having been the
devoted pupil only of that solitary and untrained teacher, himself.
However, I am not interested in him.

What I am interested in is this. Take the case of an ordinary
unbrilliant, unstupid boy who is learning to read. He has learned
to spell and read monosyllables like 'bat', 'bad', 'at', 'ring', 'sing',
etc. and some two-syllable words like 'running', 'dagger' and a

few others. We have never taught him, say, the word 'batting'. Yet we find him quite soon reading and spelling unhesitantly the word 'batting'. We ask him who taught him this word and, if he remembers, he says that he had found it out for himself. He has learned from himself how the word 'batting' looks in print, how to write it down on paper and how to spell it out aloud, so in a sense he has taught himself this word—taught it to himself without yet knowing it. How can this be? How can a boy who does not know what 'b-a-t-t-i-n-g' spells teach himself what it spells?

In real life we are not a bit puzzled. It is just what we expect of a not totally stupid child. Yet there is the semblance of a conceptual paradox here, for we seem to be describing him as at a certain stage being able to teach himself something new, which *ipso facto* was not yet in his repertoire to teach. Here his teacher was as ignorant as the pupil, for they were the same boy. So how can the one learn something from the other?

What should we say? Well, clearly we want to say that the prior things that we *had* taught him, namely words like 'bat', 'bad', 'rat' and longer words like 'butter', 'running' etc. enabled him and perhaps encouraged him to make a new bit of independent, un-coached progress on his own. We had taught him *how* to read some monosyllables, *how* to run some of them together in dissyllables, and so on. We had taught him a way or some ways of coping with combinations of printed letters, though not in their particular application to this new word 'batting'. He had made this particular application himself. So to speak, we had previously from the deck shown him the ropes and now he climbs one of them with his own hands and feet; that is to say, not being totally stupid, he was able and ready to employ this slightly general knowledge that we had given to him on a new concrete and particular problem that we had not solved for him. We had given him the wherewithal with which to think it out for himself—and this thinking out was his doing and not ours. I could just as well have taken an example from the much more sophisticated stratum where a brilliant under-graduate makes a good philosophical move that no one else has ever taught him, and maybe no one else has ever made.

Naturally, most often the boy or the undergraduate, if asked Who taught you that? would reply not that he had taught it to him-self or that he had learned it from himself, but rather that he had found it out or thought it out or worked it out for himself. Just this brings out a big part of what interests me, namely, that though in one way it is obviously impossible for one person's own discovery, whether trivial or important, to be simply what someone else had previously taught him—since it would then not be his discovery—, yet in another way it is and ought to be one main business of a teacher precisely to get his pupils to advance beyond their instructions and to discover new things for themselves, that is, to get them to think things out for themselves. I teach Tommy to read a few words like 'bat', 'run' and 'running' in order that he may then, of his own motion, find out how to read lots and lots of other words, like 'batting', that we have not taught to him. Indeed we do not deem him really able to spell or read until he can spell and read things that he has not been introduced to. Nor, to leave the schoolroom for the moment, do I think that Tommy has learned to bicycle until he can do things on his bicycle far more elaborate, speedy, tricky and delicate than the things I drilled him in on the first morning. I taught him the few elements on the first morning just in order that he might then find out for himself how to cope with hosts of non-elementary tasks. I gave him a few stereotyped exercises, and, as I had hoped and expected, in a couple of days he had developed for himself on this basis a fair wealth of boyish skills and dexterities, though he acquired these while I was away in London.

However, there remains a slight feeling of a puzzle or paradox here, and it comes, I think, from this source. A familiar and indispensable part or sort of teaching consists in teaching by rote lists of truths or facts, for example the proposition that 7×7 is 49, etc., the proposition that Waterloo was fought in 1815, etc., and the proposition that Madrid is the capital of Spain, etc. That the pupil has learned a lesson of this propositional sort is shown, in the first instance, by his being able and reasonably ready to reproduce word-perfectly these pieces of information. He gets them by heart, and he can come out with them on demand. Now every teacher knows that only a vanishingly small fraction of his teaching-day really consists in simply reciting lists of such snippets of information to pupils, but very unfortunately, it happens to be the solitary part which unschooled parents, sergeant-majors, some silly publicists and some educationalists always think of when they think of teaching and learning. They think or half-think that the request 'Recite what you have learned in school today, Tommy' is a natural and proper one, as if all that Tommy could or should have learned is a number of memorizable propositions; or as if to have learned anything consisted simply in being able to echo it, like a gramophone. As you all know, most teaching has nothing whatsoever in common with this crude, semi-surgical picture of teaching as the forcible insertion into the pupil's memory of strings of officially approved propositions; and I hope to show before long that even that small and of course indispensable part of instruction which is the imparting of factual information is grossly mis-pictured when pictured as literal cramming. Yet, bad as the picture is, it has a powerful hold over people's general theorizings about teaching and learning. Even Tommy's father, after spending the morning in teaching Tommy to swim, to dribble the football or to diagnose and repair what is wrong with the kitchen clock, in the afternoon cheerfully writes to the newspapers letters which take it for granted that all lessons are strings of memorizable propositions. His practice is perfectly sensible, yet still his theory is as silly as it could be.

Perhaps the prevalence of this very thin and partial notion of teaching and learning inherits something from the teaching and learning that are done in the nursery, where things such as 'Hickory Dickory Dock' and simple tunes are learned by heart from that mere vocal repetition which enables the parrot to pick them up too.

Well, in opposition to this shibboleth, I want to switch the centre of gravity of the whole topic onto the notions of Teaching-to so and so, and Learning-to so and so, that is, on to the notion of the development of abilities and competences. Let us forget for a while the memorization of truths, and, of course, of rhymes and tunes, and attend, instead, to the acquisition of skills, knacks and efficiencies. Consider, for example, lessons in drawing, arithmetic and cricket— and, if you like, in philosophy. These lessons cannot consist of and cannot even contain much of dictated propositions. However many true propositions the child has got by heart, he has not begun to learn to draw or play cricket until he has been given a pencil or a bat and a ball and has practised doing things with them; and even if he progresses magnificently in these arts, he will have little or nothing to reply to his parents if they ask him in the evening to recite to them the propositions that he has learned. He can *exhibit* what he has begun to master, but he cannot *quote* it. To avoid the ambiguity between 'teach' in the sense of 'teach that' and 'teach' in the sense of 'teach to' or 'teach how to', I shall now sometimes use the word 'train'. The drawing-master, the language-teacher or the cricket-coach *trains* his pupils in drawing or in French pronunciation or in batting or bowling, and this training incorporates only a few items of quotable information. The same is true of philosophy.

Part, but only part of this notion of training is the notion of drilling, i.e. putting the pupil through stereotyped exercises which

454

he masters by sheer repetition. Thus the recruit learns to slope arms just by going through the same sequence of motions time after time, until he can, so to speak, perform them in his sleep. Circus dogs and circus seals are trained in the same way. At the start piano-playing, counting and gear-changing are also taught by simple habituation. But disciplines do not reduce to such sheer drills. Sheer drill, though it is the indispensable beginning of training, is, for most abilities, only their very beginning. Having become able to do certain low-level things automatically and without thinking, the pupil is expected to advance beyond this point and to employ his inculcated automatisms in higher-level tasks which are not automatic and cannot be done without thinking. Skills, tastes and scruples are more than mere habits, and the disciplines and the self-disciplines which develop them are more than mere rote-exercises.

His translators and commentators have been very unjust to Aristotle on this matter. Though he was the first thinker, and is still the best, systematically to study the notions of ability, skill, training, character, learning, discipline, self-discipline, etc., the translators of his works nearly always render his key-ideas by such terms as 'habit' and 'habituation'—as if, for example, a person who has been trained and self-trained to play the violin, or to behave scrupulously in his dealings with other people acts from sheer habit, in the way in which I do tie up my shoelaces quite automatically and without thinking what I am doing or how to do it. Of course Aristotle knew better than this, and the Greek words that he used are quite grossly mistranslated when rendered merely by such words as 'habit' and 'habituation'. The well-disciplined soldier, who does indeed slope arms automatically, does not also shoot automatically or scout by blind habit or read maps like a marionette.

Nor is Tommy's control of his bicycle merely a rote-performance, though he cannot begin to control his bicycle until he has got some movements by rote. Having learned through sheer habit-formation to keep his balance on his bicycle with both hands on the handle-bars, Tommy can now try to ride with one hand off, and later still with both hands in his pockets and his feet off the pedals. He now progresses by experimentation. Or, having got by heart the run of the alphabet from ABC through to XYZ, he can now, but not without thinking, tell you what three letters run *backwards* from RQP, though he has never learned by heart this reversed sequence.

I suggest that our initial seeming paradox, that a learner can sometimes of himself, after a bit of instruction, better his instructions, is beginning to seem less formidable. The possibility of it is of the same pattern as the familiar fact that the toddler who has this morning taken a few aided steps tries this afternoon with or without success to take some unaided steps. The swimmer who can now keep himself up in salt water, comes by himself, at first with a bit of extra splashing, to keep himself up in fresh water. How do any formerly difficult things change into now easy things? Or any once untried things into now feasible ones? The answer is just in terms of the familiar notions of the development of abilities by practice, that is trying and failing and then trying again and not failing so often or so badly, and so on.

Notoriously a very few pupils are, over some tasks, so stupid, idle, scared, hostile, bored or defective that they make no efforts of their own beyond those imposed on them as drill by their trainer. But to be non-stupid, vigorous and interested *is* to be inclined to make, if only as a game, moves beyond the drilled moves, and to practice of oneself, e.g. to multiply beyond 12×12, to run through the alphabet backwards, to bicycle with one hand off the handlebar, or to slope arms in the dark with a walking-stick when no drill-sergeant is there. As Aristotle says, 'The things that we have got to do when we have learned to do them, we learn to do by doing them.' What I can do today I could not do easily or well or successfully yesterday; and the day before I could not even try to do them; and if I had not tried unsuccessfully yesterday, I should not be succeeding today.

Before returning to go further into some of these key notions of ability, practice, trying, learning to, teaching to, and so on, I want to look back for a moment to the two over-influential notions of teaching *that* so and so, i.e. telling or informing, and of learning *that* so and so, i.e. the old notion of propositional cramming. In a number of nursery, school and university subjects, there are necessarily some or many true propositions to be accumulated by the student. He must, for example, learn that Oslo is the capital of Norway, Stockholm is the capital of Sweden and Copenhagen is the capital of Denmark. Or he must learn that the Battle of Trafalgar was fought in 1805 and that of Waterloo in 1815. Or that $7+5 = 12$, $7+6 = 13$, $7+7 = 14$, etc.

At the very start, maybe, the child just memorizes these strings of propositions as he memorizes 'Hickory Dickory Dock', the alphabet or 'Thirty days hath September'. But so long as parroting is all he can do, he does not yet know the geographical fact, say, that Stockholm is the capital of Sweden, since if you ask him what

Stockholm is the capital of, or whether Madrid is the capital of Sweden, he has no idea how to move. He can repeat, but he cannot yet use the memorized dictum. All he can do is to go through the memorized sequence of European capitals from start through to the required one. He does not qualify as knowing that Stockholm is the capital of Sweden until he can detach this proposition from the memorized rigmarole; and can, for example, answer new-type questions like 'Of which country out of the three, Italy, Spain and Sweden, is Stockholm the capital?' or 'Here is Stockholm on the globe—whereabouts is Sweden?' and so on. To know the geographical fact requires having taken it in, i.e. being able and ready to operate with it, from it, around it and upon it. To possess a piece of information is to be able to mobilize it apart from its rote-neighbours and out of its rote-formulation in unhackneyed and *ad hoc* tasks. Nor does the pupil know that $7+7 = 14$ while this is for him only a still undetachable bit of a memorized sing-song, but only when, for example, he can find fault with someone's assertion that $7+8 = 14$, or can answer the new-type question How many 7s are there in 14? or the new-type question 'If there are seven boys and seven girls in a room, how many children are in the room?' etc. Only then has he taken it in.

In other words, even to have learned the piece of information *that something is so* is more than merely to be able to parrot the original telling of it—somewhat as to have digested a biscuit is more than merely to have had it popped into one's mouth. Can he or can he not infer from the information that Madrid is the capital of Spain that Madrid is not in Sweden? Can he or can he not tell us what sea-battle occurred ten years before Waterloo?

Notice that I am not in the least deprecating the inculcation of rotes like the alphabet, the figures of the syllogism, 'Hickory Dickory Dock', the dates of the Kings of England, or sloping arms. A person who has not acquired such rotes cannot progress from and beyond them. All that I am arguing is that he does not qualify as knowing even that Waterloo was fought in 1815 if all that he can do is to sing out this sentence inside the sing-song of a memorized string of such sentences. If he can only echo the syllables that he has heard, he has not yet taken in the information meant to be conveyed by them. He has not grasped it if he cannot handle it. But if he could not even echo things told to him, *a fortiori* he could not operate with, from or upon their informative content. One cannot digest a biscuit unless it is first popped into one's mouth. So we see that even to have learned a true proposition is to have learned *to do* things other than repeating the words in which the truth had been dictated. To have learned even a simple geographical fact is to have become able to cope with some unhabitual geographical tasks, however elementary.

We must now come back to our central question: How is it possible that a person should learn from himself something which he previously did not know, and had not, e.g. been taught by some-one else? This question is or embodies the apparently perplexing question: How can one person teach another person to think things out for himself, since if he gives him, say, the new arithmetical thoughts, then they are not the pupil's own thoughts; or if they are his own thoughts, then he did not get them from his teacher? Having led the horse to the water, how can we make him drink? But I have, I hope, shifted the centre of gravity of this seeming puzzle, by making the notions of *learning-to* and *teaching-to* the primary notions. In its new form the question is: How, on the basis of some tuition, can a person today get himself to do something which he had not been able to do yesterday or last year? How can competences, abilities and skills develop? How can trying ever succeed? We are so familiar, in practice, with the fact that abilities do develop, and that trying can succeed that we find little to puzzle us in the idea that they do.

Looked at from the end of the teacher the question is: How can the teacher get his pupil to make independent moves of his own? If this question is tortured into the shape: How can the teacher make or force his pupil to do things which he is not made or forced to do? i.e. How can the teacher be the initiator of the pupil's initiatives? the answer is obvious. He cannot. I cannot compel the horse to drink thirstily. I cannot coerce Tommy into doing spontaneous things. Either he is not coerced, or they are not spontaneous.

As every teacher, like every drill-sergeant or animal trainer knows in his practice, teaching and training have virtually not yet begun so long as the pupil is too young, too stupid, too scared or too sulky to respond—and to respond is not just to yield. Where there is a modicum of alacrity, interest or anyhow docility in the pupil, where he tries, however faintheartedly, to get things right rather than wrong, fast rather than slow, neat rather than awkward, where, even, he registers even a slight contempt for the poor performances of others or chagrin at his own, pleasure at his own successes and envy of those of others, then he is, in however slight a degree, co-operating and so self-moving. He is doing something, though very likely not much, and is not merely having things done to him. He is, however unambitiously and however desultorily, attempting the still difficult. He has at least a little impetus of his own. A corner, however small a corner, of his heart is now in the task. The eager pupil is, of course, the one who, when taught, say, to read or spell a few words like 'at', 'bat' and 'mat' travels home on the bus trying out, just for fun, all the other monosyllables that rhyme with 'at', to see which of them are words. When taught to read and spell a dissyllable or two, he tries his hand, just for fun and often but not always unsuccessfully, on the polysyllables on the advertisement hoardings; and just for fun he challenges his father to spell long words when he gets home. He does this for fun; but like much play it is spontaneous self-practising. When he returns to school after the holidays, although his spelling and reading are now far in advance of their peak of last term, he will stoutly deny that he has done any work during the holidays. It has not been work, it has been absorption in a new hobby, like exercising a new limb.

His over-modest teacher may say that he has taught this boy next to nothing—nor has he, save for the very beginnings of everything.

However, we should remember that although a total absence of eagerness or even willingness spells total unteachability, the presence of energy, adventurousness and self-motion is not by itself enough. The wild guesser and the haphazard plunger have freedom of movement of a sort, but not of the best sort. Learning how to do new and therefore more or less difficult things does indeed require trying things out for oneself, but if this trying-out is not controlled by any testing or making sure, then its adventurousness is recklessness and not enterprise. He is like the gambler, not like the investor. The moves made, though spontaneous, are irresponsible and they yield no dividends. Nothing can be learned by him from their unsuccesses or from their occasional fortuitous successes. He shoots away, but learns nothing from his misses—or from his fluke hits.

It is just here, with the notion of taking care when taking risks, that there enters on the scenes the cardinal notion of *method*, i.e. of techniques, *modi operandi*, rules, canons, procedures, knacks, and even tricks of the trade. In doing a thing that he has never done before, a person may, but need not, operate according to a method, sometimes even according to a sheer drill that he has adhered to before. If he does, then his action is still an innovation, although the pattern of his action is a familiar and inculcated one. The poet composes a sonnet, taking care to adhere to the regulation 14 lines, to the regulation rhyming scheme, to the regulation metrical pattern, or else perhaps to one of the several permitted patterns—yet, nonetheless, his sonnet is a new one. No one has ever composed *it* before. His teacher who taught him how to compose sonnets had not and could not have made him compose this sonnet, else it would be the teacher's and not the pupil's sonnet. Teaching people how to do things just *is* teaching them methods or *modi operandi*; and it is just because it is one thing to have learned a method and another thing to essay a new application of it that we can say without paradox that the learner's new move is his own move and yet that he may have learned the *how* of making it from someone else. The cook's pudding is a new one and piping hot, but its recipe was known to Mrs Beeton in the days of Queen Victoria.

Well, then, what sort of a thing is a method? First for what it is not. Despite what many folk would say, a method is not a stereotyped sequence-pattern or routine of actions, inculcatable by pure rote, like sloping arms or going through the alphabet. The parrot that can run through 'Hickory Dickory Dock' has not learned how to do anything or therefore how not to do it. There is nothing that he takes care not to do.

A method is a learnable way of doing something, where the word 'way' connotes more than mere rote or routine. A way of doing something, or a *modus operandi*, is something general, and general in at least two dimensions. First, the way in which you do a thing, say mount your bicycle, can be the way or a way in which some other people or perhaps most other people mount or try to mount their bicycles. Even if you happen to be the only person who yet does something in a certain way, it is possible that others should in future learn from you or find out for themselves the very same way of doing it. *Modi operandi* are, in principle, public property, though a particular action performed in this way is my action and not yours, or else it is your action and not mine. We mount our bicycles in the same way, but my bicycle-mounting is my action and not yours. You do not make my mince pies, even though we both follow the same Victorian recipe.

The second way in which a method is something general is the obvious one, that there is no limit to the number of actions that may be done in that way. The method is, roughly, applicable anywhere and anywhen, as well as by anyone. For, however many people are known by me to have mounted their bicycles in a certain way, I know that there could have been and there could be going to be any number of other bicycle-mountings performed by myself and others in the same way.

Next, methods can be helpfully, if apparently cynically, thought of as systems of avoidances or as patterns of *don'ts*. The rules, say, of English grammar do not tell us positively what to say or write; they tell us negatively not to say or write such things as 'A dog *are* . . .' and 'The dogs *is* . . .', and learning the art of rock-climbing or tree-climbing is, among hundreds of other things, learning never, or hardly ever, to trust one's whole weight to an untried projection or to a branch that is leafless in summer time.

People sometimes grumble at the Ten Commandments on the score that most of them are prohibitions, and not positive injunctions. They have not realized that the notice 'Keep off the grass' licenses us to walk anywhere else we choose; where the notice 'Keep to the gravel' leaves us with almost no freedom of movement. Similarly to have learned a method is to have learned to take care against certain specified kinds of risk, muddle, blind alley, waste, etc. But carefully keeping away from this cliff and from that morass leaves the rest of the countryside open for us to walk lightheartedly in. If I teach you even twenty kinds of things that would make your sonnet a bad sonnet or your argument a bad argument, I have still left you an indefinite amount of elbow-room within which you can construct your own sonnet or argument, and this sonnet or argument of yours, whether brilliant or ordinary or weak, will at least be free of faults of those twenty kinds.

There exists in some quarters the sentimental idea that the teacher who teaches his pupils how to do things is hindering them, as if his apron-strings coerced their leg-movements. We should think of the inculcation of methods rather as training the pupils to avoid specified muddles, blockages, sidetracks and thin ice by training them to recognize these for what they are. Enabling them to avoid troubles, disasters, nuisances and wasted efforts is helping them to move where they want to move. Road signs are not, for the most part, impediments to the flow of traffic. They are preventives of impediments to the flow of traffic.

Of course we can easily think of silly ways of doing things which continue to be taught by grown-ups to children and adhered to by the grown-ups themselves. Not all methods are good methods, or all recipes good recipes. For example, the traditional ban on splitting the infinitive was a silly rule. But the gratuitous though trivial bother of conforming to this particular veto was negligible compared with the handicap that would be suffered by the child who had never been taught or had never picked up for himself any of the procedures for composing or construing sentences. He would have been kept back at the level of total infancy. He could not say or

461

follow anything at all if, for example, he had not mastered conjunctions, or even verbs, and mastering them involves learning how *not* to make hashes of them.

How does one teach methods or ways of doing things? Well, there is no simple answer to this. Different arts and crafts require different kinds of disciplines; and in some one particular field, say drawing, one teacher works very differently from another. Sometimes a little, sometimes a lot can be told; there is much that cannot be told, but can be shown by example, by caricature and so on. But one thing is indispensable. The pupil himself must, whether under pressure or from interest or ambition or conscientiousness, practise doing what he is learning how to do. Whether in his exercises in the art he religiously models his strokes after Bradman, or whether he tries to win the praise or avoid the strictures or sarcasms of a feared, respected or loved coach, he learns by performing and improves by trying to better his own and his fellows' previous performances by eradicating their faults. The methods of operating taught to him become his personal methods of operating by his own criticized and self-criticized practice. Whether in spelling, in Latin grammar, fencing, arithmetic or philosophy, he learns the ropes, not much by gazing at them or hearing about them, but by trying to climb them—and by trying to climb them less awkwardly, slowly and riskily today than he did yesterday.

So far I have been, for simplicity, dividing the contributions of the teacher and the pupil by saying that the teacher in teaching how to so and so is teaching a method or way of operating, while the pupil keeps his initiative by making his own, at the start somewhat arduous, because new, applications of that method. The teacher introduces the pupil to the ropes, but it is for the pupil to try to climb them.

But now we should pay some attention to the fact that pretty soon the pupil has become familiar with the quite general fact that for lots and lots of widely different kinds of operations—spelling, say, skating and bowling at cricket—there exist different *modi operandi*. There are spelling-mistakes and there are bowling-faults, and neither spelling nor bowling can go right unless these faults are systematically avoided. So now, when he undertakes an altogether new kind of operation, canoeing, say, he from the start expects there to be *modi operandi* here too. This too will be a thing that he will have to learn how to do, partly by learning how not to do it. But this time, it may be, there is no one to teach him, and not even any other canoeist to imitate. He has got to find out for himself the way, or anyhow a way, of balancing, propelling and steering his canoe. Well, at first he tries a lot of random things, and nearly all of them end in immersion or collision; but he does after a time find out some ways of managing his craft. He may not achieve elegance or speed, but he does find out how not to topple over and how not to run into obstacles. He is trained, this time purely self-trained, regularly to avoid some kinds of faulty watermanship. But it is because he had previously learned by practice, coaching and imitation the 'hows' of lots of other things such as tree-climbing, spelling and skating that he now takes it for granted that canoeing has its 'hows' as well, which similarly can be learned by practice, trial and error, and looking for ways of avoiding the repetition of errors. Here, as elsewhere, he has to study in order to improve; but this time he has nothing to study save his own unsuccesses and successes.

His more reckless and impatient brother, though full of go, just makes a dash at it, and then another quite different dash at it, and learns nothing or almost nothing from the failures which generally result, or even from the successes which sometimes just happen to result. He is not a self-trainer.

The third brother is uninterested, slow in the uptake, scared or idle. He never chances his arm. He tries nothing, and so initiates nothing either successfully or unsuccessfully. So he never learns to canoe; never, perhaps, even regrets not having learned it or envies those who have. There is no question of his training himself in this particular art, or even, if he is a very bad case, of his being trained by anyone else; just as there was fifty years ago no real question of me training myself or of my being trained by anyone else in the arts of cricket or music.

The supreme reward of the teacher is to turn out from time to time the student who comes to be not merely abreast of his teacher but ahead of him, the student, namely, who advances his subject or his craft not just by adding to it further applications of the established ways of operating but by discovering new methods or procedures of types which no one could have taught to him. He has given to his subject or his craft a new idea or a battery of new ideas. He is original. He himself, if of a grateful nature, will say that his original idea just grew of itself out of what he had learned from his teachers, his competitors and his colleagues; while they, if of a grateful nature, will say that the new idea was his discovery. Both will be right. His new idea is the fruit of a tree that others had planted and pruned. It is really his own fruit and he is really their tree.

463

We started off with the apparent paradox that though the teacher in teaching is doing something to his pupil, yet the pupil has learned virtually nothing unless he becomes able and ready to do things of his own motion other than what the teacher exported to him. We asked: How in logic can the teacher dragoon his pupil into thinking for himself, impose initiative upon him, drive him into self-motion, conscript him into volunteering, enforce originality upon him, or make him operate spontaneously? The answer is that he cannot— and the reason why we half felt that he must do so was that we were unwittingly enslaved by the crude, semi-hydraulic idea that in essence to teach is to pump propositions, like 'Waterloo, 1815' into the pupils' ears, until they regurgitate them automatically.

When we switched from the notion of 'hydraulic injection' to the notion of 'teaching to' or 'teaching how to', the paradox began to disappear. I can introduce you to a way or the way of doing something, and still your actual essays in the exercise of this craft or competence are yours and not mine. I do not literally make you do them, but I do enable you to do them. I give you the *modus operandi*, but your operatings or tryings to operate according to this *modus* are your own doings and not my inflictings and the practising by which you master the method is your exertion and not mine. I have given you some equipment against failing, *if* you try. But that you try is not something that I can coerce. Teaching is not gate-shutting but gate-opening, yet still the dull or the scared or the lame calf does not walk out into the open field. All this does not imply the popular sentimental corollary that teachers should never be strict, demanding, peremptory or uncondoning. It is often the hard task-master who alone succeeds in instilling mistrust of primrose paths. The father may enlarge the child's freedom of movement by refusing to hold his hand, and the boxing-instructor or the philosophy-tutor may enlarge his pupil's powers of defence and attack by hitting him hard and often. It is not the chocolates and the sponge-cakes that strengthen the child's jaw-muscles. They have other virtues, but not this one.

36

THINKING AND REFLECTING

Reprinted from 'The Human Agent', Royal Institute of Philosophy Lectures, vol. 1, 1966–1967, by permission of Macmillan & Co. Ltd, The Macmillan Company of Canada Ltd. and St. Martin's Press Inc.

Just as there was a vogue at one time for identifying thinking either with mere processions or with more or less organised processions of images, so there is a vogue now for identifying thinking with something oddly called 'language', namely with more or less organised processions of bits of French or English, etc.

Both views are entirely wrong; wrong not because thinking ought instead to be identified with mere or organised processions or bits of something else instead, but because this very programme of identifying thinking with some procession or other is radically / misguided. Certainly it is often the case, and nearly always just before we fall asleep, that the thought of something bobs up, and then the thought of another thing. But their serial bobbings-up do not constitute the thoughts as thoughts; and I am not pondering or calculating if only this is happening. I can be thinking when nothing of the sort is happening.

I am going to start off by considering what sort of characterisation we are giving when we say that someone, a tennis-player perhaps, is thinking what he is doing, or that he was for a few moments so *distrait*, vacant or somnolent that he was not thinking what he was doing. References to his thinking or not thinking what he is doing are obviously carried by our characterisation of him or of his play as cautious, alert, wild, cranky, impetuous, resourceful, experimental, unimaginative, cunning, stereotyped, amateurish, and so on.

At this point I can explain why in my title I use both the word 'thinking' and the word 'reflecting'. The tennis-player is thinking what he is doing, and Rodin's *le Penseur* is obviously thinking. But while we would happily describe *le Penseur* as musing, meditating, pondering, deliberating, ruminating, reflecting or being pensive, we would rather not so describe the tennis-player—save in the unoccupied intervals between rallies, games or sets. In these intervals, certainly, the tennis-player may do what *le Penseur* is doing; he may, while his racquet is idle, ponder either about his tennis-match or else about something else, like Gödel's theorem. But while he is engaged in the game, with his mind on the game, he looks and mostly is *un*reflective or *un*pensive. We should not naturally class him as a Thinker or a *Penseur* for what he is doing now. He is not in a brown study, nor even in a series of fleeting brown studies. He does not have to be called back to the flight of the tennis-ball, as *le Penseur* may have to be called back to the starting of a shower of rain or the momentary state of the traffic around him. *Le Penseur* is in some degree detached from what is going on around him; but the tennis-player's thinking almost consists in his whole and at least slightly schooled attention being given to, *inter alia*, the flight of the ball over the net, the position of his opponent, the strength of the wind, and so on. Both are absorbed, but the tennis-player's absorption is in his and his opponent's momentary playing, while *le Penseur*'s absorption is in something detached from the rock-squatting that he is momentarily doing, and the rain-drops that are momentarily wetting him. His quick and appropriate responses to what occurs around him on the tennis-court show that the player is concentrating. His non-responses to what occurs around him show, or help to show, that *le Penseur* is concentrating. There are things, like his strokes, eye-movements, foot-movements, etc., which the tennis-player is here and now doing that he could not do, as he does them, without concentrating. They are well-timed or mistimed, concerted, wary, etc. Yet it seems that *le Penseur* is doing nothing, nothing that can be characterised as well-timed or mistimed, concerted, wary or, generally, more or less attentive, except just tackling his problem. If he is visibly doing anything, like sitting still, breathing or scratching his cheek, he is not giving his mind to doing these things. He is detached, disengaged, 'absent' from all such doings. I am, with a good deal of arbitrariness and imprecision, going for this occasion to reserve the verb 'reflecting' for the thus disengaged thinking of *le Penseur*. There will assuredly be some halfway-house cases of thinking which have some of the engagement of the tennis-player and some of the disengagement of *le Penseur*. A person doing something fairly deliberately, e.g. playing bowls or talking to his solicitor, may be in this halfway-house.

We are, of course, too sophisticated to suppose that because a verb is an active, tensed verb, in a sentence the nominative to which designates a person, therefore the person is being said to be performing an action, or doing something. The verbs to 'perish', 'inherit', 'sleep', 'resemble', 'outlive', 'succumb', 'know', 'possess' and 'forget' are conspicuous cases of active, sometimes transitive, tensed verbs which we could not be even tempted into treating as verbs of doing. I want to draw your attention to a special class, a pretty fluffy-edged class, of active, tensed verbs which we could easily be tempted into mistakenly treating as verbs of doing. I am going metaphorically to label them 'adverbial verbs', though this label is not to be taken very seriously. For one thing, I shall use the label to cover a wide range of things, with very little in common save a certain negative thing. Consider the active tensed verb 'hurry'. If told that someone is hurrying, we have not been told what he is doing, but only that he is doing whatever he is doing at an abnormally high speed. He may be hurriedly walking or typing or reading or humming or eating, and so on indefinitely. The command 'Hurry' is only the beginning of a command; it cannot yet, context apart, be obeyed or disobeyed. I label the verb 'to hurry' an 'adverbial verb', partly because any completed sentence containing it could be paraphrased by a sentence containing a proper verb of doing qualified by the adverb 'hurriedly' or the phrase 'in a hurry'. I might put the point by saying that hurrying is not an autonomous action or activity, as walking, typing and eating are. The command 'walk', 'type' or 'eat' is an obeyable command, and not the less so for being pretty unspecific. If I then eat lobster or bread or shoe-leather, I am obeying the command to eat. But to obey or disobey the command to hurry, I must do some autonomous X, like eating or humming, etc., for there to be a hurried or an unhurried X-ing that tallies with or flouts the understood command, no matter whether the command is specific or unspecific. Trying, scamping, succeeding and failing are, in generically similar ways, not autonomous activities. There must be an X-ing, if there is to be successful or unsuccessful, difficult or easy, industrious or scamped X-ing. Taking care, or being careful, vigilant or wary is, for the same general reason, not an autonomous doing. The command 'mind out' (full stop) cannot be obeyed or disobeyed unless some complement is understood. Driving with care is not doing two things, as driving with a song is. I can stop driving and go on singing, or vice versa. I can do the one well and the other badly; the one obediently and the other disobediently. But I cannot stop driving and go on exercising traffic-care. In obeying your command to drive carefully, I am not

conjointly obeying two commands, such that I might have disobeyed the first while obeying the second.

Now if a person spontaneously initiates or embarks on something—a remark, maybe—and if he does the thing with some
degree of care to avoid and correct faults and failures, and if,
finally, he learns something as he goes along from his failures and
successes, difficulties and facilities, he can claim and we shall allow
that he has been thinking what he was doing. Unlike the delirious
man, he meant at that moment to say something and not anything
else; he tried, in some measure, to satisfy already learned requirements of grammatical correctness, politeness, intelligibility, pertinence, etc., and he tried not to repeat inadequacies and faults,
and to exploit and improve on successes and adequacies. So he was
to some extent giving his in some degree trained mind to what he
was doing, and to that extent not giving his mind to extrinsic
things. He was not uttering absent-mindedly, or just raving or
nattering or saying things by rote. Some of this is sometimes put,
in philosophical circles only, by saying that his activity, in this case
that of contributing to a conversation, was 'rule-governed'. For
there were, *inter alia*, ungrammaticalities, rudenesses and irrelevances
that he avoided, corrected or withdrew because they were or
would have been such faults. He qualifies as having been thinking
what he was doing, namely making a contribution to a conversation,
not because, besides the uttering that he was doing, there was
another autonomous thing he was also doing and might have
continued doing after his uttering had stopped. There was some
degree of initiative, care and self-coaching in his talking. But none
of these elements was an autonomous action or activity. None of
them stood to his uttering as singing to driving, or even as the
steering-wheel movements to the pedal movements of driving.
His bits of uttering were not accompanied by, or interspersed with
bits of something else that he was also doing; or if they were, as
they often are, it was not for these accompaniments that he qualified
as thinking what he was saying. There are no separate chronicles
for him to give of the thinking without which his utterings would
not have been conversing, any more than the hurried breakfaster
can give us one chronicle of his breakfasting and another of his
hurrying. We can ask whether the converser was conversing in
English or in French or, if in a noisy factory, perhaps in gestures
and grimaces. We cannot ask whether the required thinking that
he did, namely thinking what to say, how and when to say it, and
how and when not to say it, was in its turn conducted in Russian,

German, gestures or images. There was no 'it' to have a separate turn of its own. Nor can we ask of a person who had been listening vigilantly whether he conducted his 'vigilating' in hand or eye movements or in Norwegian. There was no separate 'it' to conduct. If we did employ my manufactured verb to 'vigilate' it would be an adverbial verb, replaceable by our familiar adverb 'vigilantly'. Of course if, unlike the absent-minded or delirious man, a person has been doing something, thinking what he was doing, usually he can afterwards, if adequately educated, tell us what he was trying to do, and what for, what made him apologise, hesitate or stop and start again and so on. But to grant this is not to grant that to have been thinking what he was doing, X-ing, say, he must have been doing something else as well, Y-ing, say, e.g. telling himself in his head things in indicative, imperative and optative English or French sentences; or, of course, picturing things in his mind's eye either. He may in fact have been doing some bits of such Y-ing but it is not for these that he qualifies as having been thinking what he was doing. Indeed it could be because he had been doing some such bits of Y-ing that he had not been thinking what he was doing, namely the X-ing—as the centipede found who tried to run while considering how to run. In short, the thinking of the non-absent-minded, non-delirious talker is not a separate act or procession of acts, or a separate procession of anythings. The verbs 'to think', 'give one's mind to', etc., as used of him in this context, are adverbial verbs, like my manufactured verb 'to vigilate'. His thinking is not an autonomous action or activity; nor a concurrent procession of autonomous anythings. Nor is his vigilating, which is, of course, just one element in his thinking what he is saying.

I have heard part of my point put in this way, which I deprecate. It is sometimes said that while thinking does indeed need some vehicle or other, still some philosophers are so stingy about the number of eligible vehicles that they restrictively say that thinking needs for its vehicle only bits of English or French, etc.; or that it needs only images; or that it can get along only with either bits of English or French or with images. What they should do, it is suggested, is let in lots more kinds of vehicles, like the tennis-player's wrist and eye movements, the conversationalist's tongue movements and ear-prickings; the typist's finger movements; and so on. I am rejecting this vehicle–passenger model altogether. Adverbial verbs are not verbs for autonomous doings, and so not of autonomous doings which, like bicycling and strumming, need some apparatus or other. Hurrying over breakfast does require eating, but not as its vehicle; rather, to put it coarsely, as an adverb needs some suitable verb or other. Pugnacity or cunning at tennis does require strokes, but not as distemper requires brickwork or woodwork, or as marmalade requires bread or toast. Wariness in rock-climbing or taste in Latin verse composition can indeed not get along without rocks or Latin words, but not because it is left stranded or hamstrung without them, but because without them there is no 'it'.

Before moving on, let me just mention that a great many verbs of doing which can function in completed commands are in themselves partly adverbial and partly not. The verb 'scrutinise' already carries the notion of 'carefully'; and the verb 'misspell' already carries the notion of 'incorrectly'. A person who is sprinting must be running, but also he must be hurrying; and if he is guzzling, while he must be eating, he cannot be eating daintily.

But now we come to what *le Penseur* is engaged in doing. For brevity I label what he is doing 'reflecting', though the label does not naturally cover a good many of the things that *le Penseur* might be doing, such as day-dreaming, brooding, going over in his head the previously memorised dates of the Kings of England or, of course, just pretending to be reflecting.

When we think in the abstract about thinking, it is usually reflecting, calculating, deliberating, etc. that we attend to. It is from their reflectings that we grade Plato and Euclid as Thinkers; we do not so grade Bradman, Chaplin and Tintoretto. By the plural noun 'thoughts' we ordinarily refer to what *le Penseur*'s reflectings either incorporate or else are going to terminate in, if they prosper. Indeed it is just because reflecting is what we start off by considering, that we later on feel a strong pressure to suppose that for the tennis-player to be thinking what he is doing, he must be sandwiching some fleeting stretches of reflecting between some stretches of running, racquet-swinging, and ball-watching. That is, because reflecting does, or does seem to, qualify as an autonomous activity, therefore such adverbial expressions as 'on purpose', 'vigilantly', 'carefully', 'cunningly', 'tentatively', 'experimentally', 'resolutely', etc. seem to need to be construed as signifying some extra autonomous things that the tennis-player must be privily doing, besides what we see him autonomously doing. Where no one thinks that the would-be train-catcher is engaged synchronously in sprinting and also in hurrying, we are all tempted to suppose that for the tennis-player to be using his wits he must be both making muscular movements and also be doing lots of short, sharp bits of reflecting.

I think what I aim to do, if I can, is to show that it is the notion of engaged thinking, like that of the tennis-player or the conversationalist, that is the basic notion, while that of disengaged thinking or reflecting, like that of *le Penseur*, is supervenient. The notions of being pensive and having thoughts do not explain, but need to be explained via the notion of intelligently X-ing, where 'X' is not a verb of thinking.

When Plato says that in thinking the soul is debating with herself, he is grossly over-generalising, not merely from reflecting, but from one or two very special brands of reflecting, namely philosophical and perhaps also forensic reflecting. If, for example, *le Penseur* is engaged in trying to complete a limerick, or trying to recall a friend's telephone number, then, though he is certainly reflecting, he is certainly not, unless *per accidens* and *en passant*, debating with himself; and if he is, *per accidens* and *en passant*, doing a bit of debating with himself, the required limerick-ending or telephone number is not whatever, if anything, is settled by his internal debate. We are always thinking when we are internally or externally debating. We are not always debating when we are reflecting.

Sometimes philosophers and psychologists, speaking a bit less restrictively than Plato, say that in thinking, that is, what I am calling 'reflecting', the thinker must, whether in his head or *sotto voce* or aloud, be talking to himself, the coverage of their word 'talking' being a lot wider than that of the word 'debating'. For example, narrating is talking, but it is not debating. Nor is most preaching. These philosophers and psychologists put their point, sometimes, by saying that the thinker must be thinking 'in English' or 'in French', etc., or sometimes that he must be thinking 'in symbols', whatever they are.

Now there certainly are a lot of tasks on which *le Penseur* may be engaged, though he need not be, which, in one way or another, are or incorporate linguistic tasks. For example, he may be trying to compose a poem or an after-dinner speech, trying to translate a bit of Horace into English, preparing to lecture to laymen on a subject the technical terminology of which is strange to them, wondering whether to italicise or how to spell a word, and so on. Here his particular problem is the more or less difficult linguistic problem what to say and how to say or write it. He is having to think up suitable French or German phrases and sentences; and the better he is at French or German the easier it is for him to think these up. Now, he may be so good at French or German that his task is, most of the time, not difficult at all, and not even fairly easy, but perfectly easy. Then we may, in praise or envy, say that, unlike us, he can think in French or German. He no more has to hunt for the right French or German words or phrases that he needs than we, most of the time, have to hunt for the English words or phrases that we need when talking to Englishmen. When engaged in certain *ex officio* linguistic tasks, he can find the required German words and phrases without any rummaging at all.

But though *le Penseur*'s task may be, it certainly need not be a poet's task, a translator's task, an after-dinner speaker's task, or a proof-corrector's task; he need not be wondering how to say or write something. His problem is, perhaps, a historian's, a mathematician's, a mechanic's, a chess-player's, a detective's or a philosopher's problem. It is not a problem of expression, though it may carry with it some problems of expression; and these may be easy, while it is baffling, or vice versa. Solving them is not solving it. If 'Smith can think in German' means that he ordinarily finds it perfectly easy to put into suitable German what he wants to put into German, then this says nothing at all about his philosophical, mathematical or Scotland Yard reflectings, but only about his trans-frontier communicational undertakings, namely that he is good at German. It does not entail that while tackling a philosophical problem he is saying things to himself in German or in his first language, English. The view that he must be doing so has to be grounded elsewhere. I am not saying that there are no such grounds for, *inter alia*, philosophical reflecting. I do in fact think that an unworded argument belongs where an unworded quatrain belongs— nowhere. But I am not following this up, for *le Penseur* may be reflecting, though neither arguing nor composing a poem, a speech or a repartee.

I have so far sharply contrasted thinking what one is doing, e.g. conversing or playing tennis, with reflecting, e.g. what *le Penseur* is occupied in; engaged thinking with disengaged thinking. *Le Penseur* is concentrating on something, but not on sitting where and as he is sitting, or on propping his chin on the hand on which it is propped. He is, metaphorically, miles away, as the tennis-player cannot be miles away and still be playing tennis. But still, though, from this detachedness or disengagedness, in strong contrast with the tennis-player's engaged thinking, *le Penseur*'s reflecting itself, no less than tennis-playing, does require such adverbial things as trying, testing, experimenting, practising, initiative, avoidance or correction of lapses, resistance to distractions, interest, patience,

472

self-coaching, etc. Whatever *le Penseur* is engaged in that qualifies him as reflecting, he cannot, any more than the tennis-player, be absent-mindedly or deliriously or infantilely engaged in it. He, like the tennis-player, cannot be asleep or vacant, nor even an absolute beginner. Both alike must be on the *qui vive*. *Le Penseur*, no less than the tennis-player, must be, in some degree, using here and now his at least partly trained wits. He cannot not be thinking what he is doing, i.e. not be *X*-ing vigilantly, pertinaciously, etc. So even disengaged thinking, i.e. reflecting, is also, like tennis-playing, a species of engaged thinking. The adverbial verb 'to think' is presupposed by the activity-verb 'to reflect'. But where the tennis-player must be using his wits in, *inter alia*, moving his feet, eyeing the ball, swinging his racquet and so on, we seem now to be stumped to nominate any corresponding autonomous *X*-ing or *X*-ings such that *le Penseur* must be *X*-ing more or less exploratorily, tentatively, pertinaciously, pugnaciously, scrupulously or cannily. What is the *X*-ing that *le Penseur* is non-absent-mindedly, non-somnolently or non-deliriously doing which *if* done absent-mindedly or somnolently or deliriously would not then amount to pondering, calculating, etc.?

Surely part of what stumps us is our vain presumption that our bill needs to be filled by just one uniform and nominatable *X*-ing; but I am not therefore going to resort to the now over-hallowed 'family likeness' device so long before reaching, what it is for, the last resort. But certainly let us remember from the start that *le Penseur* unquestionably qualifies as reflecting or pondering as well if he is in the throes of musical composition as if he is trying to construct or destroy a philosophical or a Scotland Yard argument; or trying to find out whether the number 1,000,001 is a prime number; or trying to solve a chess-problem; or to recollect a telephone number; or to run through the alphabet backwards.

Notice here, what I hope may turn out to be relevant, that adverbial verbs may pyramid. In this way. If I am eating my breakfast, you may tell me to hurry over my breakfast. If I obey you, I do so not by breakfasting, since I am doing that already, but by accelerating the rate of my breakfasting. I am then obediently hurrying over my breakfast. If I resent your command but dare not disobey it, then I am with reluctance obeying your command to hurry over my breakfast. I am reluctantly obediently hurriedly breakfasting. I am not reluctantly breakfasting, nor necessarily reluctantly hurrying over my breakfast; I am with reluctant obedience hurrying over my breakfast, though I might have cheerfully hurried over it if you had ordered me not to do so. And so on, in principle, indefinitely. Notice that none of these adverbs can get going unless the bottom one is attached to a non-adverbial verb or a partly non-adverbial verb, in this case 'breakfasting'. This is not meant as a reminder of a bit of school-grammar; rather it is intended to bring out a corollary to one of the many things that could be meant by calling one concept 'parasitic' on another. Obeying can be parasitic on hurrying, and this in its turn on breakfasting. 'Big fleas have little fleas . . .' The notion of stealing is parasitic on the notion of owning; the notion of pretending to steal is parasitic on the notion of stealing; and the notion of rebelliously pretending to steal is parasitic on the notion of pretending to steal. And so on. When the intention with which an agent does X is ancillary to the intention with which he will or would do Y, we can say that his X-ing is an intention-parasite on his Y-ing. He has to have Y-ing in mind in order to have X-ing in mind; and he may have to have Z-ing in mind in order to have Y-ing in mind.

Now for a quite different though connected matter.

Strolling across a golf course, we see a lot of pairs and fours of golfers playing one hole after another in a regular sequence. But now we see a single golfer, with six golf balls in front of him, hitting each of them, one after another, towards one and the same green. He then goes and collects the balls, comes back to where he was before, and does it again. What is he doing? He is not playing golf. He has no opponent; he does not putt the balls into the hole; he lays the balls by hand on to the turf from which he is going to hit them. Obviously he is practising approach-shots. But what distinguishes a practice approach-shot from a real one? Several things. Negatively, he is not trying to win a match since there is no match. Nor in practising is he both making approach-shots and also doing something else as well. Positively he performs each of his strokes as a piece of self-training. Training for what? Training for making approach-shots in matches to come. But he cannot be practising without, in some way, having in mind the non-practice approach-shots of future live matches. The 'thick' description of what he is engaged in requires reference to his thoughts, in some sense, of future non-practice approach-shots. These are what it is for. His activity of practising approach-shots is parasitic on that of making match approach-shots. There are two points about practice approach-shots that need to be brought out for future use:

1. The first point is that the 'thick' description of them contains a reference to his having in mind will-be or may-be match approach-

shots. He will have practised in vain if his performance in these matches shows no improvement.

2. The second point is that the practice-shots are in some degree detached or disengaged from the conditions under which match approach-shots have to be made. The practiser can play from where he likes; he can hit without having to wait for his turn; he need not even have a green to play for; a tree-stump in a field would do. He need have only a mashie with him. Indeed he might do without golf-balls and a mashie; dandelions and a walking-stick might serve his turn. As his circumstance-dependence and apparatus-dependence decrease, so his practice-actions approximate more and more closely to being pure 'voluntaries', that is, things the doing of which is within his absolute initiative and option. I suggest already that his partial detachment from the circumstances and the apparatus of golf-matches points up the road to *le Penseur*'s total or nearly total detachment from what exists and is going on around him.

There are many activities other than practising which share with it these two cardinal features of intention-parasitism and circumstance-detachment. (*a*) The rehearsing actor is not acting, but rehearsing for acting. He is trying this morning to make himself word-perfect and gesture-perfect on 'the night'. He rehearses in vain today if he falters on 'the night'. He may rehearse in mufti; in his own room; without an audience, prompter or fellow-actors; in the dark. He is in high or low degree circumstance-detached and equipment-free in his rehearsing. Yet the 'thick' description of what he is doing, being in terms of what he is doing it for, must refer to theatre performances which, if they occur, will not be circumstance-detached or equipment-free. (*b*) The cooking-instructor teaches the making of a plum-cake by demonstrating. He can, if he likes, demonstrate with salt instead of sugar, with a cold oven, with a ten-second pause for the baking process, which in live cake-making would be an hour; and so on. His success or failure is the later production by his pupils of good or bad plum-cakes. If and when they do cake-making, they will do it under full kitchen conditions. (*c*) The boy who tries to jump the flower-bed may be neither practising to improve nor demonstrating to his friends a technique, but just experimenting, just trying to find out whether he can jump it or not. He is vexed with the grown-up who gives him a helping shove, since this stops him from finding out what he wanted to find out. He, too, enjoys a measure of circumstance-detachment. He can choose for himself when to jump, and from which side to jump. He needs no spectators. He needs only his legs, the flower-bed and maybe a decent light. Indeed, he can find out if he can jump the three-foot-wide flower-bed without even a flower-bed, since he can measure out a three-foot distance anywhere on the lawn or in the drive that he likes and try to jump that. (*d*) Some actions are preparations for others, as clearing the throat for singing, or pumping up the bicycle tyres for going for a bicycle-ride. The singing or the bicycle-ride may not take place, but the preparatory action requires for its 'thick' description a reference to the intended or expected singing or cycling. Consequently, I might clear my throat to give the false impression that I was about to sing. This throat-clearing is not a pretence throat-clearing; it is a pretence throat-clearing-in-preparation-for-singing. Its 'thick' description requires a second-remove reference to singing. Obviously I can clear my throat for singing minus the accompanist whom I shall need for my singing. (*e*) Jerking the leafless branch of the tree can be at once an experiment and a preparation. The would-be climber wants to find out if the branch is sound in order to pull himself up on it if it is sound, and not to do so if it is not. There is nothing to prevent the branch-jerking from being also a demonstration to a novice of one of the techniques of tree-climbing. The branch-tester may not be trying to climb the tree today. He wants to find out its strength for tomorrow's or for someday's tree-climbing, or for someone else's tree-climbing. Climbing the tree will require twenty minutes and suitable clothes. Testing the branch does not require all this time, or this clothing. (*f*) Pretending to X is not X-ing, but reference to X-ing has to enter into the 'thick' description of what the pretender is doing. If, what is often not the case, the pretending to X is an attempt to deceive, its success consists in the spectator thinking that the agent is X-ing or trying to X. He pretends in vain if the spectator is not taken in. Obviously the pretender to X may be free of some of the adjuncts required for X-ing. I can pretend to be rich without having a lot of money; or I can pretend to know Budapest without having been there. (*g*) Consider lastly the notion of waiting—waiting for a train perhaps. I wait in vain if the train does not arrive, or if I am on the wrong platform, or if I get into the wrong train. The 'thick' description of what I am doing on the platform requires mention of my should-be train-catching. Here there is no X-ing in particular that I must be positively doing in order to qualify as waiting. I may sit or stand or stroll, smoke or tackle a crossword puzzle, chat or hum or keep quiet. All that is required is that I do not do anything or go anywhere or remain anywhere that will prevent me catching the train. Waiting is abstaining from doings that conflict with the objective. So waiting requires no apparatus at all, and only the simple circumstance of remaining near where the train will come in and not going to sleep.

So maybe *le Penseur*'s total detachment, disengagement or remoteness from what is going on around him is *in excelsis* akin to the practising golfer's independence of lots of golf-course adjuncts; or the cookery-instructor's independence of lots of kitchen adjuncts; or the commuter's independence of almost any adjuncts, save, roughly, the right platform. We all know from our own experience how reflecting may require experimenting, testing, rehearsing, practising, and plenty of sheer waiting.

Suppose that *le Penseur* is a composer who is trying to compose a Hungarian Rhapsody, whatever that is. Yesterday he sat at a piano, trying out notes and note-sequences on the keys. The piano notes that 'thinly' he produced, 'thickly' were cancellings, modifyings, assemblings, reassemblings, rehearsings, etc. for what future trumpeters and violinists will, hopefully, be playing. Today, owing to spring-cleaning in his home, he is sitting on a rock on the hillside, half-humming notes and note-sequences, cancelling and modifying them, rehearsing them, etc. Today, unlike yesterday, he uses no instrument and he has not even to worry lest he wake the baby. Tomorrow, perhaps, he goes on composing his Rhapsody, and does this without even half-humming anything. He just 'hears in his head' his still tentative snatches and stretches of music. Now the note-sequences which he tries out, rejects, modifies, assembles, rehearses, etc., are almost totally circumstance-disengaged and totally equipment-free. They are his own 100 per cent. 'voluntaries'.

But if *le Penseur* is composing not music, but an after-dinner speech, then, whether or not he happens also to be absent-mindedly humming snatches of music, he must be producing, mostly from his own resources, candidate-words, phrases and sentences. But he is free to produce them aloud or *sotto voce* or in his head; or in ink on paper; or in 'mental' ink on 'mental' paper, or etc. Obviously his production at a certain moment of some unbegun and unfinished phrase is not all that he is 'thickly' doing. He is experimentally and suspiciously trying out, so to speak 'on appro', and quite often rejecting a candidate for what he will be delivering in the Grand Hotel tomorrow night. Or perhaps he is rehearsing, for 'the night', a now accepted candidate for inclusion; or perhaps he is operating with it as a spring-board from which to move on to its yet uncomposed sequel; or maybe he is doing several or all of these things together. But whatever he is now trying to do, his intention is frustrated if tomorrow's dinner is cancelled: and what he is now tentatively and rehearsingly doing requires no external adjuncts, apparatus, materials or circumstances—or almost none, save perhaps a dictionary and an anthology of humorous anecdotes.

If *le Penseur* is trying to solve a chess-problem he need not be humming snatches of anything or producing any words or word-sequences. He may experimentally move and re-move pieces on the chessboard in front of him, unpressed by an opponent or a clock. Or he may, like me, only much more efficiently, be considering alternative moves of visualised chessmen on a visualised chessboard; or he may in imagination, in some other manner, be experimentally making alternative moves. But whichever he is at this moment 'thinly' doing, 'thickly' he is trying to check and mate in four moves.

I now suggest that *le Penseur*'s disengagement from what exists and is going on around him does not involve that he is not, like the tennis-player, thinking what he is doing; we have seen that of course he must be doing this. Rather what he is 'thinly' doing is completely or in high degree circumstance-detached and apparatus-free. What he is 'thinly' doing, e.g. humming under his breath short sequences of notes, is entirely or almost entirely within his own initiative and option. It is a pure or nearly pure 'voluntary'. He can produce what notes he likes, when he likes and in what order he likes. He has all the freedoms that the practiser of approach-shots has, and more besides. He does not need to have 100 per cent. circumstance-emancipation in order to qualify as reflecting. I should qualify as engaged in reflection were I trying to solve a chess-problem with my eyes visibly travelling over the page of the newspaper on which the problem was set; and the composer could be fingering the keys of a real piano and still qualify as being in the throes of composition, and so as being in a brown study. His pensiveness does not require total absence of visible or audible X-ing; but the X-ing must be very much his own '*ad lib.*'.

But more than this. Not only must *le Penseur* be 'thinly' doing something which enjoys some measure of circumstance-disengagement and therefore some measure of author's optionalness; but also what he is 'thinly' doing must have a 'thicker' description. What he is 'thinly' doing must be in one or more ways and at one or more removes an intention-parasite, as the rehearsing actor's gesturings are intention-parasites on his gesturings on 'the night'; or as the tree-climber's branch-jerkings are intention-parasites on his or his son's branch-trustings or mistrustings tomorrow. The philosopher who, 'thinly', is at this moment mouthing a sentence or sentence-torso may, 'thickly' be, so to speak, jerking a tempting premiss-branch for use, or else for non-use in an argument which is not yet ready, and this would-be argument itself may in its turn be wanted for the rebuttal of some caviller's criticism. Intention-parasites may pyramid. 'Big fleas have little fleas.'

I suggest, finally, that these elements of (*a*) circumstance-detachment, author-optionalness or *ad lib*-ness and (*b*) intention-parasitism, simple or multiple, are what philosophers are trying to get under control when they say, Procrusteanly, that reflecting is, for example, 'operating with symbols' or 'using language'; or that in thinking of Folly Bridge, when I am not there, I must, instead, have in my presence some sort of proxy or token for that congested bridge—as if the gap between the tennis-player and *le Penseur* needed to be filled by a new sort of circumstance or a new sort of apparatus, only sorts which are exempted from the grosser actualities. I suggest that the gap needs to be filled by intention-parasitic and author-optional doings, of which word-producing and sentence-producing are only one species among many, though a specially important species. But this is not the time to account for its special importance.

37

THE THINKING OF THOUGHTS
WHAT IS 'LE PENSEUR' DOING?

Reprinted from 'University Lectures', no. 18, 1968, by permission of the University of Saskatchewan

I begin by drawing your attention to a special, but at first sight merely curious feature of the notion of doing something, or rather of trying to do something. In the end I hope to satisfy you that this feature is more than merely curious; it is of radical importance for our central question, namely, What is *le Penseur* doing?

Two boys fairly swiftly contract the eyelids of their right eyes. In the first boy this is only an involuntary twitch; but the other is winking conspiratorially to an accomplice. At the lowest or the thinnest level of description the two contractions of the eyelids may be exactly alike. From a cinematograph-film of the two faces there might be no telling which contraction, if either, was a wink, or which, if either, was a mere twitch. Yet there remains the immense but unphotographable difference between a twitch and a wink. For to wink is to try to signal to someone in particular, without the cognisance of others, a definite message according to an already understood code. It has very complex success-*versus*-failure conditions. The wink is a failure if its intended recipient does not see it; or sees it but does not know or forgets the code; or misconstrues it; or disobeys or disbelieves it; or if anyone else spots it. A mere twitch, on the other hand, is neither a failure nor a success; it has no intended recipient; it is not meant to be unwitnessed by anybody; it carries no message. It may be a symptom but it is not a signal. The winker could not *not* know that he was winking; but the victim of the twitch might be quite unaware of his twitch. The winker can tell what he was trying to do; the twitcher will deny that he was trying to do anything.

So far we are on familiar ground. We are just drawing the familiar distinction between a voluntary, intentional, and, in this case, collusive and code-governed contraction of the eyelids from an involuntary twitch. But already there is one element in the contrast that needs to be brought out. The signaller himself, while acknowledging that he had not had an involuntary twitch but (1) had deliberately winked, (2) to someone in particular, (3) in order to impart a particular message, (4) according to an understood code, (5) without the cognisance of the rest of the company, will rightly deny that he had thereby done or tried to do five separately do-able things. He had not *both* tried to contract his eyelids *and also* tried to do a second, synchronous thing or several synchronous things. Unlike a person who both coughs and sneezes, or both greets his aunt and pats her dog, he had not both contracted his eyelids and also done a piece of synchronous signalling to his accomplice. True, he had contracted them not involuntarily but on purpose, but this feature of being on purpose is not an extra deed; he had contracted them at the moment when his accomplice was looking in his direction, but its being at this chosen moment is not an extra deed; he had contracted them in accordance with an understood code, but this accordance is not an extra deed. He had tried to do much more than contract his eyelids, but he had not tried to do more things. He had done one thing the report of which embodies a lot of subordinate clauses; he had not done what the report of would embody several main verbs conjoined by 'ands'. There are five or more ways in which his winking attempt might have been a failure, but he was not attempting to do five things. If he is successful, he has not got five successes to put on a list, but only one.

Similarly, sloping arms in obedience to an order differs, but does not differ in number of actions from just sloping arms. It is not a conjunction of a bit of sloping arms with a separately do-able bit of obeying. It is obeying by sloping arms; it is obediently sloping arms. This adverb 'obediently' does import a big difference, but not by recording any something else, internal or external, that the soldier also did, and might have done by itself. If the officer had shouted out of the blue 'Obey', he would have given the soldier nothing to do. Obeying is not a separately orderable action, for all that obediently sloping arms does not reduce to just sloping arms. The verb 'obeyed' cannot be the sole verb in a non-elliptical report of what someone did. It functions, so to speak, in an adverbial role, and can be replaced by the adverb 'obediently' or by the adverbial phrase 'in obedience to the order'.

Come back to our winker. Perhaps, being new to the art, he

winks rather slowly, contortedly and conspicuously. A third boy, to give malicious amusement to his cronies, parodies this clumsy wink. How does he do this? Well, by contracting his right eyelids in the way in which the clumsy winker had winked. But the parodist is not himself clumsily trying covertly to signal a message to an accomplice. He is deftly trying conspicuously to exhibit something, and he fails if his cronies are not looking, or are not amused, or mistakenly suppose him to be trying covertly to signal to an accomplice. There is only one thing that he is trying to do, namely to take off the winker, and he does this just by contracting his right eyelids. Yet there is now a threefold internal complexity in his own report of what he has been trying to do. For he may say, 'I was trying (1) to look like Tommy trying (2) to signal to his accomplice by trying (3) to contract his right eyelids.' There is, so to speak, the beginning of a Chinese box of internal subordinate clauses in the parodist's report of what he was trying to do—for all that there was only one thing that he was trying to do, namely to parody the winker; and for all that the cinematograph-film records only the one eyelid-contraction. We can easily add to this nest of Chinese boxes. For our parodist, to make sure of getting his parody pat, may in solitude practise his facial mimicry. In so practising he is not yet trying to amuse anyone, for he is alone. He is rehearsing for a subsequent public performance. So he could report what he is now doing by, 'I am trying (1) to get myself ready to try (2) to amuse my cronies by grimacing like Tommy trying (3) to signal covertly to his accomplice by trying (4) to contract his eyelids.' Another box can easily be added. For our winker himself might report that he had not, on this occasion, really been trying covertly to signal something to his accomplice, but had been trying to gull the grown-ups into the false belief that he was trying to do so. So now our parodist, in practising his parody of this, would have to be described with the help of five verbs of trying—and still there is only one thing he is trying to do, and still there is only the one contraction of the eyelids that, at a given moment, the cinematograph film records. The thinnest description of what the rehearsing parodist is doing is, roughly, the same as for the involuntary eyelid twitch; but its thick description is a many-layered sandwich, of which only the bottom slice is catered for by that thinnest description. Taking the word 'only' in one way, it is true enough that the rehearsing parodist is, at this moment, only contracting his right eyelids. Taken in another way, this is quite false; for the account of what he is trying to effect by this eyelid-contraction, i.e. the specification of its success-conditions, requires every one of the successively sub-ordinate 'try' clauses, of which I will spare you the repetition.

Part of this can be brought out in another way. A person who, like most small children, cannot contract his right eyelids without also contracting his left eyelids, cannot wink. He must acquire the nursery accomplishment of separately contracting his right eyelids before he can learn to send signals by winking. The acquisition of this little muscular accomplishment is a pre-condition of the acquisition of the ability to wink. Knowing how to wink requires, but does not reduce to, being able separately to contract the right eyelids. But further. A boy who cannot wink cannot parody a wink. Knowing how to parody a wink requires, but does not reduce to, knowing how to wink. Further still. A boy trying by private rehearsals to prepare himself effectively to parody a wink must know what it is to parody well rather than badly. Else there is nothing for him to practise for or against. So we might say (1) that voluntarily contracting the right eyelids is on a higher level of accomplishment than an involuntary twitch, since the former did but the latter did not require some learning or practising; (2) that winking is on a higher sophistication-level than that of voluntarily contracting the eyelids, since more, indeed in this case a lot more, needs to have been learned for signalling to be even attempted; (3) that parodying a wink and (4) that rehearsing the parodying of a wink are in their turn on still higher sophistication-levels or accomplishment-levels. Learning a lesson of one level presupposes having learned lessons of all the levels below it. By no pedagogic ingenuities could you teach a child what stealing is before teaching him what owning is; or teach a boy to parody a wink before teaching him to wink and to recognise winks; or train a recruit to obey orders to slope arms before training him to slope arms. For future purposes we should already notice that, for the same reasons, there can be no question of my being able to direct you to Larissa before I have learned the way to Larissa; or of my being able to locate and correct mistakes in my multiplication sum before being able to multiply. Some lessons are intrinsically traders on prior lessons. Such tradings can pyramid indefinitely. There is no top step on the stairway of accomplishment-levels.

It is now time to begin to apply these ideas. I start at a stage a good long way short of that which I hope to reach in the end.

In the end I hope to be able to throw some light on the notions of *pondering, reflecting, meditating* and the *thinking of thoughts*, that is, roughly, of what *le Penseur* looks as if he is engaged in—in the end, but not straight away.

You hear someone come out with 'Today is the 3rd of February'. What was he doing? Obviously the thinnest possible description of what he was doing is, what would fit a gramophone equally well, that he was launching this sequence of syllables into the air. A tape-recording would reproduce just what he was doing, in this thinnest sense of 'doing'. But we naturally and probably correctly give a thicker description than this. We say that he was telling someone else the date. He was trying to impart a piece of wanted calendar-information, so that his attempt was unsuccessful (1) if his companion did not hear or misheard the noises, or (2) did not understand or misunderstood what he had heard, or (3) did not believe or already knew what he was told, or (4) if the speaker had himself got the date wrong. Our natural and probably correct thick description of what the utterer of the noises was up to in uttering them has to indicate success-versus-failure conditions additional to and quite different from the purely phonetic success-conditions to which the mere vocal uttering was subject. Yet the speaker could not have failed or succeeded in his attempt to give his companion the calendar-information, if, owing to catarrh, he had not succeeded in voicing the noises 'Today is the 3rd of February'. Saying, e.g. giving calendar-information, does not reduce to voicing; but it requires it or some substitute for it. Nor is saying doing two things, voicing noises and also doing something else. It is, e.g., conveying information or misinformation *by* voicing some noises.

There are, of course, alternative possible thick descriptions of what the utterer of the noises might have been trying to do. For he might have been lying, i.e. trying to get his enemy to accept a piece of misinformation; or he might have been an actor on the stage, playing the hero's part of a calendar-informant or the villain's part of a deliberate calendar-misinformant. For him to be trying to do one of these things, he must already know what it is to say things informatively; and, for that, he must already have got the ability to voice syllables. Or he may be trying to render into English a German sentence conveying correct or incorrect calendar-information. If so, the translator is not telling anyone the date, right or wrong. If faulted, he can be faulted only for mistranslation. But to give this English rendering or misrendering to the German sentence, he must already know how to tell someone the date in English when the date is the 3rd of February. Or he may be drawing a conclusion from premises given him by someone else— in which case he is not informing anyone else of the date, but arriving himself at the right or wrong date. He might regret the fallaciousness of his inference despite the fact that his conclusion happened to be true. And so on.

Under none of these alternative thick descriptions is what he is doing just voicing some syllables; yet nor is it doing some things do-able separately from that syllable-voicing. The handy umbrella-word 'saying' covers a wide variety of different things; the saying may be on any accomplishment-level above the merely phonetic one.

To give ourselves more material let us notice fairly summarily a whole run of action-describing verbs which, like the verb 'to say', cannot also function as the verbs of bottom-level or thinnest action-reports or orders.

(*a*) We have seen that there is no such action as obeying, though sloping arms in obedience to an order differs importantly from just sloping arms for fun. Complying with a request and keeping a promise are obvious parallels. If you just say 'please', there is, as yet, nothing that you have requested me to do; and if I say just 'I promise' (period) there is nothing that I have promised to do, so I have not yet even promised.

(*b*) Mimicking, parodying, pretending and shamming are also not lowest-level actions. Our parodist did mimic the winker, but only by contracting his eyelids in the way in which the winker had done so. To sham irritation I have, for example, to utter an expletive and thus sound as swearers sound. 'He is shamming (period)' cannot, context apart, tell us what he is doing. 'He is shamming irritation by voicing expletives' does.

(*c*) Doing something experimentally differs from just doing it. Doing it experimentally is trying to find out, by doing it, whether it can be done, or how to do it, or what will be the outcome of doing it. So the boy experimentally jumping the stream is vexed by a helping shove, since this interferes with his experiment. Notice that he may jump partly in order to cross the stream and partly in order to find out whether it is jumpable. So if he lands in mid-stream he has failed in part, but succeeded in part of his undertaking. But he was not making two jumps.

(*d*) Practising is rather similar. I may converse with a Frenchman just for the sake of conversation, or just to practise my French. But again I may converse with him with a sociable intent and also to give myself practice. It may turn out that the conversation was boring, but the practice was rewarding. Clearly there is no practising pronunciation without pronouncing syllables; and clearly, too, pronouncing syllables for practice is not doing two separately do-able things. I cannot just practise (period) any more than I can just obey (period). In practising pronunciation I am pronouncing with a self-drilling intention, and my pedagogic intention is not a second thing that I am doing, or a thing that I might be ordered or advised to do by itself.

(*e*) Sometimes we do things as demonstrations. The sergeant slopes arms in front of the recruits to show them how to do it. He demonstrates in vain if they do not look, or look only at his face. He, too, might in one and the same action be sloping arms, like everyone else, in obedience to the company commander's order, and also doing it as an instructive exhibition of the manual operation. If he had misheard or anticipated the order, he would have failed to obey, while still succeeding in demonstrating the motions.

Not all demonstrations are exhibitions of how to do things. The witness might tell part of his story in dumb show, i.e. with a narrative intention.

(*f*) Very many of the things that we do are steps towards or stages in some ulterior undertaking. I may walk to the village to make a purchase, or as the first stage of a walk to a second village. In the one case I have walked to the first village in vain if the shop is shut; in the other case I have walked to it in vain if a flood lies between the two villages. But I might walk to the first village with both ends in view and succeed in both, fail in both, or succeed in one and fail in the other.

(*g*) One final specimen. We do some things in cancellation or correction of other things that we have done. There is such a thing as *undoing*. We erase or cross out things miswritten, shelve what had been projected, dismantle what we have assembled, get out of skids, unsay things that we have said. There can be no unsaying or withdrawing where nothing has been said, and scrawling a line across the page is not crossing out unless there was something already written on that page.

Why have I produced this long, but far from complete series of kinds of so to speak, constitutionally adverbial verbs—active verbs that are not verbs for separately do-able, lowest-level doings?

Because, if I am right, most of them, plus others that I have not listed, are going to enter into the thick description of what *le Penseur* is doing in trying, by reflecting, to solve whatever his intellectual problem is.

It is often supposed by philosophers and psychologists that thinking is saying things to oneself, so that what *le Penseur* is doing on his rock is saying things to himself. But, apart from other big defects in this view, it fails because it stops just where it ought to begin. Very likely *le Penseur* was just now murmuring something under his breath or saying it in his head. But the question is, 'What is the thick description of what he was essaying or intending in murmuring those words to himself?' The thin description 'murmuring syllables under his breath', though true, is the thinnest possible description of what he was engaged in. The important question is 'But what is the correct and thickest possible description of what *le Penseur* was trying for in murmuring those syllables?' Was he, for example, murmuring experimentally, i.e. trying to find out something by murmuring them? And if so, just *what* would have rendered his experiment successful or unsuccessful? Or perhaps he had murmured them in cancellation of something previous; so just *what* was he wishing to cancel, and for what defects? And so on.

To say that *le Penseur* was just saying things to himself is like saying that our schoolboy parodist was just contracting his right eyelid; or that the sergeant was just fetching his rifle up on to his left shoulder; or, if you like, that the helmsman was just twiddling the helm, or the explorer was just treading on blades of grass.

Incidentally, not only is it quite wrong to say that *le Penseur* is merely voicing things to himself, in his head or under his breath, but it is also too restrictive to say that he must be saying things to himself at all. For just one example, he might be a musician composing a piece of music, in which case he might be humming experimental notes and note-sequences to himself. He would then be voicing or sub-voicing notes but not words—what words are there for him to voice which would further his work of composition? For him, too, it would be grossly inadequate to say that he is merely voicing notes. If he is composing a sonata, say, then the thinnest description of the note-voicing that he is doing would be silent about the intended musical structure and qualities of the sonata-to-be. It would be silent about what the composer is trying to accomplish by his tentative, self-critical and persevering note-voicings. It would say nothing about the composer's skills, repertoires, purposes or difficulties.

Now, I hope, we are in a position to approach the heart of our question 'What is *le Penseur* doing?' We shall approach him ladder-wise. Suppose there are, in a public park, a number of people sitting still, chin in hand, each on his rock. The first man has the job of making a count of the vehicles travelling in both directions along the road beneath him. Not merely are his eyes open, but he is carefully eyeing the vehicles in order to keep a correct tally of them. He is not just gazing, but visually keeping a tally, so he is thinking what he is doing. Nevertheless, he does not qualify as a thinker of thoughts. He is not reflecting, musing, composing or deliberating—or if he is, he thereby stops attending to his set task. Why does he not qualify? Because his attention, intentions and efforts are riveted to things going on in the adjacent outside world. Like those of a tennis-player or a car-driver, his tasks are imposed on him from external circumstances that are not of his choosing.

The occupant of the neighbouring rock is similarly not detached from external circumstances. He is listening carefully to an unfamiliar tune that is being played in his hearing by the town-band. He is lending his ears and his mind to strains of which not he but the town-band is the source. He cannot choose what to hear, or whether to hear or not.

Compare with these two men the occupant of the third rock. He is going over, in his head or under his breath or aloud, a perfectly familiar tune or poem. He is humming or murmuring it not absentmindedly but with some interest and even some degree of absorption. He can, though maybe not perfectly easily, call his tune or poem to a halt when he chooses; and in going over it he is fully detached from external circumstances. What he is giving his mind to comes out of his own resources. Yet he does not quite qualify as a *Penseur*. For the tune or poem is not his creation; and the way it runs is not subject to his choices. He cannot, or cannot easily, put his own variations into it. It runs in a rote-groove, rather as the gramophone-needle runs in a groove. Nor can we, after starting to run through the alphabet, easily insert amendments of our own; or even perfectly easily stop it at the letter 'q'.

In contrast with him, and with the occupants of the first two rocks, the occupant of the fourth rock is composing a tune, song or poem of his own. The notes or words that he voices or sub-

voices are at his own beck and call. Independent of and indifferent
to what is going on around him, he can produce his notes or
words, arrange and re-arrange them, scrap them, shelve them, and
rehearse selected sets of them under no duress either from external
circumstances or from rote-channelled grooves. He is the author
of the notes or words that he voices or sub-voices. He gives them
their existence, relegates them back into non-existence, marshals
them, memorises them, and so on, at his own sweet will. He is
in full control. So he qualifies as at least a candidate for the status
of a thinker of thoughts. For I suggest first that part of what we
require of the momentary occupation of a thinker is that it is
completely or nearly completely detached from what external
circumstances impose; and second, that the obverse side of this
detachment from alien circumstances is the thinker's uncoerced
initiation and control of his own bottom-level moves and motions,
like the word-voicings and the note-voicings of a composing poet
or musician.

Accordingly we would allow that the man on the next rock,
who is pencilling dots and lines on paper, may be engaged in
pondering. For, though he may depend on circumstances for his
possession of pencil and paper, he is free to put down what marks
he likes, which to erase, which to amend and which to connect
up, in which ways, with which others. If he is trying to design new
riggings for his yacht, or drawing from memory a sketch-map of
the foot-paths in his parish, then he is certainly meditating or
pondering just as much as a man who is voicing or sub-voicing
words in trying to compose a sermon or a lecture, or just as much
as a man who is humming notes in trying to compose a dance-tune.

The young chess-player on the next rock may be trying to
think out his next move, or his next three moves, when he is
physically waving his knight some two inches above the alternative
squares into which it might go. He is somewhat like the housewife,
(for whom I do not provide a rock) who might try to plan the
floral decoration of her dining-room by shifting and re-shifting
vases and bowls to alternative positions in the room, and by shifting
and re-shifting flowers, leaves and branches to alternative vases
and bowls. Momentary circumstances restrict her to these vases
and bowls, to these flowers, leaves and branches, and to these
tables, shelves and window-sills. But circumstances do not coerce
her into this as opposed to that arrangement. Notice that in each
case there is a thinnest description of what the person is doing,
e.g. pencilling a line or dot on paper, and that this thinnest

description requires a thickening, often a multiple thickening, of a perfectly specific kind before it amounts to an account of what the person is trying to accomplish, e.g. design a new rigging for his yacht.

However we have a long way to go yet. For the boy on the penultimate rock, trying for the first time to run through the alphabet backwards from 'Z,Y,X' to 'C,B,A', will hardly qualify as a thinker of thoughts just by being free to nominate what letters he pleases in what order he pleases, and by having a quite specific objective, together with competence to correct mis-orderings, omissions and repetitions of letters. He is thinking what he is doing, and his trying is on an accomplishment-level higher than that of being able to run by rote through the alphabet from A to Z. But its level is not high enough for what we are after. He has mastered a new trick, a trick which may or may not have utilities, but has no fertility. It is an exercise undertaken just for the sake of that exercise. Its performance leads nowhere, save towards the acquisition of a new rote-groove. What *le Penseur* is engaged in is more than this. But in requiring more than this I am not requiring that *le Penseur* be an intellectual giant, or that his intellectual problem be one of history-making dimensions. He may be an Aristotle, but he may be just one of Aristotle's students. He may be a Bismarck, but he may be just a back-bencher M.P. He may be a Beethoven, but he may be just one of us. I am going, for the sake of expository economy, to take it that in his ponderings *le Penseur* is saying things to himself; and that what he, unlike our alphabet-reverser, is trying to achieve will be a verbally formulatable theory or policy. So what I say about him will not apply directly to the thinkings of, say, a Beethoven, a Cézanne or a Mercator. These I leave on one side with a promissory and apologetic '*mutatis mutandis*'.

Still *en route* for our wanted sketch of the thick description or descriptions of what *le Penseur* is after in saying or sub-saying things to himself, let us look at the corresponding thick descriptions of three other people who are, quite likely audibly, saying things to themselves. Take (1) the meditating of the man who is now preparing an after-dinner speech; (2) that of the man who is preparing an electioneering address, and (3) that of the man who is preparing a lecture to students.

First of all, all are alike (1) in that they are not merely nattering, i.e. aimlessly voicing words and phrases; (2) in that they are not merely trying to think up conversational remarks. Conversational remarks are not circumstance-detached. What I conversationally say hinges in some measure on what you have just said; and your remark was not subject to my choice or control. Roughly, a conversation is an exchange of remarks (and not paragraphs) between two or more independent speakers. But the successive sentences of a speech or a lecture or sermon are intended by their single author to be in some measure internally threaded to their predecessors and successors, of which he himself is also the author. A remark interjected by a listener breaks the thread. So what the composing speaker or lecturer is at this moment saying to himself is meant to be a development out of and a lead towards other parts of his future speech or lecture. That it would be a digression irrelevant, repetitious, redundant or incongruous are scores on which a meditated phrase or sentence or story is dismissed. So the notion, quite popular among philosophers, that thinkers in saying things to themselves are therefore conducting something like inward conversations is not merely insufficient, it is wrong. Our composing speakers are trying to compose non-conversational, internally threaded sequences of dicta. In this respect *le Penseur*'s task is like theirs. There are not a thousand things that he wants to be able to propound. There is one thing, even if its propounding takes 1,000 sentences.

Next, unlike the composing electioneer and unlike the composing lecturer, the will-be after-dinner speaker does not aim to convert or to instruct his hearers, or not much. His speech will be a bad after-dinner speech if it is even a good harangue, lecture or sermon. It is meant to entertain, or to move, or to remind or to amuse, etc.; it is not meant to make a difference to what his listeners think or know. They are fellow-guests, not members of his congregation, his electorate or his seminar. In contrast with him the composing electioneer says what he says to himself as potential ingredients in a vote-winning harangue. He means to make new converts and to strengthen the convictions of his more faint-hearted supporters. He is out to persuade; and if sufficiently fanatical or unscrupulous he may use any persuasively effective tricks that he can think up. A plausible but bad argument may suit him better than a good but difficult one. The dominant success-condition of his undertaking is the winning and retaining, versus the losing, of votes.

In contrast with the electioneer, the will-be lecturer, at least if he cares about his subject and about his students, intends not to persuade them of anything, but to instruct them. The last thing that he wants is that his hearers should vote for his doctrine without having thought it through. He wants them to accept it for its merits, or even to doubt or reject it for its demerits. If he is a geometrician, Euclid say, he wants them to accept or reject it *qua* good geometricians in the making, and not *qua* rabid Euclideans or rabid anti-Euclideans.

In this respect *le Penseur*, if he merits our respect, is unlike the composing electioneer and like the composing lecturer. He does not want to pull wool over his own eyes, but to pull the wool from his own eyes. He wants to acquire, what the lecturer wants to help his students to acquire, a grasp or mastery of something that is not yet within reach. As what the will-be lecturer is here and now saying to himself is mooted and examined for its possible future educative effectiveness, so what *le Penseur* is here and now saying to himself is mooted and examined for its chances of being a contribution to his own conquest of his own problem. He produces a candidate-phrase, but he dismisses it for being too foggy or too metaphorical for him himself to be helped by it; or he begins to try to adapt to his own present search a line of argumentation which has worked well elsewhere, and moots one candidate-adaptation after another with growing discontentment, since each adaptation in its turn threatens him himself with new obstacles.

There is, I think, a good deal of promise in this assimilation of the thick description of what *le Penseur* is doing in saying things to himself to that of what the will-be lecturer is doing in lecture-preparingly saying things to himself. But it will not do as it stands. For there remains this huge difference between the teacher and *le Penseur*, that the teacher has already mastered what he wants his students to master. He can guide them because he is on his own ground. But *le Penseur* is on ground unexplored by himself, and perhaps unexplored by anyone. He cannot guide himself through his jungle. He has to find his way without guidance from anyone who already knows it, if anyone does know it. The teacher already knows up which paths and away from which blind alleys to beckon to his students. For him these paths and these blind alleys are already signposted. But for *le Penseur* no paths or blind alleys are yet signposted. He does not know in which directions he should, so to speak, beckon encouragingly or signal warningly to himself. To exaggerate a bit, the teacher is a sighted leader of the blind, where *le Penseur* is a blind leader of the blind—if indeed the very idea of his being or having a leader fits at all.

We are reminded of Socrates' puzzle in Plato's *Meno*: How possibly can Socrates, just by asking questions, get the geometrically innocent slave-boy to think out the right answer to a geometrical problem? Socrates' obviously unsatisfactory answer is that the slave-boy must have learned this geometrical truth in a previous existence, and that Socrates' questions had served merely as memory-floggers. The slave-boy was just, with Socratic promptings, resurrecting a piece of already acquired but submerged knowledge; and Socrates was only doing what the barrister cross-examining a witness often does, namely retrieving half-forgotten knowledge. Socrates' answer obviously will not do, since it merely postpones the question: 'How was that geometrical truth originally discovered in that supposed previous existence? Was it thought out then? Or again only resurrected?'

Consider this particular pedagogic technique of posing questions in order to tempt or provoke the students into suggesting their own incorrect or correct answers. Asking questions and then critically examining the answers, perhaps by further questions, really is one way, among many, of inducing students to think, i.e. to make their own unsteady steps forward. Now *le Penseur* does, quite likely, some of the time pose questions to himself in the hope that some of them will tempt or provoke himself into mooting tentative answers of his own for subsequent critical examination. But the huge difference between the teacher and *le Penseur* here is that the teacher knows, and *le Penseur* cannot yet know, which questions to pose, or *a fortiori* in what sequence to pose them. There is something of a method or a strategy controlling the sequence of questions that Socrates puts to the slave-boy; there can, at the start, be no such method or strategy, or hardly any, controlling *le Penseur*'s self-questionings. He does not yet know where he needs to get, or which paths will lead towards and which will lead away from where he wants to get, and which will lead nowhere at all.

But perhaps this is too pessimistic. For sometimes, from having been in partly similar jungles before, *le Penseur* may, not indeed know, but have some idea which directions look a bit more promising than which. In any particular case such a faintly promising look may prove to be a cheat; but it remains a sensible policy to try out the promising ones before trying out the unpromising ones. If from previous explorations he has acquired something of an explorer's eye for country of this general sort, then in the long run the initially promising-looking ways will have been rewarding more often than the unpromising-looking ones. Else he would not have acquired anything of an explorer's eye for country of this general sort.

So *le Penseur*, if not an absolute novice, will, in posing questions to himself, be doing so, certainly not in the teacher's knowledge that they are the right ones to ask, but also not entirely randomly. Some of his self-interrogations strike him at once, occasionally wrongly, as obviously silly questions to ask; others as not obviously silly. So we can see that the enquirer's self-questionings are indeed unlike the pupil-questionings of the teacher just in the fact that they can be only experimentally posed. His very questions are themselves, so to speak, questions 'on appro'—query-questions. They have no assured *heuristic* strategy behind them. But they are also unlike the absolute novice's self-questionings, since they really are experimentally posed. He poses them, anyhow partly, in order to find out whether or not they are the right questions to pose, that is, whether they are going to be heuristically rewarding or unrewarding. The enquirer is not saying didactic things to himself; he is experimentally saying questionably didactic things to himself. All of Socrates' questions to the slave-boy were pedagogically well chosen, and asked in a well-chosen order, since Socrates already knew Pythagoras' theorem. But Pythagoras himself, in first excogitating this theorem, had had no such guide. He got to his destination not by following signposts, but by experimentally and unconfidently following, often up blind alleys, experimentally planted signposts of his own, each with its warning question-mark inscribed on it. He had to find out by persevering trial and frequent error which of his experimental query-signposts would and which would not be misleading signposts, if read without the queries.

In short, I suggest that at least part of the thick description of what *le Penseur* is trying to do in saying things to himself is that he is trying, by success/failure tests, to find out whether or not the things that he is saying would or would not be utilisable as leads or pointers. They are not pointers, but only candidate-pointers; and most of them will have to be turned down after examination. Somewhat as my school-boy parodist was not winking but parodying winking; and somewhat as my stream-jumper was not trying to get across the stream, but to find out whether he could jump it; so, I suggest, in his pondering, reflecting, deliberating, etc. the thinker is not guiding himself anywhere, but trying to find out whether this or that track of his own making would or would not qualify as a guiding, as opposed to a mis-guiding or non-guiding, track.

Of course in real life the things said by the teacher to his students will not all or mostly be questions. He will suggest corollaries,